George Rawlinson

History of Ancient Egypt

Vol. 2

George Rawlinson

History of Ancient Egypt
Vol. 2

ISBN/EAN: 9783337329792

Printed in Europe, USA, Canada, Australia, Japan

Cover: Foto ©ninafisch / pixelio.de

More available books at **www.hansebooks.com**

EARLY EGYPTIAN STATUES, FROM MEYDOUN.

HISTORY

OF

ANCIENT EGYPT.

BY

GEORGE RAWLINSON, M.A.,

CAMDEN PROFESSOR OF ANCIENT HISTORY IN THE UNIVERSITY OF OXFORD; CANON OF CANTERBURY; AUTHOR OF "SEVEN GREAT MONARCHIES OF THE ANCIENT EASTERN WORLD."

IN TWO VOLUMES.

VOL. II.

NEW YORK:
A. L. BURT, PUBLISHER.

CONTENTS.

CHAPTER XII.
THE CHRONOLOGY.

Difficulties of the Subject—whence arising. Chronological Deficiencies of the Monuments. Schemes of Manetho, of Herodotus, of Diodorus, untrustworthy. Impossibility of an exact Chronology. Limits of the Uncertainty—(1) for the Third Period, or "New Empire:" (2) for the Second or Hyksos Period ("the Middle Empire");—(3) for the First or Earliest Period (the "Old Empire"). Possibility of an instructive History without exact Chronology, - - - 1

CHAPTER XIII.
THE OLD EMPIRE—THE FIRST BEGINNINGS.

Uncertainty of the Succession of the Early Kings—Official Order, determined on after the Expulsion of the Shepherd Kings, not to be viewed as historical. The List, as given by the chief Native Authorities. Doubts as to the Existence of Menes. Remarks on the name Athothis. Hesepti mentioned in the Ritual. Distinction attaching to Meribipu. Variations in the Lists. General Character of the Names. The traditional Notices of the Monarchs scanty and valueless. Condition of the Egyptian People at this early time. Character of their Art and of their Religion. Principal Features of their Life, - - - - - - - - - - 13

CHAPTER XIV.
THE PYRAMID KINGS.

Reigns of Seneferu, Khufu, Shafra, Menkaura, and Aseskaf, of the Fourth Dynasty; and of Usurkaf, Sahura, Kaka, Nefer-ar-kara, Ranuser, Menkauhor, Tatkara or Assa, and Unas, of the Fifth. General Condition of Egypt under these Kings. Progress of Art—of Religion—of Civilization and the Arts of Life, - - - - - - - - - - 26

CONTENTS.

CHAPTER XV.

THE SIXTH DYNASTY—CULMINATION AND DECLINE.

Marked Division between the Fifth and Sixth Dynasties—Shift of Power to the South. First Evidence of a united Egypt. Group of four Monarchs—Teta, Pepi (Merira), Merenra, and Neferkara. Probable Position of Ati. Reign of Teta. Reign of Pepi—First great War—Reflections to which it gives rise—Pepi's Pyramid and Titles—Position of Una under him—Family of Pepi. Reign of Merenra. Reign of Neferkara. Traditions respecting Nitocris. Sudden Decline of Egypt at the Close of the Sixth Dynasty. Culmination of the early Egyptian Art, and Advance of Civilization under it, - 53

CHAPTER XVI.

THE DYNASTIES BETWEEN THE SIXTH AND THE TWELFTH.

No Monuments left by any Dynasty between the Sixth and the Eleventh, which were, however, separated by an Interval. Disintegration of Egypt—Parallel Kingdoms of Memphis, Heracleopolis, and Thebes. Causes of the Disintegration and Decline; and probable Length of the Interval. Situation of Thebes. Its Antiquity, Name, and primitive Position. Rise of Thebes to Independence. Dynasty of the Antefs and Mentu-hoteps. Reign of Sankhkara. Expedition to Punt. Close of the Dynasty. Features of the Early Theban Civilization, - - - - - - - - - - 66

CHAPTER XVII.

THE TWELFTH DYNASTY.

Period of Disturbance. Accession of Amen-em-hat I.—His Military Expeditions—His great Works—His Addiction to Field Sports—He associates his Son Usurtasen, and leaves him written "Instructions." Reign of Usurtasen I.—His Obelisks—His Temples—His Cushite War—His Chief Officers, Ameni and Mentu-hotep—His Association of Amen-em-hat II. Reign of Amen-em-hat II. Reigns of Usurtasen II. and Usurtasen III. Conquest of Ethiopia, and construction of Forts at Semneh and Koommeh. Usurtasen III. the Original of the mythic Sesostris—Estimate of his Character. Reign of Amen-em-hat III.—His Throne Name—His great Irrigation Scheme—His Nilometer—His Palace and Pyramid—His other Works. Reigns of Amen-em-hat IV. and Sabak-nefru-ra. Civilization of the Period—Arts of Life. Architecture and Glyptic Art—Changes in the Religion, - - - 77

CONTENTS.

CHAPTER XVIII.

THE DYNASTIES BETWEEN THE TWELFTH AND THE SEVENTEENTH.

PAGE

The Thirteenth (Theban) Dynasty in part contemporary with the Fourteenth (Xoïte) and the Fifteenth and Sixteenth (Shepherds). Decline of Egypt at this period. Names and scanty Memorials of the Kings. Permanent Semitic Pressure on the Northeastern Frontier. Invasion brought about by previous disturbance and disintegration, - - - - - - 95

CHAPTER XIX.

THE MIDDLE EMPIRE—CONQUEST OF EGYPT BY THE HYKSOS.

Certainty of the Hyksos Conquest. Growing Power of the Tribes to the East of the Delta—the Sakti—the Kharu—the Shasu. Temptations offered by Egypt to Invaders. First Lodgments effected in her Territory. Consequent Excitement among the Eastern Tribes. Question of the Nationality of the Hyksos. Circumstances of the Conquest. Character of the Hyksos' Rule. Advantages which it conferred on Egypt. Reigns of the Hyksos Kings. Apepi's Quarrel with Ra-Sekenen. War ensues and ends in the Expulsion of the Hyksos. Supposed Synchronism of Joseph with Apepi, - 100

CHAPTER XX.

THE NEW EMPIRE—EGYPT UNDER THE EIGHTEENTH DYNASTY (ABOUT B.C. 1600-1400).

Reign of Aahmes—his War with the Hyksos—his Expedition against the South—his Buildings—his Wife, Nefert-ari-Aahmes. Reign of Amen-hotep I. Reign of Thothmes I.—his Nubian Conquests—his Syrian and Mesopotamian War—his Monuments. Short Reign of Thothmes II. Accession of Hatasu—her Buildings and other Monuments—her Fleet sails to Punt—her Association of Thothmes III., and Death. Glorious Reign of Thothmes III. His Invasion of Asia. Enemies with whom he came into contact—the Kharu, the Zahi, the Khita, the Ruten, the Nahiri. Reduction of Syria. Success in Mesopotamia—Elephant Hunt. Booty carried off. Inscriptions set up by Thothmes III. His Buildings, Statues, and Obelisks. His Employment of forced Labor. Condition of the Israelites under him. His Southern Wars. His supposed Maritime Empire. Summary of his Character. Reign of Amen-hotep II. His Wars and Buildings. Reign of Thothmes IV. His Temple to the Sphinx. His Wars. His Lion Hunts. Reign of Amen-hotep III. His Wife Taia.

Commencement of the Disk Worship. His Wars. His Buildings and Statues. His Love of Field Sports—Personal Appearance and Character. Reign of Amen-hotep IV., or Khuenaten. His strange Physiognomy. His Establishment of the Disk Worship. His new Capital. His Wars. Reigns of Sa'a-nekht, Ai, and Tutankh-amen. Restoration of the Old Religion. Reign of Hor-em-heb. Close of the Dynasty, 112

CHAPTER XXI.

THE NINETEENTH DYNASTY (ABOUT B.C. 1400–1280).

Accession of Rameses I. His Syrian War. Accession of Seti I. His Wars with the Shasu, Karu, and Khita. Peace made with the Khita. Timber cut in Lebanon. Recovery of Mesopotamia. Wars with the Libyans and Ethiopians. Seti's great Works. His Table of Kings. His Personal Appearance. His Association of his Son, Rameses. Reign of Rameses Meriamon. Over-estimate formed of him. His Wars—with the Negroes and Ethiopians—with the Hittites—with Naharain. His Treaty of Peace with the Hittites—Importance of it. He marries a Hittite Princess. His later African Wars. Large number of his Captives—Plan pursued in locating them—their Employment. Great Works of Rameses —useful and ornamental. His Personal Appearance, Domestic Relations, and Character.—Accession of his Son, Menephthah—His troubled Reign. Insignificance of his Monuments. Pacific Character of his Foreign Policy. Sudden Invasion of Egypt by the Libyans and their Allies. Proposed Identification of these Allies with European Nations. Repulse of the Libyan Attack. Relations of Menephthah with the Israelites under Moses. Troubles of his later years. Struggle between his Son, Seti II., and Amon-mes, or Amon-meses. Brief Reigns of these Monarchs.—Reign of Siphthah. Period of Anarchy. Civilization of Egypt under the Eighteenth and Nineteenth Dynasties—Architecture and its Kindred Arts—Religion—Manners and Customs—Literature. Drawbacks on the general Prosperity, - - - 154

CHAPTER XXII.

THE TWENTIETH DYNASTY (ABOUT B.C. 1280–1100).

Accession of Setnekht—his Birth and Parentage doubtful. His brief Reign. His Tomb. Setnekht associates his Son, Rameses. Reign of Rameses III. His Appellations. His new Arrangement of the Official Classes. His Wars—with the Shasu—with the Libyans—with the great Confederacy

CONTENTS. vii

PAGE

of the Tânauna, Shartana, Sheklusha, Tulsha,Uashesh, Purusata, and Tekaru—with the Mashausha—with the Negroes and Ethiopians—with the Nations of Syria. His great Works. His Planting of Trees. His Encouragement of Mining and Trade. The Conspiracy against him. His Domestic History. His Personal Appearance and Character. His Tomb. Rapid Decline of Egypt after his Death—its Causes. Reigns of Rameses IV., Rameses V., Rameses VI. and Meri-Tum, Rameses VII. and VIII. Reign of Rameses IX. and Commencement of Priestly Encroachment. Reigns of Rameses X. and XI. Rameses XII. and the Princess of Bakhtan. Reign of Rameses XIII. General View of the Period—Decline of Architecture, Art, and Literature—Deterioration of Morals—slight Changes in Civilization and Habits of Life, - - - - - - - - - - 195

CHAPTER XXIII.

THE TWENTY-FIRST DYNASTY (ABOUT B.C. 1100–975).

Accession of Her-hor, the first Priest-King. Chief Features of his Reign. His Semitic Connection. His Titles, Personal Appearance, and Character. Doubtful Reign of Piankh. Reign of Pinetem. His Son, Men-khepr-ra. re-establishes Tranquility at Thebes. Uneventful Reign of Men-khepr-ra. Later Kings of the Dynasty. General Prevalence of Peace and Prosperity. Duration of the Dynasty, - - - 219

CHAPTER XXIV.

THE TWENTY-SECOND AND CONTEMPORARY DYNASTIES (ABOUT B.C. 975–750).

The Twenty-second Dynasty not Assyrian, but Bubastite. Ancestors of Sheshonk I.—his Royal Descent—his Marriage with a Tanite Princess. His reception of Jeroboam—his great Expedition into Palestine—his Arabian Conquests. His Bas-reliefs and Buildings. His two sons—Death of the elder, and Accession of Osarkon I. Peaceful Reign of Osarkon. Reigns of Takelut I. and Osarkon II. Expedition of "Zerah the Ethiopian." Reigns of Sheshonk II., Takelut II., Sheshonk III., Pimai, and Sheshonk IV. Other Contemporary Kings. Rise of Piankhi. Disappearance of Art and Literature under the Sheshonks, - - - - - - 223

CHAPTER XXV.

THE ETHIOPIAN PHARAOHS (ABOUT B.C. 750–650).

Geography of Ethiopia, and Condition of the Ethiopians about B.C. 750. Position and Importance of Napata. Connection

of its Kings with the Egyptian Pharaohs. Sudden Rise of
Piankhi to Power, and Nature of his Rule over Egypt. Re-
volt of Tafnekht. Great Civil War and Re-establishment of
Piankhi's Authority. Revolt and Reign of Bocchoris. In-
vasion of Shabak (Sabaco). His Reign. His Monuments.
First Contest between Egypt and the Assyrian Kingdom of
the Sargonids. Reign of Shabatok. Accession of Tirhakah.
His Connection with Hezekiah. His First Assyrian War.
His Monuments. His Second War with the Assyrians. His
Death. Reigns of Rutammon and Miammon-Nut. End of
the Ethiopian Power in Egypt, - - - - - - - 231

CHAPTER XXVI.

THE TWENTY-SIXTH DYNASTY (B.C. 650–527).

Depressed State of Egypt at the Close of the Ethiopic Rule. Communications between Psammetichus I. and Gyges of Lydia.
Battle of Momemphis and Establishment of the Power of
Psammetichus over the whole of Egypt. Personal Appearance and supposed Libyan Origin of Psammetichus. Settlement of the Greeks at Bubastis. Revolt and Secession of
the "Warriors." Other Results of the Greek Influx. Psammetichus takes Ashdod. He buys off the Scyths. His
Buildings. Accession of Neco. His Two Fleets. His Ship-
canal. His Circumnavigation of Africa. His Expedition
to Carchemish. Counter-Expedition of Nebuchadnezzar.
Reign of Psammetichus II. His War with Ethiopia. Reign
of Apries. His First War with Nebuchadnezzar. His
Phœnician War. His Second Babylonian War and Deposition. His Obelisk and Inscriptions. Reign of Amasis.
Condition of Egypt under him. He conquers Cyprus and
makes alliance with Lydia. His great Works. His Wives.
Short Reign of Psammetichus III. Egypt conquered by
Cambyses. Civilization and Art under the Twenty-sixth
Dynasty. Novelties in Religion. Changes in Manners. Con-
clusion. - - - - - - - - - - - - 245

APPENDIX.

Note A. (see p. 5) - - - - - - - - - - 271
Note B. (see p. 199) - - - - - - - - - - 272
List of Authors and Editions - - - - - - - 276
Index - - - - - - - - - - - - - 281

LIST OF ILLUSTRATIONS.

FIG.	PLATE
Statues of a Man and his Wife (from Mariette's "Monuments Divers")...............*Frontispiece*	
1. Tomb near the Pyramids (from the "Description de l'Egypte")	1
2. Dog and Antelope (from Lepsius's "Denkmäler").....	1
3. Head of Egyptian Noble—early period (from the same).........	1
4. Tablet of Seneferu at Wady Magharah (from the same)........	2
5. Tablet of Khufu at Wady Magharah (from the same)........	2
6. Tablet of Sahura at Wady Magharah (from the same)........	3
7. Tablet of Pepi (from the same)...	3
8. Earliest Sandals (from the same).	4
9. Headdresses worn by Women (from the same)...............	4
10. Ornaments worn by Men (from the same)..................	4
11. Second type of Egyptian Dog (from the same)..................	4
12. Dog resembling a Turnspit (from the same)...	4
13. Tablet of Mentu-hotep II. (from the same)	5
14. Dresses worn under the Twelfth Dynasty (from the same)	5
15. Obelisk of Usurtasen I. at Heliopolis	6
16. Nefer-hotep receiving life from Anuka (from Lepsius's "Denkmäler").	8
17. House on Piles in the Land of Punt (from Dümichen's "Flotte einer ägyptischen Königin")...	8
18. Bust of Amenôphis I. (from Lepsius's "Denkmäler"),,,,,,,,,,	9

FIG.	PLATE
19. Head of Thothmes II. (from the same)...........................	9
20. Bust of Thothmes I. (from the same).......	9
21. Head of Queen Hatasu (from the same).....	9
22. Head of Queen Mutemua (from the same)	10
23. Head of Seti I. (from the same)..	10
24. Bas-relief of Menxaunor (from the Vicomte de Rougé's "Recherches"................	11
25. Head of Queen Tii (from Lepsius's "Denkmäler")..................	11
26. Head of Horemheb (from the same)........................,......	12
27. Bust of Thothmes III. (from the same)........................,..	12
28. Remarkable Capital (from the same)....................	12
29. The Twin Colossi of Amenôphis III. (called by the Greeks Memnon)	13
30. Head of Thothmes IV. (from Lepsius's "Denkmäler")	14
31. Head of Amenôphis IV. (from the same)............	14
32. Head of Menephthah (from the same)	15
33. Head of Amenôphis III. (from the same)	15
34. Novel Headdresses of Kings (from the same).....................	16
35. Head of Nefertari-Aahmes (from the same).....................	16
36. Dress of a Noble in the time of Rameses III....................	17
37. New style of Sandal (from the same),,,,,,,,,,,,,,,,,,,,,,,,	17

LIST OF ILLUSTRATIONS.

FIG.	PLATE
38. Head of Miammon Nut (from Mariette's "Monuments Divers")	17
39. Varieties of Female Apparel (from Lepsius's "Denkmäler")	17
40. Peculiar Headdress of Nefertari-Aahmes (from the same)	17
41. Throne of Egyptian King (from the same)	18
42. Ornamental Carving—Ethiopian (from the same)	19
43. Head of Set-nekht (from the same)	19
44. Head of Rameses IV. (from the same)	20
45. Head of Rameses III. (from the same)	20
46. Head of Rameses IX. (from the same)	21
47. Head of Psammetichus I. (drawn by the author from a bas-relief in the British Museum)	22
48. Head of Her-hor (from Lepsius's "Denkmäler")	22
49. Head of Shabatok (from the same)	23
50. Head of Sheshonk I. (from the same)	23
51. Head of Osarkon II. (from the same)	24
52. Head of Shabak or Sabaco (from the same)	24
53. Head of Tirhakah (from Rosellini's "Monumenti Storici")	25
54. Head of Seti II. (from Lepsius's "Denkmäler")	25
55. Capital of Pillar, belonging to time of the Psammetichi (from the same)	25
56. Piankhi receiving the Submission of Namrut and others (from Mariette's "Monuments Divers")	26
57. Bas-reliefs of Psammetichus I. (from the same)	26
58. Supposed Head of Rehoboam (from Rosellini's "Monumenti Storici")	27
59. Head of Rameses II. (from Lepsius's "Denkmäler")	27
60. Upper portion of Statue of Shafra (from the Vicomte de Rougé's "Recherches")	27
61. Head of Osarkon I. (from Rosellini's "Monumenti Storici")	27
62. Curious ornament, perhaps a Charm, worn by a Man of the Psamatik period (from Lepsius's "Denkmäler")	28
63. Dresses of a Noble and his Wife in the time of the Twentieth Dynasty (from Lepsius's "Denkmäler")	28

Map of the Fayoum (showing the Berket-el-Keroun, and the artificial Lake Moeris) ... 7

HISTORY

OF

ANCIENT EGYPT.

CHAPTER XII.

THE CHRONOLOGY.

Difficulties of the Subject—whence arising. Chronological Deficiencies of the Monuments. Schemes of Manetho, of Herodotus, of Diodorus, untrustworthy. Impossibility of an exact Chronology. Limits of the Uncertainty—(1) for the Third Period, or "New Empire;" (2) for the Second or Hyksos Period ("the Middle Empire")—(3) for the First or Earliest Period (the "Old Empire"). Possibility of an instructive History without exact Chronology.

It is a patent fact, and one that is beginning to obtain general recognition, that the chronological element in the early Egyptian history is in a state of almost hopeless obscurity. Modern critics of the best judgment and the widest knowledge, basing their conclusions on identically the same data, have published to the world views upon the subject which are not only divergent and conflicting, but which differ, in the estimates that are the most extreme, to the extent of above three thousand years! Böckh gives for the year of the accession of Menes (M'na), the supposed first Egyptian king, the year B.C. 5702, Unger the year B.C. 5613, Mariette-Bey and Lenormant B.C. 5004, Brugsch-Bey B.C. 4455, Lauth B.C. 4157, Lepsius B.C. 3852, Bunsen B.C. 3623 or 3059, Mr. Reginald Stuart Poole B.C. 2717, and Sir Gardner Wilkinson B.C. 2691.' It is as if the best authorities upon Roman history were to tell us, some of them that the Republic was founded in B.C. 508, and others in B.C. 3508. Such extraordinary divergency argues something unique in the conditions of the problem to be solved; and it is the more remarkable, since the materials for the history are abundant, and include sources of the most unimpeachable character. The best of ancient classical historians has left an important monograph on the history of the Egyptians;² a native writer of high position and intelligence[3] wrote an elaborate work upon the subject, whereof we possess several extracts and an epitome; and the monuments discovered in the country and recently deciphered contain a mass of historical information more varied, more abundant, and more curious than has been yielded by the researches made in any other of the great seats of early empire.

The chronological value of these various sources of information is, however, in every case slight. The great defect of the monuments is their incompleteness. The Egyptians had no era. They drew out no chronological schemes. They cared for nothing but to know how long each incarnate god, human or bovine, had condescended to tarry upon the earth. They recorded carefully the length of the life of each Apis bull, and the length of the reign[4] of each king; but they neglected to take note of the intervals between one Apis bull and another, and omitted to distinguish the sole reign of a monarch from his joint reign with others. A monarch might occupy the throne ten years in conjunction with his father, thirty-two years alone, and three years in conjunction with his son—in an Egyptian royal list[5] he will be credited with forty-five years, although his first ten years will be assigned also to his father, and his last three to his son. Contemporary dynasties, if accepted as legitimate, will appear in an Egyptian list as consecutive, while dynasties not so accepted, however long they may have reigned, will disappear altogether. Only one calculation of the time which had elasped between a monarch belonging to one dynasty and one belonging to another has been found in the whole range of Egyptian monumental literature, and in that—which is the (apparently) rough estimate of "four hundred years"—neither the *terminus a quo* nor the *terminus ad quem* is determined. Generally speaking, the Egyptian monumental lists are not chronological at all; the only one which is so, the Turin papyrus, exists in tattered fragments, the original order of which is uncertain, while the notices of time which it once contained are in many cases lost or obliterated. The latest historian of Egypt says of it: "As the case stands at present, no mortal man possesses the means of removing the difficulties which are inseparable from the attempt to restore the original list of kings from the fragments of the Turin papyrus. Far too many of the most necessary elements are wanting to fill up the *lacunæ*. . . . It also appears certain that the long series of the kings, which the papyrus once contained, was arranged by the author according to his own ideas and views."[6]

It may be added that the chronological element is altogether
wanting in the earlier part of the papyrus, while, as the papyrus itself belongs to the time of the eighteenth dynasty, it
furnishes no materials at all either for the chronology or the
history of the later kingdom. These many and great defects
of the Turin papyrus it is quite impossible to supply from
any other monumental source. Occasional corrections of the
numbers given in the papyrus may be made from the annals
of the kings; but there is no possibility of filling up its gaps
from the monuments, nor of constructing from them alone
anything like a consecutive chronological scheme, either for
the Early, the Middle, or even the Later Empire.[7] The
Middle Empire—that of the Hyksos—left no monuments at
all; and from the monuments alone no estimate of its duration can be formed. The Early and the Later Empires left
important monuments, but not a continuous series of them;
and the result is that, even for the last, a monumental chronology is absolutely unattainable.

Under these circumstances it is scarcely probable that modern historians would have made any attempts to reconstruct
the chronology of Ancient Egypt, had not certain schemes on
the subject descended to them from their predecessors in the
historical field, possessing, or appearing to possess, a certain
amount of authority. Herodotus, the earliest of classical in-
quirers into Eygptian history, laid it down that the monarchy
had lasted between eleven and twelve thousand years before
its destruction by Cambyses.[8] He partitioned out this time
among 347 kings, of whom, however, he mentioned nineteen
only by name. Of these one had built Memphis;[9] another
had constructed the Lake Mœris;[10] three, who were consecutive, had built the three great pyramids;[11] another had set up
the two chief obelisks at Heliopolis;[12] and so on. His chronology was very imperfect, and not altogether consistent.[13]
Still, it seemed to furnish an outline; and it contained some
important synchronisms, as one with the Trojan war,[14] and
another with Sennacherib.[15] It professed to have been derived from the Egyptian priests, men especially "well skilled in
history;" and it represented, according to the writer, not the
views of any one school, but those in which the three great
sacerdotal colleges of Thebes, Memphis, and Heliopoli- were
agreed.[16]

Another Greek writer of repute, Diodorus Siculus, while
less exact than Herodotus, seemed to furnish some important
additions to his chronological scheme, and some corrections
of it; since, while—to speak generally—following in Herod-

otus's footsteps, he occasionally added a king to the Herodotean list, and also frequently noted that several generations intervened between monarchs whom Herodotus represented as immediately succeeding one the other.

Great vagueness, however, must have characterized any chronology which should have based itself simply on the views and statements of these two authors, and had it not been for the extant remains of a third writer upon the history of Ancient Egypt, it is scarcely probable that any of the complete chronological schemes, to which we have adverted, would ever have been composed, much less published. It happens, however, that, in the third century before the Christian era, a native Egyptian priest, named Manetho, wrote for the information of the Greeks, then recently settled in Egypt as the dominant race, a history of his country, which was professedly complete and in a certain sense continuous, and which contained a vast number of chronological statements, though not (so far as appears) anything like a definite chronology. Manetho's work was not so much a history of Egypt as a history of the Egyptian kings, whom he divided into thirty dynasties, which he treated of separately, apparently without distinctly marking whether they were contemporaneous or consecutive.[17] Against each king's name was set the number of years that he reigned; and at the close of each account of a dynasty these years were added together and the total sum given.[18] The imperfection of the method was twofold. Joint reigns were counted as if they had been successive in the summation of the years of a dynasty;[19] and, contemporary dynasties not being in many cases distinctly marked, the sum total of all the years of the dynasties was greatly in excess of the real period during which the monarchy had lasted. In early times attempts were made to correct the serious chronological errors thus resulting. Eratosthenes reduced the 2,900 years [20] of Manetho's "Old Empire" to 1,076;[21] and a later writer, probably Panodorus, cut down the 5,000, or more, of the entire thirty dynasties to 3,555;[22] but it does not appear that either writer possessed trustworthy data for his conclusions, or reached them in any other way than by arbitrary alteration and a free use of conjecture. Scholars of the present day have probably quite as ample materials for criticising Manetho's scheme as either Panodorus or Eratosthenes, but are better aware of, or more ready to acknowledge, their insufficiency for the purpose.

It adds to the difficulty of eliciting a satisfactory chronology from Manetho's work, that we possess it only in epitomes, and that these epitomes are conflicting. Two writers of Christian times, Africanus, probably in the second century, and Eusebius in the fourth, professed to give a synopsis of Manetho's dynasties, with his numbers. The actual work of Africanus is wholly lost; that of Eusebius has come down to us, but only in an Armenian version. While, however, the originals of both were still in existence, they were read by a Byzantine court official, George the Syncellus (ab. B.C. 800), who embodied the main statements of both writers, as he understood them, in his "Chronography." This work is extant; and thus we have what are in fact three professed epitomes of Manetho, one by Africanus, and two rival claimants to represent the original epitome of Eusebius—the Armenian translation, and the recension of George the Syncellus. If the numbers in the three epitomes corresponded, we should be tolerably sure that we possessed Manetho's actual views; but they do not correspond—on the contrary, they differ very considerably. The total number of years assigned by Manetho to his thirty dynasties is given, in the Eusebius of the Syncellus, as 4,728; in the Armenian Eusebius as 5,205; in the Africanus of the Syncellus as 5,374.[23] The total assigned to a dynasty is very rarely the same in the three versions,[24] the difference between the totals sometimes amounting to hundreds of years. The result is that we do not know with any exactness what Manetho's real numbers were; much less what were his real chronological views, if he had any.

Finally, it has to be borne in mind that Manetho's chronological statements, even when fully ascertained by the agreement of all the epitomes, are not unfrequently contradicted by the monuments, and consequently rejected by all modern critics.[25] This occurs even in the later part of the history, where the dates are, as nearly as possible, certain. If Manetho could make mistakes with respect to the reigns of kings who were removed from his time by no more than three centuries, how can he be implicitly trusted with respect to reigns at least twenty centuries earlier?

The entire result is: (1) that Manetho's general scheme, being so differently reported, is in reality unknown to us; (2) that its details, being frequently contradicted by the monuments,[26] are untrustworthy; and (3) that the method of the scheme, the general principles on which it was constructed, was so faulty, that, even if we had it before us in its entirety, we could derive from it no exact or satisfactory chronology.

Thus the defect of the monuments is not made up to us by the chronological data which are supplied by authors. These latter are copious; but they resolve themselves ultimately into statements made by the Egyptian priests for the satisfaction of the Greeks and Romans upon points on which they felt no interest themselves, and on which their records did not enable them to give exact information. The Egyptians themselves, it can never be too often repeated, "had no chronology." It never occurred to them to consider, or to ask, how long a dynasty had occupied the throne. The kings dated their annals by their regnal years;[26] and it is probable that the dates of a king's accession and of his demise were commonly placed on record by the priests of his capital city, so that the entire length of his reign could be known; but no care was taken to distinguish the years of his sole reign from those during which he was associated with his predecessor. Neither were contemporary dynasties distinctly marked, as an ordinary rule. In one case alone did Manetho apparently note that two of the dynasties which he mentioned reigned simultaneously.[29] Yet all modern critics, or almost all, believe that several other instances of contemporaneousness occur in his list.[30] The extent to which the practice of entering contemporaneous or collateral lists is an apparently continuous line has been carried in disputed; and the divergence of the modern chronologies is due principally to the different views which have been taken on this subject. Lenormant makes two out of the thirty dynasties collateral;[31] Brugsch, five;[32] Bunsen, seven;[33] Wilkinson and Stuart Poole, twelve.[34] Until some fresh light shall be thrown upon this point by the progress of discovery, the uncertainty attaching to the Egyptian chronology must continue, and for the early period must be an uncertainty, not of centuries, but of *millennia.*

When the difficulties of Egyptian chronology are stated in this broad way, it may seem at first sight that the entire matter is hopeless, and that historians of Ancient Egypt had best drop out the chronological element from their narratives altogether, and try the experiment of writing history without chronology. But it is not necessary to adopt quite so violent a remedy. The difficulties of the Egyptian chronology are not spread uniformly over the entire period covered by the history; they diminish as we descend the stream of time, and for the period occupied by Manetho's "New Empire" are not much greater than those which meet us in Assyrian, Phœnician, or Jewish history, where it is the usual practice of historians to grapple with them and reduce them to a *minimum.* We propose, therefore, to endeavor, in the remainder of this chapter, to mark the limits of the uncertainty with

Fig. 1.—TOMB NEAR THE PYRAMIDS.—See Page 19.

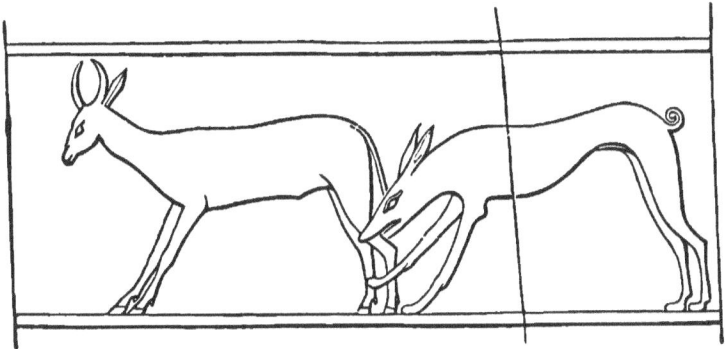

Fig. 2.—DOG AND ANTELOPE, FROM A TOMB NEAR THE PYRAMIDS.—See Page 21.

Fig. 3.—HEAD OF EGYPTIAN NOBLE (early period).—See Page 23.

Plate II. Vol. II.

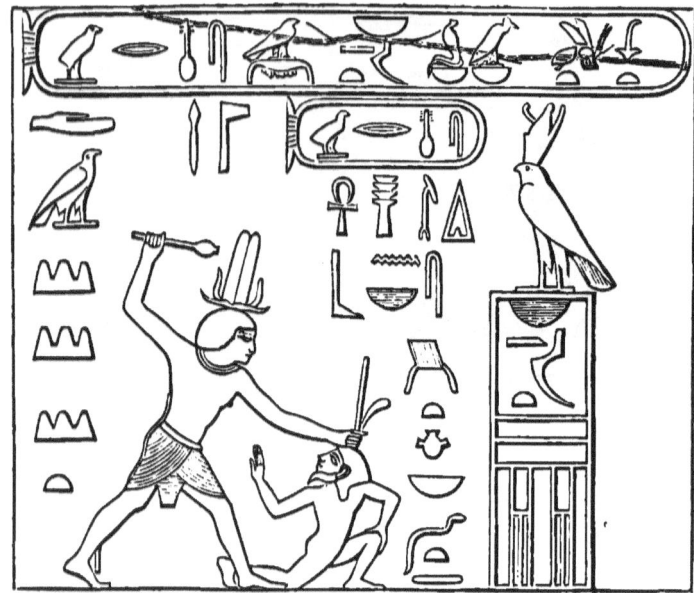

Fig. 4.—TABLET OF SENEFERU AT WADY MAGHARAH.—See Page 26.

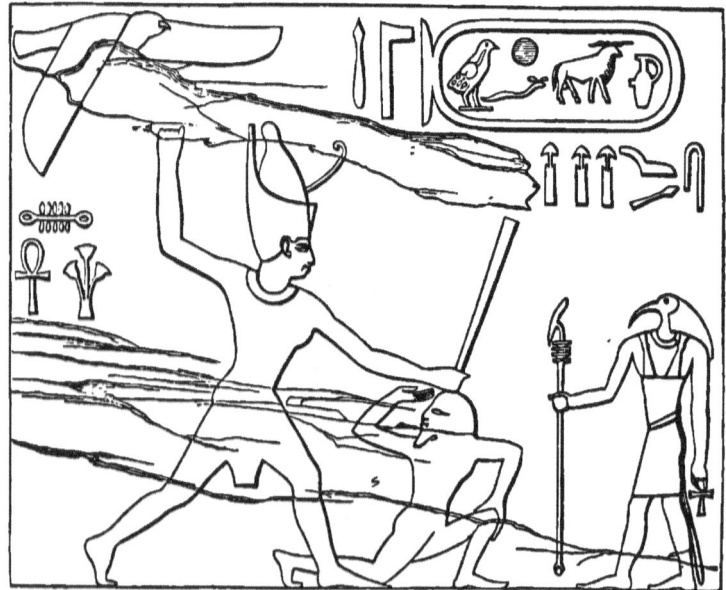

Fig. 5.—TABLET OF KHUFU AT WADY MAGHARAH.—See Page 30.

respect to each of the three periods into which it has been customary, from the time of Manetho, to divide the history of Ancient Egypt.

I. With respect to the latest period, or that of the New Empire. This period includes the last thirteen dynasties of Manetho, or, if we terminate the history of Ancient Eygpt with its conquest by Cambyses and the Persians, it reaches from the beginning of Manetho's eighteenth to the close of his twenty-sixth dynasty, containing thus the history of nine dynasties. These are the eighteenth, nineteenth, and twentieth, Theban; the twenty-first, Tanite; the twenty-second, Bubastite; the twenty-third, Tanite; the twenty-fourth, Saite; the twenty-fifth, Ethiopian; and the twenty-sixth, Saite, like the twenty-fourth. The chronology of this last-named dynasty is very nearly exact. Cambyses conquered Egypt in the year B.C. 527.[35] Psamatik III., whom he dethroned, had reigned only six months;[36] his father, Amasis, forty-four years;[37] Apries, the predecessor of Amasis, probably nineteen years;[38] Psamatik II., the father of Apries, six years;[39] Neco, his grandfather, sixteen years; and Psamatik I., the father of Neco, fifty-four years[40]—total, 145 years. Thus Psamatik I., the founder of the dynasty, ascended the throne in B.C. 672. His immediate predecessor, Tirhakah, reigned twenty-six years,[41] and we may therefore place his accession in B.C. 698. Thus far the dates are, as nearly as possible, certain. They rest mainly upon Egyptian sources, but are confirmed to a considerable extent by Herodotus, and accord with the Scriptural dates for Pharaoh-Hophra (Apries), Pharaoh-Nechoh (Neco), and Tirhakah.[42]

From the date of Tirhakah's accession we are thrown almost wholly upon Manetho. He seems to have ascribed to the two kings, who with Tirhakah, made up the twenty-fifth dynasty, either twenty-two or twenty-four years[43]—which would bring the accession of the dynasty to B.C. 720 or B.C. 722—a date confirmed by the synchronism of Shabak (Seveh or So) with Hoshea.[44]

The Saite dynasty preceding this consisted of but one king, Bocchoris, who reigned either six or forty-four years[45]—the uncertainty now beginning to take larger dimensions. His accession may have been as early as B.C. 766, or as late as B.C. 726. To the two dynasties preceding the twenty-fourth Manetho assigned a period of 209 years,[46] which would make the date for the accession of the twenty-second (Bubastite) dynasty B.C. 975 or B.C. 935. Now this dynasty was founded by the great king Sheshonk, or Shishak, who received Jeroboam as a fugitive,[47] and warred with Rehoboam.[48] It is a remarkable confirmation of the Egyptian numbers that, in the margin of our Bibles, the date for the expedition of Shishak against Rehoboam, calculated from Hebrew and Babylonian sources only, is placed in the year B.C. 971. This synchronism lends a strength and a support to the Egyptian chronology thus far, from which we may reasonably conclude that we are still upon *terra firma*, and have not entered into cloudland.

To the dynasties intervening between the twenty-second and the nineteenth Manetho is said to have given either 265, 302, or 308 years,[49] thus bringing the accession of the twentieth dynasty to B.C. 1283 as a *maximum*, or B.C. 1200 as a *minimum*. The former of the two dates is, on the whole, preferable.[50]

The nineteenth dynasty of Manetho held the throne—according to him—either a little more or a little less than 200 years.[51] It appears, however, by the monuments, that this number is exaggerated; and moderns are not inclined to allow to the dynasty a longer period than about 160 years,[52] which would give for its commencement either B.C. 1360 or B.C. 1463.

Yet greater doubt attaches to the duration of the eighteenth dynasty. Manetho's names and numbers are here in extreme confusion, and are quite irreconcilable with the monuments.[53] The time which he assigned to the dynasty was, according to Eusebius,[54] very nearly three centuries and a half; according to Africanus, a little more than two centuries and a half;[55] according to Josephus, rather less than that period.[56] Moderns vary in their estimates between 180 years and 300,[57] but incline, on the whole, to about 200. This number, if we accept it, will produce for the accession of this great and glorious dynasty, and the inauguration of the New Empire, the year B.C. 1643, for which however, Dr. Birch substitutes B.C. 1600, and Dr. Brugsch B.C. 1700.[58] There are writers who place the date as low as B.C. 1525.[59] Thus the limits of uncertainty in the "New Empire" extend, at the utmost, to somewhat less than two centuries.

II. With respect to the Middle Empire, or period of the Shepherd kings. The limits of uncertainty are here very much increased. Manetho, according to Africanus,[60] gave three dynasties of Shepherds, the fifteenth, sixteenth, and seventeenth of his list, who reigned respectively 284, 518, and 151 years, making the entire period one of 953 years. Josephus reduces this total to 511 years,[61] and the dynasties, apparently, to two. Eusebius allows only a single Shepherd dynasty, and assigns it no more than 103 years.[62] Thus the various reporters of Manetho differ here enormously, varying between one century and nine centuries and a half.

It happens, however, that in this case the monuments come to our aid. There is one which shows Apepi, or Apophis, to have been the last of the Shepherd kings, and contemporary with a certain Ra-Sekenen,[63] who immediately preceded Aahmes, the founder of the eighteenth dynasty. There is another which not obscurely intimates that Set or Saites was (as Manetho also witnesses[64]) the first of the Shepherd kings, and also gives his date as 400 years[65] before some year in the reign of Rameses II. Now the only dynasty of Shepherd kings whose names Manetho gave began with a "Saites" and ended with an "Apophis," according to both Africanus and the Armenian Eusebius; so that there are strong grounds for believing that the rule of the Shepherds really began and ended with this dynasty,[67] to which Manetho assigned 284 years, according to Africanus, or, according to Josephus, 259 years and ten months. These numbers are probably, both of them, in excess; since the dynasty consisted of only six kings, whose united reigns can scarcely have covered more than two centuries. Such an estimate produces for the accession of Saites the probable date of B.C. 1843, which is between four and five hundred years before the probable year for the accession of Rameses II. (about B.C. 1410).

If the four hundred years of the Tanis inscription be regarded as an *exact* number, which is a possible view, the only alterations required in the dates hitherto suggested would be the following. We should have to shorten the periods assigned to the seventeenth and eighteenth dynasties by twenty years each; to make the date for the accession of the eighteenth dynasty B.C. 1623 instead of B.C. 1643; and that for the accession of the seventeenth or Shepherd dynasty B.C. 1803 instead of 1843. The four hundredth year from the accession of Saites will then fall within the reign of Rameses II.

If the views here propounded be accepted, the additional uncertainty attaching to the dates of the "Middle Empire," beyond that which attaches to the earlier part of the "New Empire," will be one of some sixty or eighty years only. As, however, there are still writers of repute, who assign to the Shepherd kings a period of above five centuries, practically the additional uncertainty to the unlearned must be admitted to be one of about three centuries. The "New Empire" commenced its existence not earlier than B.C. 1700, and not later than B.C. 1520; the "Middle Empire" is thought by some o have commenced as early as B.C. 2200, by others as late as B.C. 1720. The uncertainty has now risen from two centuries to five.

III. With respect to the "Old Empire," or native kingdom anterior to the Shepherd invasion. It is in this portion of Egyptian history that the main doubts and difficulties with respect to the chronology occur, and that the uncertainty changes from one measured by centuries to one of *millennia*. Manetho assigned to his first fourteen dynasties terms of years, which, if the dynasties were in all cases consecutive, would make the whole period covered by them one of 2,905 years. Mariette Bey, who scouts altogether the idea of there being any contemporary dynasties in Manetho's list, a little diminishes this amount by corrections of a few of the numbers, and makes the "Old Empire" occupy a space of 2,790 years.[66] Brugsch Bey, who admits, but admits sparingly, the theory of dynasties being contemporary, and substitutes for Manetho's estimates of reigns a calculation by generations,[69] makes a further deduction of nearly four centuries from Manetho's sum total, and gives the old native kingdom a duration of 2,400 years. Baron Bunsen, adopting the "contemporary" idea to a much larger extent than Brugsch, and accepting a calculation of Eratosthenes by which he supposes the real length of the "Old Empire" to have been correctly fixed, reduces it to the comparatively moderate term of 1,076 years, giving for its commencement B.C. 3059.[70] Lastly, Mr. Stuart Poole and Sir Gardner Wilkinson, by still further carrying out the "contemporary" theory, effect a further reduction of about four centuries, assigning to the first native kingdom no longer a period than about six centuries and a half, whereby the commencement of monarchy in Egypt is brought down to about B.C. 2700, or a little later.[71] We have thus for the period of this First Empire an uncertainty extending to above 2,000 years, the maximum term assigned to it by recent writers being 2,790 years, and the minimum 637.

There appear to be at present no means of terminating this controversy. The monuments belonging to the ancient kingdom cluster mainly about four dynasties—the fourth of Manetho, the fifth, the sixth, and the twelfth. A few belong to the eleventh and the thirteenth. There are none which can be positively assigned to kings of the first, second, or third; and thus we have no direct proof of those dynasties having existed. Egyptian monumental history commences with Seneferu,[72] who seems to correspond to Manetho's Soris, the first king of the fourth dynasty. The fourth and fifth dynasties were certainly consecutive; and the sixth probably followed the fifth. The seventh, eighth, ninth, and tenth may have been—probably were—collateral. None of the kings belonging to them have left any monuments; Manetho has not condescended to record their names; and it cannot therefore but be suspected that they were really secondary kings, contemporary with each other, or with the monarchs of the eleventh dynasty, perhaps even with the early monarchs of the twelfth. Again, the fourteenth dynasty is as unknown as the seventh, eighth, ninth, and tenth, and must be placed in the same category. The monuments thus confirm six only of Manetho's first fourteen dynasties; and from seven to nine centuries would perhaps be a sufficient space to allow to these six.

On the other hand, the Egyptian monuments are of such a character that they scarcely ever *prove* any two kings to have been contemporary; and it is therefore quite open for an historian to maintain that all the dynasties are both historical and consecutive, in which case the conclusions of Mariette would be reasonable. The support given by the monuments to some of Manetho's early dynasties being taken to corrobate the whole, and the entire fourteen dynasties being viewed as consecutive, 2,800 years, or an average of 200 to a dynasty, will not be manifestly excessive. It is probable, therefore, that Egyptian chronologists will always be divided into the advocates of a longer and a shorter chronology, the estimate of the former class for the commencement of the monarchy exceeding that of the latter by something like two thousand five hundred years.

Exact chronology is, beyond all doubt, a most important adjunct to history; and, where the foreign relations of a state form a main element in its life, and the parallel histories of distinct countries have to be taken into account, exact chronology, or an approach to it, is a necessity for the proper understanding of the course of affairs, and of the bearing which events in one country had upon those in another. But, where a nation is isolated, or where its history at any rate is unmixed with other histories, and flows on in its own separate channel without contact with any neighboring stream, the need of exact chronology is much less, and a considerable vagueness in the dates may be tolerated. It is possible to have a very fair knowledge of the general character of a river—of the direction of its course, the hue and quality of its waters, the equableness or variableness of its flow, even of the countries upon its bank—without exact acquaintance or anything more than a very vague notion, of its length. It is the same with history. If we can obtain a clear knowledge of the condition of a people at different periods, if we can represent the different phases of its life in the order of their occurrence, if we can—to some extent, at any rate—perceive and appreciate the causes which produced the various alterations, we may present an instructive picture of them—compose an agreeable and useful history—even though we can only conjecture vaguely the length of time during which each condition lasted. It is this which an historian of *early* Egypt must aim at effecting; and if he succeeds in effecting it, he must be satisfied. The chronological riddle is insoluble. He must set it aside. But he needs not therefore to set aside that immense mass of material, possessing the highest interest, which the toils of travellers and explorers, and the patient labors of philologists, have accumulated during the last century. The "Old Empire" of Manetho is a reality. It lives and moves before us in the countless tombs of Ghizeh, Saccarah, and Beni-Hassan, on the rocks of Assouan and the Wady Magharah, on the obelisk of Heliopolis, and in numerous ancient papyri; its epochs are well marked; its personages capable in many cases of being exhibited distinctly; its life as clearly portrayed as that of the classical nations. And that life is worth studying. It is the oldest presentation to us of civilized man which the world contains, being certainly anterior, much of it, to the time of Abraham;" it is given with a fulness and minuteness that are most rare; and it is intrinsically most curious. A picture, therefore, of the Old Empire may well be required of the historian of Ancient Egypt, and will be here attempted, notwithstanding the vagueness of the chronology.

For the "Middle Empire" an approximate chronology will be given. The author is strongly convinced of the shortness of the "Shepherd" period, and cannot bring himself to assign to it a duration of above two centuries. He regards it as commencing about B.C. 1840 and terminating about B.C. 1640.

The dates for the "New Empire" will be found gradually to advance towards absolute exactness. Its commencement, circ. B.C. 1640, is doubtful to the extent already allowed," but the uncertainty of the chronology diminishes with each successive dynasty; and when we reach the twenty-second, it scarcely exceeds twenty years, since the synchronism of Sesonchis with Rehoboam fixes the commencement of that king's reign to some date between B.C. 975 and B.C. 955. From the accession of Tirhakah the chronological difficulties almost disappear, and thenceforth exact dates will take the place of those vague and merely approximate ones which are necessary for the earlier periods.

CHAPTER XIII.

THE OLD EMPIRE—THE FIRST BEGINNINGS.

Uncertainty of the Succession of the Early Kings—Official Order, determined on after the Expulsion of the Shepherd Kings, not to be viewed as historical. The List, as given by the Chief Native Authorities. Doubts as to the Existence of Menes. Remarks on the Name Athothis. Ilesepti mentioned in the Ritual. Distinction attaching to Meribipu. Variations in the Lists. General Character of the Names. The traditional Notices of the Monarchs scanty and valueless. Condition of the Egyptian people at this early time. Character of their Art and of their Religion. Principal Features of their Life.

'Ανεξέλεγκτα καὶ τὰ πολλὰ ὑπὸ χρόνου αὐτῶν ἀπίστως ἐπὶ τὸ μυθῶδες ἐκνενικηκότα.—
THUCYD. i, 21.

WHEN the great monarchs of native Eygptian blood, who bore sway in Egypt after the expulsion of the "Shepherd" kings, resolved, for the "honor of their excellent majesty," to set forth before the eyes of their subjects the long list of their royal predecessors, and for this purpose ransacked such remains of the "Old Empire" as had survived the "shipwreck" of the state brought about by those foreign invaders,[1] they undertook a task for which it may be doubted whether there existed any sufficient materials. Egyptian civilization had been annihilated by an avalanche of barbarians;[2] the whole country had been devastated; tombs had been rifled, papyri burnt or torn to shreds, even the stone monuments partially defaced and injured; how should the succession of kings from father to son during a space of even seven centuries be recovered after so complete an overthrow and destruction of all that had gone before? Royal names, rendered conspicuous by the *cartouches* enclosing them, existed no doubt in large numbers, as they exist to this day, on monuments which had escaped the wear and tear of time and the ravages of the "Tartars of the South;"[3] but what clue could there have been to their true order and proper arrangement? what means of discovering the real relationship of the kings who bore them? Egyptian monarchs did not, ordinarily, glorify their predecessors, or even put on record the name of their true father. They merged their earthly in their heavenly parentage, and spoke of Horus, or Ra, or Ammon, or Phthah as their fathers, totally ignoring the real sire from whose loins they had sprung. Private persons, in the inscriptions upon their tombs, might sometimes indicate the succession of two or three monarchs under whom they flourished; but this would be a very partial and incomplete means of arriving at the truth, and it would be altogether wanting for the earliest period.[4] It would seem that there must have been a large amount of arbitrariness in the order which was assigned to the names recovered from the monuments, as there certainly was in the number of the ancestors which the different monarchs claimed to themselves.[5]

Still a certain order, presenting fewer variations than might have been expected, seems to have been arrived at, and to have become, at any rate, the officially recognized one; and this order, though it has no claims to be regarded as historical, must, under existing circumstances, be placed before the reader, both as being the basis on which various "Histories of Eygpt" are built, and as that which is supported by the largest amount of authority. It is not certain that all the kings on the list are real personages, or that some of those who are did not reign contemporaneously; but on the whole there is ground for believing that the great majority of them were kings who actually bore sway in some part of Egypt before the erection of the pyramids; and though the bare names tell us little, and the traditions which belong to them are almost worthless, yet a certain interest attaches even to mere names of so ancient a date, and for the full understanding of the later native kingdom it is important to know what its belief was as to that more ancient monarchy from which it claimed descent, and with which it strove to establish in every way a solidarity and a continuity.

The subjoined is a tabular arrangement of the early Egyptian kings, according to the chief native authorities. It is, in its principal features, based upon the table drawn up by M. de Rougé in his interesting "Researches," but embodies corrections which he subsequently made, and a few alterations of names from other sources.

A few remarks only need be made on these names. In Mena, or M'na, the supposed first king—the Mén of Herodotus,[6] the Men-es of Manetho,[7] and the Men-as of Diodorus[8] —we have probably no real personage,[9] but a *heros eponymus*, the mythic *establisher* of the kingdom,"⁰ and founder of the first capital, Memphis. The Egyptian name, which the Greeks made into Memphis, is *Men-nofer*," 𓏠𓐍𓈖𓋴 , "the good station," or "the good establishment;" and M'na, 𓏠𓈖, is the "*establisher*" or "founder" of this "station." The name has not been discovered on any monument of the Early Empire.¹³ It first appears in the "New Table of Abydos," where it heads the list set up by Seti I., the second king

The Early Kings.

Manetho (according to Africanus).	Fragments of the Turin Papyrus.	New Table of Abydos. (Seti I.)	Table of Saccarah (time of Rameses II.)
Dyn. I.			
1. Menes	Fr. 1. { Mena	Mena	
2. Athothis	... a	Teta	
3. Kenkenes		Atet	
4. Uenephes	... a	Ata	
5. Usaphædus	Hesepti	Hesepti	
6. Miebidus	Meribipen	Meribipu	Meribipen
7. Semempses	Ati ?	Ati ?	
8. Bieneches	Fr. 20. { ... buhu	Kabuhu	Kabuhu
Dyn. II.			
9. Boêthus		Butau	Neterbiu
10. Kæechôs	.... ka	Kakau	Kakau
11. Binothris	.... nuter	Binnuter	Binutera
12. Tlas	..... es	Utnas	Utnas
13. Sêthenes	Senta	Senta	Senta
14. Chæres	(Nefer)ka		
15. Nefercheres			Neferkara
16. Sesochris	Fr. 19. { Neferka-Sokari		Sokari-neferka
17. Cheneres	(Hu)tefa		....., tefa
Dyn. III.	Beb ...	(Teti)	Bebi
18. Necherôphes	Nebka	Nebka	
19. Tosorthrus	Sar	Sar-sa	Sar
20. Tyreis	Sar-teta	Teta	Sar-teta
21. Mesochris		Setes	
22. Sôyphis		Neferkara	
23. Tosertasis			Ra-nebka
25. Aches, etc.	Huni		Huni
Dyn. IV.			
28. Soris	Seneferu	Senefera	Senefera

of the nineteenth dynasty;¹³ it is found again in the list of Rameses II., at the Rameseum;¹⁴ and appears also on a fragment of the Turin papyrus. But we have no evidence that it was known in Egypt earlier than about B.C. 1440.

Of the kings Teta, 𓏏𓏏, Atet, 𓉔, and Ata 𓅂, there is no other record than the occurrence of their names in the list of Seti I., and some supposed remains of them in the fragments of the Turin papyrus.[15] The Greeks seem to have expressed all three names by the form Athóthis[16] or Athóthes,[17] which seems like a Grecized form of the god of learning, Thoth. It was perhaps with some reference to this connection that the first Athóthis was said to have been a physician and to have written books on anatomy.[18]

The fifth king in the list of Seti I., who appears also in a fragment of the Turin papyrus, the king Hesepti or Hesep, ☷☷ (called Uasaphædus by Manetho), is mentioned in several copies of the "Ritual," or "Book of the Dead," as the author of two of its most important chapters.[19] He is also mentioned in a papyrus of the date of Rameses II., as a king anterior to Senta.[20] The context rather implies that he was immediately anterior;[21] but the expression used is to some extent doubtful. If admitted to have this meaning, it would show that, as early as Rameses II., there were different traditions as to the succession of the ancient monarchs.

The sixth king, Meribipu, the Miebidus of Manetho,[22] has the singular honor of being mentioned in the Turin papyrus, in the list of Seti I., and in that of Saccarah, as well as in the catalogues both of Manetho and Eratosthenes. The list of Saccarah places him at the head of the whole series of kings,[23] as if he had been a monarch of more than common importance. But nothing is recorded of him, either by Manetho or by any other ancient writer, to justify or account for his being held in peculiar honor; no mention is made of him in the "Ritual," nor has his name been found on any monuments of the Early Empire.

In the place of the Semempses of Manetho,[24] who is perhaps Eratosthenes' Pemphôs[25] there appears in the Turin papyrus a name greatly defaced, which M. de Rougé is inclined to read[26] as Ati, ⎜⎟⎜⎟. The New Table of Abydos has an entirely different representation, the *cartouche* containing only a single hieroglyph, which is the figure of a man standing, and holding in his hand the sceptre of a god.[27] It is scarcely possible that this single figure can represent the trisyllabic name of Manetho. That name has been identified[28] with a king, (Ra-hem)-Sementet, who appears in the lists of his ancestors given by Thothmes III., at Karnak, but is ignored by the Turin papyrus, as well as by Seti 1., and the author of the list of Saccarah. Here again we have evidence of a variety in the traditions as to the primitive times current under the early dynasties of the New Empire.

Proof of the same is also furnished by the names Butau and Teti, 〖hieroglyphs〗 in the New Table of Abydos, which are replaced by those of Neter-biu 〖hieroglyph〗 and Bebi 〖hieroglyph〗 in the list of Saccarah and the Turin papyrus,[29] as well as by the substitution of Ranebka and Huni in the Saccarah list for Setes and Neferkara in the Abydos one. The supposition that monarchs of this early period bore two names, which De Rougé makes,[30] is wholly gratuitous, and quite contrary to the monumental evidence, which shows no double name until Ra-n-user of the fifth dynasty.[31]

Of the entire list of names down to Seneferu it is to be observed, that they have an archaic and (as Dr. Brugsch expresses it) a "plebeian" character.[32] "They do not at all resemble the Pharaonic names of succeeding epochs.[33] Consisting uniformly of a single appellation, encircled by a single elliptical line, or *cartouche*, they are, with few exceptions, short, simple, severe. They express moreover, for the most part, ideas of force and terror[34]—Teta, "he who beats"—Huni, "he who strikes"—Kakau, "the chief bull," literally "the bull of bulls" —Senta, "the terrible." Into the titles of the later kings the names of divinities, whom they specially worshipped—Ra, Ammon, Thoth, Phthah, Shabak, Hor, Set—usually enter. Among the names of these early monarchs there are but three which are composed with the appellation of a god. Neferka-Sokari, 〖hieroglyph〗 the ninth in the table of Saccarah, whose name occurs also in a fragment of the Turin papyrus, Neferka-Ra, 〖hieroglyph〗, the predecessor of Seneferu, according to the New Table of Abydos, and Ranebka, or Nebka-Ra, 〖hieroglyph〗, the fourteenth in the Saccarah list, the predecessor of Huni, have a divine element in their names, the first of these names being compounded with the god Sokari, a form of Phthah,[35] and having the signification of "perfect through Sokari," the second meaning "perfect through Ra," and the third, "lord through Ra."

It cannot be said that any facts are really known of these monarchs. Tradition made Mena the founder of Memphis,[36] and his son Teta the builder of the royal palace in that city, and a writer of anatomical books.[37] Hesepti, or Hesep, was regarded as the author of some chapters of the religious work known as the "Book of the Dead."[38] Under Semempses, or

Sementet, who was perhaps a king of this period, there was said to have been a great plague.³⁹ In the time of Butau (Boêthus) the earth gaped near the city of Bubastis, and swallowed up a vast number of persons.⁴⁰ Kakau (Kæchôs) introduced the worship of the Apis-bull at Memphis, the Mnevis-bull at Heliopolis, and the sacred goat at Mendes. Binnuter (Binôthris) made a law that the crown should be allowed to descend to women.⁴¹ Nefer-ka-Sokari was a giant;⁴² and under Nefer-Ka-Ra (Nepher-cheres) the Nile flowed with honey for eleven days.⁴³ Under Necherôphes (Nebka?) the Libyans, who had revolted, made their submission on account of a sudden increase in the moon's size, which terrified them.⁴⁴ Tosorthrus (Sar-sa?) was worshipped after his death as the Egyptian Æsculapius (Aemhetp) on account of his medical skill; he paid attention to inscriptions, and was the first to construct buildings with polished stone.⁴⁵

Such are the traditions which have alone come down to us with respect to these early monarchs. Their value would be but slight, even were they to be depended on: as the case stands, it is difficult to assign them any value at all.⁴⁶ They come to us, almost without exception, from Manetho, who wrote two thousand years after the time, and who, in his accounts of far more recent reigns, is frequently contradicted by contemporary monuments. No doubt Manetho found these traditions in Egyptian authorities; but his credulity was great,⁴⁷ his critical discernment small, his diligence in research less than might have been expected.⁴⁸ To rely on Manetho is to put trust in a writer too negligent to care for truth, and, had he cared, too uncritical to discover it.

It is a relief to turn from the scanty accounts left us of (perhaps) apocryphal kings to the condition of the Egyptian people at this early period. The people certainly existed; and though not very much may be known of their condition, yet an interest attaches to all that is known very greatly beyond that which belongs to kings and dynasties. We propose to consider their condition under the three heads of art, religion, and mode of life, including manners and customs.

The history of Egypt will always be, to a very large extent, a history of art. Art had, so far as we know, its birth and earliest development in the valley of the Nile and grew up there by a natural and gradual progress without being affected to an appreciable extent by any extraneous influences. The earliest of the arts to start into being was no doubt architecture: and its first employment, there as elsewhere, was in the construction of habitations capable of affording shelter from the solar rays, and from the occasional, though not very frequent, showers of hail and rain.[49] The earliest of the Egyptian houses seem to have been of wood, which was easier to work than stone, and which was furnished in tolerable plenty by the palm groves that grew luxuriantly in ancient times, probably along the whole course of the river. Indications of the character of the houses are furnished by some of the most ancient tombs,[50] which, though constructed in stone, bear traces, like the tomb in Lycia,[51] of a preëxistent wooden architecture, which has impressed its forms upon the alien material. The rounded mass of stone which forms the lintel above the doorways of the early tombs [52] can have derived its shape from nothing but a reminiscence of the unsawn palm stem which served the purpose in the primitive mansions; the long thin pilasters and architraves are clear imitations of woodwork; and the latticed windows, most difficult to construct in stone, are such as would be produced by simplest possible arrangement of wooden bars. We may gather from the tombs that the early houses were not without ornament. Alternate pilasters and depressions, adorned with a species of panelling, extended (it would seem) along the entire façade of a house; the door was placed in the middle, and was narrow for its height; over the door was a latticed window of a considerable size, which gave light probably to a central hall, while the rooms on either side of the hall were also lighted by windows, which were small, and placed high up in the walls. The roof would appear to have been flat, and was formed probably by palm-trees split in two, and then covered with a coating of mud or cement.

From the idea of a house for the living the Egyptians passed rapidly, and at a date so early that we cannot possibly fix it, to the idea of a house for the dead. (Fig 1.) Their religious notions required that this last should be as permanent as possible; and it seems certain that, long before houses were built of any other material than wood, stone was carefully quarried and squared to be employed in the construction of the "eternal abodes"[53] of the departed. The earliest sepulchres now extant are stone buildings, looking externally like small houses.[54] They stand isolated, like the monuments in our churchyards, each consisting of an oblong chamber or chambers, enclosed with massive walls, which slope externally at an angle of 75° or 80°, but internally are perpendicular. A single door, in no way concealed, gives entrance into the interior, and it is in the ornamentation of this doorway that we have the representations of houses in wood. The chamber is roofed over with large flat stones; and, if it exceeds a certain size, the roof is supported internally by a massive square stone pier. In this simple and primitive construction we have the germ of the pyramid, which grew up out of it by a number of slight changes.

One of these changes belongs, by general consent,[64] to the period of which we are speaking. In the "tower" or "pyramid of Meydoun"[65] we see an enlarged edition of one of these early tombs, differing from them in greatly increased size and solidity, as well as in the novel feature of superimposed stories in a retreating series, the entire number of the stories being three. The Meydoun pile has a grandeur of its own. Emplaced upon an isolated rocky knoll of some considerable height, and standing in the middle of the grassy plain, "which, green as an emerald, stretches eastward to the holy stream,"[67] it has a proud and imposing appearance, and in almost any other country than Egypt would be considered a monument of high architectural importance. The base measures 200 feet each way, and the height of the edifice is little short of 125 feet. The solid contents amount to nearly three millions of cubic feet.

The great "pyramid of Saccarah," as it is called, which is also thought to belong to these early times,[68] shows a further advance in architectural skill and power on the part of the primitive builders. Like the Meydoun building, it was a tower in stages,—the number of the stages being six,—and, as in the Meydoun building, the external walls sloped inwards at a slight angle. This edifice is even more imposing than that of Meydoun,[69] since it rises to a height of nearly 200 feet, and covers an area of 135,000 square feet, instead of one of only 40,000. It is emplaced upon a rocky plateau, which has an elevation of nearly a hundred feet above the Nile valley, and is a conspicuous object on all sides.

Such, so far as appears, was the furthest point to which architectural skill was carried by the Egyptians of these early days. They did not erect a true pyramid. They did not even venture to build in perpendicular stages. They did not give to their work the minute care and finish of later times.[66] Their loftiest erections were less than half the height of those designed and executed subsequently. Gently, tentatively, the builders advanced from the small to the great, always aiming at solidity and permanence, comparatively careless of ornamentation, and looking to obtain the impressive effect, at which they aimed, by size and massiveness rather than by elegance or beauty.

Glyptic art was also known, and practised within certain limits, at this early period. The most ancient tombs are adorned internally with the sculptured forms of the owner, his wife, his children, his attendants, represented in the low relief peculiar to Egypt. These forms have all the ordinary defects of Egyptian drawing,—the hard outline, the stiff limbs, the ill-made hands, the over-long feet,—but are not greatly inferior even to those of the best epoch. There is a more marked inferiority in the representations of animals (Fig. 2), which are not only stiff but ungainly, not only conventional but absurd.[61] Grouping seems to be an unknown idea; each figure stands by itself, or is followed by its counterpart, the same form being repeated as often as is requisite in order to fill up vacant spaces on the walls of the sepulchral chambers. Sculpture "in the round" was also attempted by the primitive artists; and five or six statues exist which the best Egyptologists assign to a time anterior to that of the Pyramids.[62] Of these M. Lenormant remarks that, "on studying them, we observe a rudeness and indecision of style, which make it clear that at this period Eygptian art was still trying to find the right path, and had not yet formed itself fully."[63]

A single mosaic, supposed to be of the same early date, tends to raise the art of the time to a higher level. Brugsch says of it: "The double picture, a little smaller than the natural size, shows a man and his wife in a dignified attitude sitting by the side of one another in a chair of the form of a die. The brilliancy of the eye—imitated in shining crystal and white ivory and dark ore in a masterly manner—has all the appearance of life." On the whole, he accounts the work "a marvel of art, venerable from its antiquity, and exquisite in its workmanship."[64]

With respect to the religion of this period, the evidence that we possess is rather negative than positive. The twenty-six names of kings supposed to belong to it reveal the worship of two gods only, Ra, and Phthah, or Sokari. The name of a functionary, Thoth-hotep,[65] reveals the worship of Thoth. With regard to the other gods we have no monumental evidence to show whether at this time they were worshipped or no.[66] Certainly, temples of any pretension were not erected, or we should have some remains of them. The oldest existing Eygptian temple belongs to the reign of Chephren[67] (Shafra), the builder of the Second Pyramid; and, though the classical writers ascribe temples to earlier monarchs,[68] and several certainly existed in Khufu's time,[69] yet their fabric must have been slight, and the religion which consisted in the public worship of gods must have been secondary. No doubt Phthah, Ra, and Thoth—possibly Osiris, Isis, Athor, Horus and Set,[10]—received some worship, and there *may* have been buildings dedicated to them as early as there was monarchy in Egypt; but the real practical religion of the primitive period was that worship of ancestors, whereof we have spoken in the previous volume[11] as an important portion of Egyptian religious practice. The sepulchral chambers above described were the true temples of the period; here the worshippers met from time to time for sacred ceremonies; here hymns were sung, offerings made, and services conducted, from which both the dead and the living were expected to derive advantage. The worshippers regarded their sacrifices, libations, and offerings as contributing to the happiness of the departed, and looked to receive from them in return spiritual, or perhaps even temporal, benefits. They viewed their ancestors as still living, and as interested in the condition and prospects of their descendants; they regarded them as invested with a quasi-divinity, probably addressed their prayers to them, and, like the Chinese appealed to them for help and protection.

Hence it would seem that from the first there lay at the root of the Egyptian religion the belief in a future life, and of happiness or misery beyond the grave. Embalming was practised long before the construction of the Pyramids, and mummies were deposited in stone sarcophagi, with a view to their continued preservation.[12] The "Ritual of the Dead" had, we are told, its origin in these times;[13] and, whatever subsequent refinements may have been introduced, it would seem to be certain that the fundamental conceptions of the continuance of the soul after death, its passage through the Lower World, and its ultimate reunion with the body which it once inhabited, must have been entertained by large numbers from the very first beginnings of the nation. Whence these doctrines were derived, who shall say? There is no human name which stands in the history of Eygptian opinion where the name of Zoroaster stands in Persia, or that of Moses in the history of the Jews. The composition of the "Book of the Dead" was ascribed, in the main, to the gods.[14] How it happened that in Egyptian thought the future life occupied so large a space, and was felt to be so real and so substantial, while among the Hebrews and the other Semites it remained, even after contact with Egypt, so vague and shadowy, is a mystery which it is impossible to penetrate. We can only say that so it was; that, from a time anterior to Joseph, or

Vol. II. Plate III.

Fig. 6.—TABLET OF SAHURA AT WADY MAGHARAH.—See Page 38.

Fig. 7.—TABLET OF PEPI.—See Page 56.

Plate IV. Vol. II.

Fig. 8.—EARLIEST SANDALS.—See Page 47.

Fig. 9.—HEADDRESSES WORN BY WOMEN.—See Page 47.

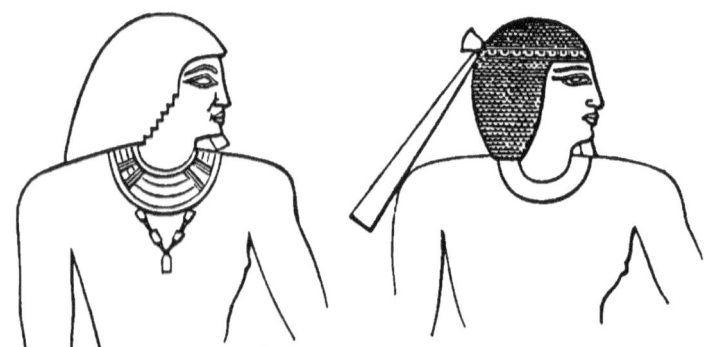

Fig. 10.—ORNAMENTS WORN BY MEN.—See Page 47.

Fig. 11.—SECOND TYPE OF THE EGYPTIAN DOG.—See Page 64.

Fig. 12.—DOG RESEMBLING A TURNSPIT.—See Page 92.

even Abraham, the children of Mizraim, in their bright and fertile land on either side of the strong-flowing Nile, thought as much of the future life as of the present; that their religious ideas clustered rather about the tomb than about the temple; and that their worship, domestic rather than national, though it included among its objects some beings regarded as wholly divine, was directed especially towards the spirits of those who had been their "fathers in the flesh," and were thought to have a natural interest in the welfare of persons sprung from their loins.

There was another worship, also of a practical character, which belongs almost certainly to this early period—the worship of the reigning monarch. Each king was regarded as an incarnation of Horus,[75] was assigned a priest or priests,[76] and a temple, or at any rate a chapel. He was styled "the victorious Horus," "the divine lord," "the ever-living."[77] His subjects worshipped him, not only during his life, but after his death. The priesthood once instituted in a king's honor was maintained ever afterwards; sacrifices were offered to the defunct sovereign at stated intervals; and in this way each occupant of the Egyptian throne, unless some revolution occurred, continued to be held in perpetual remembrance.[78]

Life in Eygpt under the early kings was simpler and less varied than it became at a later period, but not very markedly different. Towns[79] existed at the furthest date to which our materials carry us back, and the distinction between town and country life was a necessary consequence. In the town dwelt the monarch, the courtiers, the royal attendants, the artisans, the shopkeepers; in the country, large landed proprietors, their servants, agricultural laborers, cowherds, perhaps boatmen. Landed property was hereditary,[80] and an upper class was thus maintained, which regarded itself as a nobility. Royal blood often flowed in the veins of these persons, who are frequently said to be *Suten-rekh*, "grandsons of a monarch."[81] Their wealth, which was considerable, enabled them to maintain a numerous household, which consisted both of male and female servants, and reached in some instances the number of thirty.[82] Little was spent by them upon personal display. The dress of the upper class, even considerably later than the time whereof we are speaking, was wonderfully simple and unpretending, presenting little variety and scarcely any ornament.[83] The grandee (Fig. 3) wore indeed an elaborate wig, but that was indispensable for the sake of cleanliness;[84] otherwise his attire is almost unparalleled in ancient times for simplicity. A short tunic, probably of white linen, reaching from the waist to a little above the knees, was ordinarily his sole garment. His arms, chest, legs, even his feet, were naked, the use of sandals not being as yet known. The only decoration which he wore was a chain or ribbon about the neck, on which was suspended an ornament like a locket.[65] In his right hand he carried a long staff or wand, which he seems to have used as a walking-stick. Such was the great noble's ordinary apparel, his "undress" costume, to use a modern expression; when he ventured beyond this, and allowed himself to indulge in the refinement of "dress," he exchanged his tunic for a somewhat scanty robe reaching from the neck to the ankles, replaced his chain and locket by a broad collar, and, having adorned his wrist with bracelets, was ready to pay visits or to receive polite company.[66] The costume of his wife, if he happened to be married, was not a whit more elaborate. She wore her hair long and gathered in three masses, one behind the head, and the other two in front of either shoulder. On her body she had a single garment—a short gown or petticoat reaching from just below the breasts to halfway down the lower joint of the leg, and supported by two broad straps passed over the two shoulders. Her feet were bare, like her husband's, and, like him, she encircled her wrists with bracelets.[67] We have no representation or account of the houses in which these persons resided. Probably they were plain in character; but their furniture was not inartistic. The chairs on which both sexes sat—or rather stools, for they had no back—were supported on legs fashioned after those of animals, and the extremity of the seat on either side terminated in a lotus-flower.[68] Tables seem to have been round, and to have been supported by a single pillar in the centre. Couches are not represented, but they probably differed little from those of later times; and there had already been invented the peculiarly Egyptian piece of furniture known as the "head-rest."[69]

The animals domesticated at this early period were, so far as appears, the dog, the cow, the goose, and perhaps the antelope. Antelopes were, however, also hunted;[90] and it is possible that those which appear to be tame[91] were wild ones taken young and kept as pets. Pet animals seem to have been much affected, and included the jerboa, the hare, and the porcupine.[92] The only animals that can be proved to have been killed for food at this date are the ox and the goose; but we may suspect that fish, whereof several species appear in the hieroglyphics of the time, were also articles of common consumption, as they certainly were in later times.[93] Bread no doubt was the main "staff of life;" and attendants carrying baskets, which appear to contain loaves, are common."

The artisan class of the time must have included weavers, workers in metal, stonecutters, masons, carpenters, upholsterers, wig-makers, embalmers, and probably boatbuilders. Stonecutting was an art very necessary in a country where the only timber tree was one which was valued both for its shade and for its fruit. For the shaping of blocks the saw and the chisel must have been very early invented; and a metallurgy of no small merit must have formed and hardened the implements whereby materials such as those employed by the Egyptian builders and sculptors were worked with ease and freedom. Granite, indeed, was not made use of at first; a compact limestone supplied its place, and contented the primitive constructors of tombs and towers. But it was not long ere Egyptian skill and inventiveness succeeded in finding means to subdue even the most intractable materials; and we shall find the pyramic kings employing freely such stubborn substances as syenite, arragonite, red granite, and green basalt.

To conclude this brief interview of a time on which the Egyptian remains throw but a dim and uncertain light, it must be noted that the hieroglyphical system of writing was already not only invented, but elaborated, the interior of the sepulchral chambers being covered with long inscriptions, which give the titles and employments, describe the domains, and other possessions of the deceased if not with the copiousness and verbosity of a later date, at any rate with considerable fulness of detail. The hieroglyphs themselves are somewhat rude and wanting in finish; but the language is said to be completely formed; the different kinds of hieroglyphs, symbolic, determinative, phonetic, are all in use; the values of the characters are fixed; grammatical modifications are indicated by signs which for the most part continued in use; and, in a general way, it may be said that "the hieroglyphical writing reveals itself to us in the monuments of the first dynasties with all that complication which belonged to it down to the last day of its existence."

CHAPTER XIV.

THE PYRAMID KINGS.

Reigns of Seneferu, Khufu, Shafra, Menkaura, and Aseskaf, of the Fourth Dynasty, and of Usurkaf, Sahura. Kaka, Nefer-ar-kara, Ranuser, Menkauhor, Tatkara or Assa, and Unas, of the Fifth. General Condition of Egypt under these Kings. Progress of Art—of Religion—of Civilization and the Arts of Life.

"Pulcher fugatis dies tenebris."—Hor. Od. iv, ll. 39-40.

HISTORIC light dawns, and truly historic personages begin to move before us, with the accession of the dynasty which Manetho styled "the fourth." Manetho placed at the head of this dynasty a king whom he called Soris; and though the name itself corresponds rather with the "Sar" of the Turin papyrus, and of the table of Saccarah, yet, as the place assigned to him make him definitely the predecessor of Suphis (Khufu), it would seem that we may properly identify him with Seneferu, who beyond all doubt occupied that position.¹ Seneferu appears to have succeeded Huni, but to have exceeded him in the extent of his dominions.² He had the character of a good and beneficent king; and it is in harmony with this description of an Egyptian writer, that we find him in his lifetime taking the title of *neb mat*,³ or "lord of justice," which was not one commonly borne by Egyptian sovereigns. Seneferu (Fig. 4) is the first Egyptian monarch who has left behind him an inscription,⁴ and the first of whom we have monumental evidence that he made war beyond his own borders, and established the power of Eygpt over a foreign country. Thus he was great both at home and abroad; he dispensed justice to his subjects with such wisdom and impartiality as to acquire a character for beneficence; and he employed the Egyptian arms beyond his frontiers with such success that he could claim also the title of "conqueror."⁵ It must always be with a profound interest that travellers contemplate that rock-tablet in the Sinaitic peninsula which contains his name and titles, together with a representation of his prowess as he engages with and fells a foreign adversary. The chief with whom he contends is the sheikh or prince of the *Mena-nu-sat*, or "Shepherds of the East,"⁶ who at that time held the mountain country between the two arms of the

Red Sea. Attracted thither by the mineral treasures of the region,[7] the Egyptian monarch, "King of Upper and of Lower Egypt," as he proclaims himself, "Lord of Justice," and "Vanquisher of his adversary," carried all before him—defeated and dispersed the old inhabitants of the country, received their submission, and established a military and mining post in the heart of the region, which was thenceforth for centuries carefully guarded by an Egyptian garrison. The remains still to be seen in the Wady Magharah show the strong fortress within which the Egyptian troops were lodged, the deep well within the wall which secured them an unfailing supply of water, and the neighboring temples of their native deities, wherein the expatriated soldiers might have the enjoyment of the worship to which they were accustomed in their own land.[8]

It is not certain that Seneferu adorned Egypt with any buildings. The Meydoun pile has been ascribed to him,[9] but scarcely on sufficient data. Various members of his family were interred in the tombs of Ghizeh; and it is in this way that we make acquaintance with his favorite wife, Mer-ti-tefs;[10] his son, Nefer-mat;[11] his grandson, Shaf-Seneferu, the son of this latter;[12] and his eldest daughter, Nefer-t-kau, who was buried in the same tomb as her brother.[13] It has been suggested that his own mummy was perhaps deposited in the lower chamber of the Great Pyramid,[14] which in that case must be supposed to have been commenced by him; but there are no sufficient grounds for this supposition.

The Turin papyrus appears to have assigned to Seneferu a reign of nineteen years. His son, Nefer-mat, is thought to have died during his lifetime, and Shaf-Seneferu, his grandson, to have been thereupon invested with the title of hereditary prince (*erpa suten sa*), which he certainly bore;[15] but the royal dignity, instead of passing to this prince on his grandsire's demise, was obtained by Khufu. ○ ⸋ ⸋ , under what circumstances it is impossible to say. Khufu can scarcely have been a son of Seneferu, for he took to wife Seneferu's widow, Mertitefs. He was perhaps a usurper, and no relation; or possibly he may have been a brother, and have inherited the throne, because Shaf-Seneferu was not thought to be old enough to exercise the functions of royalty when Seneferu died. Shaf-Seneferu seems to have held a high place at his court, and to have died, while Khufu was still living, before the accession of Shafra.

In Khufu must be acknowledged, if not the greatest of Egyptian kings, yet certainly the greatest of Egyptian builders, and a sovereign of extraordinary energy. From the conception of the step-pyramid of Saccarah, which was the highest flight of Egyptian architectural daring at the time, to that of the Great Pyramid of Ghizeh, was so vast a stride, that the monarch who took it must be credited with a grandeur and elevation of thought approaching to genius. To more than double the height of the highest previous building, to multiply the area by five, and the mass by ten, was a venture into the untried and the unknown, which none but a bold mind could have conceived, none but an iron will could have resolved to execute. So far as conception went, Khufu may have been assisted by his architect;[16] but the adoption of a plan so extraordinarily grand, the determination to embody the conception in solid stone, this must have been wholly his own act, his own doing; and it implies a resolution and a strength of mind of the highest order. The fact must ever remain one to excite our profound astonishment, that in Egypt, almost at the commencement of its history, among a people living by themselves and deriving no instruction from without, a king —for there is every reason to believe that the whole work was begun and finished by a single monarch [17]—conceived and carried out a design so vast, completing a structure which has lasted four thousand years, which is even now among the world's chief marvels, and remains, in respect of size and mass, the most prodigious of all human constructions.[18]

A description of the Great Pyramid has been already given.[19] It must have been commenced by Khufu almost as soon as he ascended the throne, and must have been the occupation of a lifetime. Herodotus is not likely to have obtained an exactly authentic account; but his estimate of thirty years for the time consumed in constructing the pyramid itself, together with its subsidiary structures, and of 100,000 laborers as the number constantly employed upon the work,[20] is quite in accordance with the probabilities of the case, though scarcely deserving to be accepted as matter of positive history.[21] An enormous amount of unskilled human labor, gradually advancing the work by expenditure of mere brute strength, is necessitated by the circumstances of the time, and the conditions under which the pyramid was erected. A considerable employment of very highly skilled labor upon those wonderful passages and chambers, which form the true marvel of the building,[22] must also be regarded as certain; and it seems to follow that such a work could not have been carried to its completion without engaging the energies of almost the whole talent of the state, as well as almost its whole laboring population, during the period of an entire generation. Great sufferings would naturally accompany such an interference with men's natural employments, and such a concentration of vast numbers upon a limited area. The construction of the Suez Canal in the years 1865-1869 cost the lives of thousands, who perished through want and disease. It cannot be supposed that it was possible in the infancy of the world's history to execute a far vaster work without similar calamities. Hence probably the ill-repute which attached to Khufu, and the other pyramid-builders, in after times [23]—an ill-repute which, though falsely explained as resting upon religious grounds, was itself a fact, not doubtful nor disputable.[24]

In very truth, such constructions as the Pyramids, however they may move our admiration as works of art, in their kind, utterly astonishing and unapproachable. are to the politician and the moralist miserable instances of the lengths to which a paltry egotism will go for the gratification of self at the expense of others. All Egyptians had the same belief with respect to a future life—all equally desired the safe conservation of their earthly remains through many centuries.[25] Yet the bulk, even of the rich, were content to have their remains deposited in a deep pit, the mouth of which was closed and concealed from view by having one of the walls of the sepulchral chamber or chapel built over it. But the Egyptian kings, or at any rate the kings of this period, because they could command the services of their subjects, being absolute and able to employ as many of them as they chose in forced labors, would not be satisfied with the common lot. Nothing less would content them than granite chambers, sealed by portcullises, and enclosed in the centre of "artificial mountains,"[26] formed of massive blocks of stone, moved into place with sighs and groans by impressed workmen, and too often cemented with the blood of those who were maimed or crushed to death, when a block slipped, as the attempt was being made to lift and emplace it. Such accidents must have been frequent, and have occasioned a considerable loss of life; but it was easy to replace the mutilated and the killed by a fresh conscription, and so to carry out the monarch's proud design at the cost of increased suffering to his subjects. Egyptian kings did not shrink from enforcing their will at this cost. One only seems, at a certain point, to have paused in his design, and made a change, which brought his work to an earlier termination than that orginally contemplated.[27]

It must ever therefore remain a reproach to Khufu, that by the extravagance of his egotism, of his vanity, and of his ambition to excel all who had gone before or should follow him, he held his people in an intolerable bondage for a longer term of years than any other Eygptian king. We possess no representation of him that can be regarded as approaching to the nature of a portrait, or we should expect to see in his countenance indications of an iron will, a stern pride, and a cruel hardness, such as appear in the later pictures of the first Napoleon. The only bas-relief of him which exists is one at the Wady Magharah (Fig. 5), modelled after the earlier representation of Seneferu,[28] which shows him clutching an enemy by the hair of his head, and about to deal him his death-stroke with a club or mace. The relief is in a bad state of preservation, but it appears to be thoroughly conventional and not to aim at truthfulness of expression. Khufu has a face little differing from that of Seneferu, to whom in character he presented a striking contrast.

We gather from the Wady-Magharah tablet, that Khufu made two expeditions into the Sinaitic peninsula, one to take possession of the mines, on which occasion he merely set up his cartouche and his titles, calling himself "Khufu, King of Upper and Lower Egypt, the conquering Horus," and another—that commemorated on the opposite page—where he gave his name as Num-Khufu, and represented himself as "striking down one of the Pet or An foreigners in the presence of the ibis-headed god Tahuti or Thoth."[29] Both these names are found in the Great Pyramid,[30] and though some have supposed them to designate different individuals,[31] it seems to be now most commonly held[32] that they are merely two appellations of the same monarch, the successor of Seneferu, who, having been originally called Khufu, at a certain period of his life assumed the prefix of Num or Khnum, intending thereby to identify himself with the god whom the Greeks called Kneph, one of the chief objects of worship in Upper Egypt.[33]

This fact, and some others recorded on the native monuments, sufficiently refute the legend of the Greeks[34] which represented the builder of the Great Pyramid as wholly irreligious, one who shut up the temples, and was opposed to the polytheism of his subjects. The very reverse appears to have been the fact. Khufu not only took the name of Khnum, in acknowledgement of the Elephantine deity, and placed Thoth upon the trophy of victory which he set up at Wady Magharah, but called himself "the living Horus,"[35] and actually built a temple to Isis, whom (as being Horus) he called "his mother," and whose image he placed in her sanctuary, attaching at the same time to the edifice an estate by way of endowment.[36] He also, if we may trust an inscription of comparatively late date, found at the temple of Denderah, furnished the plan upon which the original edifice, dedicated to Athor on that site, was built.[37] Even the Greeks[38] inform us that Khufu, notwithstanding his alleged impiety, composed a religious work entitled "The Sacred Book," which continued to be highly valued in later ages. The extant remains certainly bear strong witness to his religious zeal, presenting him to us in the character of the first known builder of temples, the first king who is found to have acknowledged almost all the principal Egyptians gods,[39] and the first person known to have brought into use the system of religious endowments.

The family of Khufu appears to have been large. He took to wife, on his accession, Queen Mertitefs, the widow of his predecessor,[40] and had by her a number of sons and daughters whose tombs "form a crown around his pyramid."[41] Merhet, 👁️, one of his sons, is said to have been the "priest of Khufu's obelisk,"[42] whereby we perceive that this architectural embellishment, although it may not have taken an important place in the great designs of architects until the time of the twelfth dynasty, was yet already known and employed in the fourth, though probably upon a smaller scale than afterwards. Saf-hotep, another son, was (as already mentioned[43]) the "chief of the works of Khufu," and therefore most likely his head architect. A third son, Shaf-Khufu, was priest of Apis.[44] A daughter, Hents 🝆, was buried under a small pyramid in immediate proximity to the great monument of her father.[45] Two other sons, Ka-ab and Khem-tat-f, had tombs in the same vicinity.[46] Merisankh, the wife of Shafra, is thought to have been also one of his daughters.[47]

Khufu was, according to the lists of Abydos and Saccarah, succeeded by a king named Ratatf, 🝆, who is supposed to be Manetho's "Ratoises." There are several monumental evidences of this monarch's existence,[48] and the place assigned to him in the lists seems to be the correct one; but his reign must have been unimportant, and was probably extremely brief, to be counted not by years, but by months. At his demise, the throne was occupied by a son-in-law of the great Khufu, a monarch who bore the name of Shafra (Fig. 60) or Khafra, ⸺, the Chephren of Herodotu[59] and the Chabryes of Diodorus Siculus.[60]

Shafra is the first of the Egyptian kings whose personal appearance we can distinctly and fully realize. Two statues of him, in green basalt,[61] his own gift to the temple of the Sphinx, show him to us such as he existed in life, bearing upon them as they do the stamp of a thoroughly realistic treatment. The figure of the king is tall and slender—the chest, shoulders, and upper arm well developed, but the lower arm and the lower leg long and slight. The head is smallish, the forehead fairly high and marked with lines of thought, but a little retreating; the eye small, the nose well shaped, the lips slightly projecting, but not unduly thick, the chin well rounded, and the cheek somewhat too fat. The expression, on the whole, is pleasing, the look thoughtful and intelligent, but with a touch of sensuality about the under jaw and mouth. There is no particular sternness, but there is certainly no weakness, in the face, which is that of one not likely to be moved by pity or turned from his purpose by undue softness of heart.

Like his predecessor, Shafra must have made it the main business of his life to provide himself with a tomb that should be an eternal monument of his greatness and glory. He gave to his pyramid the name of *Ur*, "the great," "the principal,"[62] and though the inferiority of its actual dimensions[63] has caused it in modern times to receive the appellation of "the Second Pyramid," it is quite possible that he expected to deceive his subjects into the belief that it was a vaster edifice than that of Khufu, by the side of which he placed it. For the lie of the ground favors such a deception. The rocky platform on which the three pyramids are built rises towards the centre, and the central position of the Second Pyramid gives it a marked advantage over the first, causing its summit to attain actually a higher elevation above the level of the plain that is attained by the pyramid of Khufu.[64] In another respect also Shafra aimed at outdoing his predecessor. Not content with the compact limestone of the opposite or Mokattam range, from which Khufu drew the vast blocks with which he revetted his enormous monument, Shafra caused his workmen to ascend the Nile as far as Elephantiné, and there to quarry the hard granite of that distant locality, in order to encase, partially at any rate,[65] his own tomb with that better and far more costly material.

It is probable that Shafra also "built the small temple behind the great Sphinx,"[56] which he certainly decorated with his statues. The peculiarity of this temple is, that it is composed entirely of great blocks of the hardest materials—red granite, syenite, or aragonite—brought from the neighborhood of Syéné, or else of yellow alabaster. The stones are polished to a perfectly smooth surface, and fitted block to block "to a hair's breadth,"[57] with a skill and an exactness that provoke the astonishment of modern architects. Similar exactness appears in the masonry of the internal chambers and passages of the pyramid of Khufu,[58] and it is beyond question that the Egyptian builders of this early period had attained to a perfect power of cutting and shaping stones of the hardest quality—a power equal to that possessed at the present day by the most advanced nations. What tools were used, what methods were employed, we do not know, and can only conjecture; but the fact is certain that the stubbornness of the hardest materials was overcome; and we may add that there is nothing in the results produced to indicate that any greater difficulty was experienced in dealing with the harder qualities of stone than with the softer.

Among the titles taken by Shafra there are some which are remarkable, and which seem to indicate an advance on the bold and bald presentation of themselves to their subjects as the main Egyptian divinities, on which the kings ventured. Shafra not only calls himself "Horus, lord of the heart," and "the good Horus," but *neter aa*, "the great god," and *sa Ra*, "Son of Ra," or "of the Sun."[59] This famous title, 𓇳𓅆 so familiar to us from the cartouches of the later Pharaohs, appears in the inscriptions of Shafra *for the first time*. To him we must therefore assign the credit, or the discredit, of having invented a phrase which, exactly falling in with the vanity of subsequent kings and the adulation of their subjects, became a standing immutable title, the necessary adjunct to the proper name of every later sovereign. Shafra also added to the ordinary royal title of "conquering Horus" the prefix of *Khem*, either in the sense of "master," "ruler," or with the intention of attaching to himself another divine name, and claiming to be an incarnation of the god Khem no less than of the god Horus.

Shafra seems to have been married to a daughter of his predecessor, named Meri-ankh-s, or Meri-s-ankh.[60] Her tomb has been found at Saccarah, and has on it an inscription, by which it appears that she bore the office of priestess to Thoth, and also to one of the sacred animals regarded as incarnations of deity.[61] She claims association with the "lord of diadems,"[62] and it is thought to be not improbabale that even Shafra reigned in her right rather than in his own.[63] It does not appear from the monuments that he was in any way related to Khufu, or that he had in his veins any royal blood; and the conjecture is made that at this ancient epoch there was some special right of daughters to succeed their father, either in preference to sons, or in case of their being the elder children. A right of the kind is known to have obtained in Lycia[64] and other eastern countries; and the want of any indication of the succession from father to son in the monuments of this time raises the suspicion that some such practice prevailed in Egypt under the early Pharaohs. But however this may have been, Meri-s-ankh was at any rate a personage of great importance in Shafra's reign. She was "exalted to the highest degree of dignity to which it was possible for the wife of an Egyptian monarch to attain."[65] Associated with the "lord of diadems," she had the entire control of the royal gynæceum, or "house of the women," enjoyed two priesthood, and was deep in the confidence and high in the favor of her royal consort. She bore Shafra at least two sons. One of these, who had the name of Neb-m-akhu-t, is represented as his father's "heir."[66] He was a superior priest of the order of Heb, a sacred scribe, and "clerk of the closet" to his father. Five estates, of which he was the owner, had all been presented to him by his liberal parent, and had received names in which Shafra was an element.[67] Another son, S-kem-ka-ra, possessed fourteen such properties,[68] and must have been one of the wealthiest landed proprietors of the time. He enjoyed his wealth for a long term of years, living to a good old age under five successive kings,[69] whose escutcheons he displays upon his monument.

The immediate succession of Mencheres (Menkaura, ○ ⎯⎯⎯ 𓏌𓏌𓏌) to Shafra, asserted by Herodotus [70]and Manetho,[71] is indicated on the tomb of S-kem-ka-ra,[72] and confirmed by the table of Seti I. at Abydos.[73] Yet here again we are unable to trace by means of the monuments any blood-relationship, and can say nothing of the connection between Menkaura and his predecessors beyond the fact of there having been a tradition that he descended, not from Shafra, but from Khufu," the first and greatest of the pyramid kings. Born and bred up during the years when the whole thought and attention of Egypt was given to the construction of these wonderful edifices, he would have been more than human if he had not been carried away by the spirit of the time, and felt it his duty to imitate in some degree, if he could not hope to emulate, his predecessors. The pyramid in which he engaged was on a humble scale. As designed and executed by himself, it seems to have been a square of no more than one hundred and eighty feet, with an elevation of one hundred and forty-five feet.[75] A sepulchral chamber of no remarkable pretension,[76] excavated in the solid rock below the monument, contained the sarcophagus and coffin of the king. The sarcophagus was of whinstone, and elaborate in its ornamentation.[77] The coffin, which was of cedar wood,[78] and shaped like a mummy, but with a pedestal on which it could stand upright, was of great simplicity, being adorned with no painting, but bearing on the front two columns of hieroglyphics,[79] which are thus read by the best scholars:—"O Osiris, king of Upper and Lower Egypt, Menkaura, living eternally, engendered by the Heaven, born of Nut, substance of Seb, thy mother Nut stretches herself over thee in her name of the abyss of heaven. She renders thee divine by destroying all thy enemies, O king Menkaura, living eternally."[80] The formula is one not special to this king, but repeated on the covers of other sarcophagi,[81] and probably belonging to a ritual, though not to one of very ancient date, since the ideas embodied in it can scarcely be traced back further than the time of Mencheres himself. Before this date "the god Anubis is mentioned in the tombs as the special deity of the dead, to the exclusion of the name of Osiris;" and the coffin-lid of Menkaura "marks a new religious development in the annals of Egypt."[82] The absorption of the justified soul in Osiris, the cardinal doctrine of the "Ritual of the Dead," makes its appearance here for the first time; and we can scarcely be wrong in assigning to this monarch an important part in the doctrinal change, whereby the souls of the just were no longer regarded as retaining their individuality in the other world, but were identified each and all with Osiris himself, and were thought to be, at any rate temporarily, absorbed into his divine being.

Altogether, Mencheres left behind him the character of a religious king. According to Herodotus, he reopened the temples, which had been kept closed by Khufu (Cheops) and Shafra (Chephren), and allowed the people to resume the practice of sacrifice.[3] In the "Ritual of the Dead" it is recorded of him that one of the most important chapters of the book was discovered during his reign by his son, Hortetef, who found it at Sesennu (Hermopolis) in the course of a journey which he had undertaken for the purpose of inspecting the temples of Egypt.[4] There is such an amount of agreement in these two notices, both of which seem to imply that this monarch paid special attention to the temples, and interested himself in the cause of religion, that we shall scarcely err in assuming a foundation of truth for the king's traditional character, though the attitude of the two preceding monarchs to the established worship was certainly not that imputed to them. Mencheres was himself dedicated by his name to Ra, the sun-god, and he gave his son a name which put him under the protection of Horus. We must suppose that he sent his son on the tour of inspection mentioned in the "Ritual," thus showing himself anxious to learn what condition the temples were in; and we may conclude that he had a hand in the compilation of that mysterious treatise by the fact that Hortetef's discovery became a portion of its contents.

Nor was piety the only good quality which tradition assigned to this monarch. He was also said to have been distinguished for justice and kindness of heart.[5] The monuments of his reign are not sufficiently abundant to enable us fully to test this statement; but it is certainly in accordance with it, that we find Mencheres singling out a youth of no high birth or connection for his special favor, introducing him as an inmate into the palace, and causing him to receive his education together with his own children.[6] The youth in question, whose name was Ptah-ases, retained a lively recollection of this act of kindness, and in the inscription upon his tomb took care to commemorate the gracious favor of his royal benefactor.

Mencheres was succeeded by a monarch whose name is written ⌬, which is expounded differently by different writers, some calling it Ases-kaf and some Shepseskaf.[7] We shall adopt the former reading. Ases-kaf's immediate succession to Mencheres is indicated alike by the tomb of Ptah-ases,[8] and by that of Skemkara.[9] Ptah-ases tells us that Ases-kaf continued towards him the kind treatment commenced by his predecessor, allowed him still to receive education in the palace with the royal children, and, when he had come to years of discretion, gave him to wife his eldest daughter, Mat-sha, preferring him as a husband for her to any other man. This first act of signal favor was followed up by such a multitude of others that the modern historian is driven to remark on the antiquity of the system of pluralities,[90] and the early date at which ecclesiastical posts were assigned to court favorites for the mere purpose of enabling their holders to draw a large revenue from benefices which they must have treated as simple sinecures. Ptah-ses was prophet of Phthah, of Sokari, and of Athor, priest of the temple of Sokari, and of that of Phthah at Memphis, prophet of Ra-Harmachis, of Ma, and of Horus, as well as overseer of the granaries, royal secretary, chief of the mines, and "chief of the house of bronze."[91] He says that he was "esteemed by the king above all his other servants;"[92] and we may therefore hope that so shameless an accumulation of offices upon a favorite as that which Ptahases' tomb reveals to us was unusual.

Aseskaf, like the other monarchs of this period, built himself a pyramid, and gave it the name of *Keb*, or "refreshment."[63] This pyramid has not at present been identified among the existing sixty-six; but it is quite possible that further research may lead to its discovery. It is probably among the group known as "the pyramids of Saccarah," which became the favorite burial-place when the Ghizeh site ceased to be thought suitable, since the enormous constructions of Khufu and Shafra could not possibly, it was felt, be exceeded, and they dwarfed all ordinary erections.

The successor of Aseskaf was Uska for Usurkaf,[64] who is thought to be the Usercheres of Manetho, the first king of his fifth dynasty. An unusually close correspondence is traced between the monumental names of this period and those of Manetho's list,[65] indicative of the fact that Manetho at this point of his history has for once obtained tolerably good information. His dynastic list consists of nine kings, who are made to occupy a space of 248 years, which, however, is probably too much. The Turin papyrus reduces the period to one of 141 years only, and even this number is most likely in excess, since as many as twenty-one years are assigned to monarchs of whom the contemporary monuments show no traces, and who must be regarded as secondary associated princes.[66] The line seems really to have been one of seven kings only—Usurkaf, Sahura, Nefer-ar-ka-ra, Ranuser, Menkauhor, Tatkara or Assa, and Unas; and the time which it occupied seems a little to have exceeded a hundred years. If we assign to the four or five preceding monarchs[67] a similar term, we shall make a liberal allowance and have for the entire space from the accession of Seneferu to the death of Unas one of about two centuries.

It is difficult to conjecture any reason for Manetho's division of the kings of this period into two separate dynasties, one Memphite, and the other Elephantiné. Nothing is more distinctly shown by the monuments than the fact, that the entire series from Seneferu to Unas lived and reigned at Memphis; nor do we possess in all our ample materials the slightest trace of any break or division in the series, any change of policy, or religion, or art, to account for the fiction of two houses. It would seem that the Sebennytic priest had made up his mind to have thirty dynasties down to the close of Egyptian independence, and was not very particular how he produced them. To swell the number of years and obtain the total which he wanted, he introduced secondary associated princes into his lists by the side of the true monarchs, without distinguishing them, and from time to time he seems to have even gone the length of interpolating into his lists wholly fictitious kings. The Bicheres, Sebercheres, and Thamphthis, who close the fourth dynasty of Manetho, if not absolute fabrications, have at any rate no right to the place which they occupy. They are fictions *at that point* certainly;[98] possibly they are fictions altogether.

The reign of Usurkaf was short and undistinguished He built a small pyramid, which he calld *Uab asu*, "the most holy of all places,"[99] and established the usual worship of his own diety in connection with it, which he committed to the charge of a priest named Khnumhotep. In this worship he associated with himself the goddess Athor.[100] Among his other titles he took that of *Hor ari mat*,[101] or "Horus, the dispenser of justice," which would appear to imply that, like Seneferu,[102] he regarded it as one of his chief duties to have justice carefully and strictly administered throughout the country under his rule. Only a very few monuments belonging to his reign have been as yet discovered; but his place in the list of kings, between Aseskaf and Sahura, is certain.

The succession of Sahura (Fig. 6) o 𝟚𝟚𝟚 to Usurkaf is sufficiently established by the tomb of Skemkara,[103] and is further supported by the tables of Saccarah and Abydos,[104] as well as by Manetho,[105] if we admit his "Sephres" to represent this monarch. Sepahura followed in the steps of Seneferu and Khufu by making an expedition into the Sinaitic pe-

Vol. II. Plate V.

Fig. 13.—TABLET OF MENTU-HOTEP II.—See Page 71.

Fig. 14.—DRESSES WORN UNDER THE TWELFTH DYNASTY.—See Page 92.

Fig. 15.—Obelisk of Usurtasen I. at Heliopolis.—See Page 80.

ninsula, where he had to contend with a new enemy, the Mentu, ![glyph] who had by this time become the ruling tribe in the vicinity of the copper mines. He appears in the usual attitude of a conqueror, smiting a half-prostrate enemy with uplifted mace,[106] but wears in this representation the crown of Upper Egypt only, though another figure of him, a little behind, has the other crown instead. In the text which accompanies his sculpture he calls himself "the great god, who destroys the Mentu *and strikes down all nations*." There is, however, no evidence beyond this statement, that he carried his arms into any other region besides that of Sinai, or warred with any other nation besides the Mentu; and it is on the whole most probable that his military achievements were limited to this people and quarter, despite the grandiloquent terms of his inscription. The Egyptian kings of the period were decidedly not warlike; and we have no reason to suppose that Sahura was an exception to the general rule, or did more than repeat the former deeds of Khufu and Seneferu.

The only other fact recorded of Sahura is his erection of a pyramid, to which he gave the name of *Sha-ba*, or "the rising of the soul," to mark his belief in the resurrection.[107] This building has been identified, by the occurrence of his name on some of its blocks, with the "northern pyramid of Abousir," an edifice of some considerable pretension. It was a true pyramid, perfectly square, each side measuring 150 Egyptian cubits, or 257 of our feet, and with a perpendicular height of 95 cubits or 163 feet,[108] being thus considerably larger than the pyramid built for himself by Menkaura.[109] Directly below the apex, and a little above the level of the natural ground, was the sepulchral chamber, roofed over in the usual way, with huge blocks set obliquely, the blocks measuring in some instances thirty-six feet by twelve![110] The sarcophagus appears to have been of basalt, but had been demolished before the modern explorations; the chambers and passages are said to have been "formed, in the most skilful and artistic manner, of vast blocks of limestone from the quarries of Turah."[111] The pyramid stood in the middle of an oblong court, surrounded by a low wall or peribolus.

Sahura established as priest of his pyramid an Egyptian named An-kheft-ka, who was also priest of the pyramid of his predecessor, Usurkaf, and held other important offices.[112] Sahura's worship was continued to a late date in Egypt, his priests obtaining mention in the time of the Ptolemies.[113] It is conjectured that he was the builder of an Egyptian town called Pa-sahura,[114] but not written with the characters by which it was usual to express Sahura's name. This town was near Esneh, and is mentioned in the religious calendar of that city.

The table of Abydos places a king named Kaka, ⌐⌐⌐| in the place immediately following that occupied by Sahura;[115] and, as traces of this royal name are found in the tombs of the period,[116] it is to be supposed that there was such a sovereign, or rather perhaps such a prince, who was allowed the rank of king about this time. The real successor, however, of Sahura appears to have been Nefer-ar-ka-ra, who follows him in the table of Saccarah,[117] in the list of Manetho,[118] and in the inscriptions on several tombs.[119] We possess no particulars of this monarch's reign which have more than a very slight claim on the reader's attention. He built a pyramid which he called Ba, or "the soul."[120] He raised to high position the officials Uer-Khuu and Pahenuka, whose genius was literary, but on whom were accumulated various and sometimes most incongruous offices.[121] But otherwise we know nothing of him, except that he reigned, according to Manetho, twenty, or, according to the Turin papyrus, seven years.[122] His pyramid has not been recognized.

Nefer-ar-ka-ra was followed by Ra-n-user, or User-n-ra, as some read the name (which is expressed as follows in the Egyptian, ▭▭▭) who bore also the name[123] of An, ▭▭. He followed the example of Sahura by making an expedition against the Mentu of the Sinaitic peninsula, and represents himself at Wady Magharah in the usual form of a warrior armed with a mace, wherewith he threatens to destroy a shrinking and almost prostrate enemy.[124] He takes the proud titles of "the great god, lord of the two lands, king of Egypt, king of the upper and lower countries, conquering Horus, and son of the Sun." The device upon his ensign is *as het tati*, "place of the heart (*i. e.*, object of the affections) of the two lands." Ranuser built the middle pyramid of Abousir, which is the smallest of the three, having a base of no more than 274 feet, with an elevation of 171 feet 4 inches.[125] His sepulchral chamber occupied the usual position, in the centre of the base, and was guarded with jealous care by granite blocks and a portcullis, which, however, did not prevent the penetration and plunder of the tomb by the Mohammedan conquerors. These insatiable treasure-seekers "broke through the pyramid from the top, and split up with iron wedges most of the blocks which seemed indestructible,"[126] disappointing the hopes of the builder, who had called his pyramid *men asu*, "the (most) stable of places,"[127] and at the same time disappointing their own hopes, for they assuredly found nothing therein to repay their labors. Ranuser's reign appears to have been long and prosperous. The Turin papyrus assigns him twenty-five,[128] and Manetho forty-four[29] years. A large number of magnificent tombs belong to his time,[130] and reveal to us the names, titles, and circumstances of numerous grandees of his court, who basked in his favor while living, and, by inscribing his name upon their tombs, glorified him when dead. The finest of all these monuments is that which has been called "the marvel of Saccarah,"[131] the tomb of Ti, ▭◨◨. This monument furnished to the Museum of Boulaq some of the most admirable of the portrait-statues that it possesses,[132] and is decorated with a series of elaborate painted bas-reliefs in the best style of the early Egyptian art. We gather from the inscriptions upon its walls that the noble who erected it had at the outset of his career no advantages of birth, but rose by merit and by the favor of successive sovereigns to the highest position whereto it was possible for a subject to attain. The tomb of Ti was commenced under Kaka and finished under Ranuser,[133] who must be credited with the merit of rewarding talent and good conduct wherever he found it, whether in the ranks of the nobles or among the common people.

The immediate successor of Ranuser was Menkauhor, ⌂▬⊔⊔. (Fig. 24), who must have come to the throne when he was quite a youth, as appears by the subjoined representation of him,[134] which was found upon a slab built into one of the walls of the Serapeum at Memphis.[135]

On this monument he is called "the good god, lord of the two lands."[136] He wears the elaborate projecting tunic commonly worn by kings in the later times, and a double chain or necklace, with a broad collar, round his neck. There are traces of a bracelet upon the left wrist. Over his head hovers the protecting hawk of Horus. Almost the only other existing monument of the reign of Menkauhor is his tablet at Wady Magharah,[137] a very unpretending memorial, with no representation of his person upon it, no claim of conquest, and no title excepting the simple one "king of Egypt." Menkauhor, the Mencheres II. of Manetho,[138] must have died while still a young man, since his reign did not extend beyond eight, or at the most nine years.[139] He was buried in a pyramid called *neter asu* "the (most) divine of places;"[140] but his tomb has not yet been identified.

From Menkauhor the crown passed to Tat-ka-ra, ⸻, or Assa ⸻, the second king with two names.[141] Like his immediate predecessor, he visited, in person, or by his commissioners, the mines of Wady Magharah, where there had been some failure in one of the materials on account of which they were worked.[142] The investigations undertaken by his orders were not without result; a tablet was discovered, supposed to have been written by the god Thoth, which pointed out the exact locality where the precious *mafka* was to be found. Assa further built a pyramid which he called simply *nefer*, "the good,"[143] and introduced the customary worship of his own divinity in connection with it.[144] His favorite title was Sa-Ra, ⸻ "son of the sun."[145] The tombs of Saccarah and Ghizeh contain numerous notices of him,[146] and show that, like the other kings of the period, he was fond of accumulating offices upon his favorites without much regard to their compatibility.[147]

The most interesting of the extant memorials belonging to the time of Assa is a papyrus—"probably the most ancient manuscript in the world"[148]—written by the son of a former king,[149] who calls himself Ptah-hotep. The character used is the hieratic, and the subject of the treatise is the proper conduct of life, and the advantages to be derived from a right behavior. Ptah-hotep states that he was a hundred and ten years old when he composed the work, and that he wrote it "under the majesty of King Assa." We shall make further reference, in the later part of this chapter, to its contents.[160]

The fifth Manethonian dynasty closes, and the period of Egyptian history commencing with Seneferu terminates,[151] with a monarch called Unas, ⸻, who is no doubt the Onnos of Manetho.[152] He reigned, according to the Turin papyrus thirty, according to Manetho thirty-three, years.[153] No great reliance can be placed on these numbers; and the fact that his pyramid, the *Mustabat-el-Faraoun*, is truncated, or in other words unfinished,[154] would seem to imply that his life came to an untimely end. This edifice is an oblong building, constructed of enormous blocks of limestone, and was named by its builder *nejer asu*, "the best place."[155] Its original length from north to south was 309 feet, and its breadth 217. The height to which it had been carried up when the work ceased was no more than sixty feet.[156] There are no traces of Unas at Wady Magharah; and his reign would, on the whole, seem to have been short and inglorious.

From the brief and bald account which is all that can be given of these kings, unless we surrender the reins to the imagination, and allow ourselves to depict from fancy the scenes of their life, and their civil or military employments, we may pass once more to the general condition of Egypt during the period, and its progress in arts, in religion, and in refinement of manners.

It is the glory of the period that it carried its own proper style of architecture to absolute and unsurpassable perfection. The weak and tentative efforts of primitive times were suddenly thown aside; and the early kings of the period advanced by an audacious leap from buildings of moderate dimensions—not beyond the constructive powers of architects in most civilized countries—to those gigantic piles which dwarf all other structures, and for size and mass have, up to the present time, no rivals. Khufu and Shafra found builders willing and able to carry out their desires for tombs that should shame all past and reduce to despair all future architects. They found men who could carry up solid stone buildings to the height of nearly 500 feet,[157] without danger of instability, or even any increased risk from pressure or settlement. These builders were able, first of all, to emplace their constructions with astronomical exactness; secondly, to employ in them, wherever it was needed, masonry of the most massive and enduring kind; thirdly, to secure the chambers and passages, which were essential features of such structures, by contrivances of great ingenuity, perfectly adapted to their purpose;[158] and fourthly, by their choice of lines and proportions, to produce works which, through their symmetry and the imposing majesty of their forms, impress the spectator even at the present day, with feelings of awe and admiration, such as are scarcely excited by any other architectural constructions in the whole world.[159]

It is not surprising that the extraordinary burst of architectural power under Khufu and Shafra was followed by a reaction. Fashion, or religious prejudice, still required that the body of a king should be entombed in a pyramid;[160] and from Menkaura to Unas every successive monarch gave a portion of his time and attention to the rearing of such a mouument. But, as all felt it hopeless to attempt to surpass the vast erections which the builders of the First and Second Pyramids had piled upon the rocky platform of Ghizeh, they not unnaturally gave up all idea of even vying with those "giants of old time," and were content with comparatively moderate and unpretending sepulchres. Menkaura set the fashion of constructing for himself a modest tomb;[161] and his example was followed by the remaining kings of the period. The monuments distinctly assignable to the later kings of Manetho's fourth, and to those of his fifth dynasty, are not any more remarkable than those which may be best referred to the times anterior to Khufu.

Besides their pyramids, the kings of the fourth and fifth dynasties built temples in a solid and enduring fashion; and within the last twenty years one of these has been dug out of the sand so far as to show what were its internal arrangements and general form and design. An account of this building, together with its ground-plan, has been given in the first volume of this work.[162] It possesses the merit of great solidity and strength, and exhibits the employment of piers for the support of a roof, the original out of which grew the column. It is altogether without sculpture of any kind, the walls being perfectly plain and flat, and deriving their ornamentation entirely from the material of which they are composed, which is yellow alabaster, syenite, or aragonite. Still we are told that the effect of the whole is good. "The parts are pleasingly and effectively arranged;" and the entire building has "that lithic grandeur which is inherent in large masses of precious materials."[163]

The sculpture of the pyramid period is also remarkable. Shafra, the probable builder of the temple just described, ornamented it with several statues of himself, which at a later time were thrown into a pit or well within the building, and for the most part, most unfortunately, broken. One, however, survives, perfect in all its parts except the beard;[164] and the upper half of another is in tolerable preservation;[165] so that the glyptic art of the time can be pretty fairly estimated. Some statues belonging to the reign of the later king, Ranuser, have also been furnished by the tomb of Ti, and afford the critic further material upon which to form a judgment. The opinion of experts seems to be, that all the specimens have considerable merit.[166] The figures are well proportioned; the faces carefully elaborated with all the minuteness of a portrait; the osseous structure and the muscles are sufficiently indicated; the finish is high, and the expression calm and dignified. There is however, as universally in Egyptian sculpture, a certain stiffness, and an undue formality. The two feet are equally advanced; the arms repose side by side along the thighs; the head has no inclination to either side; the face looks directly in front of the figure; the beard is wholly conventional. If we compare the statues in question with even the archaic Greek,[167] we shall find them exceedingly inferior in all that constitutes the excellence of art. But it may be questioned whether Egyptian art, in the matter of statuary, ever went beyond, or even equalled, the productions of this early period. "Art at this time," as Lenormant justly says,[168] "attains the most remarkable degree of perfection. It is thoroughly realistic; it aims, above everything, at rendering the bare truth of nature, without making any sort of attempt to idealize it. The type of man which it presents is characterized by something more of squatness and of rudeness than are seen in the works of the later schools; the relative proportions of the different parts of the body are less accurately observed; the muscular projections of the legs and arms are represented with too much exaggeration. Still, in this first and absolutely free development of Egyptian art, however imperfect it was, there lay the germs of more than Egypt ever actually produced, even in her most brilliant epochs. The art had life—a life which at a later date was choked by the shackles of sacerdotal tyranny. If the Pharaonic artists had preserved this secret to the time when they acquired their unequalled excellences of harmony of proportion and of majesty—qualities which they possessed in a higher degree than any other people in the world—they would have made as much progress as the Greeks; two thousand years before it was reached by the Greeks, they would have attained to the absolute perfection of artistic excellence. But their natural aptitudes were to a certain extent smothered in the cradle; and they remained imperfect, leaving to others the glory of reaching a point which will never be surpassed in the future."

The principles laid down in this extract will apply, to a certain extent, to the bas-reliefs of the period, and not merely to the sculptures "in the round." While these fall short considerably of the later Egyptian efforts in variety, in delicacy of touch, and in vigor of composition, they have a simplicity, a naturalness, and an appearance of life which deserve high praise, and which disappear at a later date, when the inflexible laws of the hieratic "canon of proportions" come into force, and the artists have to walk in fetters.[169] Notwithstanding a coarseness and clumsiness in some of the human forms, and an occasional uncertainty in the delineation of the animal ones, the sculptures which ornament the tombs of Ghizeh and Saccarah, and which can be assigned almost with certainty to this period, are both interesting and pleasing. They show that Egyptian art is alive, is progressive, is aiming at improvement. The forms, especially the animal forms, are better as we proceed; they show greater freedom and variety of attitude; and the new attitudes are both graceful and true to nature. At the same time, there is no straining after effect; the modesty of nature is not outraged by the artists; there is still abundance of the simple and the conventional; the whole effect is quiet, tranquil, idyllic; we seem to see Egyptian country life reflected as in a mirror. Delicacy may be sometimes shocked by the result; but what is lost in refinement is gained in truthfulness and accuracy of representation.

In religion there is also an advance, but one that is less satisfactory. The Pantheon increases in its dimensions. Besides the gods of the primitive time,[170]—Ra, Set, Thoth, Hor or Harmachis, Osiris, Isis-Athor, Phthah or Sokari, and Anubis—we find distinct traces of the worship of Nut, Seb, Khem, Kneph, Neith, Ma, Saf, and Heka.[171] Athor also is recognized as a substantive goddess, distinct from Isis;[172] and Sokari appears to be distinguished from Phthah.[173] The esteem in which Ra is held has grown, and one half of the kings have appellations which are composed with his name.[174] The title *sa Ra*, "son of the Sun," begins to be used as a royal prefix,[175] though not yet regularly. The divinity of the kings is more pronounced. They take the designations of "the great god," "the good god," "the living Horus," "the good Horus," as well as those of "conquering Horus," and "son of the Sun." They add divine titles to their original names, as Khufu did when in the middle of his reign he became Num-Khufu. They institute the worship of their own divinity in their lifetime, appoint their sons or other grandees to the office of their prophet or priest, and load the persons so appointed with further favors. At the same time, however, they themselves worship the gods of the country, build temples to them, and assign lands to the temples by way of endowment.[176] Priests and "prophets" are attached to these buildings, and the "prophets" include persons of both sexes. The doctrine of the future life and of the passage of the soul through the Lower World acquires consistence; Osiris takes his place as the great Ruler of the Dead;[177] Anubis sinks to a lower position; and the "Ritual" receives fresh chapters.[178] Finally, the animal-worship comes to the front; Apis has his priests and priestesses;[179] and a "white bull" and a "sacred heifer" are also mentioned as invested with a divine character.[180]

An advance is also made in civilization and the arts of life. Dress, on the whole, continues much the same; but the tunic of the higher classes becomes fuller, so as to project in front, and latterly it is made considerably longer, so as to descend half way between the knee and the ankle.[181] Its color is either yellow or white, or partly one and partly the other, the yellow portion in such cases being often striped with lines of red.[182] The collars worn by men (Fig. 10) become more complicated, and have sometimes a chain and pendant attached in front. Men are also seen with fillets adorning their heads;[183] and women have headdresses (Fig. 9) of various kinds, some of which are exceedingly elegant. Their long gowns continue as scanty as ever, and are represented as either red or yellow. They wear broad collars, very much like those of the men, and have sometimes bracelets and anklets. The collars are commonly blue, or blue and white. The feet of the women are still in every case naked; those of the men show sometimes an incipient sandal (Fig. 8), which is at first a mere strap passed under the heel and secured upon the instep,[184] but afterward has a sole extending the whole length of the foot.[185]

The division of classes, and the general habits of life, continued nearly as before, but the wealth of the upper class increased, and with it the extent of their households, and the number and variety of their retainers. Large landed estates descended from father to son, of which the cultivation necessitated the employment of hundreds of laborers or slaves. These required numerous superintendents; and the general business of the farm necessitated the services of some ten or a dozen scribes,[186] who rendered their accounts to a steward or bailiff. The chief trades needed for providing the necessaries of life were established upon the estate; and the carpenter, the potter, the tailor, the worker in metal, the furniture-maker, and even the glass-blower,[187] seem to have had their place among the dependents of every opulent family, and to have worked for a single master. The estate itself consisted of two portions—arable and pasture lands; the former cultivated in grain and vegetables with great care, the latter utilized for the breeding and fattening of cattle. Domestication had by this time brought into subjection not only cows and oxen, but goats, sheep, several kinds of antelope,[188] asses, and at least seven kinds of birds.[189] These included geese, ducks, pigeons, and cranes or herons,[190] together with other species not to be distinctly recognized. The domestic fowl was, however, still unknown, and indeed remained a stranger to Egypt throughout the entire period of independence.[191] The wealth of some landowners consisted to a large extent in their animals; we find one at a very early date who possessed above a thousand cows and oxen, besides 2,235 goats, 974 sheep, and 760 asses.[192] Pet animals were also much affected, and included, besides dogs, the fox, the hare, the monkey, and the cynocephalous ape.[193]

An important produce of the farm was wine. Vines were trained artificially,[194] and the juice was expressed from the grapes either by treading,[195] or by means of a wine-press.[196] After passing through the vat, it was drawn off and stored in amphoræ. Profit was also derived from the wild creatures which frequented the marshes or the waters included within the property. Fish were caught, split, and dried in the sun,[197] after which they became an article of commerce; wild fowl were taken in clap-nets, and either killed or subjected to a process of domestication.

The ass was the only beast of burden; horses were unknown.[198] There were no wheeled vehicles; and the burdens which the asses were made to bear appear to have been excessive.[199] For heavy commodities, however, water carriage was preferred; and the Nile with its canals formed the chief means for the transportation of farming produce. Large boats were in use from a very early period, some being mere row-boats,[200] while others were provided with masts, and could hoist a big square mainsail.[201] The number of rowers was in the early times from eight or ten to eighteen or twenty, but at a later date we find as many as forty-six.[202] When the sail was hoisted, the rowers ordinarily rested on their oars, or even shipped them and sat at their ease; but sometimes both sail and oars seem to have been employed together. A heavy kind of barge without a sail was used for the transport of cattle and of the more weighty merchandise,[203] and was propelled by six or eight rowers. Light boats were also employed to a large extent for the conveyance of animals, for the saving of cattle from the inundation, and for sporting and other purposes.[204]

The amusements of the upper classes seem to have consisted mainly in hunting, fowling, and listening to music. Dogs were still of one kind only—that which has been called the "fox-dog" or "wolf-dog,"[206] which has long pricked-up ears, a light body, and a stiffly curled tail.[206] This was admitted into the house, and is commonly seen sitting under the chair of its master; but it was also frequently employed in the chase of wild animals. The antelope was no doubt the beast chiefly hunted, and the dogs must have been exceedingly fleet of foot to have run it down; but the chase appears to have included other animals also, as hares, jerboas, porcupines, lynxes, and even hedgehogs![207] In some of the hieratic papyri, packs of hounds, numbering two or three hundred, are mentioned;[208] but these belong to a later age; under the fourth and fifth dynasties we have no evidence that any individual hunted with more than three or four dogs at a time, or indeed possessed a greater number. Dogs had names, which are often written over or under their representations,[209] e. g.,

Abu, 𓃗, Ken, 𓃞, Tarm, 𓃡, Akna, 𓃥

etc., as horses had at a later time; but the other domestic pets would seem not to have enjoyed the distinction.

Fowling was practised in the way already described,[210] by entering the reedy haunts of the wild fowl in a light skiff, provided with decoy birds, probably taught to utter their note, and thus approaching sufficiently near them to kill or wound them with a throw-stick. The throw-stick of the earlier times is either the curved weapon common later, or a sort of double bludgeon presenting a very peculiar appearance.[211]

Music was an accompaniment of the banquet. It was always concerted, and in the time of the fourth and fifth dynasties consisted ordinarily of the harmony of three instruments, the harp, the flute and the pipe. Bands numbered about four or five persons, of whom two were harpers, one or two players on the flute, and one a piper. Two or three others assisted to keep time, and increased the volume of sound by the loud clapping of their hands.[212] All the musicians were men. Sometimes dancing of a solemn and formal kind accompanied the musical performance, both sexes taking part in it, but separately. and with quite different gestures.

An amusement, but a very occasional amusement, of the upper classes at this time would seem to have been literature. The composition of the ordinary inscriptions upon tombs, and in sepulchral chambers, belonged probably to a professional class. who followed conventional forms, and repeated with very slight changes the same stereotyped phrases upon monument after monument. But now and then there was a production of something which approached more nearly to a literary character. The "Book of the Precepts of Prince Ptahhotep," though the only extant work of the kind which can be referred to this period, is probably a *specimen* of performances, not very uncommon, wherewith the richer and more highly educated classes of the time occupied their leisure, and solaced their declining years. It is stated to be "the teaching of the governor, Ptah-hotep, under the majesty of King Assa—long may he live!" The object aimed at by the work was "to teach the ignorant the principle of good words, for the good of those who listen, and to shake the confidence of such as wish to infringe." It lays down, primarily, the duties of sons and of subjects, who are alike exhorted to obedience and submission. "The obedience of a docile son," says Ptah-hotep, "is a blessing; the obedient walks in his obedience. He is ready to listen to all which can call forth affection; obedience is the greatest of benefits. The son who accepts the words of his father will grow old in consequence. For obedience is of God; disobedience is hateful to God. The obedience of a son to his father, this is joy . . . such a one is dear to his father; and his renown is in the mouth of all those who walk upon the earth. The rebellious man, who obeys not," he goes on to say, "sees knowledge in ignorance, the virtues in the vices; he commits daily with boldness all manner of crimes, and herein lives as if he were dead. What the wise know to be death is his daily life; he goes his way, laden with a heap of imprecations. Let thy heart," he adds, "wash away the impurity of thy mouth; fulfil the word of thy master. Good for a man is the discipline of his father, of him from whom he has derived his being. It is a great satisfaction to obey his words; for a good son is the gift of God." And the upshot of all is—"The obedient will be happy through his obedience; he will attain old age, he will acquire favor. I myself have in this way become one of the ancients of the earth; I have passed 110 years of life by the gift of the king, and with the approval of the aged, fulfilling my duty to the king in the place of his favor." The moral level attained cannot be regarded as high; but as a composition the work is not devoid of merit. The balance of ideas and of phrases recalls the main essential of Hebrew poetry;[213] the style is pointed and terse, the expressions natural, the flow of the language easy and pleasing. If Ptah-hotep is not a great moral philosopher, he is a fair writer; there are passages in his work which resemble the Proverbs of Solomon or the Wisdom of the Son of Sirach.[214] We can well understand that in the infancy of literary composition, when there were no models to follow, or standards with which to fear comparison, men of education would find the *rôle* of author agreeable, and would devote to it a portion of their leisure time with a feeling of great satisfaction.

The advance of luxury is seen in the number and variety of the dishes served at the sacrificial feasts, where the joints may be counted by the dozen, ducks and geese by the half-dozen, loaves by the score, cakes and rolls by the hundred, amphoræ by the dozen, and where the viands provided comprise also fish, hares, onions, eggs, and fruit of a variety of kinds.[215] According to the best English authority, the Egyptian lord of this time "no more disdained the hyena for food than a modern epicure the semi-carnivorous bear; but he abhorred that universal animal, the pig, and neglected the sheep; veal and beef, not pork or mutton, were the principal meats that appeared at his table. The different kinds of venison were much prized; cranes and herons he sometimes ate, but his principal poultry consisted of different kinds of ducks and geese, the chenalopex or vulpanser amongst them. The dove and the pigeon passed into his flesh-pots, nor was the insipid fish of the Nile unknown to him. His bread was made of barley, but conserves of dates and various kinds of biscuits or pastry diversified his diet; and of fruits he had grapes, figs, dates; of vegetables, the papyrus, the onion, and other greens. Wine and beer were both drunk at the period, in addition to water and milk."[216] Among the elegancies of the banquet was the use of flowers. Lotuses were carefully gathered by his servants in the ponds and canals, were wreathed round the wine-jar and the water-jar, twisted in garlands about the head of the host and his guests, decorated many of the dishes, and were held in the hand as a nosegay.[217] Instead of the stool which had contented his ancestors, he indulged not unfrequently in a chair with a low back and a square arm, on which he rested his hand or elbow.[218] When he left the house for an airing, he was sometimes conveyed in a species of palanquin, which was placed between two poles like a sedan-chair, and borne on the shoulders of his servants.[219] He encouraged art, and employed sculptors on portrait-statues of himself or his wife,[220] which were either of wood or stone, and in the latter case were occasionally colossal. These last were sometimes erect, sometimes sitting figures, and after completion were dragged into proper position by a number of men.[221]

The condition of the lower orders was probably not very different in the primitive and in the pyramid periods, except during two reigns. While Khufu and Shafra were on the throne there must have been considerable oppression of the poor,[222] and suffering caused thereby, through the forced labor which they must have employed, the unhealthy concentration of vast masses of men on particular sites, and the accidents inseparable from the elevation into place of huge blocks of stone, when human rather than mechanical power was the motive force applied. But the lesser erections of the other kings may have been reckoned an advantage by the laboring class, as furnishing an occupation unattended with much danger, and raising the rate of wages by the demand which it produced upon the labor market. The increased wealth of the nobles, arising as it did chiefly from the great productiveness of the soil, and from skill in its cultivation, together with success in the breeding and treatment of cattle, must also have tended to raise the laborer's position, and place him above the fear of want or even of real poverty. There is reason to believe that up to this period of Egyptian history there was no large employment of slaves; wars were of rare occurrence, and when they took place, not many prisoners could be made, for the tribes upon the Egyptian borders were none of them numerous; slaves might occasionally be bought, but these passed commonly into domestic service;[223] and the result was that both the cultivation of the soil, and most of the other industrial pursuits, were in the hands of the native Egyptians, and furnished them with an ample variety of not disagreeable careers. We do not see the stick employed on the backs of the laborers in the early sculptures; they seem to accomplish their various tasks with alacrity and almost pleasure. They plough, and hoe, and reap; drive cattle or asses; winnow and store corn; gather grapes and tread them, singing in chorus as they tread; cluster round the wine-press or the threshing-floor, on which the animals tramp out the grain; gather lotuses; save cattle from the inundation; engage in fowling or fishing; and do all with an apparent readiness and cheerfulness which seems indicative of real content. It is true that the sculptures are not photographs; they *may* give a flattering picture of things, and not represent them as they were; but we do not generally find that oppressors care to conceal their oppression, or to make out that the classes which they despise are happy under their yoke. Add to this, that the Egyptian moral code required kindness to be shown towards dependents;[224] and the conclusion would seem to be at least probable, that the general contentment and cheerfulness of the laboring classes, which we seem to see in the sculptures of the pyramid period, was a reality.

CHAPTER XV.

THE SIXTH DYNASTY—CULMINATION AND DECLINE.

Marked Division between the Fifth and Sixth Dynasties—Shift of Power to the South. First Evidence of a united Egypt. Group of four Monarchs—Teta, Pepi (Merira), Merenra, and Neferkara. Probable Position of Ati. Reign of Teta. Reign of Pepi—First great War—Reflections to which it gives rise—Pepi's Pyramid and Titles—Position of Una under him—Family of Pepi. Reign of Marenra. Reign of Neferkara. Traditions respecting Nitocris. Sudden Decline of Egypt at the Close of the Sixth Dynasty. Culmination of the early Egyptian Art, and Advance of Civilization under it.

"La première civilisation de l'Egypte finit avec la sixième dynastie."—LENORMANT, *Manuel d'Histoire Ancienne*, vol. i, p. 317.

BOTH Manetho and the author of the Turin papyrus regarded the death of Unas as constituting a marked division in Egyptian history. Manetho, who made the fifth dynasty Elephantiné,¹ declared the sixth to be Memphitic,² thus affirming a separation of locality, and so probably of blood, between the two. The existing remains confirm the fact of such a separation, but exactly invert Manetho's local arrangement, connecting as they do in the strongest way the monarchs of the fifth dynasty with Memphis and its vicinity,³ while they attach those of the sixth to Middle and Upper Egypt,⁴ and exhibit them as at any rate visiting Elephantiné,⁵ if not holding their court there. The Turin papyrus is content to draw a strong line of demarcation at this point, without expressing the ground of it. On the whole, it would seem to be certain that, down to the death of Unas, Memphis was the great seat of Egyptian empire ; while with the accession of the sixth dynasty there was a shift of power to the southward. Abydos, or some place in its neighborhood, became the residence of the kings ; the quarries of El-Kaab and Hammamât were worked instead of those of Mokattam ; the vicinity of Abydos became the great burial-place of the time. There was, however, no disintegration of the empire ; Memphis continued subject to the kings who ruled in Middle Egypt ; and both the extreme north and the extreme south owned their power. Their monuments are found at Tanis and at Assouan, as well as at Hammamât, El-Kaab, and Sauict-el-Meitin ;[6] and they were evidently masters of Egypt in its widest extent, from "the tower of Syéné" to the Mediterranean.

What was the extent of the Egypt ruled by the great pyramid kings and the other monarchs of the fourth and fifth dynasties is more doubtful. As these monarchs worked the mines of Wady Magharah, we must suppose them to have held under their sway the entire low tract east of the Nile from Memphis to the Syrian Desert ; and they *may* have been masters also of the Delta, and of the Nile valley as far as the cataracts. But it is important to note that we have no proof that they were. The monarchs of what we have called "the Pyramid period" are only proved to have possessed the tract about Memphis, and the line of country connecting that tract with the mines of Wady Magharah—there are no memorials of them in the Delta, none in Upper Egypt,[7] none even in Middle Egypt—and it is possible that those tracts were not under their rule. With the sixth dynasty we have the first evidence of a united Egypt, of monarchs who reign over the entire Nile valley from Elephantiné to the marsh tract bordering upon the Mediterranean Sea.[8] At the same time we come upon the first evidence of a decidedly martial spirit,[9] of expeditions on a large scale, of elaborate military training, of the attention of the nation being turned to arms from agriculture. It is a reasonable conjecture that the kings of the sixth dynasty, more warlike than their predecessors, may have been the first to make that united Egypt which we find existing in their day, and that their foreign conquests may have been the result of a previous internal consolidation of the Egyptian power in its own proper territory.

The sixth dynasty is mainly composed of a group of four monarchs, who bore the names of Teta, Pepi or Merira, Merenra, and Neferkara.[10] The last three were near relations— Pepi being the father of both Merenra and Neferkara, who succeeded in due order to their father's sovereignty. Whether Teta belonged to the same family is uncertain. The Egyptian kings of the early period very rarely note their relationship one to another,[11] and it is quite an exceptional circumstance that we are able to trace the family connection of three consecutive monarchs in this dynasty.

Besides the four chief monarchs of the time, around whom the history clusters, we have three other monumental names, apparently belonging to the same period, the exact position

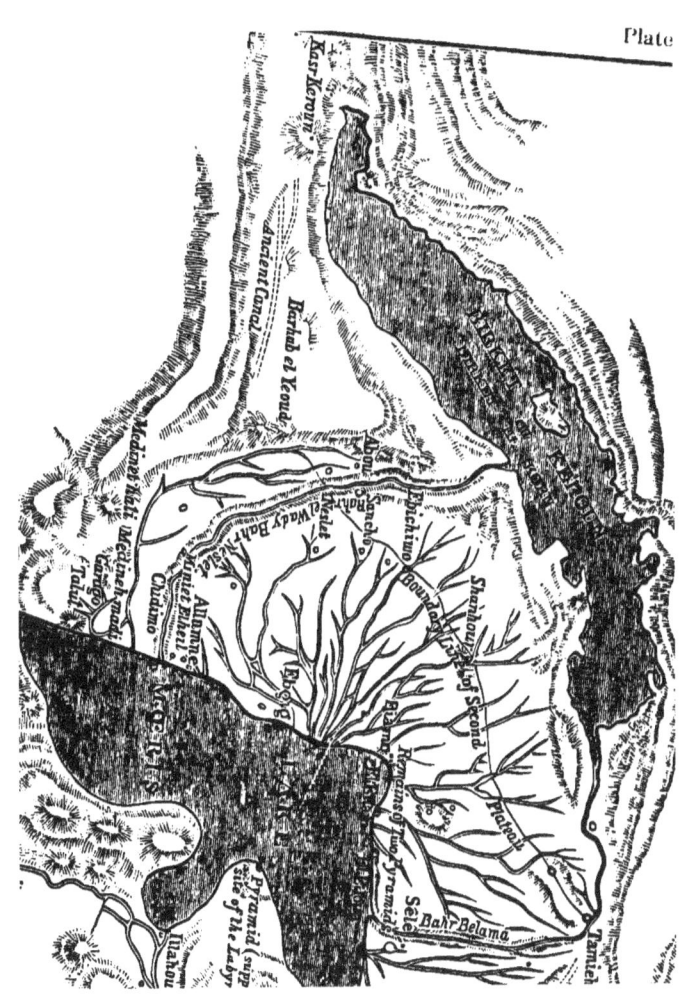

Plate VIII. Vol. II.

Fig. 16.—NEFER-HOTEP RECEIVES LIFE FROM ANUKA.—See Page 97.

Fig. 17.—HOUSE ON PILES IN THE LAND OF PUNT.—See Page 120.

of which in the list it is difficult to determine. These are Ati, Userkara, and Imhotp. Ati, 𓋹𓏏𓏭, appears in an inscription at Hammamât, set up in his first year,[12] which shows him to have built a pyramid called Bai-u, or that "of the souls." In style the inscription so closely resembles those of other kings of this time that it is supposed to prove him a monarch of the dynasty,[13] though probably one whose reign occupied but a short time and was not of any importance. What exact position should be given him is open to question. Some critics, assimilating his name to that of the Manethonian Othoës, are inclined to put him first, and to regard him as the founder of the sixth dynasty.[14] Others would give him the second place in the dynasty, directly after Teta,[15] in which case it would be natural to regard him as identical with Userkara, 𓇳𓊃𓂋𓂓, to whom the table of Seti I. at Abydos assigns that position. Inhotep, 𓅓𓊵𓏏𓊪, might in that case be relegated to the period following Neferkara, if indeed he were really a king of Egypt, which scarcely appears from his inscription.[16]

Omitting from further consideration these insignificant and doubtful monarchs, we shall regard the sixth dynasty as consisting of four chief kings—Teta, Pepi (=Merira), Merenra, his son, and Neferkara, Merenra's brother, and of a single queen, Nitocris (Net-akert), who terminated the series.

Teta, 𓍘𓏏, who succeeded Unas, either directly or after a very short interval,[17] was not a monarch of any distinction. He built a pyramid which he called *Tatasu*,[18] "the (most) lasting of places;" and he conferred favors on an officer named Sabu, or Abeba, whom he made his companion in his voyages, and otherwise distinguished above all the rest of his courtiers.[19] He also must be allowed the credit of having recognized the promise of more than ordinary talent in a youth of the official class named Una, whom he selected from the mass of candidates and attached immediately to his person. Una, who became the right hand of Teta's successor, Pepi, and of Pepi's son, Merenra, received his first promotion from King Teta, who conferred upon him the dignities of "crownbearer," "superintendent of the storehouse," and "registrar," or "sacred scribe, of the docks."[20]

Pepi (Fig. 7), the probable successor of Teta, rejoiced in the two names of Pepi, ▮▮◊◊ and Merira, ○⇌◊◊, by which he seems to have designated himself indifferently. In one tablet[21] we see two representations of him, seated back to back, and accompanied by inscriptions equally descriptive of royalty, in one of which the name of Pepi, and in the other the name Merira, is attached to the "image of his majesty." Pepi had a prosperous and a long reign, though certainly not the hundred years assigned him by Manetho,[22] since Una, who was grown to manhood and held high office in the reign of his predecessor, outlived him by several years, and was after his death in the employment of his son and successor.[23] His eighteenth year is the highest mentioned on the monuments;[24] but it is probable that he reigned longer. Pepi is the first king of Egypt who exhibits a marked warlike tendency. In his second year[25] he made an expedition against the Mentu, who had recovered possession of the Sinaitic peninsula, and, having reduced them, set up his tablet in a somewhat unusual form[26] on the rocks of the Wady Magharah. Not long after, he turned his arms against the Amu and the Herusha, two peoples living in the sands of the desert to the east of Lower Egypt.[27] Regarding these enemies as really formidable, Pepi exerted himself to collect and drill an army of unusual size, counted by tens of thousands.[28] His first levies were made in the north among the native Egyptians; but looking upon the forces thus raised as insufficient, he determined to obtain the strength that he deemed requisite by calling on the negro tribes of the south to furnish him with a contingent. The date at which these tribes were made subject to Egypt is uncertain, but it was clearly before the time of Pepi; and his power over them was so completely established that he had only to demand troops and they were furnished. From Areret, from Zam,[29] from Amam, from Ua-uat, from Kaau, and from Tattam, the swarthy bands gathered themselves together, and entering southern Egypt placed themselves at the disposition of the Pharaoh. They were no doubt a wild and disorderly crew; and it was of the first necessity to set officers over them, and subject them to a course of drill, in order to render their services of any value. The persons entrusted with this duty were a somewhat motley assemblage. They consisted of "the nomarchs, the chancellors, the close friends of the palace, the superintendents, the rulers of the nomes of the North and of the South, the superintendents of the gold region, the superintendents of the priests of the South and of the North, the superintendents of the register," and of various other " officers of the South, and of the North, and of the cities."[30] Whether the drill which took place under their auspices was effectual or not it is impossible to say. The troops, however, when regarded as sufficiently trained, were concentrated. Una, the official above mentioned, and the historian of the campaign, prepared the commissariat, "wearing out his sandals" in his assiduous performance of the task allotted him ; after a march of some considerable length, the country of the Herusha was reached, and the war began. "The warriors came," says Una, "and destroyed the land of the Herusha. and returned fortunately home ; and they came again, and took possession of the land of the Herusha, and returned fortunately home ; and they came and demolished the fortresses of the Herusha, and returned fortunately home ; and they cut down the vines and the fig-trees, and returned fortunately home ; and they set fire to the houses, and returned fortunately home ; and they killed the chief men by tens of thousands, and returned fortunately home. And the warriors brought back with them a great number of living captives, which pleased the king more than all the rest. Five times did the king send me out to set things right in the land of the Herusha, and to subdue their revolt by force ; each time I acted so that the king was pleased with me."[31] Even yet, however, the war was not over. The enemy collected in a tract known as Takheba, to the north of their own proper country, and took up a threatening attitude. Once more the Egyptian army was sent against them, this time conveyed in boats, and gained a complete victory ; the country was subdued to the extreme frontier towards the north, and acknowledged the supremacy of Pepi.[32]

The locality of this campaign is somewhat doubtful. It has been regarded as either Syria or some portion of Arabia Petræa,[33] and Pepi has been supposed to have sent his troops to their destination *by sea*.[34] But the latest critic suggests a district of the Delta as the true scene of the struggle, believing that the more northern portion of this tract, the country round Lake Menzaleh, was at this time occupied by the ancestors of the Bedouin tribes who now inhabit the desert of Suez.[35] In this case the boats employed would merely have descended the Nile, or have traversed portions of the lake just mentioned.

The circumstances of the expedition give rise to certain reflections. In the first place, it is remarkable that we find the negro races of the south already subdued without any previous notice, in any of the Egyptian remains, of the time or circumstances of their subjugation. One writer, seeing the difficulty, boldly states that "Pepi reduced these enemies to obedience:"[36] but this fact which is not mentioned by any authority, has been evolved out of his inner consciousness. We find the negroes already obedient subjects of Pepi when they are first mentioned as coming into contact with him; and his enlistment of them as soldiers to fight his battles would seem to imply that their subjugation had not been very recent. It is necessary to suppose that some monarch of the fourth or fifth dynasty had made them Egyptian subjects, without leaving behind him any record of the fact, or at any rate without leaving any record that has escaped destruction.

In the next place, it may raise some surprise, that, when there is a mention of so many nations as near neighbors to Egypt upon the south, nothing is said respecting the Cushites or Ethiopians. In later times Cushite races bordered Egypt on the south, and fierce wars were waged between the Pharaohs and the Ethiopian monarchs for the mastery of the valley of the Nile. But in the time of Pepi the Cushites were evidently at a distance. The conjecture is made that they had not yet immigrated into Africa, but still remained wholly in their original Asiatic seats, and only crossed at a later date, by way of the Straits of Bab-el-Mandeb, into the tract upon the middle Nile which they subsequently inhabited.[37] But perhaps this is too violent a supposition. The negro races mentioned in the inscription of Una need not have inhabited a very large tract of country; and the Cushites may have held all Abyssinia without obtaining mention in the inscription of Una or even attracting the attention of Pepi.

Thirdly, the question may be asked, Who were the Herusha? De Rougé translates the word "lords of the sands," and suggests that they were a Syro-Arabian race,[38] but can give no geographic or other illustrations. Of course, if the word is Egyptian and descriptive, not ethnic, it is in vain to look for parallels to it among real ethnic appellatives. Later mentions of the Herusha place them towards the north, and give them a productive land,[39] such as can scarcely be found in this direction nearer than Palestine.

Like his predecessor, Teta, and like most monarchs of the fourth and fifth dynasties, Pepi constructed a pyramid, to receive his remains when he should pass from earth. The pyramids of Pepi, and his son, Merenra, have lately been identified. They belong, as might have been expected, to the

Saccarah group, and correspond to Nos. 1 and 2 on Colonel Howard Vyse's plan. The sepulchral chambers, which contained the bodies of the kings, are covered with hieroglyphics of a religious and funereal character. The name which he gave to it was Mennefer, "the good abode"—the same designation as that of the old capital, Memphis, which had now probably ceased to be the residence of the court. The white stone sarcophagus, which he intended to occupy the sepulchral chamber of this edifice, and which no doubt ultimately received the royal mummy, was conveyed by Una, at his order, from the Mokattam quarries in "the great boat of the inner palace,"[40] with its cover, a door, two jambs, and a basin or pedestal, to the site chosen for the tomb. Other works assigned to Pepi are repairs to the temple of Athor at Denderah,[41] and one or more edifices at Tanis in the Delta, which he adorned with blocks of pink syenite brought from the quarries of Upper Egypt.[42] He also caused sculptures to be carved on the rocks of Wady Magharah[43] and Hammamât;[44] and made use of the quarries of El-Kaab,[45] where numerous inscriptions contain his name, and record his greatness. It was probably in connection with these many works that Pepi received with such extreme satisfaction the prisoners taken by his troops in their campaigns against the Herusha; he obtained thereby a most welcome addition to the body of laborers which was engaged constantly in his buildings.

The titles assumed by Pepi possess in some cases a peculiar interest. Besides the usual epithets of "King of Egypt" and "lord of the double diadem," he calls himself "lover of the two lands," "lover of his race," "son of Athor, mistress of Denderah," "lord of all life" and "the triple conquering Horus." The "two lands" are no doubt Upper and Lower Egypt, and the "race" intended may be either his own family or the nation of the Egyptians; the claim to be "son of Athor" recalls the similar claim of Khufu, who, like Pepi, adorned the temple of that goddess at Denderah;[46] "lord of all life," though not a usual title,[47] is one to which we can quite understand an Egyptian king laying claim; the only title difficult to explain is that of "the *triple* conquering Horus," which does not occur either earlier or later. De Rougé, who notes that many of the later kings assume the title of "double conquering Horus," in connection with their sway over the two Egypts," suggests that the "triple Horus" of Pepi contains an allusion to his having extended his rule over the negro territory south of Upper Egypt;[48] but it is perhaps more probable that a triple division of Egypt itself is glanced at,⁵⁴ and that Pepi, who held his court in Central Egypt—the later Heptanomis—meant to indicate his sovereignty over the Delta and the Thebaïd, as well as over that region.

The glories of Pepi's reign were, it is probable, due in some degree to his ministers. Una, who had owed his first elevation and promotion to Pepi's predecessor, Teta, continued in high favor during the whole of Pepi's reign, and held under him a number of most important appointments. He was "prophet of the royal pyramid," "royal secretary" and "keeper of the secrets," "sole companion," "superintendent of the docks," and "superintendent of the land of Khent."⁶¹ After being employed in the procuring of the royal sarcophagus with its appurtenances, he was given a commission of a military character, which associated him closely with the various expeditions against the Herusha, and gave him some ground for claiming the final success as his own.⁵² Ankh-Merira, buried at Saccarah, was "governor of the quarries opposite Memphis," and "chief director of public works" under Pepi; Pepi-Nekht was "chief *heb*" and "governor of the town of the pyramid."⁶³

In his family relations Pepi was fairly fortunate. His first wife, Amtes,⁵⁴ appears indeed to have died before him; but he did not prove inconsolable. He contracted a second marriage after a time with Ankhnes-Merira, a noble lady, though not of royal birth, who bore him at least two sons, Merenra and Neferkara, and outlived him by several years. Ankhnes-Merira was buried in the cemetery of Abydos; and her tomb bears an inscription, in which she is called "royal wife of Merira, great in favor, great in grace, great in all things, companion of Horus, mother of Merenra, king of the two Egypts; and mother of Neferkara, king of the two Egypts."⁵⁵ Her father, Khua, was loaded with favors by his son-in-law and his grandsons, who made him "chief of the town of the pyramid," "lord of the diadem," "commander of the great men both of the North and of the South," "commandant of the chief cities of Lower Egypt," and "chief of every dignity in things divine."⁵⁶

On the death of Pepi, Mer-en-ra, 🜨 ☥, the elder of his two sons, became king. Merenra's disposition seems to have been altogether peaceful. Scarcely had he mounted the throne when he gave directions to Una, whom he had made governor of Upper Egypt, to employ himself in the quarrying of blocks of stone for the pyramid, Sha-nefer, which he was bent on constructing for his own tomb, and in the obtaining of a handsome sarcophagus, together with a granite doorway

and doors for the sepulchral apartment of the pyramid."
This commission executed, Una was immediately ordered to
procure a great slab of alabaster from the quarries of Hat-nub
(Ombos?), to form a sepulchral table or altar,⁵⁸ such as appears commonly in the representations of the sacrificial feasts
in tombs. At the same time he was required to begin the
construction of docks in the country of the Ua-uat, which
were no doubt connected with the Nile, and were intended to
shelter the transports which it was necessary to employ in the
conveyance of the granite needed for the royal pyramid.
Wood was plentiful in the Ua-uat country and its neighborhood ; the negroes were friendly ; and the chiefs of Areret,
Ua-uat, Amam, and Ma furnished timber in such abundance
that four transports—probably great rafts ⁵⁹—were constructed
in the course of a year. These were loaded with the granite
blocks prepared for the pyramid, and, safely passing the cataracts at the height of the inundation, conveyed their burden
to the site which Merenra had chosen.⁶⁰ It was probably during the progress of Una's labors that the king in person visited
the quarries of Assouan near Elephantiné, and set up the
tablet, still to be seen in that locality, on which he distinctly
states that " the king himself both came there and returned." ⁶¹

It is thought that Merenra did not rule very long.⁶² He
was succeeded by his younger brother Nefer-ka-ra, ⊙⏐⏐𝖴
to whom the fragments of the Turin papyrus appear to assign
a reign of twenty years.⁶³ He too made a pyramid, to which
he gave the name of Menankh, "the abode of life," in order
to show his belief that life really, and not death, dwelt in the
tomb. Neferkara maintained the Egyptian dominion in the
Sinaitic peninsula, and sent a commission there in his second
year, which consisted of twelve persons, who have left a memorial which is still to be seen upon the spot.⁶⁴ It is remarkable that this memorial places the king and his mother almost
upon a par, as if they were both reigning conjointly. Neferkara is characterized as "King of the two Egypts, master,
and conquering Horus," his mother as "royal wife of Merira,
king of the two Egypts, and royal mother of Neferkara, king
of the two Egypts."⁶⁵ She appears to be figured upon the
rock,⁶⁶ while he is not figured at all ; and altogether her position on the tablet is quite as important and prominent as
his. We seem here to have evidence that female influence
was making itself felt in Egypt more than formerly ; and that
the way was being paved for the admission, as constitutional,⁶⁷
of exclusive female sovereignty.

The succession after the death of Neferkara is doubtful. The contemporary records fail at this point; but Manetho,[8] Herodotus,[9] and the Turin papyrus,[10] agree in referring to about this period a queen called Nitocris, ![hieroglyph] the only Egyptian female to whom a sole reign is assigned; and modern critics are inclined to accept the reign as a fact,[11] and as belonging to this dynasty. The chief event of the reign, if it be admitted as historical, is the completion of the third pyramid, begun by Mencheres. Manetho makes Nitocris its builder;[12] Herodotus who assigns it to Menkaura (Mycerinus), reports a tradition, as prevalent,[13] which made it the work of a woman. The peculiar construction of the pyramid lends itself to the theory that in its present shape it is the work of two distinct sovereigns.[14] If Nitocris is to be regarded as really the finisher of the edifice, she must be considered a great queen, one of the few who have left their mark upon the world by the construction of a really great monument. The pyramid of Mencheres, as designed and erected by him, was a building of but moderate pretensions, considerably less than many of those at Abousir and elsewhere,[15] which have conferred no fame on their constructors. It was the addition made to the pyramid by its enlarger which alone entitled it to take rank among "the Three," that ever since the time of Herodotus, have been separated off from all other edifices of the kind, and placed in a category of their own. It was, moreover, the casing of the enlarged pyramid, which was of a beautiful red granite up to half the height,[16] that caused this pyramid to be especially admired; and the casing was necessarily the work of the later builder.

The other traditions attaching to the name of Nitocris, resting as they do on the sole authority of Herodotus, can scarcely be regarded as historical. She is said to have succeeded a brother, who had been murdered by his subjects, and to have avenged his death in the following extraordinary fashion:—"Having constructed a spacious underground chamber, under pretence of inaugurating it, she invited to a banquet there those of the Egyptians whom she knew to have had the chief share in her brother's murder, and, when they were feasting, suddenly let the river in upon them by means of a secret duct of large size." Having so done, she smothered herself in a chamber filled with ashes, to escape the vengeance which she regarded as awaiting her. It is difficult to imagine that any sovereign would, under any circumstances, have pursued so roundabout a method of avenging a predecessor; it is certain that the Egyptians were wholly averse to suicide; such a suicide as that related has no parallel in mundane history, and is about as unlikely a death for any one to select as could be imagined.

Still, it is thought that, however incredible the details, they may yet mark an historic fact, viz., that about this time "murder and violence prevailed in the Egyptian kingdom,"—there were many "competitors for the throne," and their rivalry produced convulsions, amid which "the vessel of the State continually approached nearer" and nearer "to destruction,"[55]—the monarchy was disintegrated; several small kingdoms were formed; civil war raged, and monuments wholly ceased; it was only after a considerable interval—an interval which there are no means of measuring[76]—that once more a flourishing community arose in Egypt, located in a new place, which has left undying traces of itself in tablets, brick pyramids, rock sculptures and *stelæ* or tombstones, and is the not unworthy successor of the earlier kingdom, which can be traced, almost without a break, from Senoferu to Nitocris.

Before, however, the decline set in, the early civilization reached its culminating point under the kings of Manetho's sixth dynasty. Some of the best Egyptian statues, as one on which the gallery of the Louvre especially prides itself, are of this period.[78] The subjects of the bas-reliefs, the modes of representation, and the general drawing of the figures are much the same as during the previous dynasties; but the treatment is in some respects better. True relief occasionally takes the place of the peculiarly Egyptian *cavo-riliero* of the earlier time,[80] where the whole outline is deeply incised, with a hardness of effect that is unpleasing. Something more of freedom is also observable in the animal forms, and something more of life and action in the human figures.[81] Architecture, however, does not advance; the best pyramid of the period—that completed by Nitocris upon the nucleus afforded by the small construction of Mencheres—is very inferior, both in size and constructive skill, to the great monuments of Khufu and Shafra. There are no temples now remaining which can be referred to the time;[83] nor is there any novelty in the plan or ornamentation of the tombs. The forms of the gods are still absent from the "eternal houses," though they appear on the sculptured tablets of the kings.

In the arts of life we observe two or three small advances. Stools are for the most part superseded by chairs with a low back.[84] The use of sandals spreads from the grandees to their upper servants.⁸⁴ The somewhat dangerous sport of spearing the crocodile from a light boat is indulged in;⁸⁵ and the domestication of dogs (Fig. 11) has produced a new type.⁸⁶ In another direction we observe a change that is scarcely a mark of progress. War has become an element in the life of the people, and the manufacture of arms has grown into a trade. We see the fashioning of spears and bows in the sculptures,⁸⁷ and meet with occasional instances of figures where a dagger is worn in the belt.⁸⁸ Armorers are noticed as a distinct class,⁸⁹ and drove no doubt a brisk trade. The division of labor continued to extend itself; and we have mention, or representation, of at least thirty different employments.⁹⁰ Literature grew in repute, as a profession; and the skilful scribe might hope for advancement to posts of high importance. If the "Praise of Learning" is rightly ascribed to the sixth dynasty,⁹¹ we may note as an advance the increased length of literary compositions, and the employment of a form of poetry which did not consist merely in the balance of sentences. We have also to note as belonging to this period the birth of history in the shape of a biographical memoir of some length, composed by an official of high rank, and inscribed upon his tomb.⁹²

A further advance of the religion in the way of expansion and the multiplication of gods is also discernible. An altar dedicated by King Pepi, which is now in the Turin Museum,⁹³ seems to contain something like a full account of the gods recognized at this period, and something approaching to an account of the estimate which was commonly made of their relative importance. The altar is dedicated to Phthah under the form of Sokari;⁹⁴ and this god, with his wife Sekhet, occupies naturally the foremost position on the monument. It would be unsafe, however, to conclude from this, that Phthah was recognized as the chief god, since the divinity to whom an object was dedicated could not but hold the first place on that object. Next to Phthah is placed Thoth, and next to Thoth a rare deity, called Petmutf, who is said to "dwell in the houses of the Ocean."⁹⁵ These three gods are figured, and not merely named, on the monument: they occupy the first column of the inscription, which may be called "the column of the dedication," and thus stand quite separate from the remaining deities, with whom they do not enter into comparison. Thoth, however, has his place among these, appearing not in the first column only, but also in several of the remaining ones; and thus his place among the gods can be determined.

The gods generally appear to be divided into two classes, the universal and the local. The universal, or those worshipped in common by all the Egyptians, are, besides Satemi, "Hearing" (who seems to be placed first because through her the gods *hear* prayers), Tum, Khepra, and Shu, the Sun-Gods,[96] Shu being accompanied by his wife, Tafné or Tefnut;[97] then, the deities of the Osirid legend, Seb, Netpé, Osiris himself, Isis, Set, Nephthys, and Horus;[98] next Ra, with whom are joined three abstractions, Renpa, "the Year," Het, "an Age," and Jeta, "Eternity;" after these, three other abstractions—Ankh, "Life," Tat, "Stability" and Aut, "Triumph;" then, Thoth under two forms;[99] and finally, an unnamed god, called "the Great One of the five in Api-Sekhet." These deities seem to admit of the following arrangement:—

PERSONS.
1. Tum.
2. Khepra.
3. Shu.
4. Tafné.
5. Seb.
6. Netpé.
7. Osiris.
8. Isis.
9. Set.
10. Nephthys.
11. Horus.
12. Ra.

13. Thoth.
14. The Great One of the Five.

ABSTRACTIONS.
Satemi.

{ Year.
{ Age.
{ Eternity.

Life.
Stability.
Triumph.

Among the local gods, who are enumerated after these, many occur more than once, as being objects of worship in more than one city.[100] The most important of them are Phthah, worshipped in Memphis; Num or Khnum, in Elephantiné; Sabak, at Letopolis and elsewhere; Athor, at Mensa and Denderah; Bast. at Bubastis; Mentu, at Uas or Hermonthis; Neith, at Tena or This; Anubis, at Sep; Nishem,[101] at Aukaf; and Kartek, a form of Taourt,[102] at Patek. The gods of the first list also occur in the second, since many of them were the objects of a *special* local worship. Abstractions also occur in this list. and genii, such as "the Four of Amenti."[103] Altogether, including manifest abstractions, there seem to be about fifty objects of worship mentioned, of which some twenty-five or thirty are proper deities.

The list is important, as well for what it omits as for what it contains. It is very noticeable that still, though the court has moved to Abydos, and has Thebes under its sway, there is no mention of Ammon. It is also very curious that Khem is omitted, especially as Pepi is seen worshipping him in his grossest form in a tablet at Hammamât.[104] Other omissions, less surprising, but still noticeable, are those of Maut, Sati, Aten, Khonsu, Onuris, Aemhept, Anuka, Ma, Heka, and Bes. Rapid as the growth of the Pantheon has been since the date of the great pyramid kings,[105] it is not yet complete. Not only have numerous local worships yet to be absorbed into the general Egyptian religion, but fresh deities have still to be invented or discovered, fresh ideas to be developed. Ancient polytheism is a Proteus, always varying its form, and abhorrent of finality. The religion of Egypt had to pass through many different phases before it reached its final shape; and we shall still have to note various other important modifications of it in that portion of the Egyptian history with which we have to deal in these volumes.

CHAPTER XVI.

THE DYNASTIES BETWEEN THE SIXTH AND THE TWELFTH.

No Monuments left by any Dynasty between the Sixth and the Eleventh, which were, however, separated by an Interval. Disintegration of Egypt—Parallel Kingdoms of Memphis, Heracleopolis, and Thebes. Causes of the Disintegration and Decline: and probable Length of the Interval. Situation of Thebes. Its Antiquity, Name, and Primitive Position. Rise of Thebes to Independence. Dynasty of the Antefs and Mentuhoteps. Reign of Saukhkara Expedition to Punt. Close of the Dynasty. Features of the Early Theban Civilization.

"After the sixth dynasty a monumental gap, which can neither be filled up nor bridged over, occurs till the eleventh dynasty."—BIRCH, *Ancient Egypt*, p. 56.

OF the five dynasties which Manetho placed between the sixth and the twelfth, one only—the eleventh—has left any monumental traces. It has been argued by some that this dynasty was contemporary with the sixth, if not even with the fourth;[1] but the latest discoveries seem to render this theory untenable. The sixth dynasty, as was shown in the preceding chapter,[2] bore sway over the entire Nile valley, and cannot have allowed the existence of an independent monarchy in the Thebaid, which would have cut it off from the

South. There are, moreover, signs of development and advance in certain respects, under the kings of Dynasty XI., which render it almost certain that an interval of some not inconsiderable duration must have separated off the second Egyptian civilization from the first.³

It would seem that, at the death of Nitocris, the centrifugal force, which had long held the various provinces of Egypt asunder, proved stronger than the centripetal, and a disintegration of the empire took place. Memphis re-established its independence, and dynasties ruled there, to which Manetho assigned in his list the seventh and eight places. Another kingdom sprang up in the Delta, having its capital at Heracleopolis Parva, in the Sethroite nome.⁴ Here again were two successive dynasties, Manetho's ninth and tenth. In central Egypt a new power developed itself at Thebes, which rapidly acquired a superiority over the rival kingdoms, and ended by absorbing them. The eleventh dynasty has left considerable traces of itself; but of the other four there are no contemporary records, and, beyond some names of kings in the Turin papyrus, and in the lists of Karnac, Saccarah, and Abydos, which may be guessed to belong to them, we are entirely without details with respect to this period of Egyptian history.⁵

The causes of the sudden decline which accompanied the close of the sixth dynasty, and of the suspension of animation during a term variously estimated at from 166 to 740 years,⁶ are obscure, and can only be conjectured. M. Lenormant suggests⁷ an invasion and conquest of Egypt by some foreign people, which held the real dominion of the country during the interval, whatever it was, but allowed native subject monarchs to maintain a precarious and inglorious sway at Memphis and in the Eastern Delta; but Dr. Birch observes⁸ with reason, that it is "difficult to believe" in a conquest, of which there is no historical record, no trace upon the monuments. The assertion that the skulls of mummies belonging to the eleventh and later dynasties are sensibly different from those of the period terminating with Dynasty VI., and indicate a decided modification of *physique*, such as would naturally follow on the introduction into the population of a new element, with which M. Lenormant supports his theory,⁹ lacks corroboration by other writers, and is certainly not the statement of a fact generally admitted by Egyptologers. M. Lenormant himself allows the dubiousness of his theory, and winds up his remarks upon the subject with an alternative view: "It would be rash," he says,¹⁰ " to assert that the sudden eclipse which shows itself in the civilization of Egypt immediately after the sixth dynasty had not solely for its cause one of those almost inexplicable crises of weakness, wherewith the life of nations, like that of individuals, is sometimes crossed." It would seem to be best to acquiesce, for the present at any rate, in this view; and to suppose that the great burst of vigor and energy, which commencing with Seneferu, terminated, perhaps seven centuries later,[11] with Nitocris, was followed by a period of exhaustion and enfeeblement, during which no works of any magnitude were constructed, no wars of any importance carried on, no inscriptions of any sort or kind set up. Such a pause in the life of an ingenious and active people like the Egyptians cannot be supposed to have been long; and we should incline, therefore, to the lowest estimate which has been hitherto made of the probable duration of the interval.

When Egypt, after this period of torpor, once more aroused herself and began to show new signs of life, the renascent civilization developed itself from a new centre. In the long and rich valley of the lower Nile, which extends above five hundred miles from Syéné to Memphis, almost any situation might furnish a site for a great city, since, except at Silsilis and at the Gebeleïn, the valley is never less than two miles wide, the soil is always fertile, good quarries are always at hand, and lavish Nature is so bounteous with her gifts that abundant sustenance can at any point be obtained for a large population. But, in this wealth of eligible sites, there are still degrees of eligibility—spots which Nature has distinguished by special favor, and as it were marked out for greatness and celebrity. Such a position is that which the traveller reaches, when, passing through the gorge of the Gebeleïn, he emerges upon the magnificent plain, at least ten miles in width, through which the river flows with a course from southwest to northeast for a distance of some forty miles between Erment and Qobt. Here, for the first time since quitting the Nubian desert, does the Nile enter upon a wide and ample space.[12] On either side the hills recede, and a broad green plain, an alluvium of the richest description, spreads itself out on both banks of the stream, dotted with *dom* and date palms, sometimes growing single, sometimes collected into clumps or groves. Here, too, there open out on either side, to the east and to the west, lines of route, offering great advantages for trade, on the one hand with the Lesser Oasis and so with the tribes of the African interior, on the other with the **western coast of the Red Sea, and the spice region of the op-**

posite shore.¹³ In the valley of Hammamât, down which passed the ancient route to the coast, are abundant supplies of *breccia verde* and of other valuable and rare kinds of stone,¹⁴ while at no great distance to the right and left of the route lie mines of gold, silver, and lead,¹⁵ anciently prolific, though exhausted now for many ages. Somewhat more remote, yet readily accessible by a frequented route, was the emerald region of Gebel Zabara, where the mines are still worked,¹⁶ though not at present very productive.

In this favored position, partly on the left but principally on the right bank of the stream, had grown up, probably from a remote antiquity, a flourishing provincial town, to which its inhabitants gave the name of Apet,¹⁷ Apé, or, with the feminine article, Tapé, which form the Greeks represented by Thebaï,¹⁸ whence our "Thebes." The city had for ages been only one out of the many populous towns which the early Pharaohs had held under their sway; it had been, no doubt, as it always continued to be, the head of a nome;¹⁹ it had its own local peculiarities of religion, manners, speech, nomenclature, even perhaps its own modification of the generally received hieroglyphical system of writing.²⁰ But hitherto it had drawn no special attention, it had attained no notoriety. One among some scores of considerable Egyptian towns,²¹ it had been content with a subject position, had refrained from asserting itself, and had consequently remained undistinguished.

When, however, at the close of the sixth dynasty, Egypt became disintegrated, and monarchies of no great strength were established in the Delta and at Memphis, it occurred to the authorities of Apt that the city over which they presided had as much right to exercise sovereignty as Heracleopolis Parva, and that a bold asertion of independence would probably be successful, might even be undisputed. The Memphitic kings of the seventh and eighth dynasties were too weak, the Heracleopolitans of the ninth and tenth too remote to attempt interference ; and Thebes became a free city, the capital of an independent monarchy, apparently without a struggle.

Who the individual was by whom this feat was accomplished, and the foundations laid of that second and more brilliant Egyptian civilization which eclipsed the glories of the first, it is impossible even to conjecture. According to the Turin papyrus the eleventh or "first Theban" dynasty comprised six, according to Manetho²² it consisted of sixteen, Pharaohs. The monumental traces of the dynasty, discovered hitherto, appear to show a series of either six or eight monarchs[23] who bear alternately the names of Enantef or Antef, 〈hieroglyphs〉 or 〈hieroglyphs〉, and Ment-hept or Mentu-hotep, 〈hieroglyphs〉 or 〈hieroglyphs〉. But it is quite possible that the series is incomplete, and far from certain that the alternation of name was scrupulously maintained from the beginning to the end of the dynasty. A king named Sankh-ka-ra seems to have belonged to it,[24] who is not proved to have borne, besides, either of the usual appellations.

The first king of the dynasty who is known to us was an Antef, whose coffin was discovered by some Arabs in the year 1827, near Qurnah to the west of Thebes.[25] He called himself "king of the two Egypts;" and his mummy, which was found inside the coffin, bore the royal diadem on its head.[26] It was enveloped in the pasteboard covering which has been called a "cartonnage," and the coffin was of a primitive character, being scooped out of the trunk of a tree.[27] He is supposed to have been succeeded by a Mentu-hotep whose name occurs in the "Table of Karnak," but of whom we have no contemporary monument. This first Mentu-hotep was followed by Antefaa or "Antef the Great," who reigned at least fifty years,[28] and was buried in a simple pyramid of brickwork at the foot of the western or Libyan mountains, in the valley known as El-Assasif, near the ruins of Thebes.

The tomb of Antefaa, 〈hieroglyphs〉, ornamented by a sculptured tablet, of which the upper portion is lost, was recently discovered by M. Mariette. The tablet[29] shows him standing among his dogs, and waited on by his chief huntsman; from which we may conclude that, like more than one of the ancient Assyrian monarchs,[30] he delighted in the chase, and regarded with affection and pride the faithful animals who were the companions of his amusement. Each has his name engraved above him, accompanied by a brief explanation, which shows that the dogs were valued for their hunting qualities, and used in the pursuit of the antelope and other quadrupeds. They are four in number, and each is of a different kind.

A second Mentu-hotep, the fourth king of the dynasty (according to Dr. Birch),[31] who bore also the names of Neb-kher-ra, 〈hieroglyphs〉, and Ra-neb-taui, 〈hieroglyphs〉, is thought to have succeeded Antefaa. By an inscription which he set up on the rocks of Konosso, quite close to Philæ, it is shown

Vol. II. Plate IX.

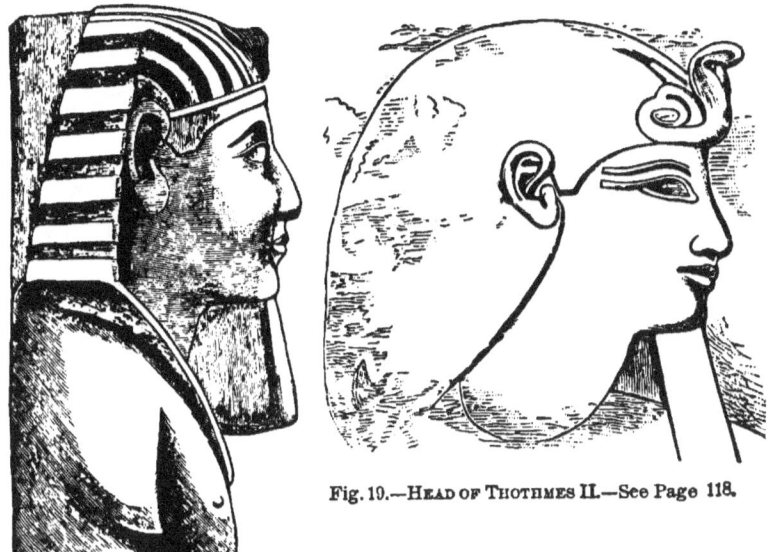

Fig. 19.—HEAD OF THOTHMES II.—See Page 118.

Fig. 18.—BUST OF AMENÔPHIS I.—See Page 115.

Fig. 20.—BUST OF THOTHMES I.— See Page 116.

Fig. 21.—HEAD OF QUEEN HATASU.—See Page 119.

Plate X. Vol. II.

Fig. 22.—HEAD OF QUEEN MUTEMUA.—See Page 141.

Fig. 23.—HEAD OF SETI I.—See Page 162.

that his dominion was not confined to the Thebaid, but extended over the whole of Upper Egypt; and at the same time it appears, by the relief chiselled upon the stone, that he claimed to be the conqueror of thirteen foreign nations,[32] probably negro tribes of the country bordering Egypt to the south. He is exhibited in the act of worshipping Khem, the special god of Kebtu, or Coptos, which appears by another tablet to have been, at any rate, his occasional residence.[33] This place commanded the entrance of the valley of Hammamât, the importance of which as a line of traffic was now for the first time fully recognized. Mentu-hotep II. sank wells in the valley, to provide water for the caravans which passed to and fro between Coptos and the Red Sea;[34] and carved a tablet on the rocks above to commemorate his operations. He also procured from a quarry in this quarter a huge sarcophagus, destined to serve as his tomb; its length was eight cubits, or twelve feet; its breadth four cubits, and its height two. The services of 3,000 men were required to transport the enormous monolith from the spot where it was quarried to the nearest wharf upon the great stream.[35] Mentu-hotep (Fig. 13) Nebkher-ra was also a patron of glyptic art. A statuary, named Iritisen, who lived under him, has left it on record in the inscription upon his tomb, that he "occupied the inmost recess of the king's heart, and made his delight all the day long."[36] This artist worked not merely in stone and marble, but "in gold, and silver, and ivory, and ebony,"[37] and was thus able to provide his royal master not only with statues, but with a vast variety of *objets de luxe*.

Mentu-hotep II. is thought to have been followed by an Antef who has left no record of his reign, but who appears in the "Table of Karnak" at this point.[38] His successor, Mentu-hotep III., continued to work the quarries of the Hammamât valley; and commissioners of his appointment set up several engraved tablets and inscriptions in that "beautiful" district.[39] These show that this monarch claimed to be the son of the god Khem, whose worship he, in common with the other kings of the dynasty, specially affected. No wars are recorded at this time, though soldiers were employed to protect the sculptors and quarrymen employed in the Hammamât district, which would seem to imply the vicinity of some enemy.

The last monarch of the dynasty appears to have borne the name of Sankh-ka-ra. He occupies the fifty-eighth place in the "New Table of Abydos."[40] An important inscription belonging to this reign has been recently discovered, and has received interpretation from M. Chabas. Sankh-ka-ra, it appears, not content with the land-trade, which had now for some time enriched the Theban monarchs and brought them in abundance the treasures of the African interior, resolved to open a new traffic by way of the Red Sea with the fertile and productive region known to the Egyptians as Punt, 𓊪𓏌𓏏𓈉. This tract has generally been regarded as a portion of "Happy Arabia;"[41] but the geographical researches of Dr. Brugsch have convinced him that Punt is to be sought, not on the Arabian but on the African side of the gulf, that in fact it is identical with the modern territory of the Somoauli.[42] "Punt," he observes,[43] "was a distant land, washed by the ocean, full of valleys and hills, abounding in ebony and other rich woods, in incense, balsam, precious metals, and costly stones; rich also in beasts, as camelopards, hunting leopards, panthers, dog-headed apes, and long-tailed monkeys. Birds with strange plumage rocked themselves on the branches of wonderful trees, especially the incense tree and the cocoa palm." Other authorities speak of it as producing benzoin, cassia, *kohl* or *stibium*, emeralds, ivory, and dogs of a good breed.[44] Sankh-ka-ra entrusted the expedition, which he sent to bring from Punt its precious wares, to a certain Hannu (Hanno?), who gives the following account of his proceedings. "I was sent," he says,[45] "to conduct ships to Punt, in order to bring back to his majesty the odoriferous gums which the princes of the red land had collected under the influence of the fear inspired by him in all countries. Behold, I left Coptos . . . . . His majesty ordained that the troops which were to accoompany me should be drawn from the southern parts of the Thebaid. . . . . I set forth with an army of 3,000 men. I passed through the red hamlet and a cultivated territory. I prepared the skins and the poles needed for the transport of the water jars to the number of twenty. Half my men each day carried loads; the other half placed the loads upon them. I dug a reservoir of twelve perches in a wood, and two reservoirs at a place called Atabet, one measuring a perch and twenty cubits, and the other a perch and thirty cubits. I made another at Ateb, measuring ten cubits each way, to contain water a cubit in depth. Then I arrived at Seba and constructed transports for the conveyance of all kinds of productions. I made a great offering there of oxen, cows, and goats. When I returned from Seba, I executed the orders of his majesty; I brought him back every sort of product that I met with in the havens of the holy land. I came back by way of Uak and Rohan, and brought with me from those places precious stones for statues in temples. Never was such a thing done since there were kings. Never was anything of the kind accomplished by any member of the royal family since the reign of the Sun-God, Ra. I acted thus for the king on account of the great affection which he entertained for me." The route pursued by Hannu as far as Seba appears to have been that which leads from Qobt or Qoft, by way of La Guitta, to Cosseir.⁴⁶ From Seba, where he built his transports, he must have proceeded southward along the African coast until he reached the fertile region with which it was his master's object to establish communications. He there probably found an *entrepôt* at which he was able to procure not only the products of the Somauli country itself, but also those which nations of the far East brought from Arabia, Persia, and perhaps even India, to be exchanged for the commodities of the regions watered by the Nile. Yemen and Hadramaut, Ophir, Bahrein,⁴⁷ Babylon, perhaps even Taprobané and Malacca, here found a mart for their valuable wares, and purchased with them the manufactures of Egypt, the hard woods of the African forests, and the swart and stalwart slaves of Nubia and Dongola. The line of traffic thus established continued in use during the whole of the Egyptian period, and even into Greek and Roman times. " It was the highway which, leading to the harbor of Leucos-limen (now Cossei ·), on the Red Sea, brought the wonders of India and Arabia to Europe ; it was the road of the merchants of all countries in the ancient world—the nations' bridge between Asia and Europe."⁴⁸

A special interest is added to Sankh-ka-ra's establishment of communications with the land of Punt by the circumstance that, according to Egyptian tradition Punt was the country from which they had derived some, at any rate, of their principal gods. Athor especially, "the mother," then "mistress of heaven," was "Queen of the Holy Land," "Mistress and Ruler of Punt."⁴⁹ Ammon was sometimes called the "Hak" or "King" of Punt, and Horus was honored as "the holy morning star which rose to the west of the land of Punt."⁵⁰ According to Brugsch, the hideous dwarf, Bes, "misshapen, and with apish countenance," was also originally a denizen of Punt, the "oldest form of the godhead" there, imported into Egypt at an early date from this distant region, and thenceforward a favorite object of domestic worship, recognized as "the god of joy, of music, and of pleasure, the divinity who chases away evil," and therefore as suited to preside over the toilet tables of great dames, and the arts by which beauty is preserved and enhanced.[51]

The eleventh, or first Theban dynasty seems to have ended in bloodshed and confusion. The first king of the twelfth dynasty tells us that, before he established himself upon the throne, Egypt had forgotten all her traditions[52]—had "become like a bull which had lost all memory of the past"[53]— that during a long term of civil war and disturbance the people of the land had suffered "affliction," and "there had been stability of fortune neither for the ignorant nor for the learned man."[54] The details of the troubles are wanting; but we can scarcely be mistaken in regarding private ambition as the disturbing force at work, and rival pretenders to the crown as responsible for the calamities of the period. The Antefs had not the prestige of long hereditary royalty; and their establishment of themselves in the kingly position might naturally create hopes and arouse jealousies, which some favorable occasion stimulated into action. Perhaps the Antef family died out ; perhaps Sankh-ka-ra had no male issue, and the husbands of his daughters disputed the succession among them. Opportunity would then arise for other claimants to come forward ; the quarrel would become more complicated, and civil war rage throughout the length and breadth of the land. It is certain that the Amen-em-hats and Usurtasens claim no connection with the Antefs and Mentu-hoteps, and all but certain that they were a new race, unconnected with their predecessors.

The "second Egyptian civilization," as it has been called,[55] differed in many respects from the first. The first was egoist, self-seeking, stately, cold, cruel. The second was utilitarian, beneficent, appealing less to the eye than to the mind, but judicious, far-sighted in its aims, and most successful in the results which it effected. The encouragement of trade and commerce, the establishment and improvement of commercial routes, the digging of wells, the formation of reservoirs, the protection of the roads by troops, the building of ships, the exploration of hitherto unknown seas—such were the special objects which the monarchs of the eleventh dynasty set before them, such the lines of activity into which they threw their own energies and the practical ability of their people. No longer aiming, like the old Memphitic kings, at leaving undying memorials of themselves in the shape of monuments that reached to heaven, but content with rude coffins and humble sepulchres, often not even of stone,[56] they were enabled to employ the labor of their subjects in productive pursuits, and to increase largely the general prosperity of the country by adding to the agricultural wealth of Egypt the luxuries and conveniences which an extensive commerce is sure to introduce. The full development of the new ideal was reserved for the dynasty which succeeded them, and is especially to be traced in the great works of utility connected with the Lake Mœris and the control of the Nile waters by means of sluices and reservoirs; but the eleventh dynasty set the example of seeking the welfare of their subjects rather than their own glorification; and when Amen-em-hat I., the founder of the twelfth, boasts that all the commands which he had ever issued had but increased the love which his people had for him,[57] he does but show that he had carried out the principles of governmental administration introduced by the Antefs and Mentu-hoteps.

It was natural that art, when such principles were in vogue, should be turned into new channels. No longer did king vie with king in the piling up of a monumental mountain; no longer was it the first aim of a monarch to "leave a memorial of himself."[58] Architecture consequently declined. The eleventh dynasty is scarcely commemorated by a single Egyptian building; and even the twelfth only left one of any great size.[59] Artistic energy was directed to statuary, to works in relief, to amulets, furniture, and ornaments of various kinds.[60] In these branches considerable progress was made. The statues of the time have no small merit;[61] the reliefs are drawn with delicacy, though wanting in variety and force. Animal forms, however, are depicted with some spirit. The four dogs of Antefaa offer a marked contrast the one with the other, and express with precision distinct canine types.[62] Two antelopes on another tomb of the same period are vigorous;[63] while the tracings of the hieroglyphs on the stelé of Iritisen, which comprise numerous figures of birds and beasts, are said to be of quite first-rate excellency.[64] Altogether, one is more struck perhaps by the persistency of Egyptian art in the same forms than by anything else in the remains of the eleventh dynasty, since even after an interval of some length, and in an entirely new and previously unknown locality, the artists give us almost identically the same designs, the same positions of the human figure, the same arrangement of their subjects, the same faces, the same furniture. Evidently, originality was either unthought of, or repressed; the canons of ancient times were considered binding; and novelty was only allowed within very narrow limits.

A greater variation from the usages of primitive times, a more distinct trace of local coloring, is to be seen in the religion of the period. From a deep and thick obscurity, the god Ammon at last begins to emerge, not yet with any distinctness, much less with that transcendent glory which made him in the best times of Thebes, most decidedly the leading god of the entire Egpytian Pantheon, but just making himself apparent as a god to whom parents think it worth while to dedicate a child.[65] Perhaps he was now for the first time introduced from Punt, which was always regarded as the locality whereto he specially belonged, and from which he made excursions from time to time,[66] like those of the Greek Zeus from Olympus. Another peculiarity of the period is the prominence given to Mentu[67] and Khem, who have hitherto been very subordinate and insignificant deities. Mentu, the god of Hermonthis, a sort of suburb of Thebes, may be called the tutelary divinity of the whole dynasty, half the kings placing their sons under his protection, and the other half bearing his name. Khem, hitherto kept for the most part in obscurity, though the special god of Coptos, takes suddenly a leading position, rears his figure upon the rocks in various quarters,[68] and shows himself in the gross and coarse form which no author of the present day could reproduce without incurring general reprobation. Other deities worshipped at the time, but with ordinary and not peculiar honors, were Osiris, Anubis, Kneph, Horus, Phthah-Sokari, Thoth, and Neith. The Sothiac festival is now also for the first time noted as in use; and feasts are also held, at stated periods, to Khem, Phthah-Sokari, and Thoth.[69]

The monuments distinctly referable to the eleventh dynasty are not sufficiently numerous to furnish us with much information as to the progress of civilization and the arts of life. There is some indication that shoes now began to take the place of sandals,[70] that glass and pottery increased in elegance,[71] and that the façades of houses were ornamented with patterns.[72] Special attention seems to have been paid to the breeding of dogs, which occur of at least four different kinds, corresponding to our greyhound, mastiff, wolf-dog, and ordinary hound.[73] The first named was used in the chase of the gazelle or antelope; the second is a house-dog, and *sits* at the foot of his master: he is of a black color, and is called *Mahats*, which is explained as meaning "blacky." The other two are employed to hunt game of various kinds. A special domestic is appointed to attend to the kennel, who seems to be regarded as an upper servant, since he wears an elegant collar.

CHAPTER XVII.

THE TWELFTH DYNASTY.

Period of Disturbance. Accession of Amen-em-hat.—His Military Expeditions—His great Works—His Addiction to Field Sports—He associates his Son Usurtasen, and leaves him written "Instructions." Reign of Usurtasen I.—His Obelisks—His Temples—His Cushite War—His Chief Officers, Ameni and Mentu-hotep—His Association of Amen-em-hat II. Reign of Amen-em-hat II. Reigns of Usurtasen II. and Usurtasen III. Conquest of Ethiopia, and construction of Forts at Semneh and Koommeh. Usurtasen III. the Original of the mythic Sesostris—Estimate of his Character. Reign of Amen-em-hat III.—His Throne Name—His great Irrigation Scheme—His Nilometer—His Palace and Pyramid—His other Works. Reigns of Amen-em-hat IV. and Sabak-nefru-ra. Civilization of the Period—Arts of Life. Architecture and Glyptic Art—Changes in the Religion.

"L'époque de la douzième dynastie fut une époque de prospérité, de paix intérieure et de grandeur au dehors."—LENORMANT, *Manuel d'Histoire Ancienne*, vol. i, p. 349.

IT has been observed in the last chapter, that the eleventh, or first Theban dynasty expired in bloodshed and confusion. A time of general disturbance followed upon the death of Sankh-ka-ra; and it was probably not till some years had elapsed that Thebes was once more able to establish her supremacy over Egypt and to give the afflicted land the blessing of a settled rule. We do not know the circumstances of the outbreak, or the causes which led to revolution; but there is some reason to suspect a general disaffection of the lower orders, terminating in open rebellion and civil war. Amen-em-hat, [hieroglyph], the individual who succeeded ultimately in re-establishing tranquillity, warns his son against seeking to win the affections of the landed lords and noblemen only, and bids him associate himself with the mass of his subjects and essay to obtain their good will.[1] It is at least probable that he had seen the evils of a contrary course, and had been induced to make himself the patron and protector of the weak and humble[2] by experience gained in the school of adversity, before he attained to sovereign power.

There is no indication of any relationship between the kings of the twelfth and those of the eleventh dynasty; and it is a conjecture[3] not altogether improbable, that the Amen-em-hat who was the founder of the twelfth was descended from the functionary of the same name, who under Mentu-hotep II. executed commissions of importance.[4] At any rate, he makes no pretension to a royal origin, and the probability would seem to be that he attained the throne not through any claim of right, but by his own personal merits. Amid a multitude of pretenders, he fought his way to the crown, and was accepted as king, because he had triumphed over his rivals. On one occasion, he tells us, his life was in extreme danger. He had taken his evening meal, and had retired to rest—stretched upon a carpet in the inner chamber of his house, he was courting sleep—when, lo! a clash of arms resounded; foes approached, hoping to assassinate him as he slumbered; he roused himself; he "woke up to fight·" and the conspirators fled in haste without waiting to exchange blows.[5] It is not quite clear whether this event occurred before or after his accession to the throne: but it reveals the stuff whereof he was made, and sufficiently explains his easy triumph over his competitors.

Once established in power, Amen-em-hat showed activity and energy. He carried on wars on every side—with the Petti, or bowmen of the Libyan interior,[6] the Sakti or Asiatics,[7] the Maxyes or Mazyes of the northwest,[8] and the Uauat and other negro tribes of the south.[9] Eagerly seconded by his young son, Usurtasen, who from his earliest youth showed an unmistakable talent for war and a positive love of fighting,[10] he inflicted blow after blow upon these enemies, and forced them to acts of submission. Still his military expeditions do not seem to have resulted in conquests, and their aim was perhaps rather to protect Egypt from predatory incursions by striking terror into the tribes upon the frontier, than to extend the bounds of the Egyptian dominion. Amen-em-hat was content to "stand on the (old) boundaries of the land, and keep watch on its borders;"[11] to rule all Egypt "from Abu (Elephantiné) to the Athu" (the marsh region of the Delta) was enough for him;[12] we do not find him establishing any military posts in the countries which he invaded; on the contrary, we find that, in one quarter at any rate, he followed up his victories by building a wall, or defensive work, upon his own frontiers, for the purpose of "keeping off the Sakti,"[13] or, in other words, of checking and repelling their incursions. This post was probable a little to the east of Pelusium, near the western extremity of the Lake Serbonis.[14]

Among extant monuments none of any great importance can be assigned to Amen-em-hat, though his activity was shown in buildings no less than in warlike expeditions. There are indications that he commenced the temple of Ammon at Karnak opposite Thebes, where fragments of a granite statue have been found on which the sculptor had engraved his name.[16] Another statue, also representing him, was erected in the Fayoum.[16] He worked the quarries of Mokattam and Hammamât,[17] adorned Memphis,[18] and constructed two considerable edifices, which have perished—a palace, supposed to have been situated at Heliopolis,[19] and a pyramid, known as Ka-nefer, 𓂋𓏤𓐪𓉴, "Lofty and Handsome."[20] Of the former, he tells us that it was "adorned with gold; its roof was painted blue; the walls and the passages were of stones fastened together with iron cramps;"[21] it was "made for eternity," he says, and not for time; but unluckily it has not fulfilled the intention of its constructor. The other, notwithstanding its proud title, was probably of moderate dimensions, like the pyramids of the Mentu-hoteps and Antefs; it was erected to contain a stone sarcophagus cut in the Hammamât quarries by Antef, son of Sabek-nekht, chief priest of the god Khem, who has commemorated the fact on the rocky wall of the Wady.[22]

A third field in which the activity of this energetic king found employment was that of the chase. He "hunted the lion," he tells us, "and brought back the crocodile a prisoner."[23] Lions, which are now not found north of Nubia, frequented in these early times the deserts on either side of the valley of the Nile,[24] and furnished a sport in which even a great king did not feel it beneath him to indulge. Crocodiles were more common, and had long been objects of pursuit to the Egyptian sportsman, who generally speared them from a boat,[25] but sometimes fished for them with a baited hook,[26] and in this way might catch them alive. Probably Amen-em-hat adopted this latter method of procedure, and on returning to his palace exhibited the victims of his skill and prowess to the nobles and officials of his court.

As he approached old age, and felt its infirmities creeping upon him, Amen-em-hat resolved to associate his son Usurtasen in the government. This prince had, as already remarked, exhibited from his earliest youth high military capacity; and it would seem that there was a party at the Court which pressed on Amen-em-hat his own abdication in favor of a successor of such merit.[27] But the aged monarch was unwilling to erase himself altogether, and saw no necessity for so extreme an act of self-abasement. Association had probably been practised from ancient times by the Egyptian kings; and it seemed to Amen-em-hat that by having recourse to this plan of action he might reconcile the demands of the discontented with his own personal inclinations. Accordingly, without descending from the throne, he allowed Usurtasen to assume the royal dignity;[28] and henceforth, for the space of ten years,[29] the father and son reigned conjointly.

Finally, before descending into the tomb, Amen-em-hat resolved to leave to his son a legacy of political wisdom in the shape of "Instructions,"[30] by the observance of which he might reign prosperously, and guide his life to a happy termination. Representing himself as speaking from the Lower World, he enjoined upon Usurtasen the practice of justice and virtue, the admission of all classes of his subjects to his presence and his affections, the avoidance of pride and exclusiveness, together with care in the selection of his intimate friends and counsellors. Briefly recapitulating the chief events of his own life, and the principles which had actuated him, he recommended to his successor persistence in the same course—the protection of the weak and humble, the relief of the afflicted, the punishment of the rebellious, the exercise of continual watchfulness and care against possible calamities, the defence of the frontier, the encouragement of agriculture, and the chastisement of foreign enemies; urging him to act even better than any of his predecessors, and reminding him that he too would have ere long to "enter the boat of Ra," and make the dread passage across the "Great Pool" into the presence of Osiris.[31] Perhaps we may attribute in some measure to this document the satisfactory and in certain respects brilliant reign which followed, and of which we have now to give an account.

Usurtasen, ⎕, who assumed the prænomen of Khepr-ka-ra, ⎕, upon his association,[32] after reigning ten years conjointly with his father in perfect amity and agreement, entered upon his sole reign when Amen-em-hat died, and continued to exercise the royal authority from that date for thirty-five years. He is remarkable at once for his constructions and for his conquests. Thebes, Abydos, Heliopolis or On, the Fayoum, and the Delta, were equally the scenes of his constructive activity; and traces have been found at all these various sites, indicative of his religious zeal and architectural eminence. Of these various works the best known, though by no means the most interesting, is the obelisk of pink granite which still stands upon the site of Heliopolis (Fig. 15), lifting itself above the verdure of the cornfields into the soft sleepy air, and pointing with silent finger to heaven. Obelisks were not previously quite unknown. We meet with the hieroglyphic form ⏐ as early as the times of the fifth dynasty;[33] and a small obelisk, erected by one of the Antefs of the eleventh, has been discovered by M. Mariette at Drah-abou'l-neg-gah.[34] But the erection of Usurtasen I. is the earliest monument of the kind, possessing any considerable grandeur,[35] which is known to us; and it has the rare advantage of still remaining on the spot where it was originally set up, and where it has witnessed the events of at least thirty-seven centuries. It rises to a height of sixty-six feet[36] above the surroundng plain, is formed of the hardest and most beautiful rose-colored granite, and contains a deeply-cut hieroglyphical legend, exactly repeated on each of its four faces. The inscription runs as follows: "The Horus-Sun, the life of those who are born, the king of the Upper and the Lower lands, Khepr-ka-ra; the lord of the double crown, the life of those who are born, the son of the Sun-God Ra, Usurtasen; the friend of the spirits in On, ever-living golden Horus, the life of those who are born, the good god, Khepr-ka-ra, has executed this work in the beginning of the thirty years' cycle, he the dispenser of life for ever-more."[37] Originally, it was beyond all doubt one of a pair[38] placed in front of the great entrance to the Temple of the Sun, the "Jachin and Boaz"[39] of the Egyptian sanctuary.

A far more interesting memorial of Usurtasen than his Heliopolitan obelisk, with its tautological epigraph, is the work of the same kind, which now lies, broken and prostrate, on the soil of the Fayoum. Considerably inferior in size, since its complete height did not much exceed forty feet,[40] this monument excels the other alike in the variety and in the artistic value of the sculptures which are engraved upon it. Usurtasen is represented, on the upper portion of the only broad face which is visible, in the act of worshipping twenty of the principal deities. Among these the most honorable positions are assigned to Ammon and Phthah, while Mentu, Ra-Harmachis, Isis, Nephthys, Sabak, Thoth, Kneph, Shu, Khem, Athor, and Sefkh are among the other objects of the monarch's adoration. The narrow sides have inscriptions, which resemble each other to a certain extent, but are far from being duplicates. In these the gods Mentu and Phthah are alone commemorated.

At Thebes Usurtasen continued the construction of the

great temple of Ammon which his father had begun, and is thought to have completed the remarkable cell,[44] which formed the inner sanctuary, or "Holy of Holies," in the temple as it existed at a later date. The original building of Usurtasen, which was probably of sandstone, appears to have been removed by Thothmes III., who, however, reproduced it in granite, and commemorated the original founder by inscribing his name upon the walls. The edifice is remarkable for the extreme simplicity of its plan, and the absence of all architectural embellishment. Usurtasen also built chambers for the priests attached to the edifice, and especially one for the "chief seer" of the temple, which continued to the time of Rameses IX., when it had to be restored, having fallen into decay.[42]

At Tanis in the Delta,[43] at Abydos,[44] and at Eileithyia,[45] Usurtasen appears to have constructed temples, which were adorned with sculptures, inscriptions, and colossal statues.[46] He also—in person or by his agents—erected memorials in the Wady Magharah,[47] and at Wady Halfa on the Nile,[48] a little above the Second Cataract. This last-named monument commemorated his principal conquest, and will conveniently introduce an account of his chief military expedition.

We have seen that, under the sixth dynasty, Egypt began to stretch out her arm towards the south,[49] and that the negro tribes of Northern Nubia were already subject to her authority. But at this time the monuments made no mention of the Cushite or Ethiopian race, which in the later period of the independent monarchy played so important a part, sometimes even ruling Egypt and coming into contact with Assyria. So late as the reign preceding Usurtasen's when Egypt warred in this quarter, the Ua-uat were still the principal tribe, and Amen-em-hat I. claimed it as his greatest military glory that he had fought with them.[50] But under Usurtasen we find a different condition of things. The Ua-uat and their immediate neighbors, have, we must suppose, been subjected; and the Egyptians, passing further south, come into contact with the veritable Cushite race—the dark-skinned nation which had early peopled the whole northern shore of the Indian Ocean, from the mouth of the Indus to the vicinity of Cape Guardafui. Usurtasen coveted the possession of the gold region, from which Nubia derived its name,[51] and, proceeding southward along the course of the Nile from the twenty-fourth to the twenty-second parallel, came into hostile collision with the Kashi, ⸺, or Cushites, who now for the first time make their appearance in Egyptian history, and gave them a severe defeat.⁵² The tribes who fought on the Ethiopian side were, besides the Cushites themselves, the Shemik, the Khesa, and the Sheat, the Akherkin,⁵³ all of whom are mentioned on the tablet which the victor set up to preserve the memory of his success. The Second Cataract was probably now made the boundary of Egypt to the south, Terminus being advanced in this direction a distance of nearly a hundred and fifty miles.

The inscription of Ameni, a general employed in this expedition, is chiefly remarkable for its statements concerning the small number of the troops under his command. They are given as 400, or at the utmost 600;⁵⁴ yet they seem to have been irresistible and to have carried all before them. We are reminded of modern African expeditions under a Stanley, a Baker, or a Gordon, where a few hundred porters and camp-followers easily disperse all the hostile forces that gather to oppose their march, and by superiority of weapons and of discipline are enabled to triumph over thousands. The account given by Ameni reveals an extreme weakness on the part of the tribes assailed, and leads us to suppose that the great nation of the Cushites was only very partially engaged in the war. Ameni's object, moreover, seems to have been booty as much as territory; he prides himself on "conducting the golden treasures" to his master,⁵⁵ and on capturing and carrying off a herd of 3,000 cattle.⁵⁶

Another remarkable personage, who claims a part in the subjugation of the tribes of the south during the reign of Usurtasen, bore the name of Mentu-hotep. This official, whose tombstone is among the treasures of the museum of Boulaq, appears to have held a rank in the kingdom second only to that of the king. He filled at one and the same time the offices of minister of justice, home secretary, chief commissioner of public works, director of public worship, and perhaps of foreign secretary and minister of war.⁵⁷ "When he arrived at the gate of the royal residence, all the other great personages who might be present bowed down before him, and did obeisance."⁵⁸ He was judge, financier, general, administrator, artist. He preserved internal peace and routed foreign enemies; instructed men in their duties, and upheld the honor of the gods. No doubt his merits had endeared him greatly to his royal master; but we may question whether he does not take too favorable a view of human nature when he says that he was equally beloved by his colleagues and the other great men.

After a sole reign of thirty-two years, Usurtasen associated on the throne his son Amen-em-hat, conjointly with whom he continued to reign for either three or four years longer.[59] He must have died at a tolerably advanced age, since, from the time of his own association by his father, he had held the royal dignity for forty-five years, and it is not likely that he would be associated before the age of twenty or twenty-five.

Amen-em-hat II., who, took the official title of Nub-kau-ra, ○ ⸺ 𓏥 was, comparatively speaking, an undistinguished prince; and but little is known of Egypt under his reign, though it extended over (at least) thirty-eight years.[60] He appears to have continued the war against the black races of the south,[61] while at the same time he extended the sphere of the Egyptian operations in the northeast. In this quarter he not only worked the old mines of the Wady Magharah, but established a new mining station at Sarabit-el-Khadim,[62] where there is a tablet which he set up in his twenty-fourth year. He repaired the tomb of one of his predecessors, called Amenu,[63] erected a statue in black basalt to his queen, Nefert, "the virtuous,"[64] and executed repairs of public buildings in several cities of the Delta. The chief official of his time was Khnum-hotep, whose rock-tomb at Beni-Hassan is one of the most remarkable and most richly adorned of those extensive excavations.[65] Amen-em-hat II. appears to have admitted the hereditary rank of this great noble, on whom he conferred a government which had been held by his maternal grandfather[66] under Amen-em-hat I. Following the example of his predecessors, Amen-em-hat II. elevated his son Usurtasen to the royal dignity, and reigned conjointly with him for six years, before he entered "the eternal abodes."

Usurtasen II., who was distinguished by the prænomen of Sha-khepr-ra;[67] ○ ✱ 𓏥, had a sole reign of thirteen years only, during which time it does not seem that there occurred any events of much importance. Egypt was flourishing, and was sought by emigrants who quitted their own less favored countries to fix their abode in the fertile valley of the Nile. Among those whose coming is recorded was a family of Amu, Semitic by all appearance, perhaps from Midian, who, to the number of thirty-seven, entered Egypt in a body, carrying their "little ones" upon asses, and sought the protection of the reigning Pharaoh through his minister.[68] Various circumstances of the scene illustrate the arrival in Egypt of the sons of Jacob; but it is not now supposed by any one to represent that occurrence.[10] Khnum-hotep remained in favor under the second Usurtasen, who appointed his son Nekht to the governorship of the Cynopolitan canton.

A third Usurtasen, distinguished by the additional name of Sha-kau-ra, ◦ ⚹⌶, now mounted the throne. We do not know his relationship to his predecessor, but it may be assumed as probable that he was either his son or his nephew. He reigned, according to Brugsch,[11] twenty-six, according to Birch,[12] thirty-eight years, and was one of the most distinguished monarchs of the twelfth dynasty. Manetho says,[13] that he was regarded by the Egyptians as the greatest of their (early?) kings after Osiris; and it is certain that he was in such high repute with the monarchs of the eighteenth dynasty, that they worshipped him as a god and built temples in his honor.[13] It would seem that these exceptional distinctions were assigned to him mainly for one reason. He was regarded as the conqueror of Ethiopia. Whatever success had previously attended the efforts of his predecessors in this direction, Usurtasen III. was the king who broke the Ethiopic power, at any rate for a time, inflicted on "the miserable Kush" a series of defeats, and permanently attached to Egypt the tract known as Northern Nubia, or the entire valley of the Nile between the First and the Second Cataract. Usurtasen began his military operations in his eighth year, and starting from Elephantiné in the month Epiphi (May) moved southward with a fixed intention, which he expressed in an inscription set up upon the Elephantiné island,[14] of reducing to subjection "the miserable land of Kashi." His expedition was so far successful that in the same year he established two forts, just below the Second Cataract, one on either side of the Nile, and set up two pillars with inscriptions warning the black races that they were not to proceed further northward, except with the object of importing into Egypt cattle, oxen, goats, or asses.[15] As, however, the tribes upon the east and south were still unsubdued, further efforts were needed. Between his eighth and his sixteenth year, Usurtasen III. continued the war with perseverance and ferocity in the tract between the Nile and the Red Sea, killing the men, carrying off the women and the cattle, setting fire to the standing crops, and otherwise conducting the struggle in a way that "reminds us of the most infamous razzias in the recent history of African warfare."[16] Far from being ashamed of these severities, he gloried in them, and pictured them on the stone columns of victory which in his sixteenth year he set up to commemorate his successes. Finally, in his nineteenth year, he again made an expedition southwards, chastised "the miserable Kush" once more, and left a record of his victory at Abydos.

The forts built by Usurtasen to protect his conquests are still visible on either bank of the Nile, a little below the Second Cataract, and bear the names of Koommeh and Semneh. They are massive constructions, built of numerous square blocks of granite and sandstone," and placed upon two steep rocks which rise up perpendicularly from the river. The columns on which he commemorated his conquests are also visible,[78] and are covered with inscriptions deeply cut into the stone. One of the inscriptions tells us that the king had permitted the erection of his statue at Semneh or the neighborhood;[79] but up to the present time no traces of this interesting monument have been found. Usurtasen worked the inexhaustible quarries of Hammamât, and set up memorials there, in which he professed himself a worshipper of the god Min, or Khem.[80] In the island of Sehel he exhibited himself as a devotee of Anka or Anuka.[81] His name appears also at Assouan (Syêné) and elsewhere.

It is not necessary to suppose that Usurtasen III., though regarded by the Egyptians themselves as one of their greatest kings, and consequently deified, was in reality a man of extraordinary ability. His actions may have contributed to form the character of that ideal Sesostris[83] whom the Egyptians paraded before the eyes of the Greeks and Romans as their great heroic monarch; but there was nothing really astonishing in them, nothing really admirable. At the head of disciplined troops he gained repeated victories over the half-armed and untrained races, in part negro, in part Ethiopic, of the south. By a "continued merciless persecution,"[84] he so far intimidated them, that they were induced to submit to Egyptian supremacy, and to endure the loss of freedom and independence. And he understood the value of fortresses as a means of establishing a dominion, of rivetting a detested yoke on a proud nation's neck, and of making revolt hopeless, if not impossible. He was also so far ambitious, so far desirous of posthumous fame, that he took care to have his deeds declared in words, and "graven with an iron pen in the rock for ever."[85] But in this respect he merely followed the previous traditional practice of the Egyptian kings, while in his conquests he only a little exceeded the limits reached by more than one of his predecessors. What gave him his fame was

Vol. II. Plate XI.

Fig. 24.—Bas-relief of Menkauhor.—See Page 41.

Fig. 25.—Bas-relief of Queen Tii or Taia.—See Page 142.

Plate XII.   Vol. II.

Fig. 26.—Bust of Horemheb.—See Page 152.

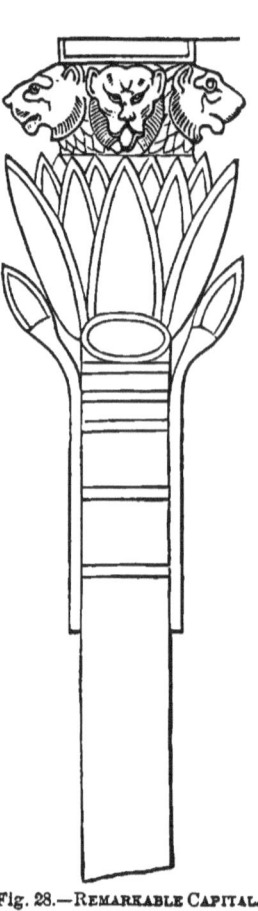

Fig. 28.—Remarkable Capital.
—See Page 192.

Fig. 27.—Bust of Thothmes III.—See Page 138.

the fact that, having finally settled Ethiopia, he was the king to whom its conquest was attributed;[16] and as this was the only considerable tract which the monarchs of the old empire subjugated, those of the new, bent upon conquest themselves, singled him out for approval and admiration. When temples had been built in his honor, and he had been put on a par with the gods Totun and Kneph,[17] mythic details naturally clustered about his name; the Sesostris legend grew up; Usurtasen became a giant more than seven feet high,[18] and the conqueror of Ethiopia, Europe, and Asia; his *stelæ* were said to be found in Palestine, Asia Minor, Scythia, and Thrace;[19] he left a colony at Colchis;[20] dug all the canals by which Egypt was in its most flourishing period intersected; invented geometry; and set up colossi above fifty feet in height![21]

According to M. Lenormant,[22] Usurtasen III. was buried in one of the brick pyramids at Dashoor; but this is not generally admitted by Egyptologists. The fragment of a cartouche found by Perring in the *débris* of the north pyramid is quite insufficient to prove the supposed interment, since the terminal element of a royal name, which was all that the cartouche contained, was one common to many monarchs.[23]

The successor of Usurtasen III. was another Amen-em-hat, the third of the name. There is monumental evidence that he held the throne for forty-two years,[24] and, as this is the exact number of years assigned to him by the Turin papyrus, we may conclude that such was the full length of his reign. The official name which he assumed on ascending the throne was Ra-n-mât, ⦿〰〰⥤⚊. This title is one of greater significance than usual, since it may be translated "the sun of justice" or "of righteousness," and would naturally imply a special desire, on the part of the monarch who bore it, to rule justly and equitably over all his subjects. Amen-em-hat's reign corresponded to this taking announcement. Instead of following in his predecessor's footsteps, and directing the forces of Egypt to the occupation of new territory, he, after one war with the negroes,[25] which was perhaps provoked by an incursion, threw the whole energy of himself and people into the accomplishment of an enterprise from which no glory was to be derived beyond that which is justly due to the conception and prosecution of wise measures tending to increase greatly the prosperity of a numerous people. Egypt depends for its productiveness wholly upon the Nile, which each year at the time of the inundation spreads a fresh deposit of the richest alluvium over the entire region to which the waters extend at their highest. The uniformity of nature, even in those operations which seem most irregular, is surprising; and the inundation not only occurs without fail year after year, but begins and ends at the same time of year almost to a day, and for the most part observes a remarkable regularity in the height to which it reaches, and the limits whereto it extends.[96] Still, there are occasions when this uniformity is broken in upon. Now and then the rains in Abyssinia, which are the true cause of the annual overflow, fall less plentifully than usual, and the rise of the river is somewhat, or even considerably, below the average. The hearts of the Eygptians under these circumstances grow faint. Only the lands close to the river bank are inundated; those at a greater distance lie parched and arid throughout the entire summer, and fail to produce a blade of grass or a spike of corn. Famine stares the people in the face; and unless large supplies of grain have been laid up in store previously, or can be readily imported, the actual starvation of thousands is the necessary consequence.[97] On the other hand, sometimes, though rarely, the fountains of the heavens are opened, and, the Abyssinian rainfall being excessive, the river rises beyond the expected height. Calamitous results at once ensue. The mounds erected to protect the cities, the villages, and the pasture lands, are surmounted or washed away; the houses, built often of mud, collapse; cattle are drowned; human life itself is imperilled, and the evils suffered are almost worse than those which follow upon a deficient flood.[98] To save Egypt from the two opposite dangers arising from an excessive and a defective Nile, hydraulic works are required on the largest scale; reservoirs have to be provided of vast extent, wherein the superfluous water of an overabundant inundation may be hoarded and detained, the pressure upon embankments being thus relieved; and from which again the precious fluid may be dispensed in the case of a deficient Nile, and the niggardliness of nature compensated by the providence and care of man. It is doubtful whether all has ever been done in this matter that might be done; but at any rate it is clear that Amen-em-hat III. made one great effort in the right direction, accomplished one most important work of the kind, and that with an engineering skill and ability that are above all praise. Taking advantage of the existence of a natural depression in the desert to the west of Egypt,[99] extending over an area of nearly 400 square miles, he formed in the southeastern part of this space a vast artificial basin or lake—known to the Greeks as Lake Mœris [100]—which extended from north to south a distance of fourteen miles,[101] and from east to west a distance varying from six miles to eleven. The area of the lake is estimated at 405,479,000 square mètres,[102] or about 480,000,000 square yards. It occupied an elevated position between two comparatively low tracts, the valley of the Nile on the one side, and the northwestern portion of the Fayoum upon the other (Fig. 16). A canal, derived from the *Bahr Yousuf*, or western branch of the Nile, cut partly in the rock,[103] supplied the lake with water, when the Nile was high, and afforded a sensible relief in times of pressure from high flood. Through the same canal water could be drawn from the lake when the Nile was low, and a large tract along the base of the Libyan range would thus be irrigated, which a low inundation did not reach.[104] At the same time, all that portion of the Fayoum which lay outside the lake, to the north and west, or about three-fourths of its surface, might be kept under constant cultivation by means of the water which could be supplied to it from the great reservoir. A vast dam or dyke, forty feet high in places, partly of solid masonary, partly of earth and pebbles, formed the boundary of the reservoir to the north and west, while southward and eastward it extended to the range of hills which separates between the basin of the Fayoum and the Nile valley. The artificial barrier ran a little east of north, from Talut in the south to Biamo in the centre of the Fayoum, a distance of fifteen miles; at Biamo it made a right angle, and was then carried in a line a little south of east from Biamo, past El Ellam and El Edoua, to the eastern range in about lat. 29° 26', making a distance of about twelve miles more. Thus the entire dyke had a length of twenty-seven miles, and, if it be regarded as averaging thirty feet in height, and at least the same in width,[105] would have contained a mass of material amounting to nearly forty-eight millions of cubic yards, or three-sevenths more than the cubic contents of the Great Pyramid of Ghizeh.[106] In connection with the canal and reservoir, a system of sluices and flood-gates was set up, whereby the flow of the water was regulated as the interests of agriculture required.[107]

At the same time special pains were taken to ascertain beforehand what the rise of the Nile was likely to be; and for this purpose a Nilometer was established at the newly occupied station of Semneh, where from the time of Amen-em-hat III. the height of the inundation was duly marked upon the rocky bank of the river, with a short inscription giving the regnal year of the monarch.[108] It is a remarkable fact that the average annual rise under Amen-em-hat at Semneh in Nubia exceeded that of the present day by more than twenty-three feet.[109] As the rise in Egypt itself seems to be nearly the same now as under the twelfth dynasty,[110] we must account for the difference at Semneh by local causes; the course of the Nile must have been anciently blocked by rocks which have given way, and the water must thus have been held back in Nubia, and prevented from flowing off rapidly. No great difference would have been produced in Egypt by the removal of the obstacles, except perhaps that the inundati n would have come on somewhat more rapidly, and its duration have been a little diminished.

While engaged in the completion of his great work of utility in the region of the Fayoum, Amen-em-hat also undertook some constructions, in its neighborhood, of an ornamental and artistic character. At a point on the eastern side of this reservoir, projecting into it towards the west, he built what seems really to have been a palace, but what the Greeks and Romans called a "Labyrinth,"[111] and believed to be an architectural puzzle."[2] It was constructed of white silicious limestone and red granite,[113] and comprised, we are told,[114] 3,000 chambers, half above ground, and half below it. Besides chambers, it possessed numerous colonnades and courts, covered with sculptures, and roofed, Herodotus says,[115] with stone. At one corner was a pyramid, 240 feet high, according to our authority, and according to modern measurements, 300 feet square at the base.[116]

To supply the materials for his constructions, Amen-em-hat had recourse to the quarries at Hammamât, where inscriptions belonging to his reign[117] record the instructions which he gave to his officers on various occasions, and in one instance his own personal presence in connection with ornamental work for the Fayoum, including a colossal statue of himself to be set up at the provincial capital.[118]

He also worked the mines of the Sinaitic region, both those of Wady Magharah and the more recently established ones of the Sarabit-el-Khadim. At both places there are tablets executed during his reign; and at the former they are numerous, and cover the period extending from his second to his forty-second year.[119] At the Sarabit-el-Khadim, they include a notice of the erection of a temple to Athor,[20] the reputed "mistress" of the country, who at once presided over the copper mines and was the "lady of turquoises." [21]

Amen-em-hat III. was succeeded by another monarch of

the same name, who Manetho calls Ammenemes,[122] and to whom he assigns a reign of eight years. The Turin papyrus gives him nine years, three months, and seventeen days, which is probably the true duration of his reign. His sister, Sabak-nefru-ra, ○ [hieroglyphs] whom he seems to have associated, reigned conjointly with him during the last four years of this period. Both appear to have interested themselves in the works of the Fayoum, where their names are found,[123] and where they are thought by some to have been interred.[124] The two pyramids crowned with colossal statues, seen by Herodotus to rise out of the waters of the Lake Mœris,[125] are identified with the stone bases now existing at Biamo,[126] at the northwestern angle of the lake, and are thought to have borne the effigies of these monarchs, whose names have been found on various blocks of stone in this region. Amen-em-hat IV. seems also to have worked the mines of the Wady Magharah and the Sarabit-el-Khadim,[127] where the labors of the workmen were still rewarded by rich yields of copper and *mafka*.[128] But the period is, on the whole, one upon which the monuments throw little light. As so often happens, a dynasty of unusual vigor and energy expires amid clouds and darkness; abnormal effort is succeeded by dulness and inaction, life and movement by exhaustion; nor is it until a considerable space has passed that the roll of history once more unfolds to us events of interest and personages of importance.

It has been said that Egypt under this dynasty enjoyed its apogee, and that its civilization attained now the fullest expansion which it ever reached under the Pharaohs.[129] There is considerable difficulty in balancing one period against another in the history of a civilized state, and in deciding when, on the whole, the highest perfection was arrived at. In our own country the Eizabethan age has its admirers; the reign of Queen Anne is by some regarded as the true Augustian period; while there is a class which maintains that no former period equals the glories of the present day. There are various grounds on which the times of the eighteenth and nineteenth dynasties may be upheld as the culminating period of Egyptian greatness, alike in arms and in arts; but the eulogy which has been passed upon the period of the twelfth, even if it be undue, has beyond a doubt some important grounds on which it may support itself.

Civilization, as observed in the preceding chapter,[130] took from the time of the eleventh dynasty, and under the presidency of Thebes, a practical and utilitarian turn. The great efforts of the principal monarchs of both the eleventh and twelfth dynasties had very markedly this character. New openings were made for trade, new routes established and provided with wells and guards, forts built to check invasion, mines worked, the Nile carefully watched and measured, and finally a huge reservoir made, and a gigantic system of irrigation established in the Fayoum and along the whole of the western bank of the river from Beni-Soeuf to the shores of the Mediterranean. Commercial intercourse was at the same time established with the Nubians, who furnished cattle, gold, and slaves; with the East African tribes (and through them with Arabia and perhaps India) for spices, gums, rare woods, precious stones, and wonderful animals; and with the Syrians for *kohl* or stibium,[131] ladanum, and balsam.[132] Foreign emigrants were readily received into the country, and brought with them novelties in dress and customs, perhaps sometimes new inventions or even new arts.[133] Luxury increased. Palaces were painted and adorned with gold;[134] carpets were spread upon their floors;[135] and the number of courts and chambers was multiplied beyond former precedent.[136] Varieties in dress were introduced. While the simple linen tunic still contented the great mass of men, there were some who affected a more elaborate style of costume (Fig. 14), and wore, besides the tunic, a cape over their shoulders, and a second tunic, of a thinner material, over the first, or even a long robe, reaching nearly to the ankles.[137] Bracelets and anklets were inlaid with precious stones, and the former worn by both men and women, but the latter by women only.[138] Men had sometimes artificial beards, which seem to have been attached to the wig.[139] The low-backed chair without arms was still in common use, but another is seen, which has a high back, and also arms.[140] Houses began to be adorned with colonnades, the pillars of which imitated the lotus blossom. Field sports were pursued with increased ardor. Gentlemen of the highest rank not only indulged in fowling, as formerly, but speared fish with their own hand, and hunted the lion[141] and the antelope. Great attention was paid to the breed of dogs (Fig. 12), and several new types were produced, more especially one with short legs, resembling the modern turnspit.[142] In moving about their estates, the grandees had themselves carried in highly ornamented litters, which were slung on two poles and borne on the shoulders of four men.[143] To amuse their leisure hours in their homes, they admitted into their apartments profes sional tumblers,[144] who were generally fair-haired and light-complexioned, and are thought to have been Libyans from the northern parts of Africa.[145]

Architecture somewhat lowered its pretensions. Instead of the enormous pyramids of the early period, the kings now constructed for their tombs either pyramids of moderate size, or merely underground chambers,[146] upon which they emplaced other buildings. The style of their temples seems to have been massive, but wanting in ornamentation. They, however, introduced certain new features into their architectural works which were striking, and employed others upon a scale which had not been previously adopted. Of the latter kind was their use of the obelisk,[147] while under the former head must be classed their erection of colossal statues upon the top of truncated pyramids.[148] In some of their buildings they fastened the stones together with metal cramps.[149] If the Labyrinth, as seen by Herodotus, was really the work of a king of the twelfth dynasty,[150] we must ascribe to the period a certain amount of architectural magnificence, though in any case the admiration of Herodotus for the edifice seems to have been overstrained and beyond its merits.[151]

The fluted columns, which have been called "Proto-Doric,"[152] belong to the times whereof we are speaking,[153] and were used in the façades of excavated tombs constructed for themselves and their families by the nobles. These tombs were of extraordinary dimensions, and in some instances most elaborately carved and painted with scenes from real life, similar in their general character to those of the Pyramid periods.[154] The reliefs are remarkable for harmony, elegance, and delicacy of workmanship,[155] but have less vigor, less reality and life, than those of the first period. Conventionalism is more apparent in them; hieratic canons are in force; and each figure is designed with strict regard to an established law of proportions. Sculpture "in the round" reaches a higher degree of excellence; and a fragment from a colossal statue of King Usurtasen I., discovered at Tanis, and now in the Berlin Museum, is viewed as "the *chef d'œuvre* of the art of the first empire," and as leaving little to be desired.[156]

The chief modifications of the religion worthy of remark are, first, the distinct elevation of Ammon to the headship of the Pantheon, indicated by the erection in his honor of the *great* temple at the capital, by the position which he occupies on the obelisk of Usurtasen I. in the Fayoum,[157] and by the frequent employment of his name as an element in the appellation of kings and other great personages;[158]

secondly, the advance of Sabak from a local and subordinate position to one of high rank among the universal divinities of the country;[159] and thirdly, the more positive and general recognition of the absolute divinity of the kings. Sabak's advance is the natural consequence of the prominence given to the canton of the Fayoum by the later monarchs of the dynasty, since the crocodile-headed god had been from a very ancient date the special local deity of that district, and the crocodile itself was always viewed as sacred there. Ammon's elevation is more difficult to account for, since he does not appear to have been *anciently* of much account in Thebes,[160] if he was even known there, which is doubtful. His position seems the result of the accident that a private individual, in whose name his was the chief element, happened to raise himself to the throne. Amen-em-hat I. at once began the temple, which gradually became the greatest in Egypt; his son, Usurtasen I., continued this work, and assigned to Ammon the first and highest place on his Fayoum obelisk; he also gave to his eldest son the name of Amen-i,[161] and to another, apparently, that of Amen-em-hat. Henceforth Ammon's place at the head of the Theban gods was well ascertained, and the predominance of Thebes in the later history gave him ultimately a pre-eminence over all the other deities throughout Egypt.

The *quasi*-divinity of the kings had always been asserted by themselves, and no doubt in the language of adulation familiar to courtiers it had occasionally been admitted, even from an early date. But it is not till the time of the twelfth dynasty that acknowledgments, made in the most *naïf* and innocent fashion, become common and seem to be a matter of course. "When I was brought to Egypt," says Saneha, "it was as though a god was in it—a land such as one which a beneficent god presides over—he spake to me, and I answered him, saying, 'Save us!' His son comes home . . . . he also is a god."[162] And again, he addresses the Pharaoh as follows,—"Thy majesty is the good god . . . . the great god, the equal of the Sun-God."[163] And when, at the invitation of the monarch, he returns to Egypt from Edom, he remarks,—"When I came near him, I fell upon my belly amazed before him. *The god* addressed me mildly."[164] Similarly, Khnum-hotep declares of Usurtasen I., "The god Tum he is himself."[165] How far these acknowledgments were mere flattery, how far they represented the sincere belief of the Egyptians, it is impossible to determine; but in either case they must have exerted an injurious influence upon the minds of the monarchs themselves, who were puffed up by the high titles bestowed on them, and became impressed with an undue sense of their own importance and dignity. The pride which made the Pharaoh of the Exodus, time after time, "harden his heart," and oppose himself to the declared will of Jehovah, was the natural consequence of a system which caused weak men to believe in the reality of their own divinity, and strong-minded men to feel an extreme contempt for others.

CHAPTER XVIII.

THE DYNASTIES BETWEEN THE TWELFTH AND THE SEVENTEENTH.

The Thirteenth (Theban) Dynasty in part contemporary with the Fourteenth (Xoïte) and the Fifteenth and Sixteenth (Shepherds). Decline of Egypt at this period. Names and scanty Memorials of the Kings. Permanent Semitic Pressure on the Northeastern Frontier. Invasion brought about by previous disturbance and disintegration.

"Vana versare in omnes opiniones licet."—LIV. iv. 20.

THE four dynasties, wherewith Manetho filled this interval, are regarded by most Egyptologists as ruling contemporaneously in either three or four places.[1] The thirteenth dynasty bore sway in Thebes, and held possession of Middle and Upper Egypt, while the fourteenth maintained itself at Xoïs in the centre of the Delta,[2] and the fifteenth and sixteenth ruled, either consecutively or contemporaneously, over some portion of the more eastern districts. Manetho's numbers for this period are untrustworthy, and, where not false, are misleading. The thirteenth dynasty may, for instance, have included sixty royal personages;[3] but we gather from the Turin Papyrus that they were pretenders to the throne, rather than real kings, and that the average time during which each one of them bore the royal title was about three or three and a half years.[4] It is not unlikely that in many instances they contended one against another; and some of them certainly, many of them possibly, reigned no more than a few months or a few days. On the other hand, there seem to have been, in the earliest part of the thirteenth dynasty, some monarchs of note; and it is thought that for a certain number of years the dynasty bore sway over the whole country, disruption not having set in until they had held the throne for two centuries or two centuries and a half.⁵ Such calculations of time are, however, exceedingly uncertain. The kings of the period, as a general rule, left no monuments; and, until forced by the curiosity of the Greeks to make chronological conjectures, the Egyptians themselves had no estimate of the duration of any dynasty, much less of these undistinguished ones.

It is difficult to conjecture the causes which, after so glorious a dynasty as the twelfth, suddenly reduced Egypt under the thirteenth to impotence and dumbness. There is no indication of foreign invasion, at any rate for a century or two after Amen-em-hat IV. and Sabak-nefru-ra set up their monuments at the edge of the Lake Mœris, but from some cause or other a gap occurs in the Egyptian records, and if it were not for a single fragile document—the papyrus of Turin—the very names of the kings would have been blotted out. Internal troubles are suggested as the most probable cause of the long silence; and the latest writer on the subject ventures to lay it down as "almost certain, that the history of Egypt at this epoch must have been made up of times of revolt and interior troubles, and murders and assassinations, by which the life and length of reign of the princes was not subjected to the ordinary conditions of human existence." ⁶ The kings appear to have maintained the practice of ruling under two names—a real personal appellative, and a throne-name, or title of honor assumed at their accession; though it is not often that both designations have come down to us. They must have maintained persistently the worship of Sabak, the crocodile-headed god, affected by the preceding dynasty, since at least seven of them bore the name of Sabak-hotep, which is translated "servant of Sabak" by Dr. Brugsch;⁷ and they must also have been devoted adherents of Ra, the Sun-God, whose name is found to have formed an element in at least two-thirds of the royal appellations of the period. Ammon, on the other hand, unless identified with Ra, of which there is no evidence, must have been in comparative disfavor, since his name occurs but once in the entire list, and then nearly at the commencement, where we come upon a Ra-Amen-em-hat. Nut and Nefer-Tum seem also to have received recognition from the dynasty, who, so far as the evidence of their names goes, admitted but a narrow Pantheon.

The dynasty commences with a Sabak-hotep, 🐝 or 𓂋𓐍𓏏, who bears the throne-name of Ra-khu-taui, ⊙𓏺𓏏, and may possibly have been a son of Sabak-nefru-ra,⁸ but who has left no monument, and is only known to us from the Turin Papyrus. He was followed after an interval by Ra-Sabak-hotep or Sabak-hotep II., whose throne-name is not known. A third Sabak-hotep, distinguished as Ra-sokhem-khu-taui, ⊙𓏺𓏏, mounted the throne soon afterwards, and left an inscription recording the height of the Nile, at Semneh, which he set up in the third year of his reign.⁹ Four kings intervened between this Sabak-hotep and the next, who was known as Ra-sokhem-sut-taui, ⊙𓏺𓏏, and left granite statues inscribed with his name at Tanis in the Delta.¹⁰ This monarch appears to have been the son of a certain Mentu-hotep who was not of royal race, and to have derived his claim to sovereignty from his mother, a princess called Aahtabu.¹¹ He married a wife, whose name was Nena, and had by her three children, all of whom were daughters. The eldest received the name of her royal grandmother, and this name is found surrounded with the cartouche, but the crown descended in the line of the third daughter, Kama, whose son Nefer-hotep appears in the Turin Papyrus as the immediate successor of Sabak-hotep IV. The genealogical tree of this family may be drawn out as follows:¹²—

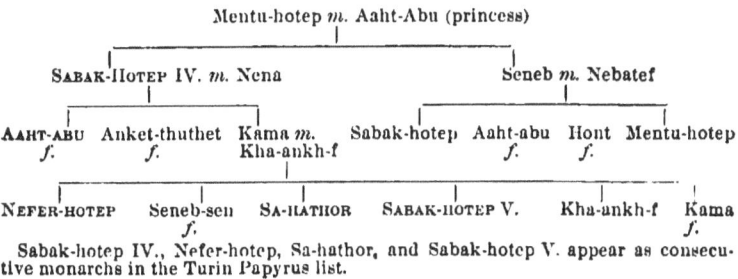

Sabak-hotep IV., Nefer-hotep, Sa-hathor, and Sabak-hotep V. appear as consecutive monarchs in the Turin Papyrus list.

More than a common interest attaches to Nefer-hotep, 𓊃𓏏 (Fig. 17). He bore the throne-name of Sha-seses-ra,

○ ⸺ 𓏝, and has left various monuments, principally in Upper Egypt. One of these is a tablet to Khem and Kneph, bearing the figures of those gods, which he set up in the island of Konosso.[13] Another, from the same locality, represents Khem, Mentu, and Sati;[14] while a third, in the island of Sehel near Philæ, represents the monarch himself receiving "life" as a gift from the goddess Anka or Anuka.[15] He also set up an inscription at Assouan,[16] on which he commemorated the members of his family.

Sabak-hotep V., who succeeded his brother Sa-hathor, and took the throne-name of Sha-nefer-ra, ○ ✱ 𓏏, left an inscription in the island of Argo near Dongola, and set up his statue at Bubastis in the Delta,[17] thus showing that he held possession of the whole valley of the Nile from the borders of Ethiopia to the Mediterranean. He was followed after a short interval by Sabak-hotep VI., who reigned as Sha-ankh-ra, and dedicated a memorial to the god Khem at Abydos, which is now in the museum of Leyden.[18]

The immediate successor of Sabak-hotep VI. was another king of the same name, distinguished by the additional designation of Sha-hotep-ra, ○ ✱ ⚍. This is the last monarch of the dynasty who bore the favorite designation. He reigned, according to the Turin papyrus, somewhat less than five years; and after his decease the crown seems to have passed to a different family.

It may have been about this time, when the dynasty had held the throne for one or two centuries, that pressure began upon the eastern frontier. A nomadic race, whose proper habitat was Syria or Northwestern Arabia, increased rapidly in power and population on this side of Egypt, and, assuming an aggressive attitude, threatened to effect a lodgment in the more eastern portion of the Delta. Already, for a considerable period, there had been on this side an influx of Asiatic immigrants chiefly of Semitic origin, Egypt offering a ready asylum to discontented or needy fugitives, who saw in the great monarchy of the South a sort of "fairyland of wealth, culture, and wisdom."[19] The immigration of Jacob's sons with their extensive households[20] is but a single instance of what was perpetually occurring in this quarter. We have already noticed[21] another example in the arrival of the thirty-seven Amu welcomed by Khnum-hotep in the sixth year of

Usurtasen II. So numerous were the incomers that Semitic names obtained a place in the geographic nomenclature of this part of the country,[22] and a certain number of Semitic words even crept into the Egyptian language.[23] The Semite deities also secured a certain amount of recognition from the Egyptian hierarchy,[24] who were never averse to an increase in the number of objects of worship, and gave as hospitable a reception to Baal, Ashtoreth, Anaïtis, Reseph, and Kiun, when they knocked at the doors of the Pantheon, as the civil rulers did to the kinsmen of Joseph or to the Amu under Abusha.[25]

The state of things thus existing was well calculated to facilitate a hostile occupation of the more eastern portion of the Delta. Already the population was half-Asiatic, and prepared to submit itself readily to Asiatic rule. So long, however, as peace reigned at Thebes, and monarchs, acknowledged as such by the whole of Egypt, had it in their power to direct the entire force of the country against an invader, invasion was not likely to take place. The Amu of the East, whether Mentu, Kharu, Khita, or Shasu, would have been powerless against a united Egypt, and their undisciplined forces would have dashed themselves in vain against the serried phalanx of the trained Egyptian troops. But when at Thebes pretender rose up against pretenders, when disturbance followed disturbance, and scarcely any prince succeeded in maintaining even the semblance of authority for more than two or three years,[26] then the failure of vital power at the heart of the nation was not slow in communicating itself to the extremities. Whether the first result was the revolt of the Western Delta, and the second the conquest by foreigners of the more eastern tract, or whether the order of these two movements was inverted, and foreign invasion produced a domestic revolt, there are no sufficient data to determine; but it would seem that, long before the feeble and multitudinous princes of the thirteenth dynasty had ceased to reign in Thebes, the Western Delta had become independent under a line of native princes who held their court at Xoïs,[27] and the Eastern Delta had been occupied by invaders of nomadic habits and probably of Semitic race. At Xoïs we are told that there were seventy-six kings in a hundred and eighty-four years,[28] which would imply a state of continual disturbance in that locality. Towards the East two Shepherd dynasties bore rule. Manetho's fifteenth and sixteenth, either contemporaneously in two adjacent kingdoms, or consecutively over the whole Eastern Delta. But the main seat of empire was still supposed to be Thebes. I was not till a fresh movement took place among the tribes upon the eastern frontier, and a fresh invasion was made in force, that the Old Empire was regarded as destroyed, and a foreign people as established in possession of the entire country.

CHAPTER XIX.

THE MIDDLE EMPIRE—CONQUEST OF EGYPT BY THE HYKSOS.

Certainty of the Hyksos Conquest. Growing Power of the Tribes to the East of the Delta—the Sakti—the Kharu—the Shasu. Temptations offered by Egypt to Invaders. First Lodgments effected in her Territory. Consequent Excitement among the Eastern Tribes. Question of the Nationality of the Hyksos. Circumstances of the Conquest. Character of the Hyksos' Rule. Advantages which it conferred on Egypt. Reigns of the Hyksos Kings. Apepi's Quarrel with Ra-Sekenen. War ensues and ends in the Expulsion of the Hyksos. Suppose Synchronism of Joseph with Apepi.

Ξένοι βασιλεῖς, οἱ καὶ Μέμφιν εἷλον, καὶ ἐν τῷ Σεθροΐτῃ νομῷ πόλιν ἔκτισαν, ἀφ' ἧς ὁρμώμενοι Αἰγυπτίους ἐχειρώσαντο.—MANETHO ap. SYNCELL. *Chronograph.* vol. i, p. 61, B.

THE conquest of Egypt by an alien people, who continued to be the dominant power in the country for above two centuries, was asserted by Manetho in the most positive terms,[1] and, though long misdoubted by modern critics,[2] has become through recent discovery an acknowledged fact. The Middle Empire of Manetho—a time of humiliation for the Egyptians, a time of stagnation, barren of art, barren of literature, barren of monuments — is at the present day admitted on all hands,[3] and controversy is shifted to the questions of the nationality of the conquerors, the true character of their domination, and the real length of the time that it lasted. Two native documents, one on stone, the other on papyrus,[4] have proved beyond a question the fact of the foreign rule ; two names of the alien rulers have been recovered from the inscriptions of the country ; and though a deep obscurity still rests upon the period, upon the persons of the conquerors and the circumstances of the conquest—an obscurity which we can scarcely hope to see dispelled—yet "the Middle Empire" has at any rate now taken its place in history as a definite reality requiring consideration, inquiry, and, so far as is possible, description.

It would seem that a dark cloud had long lain along the northeastern frontier of Egypt, in that tolerably broad tract which joins Africa to Asia, where alone the land of Mizraim was readily assailable,[5] and which it was impossible to block against a determined enemy. On this side Egypt had had her first wars. To gain and hold the mineral treasures of the Sinaitic peninsula, it had been necessary to reduce to subjection its existing occupants; and so far back as the time of Seneferu,[6] the natives of these parts, called by the Egyptians sometimes Anu, sometimes Pet, sometimes Mentu, had been attacked by the arms of the Pharaohs, despoiled of territory, and forced to make acknowledgment of subjection. At this early date the Asiatics were few and weak, and the Egyptians experienced no difficulty in maintaining their authority over the Sinaitic region and the line of road which led to it. But by the time of the twelfth dynasty population has greatly increased in these parts; and we have found[7] Amen-em-hat I. compelled to build a "wall" or fortress upon his northeastern frontier, for the purpose of "keeping off the Sakti," who had, previously to his reign, occupied the tract directly to the east of the Delta. Subsequently two other races are noticed as making their appearance in the same quarter. These are the Kharu or Khalu, a maritime and commercial people, who seem to have made their way along the coast from Philistia, or perhaps from even further north, and the Shasu, a nation of nomads, whose main habitat was the tract directly south and southeast of the Dead Sea. The word Kharu, 𓂋𓄿𓏤𓈉, is perhaps connected with the Hebrew, "Cherethite," but the ethnographic application is wider, and the Kharu may be best regarded as the Syrians generally,[8] or the inhabitants of the maritime tract extending from the mouth of the Orontes to Lake Serbonis. The Shasu, 𓈙𓄿𓋴𓅱𓈉, were most likely Arabs, and corresponded to the modern Bedouins of this region;[9] they are especially connected with Atuma or Edom,[10] and appear to have roamed over the whole of the desert region between Palestine on the one hand and Egypt upon the other, which at this time was far more productive than at present, and could support a considerable population.

Between the Kharu and the Egyptians there had long been commercial dealings;[11] and this Asiatic people had come to be well acquainted with the productiveness of Egypt and the accumulated wealth of the Egyptians, which was such as naturally to provoke the cupidity of their less fortunate neighbors. The Shasu, and the other Asiatic tribes, who were in close contact with the Kharu, and probably allied to them in blood, though differing in manner of life, would learn from these last what a variety of tempting treasures was stored up in the Egyptian palaces and temples, what countless flocks and herds cropped the rich pastures of the Delta and of the valley of the Nile, what delicate fare constituted the ordinary diet of the inhabitants, what magnificence of apparel and furniture was to be seen in their dwellings. Egypt had for centuries exercised a fascination upon the Asiatic mind, and, as we have seen,[12] had attracted to herself a continual flow of immigrants, who hoped, by adopting the Egyptian mode of life, to participate in the wealth and the luxury of the old inhabitants. The feeling which led individuals and households to quit their homes, renounce their countries, and throw in their lot with the sons of Mizraim, must have been shared in some degree by whole tribes and nations, who could not expect to be welcomed if they presented themselves *en masse* at the frontier towns, or to obtain a lodgment within Egyptian territory otherwise than by force of arms. Two such lodgments, as observed in the last chapter,[13] seem to have been effected while the thirteenth dynasty still occupied the Theban throne —at least this appears to us the most probable account that can be given of Manetho's first and second Shepherd dynasties—but the great invasion did not arrive till later. The great invasion, which resulted in a conquest of the entire country, is connected with a certain Saïtes, or Set, who belongs to a dynasty the last king of which was Apophis, a monarch whose reign almost immediately preceded that of Aahmes, the first king of the New Empire. It is impossible that two dynasties of shepherds can have followed after Apophis. We must therefore either place these dynasties in the troubled time which preceded the great invasion, or look upon them as wholly fictitious.

If some small nomadic tribes had succeeded in establishing themselves in independence within the limits of Egypt Proper, either in the Sethroïte nome, or further to the south, in the vicinity of the Bitter Lakes or of Lake Timsah, a great encouragement would have been given to the other races of the neighborhood, who had hitherto looked upon Egypt as invulnerable, and, however their cupidity may have urged them, had been prevented by their fears from venturing upon an attack. Desires long repressed would have had the rein given them, and would have blossomed into hope; a vague feeling of ex-

Fig. 29.—The Twin Colossi of Amenophis III.—See Page 144.

Plate XIV. Vol. II.

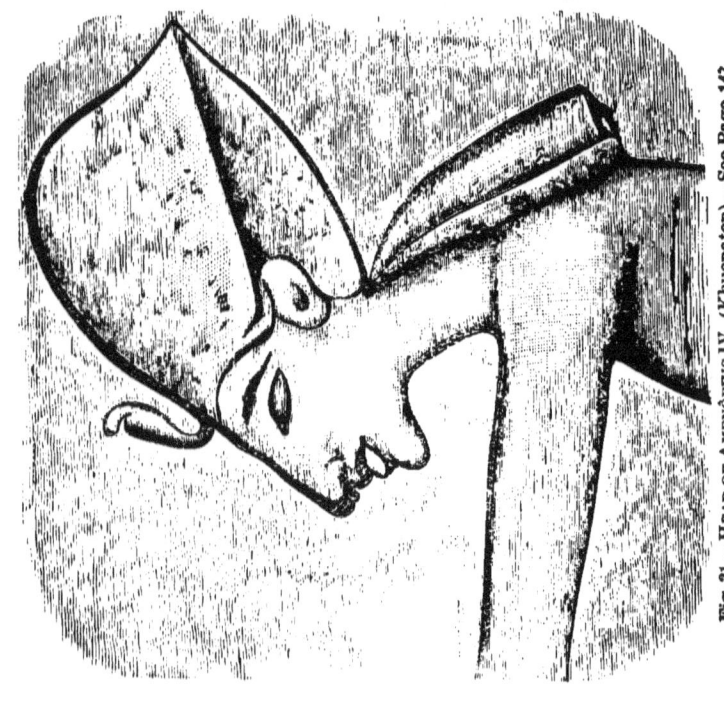

Fig. 31.—Head of Amenôphis IV. (Khuenaten).—See Page 147.

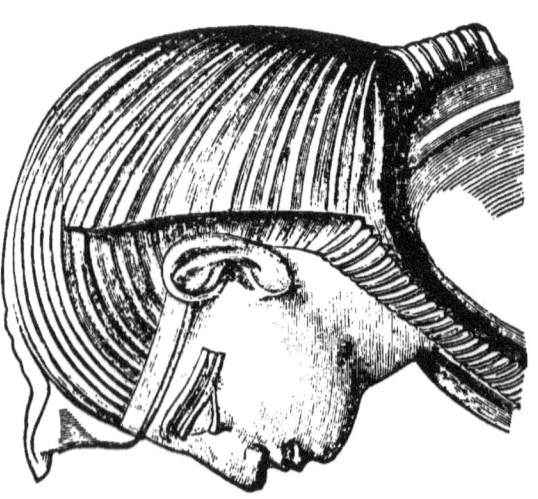

Fig. 30.—Head of Thothmes IV.—See Page 141

pectation would have been awakened among the tribes; a willingness to coalesce, a tendency towards union, would have shown itself; and, when any powerful tribe put itself forward and assumed the lead, there would naturally have been a wide-spread inclination to support the bold adventurer, and rally to a standard which was regarded as about to conduct to victory, plunder and happiness. Something like a confederacy would have been readily formed, and force would thus have been gathered which no single nation of those parts could have raised, and with which the full power of Egypt might have found a difficulty in contending, if the circumstances had been such as to allow of her full power being put forth to meet the danger.

But, as we have already seen, this was not the case. Egypt had suffered disintegration. Two native dynasties were maintaining themselves in different parts of the territory, one at Thebes, the other in the Delta. One foreign kingdom, if not two, had been set up within her borders. These kingdoms were hostile to each other, and, it is probable, were continually at war. Moreover, at Thebes certainly, and most likely at Xoïs also,[14] the state of affairs was unsettled—tumult, disturbance, civil war, open murder, secret assassination prevailed. A prey to internal disorders, Egypt invited attack from without, seeming to offer herself as a ready prey to the first comer, if only he had at his command a military force of fair quality and tolerably numerous.

That an attack came, and a conquest was made, from the tract which joins Africa to Asia, is certain, but it is not easy to determine who were the real invaders. Manetho appears to have made two conflicting statements upon the subject: he represented the invaders as Phœnicians,[15] and he represented them as Arabs.[16] The Egyptians of the time of Herodotus seem to have considered that they were Philistines.[17] Moderns have regarded them as Canaanites, Syrians, Hittites.[18] It is an avoidance, rather than a solution, of the difficulty, to say that they were "a collection of all the nomad hordes of Arabia and Syria,"[19] since there must have been a directing hand; some one tribe must have taken the lead, and have furnished the commander. Some have thought that the word "Hyksos," which comes to us from Manetho, was the best clue to the puzzle, and, expounding that word as "Shasu-kings," have settled it that the conquerors were Arabs.[20] But Manetho himself seems to have understood by "Hyksos," not "Arab-kings," but "Shepherd-kings,"[21] so that the term did not to him contain the idea of nationality. And the term itself is not found upon the monuments. Phœnicians, in the strict sense of the word, are scarcely to be thought of, since they were at no time "shepherds," and it is scarcely probable that they had as yet effected their migration from the Persian Gulf to the shores of the Mediterranean.[24] The invaders may well have been "Syrians in a large sense of that word, and may have come from Palestine, or even from the region north of it. They may have belonged to the Canaanite portion of the Syrian population, and to have been called "Phœnicians" by Manetho from that confusion between the two words which naturally followed from the Phœnician power succeeding the Canaanite in the same tract of country.[23] Among the Canaanite nations the most powerful was that of the Khita or Hittites; and, on the whole, there seem to be better grounds for regarding the invaders of Egypt at this time as predominantly Hittite than for identifying them with any other special tribe or people. Set, the leader of the invasion, bore a name identical with that of the god chiefly worshipped by the Hittites;[24] and the exclusive worship of this god is noted in the Sallier papyrus as one of the principal results of the Shepherd rule.[25] The Hittites were a really powerful people, as appears by their after struggles, both with the Egyptians and the Assyrians, and would so be more capable of measuring their strength against that of the Egyptians, and for a time obtaining the upper hand, than any other of Egypt's neighbors. A Babylonian conquest is scarcely conceivable at this early date, and is precluded alike by the name of the Shepherd kings and the peculiarities of their worship.[26]

On the whole, therefore, we lean to the belief that the so-called Hyksos or "Shepherds" were Hittites, who, pressed for room in Syria, or perhaps merely excited by a desire of conquest, moved southward, and obtaining allies from the countries along their line of route, burst like an avalanche upon Egypt. The reduction of the country was, according to Manetho, effected with the greatest ease. "Men of ignoble race," he says, "coming from the eastern regions unexpectedly, had the courage to invade Egypt, and conquered it easily without a battle."[27] They took Memphis, built themselves a city in the Sethroïte nome, and established a great fortified camp on the eastern frontier, which they called Auaris or Avaris, and occupied with a permanent garrison of 240,000 men.[28] It is not to be supposed that really no resistance was offered to the invaders by the Theban and Xoïte kings of the time; but it was readily overcome; no great battle was fought; and in a comparatively short space of time the country was subjugated, and accepted the foreign yoke. Wherever the Hyksos penetrated, they spread ruin and desolation around, massacred the adult male population, reduced the women and children to slavery, burnt the cities and demolished the temples.²⁹ But they do not appear to have cared permanently to occupy the Nile valley much beyond Memphis. After subjecting the whole of Egypt, they allowed the Theban kings to exercise a qualified sovereignty over the upper part of the Nilotic region, establishing their own court at Memphis, and from thence ruling Middle and Lower Egypt at their discretion.

The character of their rule was at the first barbaric and cruel. Professors of a religion which was monotheistic, or nearly so, the conquerors took an extreme aversion to the Egyptian polytheism, and vented their hatred by an indiscriminate destruction of all the Egyptian temples, which, according to Manetho, they absolutely "razed to the ground."³⁰ Considering how closely connected were the priests with the historical literature of Egypt, which had from the first been chiefly in their hands, we must conclude that this general demolition of edifices was accompanied by an almost complete destruction of the records of the country, which, except in the inscriptions of unopened tombs, and in papyruses buried in tombs, suffered at the hands of the Hyksos something like obliteration.³¹ Thebes, it may be, retained its monuments; but these dated only from the time of the eleventh dynasty.³² Elsewhere the flood of conquest engulfed the early literature of the country; the old civilization was, as it were, "annihilated;"³³ and a blank was produced which the clever *littérateurs* of the eighteenth and nineteenth dynasties found it impossible, excepting by the free employment of conjecture and invention, to fill.

But this purely destructive time was followed by one of reaction, and to some extent of reconstruction. The "Tartars of the South," after a certain term of years, during which they devastated Egypt from the Medtierranean to Thebes, or perhaps to Elephantiné, suffered themselves by degrees to be subjected by the superior civilization of those whom they had conquered,³⁴ and adopted their art, their official language, their titles, and the general arrangement of their court ceremonial. In Tanis especially, temples were built and sculptures set up under the Shepherd kings differing little in their general character from those of the purely Egyptian period.³⁵ The foreign kings erected their own effigies at this site, which were sculptured by native artists according to the customary rules of Egyptian glyptic art; and only differ from those of the earlier native monarchs in the headdress, the expression of the countenance, and a peculiar arrangement of the beard.[36] They built stone temples on the Egyptian model at Tanis and Avaris, wherein they worshipped Set-Nubti, or "Set the Golden," in the place of Ammon or Phthah, bringing the materials for their constructions from Assouan or Syéné,[37] and only slightly modifying established Egyptian forms, as by adding wings to the Sphinx. They lived on amicable terms with the contemporary Theban dynasty of subordinate kings, allowed their worship of Ammon-Ra,[38] and held intercourse with them by frequent embassies.

There are even certain respects in which the Shepherd monarchs appear to have been in advance of the people whom they conquered, so that "the Egyptians were indebted to the stay of the foreigners" in their country, "and to their social intercourse with them, for much useful knowledge."[39] The Shepherds had the conception of an era, and introduced into Egypt the practice of dating events from a certain fixed point, apparently the first regnal year of the first king, Set or Saïtes,[40] a practice which, had it been generally adopted, would have cleared Egyptian chronology from that uncertainty and confusion which are now its acknowledged characteristics. They "enlarged the horizon of the Egyptian artistic views"[41] "by the introduction of new forms and of greater realism into glyptic art; and they are even thought to have affected for good the language and literature of the country.[42] The language was to a considerable extent Semiticized, and an impulse was given to literature which resulted in a vastly increased activity and prolificness. Again, the Shepherds seem to have possessed a power of governmental organization not uncommonly displayed by barbaric conquerors, as by the Mongols in India and the Turks in Europe. They established throughout the territory a uniform system for military and revenue purposes, and did much to crush out that spirit of isolation and provincialism which had hitherto been the bane of Egypt,[43] and had prevented its coalescing firmly into a settled homogenous monarchy. The monarchs of the eighteenth dynasty inherited from them a united and centralized Egypt, accustomed to be directed by a single head from a single fixed centre.[44] Thus the blow by which the power of Egypt had seemed to be shattered and prostrated worked ultimately for its advancement, and the Hyksos domination may be said to have produced the glories of the Later Empire.

Of the individual monarchs belonging to the Hyksos line we know but little. According to Manetho, Set or Saïtes was not the original leader of the invasion, but a monarch whom the successful invaders placed at their head after they had overrun and conquered the entire territory.[45] He established himself at Memphis, placed garrisons in every city of importance, and fixed the tributes to be paid to him both by the Upper and the Lower country. The bulk of his troops he stationed in a city, or rather perhaps in a great fortified camp, on the eastern frontier, at Avaris, an old Egyptian town, which he rebuilt and strongly fortified. They amounted to nearly a quarter of a million of men, and were placed in this position for the purpose of repelling any attack which might be made upon the Hyksos kingdom by the Assyrians (?).[46] Set visited them every summer, with the object of renewing their supplies of grain, discharging their arrears of pay, and practising them in military exercises and manœuvres, calculated to inspire a wholesome fear among the neighboring peoples. Set took the additional title of *Aapehti,* "great and glorious," and seems also to have called himself Nubti,[47] thus identifying himself with certain deities, as had been the practice of the previous Egyptian monarchs, who had called themselves Horus, Khem. or Kneph,[48] and had been called by their wives Horus and Set.[49]

Set reigned, we are told, for nineteen years,[50] and was succeeded by a monarch whose name is given in the different manuscripts under the three forms of Anon, Bnon, and Beon. Bnon is the form generally preferred by scholars,[51] and, if accepted, may be compared with the Hebrew Benoni,[52] but the monuments have not hitherto revealed the native form of the word, and, until or unless they do, speculation upon the subject is idle. Bnon is said to have reigned either forty or forty-four years,[53] and to have been succeeded by Pachnan, or Apachnas—a king of whom we are told absolutely nothing beyond the length of his reign. which is variously reported as sixty-one years and as thirty-six years and seven months.[54]

Josephus declares that Manetho placed Apophis, or Apepi, immediately after Apachnas; but Africanus and the Armenian Eusebius are agreed that Apophis was in the Manethonian list the last king of the dynasty; and as this arrangement accords with the monumental mention of Apepi hereafter to be noticed,[55] it would seem best to follow Africanus, rather than Josephus, at this point. Africanus reported Manetho as placing between Apachnas and Apophis two kings, Staan and Archles, the former of whom reigned fifty, and the latter forty-nine years.[56] Josephus calls these kings Jannas and Assis, and places them after Apophis. Consequently, both their names and their position are to some extent doubtful; though, on the whole the representations of Africanus, who had no purpose to serve, must be regarded as more worthy of credit than those of the Jewish historians.

It results from Manetho's numbers, as reported by Africanus, that the dynasty occupied the Egyptian throne for 284 years,[57] which gives the extraordinary average of forty-seven years to a reign, or, omitting the first king, the still more extraordinary one of fifty-three years! If we regard the numbers as in any sense historical, it seems necessary to suppose that each king, soon after he came to the throne, associated a successor, and that the reigns are counted in each case from the date of the association.[58] Supposing this to have been the case, the real average of the *sole* reigns needs not have been more than about twenty-seven years; nor need the real duration of the entire dynasty have much exceeded a hundred and sixty years.[59]

Apepi, the last monarch of the line, having (it is probable) reigned in conjunction with Archles for some thirty or thirty-two years, became sole king at a mature age. Unlike Set, who had made Memphis his capital and only visited Avaris occasionally,[60] Apepi held his court permanently at the last-named city,[61] and there received the homage and tribute which were offered to him by all the various districts both of the Upper and Lower country. In Upper Egypt was established, with his consent and concurrence, a dynasty of native princes, who affected the family name of Taa, and the throne name of Ra-Sekenen. Two princes thus designated, Ra-Sekenen I. and Ra-Sekenen II., had already reigned at Thebes and been buried there in tombs which modern exploration has discovered somewhat recently.[62] A third Ra-Sekenen had succeeded, whether immediately or after an interval is uncertain, and now occupied the position of tributary dynast at the southern capital.[63] Apepi seems, for some cause or other, to have taken a dislike to his princely vassal, and to have resolved to pick a quarrel with him by preferring unreasonable demands. First of all he sent an embassy from his own court to that of the southern king, requiring him to relinquish the worship of all the Egyptian gods, except Amen-Ra, whom he probably identified with his own sole divinity, Set, or Sutech.[64] This proposition was declined, as one with which it was impossible to comply; but the refusal was couched in such terms that umbrage could scarcely be taken at it. Hereupon Apepi consulted with the most experienced of his advisers, and with their help concocted a second message, the exact purport of which is not quite clear. According to one translator,[65] it had reference to a "well for cattle;" according to another,[66] it was a demand for the stoppage of a canal. The messenger who carried the missive had orders to journey at his utmost speed, and boasts that he did not rest by day or by night till he had delivered it. Whatever the exact requirement was, it threw Ra-Sekenen into a state of extreme perplexity. He communicated the proposal to the principal men of his court—"his mighty chiefs, his captains, and expert guides"—but they had no advice to offer. "They were all silent at once in great dismay, and knew not how to answer him good or ill."[67] Then Apepi sent, it would seem, a third message, but of the purport of this nothing can be said; for the manuscript containing the narrative here most provokingly breaks off in the middle of a sentence, and we are left to conjecture the sequel.

The sequel seems to have been war. Ra-Sekenen was not prepared to submit to whatever demands might be made upon him, and when he proved intractable, compulsion was resorted to. The title of "Khen," which he assumed, signifies "victorious,"[68] and it is thought to indicate that he maintained the struggle which Apepi had forced upon him with tolerable success. The warlike energy which had characterized the invaders at the time when they made their original inroad, a century and a half or two centuries earlier, had declined. Egypt had proved their Capua; and, now that a serious conflict had arisen between them and their subjects, it was found that they were no longer the terrible foe that common fame had represented them. It must have been during the reigns of Ra-Sekenen III. and his successor, Kames, whose rule was exceedingly brief,[69] that the grasp of the Shepherds upon Egypt was shaken off, and they were forced to quit their hold and withdraw towards the east, concentrating themselves in that fortified camp on the borders of the Syrian desert, which the providence of their first king, Saïtes, had created for them. Driven out of Egypt Proper by a general uprising of the native inhabitants, at Avaris they turned to bay. They still numbered 240,000 men.[70] The Egyptians besieged them in Avaris with an army twice as numerous as theirs;[71] and after a time their efforts were crowned with success. Avaris was assaulted both by land and water. Ships of war were launched upon the canals which conveyed the Nile water to its immediate neighborhood,[72] and all its gates were blockaded and watched. After numerous assaults the place fell. The captain Aahmes, who was present at the capture, tells us the part that he took in the siege—how he "followed the king on foot when he (the king) went out on his chariot"—how, when siege was laid to the city, he "had to fight in the presence of his Majesty"—how at one time he "fought upon the canal of Patetku of Avaris, and carried off a hand;—*i.e.*, killed an enemy, and cut off his hand and carried it to camp as proof of his exploit—how a second time he did the same—how in a third engagement, he made a prisoner, and "brought him off through the water"—and how finally, at the actual taking of the town, he made prisoners of one man and three women, who were all given to him for slaves."[73] The narrator is so occupied with himself and his own adventures that he had no words to spare for any general account of the siege operations, or any connected narrative of the war. We gather incidentally from his autobiographical sketch that there was no capitulation, such as Manetho spoke of [74]—no voluntary evacuation of the city by the Hyksos army—but that the place was taken by storm; and we can perceive that the beaten enemy drew off in the direction of Palestine, whither the Egyptians pursued them, and where after a time they captured a Hyksos city called Sharhana,[75] probably the Sharuhen of the Hebrews.[76] With this event the Hyksos war appears to have terminated, and Egypt, relieved for ever from this hated enemy, entered upon a career of progress, conquest, and glory.

It is stated by George the Syncellus, a writer whose extensive learning and entire honesty are unquestionable, that the synchronism of Joseph with Apepi, the last king of the only known Hyksos dynasty, was "acknowledged by all."[77] The best modern authority accept this view, if not as clearly established, at any rate as in the highest degree probable,[78] and believe that it was Apepi who made the gifted Hebrew his prime minister, who invited his father and his brethren to settle in Egypt with their households, and assigned to them the land of Goshen for their residence. The elevation of a foreigner, and a Semite, to so exalted an office is thought to be far more likely under Hyksos than under native Egyptian rule, the marriage with the daughter of the high-priest of Heliopolis to be less surprising, and the Egyptian words and names connected with the history to point to this period.[59] If the view be allowed, a great additional interest will attach to Apepi himself, and great additional light will be thrown on the ultimate character of the Hyksos rule, which has been shown already to have been much modified and softened by contact with the old civilization of the country.[60]

For the Pharaoh of Joseph is no rude and savage nomad, but a mild, civilized, and somewhat luxurious king. He holds a grand court in a city not named, has a number of cup-bearers and confectioners,[61] sits upon a throne[62] or rides in a chariot,[63] wears a ring on his hand, has vestures of fine linen and collars of gold to bestow on those whom he favors,[64] uses the Egyptian language, and is in fact undistinguishable from a native Egyptian monarch. He does not oppress any of his subjects. On the contrary, he sustains them in a time of scarcity, when he becomes their landlord, takes a moderate rent,[65] is especially lenient to the priests,[66] and when he receives the Israelites, even concedes to his subjects' prejudice against "*shepherds.*"[67] If he is by birth and descent one of the Hyksos, he has adopted all the ordinary habits and mode of life of the Egyptians; he is even, it would seem, tolerant of their religion. This toleration may perhaps be only within certain limits; but it extends apparently to the entire priestly order.

CHAPTER XX.

THE NEW EMPIRE—EGYPT UNDER THE EIGHTEENTH DYNASTY (ABOUT B.C. 1600-1400).

Reign of Aahmes—his War with the Hyksos—his Expedition against the South—his Buildings—his Wife, Nefert-ari-Aahmes. Reign of Amen-hotep I. Reign of Thothmes I.—his Nubian Conquests—his Syrian and Mesopotamian War—his Monuments. Short Reign of Thothmes II. Accession of Hatasu—her Buildings and other Monuments—her Fleet sails to Punt—her Association of Thothmes III., and Death. Glorious Reign of Thothmes III. His Invasion of Asia. Enemies with whom he came into contact—the Kharu, the Zahi, the Khita, the Ruten, the Nahiri. Reduction of Syria. Success in Mesopotamia—Elephant Hunts. Booty carried off. Inscriptions set up by Thothmes III. His Buildings, Statues, and Obelisks. His Employment of forced Labor. Condition of the Israelites under him. His Southern Wars. His supposed Maritime Empire. Summary of his Character. Reign of Amen-hotep II. His Wars and Buildings. Reign of Thothmes IV. His Temple to the Sphinx. His Wars. His Lion Hunts. Reign of Amen-hotep III. His Wife Taia. Commencement of the Disk Worship. His Wars. . His Buildings and Statues. His Love of Field Sports—Personal Appearance and Character. Reign of Amen-hotep IV., or Khuenaten. His strange Physiognomy. His Establishment of the Disk Worship. His new Capital. His Wars. Reigns of Sa'a-nekht, Ai, and Tutankh-amen. Restoration of the Old Religion. Reign of Hor-em-heb. Close of the Dynasty.

Ἐκ σκότους τόδ' ἐς φάος.—ÆSCHYL. Ætn. Fr. 1.

THE native Egyptian monarch who drove out the Hyksos, and became the founder of the eighteenth dynasty, bore the name Aahmes, ——𓀀——, which signifies "child of the moon."[1] He is thought to have been the son of Kames (Uot-khepr-ra) and of his wife Aah-hotep, ——𓏏𓆓, whose coffin and mummy are among the treasures of the museum of Boulaq.[2] Aahmes took the throne name of Neb-pehti-ra, ⊙━𓎟, and reigned twenty-five years, more glorious than any Egyptian monarch since Usurtasen III. He probably inherited the great war, which he brought to a happy conclusion mainly by his own individual energy, but in part by the courage and conduct of his generals.[3] It is especially to be noted of this war, that it was carried on as much by water as by land, the first step towards success being the creation of a flotilla upon the Nile, which held the command of the river, and was used in the rapid and safe transport of troops to any part of the Nile valley where they were needed.[4] Aahmes, the king's namesake and favorite general, relates how he served on board one of these Nile vessels, and, descending the stream from Thebes, carried his master's arms into the Eastern Delta, and in a short time won back to his authority the entire region. As the vessels descended the river, the land force, now no more a mere infantry, but comprising certainly a body of trained chariots, and perhaps a certain amount of cavalry,[5] occupied the river bank; and Aahmes from time to time had to quit his vessel and to march on foot beside the chariot of his sovereign. Memphis must have been captured[6] before any attack could have been made upon the city of the Shepherds—the strong and vast fortress of Avaris, situated at the furthest point to which the Nile waters reached, well fortified both by walls and moats, and defended by a garrison of nearly a quarter of a million of men.[7] A lake protected the city, on one side; canals from the Nile guarded it in other quarters; while a solid rampart of baked, or perhaps merely of sun-dried brick, surrounded the whole, and rendered the position one of first-rate strength and security. However, after a siege of some considerable length, in the course of which there were several engagements,[8] the final assault appears to have been delivered with such success, that a panic seized the garrison, and they hastily fled from the place. The majority made their escape, and withdrew to Syria, but many were slain, and a considerable number taken prisoners. All captives appear to have been regarded as the property of the king; but it was a common practice to assign prisoners to those who captured them; and vast numbers of the "Shepherd" race became in this way permanently fixed in Egypt, where they intermixed with the native inhabitants and modified to some extent their physical type.[9]

The war of Aahmes with the Shepherds lasted five years.[10] It was no sooner concluded than he hastened to lead an expedition against the south, where the negro races had taken the offensive during the struggle between the Egyptians and their foreign conquerors, and apparently had re-established the independence whereof they had been deprived by the monarchs of the twelfth dynasty.[11] At first the Egyptian king carried all before him, and, regarding the country as reconquered, returned down the Nile to his capital; but ere long the tide of victory turned. A Nubian chief, called Teta-an, collected the dusky hordes under his banner, and retook the whole region of the south, carrying devastation along the Nile banks, destroying the temples of the Egyptian garrisons, and annihilating the Egyptian power. Aahmes was forced to retrace his steps, and measure his strength against this new enemy.

He engaged Teta-an twice, the Nubian being apparently each time the assailant. On the first occasion neither antagonist could claim a decisive success; but, on the second, Aahmes was more fortunate. The negro army was defeated with great loss, Teta-an made prisoner, and Egyptian authority once more established over the tract between the First and the Second Cataract.[12]

It would appear that the struggle with Teta-an must have occupied a considerable time. At any rate, it was not until his twenty-second year that the Egyptian monarch, victorious on every side, and no longer apprehensive of attack, was able to turn his attention to domestic affairs, and commence the restoration of those public edifices which had suffered either from natural decay or from hostile attack during the last two or three centuries. Rock-tablets in the quarries of Toora and Maasara of that year [13] record the fact that Aahmes at this time "opened anew the rock chambers," and employed men to "cut out the best white stone of the hill country" for the repairs of the "temple of millions of years,"—the ancient edifice dedicated to the god Phthah at Memphis,—for that of Ammon at Thebes, and for other sacred buildings. Phœnicians are thought to have been employed upon the great works thus initiated,[14] as they were some centuries later on the construction of the Temple of Solomon.[15]

Aahmes is said to have reigned altogether twenty-five years,[16] or, as Josephus expresses it more exactly, twenty-five years and four months.[17] He married a princess,[18] who took the name of Nefert-ari-Aahmes, 𓏠𓏤𓆑𓃀𓏏 , or "the beautiful companion of Aahmes,"[19] and who is represented on the monuments with pleasing features, but a complexion of ebon blackness.[20] It is certainly wrong to call her a "negress;" she was an Ethiopian of the best physical type; and her marriage with Aahmes may have been based upon a political motive.[21] The Egyptian Pharaohs from time to time allied themselves with the monarchs of the south, partly to obtain the aid of Ethiopian troops in their wars, partly with a view of claiming, in right of their wives, dominion over the Upper Nile region. Aahmes (Fig. 35) may have been the first to do this; or he may simply have "followed the example of his predecessors, who, forced by the Hyksos to the south, had contracted marriages with the families of Ethiopian rulers."[22] His queen was certainly regarded as a personage of importance. She was called "the wife of the god Ammon,"[23] and enjoyed some high post connected with the worship of that god at Thebes; Aahmes commemorated her upon his monuments;[24] during her son's reign she held, for a time at any rate, the reigns of power; while in after ages she was venerated as "ancestress and founder of the eighteenth dynasty."[25]

The successor of Aahmes was his son by this Ethiopian princess; he bore the name of Amen-hotep, [hieroglyph], which which is the Amenôphthis of Manetho.[26] On his accession he took the throne name of Tser-ka-ra; but he is more commonly known as Amen-hotep the First. Either he was of immature age at the death of his father, and therefore placed at first under the guardianship of his mother,[27] or else his attachment to her was such that he voluntarily associated her with himself in the government. Her figure appears on his monuments, drawn with the utmost care and elaboration;[28] she is joined with him in the worship of the gods;[29] she is "the lady of the two lands," as he is the "lord" of them. Little is known of the reign of Amenôphis beyond the fact that, like his father, he led expeditions to the south, and warred both with the Cushites and the negroes, seeking still further to extend the frontier of Egypt in a southern direction.[30] It does not appear, however, that much success attended his efforts beyond the capture of some prisoners and some cattle. Amen-hotep was served by two officers, Aahmes, son of Abana, and another Aahmes named Pennishem, whose tombs have been found at Thebes.[31] He took to wife an Egyptian lady, named Aah-hotep, [hieroglyph], and had a son by her whom he called Thothmes, [hieroglyph], the first prince of that celebrated name.[32] According to Manetho,[33] Amenôphis I. reigned no more than thirteen years.

The reign of Thothmes I., who succeeded Amenôphis, and took the further appellation of Aa-khepr-ka-ra, [hieroglyph], derives its chief distinction from the fact that, at this period of their history, the Egyptians for the first time carried their arms deep into Asia, overrunning Syria, and even invading Mesopotamia, or the tract between the Tigris and the Euphrates. Hitherto the furthest point reached in this direction had been Sharuhen in Southern Palestine, a city assigned to the tribe of Simeon by Joshua. Invaders from the lower Mesopotamian region [34] had from time to time made their appearance in the broad Syrian valleys and plains, had drunk the waters of the Orontes and the Jordan, ravaged the open country, and even perhaps destroyed the towns. But Syria was hitherto almost an undiscovered region to the powerful people which, nurturing its strength in the Nile valley, had remained content with its own natural limits and scarcely grasped at any conquests. A time was now come when this comparative quietude and absence of ambition were about to cease. Provoked by the attack made upon her from the side of Asia, and smarting from the wounds inflicted upon her pride and her prosperity by the Hyksos during the period of their rule, Egypt now set herself to retaliate, and for three centuries continued at intervals to pour her armies into the Eastern continent, and to carry fire and sword over the extensive and populous regions which lay between the Mediterranean and the Zagros mountain range. There is some uncertainty as to the extent of her conquests; but no reasonable doubt can be entertained that for a space of three hundred years Egypt was the most powerful and the most aggressive state that the world contained, and held a dominion that has as much right to be called an "Empire" as the Assyrian, the Babylonian, or the Persian. While Babylonia, ruled by Arab conquerors,[35] declined in strength, and Assyria proper was merely struggling into independence, Egypt put forth her arms, and grasped the fairest regions of the earth's surface. Thus commenced that struggle for predominance between northeastern Africa and southwestern Asia, which lasted for above a thousand years, and was scarcely terminated until Rome appeared upon the scene, and reduced both the rivals under her world-wide sway.

The period of aggression upon Asia commenced with Thothmes I. (Fig. 20); but his Asiatic expedition was not his first enterprise. He began his military career by an invasion of the countries upon the Upper Nile,[36] and contended in this region with the Ethiopians and Nubians, ascending the course of the river with a flotilla of ships, while his troops also, it is probable, marched along the banks, and not only directing the movements of his forces, but taking a personal part in the encounters. On one occasion we are told, "his majesty became more furious than a panther,"[37] and placing an arrow on the string directed it against the Nubian chief with so sure an aim, that it struck him and remained fixed in his knee, whereupon the chief "fell fainting down before the royal diadem."[36] He was at once seized and made a prisoner; his followers were dispersed; and he himself was carried off on board the royal ship to the Egyptian capital. This victory was the precursor of others: everywhere "the An of Nubia were hewed in pieces, and scattered all over their lands" till "their stench filled the valleys."[39] At last a general submission was made, and a large tract of territory was ceded. The Eygptian frontier was pushed on from Semneh (lat. 21° 50′) to Tombos (lat. 19°); and a memorial was set up at this latter place,[40] to mark the existing extent of the empire southward. A new officer was appointed to govern the newly annexed country, who was called "the ruler of Kush," and appears to have resided at Semneh.[41]

The expedition against the South was followed, after no long interval, by an invasion of Asia. To exact satisfaction from the races which had attacked Egypt, and for many years oppressed her, Thothmes marched an army through Palestine and Syria into Mesopotamia, engaged the natives of those regions in a long series of battles, and defeated them more than once with great slaughter. A single captain boasts that in the course of the expedition he "took twenty-one hands,"[42] or, in other words, killed twenty-one men, besides capturing a horse and a chariot. If one man could do so much, what must have been the amount of injury inflicted by the entire host! Egyptian armies, according to Manetho,[43] were counted by hundreds of thousands; and even if for "hundreds" we substitute "tens," the result must have been a carnage and a desolation sufficiently distressing. The use of the horse in war, which they had learned from their late conquerors,[44] added greatly to their military efficiency and to their power of making distant campaigns. Though unskilful riders and therefore averse to the employment of cavalry on any extensive scale,[45] they rapidly organized a strong force of chariots, which engaged with success the similar organizations of the Eastern nations, and manifested a decided superiority over them. We must suppose that the Egyptian mechanical skill carried to perfection in a short time the art of chariot-making, and that they combined lightness with strength in their vehicles to a remarkable degree. The climate of Egypt seems also to have suited the horse in these early days; and so judicious were the Egyptian breeders that the natives of Judæa and Syria,—nay, even the redoubted Hittites themselves,—imported their horses and chariots from the valley of the Nile, and paid a price for them which implies high excellence."[46] It is creditable to the spirit and adaptability of the Egyptian people, that they should so immediately have surpassed their teachers, and have been able *at once* to carry to perfection a mode of warfare which was wholly new to them, while it had long been familiar to their antagonists.

When the king returned triumphant from his Asiatic campaign,⁴⁷ with abundant booty and captives, he set up a tablet commemorative of his exploits,⁴⁸ and, to show his gratitude to the divine power which had protected him and given him the victory, proceeded further to enlarge and embellish the temple of Ammon at Thebes, commenced by Amen-em-hat I., and advanced by his son, Usurtasen. The temple at this time consisted merely of the central cell, and a certain number of chambers, built at the sides, for the priests' use. Aahmes constructed the cloistered court in front of the central cell,⁴⁹ a building 240 feet long by sixty-two broad, surrounding it by a colonnade, of which the supports were Osirid pillars, or square piers with a colossal figure of Osiris in front. At either side of the grand portal, which gave entrance to this building, he reared a granite obelisk, seventy-five feet high, on which he commemorated his piety and his worship of the gods of heaven.⁵⁰

The reign of Thothmes I. appears to have been short,⁵¹ though Manetho assigned him a period of twenty-one years.⁵² He was married to a wife, Aahmes, who is thought to have been also his sister,⁵³ and had by her a daughter called Hasheps⁵⁴ or Hatasu, ⌇⌇⌇, and two sons, both of whom bore the same name as their father. At his death the elder of the two sons ascended the throne, and ruled as Thothmes-nefer-shau; taking also the additional epithet of Aa-khepr-en-ra, ⌇⌇⌇, or ⌇⌇⌇. He is known to moderns as Thothmes II. (Fig. 19), and had a reign which was brief and undistinguished. After one expedition against the Arabs of the more northern parts of the Sinaitic peninsula, undertaken for the purpose of striking terror into those incorrigible marauders,⁵⁵ he seems to have given himself up to a life of almost complete inactivity. His sister, Hatasu, appears to have acquired great influence over him, and to have been allowed to assume the royal title and take the leading part in the government. Conjointly, the brother and sister made various additions to the great temple of Ammon at Thebes, while at the same time they busied themselves with several other buildings of importance.[56] The remarkable temple at Medinet-Abou, described in the first volume of the present work,[57] is attributed to this period, and was the result of their combined exertions. Both the brother and the sister were devotees of Ammon, whom they identified with Khem,[58] and worshipped as the source of life and lord of heaven. They also gave a prominent position to the lion-goddess, Pasht or Sekhet, whom they conjoined with Ammon and Khonsu.[59]

Hatasu (Fig. 21) is suspected of having cherished an extreme lust of power, and of having sacrificed to it affection, and even decency. The early death of her brother is laid at her door;[60] and it is certain that after his decease she strove to obliterate his memory by erasing his name from the monuments, sometimes substituting her own name, or that of her father, in its place.[61] She appears to have been a woman of great energy, and of a masculine mind, clever, enterprising, vindictive, and unscrupulous. On the death of the second Thothmes, she took entire possession of the throne, changed her name from Hatasu to Hatasu-Khnum-Ammon, took the additional throne-name of Ra-ma-ka, assumed male apparel and the style and title of a king, occupied the royal throne, and allowed her young brother, whom she suffered to live, no better place than a seat upon her footstool.[62] She is constantly represented upon the monuments in male attire, often crowned with the tall plumes of Ammon;[63] she calls herself "the *son* of the sun," "the good *god*," "the *lord* of the two lands," "beloved of Ammon-Ra, the god of *kings*." She is not, however, wholly consistent in this assumption of the masculine character. Sometimes her garb is that of a woman, her title "lady;" and her epithet, "beloved by Ammon," has the feminine suffix.[64] It may perhaps have been difficult for the sculptors always to bear in mind that the sex of the sovereign from whom they received their commission was to be concealed.

As sole monarch, Hatasu pushed forward her buildings with increased energy, and rapidly brought to completion various works of importance, which still excite the traveller's admiration. Her edifices are said to be among "the most tasteful, most complete and brilliant creations which ever left the hands of an Egyptian artist."[65] She built a temple, imposed on four steps, which is quite unique among Egyptian shrines, and is known now as that of Deir-el-Bahiri.[66] She erected obelisks at Thebes in the great temple of Ammon, which equal, alike in size and in delicacy of workmanship, the constructions of any other monarch.[67] She connected her temple at once with the older erection of Usurtasen, and with the sacred stream of the Nile, by long avenues of criosphinxes in a posture of repose.[68] She set up statues of herself in various places,[69] and inscribed her name upon the rocks of Assouan.[70] Her favorite architect was an Egyptian named Semnut, the son of Kames and Ha-nefer, to whose memory she erected a monument which is now in the Berlin Museum.[71]

But the most extraordinary of all the achievements of Queen Hatasu, and the one of which she seems to have been most proud, was the establishment of a species of sovereignty over the distant land of Punt by means of a naval expedition [72] on a scale of which we have no trace in the earlier monuments. Five ships [73] at least, manned by thirty rowers each, and having on board besides a crew of some ten or twelve, together with a detachment of Egyptian troops,[74] proceeded from some port on the western coast of the Red Sea to the southern extremity of the gulf, and landed on the shores of Punt,[75] the "Ta-neter" or "Holy Land"—the original seat of Athor and perhaps of Ammon—where a most friendly reception was accorded them. The expedition was not of a hostile, but of a purely pacific character.[76] A high official of the court accompanied the fleet as royal ambassador, and a profusion of presents for the chiefs of Punt were placed on board. The great object was to establish friendly relations, and secure both an immediate and also a continuous supply of the precious frankincense, which was consumed largely by the Egyptians in the worship of the gods, and was especially required at this time for the due honor of the great Ammon.[77] The inhabitants were quite willing to barter their highly valued product for the manufactures and for the corn of Egypt. They were simple folk, living on stages built upon piles (Fig. 17), in small cabins, which could be entered only by means of a ladder, generally built under the shadow of a grove of cocoanut palms, and in the immediate vicinity of the incense-trees.[78] It was among the objects of the expedition to procure not only incense, but a certain number of the incense-bearing trees, which the Egyptians hoped to naturalize in their own country. At their request the natives set to work and dug up as many as thirty-one of the trees, which they packed with earth about their roots in baskets, and, having slung them on poles, so conveyed them to the ships, where they were placed upon the deck under an awning.[49] Large quantities of the incense itself were also collected, and packed in sacks tied at the mouth, which were piled on the decks in various places. At the same time other valuable products of the Holy Land were put on board, especially gold, silver, ivory, ebony, cassia, kohl or stibium, apes, baboons, dogs, slaves, and leopard-skins.[80] A single tamed leopard or tigress seems to have been also embarked. Homage was done to the Queen of Egypt by Parihu, the lord of the country, and his misshapen wife,[81] who thus admitted the suzerainty of the Pharaohs; but at the same time it was distinctly stipulated that the peace and freedom of the land of Punt should be respected.[62]

The return of the embassy with its wonderful and varied treasures was made a day of rejoicing at Thebes. Twelve Nile boats of the largest dimensions conveyed the wanderers in a grand procession to the capital.[83] The whole population came out to meet them. A parade was made of the troops which had accompanied the expedition; the incense-trees, the strange animals, the many products of the distant country, were exhibited; the tame leopard, with his negro keeper, followed the soldiers; natives of the remote region called Tamahu, who had voluntarily accompanied the expedition on its return, performed their war-dance.[84] A bull was sacrificed to Ammon, and a new feast instituted.[85] Finally, to perpetuate the great occasion, and prevent its fading away from human remembrance, the entire expedition was represented in an elaborate series of reliefs on the walls of Hatasu's new temple on the western side of Thebes, where they may still be seen, not very much injured by time, by the curious traveller at the present day.

After exercising the complete royal authority for the space of fifteen years, Hatasu found herself under the necessity of admitting her younger brother to a share in the kingdom, and allowed his name to appear on public monuments in a secondary and subordinate position.[86] He had now probably reached the age of eighteen or twenty years; and his further exclusion from the throne would have been contrary to Eygptian ideas. He was therefore accepted into partnership; but this tardy recognition of his rights appears not to have contented him, and his subsequent conduct shows that he bore a deep grudge against his too jealous guardian. Actuated by a strong and settled animosity, he erased her name from her monuments;[87] and it is simply from the circumstance of his agents not having cut deep enough that we are enabled to trace his sister's career without much difficulty. Whether he proceeded to greater lengths, and directed against her person the vengeance which it is clear that he wreaked upon her inscriptions, is uncertain. The joint rule of the brother and the sister appears not to have continued for above seven years;[88] but "whether Thothmes, after reaching manhood, drove his sister by force from the throne, or whether she slept in Osiris" in the ordinary course of nature, "we cannot tell, because the monuments are silent."[89] She was probably not more than about forty years of age at her decease.

The new king, Thothmes III., crowned at length after so long a minority, took the additional title of Nefer-Khepru—"the best of beetles"[90]—to distinguish him from his father and brother, while at the same time he gave himself the throne name of Men-khepr-ra. ○▬▬𓆣, as a further distinctive appellation. Thothmes has been called "the Alexander of Egyptian history;"[91] and though the associations that this epithet awakens transcend the facts of the case, and make the expression, in the judgment of sober criticism, seem exaggerated, yet still it places a striking fact in a striking light—Thothmes III. was beyond a doubt the greatest of Egyptian conquerors. Devoid, so far as appears, of any talent for organization, as far as possible removed from the rank and position of an Alexander among persons gifted with rare administrative capacity, he had at any rate this in common with the great Macedonian, that he carried the arms of one continent into the very centre of another, overcame all hostile opposition, and brought one of the great kingdoms of Western Asia into at least a nominal submission. Considering the circumstances of the time, there is no doubt that his expeditions and the success which attended them, imply high military talent; and though the general historian must decline to rank him with the really great conquerors that the world has produced—the Alexanders, the Cæsars, the Charlemagnes—yet it must be readily allowed, and asserted, that among Egyptian conquering kings he holds the first place. No later monarch ever exceeded his glories; Thothmes III. is the nearest historical approach to the ideal Sesostris,[92] the only Pharaoh who really penetrated with a hostile force deep into the heart of Assyria,[93] and forced the great states of Western Asia to pay him tribute, if not even to acknowledge his suzerainty.

The independent public life of Thothmes (Men-khepr-ra)

appears to have commenced with the year which he reckoned as his twenty-second. Hitherto he had remained in a subordinate position, under the tutelage, or at any rate the influence, of his sister.[91] Now he was sole monarch, either by her decease or her deposition, and had the uncontrolled direction of his own actions. The natural bent of his disposition at once displayed itself: he engaged in an aggressive war with the Asiatic nations. Starting from an Egyptian post called Garu, or Zalu,[95] in the month named Pharmuthi, the eighth month of the Egyptian year, corresponding to our February, he invaded Palestine, with the object, as is distinctly stated, of "extending the frontiers of Egypt by his victories."[96] On the fourth day of the next month, Pashons (March 21), the anniversary of his coronation and the first day of his twenty-third year, he arrived at Gaza, which was a strong city even at this early time, and was regarded as the key of Syria. Here, however, he met with no resistance, the ruler being friendly to him; and having rested his troops for the night, he marched out on the fifth, and proceeded by the coast route to Jaham (Jamnia?) where he held a council of war to determine by what line the advance should continue. According to the intelligence brought in by his scouts, the enemy was collected in a position near the city of Megiddo, probably in the great plain of Esdraëlon, the ordinary battle-field of the Palestinian nations. They consisted of "all the people dwelling between the river of Egypt on the one hand and the land of Naharaïn (Mesopotamia) on the other," the Kharu (Syrians) and the Katu being the principal.[97] At their head was the king of Kadesh, a great Hittite city on the Orontes.[98] The direct route to Megiddo, which passed by Aaluna and Taanach, was strongly guarded; but Thothmes insisted on proceeding by this route, instead of making a *détour* as wished by his captains. The event justified his audacity. Megiddo was reached within a week without loss or difficulty; and on the twenty-second of Pashons (April 7) the Egyptian king attacked and completely defeated his adversaries in a pitched battle, driving them in headlong flight from the position which they occupied, and forcing them to take refuge within the walls of the city. The Syrian camp was taken, together with vast treasures in silver and gold; and the son of the king of Kadesh fell into Thothmes' hands. Megiddo itself soon afterwards surrendered, as did the towns of Inunam, Anaugas, and Hurankal or Herinokol. As many as 924 chariots and above 5,900 prisoners were captured; and much booty in the precious metals, as well as in flocks and herds, was carried off. Thothmes returned to Egypt in triumph, and held a prolonged festival to Ammon-Ra in Thebes, which he describes at great length in one of his inscriptions.[99]

The success of Thothmes in this, his first, campaign whetted his appetite for fresh conquests. Between his twenty-third and his twenty-ninth years, for which his own annals are lacking, he must have been engaged in three distinct expeditions, since he styles the campaign of the twenty-ninth year his fifth.[100] It appears from the tomb-inscription of his captain, Amen-em-heb,[101] that one of these was in Southern Judæa, or the Negeb, while in another Thothmes carried the Eygptian arms into Northern Syria, ravaged the country about Aleppo, threatened Carchemish, and even crossed the Euphrates into Upper Mesopotamia, whence he carried off a number of prisoners. It was probably at this time that he first came in contract with the Assyrians, who had recently made themselves independent of Babylon, and *claimed* at any rate the suzerainty over all Mesopotamia as far as the Euphrates. No actual collision between the troops of Egypt and Assyria, either at this time or at any later period of his reign, is recorded; but his advance to Carchemish and pretensions to conquests beyond the Euphrates must have provoked the jealousy of the Assyrian monarchs and caused alarm to be felt at the Assyrian capital. This was not now —as sometimes supposed—Nineveh, but Asshur (Kileh-Sherghat). The Assyrian monarchs, till recently subject to Babylon, were not as yet very mighty princes; the great palaces of Nimrud, Koyunjik, and Khorsabad, which have attracted so much attention in these later times, were not built; Nineveh, if it existed, was a provincial town of small repute; the kings, engaged in constant wars with the great power of the South, found the maintenance of their independence a task which taxed their strength to the uttermost, and had effected as yet no very important conquests. The Egyptian monarch, in extending his attacks into the Mesopotamian region, encountered no very great danger, measured his strength against that of no very powerful kingdom. Still, in advancing beyond the Euphrates, he was carrying his arms into unknown regions, at the distance of six or seven hundred miles from his resources, and risking an encounter with the forces of an organized state such as did not exist in the long stretch of territory which lay between Egypt and the Great River.

It is advisable, before proceeding further with the warlike expeditions of Thothmes III., to glance briefly at the general condition of the countries lying intermediate between Egypt and the great Asiatic powers of the time, Assyria and Babylonia.

The strip of territory intervening between Egypt and Mounts Taurus and Amanus, bounded by the Mediterranean on the one hand, and the Euphrates and the Syro-Arabian desert on the other, was in the time of Thothmes possessed by four principal nations.[102] These were, in the south, the Khalu or Kharu, identified by Dr. Brugsch with the Phœnicians,[103] but more probably a Syrian people; in the central parts, the Ruten or Luten (Lydians?); above them, towards the west, the Tahai or Zahi; towards the Euphrates, the Khita, or Hittites. The country of the Kharu extended along the coast from the boundary of Egypt to a place called Aup or Aupa, which seems to have been in Northern Palestine,[104] but which cannot be identified with any known site. It included within its borders the cities of Gazatu nor Gaza, Ashkaluna or Ascalon, Aaluna (Ajalon?), Sharhana or Sharuhen, Maketa or Megiddo, Taanach, and Jaham (perhaps Jamnia). Its inhabitants were addicted to mercantile pursuits, and carried on a brisk trade with the Egyptians in times of peace, being regarded by them as a respectable and civilized people. Their northern neighbors, the Ruten or Luten, held the valley of the Orontes and the coast tract as far as Aradus; among their towns were Kadesh, which seems to have been the capital, Aradus, Simyra, Argatu (Acre?), Anaugas, Inunam, and Herinokol. They are represented as of a yellowish complexion, with Jewish features and black beards and hair. It does not appear that they were a very numerous people; but they possessed a civilization of a tolerably high type, fought in chariots that were either painted or covered with plates of gold, used iron armor, had furniture of cedar-wood inlaid with ivory, and manufactured gold and silver vessels of elegant forms and delicately chased.[105] The country of the Tahai, which reached from a little north of Aradus to the Taurus mountain-range, furnished corn and wine in vast abundance,[106] as well as incense, balsam, honey, iron, lead and various kinds of precious stones.[107] Compared with the Kharu, Ruten, and Khita, the people were unimportant. East of the Tahai and northeast of the Ruten, reaching from the Antilibanus to the Euphrates, was the great nation of the Hittites, with their capital at Karikaimasha, or Carchemish, on the right bank of the great river. Their country is called in the inscriptions "the great land of the Khita."[108] Its chief cities, besides Carchemish, were

Khirabu (Aleppo), Taaranta, Pairika, Khisasap, and Sarapaina.[109] The inhabitants were fully as civilized as their neighbors, and at the same time more warlike. They had possessed from a remote antiquity a form of picture-writing, which is found not only in their own proper country, but in various parts of Western Asia,[110] from Cappadocia to the shores of the Ægean. In war the arm whereto the Khita mainly trusted was the chariot-force. Their chariots carried three each—two warriors and the charioteer[111]—whereas the Egyptian chariots carried two only; and they could bring into the field as many as 2,500.[112] Of all the Syrian nations, the Khita were the most powerful; and they maintained a separate national existence down to the time of the Sargonids.

Across the Euphrates, the rolling plain at the foot of the high mountains—the Padan Aram of Scripture—seems to have been known as Naharaïn, or "the land of the two rivers;" but the people appear to have been regarded by the Egyptians as Assyrians. There is no reason to believe that they were Assyrians in race; but it is not unlikely that, even at this early time, the Assyrian monarchs, who had thrown off the yoke of Babylon, claimed a suzerainty over the upper Mesopotamian tribes, as Babylon did over those of the lower region. In reality, the tribes were Scythic,[113] and belonged chiefly to the two races of the Nahiri and Comukha; they possessed little internal organization, and were unable to offer any serious or prolonged resistance to the forces of either Egypt or Assyria. Fluctuating between the two great powers for centuries, they were at length swallowed up by the nearer and stronger of the two, the Assyrians, who absorbed and assimilated them towards the middle of the ninth century before our era.[114]

In his fifth campaign, which fell into his twenty-ninth year, Thothmes directed his attack against the cities of the Syrian coast, took and spoiled Tunep, ravaged the land of Zahi, cut down the fruit-trees, carried off the crops, and, having laden his fleet with a variety of precious objects, sailed back to Egypt.[115] The next year he turned his arms against the more northern Ruten, took and plundered Kadesh, Simyra, and Aradus, emptied the magazines of their grain, and, to secure the permanent submission of the country, carried off as hostages a number of the young princes, whom he thenceforth retained in Egypt, requiring their relations to replace any who died by some other member of their family.[116]

A place called Hansatu on the shores of the lake Nesrana

was the chief object of attack in the ensuing year.[117] It was captured without difficulty, and yielded a booty of 494 prisoners of war and thirteen chariots.[118] It is remarkable that exploits of apparently such little importance should have been placed on record by the Egyptian monarchs with such particularity and exactness; but the fact seems to be that large populations did not exist in Syria at this period;[119] a vast number of petty chiefs divided the land among them, each ruling in his own small town or village; if confederations existed, they were of the loosest character; and it was seldom that even a temporary league united the forces of any large number of cities. Thus the wars of the Egyptians in Syria were carried on, in the main, not by great victories over numerous bodies of troops, but by a multitude of small success and petty engagements, insignificant separately, but in the aggregate sufficing to produce the submission of the inhabitants.

Of all the campaigns of Thothmes, his eighth, that of his thirty-third year, was probably the most important. Starting from the country of the Ruten,[120] he in this expedition directed his attack upon the Mesopotamian region, which he ravaged far and wide, conquering the towns, and "reducing to a level plain the strong places of the miserable land of the Naharaïn," [121] capturing thirty kings or chiefs, and erecting two tablets in the region to indicate his conquests.[122] It is possible that he even crossed the Tigris into the Zab region, since he relates that on his return he passed though the town of Ni, or Nini, which some of the best modern authorities[123] identify with Nineveh. Tribute was certainly brought him about this time from the "king of Asshur"[124] as well as from "the prince of Senkara," and the tribute included blue stone (lapis-lazuli) from Babylon, and bitumen from Is or Hit.[126] It is not to be supposed that either Assyria or Babylonia was conquered; but a raid was made into the heart of Western Asia which spread terror on every side. Assyria was actually deprived of a portion of her territory; some of her cities were temporarily, others perhaps permanently, occupied;[127] the king himself, in his fastness of Asshur, was smitten with fear, and bought off the hostility of the invader by gifts which were regarded as a "tribute," and which were repeated year after year. Even at the distant Senkara, south of Babylon, alarm was felt, and an embassy was sent to propitiate the conqueror by a present.

A curious episode of this expedition is related by the captain, Amenemheb, in the inscription upon his tomb.[128] It appears that in the time of Thothmes III. the elephant haunted the woods and jungles of the Mesopotamian region, as he does now those of the peninsula of Hindustan. In the neighborhood of Ni or Nini, large herds of the uncouth animal were to be met with; and Thothmes found leisure, in the intervals of his military operations, to hunt and kill no fewer than 120 elephants, and obtained their tusks. On one occasion, however, he was exposed to great danger. The "rogue" or leading elephant of a herd made a rush upon the royal sportman, and would probably have killed him, had not Amenemheb drawn its rage upon himself by inflicting a wound upon its trunk, and so saved his master.

The Mesopotamian campaign of Thothmes' thirty-third year was followed by one or two more in the same country, which riveted the Egyptian yoke upon the more western portion of the district, but do not appear to have much affected the more eastern parts of the territory. Nothing further is heard of Ni or Nini; no more elephants are hunted; no more tribute arrives from Senkara; the Naharaïn, over which Thothmes permanently reigned, appears to have been limited to the tract between the Euphrates and the Khabour, east of which his remains cease to be found. It was not a part of his policy to measure his strength against that of either of the great Mesopotamian kingdoms, much less to attempt the conquest of the entire territory between the Mons Masius and the Persian Gulf. He was really content a little to outdo the warlike exploits of his father, Thothmes I., and aimed simply at making the Khabour, instead of the Euphrates, the eastern limit of the empire.

The later campaigns of the great Thothmes were almost entirely in regions which he had previously overrun, and were undertaken to subdue revolt, to compel the payment of tribute, or to chastise marauders. Expeditions of this kind occupied the monarch almost continuously until his fortieth year,[129] when he appears to have allowed himself a rest from his military labors, and to have turned his attention to inscriptions, obelisks, and buildings. With an elaboration worthy of all praise, though somewhat wearisome to the student of his times, he placed on record, at Karnak and elsewhere, all the details of his several campaigns, all the particulars of the booties which he bore away, and of the tributes which he exacted from the various nations under his rule.[130] It appears that, in the way of tribute or booty, he carried off from the subject countries above 11,000 captives, 1,670 chariots, 3,639 horses, 4,491 of the larger cattle, more than

35,000 goats, silver to the amount of 3,940 pounds, and gold to the amount of 9,054 pounds. He also brought into Egypt from the conquered lands, enormous quanities of corn and wine, together with license, belsam, honey, ivory, ebony, and other rare woods, lapis-lazuli, and other precious stones, furniture, statues, vases, dishes, basins, tent-poles, bows, habergeons, fruit-trees, live birds, and monkeys! With a curiosity that was insatiable he noted all that was strange or unusual in the lands which he visited, and sought to introduce each novelty into his own proper country. Two unknown kinds of birds, and a variety of the goose, which he found in Mesopotamia and transported thence to the valley of the Nile, are said to have been "dearer to the king than anything else."[131] His artists had ordered to make careful studies of the various objects, and to represent them faithfully upon his monuments. We see on these "water-lilies as high as trees, plants of a growth like cactuses, all sorts of trees, and shrubs, leaves, flowers, and fruits, including melons and pomegranates; oxen and calves also figure, and among them a wonderful animal with three horns. There are likewise herons, sparrow-hawks, geese, and doves. All these objects appear gayly intermixed in the pictures, as suited the simple childlike conception of the " primitive artist."[132] An inscription tells the intention of the monarch. "Here are all sorts of plants and all sorts of flowers of the Holy Land, which the king discovered when he went to the land of Ruten to conquer it. Thus says the king: 'I swear by the sun, and I call to witness my father Ammon, that all is plain truth; there is no trace of deception in that which I relate. What the splendid soil brings forth in the way of productions, I have had portrayed in these pictures, with the intention of offering them to my father Ammon, as a memorial for all times.' "

Among the numerous inscriptions of this great king, none is more remarkable than that which adorns one of the chambers added by him to the grand temple of Ammon at Thebes, whereby he set forth his supposed connection with those monarchs of the Old Empire whom he acknowledged as legitimate occupants of the Egyptian throne. To Thothmes III. belongs the credit of being the first, so far as we know, to attempt the task of arranging the old kings in something like chronological order. What materials he possessed for the work, what amount of labor he expended upon it, how far it was an historical, how far an arbitrary arrangement, are points upon which various opinions may be held; but it is incontestable that out of the chaos of the past he educed a certain method and order, which in its main features came to be recognized by the Egyptians themselves as authentic and authoritative. Sixty kings, commencing with Seneferu, and comprising Assa, Pepi, several Antefs, Mentu-hoteps, and Usurtasens, were exhibited in a consecutive series as ancestors of the reigning Pharaoh, who represented himself as making offerings to them, and thus acknowledged at once their ancestral relation to himself and their divinity.[133] The "Great Tablet of Karnak," as it is called, must always remain among the most important of those documents upon which the arrangement of the early history of Egypt depends; and though by many its value is thought to be surpassed by later and fuller lists, there will always be some to whom, on account of its antiquity, it will approve itself as the most important and most trustworthy of all the early catalogues of kings.

Besides distinguishing himself as a warrior, as a record writer, as a natural historian, and as a genealogist, Thothmes III. was one of the greatest of Egyptian builders and patrons of art. The great temple of Ammon at Thebes was the special object of his fostering care; and he began his career of builder and restorer by repairing the damages which his sister, Hatasu, had inflicted on that glorious edifice to gratify her dislike of her brother, Thothmes II., and her father, Thothmes I. Statues of Thothmes I., and his father, Amenôphis, which Hatasu had thrown down, were re-erected by Thothmes III., before the southern propylæa of the temple in the first year of his independent reign.[134] The central sanctuary, which Usurtasen I. had built in common stone,[135] was next replaced by the present granite edifice under the directions of the young prince, who then proceeded to build in rear of the old temple, a magnificent hall or pillared chamber, of dimensions previously unknown in Egypt. This edifice was an oblong square, 143 feet long by fifty-five feet wide, or nearly half as large again as the nave of Canterbury Cathedral.[136] The whole of this apartment was roofed in with slabs of solid stone; two rows of circular pillars thirty feet in height supported the central part, dividing it into three avenues, while on each side of the pillars was a row of square piers, still further extending the width of the chamber, and breaking it up into five long vistas.[137] In connection with this noble hall, on three sides of it, north, east, and south, Thothmes erected further chambers and corridors, one of the former, situated towards the south, containing that "Great Tablet of Karnak" which was described in the last paragraph.

Thothmes also added propylæa to the temple on the south,[138] and erected in front of it two, or perhaps four, immense obelisks. According to an inscription which is still extant, two of these monoliths reached the quite unparalleled and almost incredible height of 108 cubits, or 162 feet, and must have weighed 700 or 800 tons.[139] Two, of which one stands to this day before the Church of St. John Lateran in Rome, attained certainly the height of 105 feet, and weighed 450 tons.[140] These last were inscribed with hieroglyphics which declared: "The king has raised these immense obelisks to the god Ammon, in the forecourt of the house of the god, on the soil of Ape, as the first beginning of the erection of immense obelisks in Thebes."[141] Finally, towards the close of his reign, he repaired and re-erected in front of the temple a second image of his father, which Hatasu had thrown down; and, either at this time or at some other, he also adorned the building with statues of himself, which are colossal and full of dignity.[142]

Other erections of this distinguished monarch are the enclosure of the temple of the Sun at Heliopolis,[143] and the obelisks belonging to the same building, which the irony of fate has now removed to Rome, England, and America;[144] the temple of Phthah at Thebes; the small temple at Medinet-Abou; a temple to Kneph, adorned with obelisks, at Elephantiné;[145] and a series of temples and monuments at Ombos, Esneh, Abydos, Coptos, Denderah, Eileithyia, Hermonthis, and Memphis in Egypt, and at Amada, Corte, Talmis, Pselcis, Semneh, and Koummeh in Nubia.[146] Large remains still exist in the Koummeh and Semneh temples,[147] where Thothmes worships Totun, the Nubian Kneph, in conjunction with Usurtasen III., his own ancestor. There are also extensive ruins of his great buildings at Denderah, Ombos, and Napata. Altogether, Thothmes III. is pronounced to have "left more monuments than any other Pharaoh, excepting Rameses II.," and, though occasionally showing himself as a builder, somewhat capricious and whimsical, yet still, on the whole, to have worked in "a pure style," and proved that he was "not deficient in good taste."[148]

There is reason to believe that the great constructions of this mighty monarch were,in part at least, the product of forced labors. Doubtless his eleven thousand captives[149] were for the most part held in slavery, and compelled to employ their energies in helping toward the accomplishment of those grand works which his active mind was continually engaged in devising. We find among the monuments of his time a representation [160] of the mode in which the services of these foreign bondsmen were made to subserve the glory of the Pharaoh who had carried them away captive. Some are seen kneading and cutting up the clay; others bear them water from a neighboring pool; others again, with the assistance of a wooden mould, shape the clay into bricks, which are then taken and placed in long rows to dry; finally, when the bricks are sufficiently hard, the highest class of laborers proceed to build them into walls. All the works performed under the eyes of taskmasters armed with sticks, who address the laborers with the words: "The stick is in my hand. Be not idle." Over the whole is an inscription which says: "Here are to be seen the prisoners, which have been carried away as living captives in very great numbers; they work at the building with active fingers; their overseers are in sight; they insist with vehemence (on the others laboring), obeying the orders of the great skilled lord (i.e., the head-architect,) who prescribes to them the works, and gives directions to the masters; they are rewarded with wine and all kinds of good dishes; they perform their service with a mind full of love for the king; they build for Thothmes Ra-men-khepr a Holy of Holies for the gods. May it be rewarded to him through a range of many years!" [161]

The scene is so graphic—the words are so forcible and suitable—that many have recognized in this remarkable picture an actual representation of the oppressed Hebrews [162] working under the tyrants who "made their lives bitter with hard bondage in mortar and in brick," beating them and ill-using them, so that "all the service, wherein they made them serve, was with rigor;" [163] but the best critics of the present day [164] are of opinion that, though the work is an excellent illustration of the sort of life led by the Israelites under the Pharaohs who oppressed them, yet, in point of fact, it depicts not their sufferings, but those of quite a different people. The laborers were persons whom Thothmes had carried off in his wars—the captives of his bow and of his spear—not members of a despised race, which he had inherited with his other subjects from his forefathers; their countenances have a Semitic cast, but are certainly not markedly Jewish; and the general character of their physiognomy is very different from that of the Jews. They have light hair, and in several instances blue eyes; [165] they are as slight in frame as the Egyptians themselves, and in few instances do they wear a beard. While, therefore, we must look with special interest on a work which brings before us the sort of suffering that befell the Israelites in their hard bondage in Egypt, we are bound to regard it as bearing only indirectly on this subject, and as primarily illustrative only of the mode in which prisoners of war were treated by the Egyptians in the palmiest days of the Empire.

It may be asked, however, with some excuse for the question, what *was* the condition of the Israelites at this time? Were they still in Egypt, or had they already gone forth? Did or did not Thothmes III. stand in any peculiar relation to them? An undying interest attaches to the Hebrew race, and Egypt herself derives from her connection with the "peculiar people" more than half the attractiveness which she possesses for the general public. Without this, she might still, through her antiquity and her mysteriousness, draw to herself the regards of the recluse student, of the philologist, and the antiquarian; but to the masses she would be simply an empire dead and gone, a closed page of old-world history, the "shadow of a great name," and nothing more. It is because "Israel sojourned in Egypt,"[156] and the house of Jacob among "a people of strange language"[157]—it is because the life and character of the Jewish race were indelibly impressed and colored by their long residence in that wonderful land, and their long contact with the wonderful Egyptian nation,—it is because for nearly eighteen centuries the histories of Egypt and Palestine were intermixed, and the Hebrew and Eygptian races acted and re-acted one upon the other, that the world at large does not regard Egyptology with indifference, or turn a deaf ear to those who seek to instruct it upon Egyptian matters. Naturally, it is at the points of contact between Egyptian and Hebrew history that the interest of the former culminates; and the historian of Egypt, when he reaches the probable period of the servitude and the Exodus, is bound to throw as much light as he possibly can on the time and circumstances of their occurrence.

We have expressed our opinion that Joseph was probably the minister of Apepi, the last Shepherd king, and that the sons of Jacob entered Egypt from Palestine under this monarch.[158] Hospitably received by a people of the same pastoral habits with themselves, the Israelites occupied the land of Goshen, a portion of the Tanitic nome,[159] lying between the Sebennytic and Pelusiac branches of the Nile, where they fed their own flocks, and at the same time superintended the herds belonging to the Egyptian king.[160] If

Joseph lived, as is commonly supposed, about seventy years after this event, he must have long outlived Apepi, whose entire reign is estimated at sixty-one years.[161] Probably he died under Aahmes, about B.C. 1600, having of course lost his position of "lord over the whole land,"[162] when the Shepherd dominion fell, but having left an undying name, which long protected his kinsmen. For many years they lived peaceably and undisturbed in the region assigned them, where they "were fruitful, and increased abundantly, and multiplied, and waxed exceeding mighty," until the land "was filled with them."[163] At length a "new king arose up over Egypt, which knew not Joseph."[164] The only question which can properly be raised at this period of the history is—Who was this? Was Thothmes III., or was any one of his predecessors of the eighteenth dynasty, the "new king," and had the oppression of the Israelites now begun, or were they still living in the quiet and retired position which they occupied from the first, "serving" the Egyptians,[165] but not ill-treated by them? Chronological considerations lead to the conclusion that the severe oppression had not yet begun. It was consequent on the very great multiplication of the Israelites, which rendered them formidable to Egypt; and this multiplication required time for its development, and cannot reasonably be thought to have attained such proportions as to call for severe measures of repression in the century, or century and a quarter, which had intervened between the reign of Apepi and that of Thothmes III.[166] The "new king" must be looked for at a date considerably later than that of this monarch, and we must regard Thothmes and all the earlier kings of this dynasty as Pharaohs under whose sway the nascent people remained quietly in Goshen, rapidly multiplying and increasing, but not to such an extent as to draw upon them, as yet, the jealous fear of their sovereign.

Among the inscriptions of Thothmes are some which seem to ascribe to him a series of victories over the nations of the south,[167] as well as over those of the north and the northeast; but his own annals are so nearly complete, and his own constant presence with the forces engaged in Syria and Mesopotamia is so distinctly marked, that it seems impossible to view these southern victories as gained by the monarch in person.[168] They were the fruit, it is probable, of campaigns carried on by his generals in the opposite quarter to that against which his own efforts were directed—campaigns which resulted in the capture of numerous prisoners and the carrying off

Vol. II. Plate XV.

Fig. 32.—HEAD OF MENEPHTAH.—See Page 181.

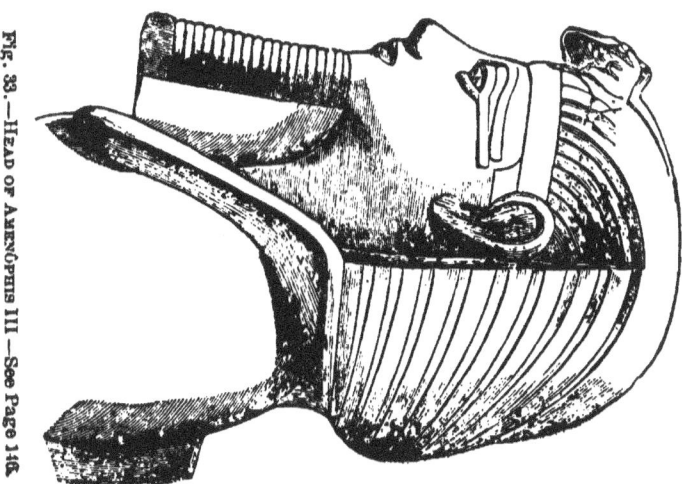

Fig. 33.—HEAD OF AMENÔPHIS III.—See Page 146.

Plate XVI.   Vol. IX.

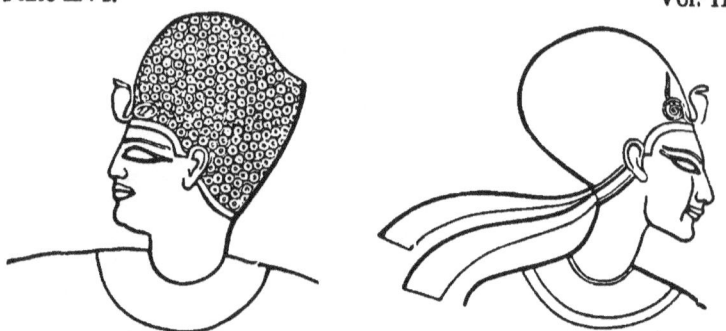

Fig. 34.—HEADDRESSES OF THOTHMES III. AND AMENÔPHIS IV.—See Page 191.

Fig. 35.—HEAD OF NEFERTARI-AAHMES.—See Page 114.

of much booty, but which did not add any new province to the Empire.

According to one writer, the maritime successes of Thothmes were almost more remarkable than those which he gained by land. "One perceives," says M. Lenormant,[169] "by the inscription upon the stélé of Thebes that the fleets of the great Pharaoh, after having first conquered Cyprus and Crete, had further subjected to his sceptre the islands of the southern Archipelago, a considerable portion of the seaboard of Greece and of Asia, and even perhaps the lower extremity of Italy. It appears to me that one ought to conclude from the same monument that the war-vessels of Thothmes III. penetrated pretty frequently into the waters of the Black Sea, where Herodotus pretends that the Egyptians had before this founded a colony in Colchis for the working of the mines.[170] I am, in fact, disposed to recognize the ancestors of the Germanic Ases—the descendants of the Ashkenaz of Genesis x.—at this time dwellers on the Palus Mæotis—in one of the tribes enumerated among the northern peoples who paid tribute to the fleet of Thothmes. In another direction the same force had made the authority of Egypt to be acknowledged along the entire seaboard of Libya. Memorials of the reign of Thothmes III. have been found at Cherchell in Algeria; and it is not at all impossible that they really mark the limit whereto the power of this prince extended on the north coast of Africa."

Now, it is certain that Thothmes was accompanied and supported by a considerable fleet in several of his expeditions into Syria;[171] and it is not at all improbable that he extended his dominion over the island of Cyprus, which at a much less flourishing period was conquered and held by Amasis.[172] But the extended maritime dominion assigned to him in this passage scarcely rests on any secure or stable foundation. It is not accepted by the more sober of modern Egyptologists,[173] nor can it be said to have probability in its favor. The spirit of maritime enterprise which animated the Greeks, the Phœnicians, and the Carthaginians, was at no time rife in Egypt; and Egyptian sailors would scarcely have confronted the perils of the inhospitable Euxine, or even of the open Mediterranean, without a much stronger inducement than any which the European coasts had at this time to offer them. It is said that they may have employed the services of Tyrian mariners;[174] but there is no evidence that Tyre was at this early date (circ. B.C. 1500) a great maritime state, or indeed that the Phœnicians proper had as yet passed from the Persian Gulf to the Mediterranean.[175] The sole foundation on which M. Lenormant's theory rests is that of the ethnic names occurring in the hymn or song of victory inscribed by Thothmes on the wall of the temple of Ammon at Thebes; but these names are of exceedingly doubtful import, and, according to Dr. Brugsch, designate none but Asiatic or African nations. The passage on which M. Lenormant rests his theory is thus translated by his German fellow-laborer:[176]—

(AMMON *loquitur*.)

I came, and thou smotest the princes of Zahi;
I scattered them under thy feet all over their lands;
I made them regard thy Holiness as the blazing sun;
Thou shinest in sight of them in my form.

I came, and thou smotest those that dwell in Asia;
Thou tookest captive the goat-herds of Ruten;
I made them behold thy Holiness in thy royal adornments,
As thou graspest thy weapons in the war chariot.

I came and thou smotest the land of the East;
Thou marchedst against the dwellers in the Holy Land:
I made them to behold thy Holiness as the star Canopus,
Which sends forth its heat and disperses the dew.

I came, and thou smotest the land of the West;
Kefa and Asebi (*i.e.* Phœnicia and Cyprus) held thee in fear ·
I make them look upon thy Holiness as upon a young bull,
Courageous, with sharp horns, whom none can approach.

I came, and thou smotest the subjects of their lords;
The land of Mathen trembled for fear of thee;
I made them look upon thy Holiness as upon a crocodile,
Terrible in the waters, not to be encountered.

I came, and thou smotest them that dwelt in the Great Sea:
The inhabitants of the isles were afraid of thy war-cry:
I make them behold thy Holiness as the Avenger,
Who shows himself at the back of his victim.

I came, and thou smotest the land of the Tahennu;
The people of Uten submitted themselves to thy power;
I made them see thy Holiness as a lion, fierce of eye,
Who leaves his den and stalks through the valleys.

I came, and thou smotest the hinder (*i.e.*) northern lands.
The circuit of the Great Sea is bound in thy grasp;
I made them behold thy Holiness as the hovering hawk,
Which seizes with his glance whatever pleases him.

I came, and thou smotest the lands in front;
Those that sat upon the sand thou carriedst away captive,
I made them behold thy Holiness like the jackal of the South,
Which passes through the lands as a hidden wanderer.

I came, and thou smotest the nomad tribes of Nubia,
Even to the land of Shat, which thou holdest in thy grasp;
I made them behold thy Holiness like thy pair of brothers,
Whose hands I have united to bless thee.

If this be a correct version of the Egyptian original, it is clear that the maritime dominion claimed is of the vaguest kind. Some "dwellers in the Great Sea" are said to have been smitten, which would be sufficiently answered by the reduction of Cyprus, or even by that of the island Tyre and of Aradus; others have heard and feared the conqueror's war-cry; he has smitten certain "northern" nations, which may point merely to the Ruten and the Tahai or Zahi; and "the circuit of the Great Sea is bound in his grasp," which would be ordinary Oriental hyperbole for obtaining the mastery over the Eastern Mediterranean. On the whole, it would seem to be most probable that the fleets of Thothmes III. traversed only the extreme eastern portion of the Levant, and that his maritime dominion did not extend further than the coasts of Egypt, Syria, Cilicia,[177] and Cyprus.

Still, it is not without reason that the latest historian of Egypt has pronounced Thothmes III. to have been the greatest of Egyptian kings.[178] Ambitous, restless, brave even to rashness,[179] equally remarkable as a warrior and as a general, successful in his naval no less than in his military operations, he spread the name and fame of Egypt through distant lands, alarmed the great empires of Western Asia, conquered and held in subjection all Syria and Western Mesopotamia as far as the Khabour river, probably reduced Cyprus, chastised the Arabs, crushed rebellion in Nubia, and left to his successor a dominion extending above eleven hundred miles from north to south, and (in places) four hundred and fifty miles from west to east. At the same time he distinguished himself as a builder. Restorer or founder of a score of temples, designer of the great "Hall of Pillars" at Thebes, by far the largest apartment that the world had as yet seen, erector of numerous gigantic obelisks, constructor and adorner of vast propylæa, author or restorer of at least five huge colossi, he has left the impress of his presence in Egypt more widely than almost any other of her kings, while at the same time he has supplied to the great capitals of the modern world their most striking Egyptian monuments. The memorial which he erected to commemorate his conquest of the land of Naharaïn looks down upon the place of the Atmeidan in the city of Constantine; one of his great Theban obelisks rears itself in the midst of the Piazza in front of the Church of St. John Lateran in Rome;[160] while the twin spires which he set up before the temple of the Sun at Heliopolis, after long adorning Alexandria, have been conveyed respectively to London and to New York, where they may check the overweening arrogance of the two proudest nations of the modern world by showing them that the art and engineering skill of ancient Egypt were in some respects unapproachable. It may be further noted that the name of Thothmes III. is found, more frequently than any other, on scarabæi and small images,[161] which were used as amulets; whence it would seem that he was regarded after his death as a sort of deity of good luck, "a preserver against the evil influence of wicked spirits and sorcerers."[162]

In person Thothmes III. does not appear to have been very remarkable. His countenance was thoroughly Egyptian, but not characterized by any strong individuality. The long, well-shaped, but somewhat delicate nose, almost in line with the forehead, gives a slightly feminine appearance to the face, which is generally represented as beardless and moderately plump. The eye, prominent, and larger than that of the ordinary Egyptian, has a pensive but resolute expression, and is suggestive of mental force. The mouth is somewhat too full for beauty, but is resolute, like the eye, and less sensual than that of most Egyptians. There is an appearance of weakness about the chin, which is short and retreats slightly, thus helping to give the entire countenance a womanish look. Altogether, the face has less of strength and determination than we should have expected, but is not wholly without indications of those qualities.

Thothmes III. died after a reign of fifty-four years,[163] according to his own reckoning,[164] probably at about the age of sixty,[165] since he seems to have been a mere infant at the death of his father, Thothmes I. He married a wife called Hatasu Merira,[166] by whom he had at least two children, a daughter,[167] Nefru-ra, and a son, Amen-hotep, who succeeded him.

Amen-hotep, the son of Thothmes III. (Fig. 27), took on his accession the throne-name of Ra-aa-khepru, and is known in history as Amenôphis II.[168] He was not a king of any great force of character or ability. During his short reign of some seven or eight years,[189] he achieved but little that is deserving of remembrance. As crown prince, it would seem that he had conducted a campaign against the Bedouins of the desert between the valley of the Nile and the Red Sea, in which he had obtained certain successes.[190] As king, his efforts were directed solely to the maintenance of the Empire acquired by his father, and the chastisement of those who rebelled against his authority. Following the usual practice of Oriental subject nations at the death of their conqueror, the tribes of Western Asia no sooner heard of Thothmes' decease than they renounced their allegiance to Egypt, and reclaimed their independence. Amenôphis in his first or second year had to undertake an expedition against the rebels, and to re-establish the authority of Egypt over the entire region which had been conquered by his father. It appears that he was everywhere successful. He rapidly overran Syria and Mesopotamia, taking the chief cities after short sieges, and even pushed his arms as far as the town of Ni, the supposed great city of Nineveh.[191] At Takhira in Northern Syria he slew, he tells us, seven kings with his own battle-club; after which he suspended their bodies from the prow of his own war-vessels, and in this way conveyed them to Egypt where he hung six out of the seven outside the walls of Thebes, and the remaining one on the wall of Napata, to serve as a warning to the negroes of the south.[192] It is remarkable that Amenôphis II. is the first king who represents himself in the act of killing several captured monarchs at one and the same time with a club or mace;[193] and the account which he gives of his proceedings raises the suspicion that the cold-blooded murder was actually accomplished by his own hand. If so, we must regard him as at once cruel and barbarous—cruel, to condemn to death so large a number, when the execution of two or three would have been equally efficacious as a warning; barbarous, to take upon himself the odious office of executioner. Modern Egyptologists have for the most part glossed over or ignored the crimes and cruelties, the defilements and abominations, which deformed the civilization of Egypt. It is not the wish of the present writer to give them undue prominence; but the interests of historic truth require that, when the occasion offers, they should be noticed, lest a false estimate should be formed of the degree of refinement and of moral development to which the Egyptians of Pharaonic times attained.

The countries which Amenôphis II. claims to have chastised and reduced to obedience are eleven in number; but some of them are very vaguely indicated. A recent writer thus enumerates them.[194] "The land of the south, the inhabitants of the Oases, and the land of the north, the Arabians or Shasu, the Marmaridæ (Tahennu), the Nubian nomad tribes, the Asiatic husbandmen, Naharaïn, Phœnicia, the Cilician coast, the upper Ruten country." If all these had rebelled, Amenôphis must certainly have had enough to occupy him during his short reign, and deserves some credit for having re-established the authority of Egypt on all sides, after it had been so seriously menaced.

As a builder, Amenôphis II. fell very far short, not only of his predecessor, but of most Egyptian kings of this period. The hall which he added to the great temple of Ammon at Thebes is on a mean scale, and poor in the character of its ornamentation;[195] his temple at Amada in Nubia has no particular merit; nor do the additions which he made to the temple of Totun at Koummeh [196] strike the traveller as having much to recommend them to his notice. The best monument of his reign is his tomb at Abd-el-Qurnah, where he is represented seated upon his throne, with a sceptre in his right hand, and wearing the peculiar headdress which characterizes the god Merula. Below him is a frieze containing the scutcheons of eleven captured kings, while in front of him are numerous relatives and attendants, bringing offerings of various kinds, stone sphinxes, colossal statues, furniture, arms, vases, mirrors, and the like.[197] His other sculptures are chiefly religious, and exhibit him as a worshipper of Harmachis, Ammon-Ra, Thoth, Kneph, Totun, and Usurtasen III., the great Nubian conqueror. They are altogether of a commonplace character.

Amenôphis was the son of Hatasu-Merira, and in one place represents her as seated behind him on a throne like his own,[198] which would seem to imply that he had associated her with him in the government. He had a son, Shæmuas or Khamus, who bore the office of chief priest of Ammon, and a grandson, Amen-hotep, or Amenôphis, with the surname of Hapu.[199] The son, however, who succeeded him on the throne, bore his grandfather's name of Thothmes, to which he added those of Men-khepru-ra, ⚬̇⚬̇𓏤𓏤, and Sha-shau, 𓏤𓏤𓏤, on his accession. It would seem that Thothmes was not the eldest son, or expectant heir of his predecessor, since he ascribes his accession to the special favor of Harmachis, and relates how that deity appeared to him as he slept, and raised his thoughts to the hope of sovereignty.[200] Naturally, when he became king, it was to the worship of Harmachis that he specially devoted himself; and identifying that god in some peculiar way with the Great Sphinx of the Pyramids,[201] he set himself to clear away the vast mass of loose sand which had accumulated round the monument, and to exhibit to his contemporaries the entire figure in all its marvellous grandeur and beauty. At the same time he set up between the fore paws of the Sphinx a massive memorial tablet, twelve feet high and nearly eight feet broad, on which he recorded the circumstances of his dream, his resolve to undertake the work of removing the immense accumulation of sand, and no doubt the happy accomplishment of his enterprise.[202] In front of his memorial tablet, and also within the paws of the monstrous animal, Thothmes constructed a small temple for the worship of the god with whom he identified it, which was recently uncovered by Dr. Lepsius, but is now again engulfed by the ever encroaching sands of the desert.[203]

As a warrior, Thothmes IV. (Fig. 30) achieved little that was remarkable. One expedition against the Hittites of Syria,[204] and another against the Cushites or people of Ethiopia,[205] are all that can be assigned to him. The former he commemorated in the great temple of Ammon at Thebes, the latter in the Nubian temple of Amada. The captain, Amen-hotep, seems to have accompanied him on both these occasions, and to have exaggerated his master's successes into a general subjection of both the South and the North.[206] Thothmes, however, in a memorial tablet at Qurnah, represents himself as smiting two enemies only.[207]

In his youth, Thothmes was addicted to field sports and manly exercises. He hunted the lion in the desert region to the west of the pyramids of Ghizeh, and practised spear-throwing for his pleasure with bronze weapons, which he hurled at a target. So swift were the horses which he was accustomed to drive in his chariot, that, according to his own statement, they outstripped the wind, and when he overtook persons as he was driving, he passed them so rapidly that they could not recognize him.[208]

Like his father, Thothmes IV. died when he was still quite a young man, having reigned not more than about eight or nine years.[209] He was succeeded by a son, Amen-hotep, or Amenôphis, who took the throne name of Ma-neb-ra,[210]

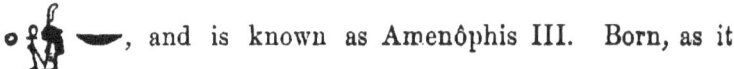, and is known as Amenôphis III. Born, as it

would seem, of an Ethiopian mother, Mut-em-ua[211] (Fig. 22), Amenôphis had a somewhat foreign physiognomy; and it was probably owing to his foreign connection that he favored changes in the State religion which were looked upon as revolutionary. He married a wife named Tii (Fig. 25) or Taia,[212] who was certainly a foreigner,[213] though of what nation is doubtful. Her father's name was Juaa, her mother's Tuaa, possibly Arabian, possibly Ethiopian appellatives. Tenderly attached to her and dominated by her influence, he leant towards that exclusive and peculiar Sun-worship which was established by his successor, and though not the direct introducer of the change, must be viewed as having paved the way to it by accustoming the Egyptians to the idea.[214] The religious history of the ancient Eastern world is a subject at once too wide and too obscure to be discussed in this place episodically; but it cannot be questioned that from a very ancient date there existed in Arabia and elsewhere a special devotion to the brilliant orb of day, which from time to time aspired to become a distinct and separate religion. In the nature worship of the Old Egyptian Empire the Sun had held no very important place. Phthah, Khem, and Kneph had been the principal deities, while Ra had occupied a quite subordinate position. With the rise of Thebes to power a change had occurred. Ammon, early identified with Ra, and known commonly as Ammon-Ra, had been recognized as the head of the Pantheon; Mentu, Shu, Tum, Harmachis, solar gods, had risen in rank and position: the solar element in the Egyptian religion had, as it were, asserted itself and come to the front. Now a further development became manifest. The theory was broached that the lord of light, the actual material sun, was the sole proper object of worship, and that the polytheism hitherto maintained as the State religion was false, wrongful, blasphemous. All adoration was claimed for one god alone out of the fifty or sixty who had hitherto divided among them the religious regards of the people. Under Amen-hotep III., indeed, the doctrine still remained veiled; but its leavening influence began to be felt from this time; and the reign of Amen-hotep III. is chiefly remarkable as conducing towards the religious revolution which so shortly followed.

But the reign is not remarkable for this only. From a military point of view, it is indeed uninteresting and of slight moment.[215] Amenôphis did not extend the power of Egypt either in the north or in the south. There are indications that he maintained in the north the dominion which had descended to him from Thothmes III.,[216] and abundant proof that he engaged personally in military operations in the south;[217] but we cannot ascribe to him any extension of the Egyptian territory even in this quarter. He was content, as it would seem, to conduct razzias on a large scale against the unhappy negro tribes,[218] and to carry off into captivity some hundreds of their members, the great majority consisting of women and children.[219] He may possibly have obtained the submission of some tribes which were not previously subject, and it is not unlikely that he once or twice defeated the Ethiopians; but it is absurd to speak of him as a conquering monarch, or to put him "on a level with the great Thothmes," in respect of military matters.

As a builder, on the contrary, Amenôphis III. is entitled to very considerable credit, and may claim a place among the most distinguished of Egyptian monarchs.[220] Tablets existing in the quarries of Toura near Memphis show that he began to excavate stone for the repairs of temples as early as his first and second year;[221] and the scale and number of his works are such as to indicate unremitting attention to sculpture and building during the whole term of his long reign of thirty-six years. Amenôphis erected the great temple of Ammon at Luxor, one of the most magnificent in all Egypt,[222] embellished that of Karnak with a new propylon, built two new temples on the same site to Ammon and Maut, and "united the whole quarter of the temples at Karnak with the new temple of Ammon at Luxor by an avenue of crio-sphinxes with the sun's disk on their heads."[223] He also built two temples to Kneph or Khum at Elephantiné, one to contain his own image at Soleb in Nu'ia, a shrine with a propylon and ram-sphinxes before it at Gebel Berkal or Napata,[224] and another shrine at Sedinga.[225] Inscribed tablets dated in his reign are found at Semneh, in the island of Konosso, on the rocks between Philæ and Assouan, at El-Kaab, at Silsilis and at Sarabit-el-Khadim in the Sinaitic peninsula.[226] Of all his edifices, that which approved itself the most highly in his own eyes was the temple, or rather perhaps the temple-palace, of Luxor. "I built on the rocky soil," he says, "a court of alabaster, of rose granite, and of black stone. Also a double tower-gateway did I execute, because I had undertaken to dedicate the most beautiful thing possible to my divine father (*i. e.* Ammon). Statues of the gods are to be seen in it everywhere. They are carved in all their parts. A great statue was made of gold and all kinds of beautiful precious stones. I gave directions to execute, O Ammon, what pleased thee well, to unite thee with thy beautiful dwelling."[247]

It was in connection with another of his temples, one built upon the opposite bank of the Nile, that Amenóphis caused to be constructed the most remarkable of all his works—the two gigantic statues which are still to be seen before the ruins of his temple, on the *dromos*, or paved way, by which it was approached.[228] These sitting figures which represent the king himself, were carved, each of them, out of a single block of solid reddish sandstone.[229] Their present height above the pavement on which they stand is nearly sixty-one feet;[230] and the original height, including the tall crown worn by Egyptian kings, is supposed to have been nearly seventy feet.[231] No other Egyptian colossi are known to have much exceeded fifty feet. A peculiar fame has attached to one of these statues, owing to the accident that during the space of about 220 years it emitted a musical sound soon after daybreak, and thus attracted to itself an inordinate share of the attention of travellers. A magical power was thought to be inherent in the "vocal Memnon"—as the statue was called—and for above two centuries travellers flocked to it, inscribed their names upon it, and added sensible or silly remarks.[232] Eminent writers also took notice of the phenomenon and spoke of it as one of the prodigies which made Egypt a land of wonders."[233] Moderns believe the sound to have been the result of the sun's rays, either upon the stone itself, or upon the air contained in its crevices.[234] Musical sounds produced by change of temperature are frequently given forth both by natural rocks and by quarried masses of certain kinds of stone; and their occurrence has been placed on record by eminently scientific persons.[235] There is no sufficient reason to doubt that the tone, "like the breaking of a harp-string,"[236] discharged by the colossus of Amenóphis (Fig. 29) was a casual instance of this natural phenomenon, neither contrived nor even understood by the Egyptian priests. It is thought to have been first given forth after the shattering of the statue by an earthquake (B.C. 27), and to have ceased upon the repair of the image by Septimius Severus, circ. A.D. 196.

The impressive appearance of the twin colossi has been frequently noticed by travellers. "There they sat," says Miss Martineau, "together, yet apart, in the midst of the plain, serene and vigilant, still keeping their untired watch over the lapse of ages and the eclipse of Egypt. I can never believe that anything else so majestic as this pair has been conceived of by the imagination of Art. Nothing, certainly, even in Nature, ever affected me so unspeakably; no thunder-storm in my childhood, nor any aspect of Niagara, or the Great Lakes of America, or the Alps, or the Desert, in my later years." And again: "The pair sitting alone amid the expanse of verdure, with islands of ruin behind them, grow more striking to us every day. To-day, for the first time, we looked up to them from their base. The impression of sublime tranquillity which they convey, when seen from distant points, is confirmed by a nearer approach. There they sit keeping watch—hands on knees, gazing straight forward; seeming, though so much of the faces is gone, to be looking over to the monumental piles on the other side of the river, which became gorgeous temples after these throne-seats were placed here—the most immovable thrones that have ever been established on this earth!" [237]

The sculptor of these wonderful colossi bore the same name as his royal master, and prided himself on their execution, conveyance, and safe emplacement as the greatest achievements of his genius. "I immortalized the name of the king," he says, "and no one has done the like of me in my works. I executed two portrait-statues of the king, astonishing for their breadth and height—their completed form dwarfed the temple-tower—forty cubits was their measure—they were cut in the splendid sandstone mountain, on either side, the eastern and the western. I caused to be built eight ships, whereon the statues were carried up the river; they were emplaced in their sublime building; they will last as long as heaven. A joyful event was it when they were landed at Thebes and raised up in their place." [238]

In brief, the works of Amen-hotep III., architectural and sculptured, are among the most striking left by any of the kings, being equally remarkable for their number, for their vast size, and for the delicacy and finish of their execution.[239] A liberal patron of all kinds of ability, he evoked the genius which he required, and covered Egypt and Nubia with masterpieces of art, in the grand and solid style for which the land of Mizraim is celebrated.

Amen-hotep was also distinguished as a lover of field sports. During the first ten years of his reign such was his ardor in the pursuit of the noblest kind of game, that he is able to boast of having slain with his own hand either 110 or, according to another authority, 210 fierce lions.[240] Later on, he presented to the priests who had the charge of the great temple at Karnak a number of live lions,[241] which he had probably caught in traps. These ferocious beasts seem occasionally to have been tamed by the Eygptians; and it is possible that they were employed to add grandeur and dignity to some of the religious processions. The lion was an emblem both of Horus and of Tum;[242] his fitness to symbolize royalty caused the employment of his image to ornament the most elaborate of the Egyptian thrones;[243] and, if we may trust the sculptures, a tame lion sometimes accompanied the king to the battle-field.[244] Africa has always been a special nursery of lions;[245] and Amen-hotep, like his father Thothmes IV.,[246] may have indulged his passion for chasing them without going beyond his own borders; or, like some of the great Assyrian kings, he may have made Mesopotamia his hunting ground, and have carried off his sporting honors in the field which at a later date supplied the noble game to Tiglathpileser and Sardanapalus.[247]

In personal character Amenôphis was remarkable for kindness, generosity, and submission to female influence. In the early part of his reign he was governed by his mother, Mutemua; in his middle and later life he deferred greatly to his wife Tii or Taia. The honors assigned to Tii in his sculptures[248] are unusual, and imply something like divided sovereignty. Amen-hotep, son of Hapu,[249] and other functionaries, as especially the vizer Khumhat,[250] were treated with much kindness and consideration by their generous sovereign, and received rewards at his hand for which they were duly thankful. Rewards were also lavishly showered on the priests and other subordinate functionaries, who do not appear to have in any way exceeded their ordinary routine of duty. The mere payment of taxes was accepted as a token of loyalty and good-will, and earned the honorable decoration of a collar or a necklace.[251] At the same time justice was carefully administered; even petty thefts did not escape inquiry and detection;[252] and conviction was followed by adequate punishment.

Amenôphis (Fig. 33) is represented with a face that is somewhat prognathous,[253] that is one which has the jaws advanced beyond the line of the forehead. He has a long nose, much rounded at the end, a short upper lip, and a projecting and somewhat pointed chin. The expresssion of his face is pensive but determined. He is sometimes beardless, but more often wears the usual long beard, not covering the chin but dependent from it, and descending to the middle of the bosom.

The reign of Amenôphis lasted at least thirty-six years.[254]

He appears by the monuments to have had four sons, whom he represented as engaged in religious worship on more than one occasion.²⁶⁵ He had also at least three daughters, called respectively, Isis, Hont-mihib and Satamon.²⁶⁶ His wife, Tii, survived him,²⁶⁷ and he left the crown to his eldest son, Amen-hotep, or Amenôphis IV., under her direction and superintendence.

Amen-hotep IV. had a physiognomy entirely different from that of any other Egyptian monarch, and indeed one altogether abnormal and extraordinary. His general appearance is rather that of a woman than of a man;²⁶⁸ he has a slanting forehead, a long aquiline nose, a flexile projecting mouth, and a strongly developed chin. His neck, which is almost unusually long and thin, seems scarcely equal to the support of his head, and his spindle shanks appear ill adapted to sustain the weight of his over-corpulent body. He is supposed to have derived this strange physique from his maternal ancestors, who are thought to have been Abyssinians of the Galla family.²⁶⁹ The throne-names which he assumed upon his accession were Nefer-khepr-ra, and Ua-en-ra; but it was not long ere he discarded these appellations, which were of the usual Egyptian type, and substituted for them the strange and wholly unheard-of designation of Khu-en-aten (Fig. 31), "Light of the Solar Disk," which thenceforward he employed in his inscriptions almost exclusively. Among his favorite epithets were Mi-Aten and Mi-Harmakhu, "friend of the solar disk," and "friend of Hor or Harmachis," whom he identified with the solar deity. He was the first king to enclose epithets of this class within his cartouche,²⁶⁰ and in this way to elongate and amplify his royal title. He was also the first openly to bring forward the disk-worship as the sum and substance of the State religion, and not only to devote himself to it with all the enthusiasm of a thoroughly Oriental nature, but to press it upon his subjects, as the proper substitute of all their ancient worships. Considering the gross character of much of the Egyptian religion, we feel strongly inclined to the belief that Amen-hotep's change was one in the right direction; that it would at once have simplified and have purified the old nature-cult had it prevailed; would have swept away much superstition, many pollutions; and would have replaced them by a belief and worship, comparatively speaking, pure and spiritual.²⁶¹ It would have been something to have substituted a form of monotheism for the multitudinous polytheism of the old creed; it would have been more to get rid of the debasing animal worship and the coarse Khem-worship so generally prevalent. If a people is too gross to rise to the spiritual conception of an immaterial deity, and *must* attach the idea of God to something of whose existence it has sensible evidence, there would seem to be in the sun an affinity and symbolic aptness which render it fitter to represent the Deity than aught else which is material.[262] In the Egyptian disk-worship, if we may judge by the small existing remains of it, there was a high tone of devotional feeling, and a conception of the Supreme Being not wholly unworthy of Him. "Beautiful is thy setting, O disk of life," says one votary;[263] "beautiful is thy setting, thou lord of lords and king of the worlds. When thou unitest thyself at thy setting with the heavenly sphere, mortals rejoice before thy countenance, and give honor to him who has created them, and pray before him who has formed them, before the glance of thy son, who loves thee, the king Khu-en-aten. The whole land of Egypt and all the nations repeat all thy names at thy rising, to magnify thy rising, in like manner as they magnify thy setting. Thou, O God, who in truth art the living one, standest before the two eyes. Thou art He who createst that which previously was not, who formest everythng, who art in everything. We also have come into being through the word of thy mouth." "Thou disk of the sun, thou living god," say another,[264] "there is none other beside thee! Thou givest health to the eye through thy beams, creator of all beings. Thou goest up on the eastern horizon of the heaven, to dispense life to all which thou has created—man, four-footed beasts, birds, and creeping things of the earth—where they live. All these behold thee; and they go to sleep when thou settest."

The religious revolution on which Amenôphis was bent, aroused, as a matter of course, the strongest hostility on the part of the priests; and the priests had it in their power to excite feelings of disaffection on the part of the people. Dr. Brugsch is of opinion that when Amenôphis, not content with the introduction of the disk-worship and its establishment as the religion of the court, proceeded to conduct a crusade against the old religion, and, as a first step, gave command for the obliteration of the names of Ammon and his wife, Maut, from the monuments, "open rebellion broke out,"[265] and the city of Ammon ceased to be a safe residence for the heretic monarch. Accordingly he deserted it, and proceeded to build for himself a new capital on a new site. Equally averse to both Thebes and Memphis, he fixed on a situation midway between the two; and in a broad plain on the right bank of the Nile, at the site of the modern Tel-el-Amarno, he rapidly brought into existence a wholly new city, which he called Khu-aten, and adorned with numerous monuments of considerable architectural pretensions.[266] The quarries of Syéné were laid under contribution, and large quantities of granite were cut in the "Red Mountain" of that neighborhood for the construction of the new metropolis.[267] A stately temple was erected on an entirely new plan in the vinicity of the royal palace; several extensive courts were built, in which fire-altars were set up; a new style of ornamentation, free in a great measure from the old conventional restraints [268] was introduced; and the city of Khu-aten rapidly attained to considerable size and beauty.

It would seem that the bold step taken by the innovating Pharaoh was thoroughly and completely successful. After his removal to Tel-el-Amarna he had no further difficulties with his subjects. He reigned for at least twelve years in unbroken peace and tranquillity, employed in beautifying the city whereof he was the founder, in setting up tablets to commemorate his own merits, together with those of his wife and daughters, and in bestowing honors and gifts on the frequenters of his court and the inhabitants of his capital.[269] In his domestic life he was especially and exceptionally happy. Deeply devoted to his mother, Tii, he received her gladly into his new city, made her a permanent resident at his court, and treated her with marked respect and honor.[270] To his wife, Queen Nefert-Tii, he was most tenderly attached, and for the numerous daughters whom she bore him his affection was almost as great. "Sweet love fills my heart," he says in one inscription,[271] "for the queen, and for her young children. Grant a long life of many years to the Queen, Nefert-Tii; may she keep the hand of Pharaoh! Grant a long life to the royal daughter, Meri-Aten, and to the royal daughter, Mak-Aten, and to their children! May they keep the hand of the queen, their mother, eternally and for ever! What I swear is a true avowal of what my heart says to me. Never is there falsehood in what I say." Altogether Nefert-Tii bore him seven children,[272] who were all daughters, and who bore a strong resemblance to their father.[273] These young princesses accompanied him when he travelled, each riding in her own two-horsed chariot.[274]

A few military expeditions of no great importance belong to the reign of Amen-hotep Khuenaten; but they do not seem to have been conducted by the monarch in person.[275] The Syrians of the North and the negro races of the South are represented as led before him by the general, Hor-em-heb,[275] who may perhaps be presumed to have gained the victories in which they were made prisoners. The triumph celebrated by Khuenaten on account of these successes is dated in his twelfth year,[276] which is the latest known year of his reign.

Khuenaten's want of male offspring caused some difficulties in respect of the succession to arise at his decease. His daughters' husbands seem to have become rival candidates for the Egyptian throne, and to have reigned in rapid succession one after another. The order of the names is disputed;[277] and it is perhaps enough to say that three monarchs, Sa'a-nekht, Ai, and Tutankh-amen, all of them more or less closely connected with Khuenaten,[278] intervened between that king and Hor em-heb, the last Pharaoh of the eighteenth dynasty. Ai and Tutankh-amen have each left memorials, by which it appears that the former held the throne for at least four years,[279] and carried on successful wars with the Asiatics,[280] while the latter received embassies both from Ethiopia and Syria with rich and costly presents, both in the shape of rare products and articles of an artistic character.[281] The Syrians brought gold, lapis lazuli, turquoises, and other precious stones, together with horses, chariots, and vases of silver, while from Ethiopia came gold chasings, golden vessels set with jewelry, chariots, ships, weapons, and oxen whose horns were tipped with ornamental carvings. Egypt, it would seem, maintained her foreign dominion unimpaired in the south, and in the north was still recognized as mistress of Syria. We may suspect, however, that she had been forced to relinquish her Mesopotamian possessions, since we have no evidence of tribute coming in from Naharaïn subsequently to the reign of Amenôphis III.,[282] and no trace of an Egyptian occupation of the tract east of the Euphrates at any later date.[283]

There is some difficulty in understanding the exact position which the three immediate successors of Khuenaten took up with respect to his religious reformation. On the one hand, it is clear that a full share of the odium which attached to the disk-worship was inherited by them, since the "avenging chisel" has mutilated their names and features almost as determinedly as those of Khuenaten himself;[284] on the other, it appears that two at least out of the three monarchs departed from his religious principles, so far at any rate as to restore the Ammon worship, and to combine it with the cult which their own inclinations may be supposed to have favored. Tutankh-amen even consented to parade his

Vol. II. Plate XVII.

Fig. 37.—EGYPTIAN TURNED-UP SANDAL.—
See Page 191.

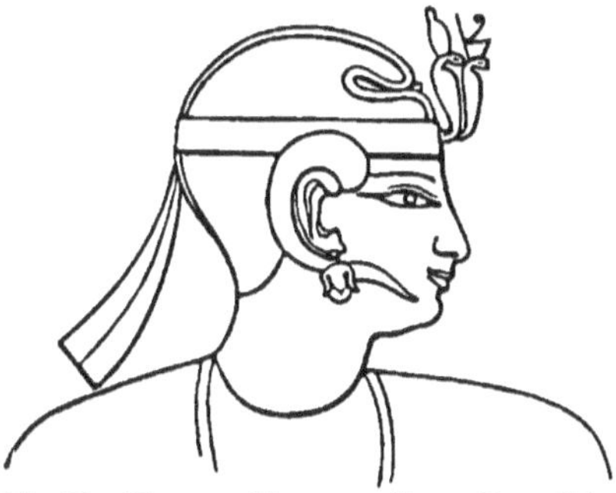

Fig. 38.—HEAD OF MI-AMMON-NUT.—Page 244.

Fig. 36.—DRESS OF A NOBLE IN THE TIME OF
RAMESES III —See Page 217.

Fig. 40.—CURIOUS HEADDRESS OF NEFERTARI-
AAHMES.—See Page 190

Fig. 39.—CHARACTER OF WOMEN'S
DRESSES.—See Page 191.

Plate XVIII.

Vol. II.

Fig. 41.—EGYPTIAN THRONE (time of the 18th Dynasty).—See Page 192.

reactionary leanings by exhibiting in his name an attachment to the Ammon worship; and Ai "sacrificed to Ammon and his associated gods according to the old traditional custom."[285] Both of these kings, moreover, reigned at Thebes, which was restored to the honor of being the state-capital, the metropolitan city of Khuenaten falling back into obscurity. On the whole, there are perhaps grounds for supposing that the successors of Amenôphis IV., finding that his reforms were odious to the priests, if not even to the great mass of the Egyptians, made an attempt at conciliating their opponents by a species of compromise. They tolerated—nay, to a certain extent patronized—the old system, but their sympathies were with the new; outwardly they returned to the ancient paths, but in their hearts they preferred the "way" introduced by Khuenaten. As commonly happens when persons "halt between two opinions," they failed to please either side; and Egypt, after a brief period of religious hesitancy, shook off their influence and returned with unabated zeal to its previous form of nature-worship.

The eighteenth dynasty terminated with Hor-em-heb-Merienammon, [hieroglyphs], who is identified with the Horus of Manetho,[286] and appears to have been a prince of vigor and ability. Though married to a sister-in-law of the heretic monarch,[287] Khuenaten or Amenôphis IV., he proved himself a staunch adherent of the ancient religion. No sooner had he mounted the throne than he set to work with a strong determination to complete the religious restoration begun under his immediate predecessors: he destroyed the edifices of such of them as he deemed tainted with heresy, obliterated in numerous cases the image of Khuenaten, recut the name of Ammon on the monuments from which it had been erased and built, of materials obtained by his demolitions a new gateway to the temple of Ammon at Karnak, to manifest his deep devotion to the great Theban deity.[288] At the same time he gave their due honors to the other gods. He represents himself as worshipping Horus, Troth, Khem, Set, Khonsu, and as specially cherished by Athor and Anuka.[289] According to an inscription which he set up at Thebes,[291] he "renewed the dwellings of the gods, from the shallows of the marsh land of Athu,[292] to the confines of Nubia. He had all their images sculptured as they had been before. He set them up, each in his temple, and had a hundred images made—all of like form—for each of them, out of all manner of costly stones. He visited the cities of the gods, which lay as heaps of rubbish in the land, and had them restored just as they had stood from the beginning of all things." He re-established for each a "daily festival of sacrifice," provided the temples with a due supply of "silver and golden vessels," of "holy persons and singers," presented to them "arable land and cattle," and gave them day by day a sufficiency of "all kinds of provisions." Gods and men were equally delighted with the new *régime*. "The heaven was in festive disposition; the land was filled with ecstasy; and, as for the divinities of Egypt, their souls were full of pleasant feelings. Then the inhabitants of the land, in high delight, raised toward heaven the song of praise; great and small lifted up their voices; and the whole land was moved with joy!"[293]

Besides accomplishing this great religious restoration, which included the rebuilding or repair of almost all the temples throughout Egypt and Nubia, Horemheb (Fig. 26) engaged in at least one important war with his neighbors upon the South. In this quarter, Ethiopia, though often defeated, and sometimes despoiled of territory, as by Usurtasen III.,[294] was still unsubdued; and, to prevent or punish predatory attacks, expeditions were from time to time necessary, which abated the pride of the "miserable Kashi," and secured Egypt a period of repose. Horemheb conducted one of these expeditions, invaded the land of Kush, bore down all opposition, and came back from his successful campaign laden with booty and accompanied by numerous prisoners. In the rock temple of Silsilis he represented himself as he was borne in triumph by his attendants on his return.[295] Seated in a palanquin, ornamented on its side by the figure of a lion, and upheld by twelve bearers, he presented himself to his admiring subjects, amid the loud cries of those who shouted: "Behold the lion who has fallen upon the land of Kush! See the divine benefactor returns home after subduing the princes of all countries. His bow is in his hand as though he were Mentu, the lord of Thebes. The powerful and glorious king leads captive the princes of the miserable land of Kush. He returns thence with the booty which he has taken by force, as his father Ammon ordered him."[296] Cawasses with sticks cleared the road by which the procession was to pass; behind the king went his chosen warriors, leading with them the captured generals as prisoners; then followed the rest of the army, marshalled in various corps, and marching in time to the sound of the trumpet's blare. A numerous company of

Egyptian officers, priests, and other officials came out to receive their monarch, and did homage to him. To complete his triumph, the unhappy prisoners were made to chant the glories of their conqueror. "Incline thy face, O king of Egypt," they said; "incline thy face, O sun of the barbarians! Thy name is great in the land of Kush, where thy war-cry resounded through the dwellings of men. Great is thy power, thou beneficent ruler—it puts to shame the peoples. The Pharaoh—life, salvation, health to him!—is truly a shining sun."[297]

It is gathered, somewhat doubtfully, from one inscription, that the reign of Horemheb lasted at least twenty-one years.[298] Manetho assigned him a still longer space, if we may believe the epitomists, who, however, vary in their accounts between twenty-eight years and thirty-seven.[299] His wife, Notemmut or Mut-notem,[300] seems to have borne him no children;[301] and thus he was unable to leave his throne to any issue of his loins. It is suspected that he reigned in right of his wife rather than by any royal rank of his own, and that she still retained the sovereignty for a while after his decease;[302] but the monuments are obscure upon the point, and the circumstances under which the glorious eighteenth dynasty came to an end, and the nineteenth succeeded it, are unknown to us.[303]

As the art and civilization of these two dynasties are similar and indeed almost identical, it is proposed to defer the consideration of these subjects to the close of the next chapter.

CHAPTER XXI.

THE NINETEENTH DYNASTY (ABOUT B.C. 1400-1280).

Accession of Rameses I. His Syrian War. Accession of Seti I. His Wars with the Shasu, Karu, and Khita. Peace made with the Khita. Timber cut in Lebanon. Recovery of Mesopotamia. Wars with the Libyans and Ethiopians. Seti's great Works. His Table of Kings. His Personal Appearance. His Association of his Son, Rameses. Reign of Rameses Meriamon. Over-estimate formed of him. His Wars—with the Negroes and Ethiopians—with the Hittites—with Naharaïn. His Treaty of Peace with the Hittities—Importance of it. He marries a Hittite Princess. His later African Wars. Large number of his Captives—Plans pursued in locating them—their Employment. Great Works of Rameses—useful and ornamental. His Personal Appearance, Domestic Relations, and Character.—Accession of his Son, Menephthah—His troubled Reign. Insignificance of his Monuments. Pacific Character of his Foreign Policy. Sudden Invasion of Egypt by the Libyans and their Allies. Proposed Identification of these Allies with European Nations. Repulse of the Libyan Attack. Relations of Menephthah with the Israelites under Moses. Troubles of his later years. Struggle between his Son, Seti II., and Amon-mes, or Amon-meses. Brief Reigns of these Monarchs.—Reign of Siphthah. Period of Anarchy. Civilization of Egypt under the Eighteenth and Nineteenth Dynasties—Architecture and its Kindred Arts—Religion—Manners and Customs—Literature. Drawbacks on the general Prosperity.

We now approach the grandest period of Egyptian history, the rule of the Nineteenth Dynasty, and the reign of the great Rameses.—P. SMITH's *Ancient History*, vol. i, p. 119.

THE founder of the nineteenth dynasty was a certain Ramses, ⊙𓉘𓏤 or Ramessu, ⊙𓉘𓏤𓀭 the first prince of that celebrated name—a name which afterwards became so glorious as to eclipse almost every other Egyptian royal title. His birth and parentage are in the highest degree uncertain; and the conjectures of the latest historians of Egypt upon the subject are so various and conflicting[1] as to increase, rather than diminish, the obscurity which hangs about his origin. The newness of his name,[2] the strangeness of his throne-name,[3] the peculiarity of the appellation which he bestowed on his son,[4] and the fact that he was the recognized head of a new dynasty, combine to establish it as almost certain that he was a *novus homo*, unconnected by blood with the monarchs of the preceding line, the Thothmeses and Amen-hoteps, one who raised himself to power at a time of political trouble and disturbance by his own talents and energy. Manetho, according to Josephus,[5] gave him a reign of only a year and four months, and we may thus regard him as prevented by an untimely end from attaining any great distinction. The circumstances which confronted him were difficult. Egypt had it would seem, during the troublous times that followed the death of Amenophis IV., lost almost all her Asiatic possessions, and fallen back into the position from which she was raised by the first and the third Thothmes. When Rameses came to the throne, he found the Hittites (Khita) masters of Syria, dominant over the whole region from Mount Taurus to Philistia. In alliance with the other Canaanite nations, with the Philistines, and even with the Bedouins (Shasu). they threatened a renewed invasion of the territory from which they had been driven by Aahmes. To meet this danger, Rameses seems to have marched an army into Syria, to have engaged the Khita in at least one battle,[6] and to have been so far successful that he induced the Hittite monarch, Seprur or Saplel, to conclude with him an offensive and defensive alliance.[7] We do not know whether he engaged in any other wars. Perhaps the prisoners whom he attached to the temple of Khem-Horus near Wady Halfa, many in number and of both sexes,[8] were the produce of his Syrian campaign, transported to the opposite limit of the empire.[9]

The coronation of Rameses I. is represented on the entrance gate of the great temple at Karnak,[10] where the monarch also exhibits himself as worshipping Mentu, Nefer-Tum, Shu, Tafné, Seb, Netpé, Isis, Osiris, and Sabak.[11] Besides these sculptures the only important work which he undertook was his tomb in the Biban-el-Moluk, or "valley of the kings" sepulchres, near Thebes, which is a rock chamber of no very large dimensions, but ornamented with a number of bas-reliefs. In one, on his descent to Amenti, he is introduced by Horus to Osiris;[12] in another he worships Nefer-Tum, represented with a scarabæus in the place of a human head;[13] in a third he takes the hand of Neith.[14] The old worship is evidently established in all its fulness during his reign; the Sun-Gods are especially revered; and a high and honorable place is assigned to Set. Rameses's regard for Set is especially indicated by the name that he gave to his eldest son, which

was Seti, or, more fully, Seti-Meriptah, , i. e.

"the Set-worshipper,"[15] beloved of Phthah."

The dangers which had threatened Egypt under Rameses, and which had been checked by his prompt invasion of Western Asia, revived under his son. Seti was scarcely settled upon the throne, when he found himself menaced upon **his northeastern frontier by a formidable combination of**

Semitic with Turanian races, which boded ill for the tranquillity of his kingdom. The redoubted Hittites, who, a century earlier, had bowed their pride before the might of Thothmes III.,[16] having recovered themselves in the hour of Egypt's weakness, were now at the zenith of their greatness, held all Syria firmly in their grasp, and are even believed by some to have extended their dominion into Mesopotamia and Asia Minor. Whatever may be thought of the fact of this enlarged dominion, or of its definite assignment to this particular period, the Hittite power *in Syria* at this time is beyond all question ; and Seti's attention was, by the necessity of the case, first turned in this direction, where he felt that the state of affairs called for a great and sustained effort. The nearest danger was from the Shasu, who "had pressed forward westward quite into the proper Egyptian territory,"[18] and made themselves masters of a considerable portion of the Tanitic canton. Seti, in the first year of his reign,[19] proceeded against these aggressors. Starting from the fortress of Khetam—the Etham of Scripture[20]—mounted himself in his war-chariot, and accompanied by a large chariot force, he marched along the coast road as far as the " land of Zahi," or the Philistine country, when he turned inland, overran the tract known in later times as Idumæa, took various fortresses, and ruthlessly slaughtered their garrisons, raging, as he himself tells us, " like a fierce lion,"[21] and wading through a sea of carnage. " The Shasu were turned into a heap of corpses in their hill country—they lay there in their blood."[22] The entire region between Egypt Proper and Canaan was subjected, the names of the strongholds were changed,[23] and Egyptian troops were placed in them.

A campaign followed against the Kharu (Syrians), who had lent some assistance to the Shasu in the recent struggle.[24] A battle was fought with this enemy at Jaham (Jamnia), in which both sides brought a large force of chariots into the field. The Kharu were defeated in the engagement; and Seti boasts that he " annihilated the kings of the land of the Syrians."[25]

The defeat of the Kharu laid Northern Syria open to invasion ; and Seti was able now to march against his principal enemy, Maut-enar, king of the Hittites, who held in subjection all the tribes from Central Palestine to the Euphrates. He proceeded first against the Ruten,[26] overcame them in several pitched battles, and, assisted by a son who fought constantly by his side,[27] slaughtered them almost to extermination.

His victorious progress brought him, after a time, to the vicinity of Kadesh—the important city on the Orontes which, a century earlier, had been besieged and taken by the great Thothmes.[28] Kadesh seems now to have belonged to the nation of the Amorites, which occupied at different time various parts of Syria and Palestine.[29] This nation was at present included among the subjects of the Hittites, and held Kadesh as their dependent allies. It would seem from one of Seti's bas-reliefs, that he had the skill, or the good fortune, to surprise this stronghold, and to become master of it by a *coup de main*. The arrival of the Egyptian army is represented as unexpected; the herdsmen are pasturing their cattle under the trees which surround the city, when the Egyptian monarch appears in his war-chariot. At once every one seeks to save himself; the herds fly with their keepers; there is a general panic and confusion. But the defenders of the town are no cowards; they sally forth from the gates, and engage the army of the invader, but are defeated with great slaughter by the warlike Pharaoh, who pierces scores of them with his arrows.[30] An attack is then made upon the fortress, which is but weakly defended, and city and people fall into the hands of Seti.

The proper territory of the Khita was now reached and invaded; and although "the well-ordered hosts of the beardless light-red Khita, on foot, on horse-back, and in chariots,"[31] gave battle to the invaders in the open field, and offered a gallant and stout resistance to the host of the Egyptians, yet here once more Seti was successful, and defeated the enemy with great slaughter, driving their squadrons before him in headlong flight, and killing a vast number of the leaders. A sculpture shows us "the miserable inhabitants of the land of the Khita" receiving from Seti this "great overthrow."[32] A song of praise was composed for the occasion, which is appended to the sculpture, and runs as follows:[33] —"Pharaoh is a jackal which rushes leaping through the Hittite land; he is a grim lion which frequents the most hidden paths of all regions; he is a powerful bull with a pair of sharpened horns. He has struck down the Asiatics; he has thrown to the ground the Khita; he has slain their princes."

The victory thus gained was followed by a treaty of peace. Seti and his great adversary, Maut-enar, entered into a solemn agreement, by which "enmity was turned to friendship,"[34] perpetual amity and good brotherhood being proclaimed between the two nations.[35] Seti then set out upon his return to Egypt. Carrying with him some scores of captured chiefs,[36] and with the heads of three leading rebels attached to the hinder portion of his chariot,[37] he proceeded in all the pomp of a triumph, through Syria and Palestine; everywhere receiving the submission and homage of the inhabitants. On his way down the broad Cœle-Syrian valley, seeing the forests of Lebanon on his right hand, and noticing the vast size and especially the great height of the cedars, he ordered a halt, and called upon the headmen of the hill tribes to set to work and fell the straightest and tallest of the trees, that he might take them with him to Egypt.[38] Assyrian monarchs at a later date acted similarly.[39] The Lebanon timber was especially suited for the fabrication of those lofty masts which were commonly placed in front of the propylæa of temples; and the delicately-scented cedar wood was thought peculiarly fitted for the material of the "Sacred Boat of Ammon," which played an important part in the Theban religious processions.[40] Seti having seen his order executed,[41] in a short time resumed his march, and, passing through the desert, returned, by way of Maktal (Migdol or Magdolon), Taa-pa-mau (Leontopolis), and Garu (Heroöpolis?) to his own country.[42]

The defeat of the Hittites appears to have involved the recovery of Mesopotamia, or, at any rate, of some portion of it. Seti, in giving an account of his expedition, declares that he "had smitten the Anu and struck to the ground the Mentu, and had placed his boundaries at the extremity of the world, and at the utmost borders of the river-land of Naharaïn."[43] In his list of the conquered countries, Naharaïn occupies a prominent place;[44] and one of its chiefs is represented among the prisoners whom he presents to Ammon, Maut, and Khonsu, on the auspicious occasion of his return.[45] As, however, no Egyptian remains of his date have been as yet discovered in Mesopotamia, it would seem to be doubtful whether he really occupied it, or did more than obtain from some of the chiefs a nominal submission.

Besides his great wars on the continent of Asia, Seti conducted important military operations both in the West and in the South. On the western borders of Egypt, in the vicinity of the Mediterranean, the blue-eyed, fair-skinned nation of the Tahennu,[46] 〈hieroglyph〉, had from time to time given trouble to the Egyptians by their raids into the Delta, and expeditions had been conducted against them by several of the more warlike kings.[47] They were a wild and uncivilized people, dwelling in caves, and having no other arms than bows and arrows. "For dress they wore a long cloak or tunic open in front;"[58] and they are distinguished on the Egyptian monuments by having all their hair shaved excepting one large lock, which is plaited and depends from the right side of the head."[49] Each warrior wore also two ostrich feathers, sloping at opposite angles, and fastened on his head at the top of the crown. Seti, accompanied by his more famous son, Rameses,[60] invaded the country of this people with an infantry and chariot force, utterly routed them in a pitched battle, and drove them to seek shelter in their caves, where they "remained hidden through fear of the king."[61] It has been supposed that these caves must have been "in the Atlas range;"[52] but there were Troglodytes in many parts of Africa much nearer to Egypt,[53] and the country about Cyrene would afford every facility for such underground abodes as are here indicated.

War was also waged under the auspices of Seti against the Cushites of the South, who had once more shown themselves troublesome; and memorials of victory were set up at Doshé and Sesebi. At the latter place Seti is made to boast that his dominion reached southward "to the arms of the Winds," as if it extended as far as Africa was inhabited. The wars in this quarter were probably not conducted by the king in person, but by the high officials who bore the title of "Royal sons of Cush," of whom two are mentioned at this period, named respectively Ani and Amen-em-apet.[55]

But the military triumphs of Seti were outdone and eclipsed by his great works. The grand "Hall of Columns" in the temple of Karnak—the chief glory of that magnificent edifice —which is supported by a hundred and sixty-four massive stone pillars, and covers a larger area than the Cathedral of Cologne,[66] was designed in its entirety, and for the most part constructed by him; and, if it had stood alone, would have sufficed to place him in the first rank of builders. It is a masterpiece of the highest class, so vast as to overwhelm the mind of the spectator, so lavishly ornamented as to excite his astonishment and admiration, so beautifully proportioned as to satisfy the requirements of the most refined taste, so entirely in harmony with its surroundings as to please even the most ignorant. Egyptian architectural power culminated in this wonderful edifice—its supreme effort—its crown and pride —its greatest and grandest achievement ; and it only remained for later ages to reproduce feeble copies of the marvellous work of Seti, or to escape comparison by accomplishing works of an entirely different description. The "Hall of Columns" at Karnak is not only the most sublime and beautiful of all the edifices there grouped together in such sort as to form one vast unrivalled temple, but it is the highest effort of Egyptian architectural genius, and is among the eight or ten most splendid of all known architectural constructions.

One might have expected that so great a work would entirely occupy the mind, and monopolize the resources, of its erector, so as to leave him neither thought nor means for other constructive efforts. But it was not so with Seti. Besides his Karnak building, he designed and commenced the striking Temple of the Rameseum [57] at Old Qurnah, opposite Thebes, in honor of his father, Rameses I.; he built a magnificent fane, in honor of Osiris, near Abydos; [58] he "erected a special temple to the goddess of the South, the heavenly Nukheb, at El-Kaab," and another similar one, in the form of a rock grotto, at the place called by the Greeks "the Cave of Artemis," [59] near Beni-el-Hassan, to Sekhet; he built also a temple at Redesieh; [60] made additions to the ancient shrines of Phthah and Tum at Memphis and Heliopolis; [61] erected at the last-named place the (so-called) Flaminian obelisk, which now adorns the Piazza del Popolo at Rome; [62] set up stelæ at Silsilis and Assouan [63] (Syêné); and left inscriptions upon tablets at Doshé, Sesebi, and elsewhere.[64] Above all, he constructed for himself a most magnificent and elaborate tomb. This excavation in the solid rock, known as "Belzoni's tomb," from the name of its discoverer, still "forms the chief attraction to all who visit the Valley of the Tomb of the Kings at Thebes,"[65] and is one of the most magnificent of Egyptian sepulchres. The lavish profusion of the painted sculptures, and the exquisite care with which everything, down to the minutest hieroglyph, is finished,[66] excite the admiration of the beholders; while the mystic character of the scenes represented,[67] and the astronomical problem involved in the roof-pictures of the "Golden Chamber,"[68] add an element of deeper interest than any comprised within the range of mere art. The tomb possesses also a mythological inscription which is exceedingly curious.[69] In the eyes of its constructer the tomb was not wholly finished, the intention of prolonging it by digging still further into the rock being apparent;[70] but still it contained, when first discovered, the alabaster sarcophagus which the king had prepared for the reception of his mortal remains, a remarkable relic of antiquity now deposited in the Sloane Museum of London.[71] Altogether, Seti's tomb, if not the most extensive, is far the most interesting and most beautiful of all those wonderful rock-sepulchres which form so important a portion of the extant Egyptian monuments. Other important works were undertaken by this great monarch, with utility, rather than ostentation, for their object. In connection with the working of the gold mines in the desert between the Nile valley and the Red Sea, he employed engineers to discover a water-source which should furnish a constant and copious supply to the miners and those employed in the carriage of the ores.[12] It has been maintained that the scientific men entrusted with the task accomplished it by boring a veritable "artesian well;"[13] but there seems to be no better foundation for this theory than the use of certain rhetorical expressions by the historiographer who placed the facts on record. "Seti," he observed,[14] "had but to say the word, and lo! the water leaped forth from the living rock—the stream flowed out in abundance." Clearly, this result, or at any rate a result capable of being thus described by a lively writer, might follow on the discovery of an ample spring by means of ordinary digging, without recourse being had to the scientific and comparatively modern operation of boring. We are certainly not justified in concluding from the expressions used that "artesian wells" were familiar to the engineering science of Seti's day, or that he did more than "happen upon" a copious source at a certain depth below the surface, in a district where there was no surface water in the shape of streams or springs.

Seti also, it is thought,[15] commenced that far more important work, afterwards accomplished by his still greater son, the formation of a canal between the most eastern branch of the Nile and the Red Sea. This canal left the Nile a little above the town of Bubastis, and ran east, or a little south of east, as far as the Bitter Lakes, when it changed its direction and was carried nearly due south into the Gulf of Suez. The length of the canal, not counting the passage of the Bitter Lakes, was about seventy miles. Its course may still be traced by a series of depressions along the line of the Wady Toumilat.[16]

The inscriptions of Seti are chiefly accounts of his campaigns and of the offerings which he made out of the spoils of the conquered nations to Ammon and the other national gods. But they comprise one document of more than ordinary historical interest. This is the "Great Table of Abydos," containing the names of seventy-five of his predecessors[17] upon the throne of Egypt, arranged in (supposed) chronological order, which he set up in the temple that he dedicated, in the desert near that city, to Osiris, the god of the dead. The list commences with Menes (Mena), the mythic founder of the empire, and is carried on through the monarchs mentioned in the text of the present work[78] to Neferarkara, the last known king of the sixth dynasty, after which it enumerates eighteen unknown monarchs,[79] who are supposed to have belonged to the sixth and eleventh dynasties, returning with the fifty-seventh name to a well-known personage, Nebkherra or Mentu-hotep II.,[80] and then following with Sankhkara, the Amen-em-hats and Usurtasens of the twelfth dynasty, the nine kings of the eighteenth, and Rameses I., the founder of the nineteenth, Seti's father. The resemblances and the differences between this list and that of Thothmes III.[81] deserve careful attention, indicating as they do, a certain settled basis of historic belief at the time, combined with a large fluctuating element of tradition or conjecture, and thereby teaching us the extreme uncertainty of the mere dynastic lists where they are not checked and confirmed by contemporary fuller documents.

In personal appearance Seti (Fig. 23) seems not to have been remarkable. He had a fairly good forehead, a rounded depressed nose, full projecting lips, and a heavy chin. The expression of his face was calm, open, and not unpleasing. In character he resembled the other Egyptian conquering monarchs, being vigorous, bold, unsparing of himself, indefatigable, but ruthless and cruel. It is difficult to decide whether his religious ardor was a genuine feeling or affected in order to secure him the gratitude and support of the priestly class, a support always of great importance to the early princes of a dynasty not yet fully recognized as in rightful possession of the throne. Certainly no Pharaoh ever showed himself more anxious to uphold the entire Egyptian religion, or more bent on paying honor to all the chief personages of the Pantheon. His material favors were freely granted to all the main national shrines, and in his bas-reliefs he exhibited himself as the worshipper of almost every generally recognixed deity. Nor does any divinity receive from Seti an undue share of attention. Ammon-Ra, Horus, Isis, Osiris, and Athor are, so to speak, his favorites ; but Egypt at this time was tolerably unanimous in assigning to these gods a pre-eminence. After these five, he honors almost equally Set, Ra, Tum, Mentu, Shu, Seb, Netpe, Nephthys, Thoth, Sabak, Ma, Maut, Khonsu, Phthah, Khem, Kneph, Sati, and Anuka.[82]

HIS RELIGIOUS ARDOR.

In his domestic relations he appears to have been fortunate. He married a wife, Tua or Tuaa, , who is thought to have been a grand-daughter of Khuenaten or Amenôphis IV.,[63] and to have thus brought a further strain of Semitic blood into the Egyptian royal house. Tua bore him at least three sons, of whom his successor, Rameses-Meriammon, was the eldest. This prince, like our own Henry VIII., united the claims and pretensions of two great rival houses—the Amen-hoteps and the Ramesides—and it was therefore of importance that he should be brought forward into political life at the earliest possible moment, since the general acceptance, of which he was assured, would add stability to the throne of his father. Accordingly, at the age of ten or twelve,[64] Seti had him crowned as king, and admitted him, at first to a nominal, and afterwards to a real, participation in the government.[65] The two appear to have borne each other a true affection; no jealousy clouded their relations; each speaks of the other with tenderness and real regard; and the son carries on with pious care all the great works left incomplete by his father.

The chronology of the two reigns has been confused and complicated by the fact of the association. It is uncertain in what year of his reign Seti made Rameses joint ruler,[66] and still more uncertain how long the joint reign continued. Seti's thirtieth and Rameses' sixty-seventh year are mentioned upon the monuments,[67] which also tell us that Rameses was ten years old when he was associated. These are all the trustworthy data;[68] and it results from them that the probable period occupied by the two reigns was about eighty years; Seti reigning twelve years alone, and an unknown number, not less than eighteen, in conjunction with Rameses, while the latter reigned as sole monarch for a long term of years after his father's death.

The full title under which the son and successor of Seti I. designated himself upon his monuments was Ra-user-ma Sotep-en-ra Ramessu-Meriamen, , thus elaborate and complicated had by this time become the royal designation. Succeeding

to the throne, in a certain sense, at the age of ten, he became
early accustomed to command, took part in the business of
the state, had a body-guard under his orders, and directed
the construction of important buildings.⁹⁰ As his father
grew old and infirm, the conduct of affairs passed more and
more into his hands, until at last—probably when he was
about twenty-eight years old—he entered upon the full sovereignty.

The greater son of a great father, Rameses II. is of all the
Egyptian kings the one whose fame has extended itself the
most widely, and whose actions have received the largest
amount of attention. This has arisen in part, from the enormous number and striking character of his monuments; in
part, from the favor in which he was held by the Egyptian
priests and the exaggerated representations which they gave
of his warlike achievements.⁹¹ In reality, he does not appear
to have shown any remarkable military genius, or to have
effected any important conquests. One great war occupied
him for many years; and, though in the course of it he no
doubt performed several brilliant exploits, yet the final result
was one of which Egypt had no cause to boast. The empire
attacked stood firm, and the war was concluded by a treaty,
of which the great principle is the exact equality and perfectly correspondent obligations of the two contracting
powers.⁹² The other wars which occasionally occupied him
were trivial, and there is no evidence that even they brought
any accession of territory to Egypt. Indeed, it would almost
seem that his object in making war was rather to obtain captives than to extend his dominions, his predominant desire
being to distinguish himself as a builder, and the services of
vast bodies of foreign laborers being necessary to carry out his
numerous and gigantic projects.⁹³

The first campaigns of Rameses II. were directed against
the negroes and Ethiopians.⁹⁴ One writer ⁹⁵ tells us that he
"pushed his arms much further into Upper Ethiopia and the
Soudân than any of his predecessors;" but proof of this
superior energy is scarcely forthcoming, and on the whole it
would seem that the southern expeditions of the son of Seti
were rather razzias, resulting in the capture of large numbers
of the unfortunate blacks, than real military operations.⁹⁶
Besides slaves, tribute and plunder were no doubt obtained in
large quantities; and Egypt was enriched by the spoils of
Ethiopia, which included gold, ivory, ebony, fruits of various
kinds, leopards' skins, lions, panthers, gazelles and other
antelopes, giraffes, and ostriches.⁹⁷

Soon afterwards occurred the first Syrian war of Rameses. The details of this campaign are wanting, but a rock-tablet at the Nahr-el-Kelb, set up in his second year,[99] indicates his personal presence on the occasion, and was erected as a token of victory. Three years later took place the second invasion. Khitasir, the son of Marasar, and grandson of Saplel, the adversary of Rameses I., was now probably at the head of the Hittites,[99] and had succeeded in effecting a league of the Western Asiatic nations against Egypt, which threatened serious consequences. Already had Seti, alarmed at the menacing combination, commenced a defensive work upon his eastern frontier,[100] probably not long before his decease. Rameses, with the ardor and audacity of youth, preferring attack to defence, in the fifth year of his sole reign [101] collected a vast army, and quitting Egypt marched "by the path of the desert along the roads of the north." [102] Khitasir, aware of his movements, summoned his allies to his aid—the peoples of Naharaïn, Khirabu, Carchemish, the Maasu, Airatu, Patasu, Kati, Leka (Lycians ?), and others [103]—and took up a position near Kadesh, his capital city, which was situated on an island in the Orontes.[104] The host was so numerous that it is said : "Their number was endless ; nothing like it had ever been before ; they covered the mountains and the valleys like grasshoppers for their number." [105] Khitasir, however, was unwilling to trust to mere numbers, and formed a scheme for deceiving Rameses as to the disposition of his troops, and so bringing him into difficulties. He sent out spies,[106] who pretended to be deserters from his army, and instructed them to say, if they were questioned, that he had broken up from Kadesh on hearing of the Egyptian advance, and had marched away to Khirabu (Aleppo), which lay far to the north. The spies fulfilled their mission, but on being examined by scourging they failed in fortitude, and confessed the truth—that Khitasir, instead of having withdrawn to Khirabu, was lying in wait to the northwest of Kadesh, hoping to fall unexpectedly on the flank of the Egyptians, if they believed the spies' tale and hurried forward on the line of his supposed retreat. Foiled in his crafty scheme, Khitasir could do nothing but quit his ambush and march openly against the Egyptians, with his troops marshalled in exact and orderly array, the Hittite chariots in front with their lines carefully dressed, and the auxiliaries and irregulars on the flanks and rear.[107] Rameses had divided his host into four portions.[108] He himself, with the brigade of Ammon, marched down the left bank of the river, while two brigades, those of Phthah and Ra, proceeded along the right bank, the division of Phthah in the centre, that of Ra some way to the eastward.[109] The position of the brigade of Set is not distinctly marked. It may have started for Khirabu before the falsity of the spies' tale was detected, or it may have acted as a rearguard to the whole army, and have been posted at some distance behind the other corps. At any rate, it took no part in the battle. Khitasir commenced the fight by a flank movement to the left, which enabled him to fall on the brigade of Ra as it was upon its march, alone and unsupported; his attack was unexpected and was irresistible; "foot and horse gave way before him;"[110] the division was utterly routed, and either driven from the field or cut to pieces. Intelligence of the complete defeat of his right wing having been received by Rameses, who had now reached the position occupied at the beginning of the day by Khitasir, he set his brigade in motion, at right angles to their previous course, eastward; but before he could reach the Orontes, the enemy, who must have crossed the river, were upon him, and the two hosts charged each other at full speed with desperate courage. The chariot of Rameses, skilfully guided by his squire, Menna, seems to have broken through the front line of the Hittite chariot force; but his brethren in arms were less fortunate; and Rameses found himself separated from his army, behind the front line and confronted by the second line of the hostile chariots, in a position of the possible danger.[111] Then began that Homeric combat, which the Egyptians were never tired of celebrating, between a single warrior on the one hand, and the host of the Hittites, reckoned at 2,500 chariots, on the other, in which Rameses, like Diomed or Achilles, carried death and destruction whithersoever he turned himself. "I became like the god Mentu," he is made to say; "I hurled the dart with my right hand; I fought with my left hand; I was like Baal in his time before their sight; I had come upon 2,500 pairs of horses: I was in the midst of them; but they were dashed to pieces before my steed. Not one of them raised his hand to fight; their courage was sunken in their breasts; their limbs gave way, they could not hurl the dart, nor had they strength to thrust with the spear. I made them fall into the water like crocodiles; they tumbled down on their faces one after another. I killed them at my pleasure, so that not one looked back behind him, nor did any turn round. Each fell, and none raised himself up again."[112]

The temporary isolation of Rameses, which is the gist of the heroic poem of Pentaour, and which the king himself recorded over and over again upon the walls of his magnificent shrines,[113] must no doubt be regarded as a fact; but it is not likely to have continued for more than a few minutes. When his companions found that he was lost to their sight, they would have made the most frantic efforts to recover him, dead or alive; and if his own prowess at all resembled the description given of it, the Hittites must have been speedily thrown into such confusion that it would have been easy for the Egyptians to come to his aid. Chariot, no doubt, quickly followed chariot through the front line of the Hittite force; the second line was engaged and defeated; soon the confusion became general. A headlong flight carried the entire host to the banks of the Orontes, into which some precipitated themselves, while others were forced into the water by their pursuers. The king of Khirabu was among the latter, and was with difficulty drawn out by his friends, exhausted and half dead, when he reached the eastern shore.[114] But the great bulk of the Hittite army perished, either in the battle or in the river. Among the killed and wounded were Grabatusa, the charioteer of Khitasir, Tarakennas, the commander of the cavalry, Rabsuna, another general, Khirapusar, a royal secretary, and Matsurama, a brother of the Hittite king.[115]

On the day which followed the battle Khitasir sent a humble embassy to the camp of his adversary to implore for peace.[116] His messenger was received with favor. Though it does not appear that any formal treaty was made, or any definite engagements entered into by the Hittite leader, yet Rameses consented not to press upon the vanquished monarch, but to withdraw his army and return to Egypt. It is possible that his victory had cost him dear, and that, until he had levied a new force, he was in no condition to venture further from his resources or to confront new perils.

The Syrian expedition of Rameses II. did not terminate with the battle of Kadesh, or with his fifth year. On the contrary, they continued certainly till his eighth year,[117] and possibly till his twenty-first, when a formal treaty of peace was concluded with the Hittites. It is difficult to determine how far during this period he carried his arms into Asia, or what extent of territory he traversed with his armies. We have no distinct evidence of any expeditions having penetrated further at this time than Northern Palestine,[118] unless it be on one occasion, when "Tunep in the land of Naharaïn," was attacked and taken.[119] But the reputation which Rameses left behind him of a warrior king,[120] the title of A-nekhtu or "Conqueror" which he bore,[121] and the general claims to victory and the success contained in his inscriptions, are thought to imply that the limits of the Egyptian power established by Thothmes III. were still in a certain sense maintained and vindicated during his reign,[122] Mesopotamia still paying tribute, and receiving Egyptian residents, if not even Egyptian garrisons, and the chiefs even of such a distant place as Singara being still content to be regarded as Egyptian subjects.[123] But, whatever vestiges remained of the old period of glory and dominion, it cannot be seriously doubted that the real power of Egypt had now considerably declined;[124] "the bonds of subjection were much less strict than under Thothmes III.; prudential motives constrained the Egyptians to be content with very much less—with such acknowledgments as satisfied their vanity rather than with the exercise of a real power.[125]

The treaty concluded with the Hittites is a strong indication of the changed circumstances of Egypt, and her inability to maintain the dominant position which she had reached under Thothmes. It was, as already observed,[126] based upon the principle of an exact equality between the two high contracting powers. Khitasir was termed "the great king of Khita, the powerful," Rameses "the great ruler of Egypt, the powerful." The genealogy of each was reckoned back to his grandfather. Both parties engaged reciprocally for their sons and their sons' sons. Friendship was pledged by the following formula: "He shall be my ally; he shall be my friend; I will be his ally; I will be his friend for ever." The stipulations of the alliance were throughout mutual. The king of the Khita engaged under no circumstances to invade the land of Egypt, and the king of Egypt engaged under no circumstances to invade the land of the Khita. Each bound himself, if the other were attacked, either to come in person, or to send his forces, to the other's assistance. Each pledged himself to the extradition both of criminals fleeing from justice, and of any other subjects wishing to transfer their allegiance. Each at the same time stipulated for an amnesty of offences in case of all persons thus surrendered. The treaty was placed under the protection of the gods of the two countries, who were invoked respectively to protect observers and punish infringers of it.[127]

It is evident that the acknowledgment of the Hittite power and the engagements to respect its territorial limits and defend it against foreign attack constituted an effectual bar to the extension of Egyptian influence in Asia, and very nearly cut Egypt off from her possessions on and beyond the Euphrates.

Little more than a nominal subjection of dependencies so remote could remain, when almost the whole of the intermediate country [128] was relinquished to a rival power. The Hittite empire must at this time have presented itself to the Mesopotamian and Syrian nations as that which was in the ascendant, and which policy required them to court. Egypt's day must have appeared to be past, and the smaller states of Western Asia must have begun to gravitate to the new centre.

A conspicuous evidence of the altered condition of things, strongly indicative of the great advance of the Hittite power, was the marriage of Rameses, in the thirty-fourth year of his sole reign, to the daughter of Khitasir, and her proclamation as queen consort by the name, which she must have newly taken, of Ur-maa-nefru-ra. "The prince of Khita, clad in the dress of his country, himself conducted the bride to the palace of his son-in-law," [129] and, after receiving hospitable entertainment, returned to his own land. It would seem that the princess had captivated the heart of the susceptible monarch by her remarkable beauty on an occasion when she had come forward in her own country to plead the cause of some captives whom he was inclined to treat harshly. "She stood forward at their head, to soften the heart of King Rameses,—a great inconceivable wonder,—not knowing the impression which her beauty made upon him." [130] The fascination of unconscious loveliness is always great ; and Rameses was apparently induced to seek the hand of the Hittite princess by the feelings which were called forth on this occasion.

Besides his great Asiatic war, to which the Hittite treaty put a happy termination, Rameses conducted a certain number of campaigns in the south and in the east. In the south he had for enemies the Cushites and the negroes, in the west the Tahennu and the Mashuash or Maxyes.[131] In both quarters he claims successes : but they do not appear to have been very decisive. In Northern Africa the power of the Maxyes was certainly not broken, for we shall find them in the ensuing reign taking the offensive and invading Egypt in force ; [132] and on the Upper Nile only small and significant tribes—the Auntom, the Hebuu, the Tenfu, the Temun, and the Hetau [133] —were subjugated. The boundaries of Egypt received no important enlargement in either quarter, nor were her Asiatic losses compensated for by African gains.

One, and perhaps the main, result of all the military operations in which Rameses II. employed himself for so many years, was the acquisition of many thousands of captives, some Asiatic, some African,—swart negroes from the Soudan, Ethiopians of equal blackness but of a higher type, blue-eyed, fair-haired Marmaridæ, light red beardless Khita, lithe Arabs, heavily-framed Ruten with black beards and features of a Jewish cast,[134] Kharu, Leka, Nahiri, Maxyes,—carried off from their homes by the grasping conqueror, whose wars were undertaken as much with the object of making prisoners as from any higher consideration. During his early years Asia furnished the bulk of these unfortunates. Later, when his Asiatic wars were terminated,—if we may trust M. Lenormant,—"man hunts were organized upon a monstrous scale throughout the whole country of the Soudan, a scale quite unknown at any former period. The aim was no longer, as under the Thothmeses and the Amen-hoteps, to extend on this side the frontiers of the Egyptian empire, so as to absorb the countries which furnished ivory and gold dust. The principal or (so to speak) sole object was to obtain slaves. Nearly every year there were great razzias, which started from Ethiopia, and returned dragging after them thousands of captive blacks of all ages and both sexes, laden with chains. And the principal episodes of these negro-hunts were sculptured upon the walls of temples as glorious exploits!"[135]

In connection with this constant introduction of large bodies of foreigners into Egypt, Rameses devised or adopted the plan,[136] so familiar to Asiatic conquerors in later times, of transporting his prisoners enormous distances, and settling them in those portions of his empire which were most remote from their original abodes. Whole tribes of negroes were removed from the Soudan into Asia; Libyans and Asiatics were planted upon the Upper Nile.[137] Flight and escape became in this way impossible, and even the yearning after a lost home tended, in course of time, to die away through the well-known inclination of the human mind to accept the inevitable.

It was, of course, in connection with his passion for "great works" that Rameses desired and obtained this vast addition to the store of "naked human strength,"[138] which on his accession he inherited from his progenitors. In the earlier times the kings had employed the great mass of their subjects in those vast constructions by which they had striven to immortalize their names.[139] But with the growth of civilization new ideas had sprung up. Some regard had come to be had for the feelings and the wishes of the lower orders;[140] and if the incubus of forced labor still legally lay upon them,[141] practically it was now well-nigh a thing of the past, and no longer an actual grievance. Slaves, captives, and subject races, not of Egyptian blood, were, at this period, the material to which kings bent upon raising great works looked for the execution of their grand projects. Of subject races there seem to have been several in Egypt under Rameses, the principal being the Sharuten or Shardana, the Apuiriu or Aperu, and the Hebrews. Of these, the Shardana were employed principally as auxiliary troops,[142] while the other two—if they were really distinct[143]—formed the main sources from which forced labor was drawn by the monarchs.[144] We know that the Hebrews at the time of the Exodus numbered 600,000 adult males;[145] the Apuiriu, if a distinct race, may have been not much less numerous; and it is a not unreasonable conjecture,[146] that in the time of Rameses II. the subject races and newly-made captives together amounted to a full third of the population. Thus the Pharaoh had an abundant stock of raw material on which to draw, without putting any pressure on his native subjects, or even seriously affecting the general labor-market.

The great works of Rameses Meriamen may be divided under the two heads of works of utility and of ornament. To the former class belong his "Great Wall," his canal from the Nile to the Red Sea, and his numerous cities; to the latter, his temples, his colossal statues, his obelisks, and his tomb. The Great Wall, commenced by his father, Seti,[147] extended from Pelusium to Heliopolis,[148] a direct distance of ninety miles, and was strengthened at intervals by the establishment of fortresses upon its line, the "treasure cities," or "store cities," mentioned in the book of Exodus as built by the oppressed Israelites, being, as it generally thought,[149] among their number. The construction of this work is a strong indication of the decline in her military power on which Egypt was now entering,[150]—a decline which, in spite of a few exceptionally brilliant periods, must be considered to have set in from this reign.

The "Great Canal"—perhaps, like the "Wall," commenced by Seti[151]—is proved by the ruins upon its banks to have been in the main the work of Rameses.[152] It was, no doubt, provided with locks and sluices,[153] as was the canal which led the Nile water into the Fayoum; and in this way the difficulties connected with the tidal changes at Suez and the variations in the level of the Nile at Bubastis were met and overcome. Dredging perhaps kept the western end of the canal open, and prevented it from being silted up by the Nile mud; but when troubles came, this practice was neglected, and the channel soon became unnavigable. Communication with the Bitter Lakes had from time to time to be reopened, and

Neco, Darius Hystaspis,[154] Ptolemy I., Trajan, and the Caliph Omar[155] are especially mentioned as having applied themselves to the work of re-establishing the waterway Various points of departure from the course of the Nile were taken at different period, the latest being at Belbays, which is about eleven miles south of Bubastis (now Tel-Basta).

Among the cities built by Rameses II., or so enlarged as to be considered his work, were Tanis—the great city of the Delta—which he made his capital;[156] Pa-Ramesu, which is probably the Raamses of Exodus; Pa-tum (Patumus or Pithom, identified by Dr. Birch with Heroöpolis); Pa-phthah, at Gerf-Hussein in Nubia; Pa-ammon at Sebua, in the same country; and Pa-ra, near Der or Dirr, above Korosko.[157] The new Tanis was situated at some little distance from the old one, where the shepherd kings had resided, and was adorned with numerous temples and obelisks, fragments of which still strew the site. A contemporary of the son of Seti thus describes the place:[168] "So I arrived at the city of Ramesu-Meriamen, and found it admirable; for nothing on the Theban land and soil can compare with it. Here is the seat of the court. The place is pleasant to live in; its fields are full of good things; and life here passes in constant plenty and abundance. The canals are rich in fish; the lakes swarm with birds; the meadows are green with vegetables; there is no end of the lentils; melons with a taste like honey grow in the irrigated gardens. The barns are full of wheat and durra, and reach as high as heaven. Onions and grapes grow in the enclosures; and the apple-tree blooms among them. The vine, the almond-tree, and the fig-tree are found in the orchards. . . . The red-fish is common in the lotus-canal; the Bori-fish in the ponds; many varieties of the same, together with carp and pike (?), in the canal of Puharotha; fat fish and Khipti-pennu fish are to be found in the pools of the inundation, and the Hauaz-fish in the full mouth of the Nile, near the City of the Conqueror. The city canal Pshenhor produces salt, the lake region of Pahir natron. Sea-going ships enter the harbor; plenty and abundance are perpetual."

The most remarkable of the temples erected by Rameses are the building at Thebes, once called the Memnonium, but now commonly known as the Rameseum (which has been already described in the first volume of this work),[159] and the extraordinary rock-temple of Ipsambul or Abu-Simbel, the most magnificent specimen of its class which the world contains. The façade is formed by four huge colossi, each seventy feet in height, representing Rameses himself, seated on the throne, with the double crown of Egypt upon his head.[160] In the centre, flanked on either side by two of these gigantic figures, is a doorway of the usual Egyptian type, opening into a small vestibule, which communicates by a short passage with the main chamber. This is an oblong square, sixty feet long by forty-five, divided into a nave and two aisles by two rows of square piers with Osirid statues thirty feet high in front, and ornamented with painted sculptures over its whole surface.[161] The main chamber leads into an inner shrine, or adytum, supported by four piers without Osirid figures, but otherwise as richly adorned as the outer apartment. Behind the adytum are small rooms for the priests who served in the temple. It is the façade of the work which constitutes its main beauty. "What shall we say," observes a modern traveller,[162] "of the rock-temple of Ipsambul, the wonderful façade of which surpasses everything which our imagination can conceive of grandeur in a human work? How small, how insignificant, in comparison with it, the petty erections of our day! There, in Nubia, on a solitary wall of rock, far removed from the dwellings of men, in hoary antiquity a temple was hewn to the great gods of the land of Egypt . . . hewn as if by *enchantment*—for this is the proper word—so bold, so powerful, so exceeding all human measure, as if giants had turned the bare rock into a living work of art! Standing before this work, achieved by the hands of men, the thoughtful child of our modern age first feels the greatness of antiquity in its all-powerful might. It was not clever calculation, not profit, nor utility, but the most elevated feeling of gratitude to God, that caused such a work to be executed; a work worthy of and fit for the immortal, inconceivable, almighty, Deity, to whom the ancients dedicated it in high veneration for the Everlasting and the Incomprehensible." After this, the judgment of the learned historian of architecture may perhaps seem tame; but its sobriety gives it a weight which is scarcely accorded to the best assorted collection of historical phrases by the modern reader. "The largest of the rock-temples at Ipsambul," says Mr. Fergusson,[163] "is *the finest of its class known to exist anywhere*. Externally, the façade is about a hundred feet in height, and adorned by four of the most magnificent colossi in Egypt, each seventy feet in height, and representing the king, Rameses II., who caused the excavation to be made. It may be because they are more perfect than any other now found in that country, but certainly nothing can exceed their calm majesty and beauty, or be more entirely free from the vulgarity and exaggeration which is generally a characteristic of colossal works of this sort."

Among the other great works of this great king were the completion of the "Hall of Columns" at Karnak,[164] of the temple begun by Seti at Abydos,[165] and of that founded but left very imperfect by Amenôphis III. at Luxor; [166] the addition of pylons and colossi to the great temple of Phthah at Memphis,[167] and the entire construction of new temples at Memphis, Heliopolis, Tanis, Biet-el-Walli, Der, Gerf-Hussein, and elsewhere.[168] At Kalabshe there is also "a small but beautiful example, belonging to the age of Rameses II., and remarkable for the beauty of its sculptured bas-reliefs, as well as for the bold Proto-Doric columns which adorn its vestibule.[169] In Nubia, Rameses introduced the practice of excavating the cells of the temples in the rock, and adding in front of the cells structural buildings consisting of courts and propylons—a combination which is extremely effective, since thus "the sanctuary has all the imperishability and mystery of a cave," while the remainder of the temple has at the same time the ample space, free play of light, and architectural effect of a building standing in the open air.[170]

In the ornamentation of his buildings Rameses especially affected the employment of obelisks and colossi. Obelisks, which have ceased to exist, adorned his Sun-temple at Heliopolis;[171] and two magnificent ones were added under his auspices to the Luxor edifice,[172] one of which has long attracted the admiration of all beholders in the commanding position which it now occupies on the Place de la Concorde at Paris. This monument, as measured by the French engineers,[173] had an elevation of eighty-two feet, and is exquisitely carved and proportioned. It is of a beautiful pink Syenite granite, and is covered with inscriptions, which have been recently translated by M. Chabas.[174]

The most imposing of all the colossi of Ramesis, and indeed of all existing colossi, are those four giant forms already described[175] which guard the portal of the great rock-temple of Ipsambul. These, however, are not, strictly speaking, statues, but figures carved in the rock. Of actual statues the largest which can be definitely ascribed to Rameses II. (Fig. 59) is that whereof the torso remains in the ruins of the Rameseum, an "image of his majesty," which was originally fifty-four feet high, and weighed nearly nine hundred tons![176] Dr. Brugsch believes it to have been one of a pair, carved to adorn the entrance court of that magnificent edifice.["] Another colossus of large dimensions was erected by Rameses in the temple of Phthah at Memphis, and is now lying, prostrate and mutilated, amid the ruins of that structure, near the modern Arab village of Mitrahenny.[178] This also represented the king himself. Colossi of Seti, his father, were erected by him at Abydos, Memphis, and Thebes;[179] and smaller ones of his favorite wife and some of his daughters have been found at Mitrahenny, a little below the surface of the soil.[180] Colossal images of gods cut in the native rock, elaborately painted, ornament the interior of the greater Ipsambul temple,[181] while the façade of the smaller one exhibits six rock-cut figures of great size, four representing Rameses himself, and two his queen, Nefer-tari-Mitenmut.[182]

The Semitic blood which flowed in the veins of Rameses[183] showed itself alike in his physiognomy and in his actions. He seems to have been the handsomest of all the Egyptian kings. A good forehead, a large, well-formed, slightly aquiline nose, a well-shaped mouth with lips not too full, and a thoughtful pensive eye, constitute an *ensemble* which, if not faultless, is at any rate vastly superior to the ordinary royal type in Egypt, and would attract attention among any series of kings.[184] Much physical vigor accompanied this beauty of face. Rameses was the father of fifty-nine sons and sixty daughters,[185] many of whom he outlived, his great natural strength enabling him, despite the strain which he put upon it by his active life and general habits, to attain almost to the full term of life assigned to man by the Psalmist.[186] He began to reign, as we have seen,[187] at the age of ten or twelve, and continued on the throne, according to the express evidence of the monuments,[188] sixty-seven years. He thus died at the age of seventy-seven or seventy-nine—a length of time which is rarely reached by Orientals.

The large number of his children makes it clear that Rameses was a polygamist. He appears to have had two principal wives, Isi-nefert and Nefertari-mitenmut.[189] one of whom he may have espoused after the death of the other. He also married, in what we must suppose legitimate nuptials, Nefrura-Urmaa, the daughter of the king of the Khita. Three wives, however, cannot have borne him 119 children between them; and it is thus clear that, besides his wives, he must have maintained a seraglio of concubines, whose number is not likely to have fallen short of twenty.[190] Such an institution was Semitic, and well-known in Asia; but hitherto it had not prevailed in Egypt, where monogamy, always compulsory on private persons,[191] had up to this time been practised also by the monarchs.

Of all his sons the one most dear to him was Shaemuas, or Khamus[192]—the child of his favorite queen, Isi-nefert—who was "a learned and pious prince, devoted especially to the religious service of Phthah," living mainly in the temple of that god at Memphis, and keeping himself aloof from state affairs "more than was quite pleasing to his father."[193] This prince was designated as his successor, and in the meantime held the office of high-priest of Phthah in Memphis, in which capacity he exerted himself to restore the worship of the holy Apis-bulls—incarnations, as it was believed, of Phthah[194]—which had fallen into desuetude. The necropolis of the bulls, the so-called Serapeum,[195] was beautified and enlarged by Shaemuas, whose buildings are celebrated in various inscriptions as "splendid works" deserving of the highest commendation. Unfortunately he died in his father's lifetime, and was thus unable to show what architectural successes he might have achieved if he had had at his disposal the revenues of a kingdom instead of the allowance of an heir apparent.

His affection for this son, and for his two principal wives, shows that the disposition of Rameses II. was in some respects amiable, although upon the whole his character is one which scarcely commends itself to our approval. Professing in his early years extreme devotion to the memory of his father,[196] he lived to show himself his father's worst enemy, and to aim at obliterating his memory by erasing his name from the monuments on which it occurred, and in many cases substituting his own.[197] Amid a great show of regard for the deities of his country and for the ordinances of the established worship, he contrived that the chief result of all that he did for religion should be the glorification of himself.[198] Other kings had arrogated to themselves a certain qualified divinity, and after their deaths had sometimes been placed by some of their successors on a par with the real national gods;[199] but it remained for Rameses to associate himself during his lifetime with such leading deities as Phthah, Ammon, and Horus, and to claim equally with them the religious regards of his subjects.[200] He was also, as already observed, the first to introduce into Egypt the degrading custom of polygamy and the corrupting influence of a harem. Even his bravery, which cannot be denied, loses half its merit by being made the constant subject of boasting; and his magnificence ceases to appear admirable when we think at what a cost it displayed itself.[201] If, with most recent writers upon Egyptian history,[202] we identify him with the "king who knew not Joseph," the builder of Pithom *and Raamses*, the first oppressor of the Israelites, we must add some darker shades to the picture, and look upon him as a cruel and ruthless despot who did not shrink from inflicting on innocent persons the severest pain and suffering.

Rameses II. was succeeded by his fourteenth[203] and eldest surviving son, Menephthah, ⸺, the Ammen-ephthes of Manetho.[204] On the death of his brother Shaemuas, he had been appointed governor of Memphis[205] and had been admitted to a share in the administration of affairs, if not actually associated,[206] by his father. On his accession he took the throne-name of Hotep-hi-ma, ⸺ "he who trusts in truth," together with the epithets Bai-en-ra,[207] ⸺, and Meri-amon, ⸺. Inheriting from his father an empire which was everywhere at peace with its neighbors, he might have been expected to have had a tranquil and prosperous reign, and to have carried on the burst of architectural energy which had manifested itself under his father and his grandfather. The power, however, which directs human affairs, wholly disappointed these expectations. The unclouded prospect of his early years gave place, after a brief interval, to storm, and tempest of the most fearful kind; a terrible invasion carried fire and sword into the heart of his dominions; and he had scarcely escaped this danger when internal troubles broke out—a subject race, highly valued for the services which it was forced to render, insisted on quitting the land; a great loss was incurred in an attempt to compel it to remain; rebellion broke out in the south; and the reign, which had commenced under such fair auspices, terminated in calamity and confusion. Menephthah was quite incompetent to deal with the difficult circumstances in which he found himself placed—he hesitated, temporized, made concessions, retracted them—and finally conducted Egypt to a catastrophe from which she did not recover for a generation.

During his early years Menephthah seems to have remained in peace and quietness, untroubled by discontent at home, unmolested by foreign enemies. At this time he employed himself in further enlarging the cities of New Tanis and Pa-Ramessu,[20] which had been built by his father, and in setting up rock-tablets at Silsilis and elsewhere.[209] He also carried on certain minor works in connection with the great temple of Phthah at Memphis, where he set up a statue of himself in black basalt, which is now in the Museum of Boulaq.[210] He nowhere, however, attempted the erection of any great edifices; and it is certainly true to say that he "does not rank with those Pharaohs who have transmitted their remembrance to posterity by grand buildings and the construction of new temples, or by the enlargement of such as already existed."[212] His monuments are indeed completely insignificant, and though widely spread and tolerably numerous, have a "mean character"[212] about them, which is especially surprising when we compare with them the noble examples accomplished by his father and his grandfather. Menephthah evidently did not inherit their ambition. He was not, however, of so elevated a temper as to be free from the blemish of personal vanity; and this defect in his character led him to be guilty of the meanness of appropriating to himself the works of former kings by the erasure of their names and the substitution of his own[213]—a practice wholly unjustifiable. Such erasures had previously been sometimes made out of hatred and as a punishment; Menephthah made them for the mere purpose of self-glorification, and was indifferent whether he wronged a friend or an enemy.

The foreign relations of Menephthah were during this period satisfactory. He maintained the alliance with the Khita which his father had concluded after the close of his great Asiatic war, and strengthened the bonds of amity by allowing corn to be exported from Egypt for the sustentation of the Hittite people,[214] when their crops failed them. He received into Egypt as new settlers several tribes of Bedouins,[215] who were desirous of exchanging their nomadic habits for a more settled life, and established them in the rich lands about the city of Pithom. He retained the foreign conquests of his predecessors in Lower Syria, Philistia, and Canaan, carefully supervising their administration by means of continual dispatches and messengers.[216] At the same time he guarded with tolerable efficiency his northwestern frontier, prevented any serious irruption of the Libyan tribes, and up to his fifth year, succeeded in maintaining general tranquillity and prosperity.

But suddenly, in his fifth year[217] he had to meet an important attack. An African chief, Marmaiu, son of Deid,[218] collected a numerous army in the tract adjacent to Egypt upon the northwest, composed in part of native Africans, in part of auxiliaries, and, crossing the Egyptian frontier, carried fire and sword over the western and southwestern Delta, even threatening the great cities of Heliopolis and Memphis. The auxiliaries consisted of five principal nations, whose names, carefully transliterated from the Hieroglyphics, would seem to have been the Aka-usha, the Tursha, the Luku, the Shartana, and the Skeklusha. It has been proposed to regard these tribes as Caucasian races, who at this time had migrated into Libya, having perhaps been previously prisoners of war, whom Rameses II. had brought from Asia to Egypt in his military expeditions;[219] but the supposed migration has no historical basis. The expeditions of Rameses II. never approached the Caucasus, and the names are only with great violence brought into accord with those of Caucasian peoples.[220] A more plausible theory identifies the races with various tribes of Europeans occupying the northern Mediterranean and supposes the auxiliaries of Marmaiu to have come by sea to his aid, and to have designed a permanent settlement in Africa. The names certainly appear at first sight to lend themselves to this view, the resemblance being considerable between Akausha and Achaioi, Tursha and Tyrseni or Tusci, Shartana or Shardana and Sardonii, Sheklusha and Sikeloi or Siceli; while Luku is not far from Ligyes or Ligures, a people of the western Mediterranean. The first appearance of European races upon the stage of history must have the greatest interest for the modern world, in which Europe plays the first part; and if the identifications of M. de Rougé[221] are allowed, it must be granted that here Europe first steps upon the scene, exhibiting herself as a great aggressive power in the fourteenth century before our era, a hundred years anterior to the earliest traditional date for the Trojan war,[222] and in the actual lifetime of Moses. So extraordinary a revelation has naturally great attractions for many minds in an age when novelty is more esteemed than sobriety of judgment, if not even than historic truth; and thus M. de Rougé's view has found many advocates among Egyptologists,[223] and has approved itself to some general scholars of distinguished reputation.[224] But the difficulties in the way of its acceptance are great; and perhaps it is as probable that the races in question were native African tribes otherwise unknown to us as that they really consisted of the Achæans, Etruscans, Sardinians, Sicilians, and Ligyans of Europe.

We have no estimate left us of the number of the invaders; but it certainly exceeded 20,000, and probably did not fall much short of 40,000 men.²²⁵ The Libyans, the Maxyes, and the Kahaka, who were Marmaiu's subjects, formed the main bulk of the force, contingents of no great size being furnished by the Akausha, Turshu, Luku, Shartana, and Sheklusha, who were not his subjects, but "foreign mercenaries." ²²⁶ The attack seems to have been made towards the apex of the Delta, and was at first completely successful. The frontier towns were taken by assault and "turned into heaps of rubbish;" ²²⁷ the Delta was entered upon, and a position taken up in the nome of Prosôpis,²²ᵇ from which both Memphis and Heliopolis were menaced. Menephthah hastily fortified these cities,²²⁹ or rather (we must suppose) strengthened their existing defences, and, making Memphis his own headquarters, proceeded to collect an army, partly of Egyptians, partly of mercenaries, wherewith to oppose the enemy. He did not, however, venture to take the command in person; but pretending an express command of Phthah, whom he had seen in vision, forbidding him to quit Memphis,²³⁰ he sent his troops under generals to encounter the enemy. A great battle was fought in the nome of Prosôpis on the third of Epiphi (May 18), in which, after the struggle had lasted six hours,²³¹ the Libyans and their allies were completely defeated and forced to fly. Marmaiu himself was among the first to quit the field; and he did so with such haste as to leave behind him not only his camp-equipage, but his bow, his quiver, and his sandals.²³² His wife and children, who had accompanied him to the fight, seem also to have escaped, together with some considerable number of his soldiers.²³³ But above eight thousand ²³⁴ were slain in the battle and the pursuit, and above nine thousand were made prisoners.²³⁵ The defeat was total and irremediable. Marmaiu's power was shattered, and he is heard of no more. The mercenaries, of whatever race they were, learned by experience the wisdom of leaving the Libyans to fight their own battles, and of not again themselves crossing swords with the Egyptians. When the next occasion came for a Libyan invasion of Egypt, no mercenaries accompanied them; and though the Sheklusha and Tursha are still occasionally found among the enemies of Egypt, the majority of the allies of Marmaiu abstained from further hostile movement. The Shartana even entered the Egyptian service, and came to hold a place among the most trusted of the Egyptian troops.²³⁶

It was probably not many years²³⁷ after this great victory

over the Libyans and their allies had raised Menephthah to a high pitch of glory, both in his own eyes and in those of his subjects, that a demand was made upon him by the chief of a subject race, long domiciled in Egypt, which must have seemed to him wholly preposterous. Moses, a Hebrew brought up in the court of his predecessor, but for many years self-exiled from Egypt, appeared before him and requested permission to conduct his people out into the desert, which bounded Egypt on the east, the distance of three days' journey, in order that they might hold a feast and offer sacrifice to their god, Jehovah.[138] Menephthah, not unnaturally, refused, fearing to lose the services of more than half a million of bondsmen, who, if they once quitted the country and found themselves free, would not be likely to return. At the same time, to punish the nation for its temerity, and to keep down its aspirations, he increased the burden of its task-work, and exacted an amount which it was impossible for them to perform."[239] Moses, however, still persisting in his demand, and alarming the king and his court by a series of "plagues," continually increasing in severity, and culminating in the "destruction of the first-born," the required permission was at length obtained; and on a certain day the nation, carefully organized by its leaders, quitted Egypt and entered the desert.[240] But Menephthah (Fig. 32) had scarcely yielded when he repented of his weakness. Gathering together all the force that he could hastily muster, horse and foot and chariots—of these last more than six hundred—he followed after the Hebrews and overtook them "encamping by the sea, at Pi-hahiroth, before Baal-Zephon."[241] It is scarcely the business of the general historian of ancient Egypt to enter into the difficult question of what sea is intended, and what route the Hebrews pursued upon quitting Egypt. The traditional belief of both the Egyptians and the Israelites that the sea was the Red Sea[242] is a fact of such vast weight that, against it, geographical speculations and ingenious explanations of names[243] sink into insignificance, and are, to say the least, quite insufficient to establish a theory which runs counter to the belief of, at any rate, three millennia. But, leaving this question on one side, we may be content to state in general terms the issue. Favored by a "strong east wind,"[244] the Hebrews made their way upon dry ground across the arm of the sea that had seemed to hem them in. On attempting to follow them along the same route, the Egyptians were overwhelmed by the returning waters; the chariot-wheels were entangled in the soft ooze; the horses

and their riders perished; the chosen captains were drowned
—"the depths covered them; they sank to the bottom as a
stone." [245] All the troops that had entered on the dangerous
path were destroyed; a great slaughter was accomplished, and
a blow received which was felt throughout the empire as a terrible calamity.

But the Pharaoh himself escaped.[246] Menephthah, with
the remnant of his host, returned to Egypt and resumed the
peaceful occupations which first the invasion of Marmaiu,
and then the Hebrew troubles, had interrupted. But now
revolt seems to have shown itself in the south.[247] A pretender, named Amon-mes or Amon-meses, [hieroglyphs] or
[hieroglyphs], belonging to a city called Hakheb or Kheb,[248]
which was situated near the modern Beni-souef, on the Nile
opposite the Fayoum, came forward, and was perhaps accepted as monarch by the Thebans. Menephthah died, leaving
his crown to his son, Seti-Menephthah [hieroglyphs], or
Seti II.; but this monarch was not generally acknowledged,[249]
and a time of confusion and disorder set in, which is characterized by Rameses III. as a period of complete anarchy, when
Egypt was without a master, and the various pretenders to
power strove with and massacred one the other.[250] Amonmes (the Ammen-e-mes of Manetho [251]) reigned for a time—
perhaps five years [252]—at Thebes, and took the title of *hak
Uas*, "King of Thebes," which he attached to his name
within his escutcheon.[253] He designed and finished his tomb
in the Biban-el-Moluk, an excavation of moderate pretensions.[254] Upon his death, Seti-Menephthah appears to have
been recognized as monarch by the Egyptians generally,[255]
and to have transferred his abode to Thebes, where he built
a small temple,[256] and erected a statue of himself, which is
now in the British Museum.[257] He also carried on a war in
the southern part of his dominions, and set up a tablet as a
conqueror on the rocks near Abu-Simbel.[258]

In countenance Seti II. (Fig. 54) was remarkably handsome. He had a long well-formed nose, nearly in line with
his forehead, arched eyebrows, a good eye with full eyelid, a
short upper lip, a cleanly cut mouth, and a delicate rounded
chin. He seems, however, to have been wanting in energy
and decision. Before he had been long seated upon

Vol. II. Plate XIX.

Fig. 42.—ORNAMENTAL CARVING (Ethiopic)—See Page 192.

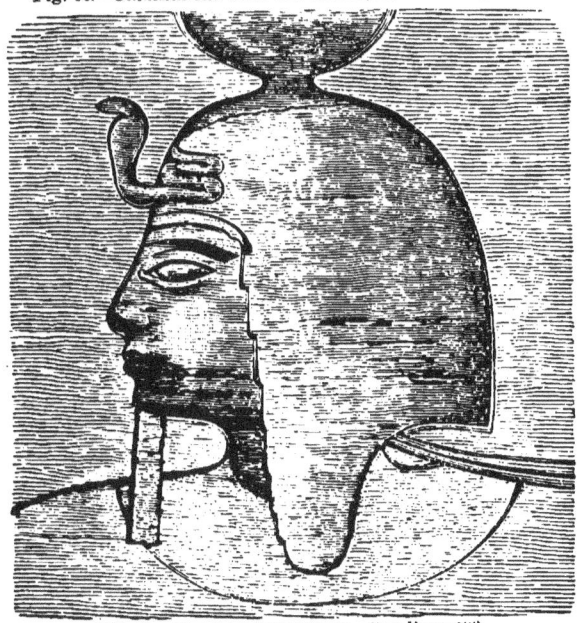

Fig. 43. HEAD OF SET-NEKHT.—See Page 196

Plate XX. Vol. II.

Fig. 44.—HEAD OF RAMESES IV.—See Page 209.

Fig. 45.—HEAD OF RAMESES III.—See Page 2⁓

the throne, a high official named Baï brought forward, as a rival claimant of the kingly power, a certain Siphthah,[259] who is thought to have been a son of Amon-mes,[260] and who was certainly a native of the same city,[261] Seti seems to have made but little resistance to this antagonist. According to one authority,[262] he accepted from him the title of "Prince of Cush," and consented to act as his viceroy in the southern provinces: but it is perhaps more probable that he was either killed in battle, or dethroned and murdered by his successful rival.

Siphthah, 𓉘𓏏𓎛𓉐, who now became king, took the epithet of Meri-en-phthah, "beloved of Phthah," and the throne name of Ra-khu-en-sotep-en-ra,[263] ⊙ 𓅃 ⎯ 𓃀 ⊙. It would seem that, to strengthen himself in his usurped position, he married a princess of the Rameside family, who may have been, but is certainly not proved to have been,[264] a daughter of Menephthah and a sister of Seti II. Her name appears on the monuments as Ta-user or Ta-usert,[265] which Manetho changed into Thuóris.[266] She seems to have shared the royal authority with her husband, and perhaps enjoyed it during the term of seven years, as Manetho (who, however, mistook her sex) recorded.[267] But the joint reign was troubled and inglorious. Siphthah did not engage in any wars; and the only important work that he completed was his tomb in the Biban-el-Moluk, which was an excavation of some pretensions.[268]

A period of anarchy followed the death of Siphthah, and separated the nineteenth dynasty from the twentieth. "For many years," we are told, "the country was without a master; the chief authority belonged to the governors of cities, who massacred one the other. After a time a certain Arsu, a Syrian, became chief among them, the whole country offering him homage; but his companions plundered all who possessed any wealth. Moreover, the gods were treated like the men; and no one any more made offerings to the temples."[269] Once more, a dynasty of the highest distinction, one which had ruled Egypt gloriously for above a century,[270] and covered the country with magnificent works, expired amid clouds and gloom. Internal rebellion and external attack combined to produce a general state of confusion and anarchy, which threatened the complete dissolution of the whole fabric of Egyptian society. For several years this state of things continued, and the sufferings of the people must have been great. Had the nation not possessed extraordinary vitality, recovery from so extreme a state of depression and exhaustion would have been impossible; but there was *that* in the Egyptian character which almost defied adverse circumstances, and enabled the monarchy to rise again and again, like the fabled giant, after being stricken to the earth, and to vindicate to itself again and again a foremost place among the leading kingdoms of the world. We shall find Egypt under the twentieth dynasty occupying almost as commanding a position as that which we have shown her to have held under the eighteenth and the nineteenth.

The civilization of Egypt under these two most important dynasties has now, according to the general plan pursued in the present work, to be considered, and will be divided under our three customary heads—Art, Religion, and Manners.

Whatever may be thought with respect to other departments of art, it cannot be questioned that Egyptian architecture reached its highest perfection under these two dynasties. The Rameseum, the temples of Medinet-Abou and Ipsambul, the palace-temples or temple-palaces of Karnak and Luxor, and the rock-cut tombs of the Biban-el-Moluk, belong alike to the period, and give it an architectural pre-eminence over every other period in Egyptian history, which only profound ignorance can doubt or extreme captiousness dispute. The latest historian of architecture has given us his verdict, that the hypostyle hall of Seti I. at Karnak is "the greatest of man's architectural works,"[271] and the entire building, of which it is a part, "the noblest effort of architectural magnificence ever produced by the hand of man."[272] The same writer has declared, though familiar with the grand examples at Ellora and Elephanta, that the rock-cut temple of Ipsambul is "the finest of its class known to exist anywhere."[273] Intelligent travellers are struck by the Theban edifices—the work almost exclusively of these dynasties—far more than by all the other constructions of the Pharaohs.[274] Most of them are disappointed by the Pyramids; there is scarcely one whose heart is not stirred by a thrill of admiration as he contemplates Karnak or Luxor.

If we inquire what exactly constituted the pre-eminence of these Pharaonic works over the remainder, the readiest answer would seem to be that they exhibited more strikingly than any others the combination of enormous mass and size with a profusion of the most elaborate ornamentation. The Pyramids are grander structures, far more massive, and—at any rate in two instances[275]—covering a larger area, but they are at present, and probably always were,[276] entirely devoid of ornament, perfectly plain constructions, intended to produce their whole effect upon the spectator by mere hugeness and solid massiveness. The Theban palace-temples have this quality in a less degree than the Pyramids, but still they have it largely. They cover nearly as much ground as the greatest of the Pyramids; they contain blocks of stone as enormous; and even their material bulk, though very inferior, impresses the mind almost as much, being more manifest and appreciable. With this quality of vast size they united a wealth of varied ornamentation to which a parallel scarcely exists anywhere else. The buildings presented a long vista of gateways, and courts, and colonnades, and pillared halls, led up to by avenues of sphinxes or of colossi, and themselves adorned with colossi or with tall tapering obelisks, which shot up above the general horizontal line of the courts and halls, as the pinnacles and towers and spires of the modern cathedral raise themselves above the line of the nave and choir. Within and without, on the massive gate-towers, on the walls of chambers and of courts, on the ceilings, on the very pillars themselves, everywhere, on every side, whithersoever the eye could turn itself, elaborate sculptures representing gods and kings, and battle-scenes, and graceful forms of vegetable life, were to be seen, all glowing with warm tints, and enchanting the eye with a blaze of gorgeous yet well-assorted hues. Form, color, vastness, multiplicity, elaboration, mystery, combined to impress, astonish, and delight the spectator who saw on every side of him stately gateways, huge colonnaded courts, long vistas of pillars, calm, silent, solemn colossi, slim obelisks—all bathed to some extent in the warm light of an Egyptian sky, and, even where the shade was deepest, resplendent with the hues of art.[277]

The combination of mass, however, with rich ornamentation is not the sole merit of the works which we are considering. There is a harmony in the forms and in the tints, a solemnity and majesty in the grand figures introduced, a skill in the employment of painting and sculpture as subsidiary to architecture, which have scarcely been surpassed as yet, and which are above all praise.[276] Moreover, the style is eminently suited to the country itself, to its climate, atmosphere, and general physical features; transport it elsewhere, and it would lose half its charm; but in Egypt, in the flat green valley of the Nile with its low wall of rock on either side, with its pellucid air, bright sun, and clear blue sky, it is as near perfection as anything human, or at least as anything within the circle of the arts. Whatever eulogy is justly bestowed on Egyptian architecture generally belongs especially to the great works of the eighteenth and nineteenth dynasties, which brought the style introduced by the monarchs of the twelfth to a pitch of excellence never exceeded, and rarely equalled, by the later Pharaohs.

In glyptic art the great glory of the period consisted in its colossi. The rock-cut images of Rameses II. at Ipsambul, the sitting figures of Amenôphis III. near Luxor, remnants (as is thought [277]) of an avenue of eighteen, and the enormous granite statue of Rameses—the pride of his Rameseum—at Karnak, are far more gigantic than any other human forms at present existing upon the earth, and impress the beholder with a feeling of combined awe and admiration, which with difficulty finds vent in expression. "Nothing which now exists in the world," says Dean Stanley, of the last-named of these colossi, "can give any notion of what the effect must have been when the figure was erect. Nero towering above the Colosseum may have been something like it; but he was of bronze and Rameses was of solid granite. Nero was standing without any object; Rameses was resting in awful majesty after the conquest of the whole of the then known world." [280] Miss Martineau's impression of the colossi of Amenôphis has been already noticed.[281] The Dean says of them: [282] "The Sun was setting: the African range glowed red behind them; the green plain was dyed with a deeper green beneath them; and the shades of evening veiled the vast rents and fissures in their aged frames. They too sit, hands on knees, and they too are sixty feet high. As I looked back on them in the sunset, and they rose up in front of the background of the mountain, they seemed indeed as if they were part of it—as if they belonged to some natural creation rather than to any work of art." The Ispambul figures are almost equally impressive. "Nothing can exceed," we are told, "their calm majesty and beauty." [283] "The wonderful façade surpasses everything which our imagination can conceive of grandeur in a human work." [284] "Standing before them, the thoughtful child of our modern age first feels the greatness of antiquity in its all-powerful might." [285]

It is the ordinary fault of colossi to be coarse and vulgar. Giants are unpleasing in actual life, and magnified representations of our fellow-men leave for the most part an unsatisfactory impression. The great colossi of the best Egyptian times are redeemed from vulgarity by their majestic pose, the stiff rigidity of their forms, and the stamp which they bear upon them of eternal changeless tranquillity. Profound repose, with something of a look of scorn, is their characteristic expression—they resemble beings above all human weaknesses, all human passions—Epicurean deities, unconcerned spectators of the lapse of ages and the follies and woes of man.

The bas-reliefs of the period have two special features—first, they are on a far larger scale than any previous ones; and secondly, they are more vigorous and animated. While domestic scenes continue to be represented in the tombs,[286] and religious ones both in the tombs and in the temples, the grand subject of war is for the first time introduced[287]—all its phases receive careful treatment, the march, the encampment, the conflict, the siege, the pursuit; vast surfaces are covered with enormous pictures, into which hundreds of figures are introduced[288]—life, action, rapid movement, energy are portrayed, infinitely varied attitudes occur; the artists seem to have emancipated themselves from all the old conventional trammels, and represent the various circumstances of battle with equal truthfulness and spirit. Especially do they succeed in the delineation of the newly-imported horses, now standing still, now trotting, now galloping at full speed; anon wounded, swerving, falling prone on the ground; or again prancing, rearing, turning round, feeding, about to lie down, extended at its ease; in every position equally well drawn and clearly studied from the life. Warfare is exhibited with all its multiform incidents. Foreign races have their various costumes, physiognomies, armature, modes of fighting, war-animals, style of chariot. Even the confusion and turmoil of a sea-fight was regarded as within the range of the artists' powers; and adverse galleys engaged in actual combat exhibit to us the facts of naval warfare about the time of Moses."[289]

It is thought that the sculptures of the period which we are considering, whether in relief or "in the round," while they comprise the highest perfection to which Egyptian art ever attained, contain also distinct traces of the commencement of a decline.[290] The change occurred in the latter part of the reign of Rameses II. It consisted in a want of care and finish, an undue elongation of the figure,[291] and an occasional rudeness and coarseness which are pronounced "barbaric."[292] To the unprofessional eye, however, the difference is not very striking, and even the sculptures of Rameses II., the second king of the succeeding dynasty, seem to fall but little short of the great masterpieces of Seti I. and Rameses II.

In the matter of religion, the most noticeable changes which occurred are connected with the disk-worship, and with the alternate elevation and depression of the god Set. The cult of the disk, favored by Amenôphis III.,[293] and fully established by his son, Amenôphis IV., or Khuenaten, is chiefly remarkable on account of its exclusive character, the disk-worshippers opposing and disallowing all other cults and religious usages. Had Khuenaten been able to effect the religious revolution at which he aimed, the old Egyptian religion would have been destroyed, and its place would have been taken by a species of monotheism, in which the material Sun would have been recognized as the One and only Lord, and Ruler of the Universe. Ammon, Khem, Kneph, Phthah, Maut, Khonsu, Osiris, Horus, Isis, Thoth, would have disappeared, and sun-worship, pure and simple, would have replaced the old complicated polytheism. But Egypt was not prepared for this change. The heiratic interest, naturally enlisted against it was strong: the popular sentiment was opposed to change, and especially to innovations which could be traced to the influence of foreigners; disk-worship never obtained any firm hold on the Egyptian people; it was a court religion, introduced and sustained by kings, for which the bulk of their subjects had neither regard nor reverence.

It was otherwise with the Set movement, which strove to elevate that god to the highest place in the Pantheon. There had been in Egypt from a remote antiquity a struggle between the devotees of Set and those of Osiris,[294] the esoteric meaning of which it is difficult to penetrate, for we can scarcely suppose that the followers of Set were actual devil-worshippers. If the myth of Osiris was originally solar, and Set was merely night, which engulfs and destroys the sun, we can understand that there would be, in such a country as Egypt, persons to whom night might seem more admirable, more divine than day; who would therefore take the part of Set, and think that he had done well to slay his brother. And the division into the two camps, once begun, would continue long after its meaning had become lost to view. The Osiris worshippers were always saying hard things of Set and seeking to depress him below the point at which he stood in the original Pantheon. The Set worshippers resisted them. During the early monarchy, Set, on the whole, maintained a fairly high place.[295] With the success of the Shepherds (Hyksôs), however, he entered on a new position. Set was the patron deity of the first Hyksôs king of Egypt, who actually bore his name; and Set-worship thus received a new impulse and a new life under the Shepherds rule, until at last it was, in Lower Egypt at any rate, established as exclusively the state religion. When the Hyksós were expelled, Set fell with them, not merely losing the position to which he had attained, but sinking to a comparatively subordinate place among the Egyptian deities. In this position he remained throughout the whole period of the eighteenth dynasty,[296] but with the accession of the nineteenth he once more came to the front. Rameses I. named his eldest son Seti—a name commonly written with the figure of the god,[297] and implying a dedication of his first-born to that divinity. Seti, when he became king, naturally brought Set forward, not only worshipping him together with the other Osirid gods,[298] but representing himself as receiving life at his hands.[299] Various princes of the Rameside house received a similar dedication with that of Seti I.,[300] and Set's high rank among the gods was maintained beyond the period of the nineteenth dynasty into that of the twentieth.

With regard to the entire period of which we are treating, nothing is more remarkable than the absence of any strong favoritism, and the equitable division of religious regard among a large number of deities. On the whole, Ammon, now almost always viewed as Ammon-Ra, maintains his pre-eminence; but great attention is paid also to Horus, Kneph, Athor, Ra, Thoth, Phthah, Osiris, Isis, Mentu, Maut, Tum, Khonsu, and Netpé. Sati also, Shu, Anuka, Seb, Tafné, and Sabak are frequently worshipped; and occasional honor is paid to Khem, Sefkh, Anubis, Nephthys, Ma, Sekhet, Neith, Taourt, Hapi, the Nile-God, Heka, Seneb, and Bes. Altogether, about forty deities appear in the bas-reliefs as objects of religious adoration during the period, which is one at which the Pantheon obtains almost its full development. To give life seems to be the prerogative of (comparatively speaking) but few deities—as Ammon. Horus, Set, Kneph, Thoth, Mentu, Athor and Netpé.[301] It belongs to Set to teach the monarch to shoot.[302] Ammon-Ra, Thoth, and Sefkh confer immortality by writing the monarch's name on the leaves of the tree of life.[303] In battle, the king is compared commonly with Mentu, Set, or (Baal),[304] and is regarded as under the special protection of Ammon-Ra.[305] Living, he is commonly entitled "the Horus," or "the living Horus;" dead, "the Osiris."

A further development of the doctrine, that the kings were actual gods,[306] also characterizes the period under consideration. Hitherto the King-worship had been one of language and sentiment;[307] now it took a material shape. Thothmes III., at Semneh and Koummeh, associated his ancestor, Usurtasen III., with Kneph and Totun on terms of complete equality,[308] figuring him on the same scale, offering to him sacrificial feasts, and representing himself as receiving "life" at his hands.[309] Amen-hotep II., his son, followed his example.[310] Other kings exalted Nefertari-Aahmes to the rank of a goddess.[311] But it remained for Rameses II. not only to represent himself as worshipped,[312] but actually to set up his own image for worship in a temple together with, and on a par with, images of three of the greatest gods,— namely, Ammon, Phthah, and Horus.[313] The deification of the reigning monarch became thus complete. It is scarcely possible that any other religious sentiment can have maintained much influence over men, when the doctrine was accepted, that in their actual monarch they had present with them a deity as great as any in earth or heaven.[314]

The arts of life made a rapid advance under the early kings of the eighteenth dynasty, and progressed steadily, though more slowly, until about the middle of the nineteenth. The costumes of kings and queens became suddenly most elaborate. King Amen-hotep I. is represented [315] with three garments over his linen tunic, which itself has a complicated and brilliant ornament in front, consisting of a broad stripe in four colors, blue, red, yellow, and green, with three pendent ends of ribbon on either side of it. He has also a broad belt, similarly variegated. His upper garments, which seem to be all made of a white, striped, very transparent muslin, are, first, a short petticoat beginning at the waist and descending to the calf of the leg; secondly, a long robe reaching from the shoulders to the ankles; and thirdly; a flowing cape. He wears further armlets and bracelets of gold, seemingly enamelled, a broad collar of many hues, white sandals, a close-fitting blue cap with a *uræus* ornament in front, an artificial black beard, two ribbons down his back, and the "tail" peculiar to kings and gods. His mother Nefertari-Aahmes (Fig. 40), who is represented with him, wears the complicated vulture-headdress which has been given above,[316] a *blue* wig, a long robe of white striped muslin, indecently transparent, and an elaborate flowing cape of the same. She has armlets and bracelets set with jewels, white sandals, a broad collar like her son's, and earrings. A broad sash, blue, red, and yellow, depends from her waist to the bottom of her robe. In another representation she has a wig with long pendants of a peculiar character.[317]

It is not often that the dresses represented are so elaborate as these; but there is, speaking generally, a marked advance in the number, complication, and variety of the garments, both of men and women. Thothmes III. introduces the tall cap, round in front and pointed at the back, which thenceforth becomes the favorite headdress of the kings, being occasionally covered with spots, which may represent pearls. Kings sometimes wear a spencer similarly spotted,[318] which covers the shoulders and reaches to the waist. One king, Amenôphis IV. (Fig. 34), wears at the base of his cap a ribbon, or diadem, terminating in two flowing ends.[319] He has also a long flowing robe, which falls behind him, and separates into two flaps, which are rounded off into points.[320] Women, no less than men, wear sandals; and both women and men wear occasionally anklets, besides armlets and bracelets.[321] The royal attendants have commonly two tunics instead of one, the inner of linen, the outer of muslin and transparent. In a few cases they wear also a muslin cape.[322] Sandals (Fig. 37) are still somewhat rare; even princes and kings are sometimes represented without them; and they are but seldom worn by persons of lower rank. The practice begins of wearing them with the toes violently turned up;[323] but this usage does not become general until the time of the twentieth dynasty. Some of the varieties in female apparel (Fig. 39) will be better understood by representation than description.[324]

The houses of the great, no doubt, became more luxurious as time went on, and one king shows us the arrangement of a royal palace, or villa,[325] from which we may obtain a tolerable notion of the general character of rich men's residences. A large square or parallelogram was enclosed within high walls, with pylonic entrances on two or more of the sides, like those of temples in miniature. The grounds were divided out into formal courts and valleys, planted with trees in rows, the trees being of various kinds, inclusive of palms and vines. Ponds or reservoirs, rectangular in shape, were frequent, and gave the charm of freshness in a climate where without constant irrigation vegetation languishes. The house itself consisted of numerous courts, surrounded with colonnaded cloisters, and entered through pylons, with here and there a group of apartments, into which light was but scantily admitted by small windows placed high up in the walls. Much taste was shown in the designs of pillars, and especially of their capitals, which combined animal and vegetable forms, after a manner that was at once curious and pleasing.[326] The number of apartments was not great, life being chiefly passed in the colonnaded courts, and in the grounds, where a sufficiency of immediate shade could be combined with the charm of remoter light and with the free play of the atmosphere. Furniture, though not very abundant according to modern notions,³²⁷ was convenient and in good taste. Animal forms were followed in the feet of chairs, fauteuils, and ottomans,³²⁸ and sometimes in other portions of the carved woodwork,³²⁹ while delicate stuffs covered the cushioned portions, adding the beauty of color to that of form.³³⁰ The elaboration of furniture culminated in the thrones (Fig. 41) constructed for the kings,³³¹ and the footstools sometimes attached to them,³³² which were carved in the richest and quaintest fashion, either with figures of captured monarchs, or with animal or vegetable forms, or with the two combined, and must have been most curious and extraordinary works of art.

Ornamental carvings or castings of an artistic character, realistic in style, were also received as tribute from some of the subject states, and served to adorn the palaces of the Pharaohs with strange and outlandish figures (Fig. 28). One such offering, brought to Tutankh-amen by the Ethiopians,³³³ is peculiarly graceful and pleasing. It represents the giraffe or camelopard amid the palm-groves of Mid Africa (Fig. 42), and expresses with much truthfulness and spirit the form of that remarkable animal.

Graceful ornamentation also characterizes the arms and chariot of the monarch, which frequently exhibit the head, or even the full form, of the lion.³³⁴ Vases are of elegant shapes, and their covers are occasionally in the forms of animals' heads.³³⁵ Figures of animals adorn the prows of vessels; and sometimes their oars terminate in representations of the heads of men.³³⁶

In social life, the introduction of the horse from Asia made a considerable change. The chariot superseded the palanquin as the ordinary mode of conveyance; and much attention was bestowed upon the equipage and the stud. Horses were great favorites, and received special names, as Ken-Amen, "strength of Ammon," Anta-hruta, "Anaïtis pleased," and the like.³³⁷ The young dandy prided himself on the strength and lightness of his vehicle, the perfect shape and condition of his carriage-horses, the beauty of their trappings, and his own skill in driving them.³³⁸ Kings generally employed a charioteer, but even they did not disdain to take the reins occasionally into their own hands and conduct their own vehicles.³³⁹ Horses bore tall plumes of ostrich feathers on their heads, had many tassels or streamers appended to them, and sometimes wore elegant housings.[340] Field-sports continued to occupy the leisure hours of most well-to-do Egyptians; and the monarchs, at any rate, added to their former pleasures of this kind the chase of the lion and the elephant.[341]

A burst of literary vigor distinguishes the period. Literature had always been held in esteem in Egypt, and had furnished a fairly satisfactory career to a considerable number of persons.[342] Men of high rank, like Ptah-hotep and Sancha, had occasionally occupied themselves with it, and even one monarch had left "Instructions" for his successor, which he had cast into a highly artificial and *quasi*-poetic form.[343] But it is not till the reign of Rameses II. and his son, Menephthah, that literary activity reaches its acme, and Egypt is able to boast of a whole "galaxy" of writers.[344] The high honor done to the "epic poet" Pentaour, whose lay of "Rameses victorious" was inscribed on the walls of half a dozen temples,[345] may have acted as a stimulus to authorship, and have given to the pursuit of knowledge and of the art of composition an attraction which it had not possessed previously. But, whatever was the cause, at least the effect is certain. Under Rameses II. and Menephthah literature flourished in all its branches—history, divinity, practical philosophy, poetry, epistolary correspondence, novels or tales, occupied the attention of numerous writers, and works in these various subjects rapidly accumulated. A public library was established at Thebes, under a director—a high official—named Amen-em-an.[346] The roll of writers included the names of Pentaour, Amen-em-api, Pan-bas, Kakabu, Hor, Anna, Meriemap, Bek-en-ptah, Hora, Amen-masu, Suanro, Serptah. Nor was original composition the sole occupation of these learned persons. The modern world is indebted to them for the careful copies which they made of earlier manuscripts, and owes to their indefatigable industry such works as "The Instructions of Amen-em-hat," "The Tale of the Two Brothers," "The Praise of Learning," and even the greater part of "The Book of the Dead."[347] Like the monks of the Middle Ages, the Egyptian hierogrammateis regarded it as a sacred duty to hand on to later ages the learning of the past, and, when the fragile papyrus of the early times was falling into decay, transcribed the perishing work upon fresh material.

Thus, in almost all respects, in arts, in arms, in literature, in the comforts and elegancies of private life, the Egypt of the fifteenth and fourteenth centuries before our era had made advances beyond the simplicity of primitive times, and attained a point which well deserves attention and even admiration. But it must not be denied or concealed that there were darker hues in the picture. The glorious achievements of the greatest of the Pharaohs in architecture and colossal statuary were not produced without much suffering among a large servile class, whose forced toil was excessive and unceasing [348]—nay, sometimes intentionally aggravated for the purpose of breaking their strength.[349] Taxation was heavy upon the lower orders of the native Egyptians, and collectors with no pity in their hearts exacted the last penny from the wretched *fellahin* by the free use of the rod.[350] Both men and women were stripped naked and subjected to the pain and indignity of the bastinado.[350] In war many cruel and barbarous customs prevailed. Captives were either reduced to slavery or put to death. The slain were systematically mutilated in order to obtain sure evidence of their numbers;[352] and conquering monarchs were not ashamed to return home from battle with the gory heads of their adversaries attached to the hinder part of their chariots.[353] Whether kings generally slew their more distinguished prisoners with their own hand is perhaps doubtful;[354] but there is distinct evidence that such an act was considered not unbecoming, and that a king could not only commit it, but boast of it.[355] The relations between the sexes did not improve as time went on. Polygamy on a vast scale was introduced into the royal household; indecency in apparel was common; and the profligacy of the women was such as to become a commonplace of Egyptian novels.[356] Altogether, it would seem that the acme of perfection in art was coincident with a decline in morals— a decline which combined increased savagery with advancing sensualism.

CHAPTER XXII.

THE TWENTIETH DYNASTY ABOUT B.C. 1280-1100.

Accession of Setnekht—his Birth and Parentage doubtful. His brief reign. His Tomb. Setnekht associates his Son, Rameses. Reign of Rameses III. His Appellations. His new arrangement of the Official Classes. His Wars—with the Shasu—with the Libyans—with the great Confederacy of the Tanauna, Shartana, Sheklusha, Tulsha, Uashesh, Purusata, and Tekaru—with the Mashausha—with the Negroes and Ethiopians—with the Nations of Syria. His great Works. His planting of Trees. His Encouragement of Mining and Trade. The Conspiracy against him. His Domestic History. His Personal Appearance and Character. His Tomb. Rapid Decline of Egypt after his Death—its Causes. Reigns of Rameses IV., Rameses V., Rameses VI. and Meri-Tum, Rameses VII. and VIII. Reign of Rameses IX. and Commencement of Priestly Encroachment. Reigns of Rameses X. and XI. Rameses XII. and the Princess of Bakhtan. Reign of Rameses XIII. General View of Period. Decline of Architecture, Art, and Literature—Deterioration of Morals—Slight Changes in Civilization and Habits of Life.

"Un prince glorieux eut jeter un dernier éclat sur les armes de l'Égypte à la veille de leur entière décadence."—LENORMANT,—*Manuel d'Histoire Ancienne*, vol. i, p. 436.

THE anarchy which supervened upon the death of Siphthah [1] can scarcely have lasted very long. Egypt was not yet reduced to such a state of exhaustion as to tolerate for many years the complete eclipse of authority and suspension of settled government. The royal race which had reigned with so much glory from the date of the expulsion of the Shepherds to the time of Seti II., was by no means extinct, nor had it even as yet shown any signs of a serious loss of vigor and governmental ability. To find a new monarch of the old blood could not have been difficult, when a recent Pharaoh [2] had been the parent of fifty-nine sons and sixty daughters. Probably, the anarchy was caused rather by a superflui‡y than a lack of candidates for the royal power, [3] since the "great men" (*ueru*) who ruled in the various towns [4] were most likely of royal descent, at any rate for the most part. It may have been difficult to decide upon the claims of the various candidates; and we can even conceive the possibility of the priests and nobles being in no hurry to make a choice, since, while the royal authority was in abeyance, their own power and dignity would be augmented. Had Egypt had no warlike neighbors, they would perhaps have temporized longer; but when a Syrian took advantage of the state of things to establish himself as prince in Egypt, and his companions robbed and plundered at their pleasure, and the Egyptian gods were treated with as little respect as the Egyptian men, and the temples were denuded of their accustomed offerings,[5] it was felt that the time had arrived for a great effort—"*the gods,*" we are told,[6] "restored the land to its even balance, as its condition properly required. They established their son, Set-nekht, as king over the whole land." It is probable that we have here a covert indication that the prime instigators of the movement which placed Set-nekht upon the throne were the priests, who, as interpreters of the will of the gods, brought him forward, and succeeded in establishing him as king of all Egypt.

The birth and parentage of Set-nekht, are in reality unknown.[7] It has been stated as an ascertained fact,[8] that he was the son of Seti II.; but the sole foundation for this is the exhibition by Rameses III. of the effigy of Seti II. among the kings whom he honors and acknowledges, in the place immediately before Set-nekht.[9] This foundation is manifestly insufficient. It gives a ground for presuming that Set-nekht was of the family of Seti II.—a presumption supported by the similarity of their throne-names[10] but none for laying down any particular relationship. Had he been actual son, it is scarcely likely that his sonship would not have been mentioned, either by himself, or by Rameses III., who gives us an account of his accession in the "Great Harris Papyrus."

Accepted as king by the priests, Set-nekht had nevertheless to establish his authority by prompt and vigorous measures. His son compares his activity with that of the god, Khepra-Sutech,[11] when he is roused to fury. "He put in order," says Rameses, "the whole land which was revolted: he executed the abominables who were in Ta-Mera (*i. e.* Egypt): he purified the great throne of Egypt: he was king of both the lands at the seat of Tum (Heliopolis?): he made the faces upright which were perverted. . . . He set up the temples, (and re-established) the divine offerings for the service of the gods, as their statutes prescribe."[12]

There is reason to believe that Set-nekht (Fig. 43) was advanced in years at his accession, and that he reigned but a short time. Ordinarily, the first task set himself by an Egyptian king was the construction of his tomb; and a shrewd guess may be given at the length of a reign by noting the extent and elaboration of the royal sepulchre. Set-nekht seems to have felt that he had not sufficient time before him to give him reasonable hope of constructing for himself a final resting-place of proper dignity, and accordingly appropriated to himself the rock-tomb of Siphthah and Taouris, merely chiselling out the names of the original owners, and replacing them by his own.[13] He thus obtained, with slight trouble, a sufficiently dignified sepulchre—one "really princelike and magnificent"[14]—while at the same time he subjected to indignity a predecessor whom he did not acknowledge to be legitimate.

It may have been also in the prospect of an early decease that Set nekht, almost as soon as he was settled upon the throne, associated with himself as king[15] his son Rameses, the third prince of the name, a youth of much promise, of whom he seems to have felt no jealousy. The two are exhibited on the rocks behind Medinet-Abou,[16] in a fashion which seems to place them on an exact equality, bearing the same royal titles and ensigns, having forms of the same size, and mentioned in the accompanying inscription exactly the same number of times. Except inscriptions of his name on the works of others, this is the sole monument which we possess of Set-nekht,[17] who had evidently not inherited the tastes of Rameses II. and Seti I.

Rameses III., known to the Egyptains as Rameses hak On, or "Rameses, lord of Heliopolis," took the throne name of Ra-user-ma-meri-amon, or "Sun, lord of Truth, beloved by Ammon." It is conjectured[18] that among the people he bore the appellation of Rameses pa-nuter, or "Rameses the god;" and that the Greeks made out of this name the Rhampsinitus of their Egyptian histories. Rhampsinitus was celebrated for his riches,[19] and Rameses III. was certainly among the wealthiest of Egyptian kings; so that the identification may be allowed, though it is not one of much value. His earliest occupation after his accession seems to have been "the restoration and demarcation of the several castes,"[20] or rather classes, into which the part of the population directly connected with the court was divided.[21] During the troublous period that preceded Set-nekht some confusion of the different orders had taken place, which Set-nekht had not had the time or the inclination to remedy. Rameses at once addressed himself to the task, and arranged the officials in five great ranks or classes, viz. 1. The *abu-en-perao*, or "councillors of the Royal House," persons who enjoyed the same dignity which was given to Joseph.[22] 2. The *ueru*, or "great princes," who are thought to have been "the governors and representatives of the king in the several nomes."[23] 3. The native soldiery, foot and horse, the latter either identical with, or at any rate including, the chariot force. 4. The foreign mercenaries, chiefly either *Shartana* or *Kahaka;* and 5. The subordinate officers and servants. The native troops are said to have amounted to some hundreds of thousands; but this is probably an exaggeration.

Having completed these arrangements in the manner which he thought most satisfactory, Rameses turned his attention to external affairs, and set himself the task of re-establishing, so far as might be possible, the authority of Egypt over those countries and districts which had passed under the dominion of foreigners during the period of revolution. It is difficult to arrange his wars in their proper chronological order, since Rameses clearly does not follow that order in his own annals,[24] but places the most important wars first. The best modern authorities are at variance upon the subject; and the order here followed, which is that of Dr. Birch, must be regarded as to some extent uncertain.

A war with the Shasu, or Bedouins of Southwestern Arabia, who had again become dominant in the region between Egypt and Palestine, is thought to have had priority over the others.[25] Rameses invaded their country, destroyed the huts or cabins (*mahar*) in which they lived, killed no doubt large numbers, and carried back into Egypt a vast booty, together with numerous prisoners, whom he made over to the priestly establishments at various temples to be employed as slaves.[26] The particular tribe of Shasu attacked in this campaign is called the "Saaru" a name in which Dr. Brugsch recognizes the inhabitants of Mount Seir,[27] or the tract south and southeast of the Dead Sea, once the special country of the Edomites, or descendants of Esau.[28]

Thus successful upon the northeast Rameses was emboldened to make a similiar expedition toward the northwest. Here, on the side of Libya, a serious encroachment had taken place upon Egyptian territory during the time of trouble. The Libyans, Maxyans, Asbystæ,[29] Auseis,[30] and other kindred tribes, had been so daring as to overstep the boundaries of Egypt proper, and to establish themselves along the whole of the left bank of the Nile, from Memphis to the shores of the Mediterranean. They had held possession of this tract for a number of years;[31] and had formed permanent settlements, where they lived with their wives and children, while their herds grazed the rich strip of territory overflowed annu-

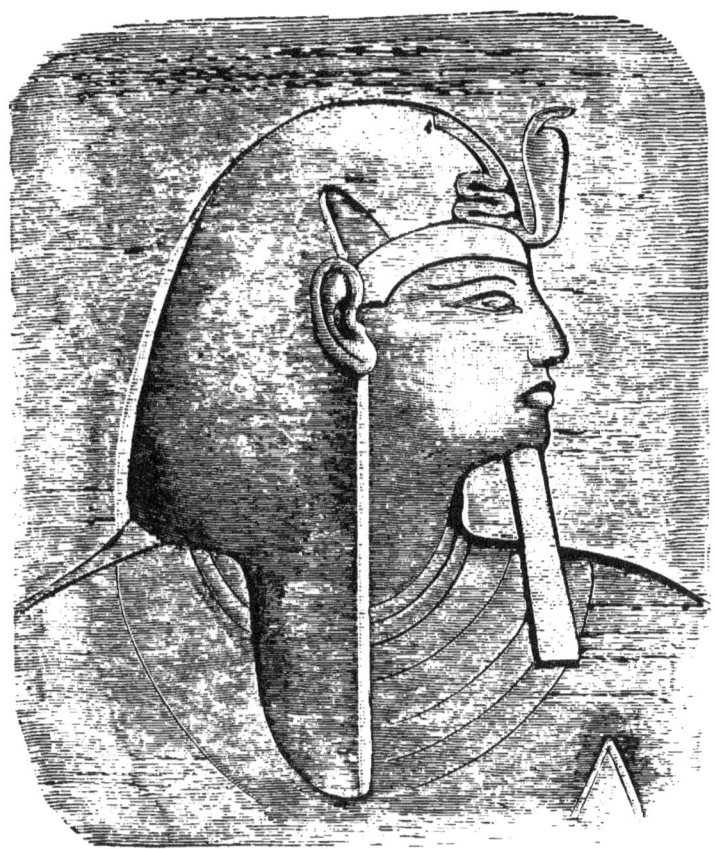

Fig. 46.—HEAD OF RAMESES IX.—See Page 212.

Plate XXII. Vol. II.

Fig. 48.—Head of Her-hor.—See Page 220.

Fig. 47.—Head of Psammetichus I.—See Page 246.

ally, and fertilized, by the inundation. Rameses fell upon them suddenly with a powerful force, and completely defeated them in a single great battle,[32] after which he drove the remnant beyond his borders, making, as he advanced, numerous prisoners, and even capturing the Libyan chief. Of the prisoners taken, some were confined in fortresses; others, after being branded with a red-hot iron,[33] were pressed into the naval service and forced to act as mariners on board the Egyptian fleet. Slavery was the portion of the women and children; the cattle, which were too numerous to count, increased the wealth of the priest-college attached to the great temple of Ammon at Thebes.

The first war with the African nations is fixed by an inscription to the fifth year of Rameses.[34] He would, apparently, have been content with the laurels gained in these two minor campaigns, and would have tempted fortune no further, had he not been forced in self-defence to meet two terrible attacks, which, in his eighth and again in his eleventh year, threatened Egypt with destruction. Few things in history are more extraordinary than the aggressive movements, which suddenly, in the eighth year of Rameses III., spread the flames of war over all the East from the skirts of Taurus to the mouths of the Nile. There is great difficulty in identifying the particular nations which took part in the expedition;[35] but it can scarcely be doubted that a league was formed between a number of widely separated peoples, partly dwellers in Asia Minor, partly inhabitants of the coasts and islands of Europe, and a combined attack organized, at once by land and by sea, having Syria for its immediate and Egypt for its ultimate object. The isles and shores of the Mediterranean gave forth their piratical hordes—the sea was covered with their light galleys, and swept by their strong oars—Tânauna, Sharuten, Sheklusha, Tulsha, Uashesh, combined their squadrons into a fleet, while Purusata and Tekaru advanced in countless numbers along the land. "No people stood before their arms."[36] Bursting forth from the passes of Taurus, the hordes spread themselves over Northern Syria, wasted and plundered the entire country of the Khita, proceeding eastward as far as Carchemish; descended upon Palestine, and were about to press on into Egypt, when they were confronted by Rameses at the head of the Egyptian army. Calling in the aid of stratagem, the Pharaoh, who was probably out-numbered, succeeded by means of an ambush in defeating his assailants, threw their host into confusion, and after an immense slaughter drove the remnant of the broken army from the field. But the struggle was even yet not over. Though the attack by land had failed, the allied fleet gallantly persevered. Quitting their defeated friends, the Tánanua, with their confederates, made sail for the nearest mouth of the Nile, hoping to find it unguarded, and intending in that case to ascend the stream to Memphis, or to ravage far and wide the fertile region of the Delta. But Rameses had made preparations against this peril. He had established a "defence on the water, like a strong wall, of ships of war, of merchantmen, of boats and skiffs;"[37] in other words, he had left a fleet to guard the Pelusiac mouth of the great river, and prevent the Tûnauna from entering it. He also hurried in person to the probable scene of action, and arrived in time to take part in the great battle which frustrated the last hopes of the invaders, and placed Egypt once more in safety. While his naval force contended with the enemy in the shallow waters of the Pelusiac lagoon, he himself with four of his sons and his best warriors lent their aid to complete the discomfiture of the assailants by shooting them down with arrows from the shore.[38] If we rightly read the king's meaning in the vainglorious inscription which he set up to celebrate his victory, the Tánauna were so far successful as to break through the opposing vessels of the Egyptians, and to force their way to the shore. But here their progress was arrested. "A wall of iron shut them in upon the lake." The best troops of Egypt lined the shores of the lagoon; and wherever the invaders attempted to land, they were foiled. Repulsed, dashed to the ground, hewn down at the edge of the water, they were slain "by hundreds of heaps of corpses." After a while resistance ceased, and large numbers were made prisoners. The empty ships, stuck fast in the Nile mud, or floating at random upon the still water, became the prize of the victors, and were found to contain a rich booty. Thus ended this remarkable struggle, in which nations widely severed and of various bloods—scarcely, as one would have thought, known to each other, and separated by a diversity of interests—united in an attack upon the foremost power of the whole world, traversed several hundred miles of land or sea successfully, neither quarrelling among themselves nor meeting with disaster from without, reached the country which they had hoped to conquer, but were then completely defeated and replused in two great engagements— one by land, the other partly by land and partly by sea—so that "their spirit was annihilated, their soul was taken from them."[39] Henceforth no one of the nations which took part in the combined attack is found in arms against the power that had read them so severe a lesson.

It might have been hoped that Egypt, raised in repute by her double victory, would now have been left in peace, and have entered on a prolonged period of repose. But no—this was not to be—her trials were not yet over. Within little more than two years of the events just narrated, another furious attack was made upon her territory by a powerful enemy, seeking, like the Tekaru and Purusata, to effect a permanent lodgment within her borders, and therefore accompanied by their wives and families, their boys, their girls, their slaves, and even their cattle."[40] This time the invaders were the Mashauasha, or Maxyes, who appear to have inhabited the region called Marmarica, or "the Cyrenaica," the only fertile tract interposed between Egypt and the Beylik of Tunis. Already, in the reign of Menephthah, they had made one great attack upon the more western portion of the Delta, and had been defeated with fearful slaughter by that monarch.[41] Subsequently they had adopted a system of gradual encroachment upon Egyptian territory, and had found that system tolerably successful until, in the earlier part of his reign, Rameses III. drove them out. Now, in his eleventh year, probably under pressure from the west, they resolved upon a new invasion, perhaps hoping to find Egypt weakened by the recent contest. Their leaders were Kapur, and his son Mashashal, brave men who imperilled their lives in a well-nigh desperate undertaking. Compared with the Tekaru and Tânauna they were an insignificant enemy; and Rameses easily defeated them in a great battle on the Canopic branch of the Nile, wherein they lost about 2,000 killed, and almost an equal number of prisoners. Kapur was captured in the course of the engagement, and after his capture put to death.[42] Mashashla surrendered to Rameses, with such troops as had survived the fight, unconditionally. It is to be hoped that he received more merciful treatment than his father.

Of the remaining wars of Rameses III. we possess no details. From the representations upon his sculptures there is reason to believe that he conducted at least one campaign in the extreme south, and another in the remote northeast, and that in both his efforts were crowned with all the success that he anticipated. Beyond his southern frontier he attacked and defeated the Ethiopians, together with the negro tribes of the Taraura and the Amar.[43] In Western Asia he seems to have overrun the entire territory between Egypt and the chain of Amanus, carrying off as prisoners thirty-eight chiefs, among whom were those of Carchemish and Aleppo," and forcing the natives generally to resume that position of dependence upon Egypt which had been originally established by the great Thothmes. We are even told [45] that he claims in some of his sculptures supremacy over Naharaïn or Western Mesopotamia, as well as over Punt, Kush, and Cyprus; but it is—to say the least—doubtful whether his dominion really extended over any of these distant regions.

The reign of Rameses III. extended over the long period of thirty-one years,[46] and he had thus ample time, after his defensive wars were concluded, to direct his attention to those material works and interests on which the prosperity of a country, and the fame of its monarch, to a large extent depend. Of all his constructions the most magnificent was the "beautiful" temple of Ammon," which he built at Medinet-Abou opposite Thebes, and which he adorned with painted sculptures commemorative of his great victories. Here are to be seen the series of drawings which represent the grand campaign of his eighth year,[48] exhibiting him as haranguing his troops before setting out, as accompanying them upon the march, as conquering at their head in the great land battle, as hunting the lion, by way of refreshment after his warlike toils, as taking part with his sons in the sea-fight, and as returning in triumph with his numerous captives to Thebes. Here also is the "Treasury," celebrated by Herodotus, on the walls of which are depicted and recorded his riches.[49] Here, further, is the calendar of feasts for the first five months of the Egyptian year,[50] which shows that on the average more than one day in five was held to be sacred. Though less imposing than the vast structures at Luxor and Karnak, the temple of Rameses III. at Medinet-Abou has considerable architectural merit, while its sculptures are executed in "a lifelike and artistic style."[51] It is a work of which even a great monarch might be proud, and not unworthily closes the long list of magnificent temples with which the Rameside kings adorned the cities of Egypt.

Minor shrines were also erected by Rameses III. at Thebes itself to Khonsu, at This to Onuris or Hanher, at Abydos to Osiris, and at Raamses to Sutech.[52] He likewise made an addition to the great temple of Ammon at Karnak; but this building is said to be a "very ordinary piece of architecture, almost worthless in an artistic point of view." [53]

More important than these minor shrines, and far more useful to those who dwelt in its vicinity, was the great reservoir which he constructed in the country of Aina,⁵⁴ by some supposed to have been at Beersheba,⁵⁵ by others near Suez,⁵⁶ which was sunk in the earth to a depth of fifty-two feet, the sides being lined with stone, and the whole basin edged with a quay, and walled in, so that only those who were admitted by the authorities could use the water.

Another work of utility in which this beneficent monarch engaged was the planting of trees. "Over the whole land of Egypt," according to his own account,⁵⁷ "he planted trees and shrubs, to give the inhabitants rest under their cool shade." In a climate like that of Egypt, and a country where indigenous trees are few, no labor could be more serviceable, or more grateful to the mass of his subjects, than that which is here indicated. Rarely do we find despotic monarchs so sympathetic with their people, so thoughtful on their behalf, so anxious to benefit them, as he would seem to have been. It was the crowning satisfaction of his life, that by his domestic administration and his military successes he had brought Egypt into such a condition, that "the weakest woman could travel unmolested whithersoever she wished; the mercenary soldiers might repose at ease in their cities; no enemy invaded the land; the people ate and drank in jubilee, their wives with them, and their children at their side; they did not look behind them (suspiciously); their hearts were content." ⁵⁸

It was perhaps partly in his own interest, but it may have been also with a view to his subjects' advantage that he encouraged mining operations and trade. The turquoise mines of the Sarabit-el-Khadim were once more worked during his reign, and produced abundantly.⁵⁹ A commerce was established with a copper-producing country not previously heard of, called Ataka, and the ore was brought to Egypt in vast quantities, partly on shipboard, partly on the backs of asses.⁶⁰ A fleet was built near Suez and launched upon the Red Sea, which made voyages to the coast of Punt, and there exchanged the productions of "the land of Ham (Khemi)" for the gums and spices, more especially the frankincense, of that remote region.⁶¹ The caravan route from Coptos to Cosseir was reopened, and the riches of the East once more flowed freely into Egypt from the various regions that bordered the Indian Ocean. The general wealth of the country largely increased, and, the revenue rising with the advance in the national prosperity, Rameses was able to make those enormous offerings to the principal temples, which are recorded in the document known as "The Great Harris Papyrus."⁶²

It is with a pardonable pride that Rameses exclaims, toward the close of his long reign: "The land (of Egypt) was well satisfied under my rule—I did well to gods and men also."[63] Having repulsed two foreign invasions, having restored the land's ancient boundaries, having encouraged commerce, having stimulated production, having even provided for his people's comfort by giving them everywhere the pleasant shade of trees, he might well expect to be popular, and to terminate his time on earth, and "join the circle of the gods in heaven,"[64] without suffering from that curse of despotism, conspiracy. But in a corrupt society the best have most to fear; and there is reason to believe that the Egyptian court, since the introduction of polygamy by Rameses II., had become a hotbed of intrigue and vicious sensualism. Eunuchs had in all probability been given the charge of the royal harem,[65] and had brought with them into the palace the trickery and shamelessness for which that unhappy class is noted. Moreover, a belief in magic prevailed; and as in the time of the early Roman Empire,[66] so now men really thought that they could compass the death of one who stood in their way, bewitch his mind, or paralyze his limbs, by the use of figures in wax, and of certain traditional *formulæ*.[67] What the *exact* object of the conspirators was does not appear; but it is certain that the reign of Rameses III. was, ere it closed, disturbed by a conspiracy in which many of the highest court officials and a certain number of the royal concubines were mixed up,[68] and which can scarcely have aimed at anything less than the death or deposition of the monarch. The chief conspirator seems to have been a certain Bakakamen, house-steward, or major-domo of the palace. His position giving him access to all parts of the royal residence, he succeeded in drawing over to his interests a number of councillors, scribes, and commanders of the mercenary troops, as well as certain women of the harem, and among them a lady named Ti or Taia, whom Dr. Brugsch believes to have been a wife of the king.[69] Among the male conspirators was one who professed a knowledge of magical arts, and who not only furnished Bakakamen with formulæ that were supposed to ward off ill-luck, but supplied him also with waxen images, some of men and some of gods, the proper use of which would, it was believed, induce paraylsis.[70] Thus much we learn from our documents—the rest we can only conjecture. Taia had a son engaged in the conspiracy, named Pentaour. Was it the intention of the conspirators to paralyze and then kill the monarch—to proclaim Pentaour as his successor, and make Taia queen-mother? Or did they merely wish to reduce the king to imbecility, and themselves exercise the royal authority in his name? It is remarkable that nothing is said of any intention to seek the king's life ; but there is an Oriental reticence on the subject of death where kings are concerned, which may account or this omission.

After the conspiracy had reached a certain point, but before it had effected anything, by some means or other it was discovered. Too many persons had been taken into counsel for secrecy to be long maintainable; and if the conspirators really trusted to their silly enchantments, they may have delayed imprudently. Anyhow, the plot was found out. Some four-and-thirty persons were immediately arrested; and Rameses appointed a court of twelve high functionaries to try them. It is to his credit that in giving them their commission, he warned them against unfairness toward the accused. "Regarding the discourses which are held about these men," he said, "which are (to me) unknown, you shall *institute an inquiry* about them. They shall be brought to a trial, *to see if they deserve death*. . . . If that which has been done was actually done by them, then let their doings be upon their own heads. I am the guardian and protector forever, and bearer of the royal insignia of justice, in presence of the god-king, Ammon-Ra, and in presence of the Prince of Eternity, Osiris."[11]

We have no account of the proceedings at the trial. The report which the judges made on concluding their investigations is a formal and dry document, giving *seriatim* the names of the prisoners, the exact degree of their participation in the conspiracy, and the sentence which was passed upon them. It appears that thirteen persons, including Bakakamen and Pentaour, were adjudged to have been principals in the conspiracy, while twelve others were condemned as accessories, having been aware of what was going on and given no information to the authorities. No difference, however, was made in the punishment of the two classes. All equally suffered death, the sentence upon them being that they should kill themselves with their own hand. We learn by this that "the happy dispatch," which we have been accustomed to associate especially with one somewhat barbarous kingdom, was an institution of the Egyptians."[12]

Lighter punishments were inflicted on the females who had compromsied themselves, and on some of those who had turned king's evidence, but had failed to make satisfactory depositions. The latter underwent mutilation, having their noses and their ears cut off.[73] The former seem to have been condemned to the penal servitude of keeping a beer-house,[74] which was thought sufficient punishment for ladies of delicacy and refinement.

Finally, it would seem that, while the inquiry was in progress, the complicity in the conspiracy of some of the very persons appointed to conduct the investigation was detected. A brief appendix [75] to the report of the judges states, that five persons, of whom three had been previously mentioned as members of the court, were also adjudged to have been accomplices in the crime, and were sentenced to expiate their guilt by death. With this strange transformation of the judges into the condemned the trial terminated; and Rameses, relieved from the fears and doubts that must have harassed him during its continuance, proceeded to secure the tranquillity of the kingdom in the event of his death by making arrangements for the succession.

The legitimate wife of Rameses III. was a certain Hesi, or Isis, who bore also the foreign name of Hemarozath, and was the daughter of a certain Hebnan-rosanath. It is suggested that she was a Hittite or an Assyrian princess;[76] but the latter supposition, at any rate, is improbable.[77] We are not accurately informed whether she was the mother of any of the king's numerous children; but it is tolerably certain that she was not the mother of all, since they consist of eighteen sons and fourteen daughters.[78] Rameses, it is clear, must have had many secondary wives, each of whom no doubt wished that one of her own children should succeed him. He appears, however to have been swayed by no partiality or favoritism, but to have simply admitted the claims of nature, and given the preference to his first-born. Prince Rameses-Meriammon, hitherto commander of the infantry, was selected by his father from among his numerous sons, and associated with himself upon the throne under the title of Rameses-hakma-meri-Ammon,[79] or "Rameses, Lord of Truth, beloved by Ammon." His other sons were given high military or priestly dignities; and, in course of time, as many as four of them attained to the throne.

In person Rameses III. (Fig. 45) appears to have been much favored by nature. His figure in the sculptures is noble and dignified;[80] his features pleasing, his expression amiable. Something of the feminine look which we observe in so many of the Egyptian monarchs,[81] characterizes the countenance, which is more remarkable for sweetness than for any signs of strength or energy. In his actions, however, the king showed a firmness and a daring which his features belie, and proved himself a worthy descendant of Rameses the second and Sethos the first, of the third Thothmes and the third Amenôphis. Less distinguished certainly than these greatest of Egyptian monarchs, he yet inherited something of their spirit, and in an age when degeneracy had set in, it was his lot to prolong the period of Egyptian greatness, and to revive the glories of a summer-time that was gone by an autumnal burst of brilliant, if short-lived sunshine. It is perhaps true,[2] that, like many an Oriental monarch, he tarnished the glory of his military career, by sensual indulgence within the walls of the palace, and thus laid himself open to those attacks which we find to have been directed against him by the caricaturists of his day. But, if we remember how the great in all ages are pursued by the scurrilous abuse of the mean and the malignant, we shall hesitate to attach serious importance to the "album of caricatures" reflecting upon this monarch,[3] which, after all, may be only an accidental survivor of a class of works similiar to those which in modern Europe load with ridicule each sovereign, or each ministry, successively.

After a reign which exceeded thirty-one years, the third Rameses was gathered to his fathers. He had prepared for himself a tomb of no great pretensions in the rocky mountain opposite Thebes which was at this time the cemetery of the kings. It consisted of the usual long tunnel in the rock, divided into chambers, passages, and halls, and had no peculiar feature, unless it were that of "a range of side-chambers, in which, among other things, all the possessions of the king, such as weapons, household furniture, and the like, were represented in colored pictures, just as they were once actually deposited in the rooms apportioned for them" in the palace."[4] A granite sarcophagus, the lid of which is now to be seen in the Fitzwilliam Museum at Cambridge, was placed in the innermost chamber, and received the royal remains.

With Rameses III. terminated the palmy period of Egyptian greatness and glory, which, commencing with Aahmes, the founder of the eighteenth dynasty, about B.C. 1600, continued for above three centuries, till the death of the son of Set-nekht, about B.C. 1280.[5] It is, of course, readily intelligible that a period of prosperity should be succeeded by one of decline, since the same law which governs individual life seems to have been appointed to rule also the destinies of nations; but it is difficult to understand, and account for, the suddenness and completeness of the collapse in this particular case, where all the vital powers seem at once to have failed, though the failure was not total, and a long and lingering decay preceded the final dissolution. The lack of contemporary monuments, which is one out of many signs of the decline, adds to the difficulty of tracing out the causes which led to it, and must render any attempt at their analysis to a considerable extent speculative and conjectural.

The strength of Egypt had, from the first, consisted in its isolation and its unity. A single homogeneous people was spread along the valley of the Nile from the tower of Syéné to the shores of the Mediterranean. The people was almost without neighbors, since the Nile valley was shut in on either side by arid tracts very sparsely inhabited; the sea bounded it upon the north; the Nubian desert almost cut it off from the south. United by the ties of a common religion, a common language, common ideas and customs, the people was emphatically one, had a strong national sentiment, despised foreigners, and held itself infinitely superior to all the other nations of the earth. For centuries upon centuries the policy of isolation was maintained—the negroes were not allowed to descend the Nile [16] or the Greeks to ascend it [17]— the Soudan and the Sinaitic peninsula were the limit of the Egyptian arms—Europe and Asia were unknown regions to the sons of Ham—foreign manners, foreign ideas, foreign gods were either unheard of or studiously ignored. But with the accession of the eighteenth dynasty all this was changed. The Thothmeses and Amenóphises carried their arms deep into Asia—Hatasu encouraged commerce with Punt—Set and Rameses II. filled Egypt with foreign captives —later monarchs established large corps of foreign mercenaries —the "gilded youth" of the upper circles took to indulging in foreign travel [68]—and, as a natural result, foreign manners crept in—the language was corrupted by a large admixture of Semitic words—the Pantheon was invaded by a host of Semitic or Scythic deities; and the old national exclusive spirit, sapped and weakened by these various influences, decayed and died away.

A second cause of the decline would seem to have been the fact that the Rameside race was exhausted, and that, the longer it continued, the weaker were the princes born of the Rameside stock and so entitled by hereditary descent to rule over Egypt. It is the fatal drawback on the many advantages of "legitimate" monarchy, that a time must arrive when the original vigor of the ruling race, whatever it was, must fail, its powers decline, and its fitness for its position come to an end. "There is a run in families," says Aristotle very acutely;" "after a few generations, transcendent genius develops into madness, while solid parts become stupidity." The Rameside *physique* declines manifestly in the monuments as time goes on, and by the date of Rameses IV. (Fig. 44) has reached a point beyond which there could scarcely be much deterioration.

One further ground of internal weakness, and therefore cause of decline, is to be found in an essential feature of the Egyptian political system, whereby a considerable but indefinite power was lodged in the hands of the priests. A hieratic system may no doubt be as long-lived as any other; but a system that is half hieratic, half monarchical, carries within it the seeds of its own destruction, and contains an element of weakness from which a thorough-going despotism is free. A time was sure to arrive, earlier or later, in Egypt, when the *pontificale* and the *regale* would come more or less into collision, when the kings, growing jealous of the priests, would seek to curtail their power at the risk of internal revolution, or the priests, losing respect for the king, would stealthily creep into their places. The actual march of events in Egypt was in the latter direction. The hieratic chiefs, the high-priests of the god Ammon at Thebes, gradually increaed in power, usurped one after another the prerogatives of the Pharaohs, by degrees reduced their authority to a shadow, and ended with an open assumption not only of the functions, but of the very insignia of royalty."[60]

A space of nearly two centuries elapsed, however, before this change was complete. Ten princes of the name of Rameses, and one called Meri-Tum, all of them connected by blood with the great Rameside house, bore the royal title and occupied the royal palace, in the space between B.C. 1280 and B.C. 1100. Egyptian history during this period is almost wholly a blank. No military expeditions are conducted—no great buildings are reared—art almost disappears—literature holds her tongue. If at any time the silence is broken, if the stones occasionally lift up their voice and speak, it is either in dry utterance of old and well-worn official phrases and *formulæ*, or in audacious plagiarisms from the compositions of an earlier age. The writers of the twelfth and thirteenth centuries, aware that they are destitute of originality, contentedly reproduce, with slight changes, the masterpieces of the fourteenth and fifteenth."[61]

The immediate successor of Rameses III. was his eldest son, Rameses IV., who bore the throne names of Hak-ma and Ma-ma.⁹² Nothing is known of him excepting that he worked with great vigor the quarries of the valley of Hammamât ⁹³ and the adjoining rocky and sterile regions, which produced many excellent varieties of hard stone. What use he made of these materials it is impossible to say, since neither any one great edifice, nor any large number of small ones, bear his name. He set up some magnificent sculptures in the great temple of Ammon at Karnak,⁹⁴ and made some small additions to his father's temple of Khonsu at Thebes; but beyond these, and some rocky-inscriptions in the Hammamât region, no monuments of his reign have been identified.⁹⁵ It appears by the Hammamât inscriptions that he held the throne for at least eighteen years, and we may conjecturally assign him the space between B.C. 1280 and B.C. 1260.

The successor of Rameses IV. was neither his son nor his brother, nor even perhaps a member of the Rameside family. He took the quite new throne-name of Ammon-hi-khopeshef, but also called himself Rameses, and is known as Rameses V.⁹⁶ Some suppose him to have been a descendant of Siphthah;⁹⁷ but this is wholly uncertain. His only records are his tomb in the Biban-el-Moluk, afterwards appropriated by his successor, Rameses VI., and a single inscription at Silsilis, couched in inflated terms, which represents all Egypt as enraptured at his coronation, and the country as flourishing under his rule.⁹⁸ It is certain that no dependence can be placed on such self-laudation, and not impro'able that it covers an uneasy feeling, on the part of the monarch who has recourse to it, that his rule is the reverse of popular.

On the death of the usurper the throne was regained by the Rameside family, and occupied (it is thought) by two princes, sons of Rameses III., who ruled conjointly.⁹⁹ These were Rameses, his second, and Meri-Tum, his seventh son, who bore the office of high-priest of Ra in Heliopolis. It is suggested that while Rameses VI. reigned in Thebes and bore sway over the Upper Country, his younger brother held his court at the City of the Sun, and ruled over the Delta. In the tomb which the elder prince appropriated from his usurping predecessor, an astronomical ceiling is thought to furnish the date of B.C. 1240 for the time of its ornamentation,¹⁰⁰ so that that year may be regarded as included in the sixth Rameses's reign. No historical events can be ascribed to it, but we have evidence that the Egyptian dominion still extended over the distant South, where a "Prince of Kush" still ruled as the Pharaoh's viceroy, with Adons of the various districts under him, and the Pharaoh's suzerainty was marked by the erection of statues in his honor, and the settlement upon them in perpetuity of landed estates.[101]

Conjointly with these two princes, or after their decease, two other sons of Rameses II. assumed the royal title, and are ranked as Pharaohs under the names of Rameses VII. and Rameses VIII. The latter bore the throne name of Set-hi-khopeshef,[102] which would seem to indicate that he was a votary of Sutech, whose worship was, it is clear, always held in respect by the Rameside monarchs. Nothing is recorded of Rameses VII. and VIII. beyond their names. We may perhaps assign them, conjecturally, the space between B.C. 1230 and B.C. 1220.

With Rameses IX. we bid adieu to the immediate issue of Rameses III., and descend, at least a generation, to a grandson or great-grandson of the last warlike monarch. This king took the throne name of Neferkara-sotep-en-ra,[103] and held the throne for at least nineteen years,[104] thus bringing us nearly to the close of the thirteenth century. His reign is remarkable for two novel circumstances. One of these was the trial of a number of sacrilegious malefactors, who had invaded the sanctity of the royal burial-places, plundered the royal mummies of their golden ornaments, burnt the coffins, and thrown the corpses on the ground. Kings and queens had alike suffered: Antefs of the eleventh dynasty, Sabak-adorers of the thirteenth, a queen Isis, a Ra-Sekenen, and even an Amenôphis, the first of the name.[105] All belief in the "divinity that hedged a king," according to the Egyptian religious system, must have passed away when a "thieves' society was formed for the special purpose of secretly opening and robbing the tombs of the kings, in which even sacerdotal persons took a part."[106] We may perhaps trace in the proceedings a concealed purpose of bringing royalty into contempt; we cannot be mistaken in gathering from them a weakening of the old superstition which viewed the kings as gods. As yet, however, the new ideas had the general public sentiment against them. Opinion was greatly shocked by the disclosures made, and officials of the highest rank were nominated to form a court of inquiry which should investigate the business, and inflict condign punishment upon the guilty. Amen-hotep, the high-priest of the Great Temple of Ammon at Thebes, the chief of the Egyptian hierarchy, presided over the court, and, after acquitting a certain number of the accused, not perhaps the least guilty, condemned eight persons as the real culprits, who were either bastinadoed, or else put to death.[107]

The other novelty, which documents of the time put before us, is the new position, relatively to the king, that the high-priest of the Theban Ammon seems now to begin to occupy. An acute observer, familiar with all the monumental evidence, makes indeed the remark, that *"from the time of Rameses III.*, the holy fathers, who bore the exalted dignity of chief priest in the temple-city of Ammon, were always coming more and more into the foreground of Egyptian history. Their influence with the kings assumed, step by step, a growing importance."[108] But even he does not note any tangible change until the reign of Rameses IX. (Fig. 46), when for the first time the high-priest of Ammon at Thebes steps forward as the great guardian, protector, and restorer of his shrine, and, "whereas formerly it was the priests who expressed in the name of the gods their thanks to the kings for the temple-buildings at Thebes," now this is reversed, and "it is the king who testifies his gratitude to the chief priest of Ammon for the care bestowed on his temple by the erection of new buildings and the improvement and maintenance of the older ones."[109] The office of high-priest has become hereditary, and in the tenth year of Rameses-neferkara-sotepenra, Amen-hotep, who has recently succeeded his father, Ramessu-nekht, who appears on the walls of the temple as the first person in a scene where the king has simply to assign him his reward, and to see it conferred upon him by his great dignitaries.[110] A titular superiority still attaches to the Pharaoh, who is "the fountain of honor" and whom Amen-hotep frequently acknowledges to be "his lord;" but practically there can be no doubt that Amen-hotep plays the principal part. He is "the teacher of the king;" he has "found the holy house of Ammon hastening to decay, and has taken in hand its restoration ;" he has "strengthened its walls," has "built it anew," has "made its columns," has "inserted in the gates the great folding doors of acacia-wood."[111] The high-priest is the active mover in the whole business; the king is passive; he looks on, "sees and admires what is done;" approves it, and rewards it. But the initiative has passed into the hands of his nominal subjects; and it is easy to see that ere long there will be a division of the royal authority, and the Pharaoh will possess its shadow, the high-priest its substance.

Still the royal authority in Egypt died hard, and, as we shall find soon revived. The reign of Rameses IX. brings us, as we have seen,[112] to the close of the thirteenth century. It is not until the opening of the eleventh that we find the high-priests of Ammon completely established in the position of actual rulers of the country. An entire century thus passed between the first beginning of serious encroachment upon the Pharaoh's position and the transfer of their authority to the priests of Ammon. During this century four other kings, bearing the name of Rameses, and distinguished by special epithets, seem to have occupied the throne—viz., Rameses X., bearing the further names of Khepr-ma-ra Sotep-en-ra, ⭕👤🐝⭕〰️, and Ammon-hi-khopeshef;[113] Rameses XI., known as Sesha-en-ra[114] Meriammon 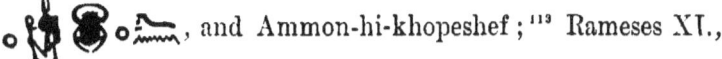; Rameses XII., called User-ma-ra[115] Sotep-en-ra; and Rameses XIII.[116] The twelfth Rameses reigned at least thirty-three years,[117] and the thirteen at least twenty-six years,[118] thus holding the throne, between them, for considerably more than half a century. Their predecessors may have been almost as long-lived; and the four reigns may well have occupied the space between B.C. 1200 and B.C. 1100.

One event only can be assigned to this obscure period. An inscription set up in the temple of Khonsu, founded at Thebes by Rameses III., relates a tale which must undoubtedly have had an historical foundation, though its details may have received much amplification and embellishment. The document belongs to the time of Rameses XII. It relates[119] that, once upon a time, when this prince was in the land of Nehar,[120] collecting the revenues or tributes that were willingly rendered to him annually by the territorial chiefs of those parts, one of them, called the chief of Bakhtan, placed his daughter among the tribute-bearers, and thus drew the king's attention to her beauty, which was so great that he immediately made her his wife, and advanced her to the first rank in his harem. Some time after this, Rameses XII. was in Thebes, performing his religious duties in the great temple of Ammon, when an extraordinary embassy from his father-in-law sought his presence, and requested that the Egyptian monarch would send the best-skilled man of his court to recover the queen's sister, Bentaresh, who was struck down by a sudden sickness. Rameses complied. The man supposed to be most skilful, the scribe, Thoth-em-hebi, was selected, and sent back with the envoys to Bakhtan, with orders to place all the knowledge that he possessed at the disposal of the chief of the country. We are told that, on his arrival, he pronounced the case of Bentaresh to be one of possession by an evil spirit,[121] but that after various attempts he was forced to acknowledge himself unable to cope with the demon. Upon this it would seem that he returned to Egypt, and the chief of Bakhtan sought assistance elsewhere. But eleven years later[122] he once more had recourse to his son-in-law. This time his envoy requested that the god Khonsu, the expeller of evil spirits, might be sent from Thebes to Bakhtan[123] for the relief of the possessed princess. Rameses hesitated, but after consulting the oracular shrine of Khonsu in the Theban temple, and receiving a favorable reply, he dispatched the image of Khonsu in a sacred ark, borne on the shoulders of ten priests,[124] and escorted by a troop of cavalry, from Thebes to Bakhtan, in order that a second attempt might be made to cure the princess. After a journey which lasted seventeen months,[125] the ark arrived, was joyfully received by the afflicted prince, and brought into the presence of his daughter, from whom it at once expelled the demon. Great joy now prevailed in Bakhtan; for the spirit departed,[126] and the recovery of the princess was complete. It might have been expected that the ark which had wrought the cure would have been immediately restored to its Egyptian owners with grateful thanks for the loan of it; but the power shown seemed to the prince of Bakhtan so valuable that he was loth to lose possession of so great a treasure. Accordingly he resolved to retain the ark in his own capital, and actually had it in his keeping for three years and nine months,[127] at the end of which time he was induced to relinquish it under the following circumstances. He dreamed that he saw the god Khonsu, in the shape of a golden sparrowhawk, quit the ark, and fly away in the direction of Egypt. Waking up in a state of great agitation,[128] he summoned the priest attached to the ark, and, declaring to him what he had seen, announced his determination to send the holy structure back, and desired him to make the needful preparations. The return journey seems to have taken even a longer time than the journey from Egypt; for it was not until the thirty-third year of Rameses[129] that the ark of Khonsu was once more safely replaced in its proper chapel in the temple at Thebes.

The interest of this narrative is considerable and of a varied character. If we accept the identification of "Nehar" with Naharaïn, we shall have to regard it as indicating the retention to so late a date as about B.C. 1130 of Egyptian supremacy over Mesopotamia;[130] and we must ask ourselves, Who is this king of Bakhtan who dwells at such a remote distance from Egypt, yet regards himself as in some sort an Egyptian tributary, and where is this Bakhtan, not elsewhere mentioned in the Egyptian records, yet apparently a place of considerable consequence? Bagistan (now Behistun) and Ecbatana (now Hamadan) have been suggested ;[131] but these seem too remote, and the latest historian thinks that a town of no great importance in Syria, called elsewhere Bakh or Bakhi, may be intended.[132] Some have gone so far as to suppose that the "prince of Bakhtan" who detained the ark was Tiglath-Pileser I., the first great Assyrian conqueror[133] (about B.C. 1130–1110); but, besides the want of correspondence between the names "Bakhtan" and "Asshur,"[134] the entire position of the prince of Bakhtan in relation to Egypt is one which we cannot conceive Tiglath-Pileser occupying. Tiglath-Pileser was an independent and warlike monarch who bore sway (about the close of the twelfth century B.C.) over the entire tract between Babylonia on the one hand and Phœnicia on the other. He perhaps on one occasion made Egypt pay him tribute,[135] and it is incredible that he should, a little time before or a little time after, have paid tribute himself to Egypt, and sent his daughter to be a secondary wife of the Egpytian monarch. The greatness of Assyria began about B.C. 1300; and it is unlikely that Egypt maintained her Mesopotamian conquests much beyond that date. We have already noted the decline of the Egyptian power in this quarter,[136] and the improbability that even Rameses III. possessed any real authority in the countries east of the Euphrates. Supposing that he did, his weak successors must almost certainly have lost it. Chushan-Risathaim, who was independent king of Mesopotamia within a century of the Exodus,[137] must have been long anterior to Rameses XII., and Egyptian rule, even over Syria, must have been lost before he could conquer Palestine. We incline therefore to believe that "Nehar" in the tablet of Rameses XII. is not Naharain; that Bakhtan is not a country very remote from Egypt; and that the long time spent upon the road by the envoys who carried the ark was owing to the difficulty of conveying so large and unsteady a structure on the shoulders of a few priests along the rough tracks of the country.

The Rameses who closes the long list, and is reckoned the last king of the twentieth dynasty, was Rameses XIII., who, as if an exuberant amount of titles could make up for a deficiency in power, called himself Men-ma-ra, Sotep-en-ptah, Shaemnas, Meri-ammon, Ramessu, Neter-hak-on.[138] His principal monuments are found in the temple of Khonsu at

Thebes, which he appears to have delighted in ornamenting.[139] The other indications of his reign are scattered and fragmentary;[140] they scarcely contain a single notice of historic interest. By one of them, however, we learn that, weak and insignificant as he was, Rameses XIII. held the throne of Egypt for above twenty-six years.

The decline of Egypt under this dynasty was not merely a decline in power. Architecture, glyptic art, literature, morals—all suffered, and suffered almost equally. After the death of Rameses III. not a single great building was set on foot by any of the Egyptian kings, much less was any architectural novelty attempted. The monarchs contented themselves with making small additions to old edifices, having no pretension to originality, and inferior in every respect to the buildings whereto they were appendages. The grand features of ancient times were not even imitated. No more hypostyle halls, like those at Luxor and Karnak—no more gigantic colossi—no more mighty obelisks. The greatest works which the kings undertook were their tombs. These were still "hypogees," or subterraneous galleries excavated in the rock, and divided into a number of halls, passages, and chambers. They still attained a considerable length, and were ornamented with interesting paintings. But neither in the size nor in the finish of their ornamentation did they rival the similar works of former days—such as the tombs of Amenôphis III., of Seti I. and Rameses II. They ceased to have any architectural features, such as columns, or piers, or chambers with arched roofs.[141] Even the paintings were, on the whole, less interesting than those of an earlier age.

In glyptic art, connoisseurs detect a falling off as early as the latter part of the reign of Rameses II.;[142] but the decline is not palpable until the reign of Rameses III. is past. Then the "grand style" disappears. The great compositions, covering entire pylons, and comprising hundreds of figures, come to an end—no new scenes are portrayed—rather, a wearisome sameness, a repetition *usque ad nauseam* of the same stereotyped religious groups, meets us and disgusts us. If there is any change, it is in the grossness of the religious representations, which increases.[143] Again, the range of art is narrower. Domestic and military scenes almost drop out; but few animals are depicted; we have no banquets, no gardens, no fishing, no fowling, no games. And the drawing certainly deteriorates; there is a feebleness and clumsiness in the outlines, a rigidity in the forms, as well as a want of variety, which are unpleasing.

Statuary also falls off. The figures become unduly elongated, and are finished with less care.[144] They have no longer the truth to nature which is possessed by the earlier statues, while they are certainly in no respect idealized. Moreover, unless we include statuettes, they become, comparatively speaking, rare, as if they had gone out of fashion, and were no longer demanded from the artists.

The decline of literature is even greater and more surprising. After the galaxy of talent which clustered about the reigns of Rameses II. and Menephthah,[145] after the masterpieces of Pentaour, Kakabu, Nebsenen, Enna, and others, suddenly there comes a time when literature is almost dumb, when "the true poetic inspiration appears to have vanished, and the dry official tone to have taken its place"[146]—when abstracts of trials,[147] lists of functionaries,[148] tiresome enumerations in the greatest detail of gifts to the gods,[149] together with fulsome praises of the kings, either by themselves or others,[150] form the substance of the written compositions which survive, and which we have every reason to believe a fair sample of the literary produce of the age. Not a single name of an Egyptian writer belonging to this dreary period remains on record; not a single work of imagination can be ascribed to it. Astronomy may ultimately owe something to the tables of the hours and of the risings of the stars which decorate the tomb of the sixth Rameses in the Biban-el-Moluk;[151] but literature, in the proper sense of the word, can never receive any enrichment from the curt and dry records, the legal *formulæ*, the endowment deeds,[152] the royal orders,[153] or the religious mysticism,[154] which constitute the whole that remains to us of Egyptian literature during the twelfth and thirteenth centuries.

In morals, the decline had begun under Rameses II., with the introduction of polygamy. It advanced under Rameses III. (Fig. 36), when the court became a hotbed of intrigue and conspiracy, the highest officials combining with the women of the harem to seek the life of the king, or reduce him to an imbecile condition, by magical arts,[155] enchantments, and "all sorts of villainy."[156] The grossest license appears in the caricatures of the time, which assume that the king is a voluptuary, and satirize his weakness with a shameless disregard of decency.[157] Not long afterwards sacrilege becomes fashionable, and a "thieves' society" is formed, containing several members of the sacerdotal order, for the purpose of opening and plundering the ancient tombs, without even sparing those of royal personages.[158] Inquiry on the subject is baffled for a considerable period, probably through the high position of some of those engaged in the transactions.[159] These transactions included the grossest ill-usage of the dead bodies, which Egyptian notions made almost the extreme of wickedness. When at last punishment overtakes some of the offenders, it is inadequate, the greater number of the condemned merely suffering the bastinado.

Civilization and the arts of life reached perhaps their highest development under Rameses III. It is then that we find the most luxurious fauteuils and ottomans,[160] the richest dresses, the most gorgeous river-boats,[161] the most elaborately carved musical instruments.[162] After his time, Egypt became, comparatively speaking, poor; and, while the general mode of life continued much the same as before, there was a falling off in grandeur and magnificence. Dresses (Fig. 63) became somewhat more complicated,[163] but less splendid. Anklets were no longer worn, earrings became rare, and bracelets ceased to be jewelled. On the other hand, the wigs of men and the hair of women (if it is indeed their own) were worn longer, and arranged more elaborately.[164] The absurd fashion still continued of turning up the toes of sandals to a height of two or three inches. Monkeys continued to be kept as pets;[165] the lotus blossom was still the usual adornment of the head for ladies at feasts, and lotus collars were still placed round the necks of guests. Music appears in the sculptures rather as an accompaniment of sacred ceremonies than as a means of amusing and entertaining company.[166] The domestic scenes of the period are, however, so few, that we cannot pretend to anything like a full knowledge of Egyptian private life at the time; and, on the whole, it is perhaps most probable that (in the main) it retained under the twentieth dynasty the general character which it had acquired under the great kings of the eighteenth and nineteenth.

CHAPTER XXIII.

THE TWENTY-FIRST DYNASTY (ABOUT B.C. 1100-975).

Accession of Her-hor, the first Priest King. Chief Features of his Reign. His Semitic Connection. His Titles, Personal Appearance, and Character. Doubtful Reign of Piankh. Reign of Pinetem. His Son, Men-khepr-ra, re-establishes Tranquillity at Thebes. Uneventful Reign of Men-khepr-ra. Later Kings of the Dynasty. General Prevalence of Peace and Prosperity. Duration of the Dynasty.

"Les grands prêtres d'Ammon à Thèbes se mettent á jouer le même rôle que plus tard les maires du palais sous nos derniers rois mérovingiens."—LENORMANT, *Manuel d'Histoire Ancienne*, vol. i, p. 446.

THE bold priest, who, biding his time, by cautious steps advanced himself into the rank and position of "King of Upper and Lower Egypt," bore the name of Pe-hor or Herhor, According to Manetho,[1] he was a native of Tanis, one of the chief cities of the Delta, the favorite residence of the Hyksos or Shepherd Kings.[2] How he became high-priest of Ammon at Thebes is not clear, since that office seems ere this to have been hereditary;[3] but, having once attained that position, he speedily conciliated to himself the favor of the reigning monarch, Rameses XIII., and received from him the additional titles and offices of "chief (*uer*) of Upper and Lower Egypt," "royal son of Kush," "fanbearer on the right hand of the king," "chief architect," and "administrator of the granaries."[4] Having thus managed to get all the most important offices of the government into his own hands, he succeeded, probably at the death of the king without issue,[5] in quietly stepping into his place. No doubt, his position as head of the priestly order secured him important support in every city of the empire; but had not the Egyptians generally, and the military class in particular, been weakened and demoralized by their long abstention from war under the last ten Rameside kings, he would scarcely have settled himself upon the throne without a struggle. Of this, however, there is not the slightest trace. Her-hor appears to have been troubled by no internal disturbances. He adorned Thebes with sculptures,[6] led the forces of Egypt beyond the frontier to the more distant portion of Syria,[7] obtained military successes, and left his crown to his son or his grandson, who succeeded to his authority without difficulty.

It is thought that Her-hor, in order to strengthen his power, allied himself with a foreign monarch. The names of his wife, Netem, and of his children,⁸ are non-Egyptian, and have been pronounced Semitic,"⁹ but perhaps with scarcely sufficient evidence. The positive statement that "he allied himself closely with one of the kings of Nineveh, in whose friendship he sought a support to his usurpation,"¹⁰ is one of those bold assertions in which modern historiographers indulge because it is impossible absolutely to refute them. The assertion is simply without one atom of foundation. There were plenty of Semites within the limits of Egypt, with whom Her-hor might intermarry if he so pleased, and the population of Syria was in the main Semitic, so that he had no need to go to the distant Assyria for a Semitic wife. Netem, his consort, is never said to have been of royal birth. She is the *sutem hemt eur*, or "great royal consort," but not *suten sat*, "king's daughter" or "princess." Moreover, neither the name of his wife, Netem, nor the names of any of his sons,¹¹ are definitely Assyrian. Her-hor was probably married, long before he ascended the throne, to one of those Semitic Egyptians who abounded in the northeastern provinces,¹² and allowed his wife to give her children Semitic names, such as were common in those regions.

It is remarkable that, on assuming the royal title, he did not at first lay aside the designation of "high-priest of Ammon," but bore that descriptive epithet regularly in one of his royal scutcheons,¹³ while in the other he took the title of

Si-Ammon, ▭, or "son of Ammon," which was subsequently claimed and borne by Alexander. Later, he called himself Si-Ammon only.¹⁴ It would seem that when he relinquished the priesthood for himself, he devolved it upon his

eldest son, Piankh, ▭, thus securing its continued

connection with the crown, and stamping his dynasty with a permanent hieratic character.

The personal appearance of Her-hor (Fig. 48) was pleasing. In the sculptures his features are delicate and good; his expression mild and agreeable.¹⁵ Though he claims to have reconquered the Ruten, we cannot suppose him to have been much of a warrior; and he certainly did not revive the glories of the empire to any considerable extent, or re-inspire the Egyptians with military ardor. On the whole, he would seem to have been a mild prince, not much more energetic than his Rameside predecessors; and we may suspect that he took the bold step of usurping the crown, rather at the prompting of his order than inspired by any personal ambition.

It is uncertain whether Her-hor's son, Piankh, or his grandson, Pinetem, was his successor. Bunsen and Brugsch accord to Piankh the title of king;[16] but it is admitted that he has neither the cartouche surrounding his name, nor the royal title affixed to it, in any of the monuments. The monuments are so scanty,[17] that the negative argument is perhaps not of very much weight; and it is just possible that Piankh, the son of Her-hor, succeeded his father, and held the crown for a few years before the accession of Pinetem.

Pinetem, the grandson of Her-hor and son of Piankh, whose name is expressed in the hieroglyphics by  took to wife a princess of the Rameside house named Ramaka or Rakama,[18] and so strengthened his title to the crown, which is thought to have been disputed by the male descendants of the old Rameside stock, who had been banished with their partisans to the lesser Oasis. Pinetem had fixed his court at Tanis in the Delta,[19] the native place of his grandfather, and had probably thereby offended the Thebans, who, to vent their spleen, took the part of the Rameside pretender. Hereupon Pinetem, in the twenty-fifth year of his reign, despatched his son Ra - men - khepr, or Men - khepr-ra, on whom he had devolved the office of high-priest of Ammon, to the southern capital, to persuade or coerce the disaffected.[20] After punishing a certain number, he appears to have received the submission of the rest, but at the same time to have accepted their view, that clemency rather severity was the proper course to be pursued towards the rebels, and that the first step necessary to be taken was the recall of the exiles from the Oasis. These are said, in the hyperbolical language of the East, to have amounted to a hundred thousand; and though this is no doubt an exaggeration, it is one which implies that they must have been in reality very numerous, and that the internal troubles, to which the usurpation of the high-priests had led, must have become ultimately of a very serious character indeed. Men-khepr-ra, as Pinetem's representative, allowed the exiles to return, and pledged his word that the practice of banishment for political offences should be discontinued. After this we do not hear of any more disturbances, and we may conclude that the policy of conciliation was successful.

Men-khepr-ra must, soon afterwards, have become king. His name occurs, enclosed in the royal cartouche, on bricks brought from the city of Kheb in the Heptanomis,[21] on which we find almost the name of his wife, Hesi-em-kheb;[22] but we cannot ascribe any events to the period during which he occupied the throne. The supposition of a great Assyrian attack upon Egypt under a king, Sheshonk, and his son Nimrud, which has the authority of one important name in its favor,[23] is not generally accepted, and seems to lack evidence.

Other eventless reigns belonging to the dynasty[24] are those of Pa-seb-en-sha, [hieroglyph], Pinetem II., and Hor-Pasebensha, [hieroglyph]. It is generally agreed that these kings belonged to the same family with those already enumerated, but their exact relationship one to another and even the order of their succession are uncertain. Egyptian history is a blank during this space. We only know that friendly relations were established during the course of it between Egypt and Palestine, where an important kingdom had been set up by David and inherited by Solomon; that a monarch of the Tanite line consented to give one of his daughters in marriage to the latter prince;[25] and that, under these amicable relations of the two powers, a brisk trade was carried on for horses and chariots between the Egyptians on the one hand and the Syrians and Hittites on the other.[26] Egypt was at the same time, as no doubt it was always, open as an asylum to the political fugitive; and the Hadad, prince of Edom, who fled from David, found a refuge with some monarch of the Tanate dynasty,[27] just as Jeroboam, at a later date, found a refuge with Shihsak.[28] The country was quiet, without disturbance from within or menace from abroad; the kings were peaceful, never forgetting that they were priests as well as sovereigns; the people were satisfied to apply themselves generally to useful trades and productive employments; they were no longer assailed either from the west or from the north, since the Libyans had been taught a lesson, and the "war of Troy" had changed the condition of the powers of the Mediterranean; they were safe upon the side of the east, since they had a bulwark in the new empire raised up by tne kings of Israel; and on the side of the south the Ethiopians as yet gave no sign. Cloud and tempest were gathering, and would burst in fury upon the land at a not very distant future; but as yet the atmosphere was serene—thunder did not even mutter in the distance—the calm prevailed which is generally thought to a portend storm.

The duration of the dynasty is calculated by Manetho[20] at 130 years; and, having regard to the synchronism between Sheshonk and Solomon, we may assign it, without much chance of serious error, the space between B.C. 1100 and B.C. 975.

CHAPTER XXIV.

THE TWENTY-SECOND AND CONTEMPORARY DYNASTIES (ABOUT B.C. 975-750).

The Twenty-second Dynasty not Assyrian, but Bubastite. Ancestors of Sheshonk I. —his Royal Descent—his Marriage with a Tanite Princess. ' His reception of Jeroboam—his great Expedition into Palestine—his Arabian Conquests. His Bas-reliefs and Buildings. His two sons—Death of the elder, and Accession of Osarkon I. Peaceful Reign of Osarkon. Reigns of Takelut I. and Osarkon II. Expedition of "Zerah the Ethiopian." Reigns of Sheshonk II., Takelut II., Sheshonk III., and Sheshonk IV. Other Contemporary Kings. Rise of Piankhi. Disappearance of Art and Literature under the Sheshonks.

"If the history of the twenty-first dynasty is obscure, that of the twenty-second, or Bubastite dynasty, as it has been called, is not less difficult."—BIRCH, *Egypt from the Earliest Times*, p. 135.

WE are asked to see in the establishment of the twenty-second dynasty the effect of the absolute conquest of Egypt by the Assyrians,[1] which resulted in the establishment of a junior branch of the Assyrian royal family upon the Egyptian throne, and the subjection of the country for nearly two centuries to a foreign yoke. But a large number of important considerations oppose themselves to the reception of this novel theory, which has not, so far as we are aware, been accepted by any Egyptologist of repute, except its propounder. In the first place, the Assyrians appear to have been at the time in question exceptionally weak;[2] and whereas, rather more than a century earlier (B.C. 1100), they carried their victorious arms across the Euphrates into Northern Syria,[3] and a century later (B.C. 875) reduced the Phœnician towns to subjection,[4] in the interval—from B.C. 1100 to B.C. 900— they were in a depressed and debilitated condition, quite incapable of making extensive foreign conquests. Secondly, it is certain that the Egyptians neither speak with any distinctness of any foreign attack upon their independence at this time, nor use the term "Assyrian"—with which they were well acquainted[5]—in any connection with the kings of this dynasty. The term used in such connection, and supposed to designate "Assyria," is *Mat*,[6] which may perhaps mean "the peoples," but which has no more connection with the word Assyria than with Palestine, or Babylon, or Persia. Further, the new names which now come into Egyptian history, and which are thought to support the Assyrian theory, are decidedly non-Assyrian, and, so far as is known, were never borne by any Assyrian person.[7]

Manetho, who, living under the Ptolemies, had no false shame leading him to conceal the subjection of Egypt by her neighbors—who called the seventeenth dynasty Phœnician or Arabian,[8] the twenty-fifth Ethiopian,[9] and the twenty-seventh Persian[10]—declared the twenty-second to be Bubastite,[11] and therefore native Egyptian. His statement is confirmed by the fact, that two of the kings[13] called themselves *Si-Bast*, or "Son of Bast;" the goddess from whom Bubastis took its name, and who was especially worshipped there. It appears[13] that a certain Sheshonk (Fig. 50), a Bubastite contemporary with one of the later kings of the twenty-first dynasty, took to wife a princess of the Tanite House,[14] named Meht-en-hont or Meht-en-usekh,[15] and had by her a son, Namrut, who became the father of a second Sheshonk . This second Sheshonk, having royal blood in his veins, was selected by a later Tanite king as a fitting husband for his daughter, Keramat, , and was thus led to raise his thoughts to the crown. Whether he usurped it, or succeeded, in right of his wife, on the failure of heirs male in the Tanite line,[16] is doubtful; but perhaps it is not probable that he was regarded as the rightful heir. Shortly after his accession, he took the throne-name of Hut-khepr-ra-sotep-en-ra, and bore this name in his second shield on most occasions."

It was probably not long after his accession that he received a fugitive of importance from the neighboring country of Palestine, where Solomon still occupied the throne of his father David. This was Jeroboam, the son of Nebat, an officer who had held high employment under Solomon,[18] but had become an object of suspicion because it had been prophesied that he would one day be king of ten out of the twelve tribes of Israel. To prevent the accomplishment of this prophecy, Solomon wished to put Jeroboam to death ;[19] he, however, contrived to effect his escape, and became a refugee at the court of Sheshonk, where, according to tradition,[20] he was well treated. When Solomon died some time after, Jeroboam returned to his native land; and the prophecy of Ahijah was fulfilled under the circumstances related in the First Book of Kings.[21] The Israelites elected Jeroboam to be their sovereign; but he propably felt his tenure to be insecure, and consequently made representations to Sheshonk which caused that monarch to undertake an important military expedition. The Egyptians had for several centuries known nothing of war ; but a number of mercenary soldiers had been maintained as a sort of police, and there was thus a standing army of a certain amount, consisting mainly of the Libyans of the west and the negroes and Ethiopians of the south, which preserved internal order, guarded the frontiers, and might be employed, if need were, beyond them. Sheshonk, a new king of a new dynasty, might be anxious, like Her-hor when he attacked the Ruten,[22] to impress the nation favorably by the display of energy and military daring. If he could count on the friendship of Jeroboam, he would be exposing himself to little danger, and he might gather laurels, such as had been unheard of for above a century, without any risk of a reverse. Accordingly he determined on a great expedition into Palestine. Collecting the whole body of the mercenaries, and adding to them probably some Egyptian levies, he was able to raise a force of twelve hundred chariots, sixty thousand horse,[23] and footmen "without number," at the head of which he entered the Holy Land—"in three columns," as has been supposed[24]—and, spreading his troops far and wide over the country, "took the fenced cities which pertained to Judah and came to Jerusalem."[25] Now for the first time since they entered the "Land of Promise" had the Jews to contend with their great southern neighbor—now for the first time did they come in contact with huge masses of disciplined troops, armed and trained alike, and soldiers by profession. The clouds of horse, the vast body of chariots, the countless number of the footmen which swarmed over the land, seem to have overawed their minds, and prevented the very thought of an organized resistance. In vain had Rehoboam, immediately after Jeroboam's revolt, fortified a number of the towns of Judæa,[26] especially those towards the south and southwest,[27] in anticipation of an Egyptian inroad. At the sight of the advancing host the cities opened their gates, or fell after brief sieges;[28] and in an incredibly short space of time the triumphant Pharaoh appeared before the Jewish capital, which yielded at discretion. Sheshonk entered the city, stripped the temple of its most valuable treasures, and plundered the royal palace,[29] but accepted Rehoboam's submission, allowed him to remain in Jerusalem as tributary prince,[30] and marched away his troops to further conquests.

Jeroboam, it would seem, had work for his ally to do, not in Judæa only, but also in his own territory. The Levitical cities, scattered about the land, were hostile to him;[31] and many of the Canaanitish towns had either never been subdued, or had taken advantage of the disruption of the kingdom to reclaim their independence.[32] Sheshonk is found, by the list of the conquered cities and tribes which he set up on his return home, to have carried his arms over the kingdom of Israel no less than over that of Judah, and to have captured in the former a large number of Levitical cities, such as Rehob, Gibeon, Mahanaim, Beth-horon, Kedemoth, Bileam or Ibleam, Alemoth, etc., and a certain number of Canaanite ones. He may even be traced across the Jordan valley, where he took Beth-shan, into the trans-Jordanic region, where he captured Mahanaim and Aroer, and thence into northwestern Arabia, where he reduced the Edomites, the Temanites (?), and several tribes of the Hagarenes.[33] Thus his expedition, though not to be compared with the great campaigns of Thothmes I. and III., of Seti I. or Rameses II., had a considerable success. Jeroboam, the friend and ally of Egypt, was strengthened and helped; Rehoboam (Fig. 58) was made a tributary; and the Arab tribes south and east of Palestine were reduced to dependence.

On his return to Thebes from Asia, with his prisoners and his treasures, it seemed to the victorious monarch that he might fitly seek to emulate the glories of the old Pharaohs, not only in war but in the arts of peace. Seti and Rameses had eternized their victories by inscribing them upon imperishable stone at Thebes—why should he not follow their example, and set up his memorial in the same place? He was "high-priest of Ammon in Apt,"[34] and the Great Temple of Karnak was thus under his special care; it was therefore at that place that he resolved to impress upon the stone the image of his own person and the record of his successes. On the external southern wall of this building, in the so-called portico of the Bubastites, he caused himself to be represented twice—once holding by the hair of their heads thirty-eight captive Asiatics and threatening them with uplifted mace,[35] and a second time leading captive 133 cities or tribes, each specified by name, and personified in an individual form, though the form is incompletely rendered.[36] Out of all these, the greatest interest will always attach to that which bears the inscription, "Yuteh Malk," and represents either the captive Judæan kingdom, or Rehoboam himself.[37]

Besides engraving his bas-reliefs on a part of the old Temple of Ammon, Sheshonk "built a sort of entrance hall, which leads from the south, close by the east wall of the sanctuary of Rameses III., into the great front court of the temple."[38] A record in the quarries of Silsilis shows that he drew the stone for this edifice from that locality, and that he gave the order for the stone to be hewn in the twenty-first year of his reign.[39] As no higher date than this is found on his monuments, and as Manetho gave him exactly twenty-one years,[40] we may assume as highly probable that his reign was not much further prolonged, and assign him the period from about B.C. 975 to B.C. 953.

Two sons of Sheshonk I. are known to us. The eldest, who was named Shupot or Aupot, 🝰🝱🝲🝳), received during his father's lifetime the titles of "high priest of Ammon-Ra in Thebes" and "commander-in-chief of the Theban soldiers."[41] He also presided over the working of the quarries at Silsilis.[42] Apparently, however, he died before his father, and so made way for the second son Osarkon,

🝰🝱🝲🝳 , who took the throne name of Sokhem-khepr-ra-sotep-en-ra,[43] and held the throne, according to Manetho, for fifteen years,[44] from about B.C. 953 to B.C. 938. It is thought by some[45] that, like his father, he was ambitious of military glory, and that he followed his father's example by making a great expedition into Palestine, being, in fact, the Zerah, or Zerach, זֶרַח, who invaded Judæa in the reign of Asa, the grandson of Rehoboam.[46] But the dates of the two expeditions, which fell thirty years apart, and the epithet of Zerah, "the Cushite," הַכּוּשִׁי, are against the view. Osarkon I. (Fig. 61) cannot possibly have been termed "the Cushite," since his father and mother were both native Egyptians; and as Shishak's expedition was made tolerably late in his reign,[47] and Osarkon probably did not outlive him above fifteen years, the date of Zerah's expedition would not be reached until Osarkon's reign was over. There is every reason to believe that he was a peaceful and wholly undistinguished prince, content to add a few sculptures to the "Bubastite portico" of his father,[48] and to rule Egypt in quietness during such term of life as Heaven might allow him. His portrait, as given by Rosellini,[49] is that of a mild prince, not remarkable for energy or determination..

Osarkon I. was followed upon the throne by his son Takerut or Takelut, 〕 who assumed the title of Si-Hesi, "son of Isis," and further took the throne-name of Hut-ra-sotep-en-Ammon-neter-hak-uas. It is thought[50] that, in the early part his reign, he was engaged in a struggle with his younger brother, Sheshonk, the son of Osarkon I. by a Tanite princess, Keramat, and that, although successful, he had to concede to the cadet of his house the new and high title of "Lord of Upper and Lower Egypt," which is found attached to his name in the inscriptions. Sheshonk was also recognized as "high-priest of the Theban Ammon," and thus enjoyed a dignity not much inferior to that of his brother. He likewise bore the office of "commander-in-chief of the troops." Takelut had a short[51] and undistinguished reign. He has left no monuments, and is only known through the Apis stelæ, which give him a wife called Kapes, and a son Osarkon,[52] who succeeded him.

The second Osarkon reigned at least twenty-two years.[53] He called himself Si-Bast, or "son of the goddess Bast," the queen of Bubastis, and also took the throne-name of User-ma-ra-sotep-en-Ammon. Chronological considerations[54] make it probable that the great expedition into Palestine, ascribed in the Second Book of Chronicles to "Zerah the Ethiopian," took place in his reign, either under his own auspices, or under those of an Ethiopian general, to whom he entrusted the command of his army. The Hebrew Zerach, זרח, may possibly represent the Egyptian O-sark-on, and Osarkon II. may be called an Ethiopian, because his mother, Kapes, was an Ethiopian princess;[55] or the Pharaoh, whose mercenary troops were largely Ethiopian, may have placed the invading army under a leader of that nation. The object of the expedition was to bring back Judæa, which had revolted,[56] to the subject position which had been imposed upon her by Sheshonk (Shishak). The attack, however, completely failed. Inspirited by the words of Shemaiah, which assured him of victory, the Jewish king Asa, the grandson of Rehoboam, boldly met the invader in the open field, engaged his numerous host, which is vaguely estimated at a "thousand thousand," and completely defeated it in a great battle.[57]

Osarkon II. (Fig. 51) appears to have had three wives.[58] The chief of these bore the same name as the queen of Sheshonk I., Keramat, and was probably by birth a princess of the royal house. She was the mother of Sheshonk II. (who, in his father's twenty-third year, was old enough to exercise the functions of royalty at Memphis), and must therefore have been taken to wife by Osarkon before, or soon after, he ascended the throne. Another of his wives, named Hesi-em-kheb, bore him the princess Thes-bast-per, while a third, Mut-at-ankhes, was the mother of prince Namrut, who became "overseer of the prophets and commander of the soldiery at Heracleopolis Magna,"[59] governor of the Thebaïd, the high-priest of Ammon at Thebes.

The crown-prince, Sheshonk, as governor of Memphis, celebrated the funeral rites of a deceased Apis bull in his father's twenty-third year,[60] and probably ascended the throne soon afterwards. He was even less distinguished than his predecessors, and apparently had but a short reign.[61] The throne-name which he assumed, and which distinguished him from the other Sheshonks, was Seses-khepr-ra-sotep-en-Ammon.

The remaining monarchs of the dynasty were Takelut II., called Si-Hesi, or "son of Isis," like the former prince of the name, and also Hut-khepr-ra-sotep-en-ra; Sheshonk III., known as Si-Bast and User-ma-ra-sotep-en-ra; Pamai,

 called User-ma-ra sotep-en-ammon ; and Sheshonk IV., called Aa-khepr-ra. These four princes are thought to come in the regular line of succession[62] from Sheshonk II., and, together with Sheshonk I., Takelut I., and the two Osarkons, to make up the nine monarchs whom Manetho assigned to this royal house.[63] Egypt rapidly declined under their government and once more suffered disintegration; rival dynasties established themselves at Thebes, Tanis, Memphis, and elsewhere;[64] Ethiopia acquired a preponderating power in the south, and the empire tended to dissolution. Disturbances are spoken of as occurring as early as the reign of Takelut II., both in the south and in the north;[65] and very soon the entire attention of the rulers was diverted from public works and

foreign expeditions to internal quarrels and dissensions. The descendants of the great adversary of Rehoboam still claimed the royal title, and exercised a precarious authority at Thebes, while the twenty-third dynasty of Manetho reigned at Tanis and Bubastis,[66] and an upstart prince, called Tecnaphthus or Tafnekht, held Memphis and the Western Delta. At Napata, on the Upper Nile, a certain Piankhi obtained sovereign power, and by degrees established a sort of protectorate or suzerainty over the whole of Egypt. As this change marks one of the main crises in Egyptian history, and is connected closely with the period of the twenty-fourth, or Ethiopian dynasty, its consideration is deferred to the ensuing chapter.

Art under the Sheshonks did not so much decline as disappear. A certain number of porticoes and bas-reliefs[67] were indeed added to the Temple of Karnak by the earlier monarchs; but these weak efforts are wholly devoid of artistic value; and after a time they are discontinued, as though the kings were ashamed at the contrast between their own feeble performances and the great works of former sovereigns. The Apis stelæ continue, but are rude memorial stones, with no pretension to rank as works of art.[68] Stagnation and deadness characterize the tombs of the time, which repeat antique forms, but without any of the antique spirit. Statuary almost entirely ceases;[69] a certain number of statuettes may belong to the time,[70] but life-sized figures are almost wholly wanting.

The condition of literature under the dynasty is similar. Excepting a few official tablets without the slightest literary merit,[71] and some magical texts and spells,[72] nothing seems to have been written. The literature of the time is reduced to the two branches of the mystic and the commonplace. On the one hand, we are gravely informed that "when Horus weeps, the water that falls from his eyes grows into plants producing a sweet perfume. When Baba (Typhon) lets fall blood from his nose, it grows into plants changing to cedars, and produces turpentine instead of the water. When Shu and Tefnut weep much, and water falls from their eyes, it changes into plants that produce incense. When the Sun weeps a second time, and lets water fall from his eyes, it is changed into working bees; they work in the flowers of each kind, and honey and wax are produced instead of the water."[73] On the other hand, the eternity of inscription on hard stone is bestowed on statements that "King Sheshonk caused a new quarry to be opened to begin a building,"[74] or that "in the

Vol. II. Plate XXIII.

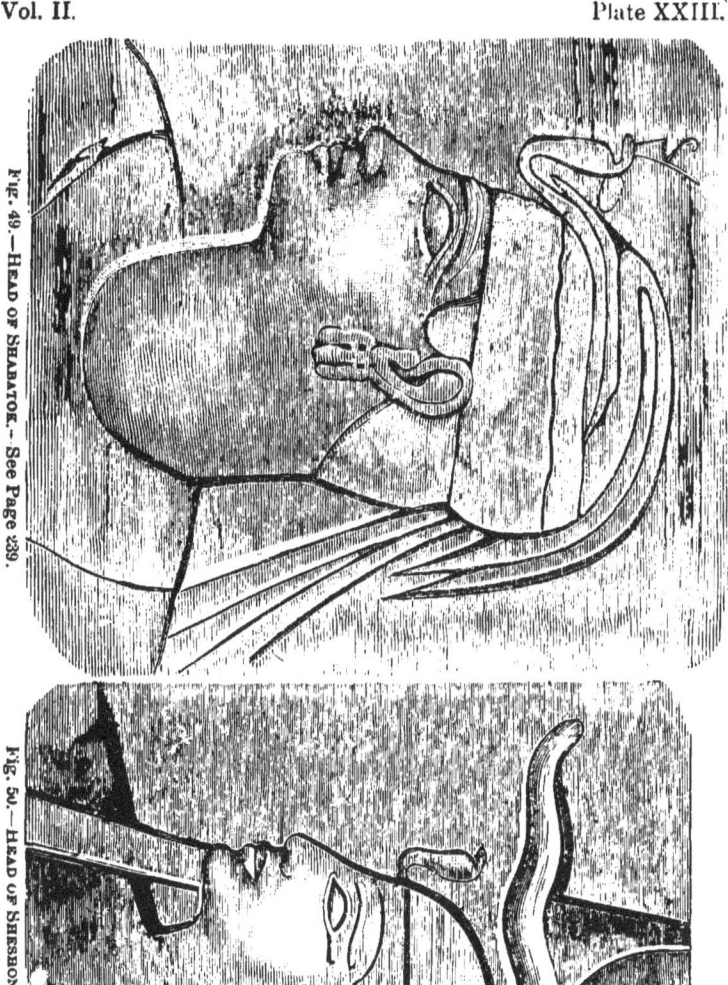

Fig. 49.—HEAD OF SHABATOK.— See Page 239.

Fig. 50.—HEAD OF SHESHONK I. (Shishak).— See Page 224.

Plate XXIV.   Vol. II.

Fig. 52.—Head of Shabak.—See Page 238.

Fig. 51.—Head of Osarkon II.—See Page 229.

year 2, the month Mechir, on the first day of the month, under the reign of King Pimai, the god Apis was carried to his rest in the beautiful region of the west, and was laid in the grave, and deposited in his everlasting house and his eternal abode. He was born in the year 28, in the time of the deceased king Sheshonk III. His glory was sought for in all places of Lower Egypt. He was found after some months in the city of Ha-shed-abot. He was solemnly introduced into the temple of Phthah, beside his father, the Memphian god Phthah of the south wall, by the high priest in the temple of Phthah, the great prince of the Mashuash, Petise, the son of the high-priest of Memphis and great prince of the Mashuash, Takelut, and of the princess of royal race, Thesbast-per, in the year 28, in the month Paophi, on the first day of the month. The full lifetime of this god amounted to twenty-six years." [76] Such are the highest efforts of Egyptian authorsihp in the two centuries and a quarter which intervene between B.C. 975 and B.C. 750.

CHAPTER XXV.

THE ETHIOPIAN PHARAOHS.

Geography of Ethiopia, and Condition of the Ethiopians about B.C. 750. Position and Importance of Napata. Connection of its Kings with the Egyptian Pharaohs. Sudden Rise of Piankhi to Power, and Nature of his Rule over Egypt. Revolt of Tefnekht. Great Civil War and Re-establishment of Piankhi's Authority. Revolt and Reign of Bocchoris. Invasion of Shabak (Sabaco). His Reign. His Monuments. First Contest between Egypt and the Assyrian Kingdom of the Sargonides. Reign of Shabatok. Accession of Tirhakah. His Connection with Hezekiah. His First Assyrian War. His Monuments. His Second War with the Assyrians. His Death. Reigns of Rutamen and Miamen-Nut. End of the Ethiopian Power in Egypt.

"The land shadowing with wings, which is beyond the rivers of Ethiopia!"
ISAIAH xviii. 1.

THE slight sketches given of Ethiopia and the Ethiopians[1] in the first volume of the present work are scarcely sufficient to enable the reader fully to comprehend the relations in which Egypt had come to stand towards her southern neighbor, or the nature of the subjection with which she was now threatened from that quarter. Ethiopia, in the ordinary and vague sense of the term, was a vast tract extending in length above a thousand miles, from the ninth to the twenty-fourth degree of north latitude, and in breadth almost nine hundred miles, from the shores of the Red Sea and Indian Ocean to the desert of the Sahara.[2] This tract was inhabited for the most part by wild and barbarous tribes—herdsmen, hunters, or fishermen—who grew no corn, were unacquainted with bread, and subsisted on the milk and flesh of their cattle, or on game, turtle, and fish, salted or raw.[3] The tribes had their own separate chiefs, and acknowledged no single head, but on the contrary were frequently at war one with the other, and sold their prisoners for slaves. Such was Ethiopia in the common vague sense; but from this must be distinguished another narrower Ethiopia, known sometimes as "Ethiopia Proper" or Ethiopia above Egypt,"[4] the limits of which were, towards the south, the junction of the White and Blue Niles, and towards the north the Third Cataract.[5] Into this tract, called sometimes "the kingdom of Meroë," Egyptian civilization had, long before the eighth century, deeply penetrated. Temples of the Egyptian type, stone pyramids, avenues of sphinxes, had been erected;[6] a priesthood had been set up,[7] which was regarded as derived from the Egyptian priesthood; monarchical institutions had been adopted: the whole tract formed ordinarily one kingdom; and the natives were not very much behind the Egyptians in arts or arms, or very different from them in manners, customs, and mode of life. Even in race the difference was not great. The Ethiopians were darker in complexion than the Egyptians,[8] and possessed probably a greater infusion of Nigritic blood; but there was a common stock at the root of the two races—Cush and Mizraim were brethren.[9]

In the region of Ethiopia Proper a very important position was occupied in the eighth century by Napata. Napata was situated midway in the great bend of the Nile, between lat. 18° and 19°, where for a time the mighty stream ceases to flow to the north, and takes a course which is considerably south of west. It occupied the left bank of the river in the near vicinity of the modern Gebel Berkal. Here, as early as the time of Amenóphis III., a great sanctuary was raised to Ammon by that distinguished king;[10] and here, when the decline of Egypt enabled the Ethiopians to reclaim their ancient limits, the capital was fixed of that kingdom, which shortly became a rival of the old empire of the Pharaohs, and aspired to take its place. The city increased in size; new temples were raised to Osiris and other Egyptian gods; avenues of sphinxes adorned the approaches to the temples; sepulchral monuments were erected in the shape of pyramids; the entire city had a thoroughly Egyptian aspect; and Egyptian ideas dominated the minds of the inhabitants. "The Theban god, Ammon-Ra, was recognized as the supreme god of the country. The king's full name was formed exactly according to the old Egyptian pattern. The Egyptian language and writing, division of time, and everything else relating to manners and customs, were preserved."[11] Though an Ethiopian city, Napata had all the appearance of an Egyptian one; and nothing showed its foreign character but a certain coarseness and rudeness in the architecture, and an entire absence of any attempt at originality in the artistic forms or in the mode of employing them.

Napata was also a place of much wealth. The kingdom of Meroë, whereof it was the capital, reached southward as far as the modern Khartoum, and eastward stretched up to the Abyssinian highlands, including the valleys of the Atbara and its tributaries, together with most of the tract between the Atbara and the Blue Nile. This was a region of great opulence,[12] containing many mines of gold, iron, copper, and salt, abundant woods of date-palm, almond-trees and ilex, some excellent pasture-ground, and much rich meadow-land suitable for the growth of *doora* and other sorts of grain. Fish of many kinds and large turtle[13] abounded in the Atbara and other streams'; while the geographical position was favorable for commerce with the tribes of the interior, who were able to furnish an almost inexhaustible supply of ivory, skins, and ostrich feathers. Napata continued down to Roman times a place of importance, and only sank to ruin in consequence of the campaigns of Petronius against Candacé in the first century after our era.[14]

It is thought that during the troubles which issued in the supersession of the first Tanite dynasty by that of the Sheshonks, a branch of the family of Her-hor transferred itself from Thebes to Napata, and intermarrying there with the principal Cushites of the place, was accepted as a royal house, and founded the northern Ethiopian kingdom, which after a time became dangerous to the Egyptians. The "princes of Noph"[15] at first were of no great importance; but as Egypt became more and more disorganized and decentralized, their power grew relatively greater, until at last they found themselves able to assume the protectorate of one Egyptian kingdom after another, and ultimately about B.C. 750, to exercise a species of lordship over the whole country. The individual who is first found occupying this novel

position is a certain Piankhi, ⊐𓇋𓏺𓂝𓈖𓐍𓏭, who calls himself Mi-
Ammon or Meri-Ammon, "beloved of Ammon," and is
thought to have been a descendant of Her-hor." On a stélé
found at Gebel Berkal, the ancient Napata, this prince, who
assumes the ordinary Pharaonic titles, "Son of the Sun," and
"King of Upper and Lower Egypt," states that in his twenty-
first year, a great revolt broke out in Egypt against his authority.[18] By the account which he gives of the revolt we find
that, previously to it, Egypt was divided into at least seven
kingdoms, each ruled by a native Egyptian king, who however was not independent, but owed allegiance to Piankhi.
Tafnekht ruled in the Western Delta, and held Saïs and
Memphis; Osarkon was king of the Eastern Delta, and kept
his court in Bubastis; Petisis was king of Athribis, also in the
Delta, and Aupot ruled in some portion of the same region ;
in middle Egypt the tract next above Memphis formed the
kingdom of Pefaabast, who had his residence in Sutensenen, or
Heracleopolis Magna; while above this was the dominion of
Namrut, extending beyond Sesennu (or Hermopolis), his capital. Bek-en-nefi had also a principality, though in what
exact position is uncertain. Other chiefs appear to have held
cities, but probably under one or other of the seven princes
above mentioned. There were also various generals of mercenaries in different parts of the country, who had independent commands,[19] owing allegiance only to Piankhi. Upper
Egypt, from the vicinity of Hermopolis (lat. 27° 47'), appears
to have been completely absorbed into the kingdom of Napata, and to have had no subordinate or tributary monarch.
    It is impossible to say at what time in Piankhi's reign,
prior to his twenty-first year, the original establishment of his
authority over Egypt took place; but his stélé contains no
indication that the date was recent. On the whole, it would
seem to be most probable that he began to extend his sway over
Upper Egypt soon after his accession,[20] which cannot have
been much later than B.C. 755,[21] and, gradually advancing towards the north, became master of the Delta, and so of all
Egypt, by B.C. 750. He may then have reigned quietly and
peacefully for fifteen or sixteen years, and so have reached
the twenty-first year of his sovereignty when the revolt broke
out. At that date, Tafnekht, the ruler of Saïs and Memphis,
suddenly resolved to throw off his allegiance, trusting perhaps partly in his power, partly in his remoteness from
Napata. Sailing up the Nile, "with multitudes of warriors

from the whole (western) land following him,"[22] he occupied the country on both sides of the river, including the Fayoum,[23] as far as Heracleopolis Magna (lat. 29° 11′), without—so far as appears—encountering any opposition. "Every city, both of the west and of the east, opened its gates to him."[24] Heracleopolis seems to have ventured to stand a siege,[25] but was taken. Tafnekht then advanced on Hermopolis, and so alarmed the king, Namrut, that, after razing one of his forts in order to prevent it from falling into the enemy's hand, he gave up the idea of resistance, and joined the rebellion.[26] About the same time, several other of the subject monarchs, as Osarkon of Bubastis, Bek-en-nefi, and Aupot,[27] gave in their adhesion to Tafnekht, and brought their forces to swell the number of his army.

Meanwhile, Piankhi, having received intelligence of the revolt, sent a strong body of troops down the Nile under the command of two generals, who would, he hoped, be able to defeat and disperse the rebels without his own intervention.[28] This expedition was at first successful. On its way down the river, below Thebes, it fell in with the advancing fleet of the enemy and completely defeated it. The rebel chiefs, abandoning Hermopolis and the middle Nile, fell back upon Sutensenes, or Heracleopolis, where they concentrated their forces and awaited a second attack. This was not long deferred. Piankhi's army, having besieged and taken Hermopolis,[29] descended the river to Sutensenen, gave the confederates a second naval defeat, and disembarking followed up their success with another great victory by land, completely routing the enemy, and driving them to take refuge in Lower Egypt or in the towns along the banks of the Nile below Heracleopolis. But now a strange reverse of fortune befell them. Namrut, the Hermopolitan monarch, hearing that his capital was in the enemy's power, resolved on a bold attempt to retake it, and, having collected a number of ships and troops, quitted his confederates, sailed up the Nile, besieged the Ethiopian garrison which had been left to hold the city, overpowered them, and recovered the place.[30] Hereupon Piankhi made up his mind that his own personal presence was necessary in order to quell the revolt. Quitting Napata in the first month of the year, he reached Thebes in the second,[31] and after performing sundry religious ceremonies in honor of the great god, Ammon, advanced against Hermopolis, pitched his camp to the southwest of the city, and prepared to take it by storm. Towers were raised to a greater height than the walls, from which the archers shot into the city, and the catapult-men hurled stones into it, with such effect, that in a short time the inhabitants could not bear the stench of the corpses³⁴ and insisted on a surrender. Namrut consented. (Fig. 56). Having first softened the great king's heart by sending his wife as a suppliant to Piankhi's harem, to prostrate herself before his wives, daughters, and sisters, and beseech their intercession in his favor, he himself came forth from the city, and presented himself before Piankhi in equally humble fashion, leading his horse with his left hand, and holding a sistrum in his right—the instrument wherewith it was usual for worshippers to approach a god. Piankhi had this scene engraved at a later date on the monument which he set up to record his victories;³³ but at the time he seems not to have been much impressed by it, and to have declined to receive Namrut into favor.

Pefaabast, king of Heracleopolis Magna, who shortly afterwards surrendered, was treated with equal coldness. Piankhi seems to have felt himself strong enough to suppress the revolt without the help of any of the subject princes, and reserved the question of punishing or condoning their offences until the struggle should be over.

Bent on putting down all opposition, Piankhi now proceeded from Heracleopolis along the course of the Nile towards Memphis, receiving the submission of the cities on either bank of the river upon his way, and in a short time appeared before the southern capital, and summoned it to surrender at discretion.³⁴ But Tafnekht had recently paid the city a visit, strengthened its defences, augmented its supplies, and reinforced its garrison with an addition of 8,000 men, thereby greatly inspiriting its defenders. Resistance was therefore resolved upon; the gates were closed, the walls manned, and Piankhi challenged to do his worst. "Then was his Majesty furious against them like a panther."³⁵ Collecting vessels of every sort and size, and taking the command in person, he attacked the city from the water, brought the ships close to the houses, and, using the masts and yards of the vessels for ladders, succeeded in forcing an entrance, and captured the place after a great slaughter. Aupot, Petisis, and Merkaneshu, a leader of mercenaries, upon this surrendered, and armed resistance to the authority of Piankhi ceased. Two chiefs, however, had still to make their submission, Tafnekht, the leader of the rebellion, and Osarkon, the prince of Bubastis. Proceeding against the latter, Piankhi had reached Heliopolis, where he was received with acclamations and hailed as "indestructible Horus,"³⁶ when Osarkon, seeing that resistance was hopeless, came into his camp and did homage. Nothing remained but that Tafnekht should bow to fortune. That prince, after the capture of Memphis, had fled beyond the seas,—to Cyprus, as one writer conjectures,[37]—and was thus in no personal danger; but the condition of a refugee is irksome, and Piankhi had shown himself so clement to the other chiefs, that even the arch-rebel felt he might perhaps be forgiven. Tafnekht, therefore, from his island refuge sent an embassy to Piankhi, with a sufficiently humble message,[38] desiring pardon and proffering a new oath of allegiance. The Ethiopian monarch accepted the overture; the oath was taken, the pacification of Egypt effected; and, amid music and song,[39] the conqueror re-ascended the Nile, and returned, laden with the good things of Egypt, Syria, and Arabia, to his own capital city, Napata.

It would seem that Egypt now returned to its previous condition, all the rebel chiefs being allowed to resume their several governments and to exercise the same powers as before. Piankhi showed himself of a mild and merciful disposition, deposed no one, deprived no one of any portion of his territories, did not even take hostages, but trusted that their experience of the futility of revolt would prevent the chiefs from making any further efforts.

It is uncertain whether or no he personally witnessed the disappointment of his expectations. Egypt revolted and threw off the Ethiopian yoke within a few years of its reimposition, but perhaps not until Piankhi himself had been gathered to his fathers. The leader of the rebellion on this occasion was a certain Bek-en-ranf, 𓃀𓂝𓎡𓈖𓂋𓆑, whom the Greeks called Bocchoris or Bonchoris,[40] a native of Saïs, and perhaps a son of Tafnekht.[41] The circumstances of his revolt are wholly unknown to us, since the monuments are silent, barely mentioning his name,[42] and neither Manetho nor the native Greek writers were aware of the subjection of Egypt by Piankhi. Bocchoris is regarded by the Greeks as a somewhat remarkable personage, feeble in body and avaricious, but with a certain renown for wisdom, and the author of laws which had the approval of his countrymen.[43] According to Africanus,[44] Manetho gave him a reign of six years only, and as this number is found also upon one of the Apis stelæ,[45] we may accept it as probably marking the real duration of his reign. The Ethiopians, evidently stronger at this period than the Egyptians, are not likely to have allowed him a long respite, and when Sabaco, who had succeeded Piankhi at Napata, reclaimed the dominion which Piankhi had held, it is evident that Bocchoris was unable to make a prolonged resistance. Sabaco, a genuine Ethiopian,[46] not (like Piankhi) more than half an Egyptian, used his rights of conqueror to the full, employed large numbers of the inhabitants in forced labors,[47] and, by way of a warning to others, burnt Bocchoris alive for his rebellion.[48]

The reign of Shabak, [hieroglyph] or Sabaco, over Egypt, is estimated by Manetho at twelve years; and this date is also found upon the monuments[49] as a *minimum* one, which may have been exceeded. According to Herodotus,[50] he transferred his residence from Ethiopia to Egypt, where he certainly set up memorials, both at Thebes and at Memphis.[51] It was probably soon after his accession[52] that he received an embassy from Hoshea, king of Israel, entreating his assistance against Assyria, and had to consider whether he would venture to provoke the hostility of that mighty empire.

A time had been when Egypt was the aggressor, and carried her arms deep into Asia, robbing (as we have seen)[53] Assyria of a province, and forcing her kings to pay an annual tribute. But that time was a very distant one; seven centuries, or more, had passed away since the great Pharaohs of the eighteenth dynasty harried the Mesopotamian plains and struck terror into the hearts of the kings of Asshur. Now for above a century and a half the power of Assyria had been in the ascendant;[54] she had continually advanced her limits; the Euphrates had been crossed; Upper Syria, Phœnicia, Hamath, the kingdom of Damascus, brought under subjection; and at length an attack was made upon that country which Egypt might well consider almost her last bulwark upon the northeast, which she looked upon as properly her own, and over which, so late as the time of Sheshonk I., she had actually exercised sovereignty. Shabak, as an Ethiopian, might not feel keenly the change in the relative position of the two countries; but he had enough of political sagacity to perceive the peril of the situation, and enough of boldness to resolve on meeting it halfway, and not remaining wholly upon the defensive. He encouraged Hoshea to defy the power of the Assyrians; and though, from circumstances which are unknown to us, he did not march to his aid, yet, a year or two later (B.C. 720), he met the advancing tide of Assyrian conquest on the southern limits of Palestine, and fought a great battle in defence of the country whereof he had become king.⁵⁵ The battle of Raphia is one of the turning-points in the world's history. Then for the first time was the relative strength of Asia and Africa tested in open combat on a fair field. It was ominous of the future that Africa succumbed. Shabak was completely defeated by the great Sargon, the builder of Khorsabad, and founder of the last and greatest Assyrian dynasty. His army was routed, and he was forced to seek safety in flight. It was probably soon afterwards that he concluded that treaty with the Assyrians, the seal of which, containing his cartouche, was found by Layard on the site of Nineveh.⁵⁶

If Shabak reigned twelve years only, he must have been succeeded by Shabatok (Fig. 50), [hieroglyphs], about B.C. 712. Sargon was at this time still king of Assyria, and at the zenith of his power. In B.C. 715, he had conquered part of Arabia, and received tribute from Egypt;⁵⁷ in B.C. 711, "he took Ashdod," as noticed by Isaiah.⁵⁸ In the same year he claims to have received the submission of Ethiopia. "The king of Meroë," he says, "who dwelt in the desert, and had never sent ambassadors to any of the kings, my predecessors, was led by the fear of my majesty to direct his steps towards Assyria, and humbly bow down before me."⁵⁹ Shabatok is probably the monarch intended; and it would seem that, through fear of the Assyrian power, he must have undertaken a journey into some part of Sargon's dominions⁶⁰ for the purpose of bowing down before his footstool and doing him homage.

Shabatok probably reigned about fourteen years,⁶¹ from B.C. 715 to B.C. 698. He has left very few memorials of himself. In a sculpture, given by Rosellini,⁶² he makes an offering to Ammon-Ra and Maut; in one, given by Mariette,⁶³ he receives life from Neith; and a sitting statue of him, much broken, has been found on the site of Memphis.⁶⁴ On this last he calls himself Mi-Phthah, "lover of Phthah;" but his more ordinary epithet was Meri-Ammon, "beloved by Ammon." In personal appearance he would seem to have much resembled Shabak, who was probably his father; but his eye was larger, his nose shorter, and he represents himself as without a beard. It is remarkable that both he and his predecessor went back for their throne-names to the early period of Egyptian history, Shabak calling himself Nefer-ka-ra, 𓋋, a form of name not borne by any king since the tenth dynasty,[65] and Shabatok Tatkaura, 𓋋, one not borne since the fifth.[66]

The immediate successor of Shabatok appears to have been Tirhakah, whom Manetho made the third Ethiopian king. The form of his name in Egyptian is Tahark or Tahrak, 𓏤𓆎, which Manetho rendered by Tarakos[67] and the later Greeks by Tearchon.[68] His monuments are found at Memphis, at Medinet-Abou, at Thebes, and at Napata. It is not improbable that from Napata he exercised the supreme authority over Egypt even during the reign of Shabatok, and it appears to have been with him that Hezekiah negotiated,[69] when the continued existence of Judæa was menaced by Sennacherib. Sennacherib had in B.C. 701 taken Ascalon and Ekron, defeated an Egyptian army which marched to the relief of the latter city;[70] invaded Judæa, and made Hezekiah tributary,[71] after which he had returned to Nineveh. The Jewish monarch took advantage of his absence to send an embassy to Egypt, and received such encouragement that, in the next year, Sennacherib deemed it necessary to march a second time[72] into Palestine (B.C. 699) for the purpose of chastising both Judæa and Egypt. Regarding the Egyptians as his main enemy, and hearing that Tirhakah was on his way to oppose him, he marched past Jerusalem, by way of Libnah and Lachis towards Pelusium,[73] and found there an Egyptian army encamped under a leader whom Herodotus calls Sethos, possibly Shabatok, but more probably[74] another Egyptian sub-king, whom Shabatok or Tirhakah had established at Memphis. The two hosts were encamped opposite each other, when in the night occurred that terrible calamity, explained by different writers in different ways,[75] whereby the Assyrians were utterly discomfited, their invasion brought to an end, and Egypt for the present relieved from any danger of further attack. Sabatok having soon afterward died, Tirhakah established himself as sole ruler of Egypt (B.C. 698), and probably transferred his abode from Napata to Memphis, where so many of his memorials have been discovered.

It is chiefly in a religious character that Tirhakah appears in his sculptures and inscriptions. In a temple which he built to Osiris-Phthah at Memphis, he represents himself in one tablet[76] as cherished by Isis, whom he calls "the great goddess," "the mother of all the gods," while in another " he receives life from Mentu, and in a third pours a libation to Osiris Phthah.[76] An Apis is recorded as having died in his twenty-fourth, and another as having been born in his twenty-sixth year.[79] He is, however, exhibited at Medinet-Abou in the dress of a warrior,[80] smiting numerous captive enemies with his mace, and celebrated in Greek tradition as a great conquering king who carried his victorious arms along the whole of North Africa as far as the Pillars of Hercules;[81] but it is quite uncertain whether these traditions have any basis of truth. We have no native accounts of the circumstances of his reign, which *seems* to have been eventless, or nearly so, from the destruction of Sennacherib's army to the great invasion of Egypt by Esarhaddon.

Esarhaddon, the son of Sennacherib, succeeded him upon the Assyrian throne in B.C. 681. He was one of the most warlike of all the Assyrian monarchs,[82] and having, during the first nine years of his reign, established the authority of Nineveh over Armenia, Babylonia, Cilicia, Phœnicia, and Arabia, he in B.C. 672 determined on wiping out the memory of his father's Pelusiac disaster by effecting, if possible, the conquest of Egypt. Marching from Aphek in Lebanon along the coast of Palestine to Raphia, and obtaining, like Cambyses at a later date,[83] supplies of water from an Arabian sheik.[84] he passed the desert in safety, and, invading Egypt, gained a great battle over the forces of Tirhakah in the lower country, took Memphis and Thebes, and drove Tirhakah to take refuge in Ethiopia. Having thus made himself master of the country, he broke it up into twenty governments, appointing rulers—some Assyrian, but most of them native Egyptians—in the twenty most important cities or districts.[85] These were Thebes itself, Memphis and Saïs, which were united, Tanis, Sebennytus, Athribis, Natho, Pisapti, Heracleopolis, Mendes, Busiris, Momemphis, This, Hermopolis, Lycopolis, etc. Among the rulers were a Sheshonk, probably descended from the kings of the twenty-second dynasty, a Tafnekht, a Petubastes, and a Neco. The last-named chief, who was ruler of Saïs and Memphis, is no doubt the father of the first Psamatik [86] and we may presume that, not very long after his accession, he associated that prince upon the throne, since Psamatik counts the years of his reign from B.C. 667.[87] Egypt remained for three years in this condition—subject to Assyria, and split up into twenty governments or states. Tirhakah's reign appeared to have come wholly to an end, and the Ethiopian dominion to have terminated.

But the Ethiopians were merely biding their time. Tirhakah had withdrawn to Napata or to Meroë, where he kept watch upon events. No sooner did Esarhaddon, in B.C. 669, shows signs of physical decay, than Tirhakah "issued from his Ethiopian fastnesses, descended the valley of the Nile, expelled the kings set up by Esarhaddon, and re-established his authority over the whole country." [68] The kings fled to Nineveh, where they found Asshurbanipal, the son of Esarhaddon, established in power. Learning from them what had happened, he at once put his forces in motion, and in B.C. 668 led them throuh Syria and Palestine into Egypt, defeated the Egyptians and Ethiopians in a great battle near Karbanit, stormed Memphis and Thebes, and forced Tirhakah once more to take refuge in his own proper country.[89] After this he retired, having first reinstated the princes, in the former governments and strengthened the Assyrian garrisons in the various towns.

But the contest was not yet over. The tributary monarchs themselves had grown weary of the Assyrian yoke, and were inclined to prefer the Ethiopians, if subjection to one power or the other was a necessity. They intrigued with Tirhakah; and though some of them were arrested and sent to Nineveh,[90] yet the rebellious spirit smouldered on; and, Lower Egypt being in a state of disturbance, Tirhakah (Fig. 53) again invaded the upper country, took Thebes, and prepared to march upon Memphis. Neco was sent from Nineveh to oppose him, and Tirhakah in alarm evacuated Thebes, and retiring to Napata, there died (B.C. 667). His stepson, Rut-ammon, the Urdamané of the Assyrian inscriptions,[91] succeeded him and immediately applied himself to the task of maintaining the Ethiopian power. Descending the Nile, he reoccupied Thebes and Memphis, cleared Egypt of the Assyrians, and made himself master of the whole country. Asshurbanipal, upon this, undertook the conduct of the war in person, marched an army into Egypt, drove Rut-ammon from Memphis to Thebes, and from Thebes to Kip-kip, an unknown town of Nubia—thus, for the fourth time, establishing the Assyrian authority over the country. It would seem that Rut-ammon, shortly after this, died in Nubia, and was succeeded by Mi-ammon-Nut,[92] who was perhaps a son of Tirhakah.[93]

Mi-ammon-Nut tells us[94] that in the year of his accession to the throne (about B.C. 660) he had a remarkable dream in the night. Two serpents[95] appeared to him, the one on his right hand, the other on his left. He woke to find that they had vanished, and at once consulted the interpreters as to the meaning of the vision. It was expounded to signify that all Egypt would one day be his—the Lower country as well as the Upper; the land was given to him in its length and in its breadth; Ammon would be with him and prosper him.[96] Mi-ammon-Nut accepted the interpretation, and marched upon Egypt at the head of a hundred thousand men.[97] In Upper Egypt it would seem that he was hailed as a deliverer. Under the Assyrians, who were probably still dominant, though nothing is said of them, the temples had gone to decay, the statues of the gods were overturned, the temple revenues were confiscated, and the priests restrained from the exercise of their offices. Mi-ammon-Nut proclaimed himself the champion of religion. He visited the temples, led the images in procession, offered rich sacrifices, and paid every respect to the priestly colleges. Accordingly "even those whose intention had been to fight were moved with joy."[98] Acclamations were everywhere raised. "Go onward in the peace of thy name," they said, "go onward in the peace of thy name! Dispense life throughout all the land—that the temples may be restored which are hastening to ruin; that the statues of the gods may be set up after their manner; that their revenues may be given to the gods and goddesses, and the offerings for the dead to the deceased; that the priest may be established in his place, and all things be fulfilled according to the holy Ritual."[99] It was not until he reached Memphis that any opposition was made. There a battle was fought without the walls, and a decisive victory gained,[100] after which Memphis was occupied, and the enlargement and beautification of the temple of Phthah commenced. The chapel to Phthah-Sokari-Osiris, recently uncovered by M. Mariette, which is full of Mi-ammon-Nut's sculptures and descriptions,[101] was no doubt taken in hand and highly decorated, its stones being inlaid with gold, its panelling made of acacia-wood scented with frankincense, its doors of polished copper, and their frames of iron.[102] Still the princes of the Delta, Assyrian feudatories, hesitated to come in; and Mi-ammon-Nut after a while proceeded against them with his troops. The princes shut themselves up in their towns; and unwilling to waste his time in sieges, the Ethiopian returned to Memphis, and probably commenced separate negotiations with the various chiefs. The result was that ere long they made up their minds to submit, and by the mouth of Paqrur, king of Pi-sapti, placed themselves, their lives, and their possessions, at his disposal. The act of humiliation was accepted; their lives were spared; and after receiving hospitable entertainment they were sent back to their several towns, to govern them as Ethiopian and no longer as Assyrian vassals. Finally, Mi-ammon-Nut (Fig. 38), having (as he thought) firmly established his power, sailed up the Nile amid general rejoicing, and returned to Napata.[103]

But this expedition, which had seemed to rivet the Ethiopian yoke on the necks of the Egyptians, led in fact to their shaking it off. On the one hand, the attack showed the princes the evils of divided empire, and suggested the idea of their placing themselves under a chief. On the other, the non-interference of the Assyrianss in the quarrel rendered it plain that their power was on the decline, and that the Egyptians had not much to fear from them. After having been a shuttlecock between Ethiopia and Assyria for some ten or twelve years, Egypt resolved on an endeavor to detach herself wholly from both. How Mi-ammon-Nut's authority was shaken off we do not know. Perhaps he died, and left no successor of sufficient energy to attempt the difficult task of holding in subjection a great nation, possessed of a higher civilization than that of his own. Perhaps he made a struggle to retain his authority, but was worsted. All that is known is, that, from about the year B.C. 650, the Ethiopian dominion over Egypt ceased. It had lasted, with interruptions, a little more or a little less than a century.[104] Egypt had derived no advantage whatever from the connection, had improved neither in arts nor arms, and could show not a single monument of any splendor or artistic excellence for which she was indebted to her conquerors.[105] The influence of the great Nigritic power was altogether depressing and debasing; and if under the new dynasty, which succeeded, the Egyptians showed any advance in civilization or in any of the arts, it was owing, not to the closer contact with their southern neighbors, but to an effluence which reached them from the north.

CHAPTER XXVI.

THE TWENTY-SIXTH DYNASTY (B.C. 650-527).

Depressed State of Egypt at the Close of the Ethiopic Rule. Communications between Psammetichus I. and Gyges of Lydia. Battle Momemphis and Establishment of the Power of Psammetichus over the whole of Egypt. Personal Appearance and supposed Libyan Origin of Psammetichus. Settlements of the Greeks at Bubastis. Revolt and Secession of the "Warriors." Other Results of the Greek Influx. Psammetichus takes Ashdod. He buys off the Scyths. His Buildings. Accession ot Neco. His two Fleets. His Ship-canal. Circumnavigation of Africa. His Expedition to Carchemish. Counter-Expedition of Nebuchadnezzar. Reign of Psammetichus II. His War with Ethiopia. Reign of Apries. His First War with Nebuchadnezzar. His Phoenician War. His Second Babylonian War and Deposition. His Obelisk and Inscriptions. Reign of Amasis. Condition of Egypt under him. He conquers Cyprus and makes alliance with Lydia. His great Works. His Wives. Short Reign of Psammetichus III. Egypt conquered by Cambyses. Civilization and Art under the Twenty-sixth Dynasty. Novelties in Religion. Changes in Manners. Conclusion.

THE long struggle of the Ethiopians and Assyrians for the mastery over Egypt, the rapid advances and retreats executed by the armies of both powers in the course of the various campaigns—advances and retreats which generally commenced at one extremity of the Nile Valley and terminated at the other—must have inflicted an amount of injury on the country and people which can scarcely be estimated, must have half ruined the towns, and have carried desolation over the broad and fertile plains on either side of the river. The great city of Thebes, so long the admiration of the Greeks,[1] and probably for many ages quite the most magnificent city in the world—passed into a byword for depression and decay in consequence of the long-continued troubles. "Art thou better than populous No," Nineveh was asked,[2] "that was situate among the rivers, that had the waters round about it, whose rampart was the flood? Yet she was carried away—she went into captivity." And the fate which befell Thebes was shared by Memphis, Heracleopolis, Hermopolis, Hasebek,[3] and by the great majority of the other towns. Nor could the ruin be readily repaired. The petty princes, vassals either of Assyria or Ethiopia, were neither sufficiently assured of their position, nor sufficiently rich, to undertake works of the cost and magnitude needed in order to restore the ruined edifices and obliterate the marks of invasion. Thus Egypt, towards the middle of the seventh century B.C., was reduced to a condition of extreme wretchedness and depression, for which it could scarcely have been anticipated that a revival would ever take place—far less so rapid and complete a revival as that which was actually effected under the Saïtic monarchs of the great twenty-sixth dynasty.

The signal for the movement which resulted in this revival was given in the far-off country of Babylonia. There, about B.C. 650,[4] a brother of the great Assyrian monarch, Asshurbanipal, raised the standard of revolt against his suzerain, and, in conjunction with the neighboring country of Elam or Susiana, commenced a struggle for independence. At the same time, in order to distract the efforts of his adversary, he sent emissaries to various distant countries, and among them to Egypt,[5] with the object of exciting the subject nations to throw off the Assyrian yoke, pointing out to them that they had now an excellent opportunity of regaining their freedom. It seems to have been this invitation, rather than any quarrel with his brother princes,[6] that caused Psammetichus, at this time king of Saïs, to form the project of reuniting Egypt into a single monarchy, and at the same time of releasing his country from any, even nominal, dependence on Assyria. Before, however, manifesting his intention by any overt act, he took the precaution of strengthening himself by a distant and powerful alliance. Having learnt that Gyges, king of Lydia, a rich and warlike monarch, was ill-affected towards the Assyrian power,[7] which had recently been extended over his country, he sent an embassy to Sardis, with a request for a contingent of troops. Gyges assented;[8] and a body of soldiers, drawn chiefly from the Carians and the Ionian Greeks[9]—who were at this time in his service[10]—was dispatched from Asia to Africa, to help Psammetichus against the Assyrians and the Assyrian vassal-kings. By the aid of these foreign auxiliaries, the Saïte monarch was completely successful. In a battle near Momemphis[11] the modern Menorf —he signally defeated the combined forces of the vassal monarchs, and, as the result of his victory, placed on his head the double crown, and proclaimed himself "lord of the two Egypts, the upper and the lower country."

It is suspected[12] that Psammetichus (Fig. 47)—or Psamatik, ▪𓊪𓋴𓌳𓍿𓎡, to give him his native name—was of Libyan descent, connected with the family of which the arch-rebel against the Persians, Inarôs, was also a member.[13] The names Psamatik and Neco, 𓈖𓃡𓂓, are unknown in the Egyptian nomenclature up to this date, and have no Egyp-

Vol. II.   Plate XXV.

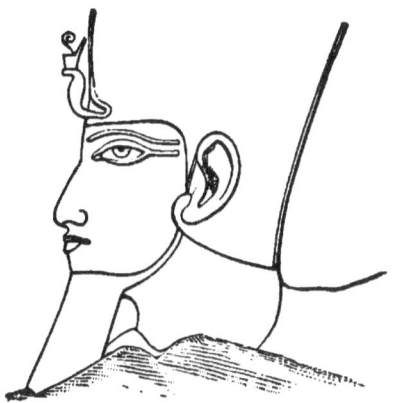

Fig. 53.—HEAD OF TIRHAKAH.—See Page 242.

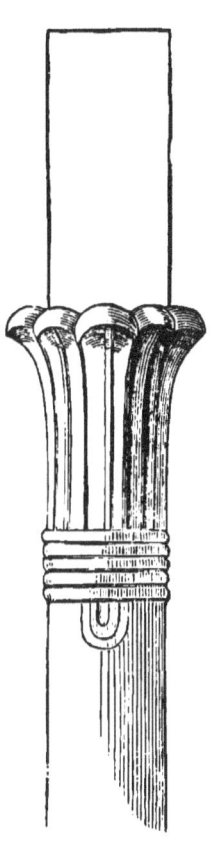

Fig. 55.—CAPITAL OF PILLAR
(time of the Psammetichi).
—See Page 268.

Fig. 54.—HEAD OF SETI II.—See Page 183.

Plate XXVI.   Vol. II.

Fig. 56.—PIANKHI RECEIVING THE SUBMISSION OF NAMRUT AND OTHERS.—See Page 236

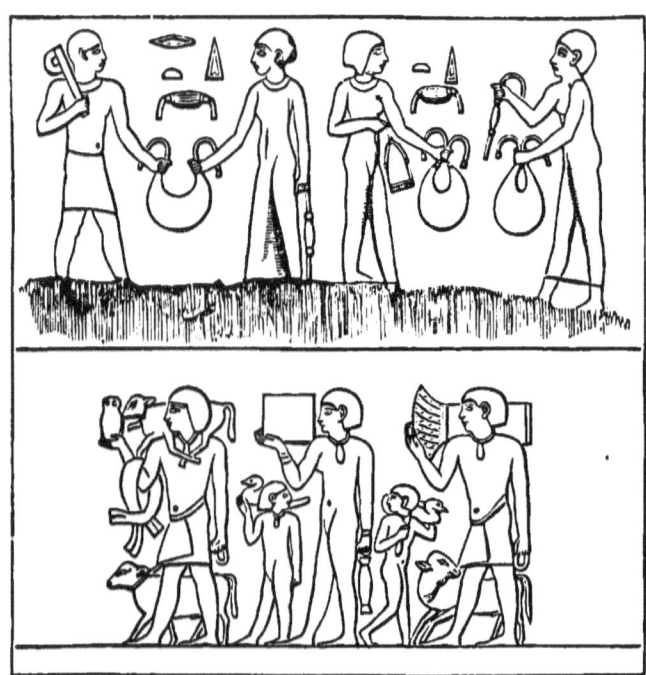

Fig. 57.—BAS-RELIEFS OF PSAMATIK I.—See Page 268.

tian etymology. Moreover, the Western Delta was, as we have already seen,[14] peculiarly open to Libyan invasion, and Saïs, the chief city of this region, would naturally contain in its population a large Libyan infusion. It is not to be supposed, however, that the Psammetichi were recent immigrants—they had no doubt been long settled in the region, and had gradually raised themselves to a high position among the nobles of Saïs. But the physical type of the family was markedly non-Egyptian. Psammetichus had a more open eye than the ordinary Egyptian one, a nose the reverse of the Egyptian form, which is aquiline and depressed, lips of moderate thickness, and a large but retreating chin. His skull seems to have been of the shape called "dolichocephalous," with a very small development behind the ears.[15] He bore his foreign origin in his very aspect, and therefore hastened to cover this defect, and legitimate himself in the eyes of his subjects, by marrying an Egyptian princess, Shepenput,[16] the daughter of a "King Piankhi," who traced his descent to the unfortunate Bekenranf or Bocchoris,[17] the earliest Saïtic monarch in the dynastic lists.

Having thus strengthened his right to the throne, the prudent ruler proceeded to secure himself the still more important support of might, by permanently engaging the services of those mercenary troops to whose strong arms he felt that his success was owing; and, having induced them to enlist regularly under his banner, he settled them within a moderate distance of his capital in two great fortified camps on either side of the Pelusiac branch of the Nile below Bubastis.[18] This proceeding appears to have given offence to the Egyptian warrior class, which was chiefly concentrated in three localities, Daphnæ or Tahpenes, near Pelusium, Marea on the Lacus Mareotis, and Elephantiné.[19] It was either forgotten that mercenaries had been freely employed by the Ramesides and the Sheshonks, or there was something in the extent and character of the new arrangement which made it peculiarly unpalatable. A large secession of the "warriors" took place[20] soon after the settlement of the Carians and Ionians in their new "camps;" and though Psammetichus pursued the deserters into Nubia and sought to arrest their march, he failed to persuade them.[21] Above two hundred thouand of the soldier class, if we may believe Herodotus[22] and Diodorus,[23] having quitted Egypt, made their way up the Nile to Ethiopia, and were settled by the reigning monarch high up the course of the river, apparently upon the White Nile,[24] about lat. 9°. Here they were known as the Asmach or Automoli, under which latter name they are often mentioned by the geographers.[25]

The introduction into Egypt of a large body of Asiatic Greeks, warlike and yet civilized and refined, and the close relationship in which they henceforth stood to the king, of whose throne they must have been the chief physical support, were events of considerable importance in their effect upon Egyptian art, manners, and habits of thought. The spirit of inquiry was suddenly awakened in the inert Egyptian mind, which had hitherto been content to work in a traditional groove, and had eschewed all needless speculations. Psammetichus himself had his curiosity aroused, and began experiments and investigations. A strong spring, which welled forth from the rock in the neighborhood of Elephantiné, and was called by some—absurdly enough—the true source of the Nile, was reputed to be unfathomable. Psammetichus brought a measuring line, with a heavy weight attached to it, and had the fountain sounded, but failed to reach the bottom.[26] A question having been raised, probably by some of the newcomers, as to the relative antiquity of different races of mankind, Psammetichus had two children isolated from their species, brought up by a dumb herdsman,[27] and suckled by a goat, in order to see what language they would speak, since he presumed that, if they never heard a word uttered, they would revert to the primitive type of speech. The result of his experiment was thought to prove the Phrygians to be the most ancient nation; and the Egyptians, we are told,[28] thenceforth acquiesced in that conclusion as an established one.

A second consequence of the Greek influx was the establishment of a class of "interpreters," who acted as intermediaries between the Greeks and the native Egyptians in business transactions, being equally conversant with the languages of both nations.[29] The Greeks, with that self-conceit which characterized them above all the other peoples of antiquity, declined to speak or understand any language but their own, and thus depended on the interpreters—persons in a humble position—for all their knowledge of the history, antiquities, and religious opinions of the Egyptians. Hence probably the frequent mistakes which disfigure their accounts of these matters, and detract so largely from their value.

It would seem[30] that another consequence was the opening of free communication and commercial intercourse between Egypt and Asiatic Greece, such as had certainly not existed previously. The Egyptians had hitherto been jealous of foreigners, and scarcely allowed them to land upon their coast." Now Greek trade and even Greek settlements were encouraged. The Milesians established a fortified port on the Bolbitine mouth of the Nile, and shortly afterwards founded Naucratis on the western or Canopic branch.[32] That city became an important *entrepôt* of Greek commerce, and the monopoly of the lucrative traffic thus established was not long confined to a single state. Chios, Phocæa, Rhodes, Halicarnassus, Mytilênê, Egina, Samos claimed a share in the Egyptian trade,[33] and Naucratis shortly received immigrants in considerable numbers from these and other Greek cities. The wines of Greece were highly appreciated by Egyptian epicures;[34] and Greek pottery and glyptic art attracted a certain amount of favor. Greek courtesans, moreover, established themselves at Naucratis, and accumulated immense fortunes.[35] Thus the influence exercised upon Egypt by the Greek settlement was one not altogether for good; but on the whole it is probable that the benefits which resulted from it outweighed the disadvantages.

The loss of military strength consequent upon the desertion of the "warriors" did not deter Psammetichus from attempting, like other founders of dynasties, to obtain for himself the *prestige* which is derived from foreign conquests. The Assyrian power declined rapidly in the decade of years which followed the loss of Egypt.[36] Western Asia became disorganized, and a tempting opportunity was thus offered for Egypt to claim once more dominion over Syria. Psammetichus, if there is any ground at all for the statement of Herodotus that he besieged Azotus (Ashdod) for twenty-nine years,[37] must have commenced his aggressions in this quarter very soon after he became king of all Egypt.[38] Ashdod was the key of Syria upon the south, and was a city of great strength, as indeed the name implies.[39] Psammetichus can scarcely have blockaded it continuously for the time mentioned,[40] but he may have attacked it frequently, or indeed annually,[41] during that space, and his efforts may only have been crowned with success in the twenty-ninth year from the date of his first assault. The Jewish history of the time shows that he did not carry his arms inland, or make any attempt to interfere with Manasseh, Amon, or Josiah; but it would seem that from Ashdod he proceeded northwards along the Syrian coast, and reduced Phœnicia to a species of vassalage, establishing the Egyptian power over the coast line as far north as Aradus, where he built a temple to the Egyptian goddess, Sechet or Bast, and left a statuette inscribed with his name.[42]

It was probably after Ashdod had fallen, and when Psammetichus regarded his power as firmly fixed in Philistia and Phœnicia, that a sudden danger manifested itself which no wisdom could have foreseen and no statesmanship have averted. Breaking through the great barrier of the Caucasian range, a horde of fierce barbarians—Ugrian or Tatar—spread themselves (about B.C. 630-620) over Armenia and Mesopotamia,[43] defeated the armies sent against them by the civilized nations of those parts,[44] became complete masters of the open country, and, having desolated and exhausted one region after another, finally descended upon Syria, and threatened to invade Egypt. Baffled by the high walls which for the most part defended the towns, it was their ordinary practice to pass them by, and to ravage only the unwalled villages and the cultivated plains;[45] but occasionally a weak town, reputed rich, tempted their attack, and succumbed to it. Pressing towards Egypt along the coast route, they must have come upon Ashdod; but Ashdod was too strong for them to meddle with. They passed on and reached Ascalon, an ancient city,[46] famous for its temple of Derceto, the Philistine Ashtoreth. This place fell into their hands, and proved so seductive that in a short time the invading host was reduced by its excesses to such a condition as made it little better than an army of women.[47] Psammetichus, under these circumstances, found no difficulty in persuading the chiefs, on receipt of a moderate bribe, to give up their project of invading Egypt, and even evacuate the portion of southern Syria which they had occupied. Whither they retired is uncertain;[48] but there is reason to think that from the time of their stay at Ascalon their power declined—the Philistine city proved their Capua—and Western Asia in a short time was able to rid itself of its oppressors.

During the later years of his life, Psammetichus would seem to have devoted his attention to art and architecture. Herodotus tells us that he built the southern gateway, which gave entire completeness to the great temple of Phthah at Memphis,[49] and also "made a court for Apis, in which Apis was kept whenever he made his appearance in Egypt."[50] This latter was surrounded by a colonnade, adorned with Osirid figures eighteen or twenty feet high. Psammetichus also made a new gallery for the reception of the Apis bulls after their death, in the burial-place of Saccarah,[51] piercing the solid rock with arched embrasures, in each one of which at least one Apis was to be deposited. He likewise adorned Memphis with a new temple to Sechet,[52] where she was long honored as the wife of Phthah and the Goddess of Life. In Thebes he restored those portions of the great temple which had been injured by the Assyrians,[53] and at Medinet-Abou he constructed works which attracted the attention of later ages.[54] Saïs, Mendes, Philæ, and Heliopolis were likewise objects of his care; and their sites have yielded specimens of the arts which he fostered and encouraged.[55] An invention of his reign,[56] which cannot, however, be assigned to the initiative of the monarch, was the later *enchorial* or *demotic* writing, which superseded the hieratic, being simpler and easier to write rapidly, though somewhat more spread out over the paper.

Besides his wife, Shepenput, the daughter of King Piankhi, Psammetichus is thought to have been married to a lady called Hent or Hont,[57] who was the mother of his eldest, if not his only son,[58] Neku—the Nehoc of Scripture. By Shepenput he had a daughter, whom he called Netakert-mimaut, or "Nitocris beloved of Maut;" and this princess was taken to wife by her half-brother. Neco.[59] Thus the legitimacy supposed to attach to the descendants of Bocchoris was transferred to this prince, who reigned partly in his own right, partly in that of his wife.

Neco, —, who must have been tolerably advanced in years when he ascended the throne,[60] was nevertheless one of the most enterprising and energetic of Egyptian rulers. Inheriting his father's designs against Syria and Phœnicia, and convinced that the successful prosecution of such an enterprise as the conquest of those countries required the employment of a powerful fleet,[61] his first efforts[62] were directed towards the construction of a navy capable of contending with any that the Phœnician monarchs could bring against him. As Egypt was washed by two seas, and he had ports on both, dock-yards were established and ship-building actively pursued simultaneously in the two quarters, the work being pushed with such vigor that in a short time he possessed two fleets of *triremes*,[63] one in the Mediterranean and the other in the Red Sea. Egyptian fleets had hitherto consisted of vessels having one rank of rowers only;[64] but biremes, or vessels with two ranks, had been built by the Phœnicians[65] as early as B.C. 700, and triremes had been invented by the Greeks at about the same date.[66] Neco's Greek and Carian mercenaries were probably well acquainted with them, and would recommend them to their master as excelling all other vessels of war. The vessels in which they, or rather their predecessors, had reached Egypt forty years earlier, and which were laid up in dry docks near Bubastis,[67] may have been of this class and have served the shipwrights of Neco as patterns. At any rate two fleets of triremes were built on the two Egyptian seas, and their active services were put[67] in request, Herodotus tells us, on more than one occasion.[68]

Closely connected with these naval projects and aspirations was, beyond all doubt,[69] another enterprise in wh'ch the active-minded monarch engaged at the same period. The great kings of the nineteenth dynasty had, as we have seen,[70] established water communication between the two Egyptian seas by means of a canal carried across from the Nile near Bubastis to the Bitter Lakes, and thence to the head of the Gulf of Suez. But this work had been intended for commercial, not military, purposes, and had been constructed on a moderate scale, the width of the cutting being probably not much greater than that of the canals of our own country. Neco's designed was of a far grander character. He wished to construct a ship-canal, along which his triremes might pass, and designed it on a scale which would have allowed of two vessels of this class being rowed along it abreast,[71] and therefore of their meeting and crossing each other without shipping their oars. Had the work been successfully completed, it would have been feasible to unite the two fleets on any occasion when it seemed desirable, and to employ the entire naval force of the kingdom, either in the Mediterranean or the Red Sea, against Phœnicia or Arabia. Unfortunately the enterprise failed. According to Herodotus,[72] it was stopped by an oracle which warned Neco that he was doing the work of the foreigner. But, if any such prophetic announcement was really made,—which is, to say the least, doubtful[73]—the priestly warning was probably itself based upon another quite separate fact—namely, the loss of life which occurred when the king attempted to put his plan into execution. In a climate like that of Egypt, and still more of the deserts which border it, hard labor under the scorching sun is itself dangerous; the concentration of many laborers on one spot increases the peril; insufficient provision of supplies and shelter multiplies it. So small a work as the Alexandrian canal costs Mehemet Ali the lives of 10,000 men ;[74] how many were sacrificed in the construction of the great cutting of M. de Lesseps will probably never be known. Neco is said to have lost, before he desisted, 120,000 of his laborers.[75] The number may be an exaggeration, but it indicates a fact. Excavators having been unwisely concentrated, or too much labor required of them, or an insufficient provision having been made of the necessary supplies, a fearful mortality was the consequence. Thousands perished in the course of a few months; and either compassion for his subjects' woes, or fear of their resentment, induced the monarch reluctantly to forego his purpose, and leave his great work unaccomplished.

But the idea of uniting his two navies still haunted him. If it could not be effected in one way, might it not in another? His Greek friends would tell him that the Ocean surrounded the whole of the earth,[76] and he might conclude from this that Africa was a peninsula. If so, might it not be circumnavigated? To obtain an answer to this question, Neco despatched from a port on the Red Sea a body of Phœnician mariners, who, starting with abundant supplies, sailed southward until they reached the extremity of the African continent, rounded the Cape of Storms, and returned, by way of the Atlantic, the Straits of Gibraltar, and the Mediterranean, to the country from which they had taken their departure.[77] The attempt was a success; but the success involved a disappointment. So much time was taken up by the voyage that the junction between the two seas, thus proved to exist, was of no practical service. Neco had to content himself with the glory of a geographical discovery, and to relinquish wholly his project of uniting his two fleets into one.

Having occupied in these enterprises the first two or three years of his reign,[78] Neco, in B.C. 608, proceeded to commence active military operations,[79] invading Syria with a large army by land,[80] while no doubt his fleet co-operated by advancing along the shore. Already possessed of Ascalon and Ashdod, he found no difficulty in penetrating by the coast route[81] as far north as the city of Megiddo on the border of the great plain of Esdraëlon. There, however, he was confronted by a hostile force, which blocked his way. Josiah, king of Judah, an energetic monarch, who had taken advantage of the fall of Nineveh, and the general unsettlement of Western Asia consequent thereupon, to reunite under his sway the greater part of the old kingdom of David,[82] determined on opposing the further progress of the Egyptian army,[83] either from a sense of duty, because he regarded himself as a Babylonian feudatory, or from a suspicion that, if the Egyptians became lords of Syria, they would not allow him to retain his sovereignty. In vain Neco tried to disarm his opposition, and induce him to retire, by an assurance that he had no hostile intentions against Judæa,[64] but was on his way to Carchemish, the great stronghold upon the Euphrates, where he hoped to meet and engage the forces of Nabopolassar, king of Babylon. Josiah was obdurate. Even Neco's assurance that God was with him, and had commanded the expedition,[65] failed to alter his resolution. A battle was thus forced on the Egyptian monarch, who would gladly have avoided one; and the hosts of Egypt and Judæa met, for the first time since the days of Asa, in the neighborhood of Megiddo, the scene of so many conflicts. As might have been expected, the Jewish king, not being miraculously helped, as Asa was against Zerah,[66] very soon succumbed; his army was completely defeated, and he himself mortally wounded by an arrow. Hastily quitting the battle-field, he made his way to Jerusalem, where he shortly afterwards died of the hurt received at Megiddo.[67] The Egyptian monarch, having brushed away the obstacle in his path, pursued his march through Galilee and Cœle-Syria to the Euphrates. Whether he fought any more battles or no is uncertain; but it appears that his expedition was entirely successful, and that the whole country submitted to him as far as Carchemish (Jerabolus). Three months sufficed for the conquest,[69] and at the expiration of that time the victorious monarch returned to Egypt, taking Judæa on his way, and making new arrangements for its political status and government. As a king had been set up in the place of Josiah without his authority, he deposed him, loaded him with chains, and carried him to Egypt as a prisoner.[80] He did not, however, abolish the Jewish state. On the contrary, he selected from the family of Josiah the prince who had the best title to the throne,[91] and established him at Jerusalem as subject or tributary monarch. He then fixed the tribute[92] which Judæa should pay at a hundred talents of silver (40,625*l*.), and a talent of gold (11,000*l*.). which may be consdereid a very moderate requirement, and returned to his own country.

The subjection of Syria to Egypt continued for three years.[93] But in B.C. 605 Nabopolassar, king of Babylon, having perhaps associated his eldest son, Nebuchadnezzar,[94] sent him at the head of a large army to win his spurs in a campaign against King Neco. That monarch, aware of what was intended, marched in person to the defence of his newly acquired territory, and took up a position resting upon Carchemish.[95] where he awaited the onset of the enemy. The Egyptian force comprised, as usual, a large body of chariots, consisting besides of horsemen and footmen. It was an immense host, and is described under the metaphor of a flood, whose waters toss to and fro, and cover the face of the earth.[96] Seemingly the Greeks and Carians did not on this occasion form any part of the expedition. African auxiliaries alone being employed—Ethiopians, Nubians, and Marmaridæ.[97] It was not long before Nebuchadnezzar made his appearance, and joined battle with his adversary. We have no particulars of the engagement, but its result is abundantly apparent. Neco suffered a complete and shameful defeat. His "valiant men were swept away;"[98] they "fled apace,"[99] and stumbled one over another."[100] The prestige of Egypt, which lately stood so high, was utterly lost. The cry went forth, "Pharaoh, king of Egypt, is but a noise," an empty sound, and nothing more; "he has passed the appointed time," outlived his energies, and is no longer formidable.[101] The victorious Babylonians carried all before them, swept down the Cœle-Syrian valley, overran Galilee and Samaria, and appeared shortly before Jerusalem. Jehoiakim resisted them, and the city stood a siege, but was quickly taken and plundered by the irresistible invaders.[102] Nebuchadnezzar then continued his march southwards, with the intention of attacking Egypt, and would probably have made himself master of the country, had he not been suddenly called away to Babylon by intelligence of the decease of his father. Leaving his prisoners and the bulk of his troops to make the long march by the ordinary circuitous route, he himself with a few light-armed troops crossed the desert and hurried to the capital.[103]

Neco thus obtained a respite, and was able in some measure to repair his losses and redeem his position, before Nebuchadnezzar found himself at leisure to return into Syria, and see to the consolidation of his power in that distant and not very submissive region. The Egyptian monarch saw clearly that it was of the utmost importance to raise up opponents to the Babylonians in the Syrian territory, and prevent them from obtaining quiet possession of a tract which would bring them to the very doors of Egypt. He therefore intrigued with Judæa,[104] and probably also with Phœnicia, inciting the newly subjected kings to rebel and throw off the Babylonian yoke. In two instances he was successful. Jehoiakim, after three years of submissive endurance, in B.C. 602, declared the independence of his country;[105] and the king of Tyre, a few years later,[106] followed the example of his Jewish brother. Nebuchadnezzar had to begin the conquest of Syria afresh, and recognizing the importance of the crisis, made preparations accordingly. Collecting an army of above 300,000 men, partly composed of his own subjects, partly of Median allies,[107] he, in the year B.C. 598, marched for the second time westward, crossed the Euphrates, and led his troops into Palestine. Dividing his army into two portions, he formed the sieges of Tyre and of Jerusalem simultaneously.[108] Jerusalem was soon reduced, but Tyre resisted with the utmost stubbornness. For thirteen years[109] the further progress of the Babylonian arms was arrested by a single city of no great size, but strong in her wealth and her situation. Under these circumstances, Egypt escaped all further attack; and Neco must have felt that his intrigues had had a success which he had scarcely dared to anticipate.

From B.C. 605—the year of the battle of Carchemish—to B.C. 596, when he died, Neco undertook no military expeditions, but nursed his strength, and remained persistently on the defensive. It was probably during this interval that he occupied himself with the buildings which are mentioned in some of his inscriptions. Though not a monarch who greatly interested himself in architecture or art, Neco still regarded it as incumbent upon him to leave some memorials of his reign. He made additions to the temples of Phthah and Neith at Memphis,[110] embellished Saïs,[111] and set up tablets in the quarries of Toora and in the valley of Hammamât. A statue, which represents him on his knees making an offering, adorns a private collection in Paris.[113] Several vases and scarabæi bear his name;[114] but, on the whole, he must be placed among the kings whose remains are scanty and insignificant. He is thought to have been buried at Saïs,[115] whence, early in the last century, was brought a scarabæus, taken from a mummy, which bore his name and had probably been placed by the embalmers upon the region of his heart.[116]

According to Lepsius,[117] Neco had two wives, Net-akert-mimaut, his half-sister, and Takhuat or Takhot. It was the latter who bore him the son by whom he was succeeded,[118] and whom he named after his own father, Psamatik. This prince, called by Herodotus Psammis,[119] and known to modern historians as Psammetichus II., was distinguished from his grandfather by the throne-name[120] of Nefer-ap-ra,

◯ ◌ ✧, the throne-name of Psammetichus I. having been Ua-ap-ra, ◯ ◌ ✧. His short reign of six years, or rather of five years and a half,[121] was not very eventful. As Tyre still baffled all the efforts of Nebuchadnezzar,[122] there was for the time no danger of the Babylonians troubling Egypt; and Psamatik seems to have felt himself so secure upon this side that he ventured to employ the main strength of the empire in the directly opposite quarter. Herodotus tells us that he made an expedition into Ethiopia;[123] and his own monuments give numerous indications of his presence and directing energy upon the Ethiopian border. Two inscriptions on the rocks at Elephantiné, one in the island of Bigeh or Beghe, two at Philæ, and one in the island of Konosso,[124] imply a stay of some considerable length at the extreme south of his own proper territory. If we refer to his reign the celebrated archaic Greek inscrition of Abu Simbel,[125] we may consider that we have actual evidence of his Ethiopic expedition having penetrated deep into Nubia, under the joint command of a Greek and an Egyptian general, in the latter of whom we may perhaps recognize the later Egyptian monarch, Amasis.[126] Whether a contingent of Jews also lent their aid to the Egyptian monarch, as stated by Aristeas,[127] is perhaps more doubtful, yet is certainly not beyond the range of posibility. Egypt and Judæa were at this time closely drawn together by common fear of Babylon; and though Zedekiah, the king of Judæa contemporary with Psamatik II., was a Babylonian feudatory, yet in his heart he was thoroughly disaffected, intended to revolt, and looked to Egypt to support him. The friendly act of sending some of his own subjects to aid Psamatik would strengthen his claim for a return in kind when the fitting hour came, and may thus be accepted, though the authority upon which it rests is weak.

Psamatik would seem not to have brought the Ethiopian war to an end. An inscription upon a statue now in the Louvre tells us that an Egyptian general, named Hor or Horus, was engaged in a struggle with the "miserable Kush" in the first year of Apries, and completely vanquished them, thus terminating the war which had been commenced by that king's predecessor.[128]

Though little distinguished as a warrior or as a statesman, as a patron of art Psamatik II. followed worthily in the footsteps of his grandfather. He adorned with bas-reliefs the temples of Abydos and Philæa[129] made additions to the great fane of Ammon at Thebes,[130] erected an obelisk (or obelisks)[131] to Ra-Harmachis and Tum, probably at Heliopolis, and adorned Saïs with a statue of himself and another of the goddess Neith.[132] Statuary seems to have received great attention during his reign. Besides the two figures already mentioned, the museums of Europe and Africa contain at least five others, mostly, however, incomplete, which belong to this period.[133] One of these, in the collection of the Vatican, is said to be remarkable for its beauty.[134]

The wife of Psamatik II. was a Nitocris, distinguished as Seret-pi-Mentu,[135] the daughter of Neco and Nitocris-Mimaut. She bore him two children, a son, to whom was given as a name the throne-name of his great-grandfather, Ua-ap-ra, and a daughter, called Ankhnes-neferapra.[136] The son succeeded, and was known among the early Greeks as Apries,[137] among the later as Uaphris.[138] He was a vigorous and enterprising prince, not afraid of measuring his strength against that of Babylon, and having it for his especial aim to re-establish Egyptian influence over the Asiatic regions formerly held by the great kings of the eighteenth, nineteenth, and twentieth dynasties, and recently occupied for three years by Neco. Having rapidly brought the Ethiopian war commenced by his father, Psamatik, to a successful conclusion [139] (B.C. 591-0), he lent a ready ear, in B.C. 588 to the ambassadors of Zedekiah, king of Judæa, who proposed a close alliance between the two countries, and engaged that Zedekiah should throw off the Babylonian yoke and openly rebel, if Apries (Hophra) would agree to support the movement by a considerable army.[140] A treaty was at once concluded on these terms; Judæa revolted; and towards the close of the year Nebuchadnezzar laid siege to Jerusalem, building forts around it,[141] and blockading it so strictly that no one could either quit the city or enter it. Apries, under these circumstances, redeemed his pledged, levied an army, and, quitting Egypt, marched to the relief of the beleaguered city, and actually raised the siege.[142] The Babylonian monarch did not wait to be placed between two fires, but broke up from before Jerusalem, and proceeded southward to meet the more important enemy. Hophra, advancing along the coast route, had, it would seem, taken Gaza,[143] and perhaps Ascalon,[144] when he received intelligence of the approach of the Babylonians. It is generally supposed that he at once withdrew into Egypt, so avoiding a battle;[145] but so sudden a change of mind seems improbable, and Josephus distinctly asserts that an engagement was fought in which Nebuchadnezzar was victorious.[146] Apries, worsted in the fight, had to retire, and made no further effort. The blockade of Jerusalem was re-established, famine set in, the Holy City fell in B.C. 586, and the last remnant of the Jewish people was led away into captivity.[147] Tyre surrendered in the next year,[148] and the schemes of Apries, for the moment, came to nought. Babylon triumphed; the great king returned in B.C. 585 to Babylon, with more than one conquered monarch in his train, victorious over Egypt, Phœnicia, and Judæa, master of Asia from the range of Zagros on the one hand to the "river of Egypt" on the other. But success is apt to beget security, and periods of exertion are, in the East especially, apt to be followed by periods of repose and indolence. Nebuchadnezzar, when he returned home from the captures of Tyre and Jerusalem, must have reached an age at which the physical powers begin to decay, and when rest becomes an object of desire to most men.[149] The silence of the Babylonian historian[160] and of the Babylonian monuments with respect to military expeditions at this period of his reign gives rise to the suspicion that, having, as he thought, done enough for glory, he now proceeded to console himself for the hardships of warfare by giving himself up to the seductive enjoyments of an Oriental court. In any case, Apries seems to have been emboldened to resume his projects of aggrandizement, and to have attacked Syria with a combined fleet and army.[161] We are told by Herodotus that he fought a battle with the king of Tyre at sea, and sent an expedition against Sidon by land.[162] Diodorus adds that he took Sidon, and defeated the combined fleet of Phœnicia and Cyprus in a great engagement.[153] These grand successes so elated him that he is said to have defied the gods to cast him down,[154] just as at an earlier date he had called the Nile his own creation—"the stream which he had made for himself."[155]

It was, however, in the counsels of Providence, that he should suffer a severe reverse of fortune and perish miserably.[156] What degree of credence, indeed, we ought to attach to the story told by Herodotus of the circumstances under which he was deposed and put to death, is doubtful. Herodotus was informed by the Egyptians that the revolution which brought his reign to an end arose out of an unsuccessful expedition against Cyrêné, in which he was thought to have intentionally sacrificed the lives of some thousands of his soldiers;[157] but Josephus believed that he was put to death by Nebuchadnezzar.[158] Inscriptions have recently been discovered which show that Nebuchadnezzar did really invade Egypt in his thirty-seventh year (B.C. 568), a date which falls within the lifetime of Apries,[159] and coincides so nearly with the accession of Amasis as to render it highly probable that the two events were connected. The Babylonian monarch, it appears, overran the whole of Egypt as far as Syêné, and only there encountered the Egyptian troops,[160] who were under the command of the general Hor, the hero of Apries's

Ethiopian campaign.[161] This commander claims the merit of having inflicted a check on the Babylonian arms, and caused Nebuchadnezzar to retire; but he does not dispute the fact that all Egypt lay at his mercy, and that he had it in his power to remodel the government as he pleased. To depose one monarch and set up another was the usual practice of the Babylonians—to execute a prince who had offended against their code of international law was a proceeding not unknown to them;[162] it cannot but be suspected, more now than ever, that the true course of events was concealed from Herodotus by the self-love of the Egyptians, and that, whatever discontent may have arisen from the failure of the Cyrenaic expedition, Apries was really deposed and executed, and Amasis made king in his stead by Nebuchadnezzar.

The victim of a monarch's offended dignity, or, if we are to believe Herodotus, of a mob's hatred, was not deprived of the funeral honors to which his birth entitled him. His body was embalmed, and buried in the royal burial-place, inside the temple of Saïs, very near the sanctuary.[163] The passions which had pursued the living man calmed themselves in the presence of death, and the last monarch of the line of Psammetichus I. was allowed to find a resting-place in the sepulchre of his fathers.

Apries was wholly undistinguished as a builder, and cannot be said to have been ever a liberal patron of art. We have no evidence of his having employed more than a single sculptor on a single occasion in the highest kind of glyptic art, namely statuary.[164] His stelæ are, however, common, and are sometimes adorned with bas-reliefs;[165] but these have little merit. Nor can more praise be given to the wall fragments belonging to his reign which have been found at Nahariyeh[166] and elsewhere. His most noted work is that small obelisk which now stands in the Piazza Minerva at Rome, placed by the fantastic Bellini on the back of an elephant.[167] It is one of a pair,[168] which the Romans brought from Egypt to adorn the temple of Isis and Serapis, when they adopted the worship of those Egyptian deities. Originally dedicated to Neith,[169] and erected probably at Saïs, it became the symbol of a very different and far lower worship in a remote and alien capital.

If Apries, however, cared little for artistic memorials, he did not neglect to leave behind him numerous records of his reign in the way of inscriptions. At least six inscribed stelæ belonging to his time are still extant;[170] and he has left rock inscriptions at the Biban-el-Moluk,[171] at Silsilis,[172] at the island of Bigeh,[173] at Philæ,[174] and at the island of Konosso.[175]

His most important memorial is one found on the site of the temple of Phthah at Memphis, which has been translated by Dr. Wiedemann.[176] It secures the rights and privileges of the god Phthah, and of the priests attached to the worship at Memphis, in very stringent terms, requiring all officials to protect the priests in the possession of the temple-lands, to impress for the public service none of their slaves or peasants, and even to maintain in good repair the canals by which the temple-lands were intersected. It is evident that under Apries the priest class retained its ascendency, and that even a monarch, who thought no god could cast him down, regarded it as prudent to court priestly favor.

It is agreed on all hands that Aahmes, ⸺𓏌𓊪, or Amasis, who succeeded Apries, was entirely unconnected by blood with the Psamatik family. According to Herodotus, he was a native of Siouph, a small town in the neighborhood of Saïs,[177] and was not even a member of a distinguished house, but a man who sprang from the middle class. This is not disproved by his possession of high military rank, even if he was an officer under Psammis;[178] since in the Egyptian military service advancement was obtained solely by merit. Various tales were told, not greatly to his credit, of the conduct pursued by Amasis in his younger days,[179] when he was "sowing his wild oats;" but it is questionable whether much credit should be attached to them. Even the anecdotes of his behavior as king[180] are of the legendary type, parallel to those which the early Persians loved to tell of Cyrus, and the later ones of Artaxerxes, son of Babek, the historical value of which is about equal to that of the tale, with which each English child is made familiar in the nursery, of King Alfred having his ears boxed by the neatherd's wife. We may perhaps conclude, from the general tone of the tales, that among the characteristics of the monarch was a rough and not overdelicate humor, which pleased the common people but shocked the more refined among his subjects. He compensated, however, for this unseemly trait by numerous good qualities. He was active and energetic, exemplary in his devotion to business, distinguished as a builder, as a conqueror, as a legislator, and above all as an administrator. If he began his reign under discreditable circumstances, holding his crown as a Babylonian feudatory, and bound probably to the payment of a tribute, he ultimately succeeded in raising Egypt to a high pitch of prosperity and a lofty position among the nations. The decline and fall of Babylon,[181] complete in B.C.

538, gave Egypt wholly into his hands, and enabled him to pursue a policy of his own devising, which, whatever its effect on the national spirit and on the ultimate fate of his country, had at any rate the immediate result of enormously developing Egypt's resources and increasing her wealth and population. Herodotus declares that Egypt had in his day 20,000 inhabited cities;[182] and though this statement may by pronounced impossible, yet it is strongly significant of the extremely flourishing condition of the country under the rule of Amasis. A series of high inundations is said to have intensified the productive power of the land,[183] while an active commerce[184] encouraged the chief Egyptian industries, led to the accumulation of fortunes, and rendered easily procurable a great variety of luxuries. Amasis induced the Greeks to settle in large numbers at Naucratis, and to adorn the town and neighborhood with temples of the peculiar Grecian type. He had friendly dealings with the important Greek state of Cyrêné, and even took for one of his secondary wives a Cyrenæan lady, called Ladicé, whom he treated with especial favor.[185] He also removed the Greek mercenaries from the position assigned to them by Psammetichus I., and brought them to the capital city of Memphis,[186] where he made them the garrison of the place. To mark his affection for the Greeks, he offered rich presents to Delphi,[187] Samos, Lindus, and Cyrêné, sending to the last-mentioned place a statue of Athêné covered with plates of gold, as well as a painted likeness of himself.[188]

The only warlike expedition in which Amasis is known to have engaged was one against Cyprus. That important island had formed a part of the Egyptian dominions under the eighteenth dynasty,[189] and was now again subjected and forced to pay tribute.[190] Its reduction implies the temporary weakness of Phœnicia, which always threw the ægis of its protection over its near neighbor, when sufficiently strong to do so, and frequently claimed and exercised a certain authority over the whole island. It would seem that the long war of Nebuchadnezzar against Tyre and the subsequent expedition of Apries against both Tyre and Sidon had so brought down the Phœnician power at this time, that no help could be given to the Cypriots. To suppose, however, that Phœnicia itself was subject to Amasis, is to intrude into the narrative a fact of which there is absolutely no evidence,[191] monumental or other; while to state[192] that "he led an army into Syria and made himself master of the Phœnician towns,"

Vol. II. Plate XXVII.

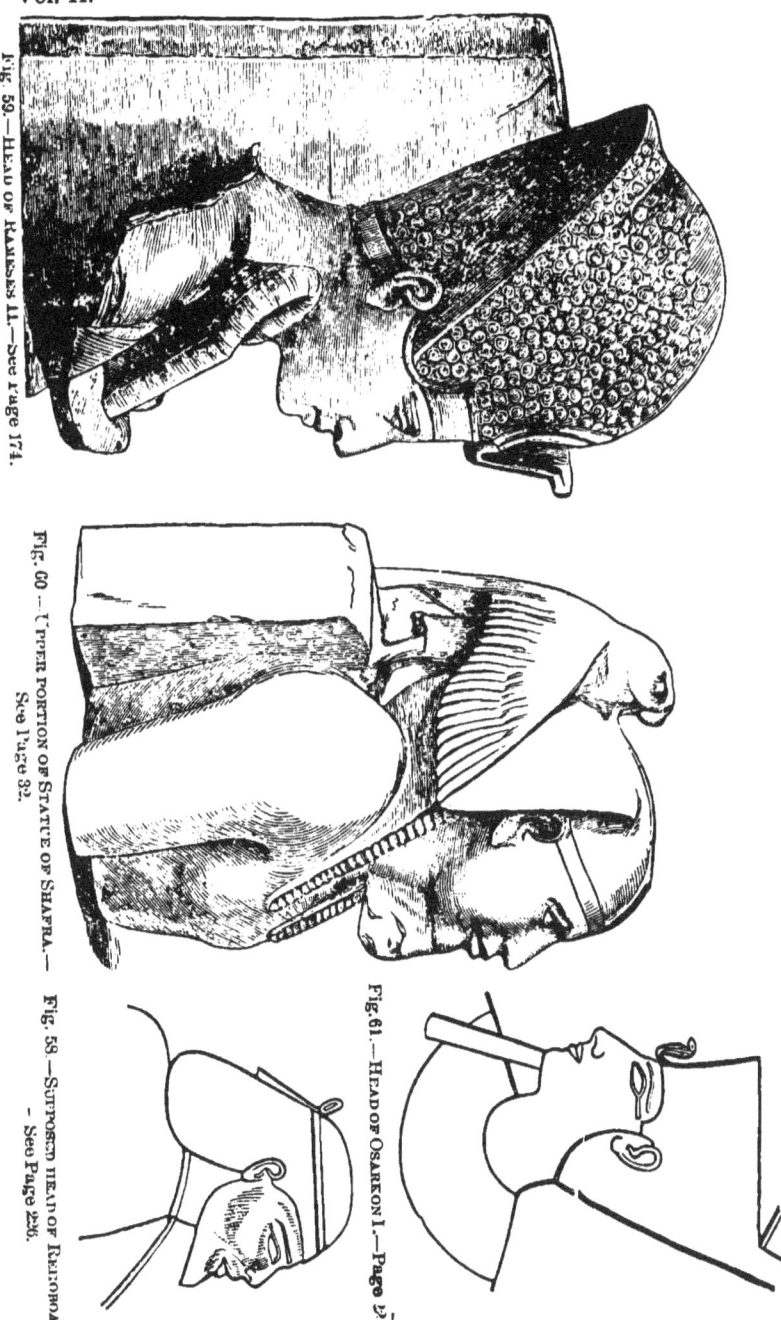

Fig. 59.—Head of Rameses II.—See Page 174.

Fig. 60.—Upper portion of Statue of Shafra.—See Page 32.

Fig. 58.—Supposed Head of Rehoboam.—See Page 226.

Fig. 61.—Head of Osarkon I.—Page 9.

Plate XXVIII. Vol. II.

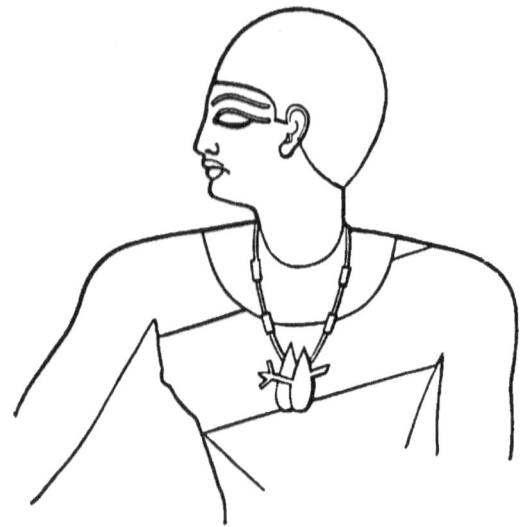

Fig. 62.—Curious Ornament worn by a man of the Psamatik period, perhaps a charm.—See Page 269.

Fig 63.—Dresses of an Egyptian Noble and his Wife (20th Dynasty.)—See Page 218.

is to indulge in a flight of fancy scarcely worthy of a serious historian.

Amasis lived at a time in the world's history when vast changes were impending, when the entire East was in a condition of ferment and transition, old things being on the point of vanishing away, and all things of becoming new. It is doubtful whether any amount of political wisdom could have enabled him to pursue such a course as would have saved Egypt from invasion and conquest, and the kingdom of the Pharaohs from extinction. As it was, the mere shrewd common sense with characterized him was a very insufficient guide amid the difficulties of situation; and the course which he actually took was one certainly not calculated to keep him free from entanglements, and master of the situation. In the year B.C. 555, yielding to the representations of the Lydian king, Crœsus, he allowed himself to be drawn into a tripartite treaty,[193] which bound up his fortunes irrevocably with those of two Asiatic kingdoms, exposed to far more immediate danger than his own. The rise of the Perso-Medic power was a new feature in Asiatic history, and might have been expected to revolutionize Asia; but its effects did not necessarily flow on into another continent. Prudence should have suggested to a monarch geographically isolated to pursue a policy of abstention. Instead of so doing, Amasis was tempted by the apparent advantage of uniting three powers against one, to join with Lydia and Babylon in the alliance against Persia, and so to give Cyrus, the Persian king, a ground of quarrel with him. Whether he actually sent troops to the assistance of Lydia, or not, is perhaps doubtful, being denied by Herodotus[194] and asserted by Xenophon.[195] Subsequently, however, when he attacked Cyprus, he clearly took a second step on the road to hostilities with Persia, since, after conquering Babylon (B.C. 538), Cyrus undoubtedly regarded himself as inheriting the whole of the Babylonian empire, which embraced Phœnicia, and Cyprus, as depending on Phœnicia. It would appear that Cyrus at once took umbrage, and with hostile intent sent an embassy to Egypt, with the demand that Amasis should give him one of his daughters as a secondary wife.[196] Such a demand, made by equal of equal, was an insult. Amasis, however, did not dare openly to reject it. He devised a sort of compromise, and sent a princess of the house of Apries, under pretence of her being his own daughter, to take the discreditable position. The fraud was discovered after a time, and a further cause of quarrel was thus added to those existing before.

Actual invasion did not, however, befall Egypt in Amasis' time. Cyrus, soon after his conquest of Babylon, became involved in a war on his northeast frontier,[197] which terminated disastrously. He died in B.C. 530-529, and his son Cambyses was at first occupied with a disputed succession.[198] Thus Egypt had a respite. It was not till after the death of Amasis in B.C. 528-7, that war actually broke out between the two powers, and the hosts of Persia made their attack on the kingdom of the Pharaohs.

During his long reign of forty-four years,[199] Amasis found abundant time to encourage art and architecture. The chief object of his fostering care was his capital city of Saïs, which owned to him much of its ornamentation. He added a great court of entrance to the temple of Neith in that city, with propylæa of unusual dimensions, adorned the dromos conducting to it with numerous andro-sphinxes, erected colossal statues within the temple precincts, and conveyed thither from Elephantiné a monolithic shrine or chamber of extraordinary dimensions.[200] The length of the chamber was, according to Herodotus, twenty-one cubits, or thirty-one feet six inches; its width, twelve cubits, or eighteen feet; and its height five cubits, or seven and a half feet. It must have weighed several hundreds of tons.[201] Another similar shrine, but of smaller dimension, was erected by Amasis at Thmuïs, or Leontopolis, and still remains *in situ;* the length of this is about twenty-two feet, the breadth thirteen, and the height eleven.[202]

Amasis also adorned Memphis with statues and buildings. A colossal work of the former class reached the great height of seventy-five feet, and is said by Herodotus[203] to have been "recumbent," the truth perhaps being that it had never been erected. This statue, in the time of Herodotus, lay in front of the great temple of Phthah, where it seems to have been also seen by Strabo.[204] Two lesser colossi were placed by Amasis on either side of the same temple.[205] The temple of Isis, which he erected at Memphis, was a large and handsome building.

Thebes, Abydos, and Bubastis were also scenes of his architectural activity. At Thebes the great Karnak temple is said to have been "restored" by Amasis;[206] at Abydos that of Osiris was beautified;[207] at Bubastis, that of Bast or Pasht was adorned.[208] Materials for the restorations and embellishments were derived from the quarries of Toora, of Hammamât, and of Silsilis, in all which places there are inscriptions dated in this monarch's reign, set up apparently by his officers.[209]

Statuary received its full share of attention at this period, and the king himself was among those who gave this highest form of art the greatest encouragement. Besides his colossi, Amasis caused numerous statues to be made of himself, some of which have come down to our day. There is one, much injured, in the Villa Albani at Rome; another, in a still worse condition, at the Hague; and a third, or rather the head of a third, in the Museum of Boulaq.²¹⁰ To his reign belong also the statue of Pefaanet in the Museum of the Louvre, that of Nefau-mencht in the Museum of Berlin, and those of Psamatik, Uta-hor-suten-net, and Henáatá, in the Museums of Florence and London.²¹¹ Statues are also mentioned among the presents which he bestowed upon Greek communities, as Cyréné, Samos, and Lindus.²¹² Some were in stone, others in wood, a material very commonly used by the Egyptians.

The picture of himself, painted on panel, which Amasis presented to the Cyrenæans,²¹³ shows that he did not confine his attention to statuary, but was likewise a patron of the sister art of painting. Wilkinson says²¹⁴ that works of art belonging to this class were produced by the Egyptians as early as the twelfth century; but it may be doubted whether painting at that early date was not limited to the coarse coloring of bas reliefs, and whether portraits on a flat surface were not, at the time of Amasis, of recent introduction into Egypt from Asiatic Greece or Lydia, where the art seems to have originated.²¹⁵

Amasis appears to have had at least three wives.²¹⁶ The most important of them was Ankhnes-neferapra, daughter of Psamatik II. and of Nitocris, the sister of Apries, by espousing whom he sought to acquire a legitimate title to the throne of the Pharaohs. Another, as we have seen,²¹⁷ was Ladicé or Laodicé, the daughter of a Greek of Cyréné, whom he wedded to cement his friendship with that state. A third, named Tentkheta, was the daughter of an Egyptian priest of Phthah, Petnit, or Patu-nit.²¹⁸ The last-named of these royal ladies bore him the prince who succeeded him upon the throne under the name of Psamatik Ankh-ka-en-ra,

Ankhnes-neferapra seems to have held the principal rank in the royal harem. She alone of the royal wives was allowed to exhibit herself upon the walls of temples, where she appears sometimes alone, sometimes accompanied by her husband, sometimes attended by an official called Sheshonk.²¹⁹ Her sarcophagus in black marble is of the finest quality, covered with hieroglyphics, and wrought with care and delicacy. It was found at Luxor, behind the Rameseum, in a deep pit, by the French expedition of the beginning of the present century,[220] and is now to be seen in the great Egyptian gallery of the British Museum.[221]

Amasis was buried at Saïs, in a tomb which he had prepared himself within the precincts of the temple of Neith.[222] It was a sepulchral chamber, opening out of one of the cloistered courts, with folding doors, and with the tomb at the further end. Though violated by Cambyses,[223] it was not destroyed, but appears to have been seen by Herodotus in its pristine condition. There are, however, at present no remains to be seen of it.[224]

Psamatik III. succeeded his father at a time when the Persian invasion was a thing that could not be arrested. As his whole reign did not exceed six months,[225] and the expedition must have been some months upon the march, we may presume that it was on its way at the time of his accession. All that he could do, therefore, was to make preparations for a stubborn resistance. He gathered his Greek and Carian mercenaries together, and took up a position near Pelusium,[226] the point at which an invader from the northeast necessarily approached Egypt. The foreign corps was supported by a large army of native Egyptians; but it may be suspected that the two elements did not very heartily coalesce, and the result was a crushing defeat which decided the fate of the empire. If we may believe Ctesias,[227] the loss on the Egyptian side was 50,000 men, which implies a complete rout; while, as the Persians lost 7,000, there must have been some stiff fighting before the rout began. No doubt the Greeks fought well; but in the broad plain wherein the battle took place they would be outflanked, surrounded, and overpowered by numbers. The Persians were at no time contemptible soldiers, and they were now at the height of their national vigor; they had recently conquered the whole Western Asia, were full of confidence in themselves, hardy, strong, and accustomed to fighting. The Greeks, on the other hand, had acted as a mere civic guard for nearly half a century, and the native Egyptians were still more unaccustomed to warfare, having seen but little active service[32n] since the time of Psamatik I. It is not surprising, therefore, that the army of Egypt was defeated, and driven in headlong flight from the field; nor can we wonder that no second stand was made in the open, since it must have been felt that the same causes which had given Persia the victory on the Pelusiac plain would secure her arms success in any other similar encounter.[229]

Nothing then remained for Psamatik but to place his troops behind walls, and see if in this way he could baffle or tire out the invaders. Memphis was a strong city, and, had it been well provisioned or able to maintain its communication with the sea, might have stood a prolonged siege.[230] But no special preparations for a siege seem to have been made; and Cambyses had taken care to bring with him a strong fleet,[231] which blockaded the mouths of the Nile, and even mounted the river to the vicinity of the capital.[232] Thus it was impossible to continue the defence very long. After murdering the crew of a Greek vessel, sent to summon them to surrender, and thus deservedly incurring the extreme displeasure of Cambyses, the entire garrison, regarding resistance as hopeless, gave themselves up. Cambyses punished the deed of blood severely. He selected from the Egyptians who had surrendered themselves two thousand chief men—ten for each of the murdered Greeks[233]—and condemned them to be publicly executed. A son of the fallen monarch shared their fate. As for the king himself, it would seem that at first his life was spared,[234] and that he was even treated with some favor; but it was not long before suspicion arose. Psamatik was accused of having taken part in a conspiracy against Cambyses, and was forthwith put to death. Thus perished this unfortunate monarch, the last of the long line of Pharaohs, which commencing with Menes, or at any rate with Seneferu,[235] had ruled Egypt, as a great independent monarchy, for not less than twenty centuries.

It is not within the scope of the present history to pursue the fortunes of the Egyptian people any further. Frequent revolts characterized the period of their subjection to Persia; and from time to time it probably appeared to the people themselves that the throne of the Pharaohs was re-established. But again and again the Persians proved their superiority in the field, and forced the Egyptians to submit to them. Thus during the Persian period—from B.C. 527 to B.C. 322—Egypt must be considered to have occupied in the main, the position of a Persian province;[236] and her revolts and re-subjugations belong therefore to the history of Persia. The present writer, in his "Fifth Ancient Monarchy," has already treated of them;[237] and the reader who desires to pursue the subject may be referred to that work for information.

Still, it remains to touch briefly upon the art and civilization of this final period, which have peculiar features not destitute of interest. The time is one of revival, and has been called 'the Egyptian *renaissance.*'[238] Under the

Ethiopians, and still more under the Assyrians, Egyptain art had declined, nay, had almost sunk into abeyance. Such indications of it as we possess are coarse and tinged with foreign ideas. It was the object of the Psammetichi to re-establish a true native school (Fig. 55). We have small remains of their architecture, but enough to show clearly that it went upon the old lines; and we know that it included colossal statues, obelisks, enormous propylæa, pillared courts,[239] and the other main elements of early Egyptian architectural effect. Some novelties in the ornamentation are pleasing.[240] Of their plastic art, on the contrary, we have abundant specimens; and we can see that it aims at a "return to the good old times,"[241] the representations calling vividly to remembrance the masterpieces of the old empire. True relief is used, instead of the *cavo rilievo* which was in fashion under the eighteenth and nineteenth dynasties. "An extreme neatness of manipulation in the drawings and lines, in imitation of the best epochs of art in the earlier times, serves for the instant recognition of the work of this age, the fineness of which often reminds us of the performances of a seal-engraver."[242] Extreme delicacy and extreme elaboration are the main characteristics of the plastic art of the period. Faces are finished with great care, the ear and nose being well rendered, and the hair worked out in the utmost possible detail.[243] Some of the bas-reliefs (Fig. 57) seem to show traces of Greek influence. There rest upon these works, as has been well said, "a gentle and almost feminine tenderness, which has impressed upon the imitations of living creatures the stamp of an incredible delicacy both of conception and execution."[244] Wood-engraving is incapable of expressing such soft and tender treatment;[245] but the accompanying illustrations will perhaps help to give some slight idea of the art in question—of its beauty, delicacy, and approximation to the Greek type.

Similar refinement is observable in the statues and statuettes. The Pastophorus of the Vatican, the Horus of the Louvre, the bronze statuette of Ammon-Arsaphes in the British Museum, the "little statues, holding a shrine of the Saïte dignitary, Pitebhu,"[246] the "famous cow of the celestial Hathor, and the statues of Osiris and Isis, the offerings of a certain Psamatik, which now form the admired masterpieces of the collection at Boulaq; the numberless standing images in bronze of the goddess Neith of Saïs—these, and a hundred similiar works of sculpture, furnish instructive examples of **the refinement and delicacy of the monuments which came** from the hands of the artists of this period."[247] The proportions of the figures are defective, the limbs being too long and slim; the muscular development is but slightly indicated;[248] and the whole result is wanting in strength and vigor; but grace, softness, tenderness, characterize the period, and give it a beauty and elegance which are charming."[249]

But, while in artistic matters there was thus an effort—albeit only moderately successful—to return to antiquity and to produce works of an archaic type, in religion and in manners the spirit of the age was different, and exhibited an unwholesome craving after what was strange and novel. "Besides the great established gods of the old Egyptian theology, there now come forward upon the monuments," says Dr. Brugsch,[250] "monstrous forms, the creations of a widely-roving fancy, which peopled the whole world—heaven, earth, and the subaqueous and subterranean depths—with demons and genii of whom the older age with its pure doctrine had scarcely an idea." By the time of Nectanebo I. half the gods of the Pantheon were new;[251] and though this extreme development was the work of a later age than that of the Psammetichi, the spirit from which it proceeded was already abroad. Asia poured the fetid stream of her manifold superstitions into Africa, and to the old theology was added a wild and wierd demonology which proved wonderfully attractive to the now degenerated Egyptians. At the same time the belief in magic and witchcraft became general. "Exorcisms (Fig. 62) of the demons in all manner of forms, from wild beasts with their ravening teeth to the scorpion with his venomous sting, form henceforth a special science, which was destined to supersede the old and half-lost traditional lore of past ages. The demon-song of 'The old man who regained his youth, the hoary one who became young again,' the exorcisms of Thoth and the powers of witchcraft in league with him, are the favorite themes which cover the polished surfaces of the monuments of this remarkable time."[252] Apis worship became also more pronounced. Ever-increasing honors were paid to the sacred bulls, as time went on. The tablets recording their birth, life, and burial grow in length;[253] the ceremonies accompanying their sepulture become more complicated and more expensive,[254] and the adornment of their tombs more magnificent. Granite sarcophagi were provided for them; and these were cut and polished with great care;[255] they were from twelve to thirteen feet high and from fifteen to eighteen feet long; the smallest did not weigh **less than sixty-four tons.**

Manners likewise suffered a transformation. The women were degraded by having the heavier forms of labor thrown upon them,[256] and were otherwise burdened and placed under restrictions.[257] The men were demoralized by being cut off from military training, and from the bracing effects of active service both upon mind and body. National spirit was sapped by the devolution of the royal favor on a race of foreigners, to whom Egyptian customs and Egyptian ideas were abhorrent, and who no doubt openly showed their contempt for the unwarlike nation which had hired their services. Commerce with Greece and with Asia unsettled all the old Egyptian opinions and habitudes, and introduced a thousand novelties of belief, dress and behavior. The Saïtic kings had thought to renovate the old monarchy by an infusion of fresh blood into its veins.[258] But the experiment, always hazardous, failed, since the patient was too weak to bear so violent a remedy. The civilization of the Egyptians had grown up under circumstances which completely isolated it. Its continuance depended on the isolation being continued. The basis upon which it rested was immobility. From the time that it was brought into contact with the spirit of progress, as embodied in the Greek race and the Grecian civilization, it was necessarily doomed to perish. It did not possess the vigor or vitality which could enable it to start afresh on a new path; nor was it sufficiently solid and self-poised to remain unaffected by the new ideas. Like a building, grown old and unstable through the long lapse of years, which it is attempted to restore and renovate by new work alien in character, the Egyptian civilization collapsed under the difficulties of the times and the experiments made upon it, disappearing from the ken of man in a heap of unsightly ruins. That it had a revival under the Ptolemies is what we should not have expected, and must be regarded as an indication of its having possessed an extraordinary force and power—a force and power which enabled it to rise from the grave after a trance of two centuries and become once more for nearly three hundred years a living entity.

APPENDIX.

NOTE A. (See p. 5.)

THE fragments of the Turin "Papyrus of the Kings," after all the care and labor bestowed on them by Seyffarth,¹

MANETHO, according to.   TURIN PAPYRUS.

Names of Kings	Africanus	Armenian Eusebius	Eusebius of Syncellus	Names of Kings	Years	Months	Days	Authorities
	Yrs.	Yrs.	Yrs.					
2ND DYNASTY								
Nephercheres	25	—	—	Neferka-Sokari	8	8	0	De Rougé & Brugsch
Sesochris	48	48	48	Hutefa	11?	8	4	"
Cheneres	—	—	30	Beb(l)	27	2	1	"
3D DYNASTY								
Necherophes	28	—	—	Nebka	19	?	?	"
Tosorthros	29	—	—	Sar	19	1?	0	"
4TH DYNASTY								
Soris	29	—	—	—	19	0	0	Brugsch
Souphis	63	—	—	—	6	0	0	"
Souphis II	66	—	—	***zaf	6	0	0	"
Mencheres	63	—	—	—	24	0	0	"
Rutoises	25	—	—	—	24	0	0	"
Bicheres	22	—	—	—	23	0	0	"
Sebercheres	7	—	—	—	8	0	0	"
5TH DYNASTY								
Usercheres	28	—	—	—	18	0	0	"
Sephres	13	—	—	—	4	0	0	"
Nephercheres	20	—	—	—	2	0	0	"
Sisires	7	—	—	***ka	7	0	0	"
Cheres	20	—	—	—	12	0	0	"
Rathures	44	—	—	—	7	0	0	"
	—	—	—	—	—			"
	—	—	—	—	21	0	0	"
Mencheres	9	—	—	Menkahor	8	0	0	—
Tancheres	44	—	—	Tat	28	0	0	—
Onnos	33	—	—	Unas	30	0	0	—
6TH DYNASTY								
Othoës	30	—	—	—				De Rougé & Hincks
Phios	53	—	—	—	?	6	21	"
	—	—	—	—	20	0	0	"
Methusouphis	7	—	—	—	14	?	0	"
Phiops	94	—	—	—	90	0	0	"
Menthesouphis	1	—	—	—	1	1	0	"

APPENDIX.

MANETHO, according to.   TURIN PAPYRUS.

Names of Kings	Africanus	Armenian Eusebius	Eusebius of Syncellus	Names of Kings	Years	Months	Days	Authorities
	Yrs.	Yrs.	Yrs.					
12TH DYNASTY								
Amenemes .	16	16	16	—	—			Wilkinson
Sesonchosis	46	46	46	—	45	0	0	"
Ammanemes	38	38	38	—	10 at least			"
Sesostris . . .	48	48	48	—	19	"	"	"
Lachares . . .	8	8	8	—	30	"	"	"
Ameres . . .	8			—	40	"		"
Amenemes . .	8	42	42	—	9	3	27	Wilkinson
Skemiophris .	4			—	3	10	24	& Brugsch

N. B.—It will be seen that of the thirty-seven reigns estimated by both authorities, three only are alike ; six more come within one year, while twenty-eight differ still more widely. Taken altogether, Manetho's numbers are greatly in excess, amounting, when added together, to 984 years ; whereas the numbers of the papyrus amount to less than 615 years.

Lepsius,[2] and Wilkinson,[3] admit still of so much variety of arrangement, that only in a comparatively few cases can we compare with absolute certainty its statements as to the length of kings' reigns with those of Manetho. In far the greater number of cases where such a comparison has been regarded as possible, the possibility rests upon a hypothetical arrangement of the fragments, which is more or less probable ; and thus an element of uncertainty comes in. We have, therefore, in the above comparative list, distinguished the certain from the doubtful cases by printing the former in italics. With regard to the latter, which are printed in the ordinary Roman type, we shall in each case give in a separate column the authority by whom the arrangement producing the result has been made.

NOTE B. (See p. 199.)

Most Egyptologists accept the identifications of De Rougé and regard the Tânauna as Danaans, the Sharuten as Sardinians, the Sheklusha as Sikelians or Sicilians, the Tulusha as Tuscans, the Uashash as Oscans, the Purusata as Pelasgians, and the Tekaru as Teucrians.[4] But there is scarcely any case, excepting the last, where the identification is etymologically satisfactory.

APPENDIX. 273

Tánauna. ⟶ 𓀀𓏌𓂝𓅐. Rendered letter for letter, this word is *Ta-a-na-u-na*, hardly a natural equivalent for the Greek Dănăoi. The hand may no doubt represent *d*; but the double *a* which follows corresponds but ill with the short Greek alpha. The *u* is altogether superfluous, as also is the *n* of the final syllable. By saying that *Tánauna* represents the "Danaans," this surplusage is concealed, since "Danaan" has an *n*; but the *-an* is an English adjectival ending, to which there is no equivalent in the Greek Danaoi. It has been sought to remove the objection from the double *a* by supposing Daunii, and not Danai, to be meant;[5] but the second *n* remains superfluous in this case no less than in the other.

Sharuten. 𓉐𓅐𓏤𓈖. Here again the final *n* is superfluous. The people of Sardinia were known to the Romans always as Sardi, to the Greeks generally as "Sardooi."[6] It is true the Greeks called them "Sardonioi" occasionally;[7] but their own name for themselves is likely to have had a form like the Latin.

Sheklusha, 𓉐𓂝𓏤𓅐. In this word the last *two* signs are superfluous. In Sikeloi, Siculi, there is no second *s*; and the best Egyptian equivalent would be Sheklu, or rather Seklu, 𓉐𓂝, there being no necessity of changing the initial *s* into *sh*.[8]

Tulusha, ⟵𓅱𓃭𓉐𓅐. The lion may no doubt be read as *r* no less than as *l*; and *Turusha* may be the proper articulation. It is said that that word well represents the *Tusci* of the Romans, or still better the *Tursce, Turscer,* of the Eugubine Tables.[9] We are told, however, that the Tuscans or Etruscans called themselves *Rasena,*[10] so that the initial *t* would appear not to be a root letter of the name.

Uashasha, 𓊪𓅐𓉐𓅐𓉐𓅐. If the name "Osci" is a contracted form of "Opici" (through Opisci),[11] and *p* consequently a root letter of the name, we should expect the *p* to appear in an Egyptian representation of the word bearing date about B.C. 1300. Further, the second *sh* is superfluous, " Osci " having one *s* only.

Purusata, [hieroglyphs]. Here the difficulty is admitted to be considerable, since, if the Pelasgi are meant, the *l* of the last syllable is inexplicable. It is true that the Egyptians had no *g;* but they had several forms of *k*, and would naturally have expressed the *g* in Pelasgi by one of them." There would also have been no reason why they should have used the long *u*, ρ to express the Greek epsilon in Πελασγοί. These grounds of objection to the proposed identification are so strong, that many think them insuperable, and suggest that the *Purusata* are really the Philistines,[13] פְּלִשְׁתִּים, Φυλιστιείμ, whom they suppose to have migrated from Crete at this time, and, after their repulse by Rameses, to have been settled by him in Gaza, Ashdod, and Ascalon. This view, however, if free from etymological, is beset by historical difficulties;[14] and the result is that the Purusata, like most of the other tribes named, remain an enigma for future ages to unriddle.

Tekaru, [hieroglyphs]. The identification of the Tekaru with the Teucri (Τευκροί) is wholly unobjectionable. Etymologically the two words are exact equivalents, while historically the Teucri are known as powerful and bold adventurers, dissatisfied with their old settlements in Asia, and desirous of spreading themselves into remote countries. The Teucrian and Mysian invasion of Europe, mentioned by Herodotus,[15] which began at the Canal of Constantinople and ended at the Adriatic, is a fair parallel to the expedition of the Tekari and Purusata in the eleventh year of Rameses III., which began in Asia Minor and terminated on the confines of Egypt.

The argument which has the greatest force in favor of the proposed identifications is the cumulative one. While, severally and separately considered, the identifications are in almost every case doubtful, they lend support to each other by the way in which they blend into an harmonious whole. No counter theory has been proposed which is nearly so plausible. Dr. Brugsch's " Carian-Colchian " invasion, in which the natives proceed from Armenia and Cilicia, partly by land through Asia Minor, and partly by water on the Mediterranean,[16] in which the Uashasha are the Ossetes of the Caucasus,[17] the Tekaru and the Purusata Zygritæ and Prosoditæ from Cyprus,[16] the Turusha people of Mount Taurus,[19] the

Sharuten Colchio-Caucasians, and the Sheklusha the people of Zagylis,[20] has no coherency, and approves itself to no one. In the theory of De Rougé, adopted by M. Chabas and Dr. Birch, there is the double charm of consistency and of surpassing interest. The nations form a group, widely dispersed yet still continuous, extending from Sardinia and Sicily on the one hand to northeastern Asia Minor on the other. They represent the chief nations of these parts and leave no manifest gap. The parts, by land and sea, are distributed as we might expect. And the result is that most minds accept the view as probably not far from the truth. They delight to think that the European nations, so far back as the thirteenth century B.C., showed signs of their inherent vigor, possessed fleets, fought naval battles, and contended with the most advanced and the most powerful of the then existing monarchies. They cannot but feel that the entire subject is encompassed with difficulties; but the theory which has been put forth attracts them, and they embrace it with entire satisfaction. If it is not true it ought to be. *Se non è vero è ben trovato.*

LIST OF AUTHORS AND EDITIONS

QUOTED IN THE NOTES.

ABD-ALLATIF, Relation de l'Egypte, traduite et enrichie de Notes par M. Silvestre de Sacy, Paris, 1810, 4to.
ACHILLES TATIUS, ed. Jacobs, Lipsiæ, 1821.
ÆLIAN, Natura Animalium, ed. Jacobs. Jenæ, 1832.
AGATHARCIDES, in C. Müller's Geographi Minores, Parisiis, 1855-1861.
AFRICANUS, Fragments, in the Chronographia of Syncellus. (See SYNCELLUS.)
ALEXANDER, Bishop, Bampton Lectures, London, 1877.
ALEXANDER, POLYHISTOR, in the Fragm. Hist. Græc. of C. Müller, vol. iii, Parisiis, 1849-51.
ALISON, Sir A., History of Europe, Edinburgh and London, 1852.
AMMIANUS MARCELLINUS, ed. Gronovius, Lugd. Batav., 1693, 4to.
ANDERSON, Geography for the Use of Schools, London, 1858.
ARISTOTLE, Opera, ed. Acad. Reg. Boruss., Berolini, 1831.
ATHENÆUS, Deipnosophistæ, ed. Schweighaüser, Argentorat. 1801, etc.

BAKER, Sir S., Albert Nyanza. London, 1866.
—, Sir S. Nile Tributaries, London, 1867.
BARTH, Dr., Wanderungen, etc., Berlin, 1849.
BEHISTUN INSCRIPTION, ed. H. C. Rawlinson, in the Journal of the Asiatic Society, vols. x and xi, London, 1847-8.
BELON, Nature des Oyseaux, Paris, 1555, folio.
BELZONI, G., Operations and Discoveries in Egypt and Nubia, London, 1822, 4to.

BEROSUS, in C. Müller's Fragm. Hist. Græc., vol. ii, Parisiis, 1848.
BIRCH, Dr. S., Ancient Pottery, London, 1873.
—, Egypt from the Earliest Times,[1] London (no date, about 1875).
—, Egyptian Grammar, in Bunsen's Egypt's Place, vol. v, London, 1867.
—, Guide to First and Second Egyptian Rooms,[2] London, 1874.
—, Guide to Egyptian Galleries, London, 1874.
—, Hieroglyphical Dictionary, in Bunsen's Egypt's Place, vol. v, London. 1867.
BLAKESLEY. Dean, Herodotus with a Commentary, London, 1854.
BOECKH, Corpus Inscriptionum Græcarum, Berolini, 1828, etc., folio.
BRUCE, Travels to Discover the Source of the Nile, 3d ed., Edinburgh, 1815.
BRUGSCH, Dr. H., Études sur un Papyrus Médical de Berlin, Leipzig, 1853.
—, Geographische Inschriften altägyptischer Denkmäler, Leipzig, 1857-60.
—, Grammaire Démotique, Berlin, 1855, folio.
—, Geschichte Aegyptens unter den Pharaonen, Leipzig. 1878.
—, Histoire d'Egypte, 2ième édition, Leipzig, 1875.
—, History of Egypt under the Pharaohs, translated by H. D. Seymour and P. Smith, London, 1879.
—, Hieroglyphisch-demotisches Wörterbuch, Leipzig, 1867-8, folio.
—, L'Exode et les Monuments Egyptiens, Leipsig, 1875.
—, Recueil de Monuments Egyptiens, Leipsic, 1859-63, 4to.
—, Scriptura Ægyptiorum demotica. Berolini, 1848, 4to.

[276]

[1] Quoted sometimes in this work as "Ancient Egypt."
[2] Quoted as "Guide to Museum."

LIST OF AUTHORS.

BUNSEN, Ch. C. J., Egypt's Place in Universal History, translated by C. H. Cottrell, with additions by Dr. S. Birch, London, 1848-67.
BURCKHARDT, Travels in Nubia, 2d ed., London, 1822.
BURTON, Excerpta Hieroglyphica, Cairo, 1825-37.

CALLIMACHUS, ed. Ernesti, Lugd. Bat., 1761.
CAMBRIDGE ESSAYS, London, 1855-8.
CENSORINUS, ed. Haverkamp, Lugd. Bat., 1767.
CHABAS, F. J., Études sur l'Antiquité Historique, Paris, 1872.
—, Le plus ancien Livre du monde, Paris, 1857.
—, Les Pasteurs en Égypte, Amsterdam, 1868, 4to.
—, Mélanges Egyptologiques, Séries I. et II., Paris, 1862-4.
—, Mélanges Egyptologiques, Série III., Paris, 1870-3.
—, Recherches pour servir à l'Histoire de la XIXme Dynastie, et spécialement à celle des temps de l'Exode, Paris, 1873, 4to.
CHAMPOLLION-LE-JEUNE, Dictionnaire Egytien en Écriture Hiéroglyphique, Paris, 1841-4, folio.
—, Grammaire Egyptienne, Paris, 1836-41, folio.
—, Lettres écrites d'Egypte et de Nubie en 1828 et 1829, Paris, 1868.
—, Notices Descriptives des Monuments de l'Egypte et de la Nubie, Paris, 1835-45, folio.
CICERO, ed. Ernesti, Londini, 1819.
CLAUDIAN, ed. Heber, Londini, 1836.
CLEMENS ALEX., ed. Potter. Venetiis, 1757.
CONTEMPORARY REVIEW, London, 1879.
CORY, Ancient Fragments, London, 1832.
CTESIAS, ed. Bähr, Frankfurtii, 1824.
CUDWORTH, Intellectual System of the Universe, London, 1678, folio.
CURTIUS, Q., Vita Alexandri Magni, ed. Pitiscus, Hague, 1708.

D'ANVILLE, Mémoires sur l'Égypte Ancienne et Moderne, Paris, 1766, 4to.
DECREE OF CANOPUS, in the "Records of the Past," vol. viii. (See RECORDS.)
DESCRIPTION DE L'EGYPTE, publiée sous la Direction de M. Jomard, original edition, Paris, 1802-29, folio.
DEVERIA, Mélanges d'Archéologie Egyptienne, Paris, 1857.
DICTIONARY OF LANGUAGES, a Rudimentary Dictionary of Universal Philology, London, 1873.
DIO CASSIUS, ed. Reimer, Hamburgh, 1752, folio.
DIODORUS SICULUS, ed. Dindorf, Parisiis, 1843-4.
DIOGENES LAERTIUS, ed. Wetstein, Amstelodami, 1692.
DIONYSIUS HALICARNASSENSIS, ed. Reiske, Leipsic, 1774-7.

DIOSCORIDES, Materia Medica, ed. Kuhn, Lipsiæ, 1829.
DÖLLENGER, Dr., Jew and Gentile, translated by N. Darnell, London, 1862.
DÜMICHEN, Die Flotte einer ägyptischen Königin, Leipsig, 1868.
—, Historische Inschriften alt-ägyptischer Denkmäler, Leipzig, 1867, folio.

ENCYCLOPÆDIA BRITANNICA, 8th ed. Edinburgh, 1853-60.
ERATOSTHENES, in the Chronographia of Syncellus. (See SYNCELLUS.)
EUSEBIUS PAMPHILI, Chronicorum Canonum libri duo, ed. Maius et Zohrab, Mediolani, 1818.
—, Præparatio Evangelica, ed. Gaisford, Oxonii, 1843.
EUSTATHIUS, Comment. ad Dionys. Perieget., ed. H. Stephanus, Parisiis, 1577.

FALKENER, Ephesus, and the Temple of Diana, London, 1862.
FELLOWS, Sir C., Travels in Asia Minor, London, 1839.
—, Travels in Lycia, London. 1841.
FERGUSSON, J., History of Architecture, 1st ed., London, 1865; 2d ed., London, 1873.
FORSKAL, Descriptiones Animalium, Avium, etc., ed. C. Niebuhr, Havniæ, 1775, 4to.

GATTY, C., Catalogue of Mayer Collection, Liverpool, 1877.
GEMINUS, Elementa Astronomiæ, Altorfii, 1590.
GENTLEMEN'S MAGAZINE, London, 1800 et seqq.
GLADSTONE, W. E., Homeric Synchronisms, London. 1876.
—, Juventus Mundi, London. 1869.
GROTE, G., History of Greece, London, 1862.

HASSELQUIST, Voyages and Travels in the Levant, London, 1766.
HECATÆUS, Fragments, in C. Müller's Fragm. Hist. Græc., vol. i, Parisiis, 1846.
HEEREN, Works, translated by Talboys, Oxford, 1833.
HELLANICUS, Fragments, in C. Müller's Fragm. Hist. Græc., vol. i, Parisiis, 1846.
HENGSTENBERG, Aegypten und Mose, Berlin, 1840.
—, Egypt and the Pentateuch, translated from the above by Mr. Robbins, with additional notes by Dr. Cooke Taylor, Edinburgh, 1845.
HERODOTUS, ed. Bähr, Lipsiæ, 1856-61.
—, ed. Blakesley, London, 1854.
—, History of, a new English Version, by Canon Rawlinson, assisted by Sir H. Rawlinson and Sir Gardner Wilkinson, 2d ed., London, 1862; 3d ed., London, 1875.
HIERONYMUS, Opera, Benedictine ed., Paris, 1693, folio.
HIPPOCRATES, ed. Kuhn, Lipsiæ, 1826.

278 LIST OF AUTHORS.

HOMER, Iliad, ed. Heyne, Lipsiæ, 1802.
—, Odyssea, ed. Löwe, Lipsiæ, 1828.
HORACE, ed. Döring, Oxonii, 1838.
HORAPOLLO, Hieroglyphica, ed. De Pauw, Traject. ad Rhen., 1727, 4to.
HUMBOLDT, Asie Centrale, Paris, 1843.

ISOCRATES, in the Oratores Attici of Baiter and Saupp, Turici, 1850.

JAMBLICHUS, De Vita Pythagoræ, ed. Kiessling, Lipsiæ, 1815.
JOSEPHUS, Opera, ed. Hudson, Oxonii, 1720.
JOURNAL OF ASIATIC SOCIETY, Lincoln, 1846, et seqq.
JOURNAL OF GEOGRAPHICAL SOCIETY, London, 1840, et seqq.
JUNKER, Forschungen aus der Geschichte des Alterthums, Leipzig, 1863.
JUSTIN, ed. Gronovius, Lugd. Bat., 1760.
JUVENAL, ed. Ruperti, Lipsiæ, 1819-20.

KALISCH, Historical and Critical Commentary on Exodus, London, 1865.
KENRICK, Ancient Egypt under the Pharaohs, London, 1850.
KURTZ, History of the Old Covenant, trans. by J. Martin, Edinburgh, 1859.

LACTANTIUS, Opera, ed. Bauldri, Traject. ad Rhenum, 1692.
LANE, Modern Egyptians, London, 1836.
LARCHER, Histoire d'Hérodote, Paris, 1786.
LAYARD, Sir H., Nineveh and Babylon, London, 1853.
LEEMANS, Monumens Egyptiens du Musée d'Antiquités des Pays-Bas à Leide, Leide, 1839-76, folio.
—, Lettre à Salvolini, Leide, 1838.
LENORMANT, Manuel d'Histoire Ancienne de l'Orient, 3me ed., Paris, 1869.
—, Frammento di Statua, di uno dei Pastori di Egitto, Roma, 1877.
LEO AFRICANUS, Africæ Descriptio, Antverpiæ, 1556.
LEPSIUS, Dr. R., Denkmäler aus Aegypten und Aethiopien, Berlin, 1849-58, folio.
—, Chronologie der Aegypter, Berlin, 1849, 4to.
—, Grundplan des Grabes König Ramses IV., Berlin, 1867, 4to.
—, Königsbuch der alten Aegypter, Berlin, 1858, 4to.
—, Lettre sur l'Alphabet Hieroglyphique, Rome, 1837.
—, Todtenbuch der Aegypter, Leipzig, 1842, 4to.
—, Ueber die XXII. ägyptische Königsdynastie nebst einigen Bemerkungen zu der XXVI. und andern Dynastien des neuen Reichs, Berlin, 1856, 4to.
LEWIS, Sir G. C., Astronomy of the Ancients, London, 1862.
LETRONNE, Statue Vocale de Memnon, Paris, 1833, 4to.
LINANT DE BELLEFONDS, Mémoire sur le Lac Mœris, Alexandria, 1843, 4to.

LIVY, ed. Travers Twiss, Oxonii, 1840-41.
LUCAN, Pharsalia, ed. Oudendorp, Lugd. Bat., 1728.
LUCIAN, ed. Hemsterhuis, Biponti, 1789 et seqq.

MACROBIUS, ed. Gronovius, Lugd. Bat., 1670.
MANETHO, Fragments, in C. Müller's Fragm. Hist. Græc., vol. ii, Parisiis, 1848.
MANILIUS, ed. Stöber, Argentorat., 1767.
MARIETTE, Choix de Monuments et de Dessins découverts ou exécutés pendant le déblaiement du Sérapéum de Memphis, Paris, 1856, 4to.
—, Fouilles exécutées en Egypte, en Nubie, et au Soudan d'après les ordres de S. A. le Viceroi d'Egypte, Paris, 1867, folio.
—, Monuments d'Abydos, vol. iii, Paris, 1880, 4to.
—, Monuments Divers recenillis en Egypte et en Nubie, Paris, 1872-7, folio.
—, Renseignements sur les soixante-quatre Apis trouvés au Sérapéum, Paris, 1855.
—, Sérapéum de Memphis, Paris, 1857, folio.
MARTIAL, Epigrammata, ed. Mattaire, Londini, 1716.
MARTINEAU, H., Eastern Life, Present and Past, London, 1848.
MEGASTHENES, in the Fragm. Hist. Gr. of C, Müller, vol. ii, Paris, 1846-51.
MELA, De Situ Orbis, ed. H. Stephanus, Parisiis, 1577.
MERIVALE, Dean, History of the Romans under the Empire, London, 1865.
MORELL, Thesaurus Morellinus, ed. Haverkamp, Amstelodami, 1734.
MOSHEIM, Latin Translation of Cudworth's Intellectual System of the Universe, Jenæ, 1733, folio.
MULLER, C., Fragmenta Historicorum Græcorum, Parisiis, 1846-70.
—, Geographi Minores, Parisiis, 1855-61.
MÜLLER, K. O., Ancient Art, translated by Leitch, London, 1852.
MÜLLER, MAX, Languages of the Seat of War, 2d ed., London, 1855.
NIEBUHR, B. G., Vorträge uber alte Geschichte, Berlin, 1847.
—, History of Rome, E. T., Cambridge, 1831-42.
—, C., Description de l'Arabie, Amsterdam, 1774.

OPPERT, Expédition Scientifique en Mésopotamie, Paris, 1859—63.
—, Inscriptions des Sargonides, Versailles, 1863.
OVID, ed. Bipont., Argentorat., 1807.

PALMER, W., Egyptian Chronicles, London, 1861.
PAUSANIUS, ed. Siebelis, Lipsiæ, 1822.
PICKERING, Races of Man, London, 1851.
PLATO, ed. Stallbaum, Lipsiæ, 1821-5.

PLINY, Hist. Nat., ed. Sillig, Hamburgi et Gothæ, 1851-7.
PLUTARCH, Opera (ex-officina Hack), Lugd. Bat., 1669.
POLYÆNUS, ed. Luchtmans, Lugd. Bat., 1690.
POLYHISTOR, Alex., in C. Müller's Fragm. Hist. Græc., vol. iii, Parisiis, 1849.
PORPHYRUS, De Abstinentia, ed. De Rhör, Traject. ad Rhenum, 1767.
PRISSE D'AVENNES, Monuments Egyptiens, Paris, 1830-37, folio.
PROPERTIUS, in the edition of Baskerville, Birminghamiæ, 1772.
PTOLEMY, Geographia, ed. Bertius, Amstelodami, 1618.

QUARTERLY REVIEW, London, 1831-75.

RAWLINSON, G., Ancient Monarchies, 1st ed., London, 1862-7 : 2d ed., London, 1871.
—, History of Herodotus. (See HERODOTUS.)
—, Historical Illustrations of the Old Testament, London, 1877.
—, Origin of Nations, London, 1877.
—, Seventh Great Oriental Monarchy, London, 1876.
RAWLINSON, Sir H., Cuneiform Inscriptions, in the Journal of the Royal Asiatic Society, vols, x, xi, etc.
RECORDS OF THE PAST, ed. Dr. S. Birch, London, 1873-8.
REPORT OF BRITISH ASSOCIATION, London, 1875.
REVUE ARCHÉOLOGIQUE, Paris, 1863, et seqq.
REVUE ASIATIQUE, Paris, 1830, et seqq.
REYNOLDS, Sir J., Discourses before the Royal Academy, London, 1798.
RICHARDSON, Travels along the Mediterranean and Parts Adjacent, London, 1822.
RITUAL OF THE DEAD, translated in Bunsen's Egypt's Place, vol. v. (See BUNSEN.)
ROBERTS, D., Egypt and Nubia, London, 1846, folio.
ROSELLINI, Ippolito, Monumenti, Civili, Pisa, 1844-6, 8vo and folio.
—, Monumenti del Culto, Pisa, 1844, 8vo and folio.
—, Monumenti Storici, Pisa, 1832, 8vo and folio.
ROSETTA STONE, in the Records of the Past, vol. iv. (See RECORDS.)
ROUGÉ DE, Catalogue des Monuments Egyptiens de la Salle du Rez-de-chaussée, Paris, 1849.
—, Études sur le Rituel Funéraire des anciens Egyptiens, Paris, 1861-4, folio.
—, Inscription Historique du Roi Pianchi-Meriamoun, reprinted from the Revue Archéologique, Paris, 1863.
—, Recherches sur les Monuments qu'on peut attribuer aux six premières Dynasties de Manéthon, Paris, 1866, 4to.
RUSKIN, J., Stones of Venice, London, 1851-3.

RUSKIN, J., Seven Lamps of Architecture, London, 1849.
RUSSELL, Dr., Ancient and Modern Egypt, published in the Edinburgh Cabinet Library, Edinburgh, 1830-4.

ST. HILAIRE, J. B., Egypt and the Suez Canal, a Narrative of Travel, London, 1857.
ST. LEON, E. de, Egypt and the Khedive, London, 1877.
SCHOLIA AD ARISTOTELEM, in the edition of Aristotle's Works published by the Acad. Reg. Boruss., vol. iv, 1836.
SCHOLIA AD ARATUM, in the Phenomena of Aratus, ed. Buhle, Lipsiæ, 1793.
SCHWEINFURTH, Heart of Africa, London, 1873.
SCYLAX, Periplus, in the Geographi Minores of C. Müller, Parisiis, 1855-61.
SENECA, Opera, ed. Gronovius, Amstelodami, 1672.
SHARPE, S., History of Egypt from the Earliest Times to the Conquest of the Arabs, London, 1859 (4th edition).
—, Egyptian Inscriptions, London, 1836-56, folio.
SHAW, Dr., Travels in Barbary and the Levant, Oxford, 1738.
SMITH, Dean Payne, Bampton Lectures, London, 1869.
SMITH, Dr. W., Dictionary of Greek and Roman Antiquities, 2d ed., London, 1853.
—, Dictionary of the Bible, London, 1863.
—, Dictionary of Greek and Roman Geography, London, 1854.
SMITH, George. History of Asshurbanipal, London, 1871.
SMITH, Philip, Ancient History from the Earliest Records to the Fall of the Western Empire, London, 1865.
SMYTH, C. Piazzi, Antiquity of Intellectual Man, Edinburgh, 1818.
—, Astronomical Observations, Edinburgh, 1847-53.
SOLINUS, Polyhlstor, ed. H, Stephanus, Parisiis, 1577.
SOPHOCLES, ed. Brunck, London (Valpy), 1824.
SPANHEIM, De præstantia et Usu Numismatum, Romæ, 1664, 4to.
SPEAKER'S COMMENTARY, London, 1870-80 (continuing).
STANLEY. Dean, Sinai and Palestine, London, 1856.
STEPHANUS BYZANTINUS, ed. Berkel, Lugd. Bat. 1694.
STRABO, ed. Kramer, Berolini, 1844-52.
SYNCELLUS, Georgius, Chronographia, ed. B. G. Niebuhr, Bonn, 1829.
SYNESIUS, Opera omnia, Paris, 1612.

TACITUS, Opera, ed. Walther, Halis Saxonum, 1831.
THEOCRITUS, Idyllia, ed. Kiessling, London, 1829.
THEOPHRASTUS, De Lapidibus, in his Works, ed. Heinsius, Lugd. Bat., 1613.

THEOPHRASTUS, Historia Plantarum, ed. Stackhouse, Oxonii, 1813.
THUCYDIDES, ed. Becker, Oxonii, 1824.
TRANSACTIONS OF THE ROYAL SOCIETY OF LITERATURE (New Series), London, 1830 et seqq.
TRANSACTIONS OF THE SOCIETY OF BIBLICAL ARCHÆOLOGY, vols. i-vii, London, 1872–80.
TRANSACTIONS OF THE SOCIETY OF BRITISH ARCHITECTS, London, 1854 et seqq.
TREVOR, Canon, Ancient Egypt, its Antiquities, Religion, and History, London, 1863.
TRISTRAM, Canon, Land of Israel, London, 1865.

VALERIUS MAXIMUS. ed. Redmayne, Londini, 1673.
VALÉRY. Historical, Literary, and Artistical Travels in Italy, translated by C. E. Clifton, Paris, 1839.
VIRGILIUS, Opera, ed. Forbiger, Lipsiæ, 1836–9.
VISCONTI, Museo Pio-Clementino, Romæ, 1782–98, folio.
VITRUVIUS, ed. De Laet, Amstelodami, 1649.
VYSE, Col. Howard, Pyramids of Gizeh, London, 1840–2.

WIEDEMANN, Geschichte Aegyptens von Psammetich I. bis auf Alexander den Grossen Leipzig, 1880.

WILKINSON, Sir J. G., Architecture of Ancient Egypt, London, 1850.
—, Hieratic Papyrus of Turin, London, 1851, 4to.
—, Manners and Customs of the Ancient Egyptians, 1st ed., London, 1837–41; New Edition by Dr. S. Birch, London, 1878.
—, Materia Hieroglyphica, Malta, 1824–30, 4to.
—, Notes and Essays in Rawlinson's History of Herodotus (q. v.).
—, Topography of Thebes, London, 1835.
WINCKELMAN, History of Ancient Art, E. T., London, 1850.
WINER, Realwörterbuch, 3d ed., Leipzig, 1847–8.

XANTHUS LYDUS, Fragm. in the Fragm. Hist. Gr. of C. Muller, vol. i, Parisiis, 1846.
XENOPHON, Opera, ed. Schneider et Dindorf, Oxonii, 1817 et seqq.

ZEITSCHRIFT FUR ÄGYPTISCHE SPRACHE UND ALTERTHUMSKUNDE, ed. Lepsius. Berlin, 1860–80 (continuing).
ZOEGA, Numi Ægyptii, Romæ, 1787. 4to.
—, De Origine et Usu Obeliscorum, Romæ, 1797, folio.

NOTES TO HISTORY OF ANCIENT EGYPT.

CHAPTER XII.

[1] Compare the list given by Brugsch (*History of Egypt*, vol. i, p. 30* E. T., 1st ed.) with that of the author in his *Origin of Nations*, p. 21.

[2] Herodotus, book ii.

[3] Manetho of Sebennytus, priest of On, or Heliopolis.

[4] It would seem that a king did not become a god until he ascended the throne.

[5] This is the case with Usurtasen I. according to Brugsch (*History*, vol i, p. 120, 1st ed.), who is given in the Turin papyrus forty-five years.

[6] Brugsch, *History of Egypt*, vol. i, pp. 36-7, 1st ed.

[7] This is confessed by most Egyptologists, though not as yet very clearly apprehended by the general public. Brugsch says: "It is only from the beginning of the twenty-sixth dynasty that the chronology is founded on data which leave little to be desired as to their exactitude" (ibid. p. 32*). Bunsen: "History is not to be elicited from the monuments; not even its framework, chronology" (*Egypt's Place in Universal History*, vol. i, p. 32). Stuart Poole: "The evidence of the monuments with regard to the chronology is neither full nor explicit" (*Dictionary of the Bible*, vol. i, p. 506). Lenormant: "Le plus grand de tous les obstacles à l'établissement d'une chronologie égyptienne régulière, c'est que les Egyptiens eux-mêmes, n'ont jamais eu de chronologie" (*Histoire Ancienne de l'Orient*, vol. i, p 322).

[8] Herod ii, 100, 142.

[9] Ibid. § 99.

[10] Ibid. § 101.

[11] Ibid. §§ 124-34.

[12] Ibid. § 111.

[13] Mœris, he says, lived 900 years before his time (ii, 13), Sabaco 700 (ibid. § 140); yet nine kings intervened, to whom his method of calculation would assign three centuries.

[14] Ibid §§ 112-20.

[15] Ibid. § 141.

[16] Ibid. § 3.

[17] At the commencement of his account of Manetho's dynasties, Eusebius says: "If the quantity of time (covered by these kings) is in excess, we must remember that there were, perhaps, at one and the same time, several kings in Egypt, for *we are told* that the Thinites and Memphites reigned simultaneously, and likewise the Ethiopians and the Saïtes, *and others also*. Moreover, some seem to have reigned in one place, some in another, each dynasty being confined to its own canton; so that the several kings did not rule successively, but different kings reigned at the same time in different places" (*Chron Can*. i, 20, § 3). The expression "we are told" is of special importance, as showing that Eusebius did not himself invent the theory of contemporary dynasties in Egypt; but it is unfortunately vague, and does not enable us to determine whether Manetho, or some commentator on his history, whose work Eusebius had read, is referred to.

[18] The sum total does not generally agree with the items; but it is sufficiently near to make it probable that it was arrived at by simple addition.

[19] See Brugsch, *History of Egypt*, vol. i, p. 120, 1st ed. Errors of this kind, Dr. Brugsch says, make him "despair of putting together a chronological table of the Old Egyptian Empire."

[20] This is the number produced by adding together the years assigned to the first fourteen of the Manethonian dynasties by Africanus. The Armenian Eusebius raises the number to 3,023.

[21] See Bunsen's *Egypt*, vol. i. pp. 119-125.

[22] Ibid p. 86. Compare Müller, *Fragm Hist. Gr.* vol. ii, p 537.

[23] Results slightly differing from these are given by Bunsen (*Egypt*. vol. i, p. 82). Differences in the MSS and in the statements made by the Syncellus make absolute accuracy impossible.

[24] In six only out of the thirty dynasties is the number exactly the same in all the three versions.

[25] E.g. Manetho, according to all the three versions, assigned six years only to Neco, the Pharaoh Nechoh of Scripture. But an Apis *stela* assigns him sixteen years; and this is regarded as settling the matter.

[26] It is especially remarkable that the numbers of the Turin papyrus differ so greatly from Manetho's, showing that the Egyptians had no one definite, generally admitted scheme. As this is a very important point, the details are given in the Appendix (Note A).

[27] Lenormant, *Histoire Ancienne de l'Orient*. vol. i. p. 322.

[28] *Records of the Past*, vol. ii. pp. 19, 21; vol. iv, p. 27; vol. vi, pp. 23, 43, 44, 63, etc.

[29] Manetho's seventeenth dynasty consisted of an equal number of The

ban and Shepherd kings, whom he represented as reigning side by side during the space of 151 years (Syncell. *Chronograph*, p 61).

[30] Even Lenormant admits that in one part of his work, "Manéthon, pour comble d'obscurité, avait *indubitablement* (le témoignage des chronographes est formel) admis dans ses listes des dynasties collatérales, mais qu'en même temps, dans les extraits que nous en avons, aucune indication positive n'indique celles qui furent contemporaines" (*Manuel d'Histoire Ancienne de l'Orient*, vol. i, pp 355-6).

[31] The eleventh with the ninth and tenth (ibid. p 348); and the thirteenth with the fourteenth (p. 358)

[32] *History of Egypt* (1st ed.), vol. i, pp. 107-119, 181; vol ii, pp. 313-14.

[33] *Egypt's Place*, vol. ii, pp. 106, 208, 239; vol. iv, pp. 499, 500, 510-12.

[34] See the author's *Herodotus*, vol. ii, p. 338, 3d edit.

[35] Cambyses died in B.C. 521, having reigned six years in Egypt (Brugsch, *History of Egypt*, vol ii, p 305, 1st ed.), which he must therefore have conquered in B.C. 527, not in B.C. 525, as generally supposed.

[36] Herod. iii, 14, ad init.; Manetho ap. Syncell. *Chronograph* vol i. p. 75, D.

[37] So Herod. iii, 10 Manetho (according to Africanus) gave the same number, but, according to Eusebius, forty-two years only.

[38] Herod. ii, 161, and Manetho, according to Eusebius. But, according to Africanus, Manetho's number was nineteen.

[39] This is proved by one of the Apis *stelæ* (Mariette, No. 40; Brugsch, vol ii, p. 287, 1st ed.), which also makes certain the sixteen years of Neco.

[40] Another of the *stelæ* (No. 39 of Mariette) determines the reign of Psamatik I. to fifty-four years.

[41] The fifty-four years of Psamatik I. were counted from the end of the twenty-six years of Tirhakah, as appears from stelæ No. 37 of Mariette, which is given also by Brugsch (vol. ii, p 285, 1st ed.). Manetho assigned to Tirhakah only eighteen or twenty years.

[42] Pharaoh Hophra appears in Jeremiah as the Egyptian antagonist of Nebuchadnezzar, and as contending with him after the time when Jeremiah was taken into Egypt. This was about B.C. 585, which would be the twelfth year of Apries, according to the numbers in the text. Pharaoh-Nechoh warred with Josiah of Judah, and caused his death in the fourth year before the accession of Nebuchadnezzar, according to the Second Book of Kings, or B.C. 609. Neco, according to the above numbers, reigned from B.C. 618 to 602. Tirhakah is in Scripture contemporary with the great expedition of Sennacherib against Hezekiah, which

fell in the earlier part of Sennacherib's reign, probably about B.C. 698.

[43] Twenty-two, according to Africanus (Syncell. *Chronograph*, vol. i, p. 74, B); twenty-four, according to Eusebius (ib. p. 75, B).

[44] It is generally allowed that the So or Seveh אסֹ of 2 Kings xvii. 4, represents Shabak, in whose name the *k* is unimportant, being merely the suffixed article (Brugsch, *Hist. of Egypt*, vol. ii, p 275, 1st ed.). This king was called in to aid him by Hoshea, a short time before the capture of Samaria, which was in B.C. 722 or B.C. 721.

[45] Six, according to the Manetho of Africanus (Syncell *Chronograph*, vol. i, p. 74, B); forty-four, according to the same author, as reported by Eusebius (ibid. p 75. A).

[46] So Africanus (ap. Syncell. pp. 73-4). The numbers, as reported by Eusebius, scarcely come into competition here; since he assigns identically the same number of years (forty-four) to three dynasties in succession—the twenty-third, twenty-fourth, and twenty-fifth.

[47] 1 Kings xi, 40.

[48] Ibid. xiv, 25, 26; 2 Chr. xii, 1-9.

[49] Two hundred and sixty-five, according to Africanus (Syncell. pp. 73-4); but 302, according to the Armen. Eusebius, and 308, according to the Eusebius of Syncellus (pp. 74-5).

[50] Minimum are generally to be preferred to maximum numbers in the Egyptian lists, on account of the tendency to swell the totals by counting in the entire reigns of kings who were at first associated with their fathers. But the evidence of the monuments at this point tends to show that even the highest estimate of Manetho's numbers is here insufficient.

[51] Manetho's total, according to Africanus, was 200 years; according to Eusebius, 194 years (Syncell. pp. 72-3).

[52] Wilkinson, in the author's *Herodotus*, vol. ii, pp. 364-71, 3d edit.; Brugsch, *History of Egypt*, vol. ii, p. 314, 1st ed.; Lenormant, *Manuel d'Histoire Ancienne*, vol. i, p. 321, etc.

[53] The four kings named Thothmes have but one certain representative in Manetho's list, his Tuthmosis; the three or four Amunophs (Amenhoteps) are reduced to two. Horus, really the last king of the dynasty, is followed by six or seven others; a "Chebros" is interpolated between Aahmes and Amunoph I. Manetho's numbers are insufficient for some of the kings, in excess for others. If the dynasty be closed with Horus, the sum total will not amount to 200 years, according to any computation, and according to one—that of the Armenian Eusebius—will be only 165 years.

[54] Ap. Syncell, vol. i, p. 73, A. The summation of the reigns is given as 348 years, though the actual sum of the

CH. XIII.] THE OLD EMPIRE—THE FIRST BEGINNINGS. 283

years assigned to the kings is, at the most, 325 years
[55] Two hundred and sixty-three years (ap. Syncell. pp. 62, 69, 70).
[56] Two hundred and forty-six years, if we take Rameses I. as heading the nineteenth dynasty (Joseph. c. Apion. § 14).
[57] Mariette and Lenormant give 241 years (Manuel d'Histoire Ancienne, vol. I, p 321); Brugsch, 300 years (History of Egypt, vol. ii, p. 314, 1st ed.); Wilkinson, 190 years (Rawlinson's Herodotus, vol. ii, pp 352, 364); Bunsen, 221 years, etc.
[58] Birch, Ancient Egypt, p. 78; Brugsch, History of Egypt, l.s.c.
[59] Stuart Poole in Dr. Smith's Dictionary of the Bible, ad voc. EGYPT (vol. i, p. 510).
[60] Ap. Syncell. Chronograph. vol. i, p. 61.
[61] Contr. Apion. i, § 14.
[62] Chron. Can. i, 20, § 5; ap. Syncell. Chronograph. vol. i, p. 62, A. The two agree exactly.
[63] See Records of the Past, vol. viii, pp. 3, 4; Brugsch, History of Egypt, vol. i, pp. 239-41, 1st ed
[64] All the reporters of Manetho agree that he made Saites (Salatis) the first of the shepherd kings.
[65] See the "Tablet of 400 years," given in the Records of the Past, vol iv. pp. 35-6; and compare Birch, Ancient Egypt, pp. 75-6, and 126.
[66] Ap. Syncell. Chronograph. pp. 60-1. It is true that Josephus deranges the names (Contr. Ap. l.s.c.), making Apophis the fourth instead of the sixth king; but Africanus and the Armenian Eusebius together must be taken to outweigh his authority.
[67] This point has been well argued by Canon Cooke in the Speaker's Commentary (vol. i, part i, pp. 447-8). His arguments seem to me quite irresistible.
[68] See the table given by Lenormant on the authority of Mariette (Manuel d'Histoire Ancienne, vol i, p. 321).
[69] Hist. of Egypt, vol. i, pp. 33-4; vol. ii, pp. 311-15, 1st ed Calculations founded upon generations are, by the nature of the case, exceedingly uncertain, and become a source of large error, if the ordinary length of a generation in the time and country for which the calculation is made is improperly estimated. Brugsch allows 33⅓ years for his Egyptian generations, which is an over-estimate of at least one third. A correction of this error would reduce his 2,400 years to 1,600.
[70] Egypt's Place, vol. v, p. 62.
[71] See the author's Herodotus, vol. ii, pp. 340-1, and Dr. Smith's Dictionary of the Bible, vol. i, p 508.
[72] Brugsch, History of Egypt, vol. i. p. 63, 1st ed.; Birch, Ancient Egypt, p. 31; De Rougé, Recherches, etc , p. 39.
[73] No historian of Egypt places Abraham before the twelfth, or the later part of the eleventh dynasty. One (Lepsius)

regards his sojourn in Egypt as belonging to the time of the eighteenth dynasty.
[74] See above, p. 8.

CHAPTER XIII.

[1] See Lenormant, Manuel d'Histoire Ancienne, vol. i, p. 360: "Nous assistons donc, sous la quinzième et seizième dynasties, à un nouveau naufrage de la civilisation égyptienne."
[2] Ibid. p. 363: "La civilisation égyptienne, d'abord comme anéantie par l'invasion, reprit ainsi le dessus dans la Thébaïde." etc.
[3] See Lenormant, Manuel, vol. i, p. 362: "Les Pasteurs dans la Basse-Egypte, comme les Tartares en Chine, se laissèrent," etc.
[4] No names of kings have been found on the tombs of individuals anterior to the times of the fourth dynasty (De Rougé, Recherches, etc., pp. 12-36).
[5] Thothmes III. exhibits sixty-one of his in the "Hall of the Ancestors" at Karnak (Bunsen's Egypt, vol. i, p. 44); Seti I. exhibits seventy-seven, though living only three generations later (De Rougé, p. 14); while Rameses II., the son of Seti I., exhibits only fifty-two (Bunsen, vol. i, pp. 50-1)
[6] Herod. ii, 99. Herodotus does not actually give this form; but his dative Μηνι and his accusative Μηνα imply it.
[7] Ap. Syncell. Chronograph. vol. i, p. 54, B.
[8] Diod. Sic. i. 45.
[9] Dr. Birch says with equal judgment and force: "Nothing known to have been made at the time of Menes remains; and he must be placed among those founders of monarchies whose personal existence a severe and enlightened criticism doubts or denies" (Ancient Egypt, p. 25).
[10] Compare the "Theseus" of Athenian legend, whose name meant "disposer," "founder," "law-giver."
[11] Brugsch, Histoire d'Egypte. p. 31; Birch in Bunsen's Egypt, vol. v, p. 585.
[12] Birch, Ancient Egypt, p. 24: "No contemporary monument is known of his age or inscribed with his name "
[13] De Rougé, Recherches, etc., p. 17, and pl. 2 at the end of the book.
[14] Bunsen, Egypt, vol. ii, p. 54.
[15] These remains appear to be so slight as to make it quite uncertain whether the papyrus really contained them (De Rougé, Recherches, etc., p. 18, note).
[16] Manetho ap. Syncell. Chronograph. vol i. p. 54, c; p. 55, B.
[17] Eratosth. ap. eund. p. 91, D.
[18] Manetho ap. eund. p. 54, c.
[19] Chs. lxiv and cxxx. See De Rougé, Recherches, etc . p. 30, note ¹.
[20] Brugsch, History of Egypt, vol. i, p. 58, 1st ed.
[21] The passage runs as follows:—"This is the beginning of the collection of receipts for curing leprosy. It was dis-

covered in a very ancient papyrus, enclosed in a writing case, under the feet of the god Anubis, in the town of Sochem, at the time of the reign of his majesty the defunct king. Hesepti. After his death it was brought to the majesty of the defunct king Senta, on account of its wonderful value" (ibid. l.s c).

[22] Ap. Syncell. Chronograph. vol. i, p. 54. c.
[23] De Rougé, Recherches, etc., pl. 1, No. 1.
[24] Ap. Syncell. l.s.c.
[25] Ibid. p. 96. c.
[26] Recherches sur les monuments qu'on peut attribuer aux six premières dynasties. p 20.
[27] Ibid. pl. ii, No. 7.
[28] By Bunsen (see his Egypt, vol. ii, p. 61). Dr. Birch appears to take the same view, when he says (Ancient Egypt, p. 26) that the name of Semempses "is found both in the Egyptian and the Greek lists."
[29] De Rougé, Recherches, etc., pp. 21, 24.
[30] Ibid. p. 21.
[31] That Ka-n-user was also called An will appear in its proper place.
[32] History of Egypt, vol. i, p. 55, 1st ed.
[33] Ibid.
[34] Ibid. p. 56.
[35] See above, vol. i. p. 159.
[36] Herod. ii, 99. Diodorus, however, ascribes the foundation to a later king, Uchoreus (i, 50).
[37] Manetho ap. Syncell. Chronograph. vol i, p. 54. c.
[38] See above, p. 16.
[39] Manetho, l.s.c.
[40] Ibid. p. 54, D.
[41] Ibid.
[42] Ibid. p. 56, A.
[43] Ibid. p. 55, A.
[44] Ibid. p. 56, B.
[45] Ibid.
[46] Brugsch says: "Here ends, according to the Manethonian writing, the information — half fable, half true — of the first rulers of Egypt. It teaches us little. We are still waiting for the door of the chamber of the ancestors of the most ancient kingdom to be opened to us" (History of Egypt, vol. i, p. 62, 1st ed.)
[47] He believed in the Nile flowing with honey, in Mena being devoured by a hippopotamus, and in a lamb speaking!
[48] A very small amount of inquiry must have taught Manetho that Neco reigned sixteen and not six years.
[49] See above, vol. i, p. 24.
[50] Compare fig. 36, pl. xii, and fig. 44, pl. xv, of vol. i.
[51] Fellows, Travels in Asia Minor, pls. opp. pp. 220 and 238; Lycia, pls. opp. pp 128, 129, 130, etc.
[52] Well represented by Lepsius. Denkmäler, vol. iii, pt. ii, pls. 3, 8, 13, etc.
[53] Diod. Sic. I, 51.

[54] Fergusson, History of Architecture, vol. i, p. 102.
[55] See Birch, Ancient Egypt, p. 29; Brugsch, History of Egypt, vol. i, p. 66, 1st ed.; Fergussou, History of Architecture, vol. i, p. 100.
[56] See above, vol. i, note [10] Ch. vii, and for a representation of the "tower," or "pyramid," see fig. 38, pl. xiii, vol. i.
[57] Brugsch, l.s.c.
[58] Lenormant, Manuel d'Histoire Ancienne, vol. i, p. 332; Birch, Ancient Egypt, p. 25; Bunsen, Egypt's Place, vol. ii, p. 380; Brugsch, History of Egypt, vol. i, p. 59, 1st ed.
[59] For a representation see above, vol. i. figs. 39, 40, pl. xiii, and for the exact measurements see p. 93.
[60] Birch, Ancient Egypt, l.s.c.
[61] See the tomb of Amten, whence the above illustration is taken (Lepsius, Denkmäler, vol. iii, pt. ii, pl. 6).
[62] Three of Sepa and his sons, discovered near the Pyramids and now in the Museum of the Louvre; two others, "with a European cast of features," found at Meydoum, and forming a part of the same collection, and a statue of Amten in the Museum of Boulaq. (See Birch, Ancient Egypt, p. 30.)
[63] Manuel d'Histoire Ancienne, vol. i, p. 333
[64] History of Egypt, vol. i, p. 66, 1st ed
[65] Lenormant. l.s c.; Birch, l.s.c.
[66] Anubis is mentioned as a god of the early times by a writer of the age of Rameses II. (Brugsch, History of Egypt, vol. i, p. 58, 1st ed.).
[67] For a description of this temple, see vol. i, pp. 101–102.
[68] Herod. ii. 99; Diod. Sic. i. 45, 46, etc.
[69] An Inscription given by M. de Rougé in his Recherches (pp. 46–9) attributes to Khufu the erection of a temple to Isis, and speaks of temples of Osiris and of the Sphinx, who is identified with Horus (Harmachis), as previously existing.
[70] Athor (identified with Isis) is mentioned as having a temple in the same inscription (p. 47). Horus and Set are mentioned as objects of veneration to Khufu's mother. The religious practice of the primitive times is not proved by these texts, but is not likely to have been very different.
[71] See vol. i, pp. 200.
[72] Birch, Guide to British Museum, p. 54.
[73] See above, p. 16.
[74] Compare vol. i, p. 70.
[75] Seneferu, the earliest king of whom we possess any monument, calls himself "the crowned Horus," and "the victorious Horus" (De Rougé, Recherches, pp. 32, 33; Lepsius, Denkmäler, vol. iii, pt ii, pl. 2, a).
[76] De Rougé, Recherches, pp. 30, 34, etc.
[77] Ibid. p 33; Records of the Past, vol. ii, pp. 3, 6, etc.

⁷⁸ Priesthoods of Mena and Teta continued down to the latest time of Egyptian ind-pendence. Senta, Ranebka, and Sar (Soris?) are also found to have had priests attached to their worship long after their decease (De Rougé, *Recherches*, p. 31; Brugsch, *History of Egypt*, vol. i, p. 48, 1st ed.).

⁷⁹ Teni or This, and Men-nofer or Memphis, are connected with the earliest of the traditions. The early tombs belong mainly to the necropolis of the latter city.

⁸⁰ De Rougé, *Recherches*, p. 40; Birch, *Ancient Egypt*, p. 44.

⁸¹ De Rougé, pp. 41, 44, etc.

⁸² See Lepsius, *Denkmäler*, vol. iii, pt. ii, pls. 3–7. The exact number of attendants represented on the walls of the sepulchral chamber of Amten is thirty-three.

⁸³ Compare the entire series of drawings in the *Denkmäler*, vol. iii, pt. ii, which descend as low as the time of the fifth dynasty.

⁸⁴ Herod. ii, 36.

⁸⁵ See Fig. 3.

⁸⁶ Lepsius, *Denkmäler*, vol. iii, pt. i, pl. 3 (upper figure).

⁸⁷ Lepsius. *Denkmäler*, vol. iii, pt. i, pl. 7. Compare pls 20, 29, etc.

⁸⁸ Ibid. pls. 3 and 6.

⁸⁹ See above, vol. i, pl. lxvii, fig. 167, and compare Lepsius, *Denkmäler*, vol. iii, pt. ii, pl. 4, line two on left, where an attendant carries a head-rest in his left hand.

⁹⁰ See Fig. 2.

⁹¹ Lepsius, pl. 4. Two antelopes, which make no struggles to free themselves, are carried in the arms of attendants, who bring them to their master.

⁹² Ibid. pl. 3.

⁹³ Supra, vol. i, p. 258.

⁹⁴ Lepsius, pls. 5 and 7. Loaves also appear above the sacrificial table, where Amten is seated, as at a feast They are small, and are arranged in two baskets (pl. 3).

⁹⁵ Lenormant, *Manuel d'Histoire Ancienne*, vol. i, p. 334: "L'écriture hiéroglyphique se montre à nous dans les monuments des premières dynasties avec toute la complication qu'elle a conservée jusqu'au dernier jour de son existence."

CHAPTER XIV.

¹ The succession of Khufu to Senoferu is shown most clearly on the tomb of Mertitefs, who was successively the favorite wife of each (De Rougé, *Recherches*, p. 37).

² In the Prisse papyrus we read: "Lo! the majesty of King Huni died: and lo! the majesty of King Seneferu became a beneficent king for the *entire* country" (ibid. p. 29).

³ See the woodcut Fig 4, where the third title, [symbol] has this meaning.

⁴ See Birch, *Ancient Egypt*, pp 30 1: "It is with the fourth Memphite dynasty that the history of Egypt begins to assume greater importance; the events recorded are no longer dependent for their remembrance on the glosses or curt notices of Greek epitomists, but the monuments of the country contain exact and contemporary accounts of the events which took place." De Rougé, *Recherches*, p. 30: "J'ai fait remarquer depuis longtemps que le plus ancien monument connu jusqu'ici est le trophée de la campagne du roi *Snefru* contre les populations qui occupaient la presqu'île du Sinaï."

⁵ The fourth title in the inscription of Wady Magharah, the hawk of Horus perched upon the sign for gold [symbol], is translated on the Rosetta Stone by "vanquisher of his adversaries."

⁶ Birch, *Ancient Egypt*, p. 31.

⁷ Brugsch supposes mines of turquoise to have been the great attraction of this region (l.s c.); but most Egyptologists consider, that the tract was occupied on account of its copper mines (Wilkinson, in the author's *Herodotus*, vol. ii, p. 344, 3d edit.; De Rougé, *Recherches* p. 31; Bunsen, *Egypt's Place*, vol. iii, p. 383; etc.).

⁸ Brugsch, *History of Egypt*, vol. i, p. 65, 1st ed.

⁹ By Brugsch, conjecturally (*History of Egypt*, vol. i, p. 66, 1st ed.)

¹⁰ See a paper by M. Mariette in the *Revue Archéologique* for September, 1864.

¹¹ Lepsius, *Denkmäler*, vol. iii. pt. ii, pl. 16; De Rougé, *Recherches*, p. 38.

¹² *Denkmäler*, vol. iii, pt. ii, pl. 17.

¹³ The tomb, No 56 at Ghizeh, of which a representation is given in the *Denkmäler*, vol. iii, pt. ii, pl 16.

¹⁴ De Rougé, *Recherches*, p. 41, note ².

¹⁵ Ibid p. 39.

¹⁶ Khufu seems to have employed his son, Saf-hotep, as his chief architect; at least, this son takes the title of "chief of the works to the king" (De Rougé, *Recherches*, p. 43). He is buried in a tomb close to the Great Pyramid (ibid.).

¹⁷ De Rougé has suggested that Seneferu may have begun, and Khufu have completed, the Great Pyramid (*Recherches*, p. 41). But there is no sufficient reason for connecting Seneferu with it.

¹⁸ Lenormant, *Manuel d'Histoire Ancienne*, vol. i, p. 335 (quoted above, vol. i, p. 205, note ²).

¹⁹ Supra, vol. i, pp. 97–101.

²⁰ Herod. ii, 124. The laborers are said to have been relieved every three months, so that 400,000 were employed in the course of each year.

[21] So Birch, *Ancient Egypt*, p. 34.
[22] Supra, vol. i, p. 101.
[23] Herod. C. 124-9.
[24] The identification of the pyramid-builders with the "Shepherds" (Herod. ii, 128), unhistorical as it was, indicated the abhorrence in which their memories were held; for the "Shepherds" were detested by the Egyptians of the New Empire.
[25] See above, vol. i, pp. 150, and 237.
[26] Lenormant, *Manuel d'Histoire Ancienne*, vol. i, p. 335.
[27] See the description of the southern stone pyramid of Dashoor in vol. i, pp. 336.
[28] See the woodcut, Fig. 4.
[29] Birch, *Ancient Egypt*, p. 36.
[30] Lepsius, *Denkmäler*, vol. iii, pl. 1; Bunsen, *Egypt's Place*, vol. ii, p. 188
[31] As Bunsen (*Egypt's Place*, l.s c.) and Wilkinson (in the author's *Herodotus*, vol. ii, p. 204, note ¹, 3d ed.).
[32] Birch, *Ancient Egypt*, pp. 32-8; Brugsch, *History of Egypt*, vol. i. pp. 69-76, 1st ed.; Lenormant, *Histoire Ancienne*, vol. i, p. 237; De Rougé, *Recherches*, pp. 41-54.
[33] Supra, vol. i, pp. 155-157.
[34] Herod. ii, 124; Manetho ap. Syncell. *Chronograph*. vol. i, p. 56, D.
[35] De Rougé, *Recherches*, p. 46. It is possible that this inscription may be of a later date, as De Rougé suspects, and Dr. Brugsch (*History of Egypt*, vol. i, p. 81, 1st ed.), pronounces; but, if so, it was at any rate modelled on the lines of some inscription of the time, the phrases of which it probably reproduced without much alteration.
[36] De Rougé, p. 47. Brugsch, however, translates differently (*History of Egypt*, l.s.c.).
[37] Birch, *Ancient Egypt*, p. 37.
[38] *I.e.* the Greek epitomists, Africanus and Eusebius (see Syncell *Chronograph*, vol. i, pp. 56, D. and 57, c)
[39] Khufu connects with himself especially Horus and Kneph. He represents Thoth on his tablet at the Wady Magharah. His wife regards him as an impersonation of Horus and Set (De Rougé, *Recherches*, p. 45). He builds a temple to Isis, whom he identifies with Athor; and he mentions with respect the temples of Osiris and of Harmachis, or the Sphinx (ibid. pp 46-7).
[40] De Rougé, *Recherches*, p. 37.
[41] De Rougé, *Recherches*, p. 42. Compare, for the fact, Brugsch (*History of Egypt*, vol. i, p 76, 1st ed.).
[42] Lepsius, *Denkmäler*, vol. iii, pls. 18-22.
[43] Supra, note 16.
[44] De Rougé, *Recherches*, p. 44.
[45] Ibid. p. 47. Compare Herod ii, 126.
[46] Lepsius, *Denkmäler*, vol. iii, pls. 23 and 33.
[47] De Rougé, *Recherches*, pp. 57-61.
[48] These have been carefully collected by De Rougé, and will be found in his *Recherches*, pp. 52-4.

[49] Herod. ii, 127.
[50] Diod. Sic. i, 64.
[51] I am indebted for my knowledge of these statues to M. de Rougé's valuable work, *Recherches sur les Monuments*, etc., where two photographs are given, from one of which the accompanying illustration has been taken. The statues themselves are in the Museum of Boulaq.
[52] De Rougé, *Recherches*, p. 56. Compare Brugsch, *History of Egypt*, vol. i, p. 77, 1st ed.
[53] See above, vol. i, pp. 96, 99.
[54] Ibid. p. 203 The difference in the actual height of the edifices was one of 20½ feet in favor of the pyramid of Khufu. The difference in elevation of the summits above the plain was one of 6½ feet in favor of the pyramid of Shafra.
[55] Birch, *Ancient Egypt*, p. 38; Wilkinson in the author's *Herodotus*, vol. ii, p. 204, note ², 3d edit.
[56] Birch, l.s c. On the other hand, it is quite possible that this temple may have been an older construction, and that Shafra only added to its ornamentation.
[57] Brugsch, *History of Egypt*. vol. i, p. 77, 1st ed.
[58] See above, vol i, p. 101.
[59] De Rougé, *Recherches*, p. 56.
[60] Ibid. pp. 57-61.
[61] On these animals, see above, vol. i, pp. 195-197. It is uncertain to which of these Merisankh was priestess, as the expression used upon her tomb is ambiguous.
[62] De Rougé, *Recherches*, pp. 58-9.
[63] Ibid. pp. 61-2.
[64] Herod i, 173.
[65] De Rougé, *Recherches*, p. 59.
[66] Ibid. p. 75.
[67] Lepsius, *Denkmäler*, vol. iii, pt. ii, pl. 12 b.
[68] Ibid pl. 42 a.
[69] Shafra, Menkaura, Aseskaf, Uskaf, and Sahura (Lepsius, l.s.c., pl 42. Compare De Rougé, *Recherches*, p. 77).
[70] Herod. ii, 129.
[71] Ap Syncell. *Chronograph*. p. 56, D.
[72] *Denkmäler*, l s c.
[73] De Rougé, *Recherches*, pl. 2 at the end of the volume, Nos. 23 and 24.
[74] Herod. l.s.c.
[75] See above, vol. i, p. 96. These dimensions are considerably less than those of the step-pyramid of Saccarah, and indicate an entire abandonment of the magnificent ideas of Khufu and Shafra.
[76] That is, as compared with the remarkable chamber of Khufu (see vol. i, p. 99. Otherwise, the construction is curious and worthy of notice. (Compare vol i, pls. xiv, xv, figs. 42, 44.
[77] See above, vol. i p.
[78] Birch, *Ancient Egypt* p. 40.
[79] There is a good representation of the lid of Menkaura's coffin in Col. Vyse's *Pyramids of Gizeh*, vol ii, opp.

p. 94, and another in Lepsius's *Denkmäler*, vol. iii. pt. ii, pl. 1.
⁶⁰ Translations, varying in a few particulars, are given by De Rougé, *Recherches*, p. 65; Brugsch, *History of Egypt*, vol. i, pp. 3-4, 1st ed.; and Birch, *Ancient Egypt*, p. 40. I have followed these authorities where they agree, and referred to the text of Lepsius where they differ.
⁶¹ Brugsch, *History of Egypt*, vol. i, p. 84. 1st ed.
⁶² Birch. *Ancient Egypt*, p. 41.
⁶³ Herod. ii. 129.
⁶⁴ See the " Rubric" at the end of ch. lxiv (Bunsen, *Egypt's Place*, vol. v, pp. 209-10).
⁶⁵ Herod. ii, 129.
⁶⁶ De Rougé, *Recherches*, pp. 66-7.
⁶⁷ De Rougé prefers the form Aseskaf (*Recherches*, pp 66-75); Brugsch the form Shepses-kaf (*History of Egypt*, vol. i. pp. 85-7, 1st ed.). Dr. Birch allows either reading (*Ancient Egypt*, p. 41).
⁶⁸ De Rougé p. 67.
⁶⁹ Lepsius, *Denkmäler*, vol. iii, pt. ii, pl. 42.
⁹⁰ Birch, l s.c.
⁹¹ De Rougé, *Recherches*, pp. 68-72.
⁹² Ibid. p 67.
⁹³ De Rougé, *Recherches*, p. 72. Brugsch reads the word Qebeh, but gives it the same meaning (*History of Egypt*, vol. i. p. 87. 1st ed.)
⁹⁴ Usurkaf, according to Brugsch (*History of Egypt*, vol. i. p. 87); Usurkaf, according to De Rougé (*Recherches*, pp. 75-80) and Birch (*Ancient Egypt*, p. 47).
⁹⁵ See De Rougé's table in the *Recherches*, p. 75.
⁹⁶ Ibid. p. 76. De Rougé compares these princes to the " Cæsars" of the time of Diocletian and Constantine.
⁹⁷ Seneferu, Khufu. Shafra, Menkaura and *perhaps* Ratatf, who, however, may have been a " Cæsar."
⁹⁸ De Rougé says: " Il résulte de notre inscription que les trois derniers noms de la quatrième dynastie, dans la liste d'Africain, n'ont pas de place chronologique sur les monuments: Bichérès, Sébèrchérès et Tamphthis sont évidemment interpolés dans cet endroit" (p. 78).
⁹⁹ Ibid. l.s.c.
¹⁰⁰ Ibid. p. 80.
¹ ¹ Mariette (in his *Monuments Divers*, pl. 54, e) gives a representation of a cylinder. now in the Museum of Boulaq, where the cartouche of Usurkaf is twice accompanied by this title, which

is written thus: .

De Rougé translates it by " le dieu faisant justice" in his *Recherches*, p. 79.
¹⁰² See above. p. 26.
¹⁰³ Lepsius, *Denkmäler*, vol. iii, pt. ii, pl. 41 a.
¹⁰⁴ De Rougé, *Recherches*, pl. i, No. 23; pl. ii. No. 27.

¹⁰⁵ Ap. Syncell. *Chronograph*. vol. i, p. 57, D.
¹⁰⁶ Lepsius, *Denkmäler*, vol. iii, pt. ii, pl 39 f.
¹⁰⁷ De Rougé, p. 81.
¹⁰⁸ Bunsen. *Egypt's Place in Universal History*, vol. ii, p. 103; and compare the table at the end of the volume.
¹⁰⁹ See above, pp. 34, 35. The original Third Pyramid of Ghizeh is here meant, not the later enlarged one.
¹¹⁰ Bunsen, l.s.c.
¹¹¹ Bunsen, *Egypt's Place*, vol. ii, p. 104
¹¹² De Rougé, *Recherches*, p. 82.
¹¹³ Ibid. p. 83.
¹¹⁴ Brugsch, *History of Egypt*, vol. i, p. 88, 1st ed.; De Rougé, *Recherches*, l. s.c.
¹¹⁵ De Rougé, *Recherches*, pl. ii, at the end of the volume, No. 28.
¹¹⁶ Some of the blocks in the interior of the tomb of Ti had the name of Kaka on them, roughly painted in red by the masons (De Rougé, p. 97). It occurs also on the tomb of Senothemhet (*Denkmäler*, vol. iii, pt. ii, pl 75) and on a vase found at Saccarah (De Rougé, p. 84).
¹¹⁷ See De Rougé's table, No. 24.
¹¹⁸ Under the form Nefercheres. (Syncell. *Chronograph*. vol i, p. 57, D).
¹¹⁹ *Denkmäler*, vol. iii, pt. ii, pls. 43-49.
¹²⁰ De Rougé, *Recherches*, p 85.
¹²¹ Ibid. pp. 86-8. Uer-khuu, besides being " scribe of the palace," " keeper of the writings," and " head receiver of petitions," was also " chief of the granaries," and " commander of the corps of recruits for the infantry service" (ibid. p. 86).
¹²² De Rougé, *Recherches*, p. 75.
¹²³ This is the first instance of an Egyptian king with two names, one that given to him when he was a child, the other assumed at his accession. Persian monarchs had sometimes, in the same way, an original and a throne name (*Ancient Monarchies*, vol. iii, p. 485. 2d ed).
¹²⁴ *Denkmäler*, vol iv. pt. ii, pl 152 a.
¹²⁵ Bunsen, *Egypt's Place*, vol. ii, p. 101
¹²⁶ Ibid. p. 102.
¹²⁷ De Rougé, *Recherches*, p. 89.
¹²⁸ Ibid. p 75.
¹²⁹ Ap. Syncell. *Chronograph*. vol. i, p. 58, A.
¹³⁰ *Denkmäler*, vol. iii, pt. ii, pls, 55-59; De Rougé, *Recherches*, pp. 89-92.
¹³¹ De Rougé, p. 92.
¹³² Ibid. p. 93.
¹³³ Ibid. p. 97.
¹³⁴ Birch says, with reference to this portrait: " He appears to have been youthful, with a good profile and rather a full face" (*Ancient Egypt*. p. 48). De Rougé (*Recherches*. p. 99): " Il paraît jeune et son profil est très-fin."
¹³⁵ Brugsch. *History of Egypt*, vol. i, p. 91; De Rougé, l.s.c.

[135] See the plate in M. de Rougé's *Recherches,* opp. p. 98, where I read these titles.
[137] *Denkmäler,* vol. iii, pt. ii, pl. 39 c.
[138] Ap. Syncell. *Chronograph.* l.s.c.
[139] The Turin papyrus gives the former, Manetho the latter number (De Rougé, *Recherches,* p. 75).
[140] Ibid. p. 99.
[141] See above, p. 40.
[142] Birch, *Ancient Egypt,* p. 48. Compare the *Denkmäler,* vol. iii, pt. ii, pl. 39 d.
[143] De Rougé, *Recherches,* p. 100.
[144] Ibid. pp. 100-1.
[145] This title is found at Wady Magharah, and also in a legend quoted by De Rougé (*Recherches,* p. 100, note [1]). It was not as yet at all an ordinary title of the kings.
[146] *Denkmäler,* vol. iii, pt. ii, pls. 60-72, and 76-8.
[147] Khut-hotep, for instance, was "priest of the pyramids of Ranuser, Menkauhor, and Tatkara," "lord of the double treasury," "commandant of the granaries," "keeper of the records," and "governor of Memphis" (De Rougé, *Recherches,* pp. 101-2).
[148] Brugsch, *History of Egypt,* vol. i, p. 92, 1st ed.
[149] Dr. Brugsch calls him "the son of Unas" (l.s.c.); but De Rougé had pointed out the impossibility of this (*Recherches,* p. 102), since he wrote his book while Unas was still alive, and when his own age was 110.
[150] See below, p. 50.
[151] This is an important point The first marked division in the list of kings which appears in the Turin papyrus was after Unas, when there was an enumeration of the kings from the time of Menes, and of the sum total of the years of their reigns. (See De Rougé, *Recherches.* p. 105.)
[152] Ap. Syncell, *Chronograph.* vol. i, p. 58, A.
[153] Ibid Compare De Rougé, *Recherches.* p 75.
[154] De Rougé observes very pertinently: "Si le Mustabat-el-Faraoun avait dû avoir primitivement la forme de pyramide tronquée, on ne voit pas pourquoi cette forme n'apparaîtrait pas comme déterminatif de la pyramide *Nefer-asu*" (*Recherches,* p 103, note [1]). But the determinative is the ordinary complete pyramid,

[155] Ibid. p. 103.
[156] Vyse, *Pyramids of Gizeh,* vol. iii, p. 53.
[157] See above, vol. i, p. 97.
[158] Ibid. pp. 95, 99, etc.
[159] Vyse, *Pyramids of Gizeh,* vol. i, p. 176.
[160] We must not make the mistake of converting this proposition, and assuming that "every pyramid is the tomb of a king" (Brugsch, *History of Egypt,* vol. i, p. 72, 1st ed.). Many, it is probable, cover the bodies of mere princes and princesses. (See Herod. ii, 126.)
[161] This would be true, even if the entire Third Pyramid were the work of Menkaura, for it is less than one-seventh of the size of the Second. But it is still more strikingly true, if we regard the original nucleus of the pyramid (see above, vol. i, Ch. vii, note [8b]) as alone the work of Mencheres
[162] See vol. i, pp. 104-5.
[163] Fergusson, *History of Architecture,* vol. i, p. 106.
[164] An excellent representation of this statue, taken from a photograph, will be found in the work of M. de Rougé so often quoted (*Recherches sur les Monuments,* etc , opp. p. 54).
[165] See the woodcut Fig. 61 of this volume.
[166] Birch, *Ancient Egypt,* pp. 38, 43; De Rougé, *Recherches,* pp. 54, 93; Lenormant, *Manuel d'Histoire Ancienne,* vol. i, p. 337; Brugsch, *History of Egypt,* vol. i, p. 78, 1st ed.; etc.
[167] As with the Æginetan marbles in the Glyptothek at Munich. Some from Branchidæ in the British Museum are more on a par with the Egyptian.
[168] *Manuel d'Histoire Ancienne,* vol. i, pp 340-1.
[169] Birch holds that there was a "canon of proportions" always, but that it varied at different periods (Wilkinson's *Ancient Egyptians,* vol. ii, p. 270, note, edition of 1878). Lenormant is of opinion that at first the artists were free (*Manuel,* vol i. p. 340).
[170] See above. pp. 21-2.
[171] Of Nut and Seb on the coffin-lid of Menkaura, of Khem in the name Khemten (De Rougé, *Recherches.* p 50) and in the title taken by Shafra (supra, p 63), of Knĕph in Khufu's prefix, of Neith and Ma in the mention of their prophetesses (De Rougé, pp. 86, 88, 91, 97, etc.), of Saf in the name Saf-hotep (ib p. 43) and in the appellation *Saf-meri,* "beloved of Saf," applied to a certain Akauhor (ib. p. 84), and of Heka in one of the employments of Pahenuka which includes her name (Ib. p 88).
[172] De Rougé. pp. 72, 80, etc.
[173] Ptah-ases, the favorite of Menkaura and Asesskaf, was priest both of Phthah (Ptah) and of Sokari (ib. p. 71).
[174] Rataff, Shaf-ra, Menkaura. Sahura, Neferarkara, Ranuser, and Tatkara.
[175] Supra. pp. 33 and 42.
[176] De Rougé. *Recherches,* p. 47.
[177] Ibid. p. 65. Compare Birch, *Ancient Egypt,* pp. 41-2.
[178] Supra, p. 35.
[179] De Rougé. *Recherches,* pp. 44, 58-61, etc. Perhaps the females attached to the worship of Apis should be called "prophetesses" rather than "priestesses." Their title is *neter hon-* not *ab*.

¹⁸⁰ Ibid. p. 51.
¹⁸¹ See the *Denkmäler*, vol. iii, pt. ii, pls. 78, 79.
¹⁸² *Denkmäler*, vol. iii, pt. ii.
¹⁸³ Ibid. pls. 73, 97. This, however, is very unusual.
¹⁸⁴ See the *Denkmäler*, vol. iii, pt. ii, pls. 13, 50 b. The former of these two monuments belongs to the time of Shafra.
¹⁸⁵ Ibid. pl. 80 c.
¹⁸⁶ Scribes are seen at work from the time of Shafra. They have a pen or paint-brush in the right hand and one or two behind the ear. With their left hand they hold their paper and palette. They commonly sit or squat at their work. (See the *Denkmäler*, pt. ii, pls. 9, 11. 19, 51, etc.)
¹⁸⁷ For glass-blowing, see the *Denkmäler*, vol. iii, pt. ii, pls. 28 and 74; and for the other trades named, see especially pl. 49 of the same work.
¹⁸⁸ Domesticated antelopes are frequently represented in the tombs. (See *Denkmäler*, pt. ii, pls. 12 b, 17 b, 23, 80, 140, etc.)
¹⁸⁹ Seven kinds of domesticated birds, with their respective names, are figured on a tomb, given in the *Denkmäler*, pt. ii, pl. 70.
¹⁹⁰ Cranes or herons are also very frequently represented among the poultry of a farm (ibid. pls. 17 b, 45 c, 50 b, etc.).
¹⁹¹ Birch, *Ancient Egypt*, p. 45.
¹⁹² *Denkmäler*, vol. iii, pt. ii, pl. 9.
¹⁹³ Foxes appear in pls. 11, 14 c, 15 b, 45 c, etc.; hares in pls 3, 12 b, and elsewhere; the common small monkey in pls. 36 b and c; and the cynocephalous ape in pl 13
¹⁹⁴ See above, vol. i, p. 36.
¹⁹⁵ *Denkmäler*, pt. ii, pl. 96 s.
¹⁹⁶ Ibid. pls. 13, 49, 16 s, etc.
¹⁹⁷ Ibid. pls. 12 b and 46.
¹⁹⁸ Birch, *Ancient Egypt*. p. 44.
¹⁹⁹ See the *Denkmäler*, pt. ii, pls. 43 a, 47, 56, 80 c, 106 b, etc.
²⁰⁰ Ibid. pls. 10, 12 a, 22 d, etc.
²⁰¹ Ibid. pls. 22 d, 45 a, 64 bis, etc. For a representation, see above, vol. i, pl. lxxiv, figs. 188, 189.
²⁰² See the *Denkmäler*, pt. ii, pl. 45 b.
²⁰³ Ibid. pls. 62, 103, and 104. Compare Herod. ii, 96.
²⁰⁴ Lepsius, *Denkmäler*, pt. ii, pls. 12 b, 60, 77, etc.; Mariette, *Monuments Divers*, pl. 17.
²⁰⁵ Wilkinson, *Ancient Egyptians*, vol. ii, pp. 99-100 (edition of 1878), and Birch's note.
²⁰⁶ For one representation, see above, pl. i, fig. 2; and for another, see vol. i, pl. iii, No. 2.
²⁰⁷ *Denkmäler*, pt. ii, pls. 12 and 46.
²⁰⁸ Birch in Wilkinson's *Ancient Egyptians*, vol. ii, p. 100, note.
²⁰⁹ *Denkmäler*, pt. ii, pls. 17 c, 36 a, 42 and 52.
²¹⁰ See above, vol. i, pp. 253.
²¹¹ *Denkmäler*, pt. ii, pl. 12 b.
²¹² *Denkmäler*, pls. 36 b, 52, 74 c, etc.

²¹³ See the *Bampton Lectures* of the present Bishop of Derry, pp. 177-80.
²¹⁴ As, for instance, the following:
1. "If thou art become great after thou hast been humble, and if thou hast amassed riches after poverty, and art come to be the first man in thy city; if thou art known for thy wealth, and hast become a great lord, let not thy heart grow proud because of thy riches; for it is God who has given them unto thee."
2. "Despise not another who is as thou wast; be towards him as towards thine equal."
3. "Happiness makes one content with any abode; but a small disgrace darkens the life of a great man."
4. "Good words shine more than the emerald which the hand of the slave finds among a heap of pebbles."
5. "The wise man is satisfied with what he knows; content dwells in his heart, and his lips speak words that are good."
6. "Let thy face be cheerful as long as thou livest. Has any one, who has once entered the grave, come forth from it?"
²¹⁵ *Denkmäler*, pt. ii, pls. 52, 57 b, 61 a, etc.
²¹⁶ Birch, *Ancient Egypt*, p. 45.
²¹⁷ Lepsius, *Denkmäler*, pt. ii, pls. 12 b, 27, 30, 36 c, 67, 68, etc.
²¹⁸ Ibid, pls. 57 b, 61 a, 69, 71 a, etc.
²¹⁹ Lepsius. *Denkmäler*, pt. ii, pls. 50 and 98 b. In the former representation the number of the bearers would seem to be twelve. In the latter twenty-six. The primitive palanquin is of a ruder kind than that represented in vol. i, p. 535, which belongs to the time of the twelfth dynasty.
²²⁰ See Mariette, *Monuments Divers*, pl. 20, and compare the illustration facing p. 85. For a wooden head of this period, see Brugsch, *History of Egypt*, vol. i, opp. p. vii, 1st ed.
²²¹ Lepsius, *Denkmäler*, pt. ii, pls. 64 bis, b, and 104 c.
²²² See above, p. 30.
²²³ As Joseph did (Gen. xxxix. 1-4).
²²⁴ Birch, *Ancient Egypt*, p. 46.

CHAPTER XV.

¹ Ap. Syncell. *Chronograph*. p. 57, D.
² Ibid. p. 58, A.
³ De Rougé, *Recherches*, pp. 76-7.
⁴ Ibid. p. 114. Compare Brugsch, *History of Egypt*, vol. i, p. 96, 1st ed.; Birch, *Ancient Egypt*, p. 51.
⁵ *Records of the Past*, vol. ii, p. 4.
⁶ Brugsch, *History of Egypt*, vol. i, pp. 98-101, 1st ed.; Lepsius, *Denkmäler*, vol. iv, pl. ii, pls. 105-117.
⁷ No doubt the granite, syenite, etc., used in the pyramids and other constructions of these kings, must have been obtained from Upper Egypt, and the free employment of these materials makes it probable that their authority

extended to Syênê; but this probability falls considerably short of a proof. It is quite possible that they imported the granite from the dominions of other friendly kings.

⁸ It is conceivable, however, that even at this time there may have been independent kings in the western part of the Delta, at Saïs, for instance, or Xoïs, or even at Sebennytus (Semnood).

⁹ The only indications of war furnished by the pyramid period are the tablets of Seneferu, Khufu, Sahura, and Ranuser at Wady Magharah, and the employment of certain military hieroglyphs. (De Rougé, Recherches, pp. 91, 104, etc.).

¹⁰ These four monarchs form a connected group in the monuments (De Rougé, pp. 148-9), and in the table of Saccarah. The inscription of Una closely unites three of the four, Teta, Pepi, and Merenra (Records of the Past, vol. ii. pp. 3 and 6).

¹¹ Each king is so absorbed in the glories of his divine ancestry as to neglect all reference to his human progenitors. The kings generally seem ashamed of acknowledging that they had any earthly father.

¹² Lepsius, Denkmäler, vol. iv, pt. ii, pl. 115 f.

¹³ De Rougé, Recherches, p. 149.

¹⁴ As Lenormant (Manuel d'Histoire Ancienne, vol. i. p. 343).

¹⁵ Brugsch, History of Egypt, vol. i, p. 97. 1st ed. De Rougé (l.s.c.) thinks Ati may have held either position.

¹⁶ Denkmäler, vol. iv, pt. ii, pl. 115 h. The name has the cartouche certainly; but it is not preceded or followed by any royal title.

¹⁷ Una's inscription (Records of the Past, vol. ii. p. 3) is sufficient proof of this.

¹⁸ Or "Tat-setu," according to Brugsch (l.s.c.). Its position is at present unknown.

¹⁹ De Rougé, Recherches, pp. 110-11.

²⁰ Records of the Past, l.s.c.

²¹ Lepsius, Denkmäler, vol. iv, pt. ii, pl. 115 a.

²² Ap Syncell. Chronograph. vol i. p. 58, B. This has generally been understood to be Manetho's view, according to Africanus. Eusebius, however, makes Manetho say that Pepi (Phiops) ascended the throne at the age of six, and lived to be a hundred (ib. 58, D).

²³ Records of the Past, vol. ii. pp. 6-8.

²⁴ Lepsius, Denkmäler, vol. iv, pt. ii, pl. 116 a.

²⁵ Birch, Ancient Egypt, p. 52; Denkmäler, l.s.c.

²⁶ The tablet consists of two parts. In the left-hand compartment Pepi is represented as king of Upper Egypt, slaying one of the Mentu; in the right-hand one he appears as king of Lower Egypt, bearing the flagellum and running.

²⁷ So Brugsch, History of Egypt, vol. i, p. 99, 1st ed. Compare De Rougé, (Recherches, p. 122) and Birch (Ancient Egypt, p. 52).

²⁸ Records of the Past, vol. ii, p. 4, line 14.

²⁹ So Brugsch reads the word (History of Egypt vol. i, p. 100. 1st ed.). Others give the name as "Nam" (Records of the Past, vol. ii. p. 41, line 15).

³⁰ Records, vol. ii, p. 5. Compare De Rougé, Recherches. p. 124.

³¹ De Rougé, Recherches, p. 125.

³² Records of the Past, vol. ii, p. 6.

³³ De Rougé, Recherches, p. 127.

³⁴ Ibid. p. 126.

³⁵ Brugsch, History of Egypt, vol. i, p. 101. 1st ed.

³⁶ Lenormant, Manuel d'Histoire Ancienne, vol. i, p. 344.

³⁷ Lenormant, Manuel d'Histoire Ancienne, vol. i. p. 344.

³⁸ Recherches, p. 127, note.

³⁹ Records of the Past, vol. vi, p. 19.

⁴⁰ Records of the Past, vol. ii, p. 3.

⁴¹ De Rougé, Recherches, p. 116, note.

⁴² Ibid p. 115.

⁴³ See above, p. 56.

⁴⁴ Lepsius, Denkmäler, pt. ii, pl. 115 a, e, f, i.

⁴⁵ Ibid. pl. 117.

⁴⁶ Brugsch, History of Egypt, vol. i, p. 98, 1st ed.

⁴⁷ Pepi takes it again at Wady Magharah (Denkmäler, pt. ii, pl. 116 a), and it is assumed also by Kanuser (ib pl. 152 a). Compare Ptah-hotep's acknowledgment: "I have passed 110 years of life by the gift of the king" (supra, p. 50).

⁴⁸ Recherches, p. 116. He omits to note that it occurs as early as the time of Khufu. (See the Denkmäler, part ii, pl. 2 b.)

⁴⁹ Recherches. p. 117.

⁵⁰ On the recognition of this division, see above, vol. i. p. 113, note ¹⁰⁵.

⁵¹ Records of the Past, vol. ii, pp. 3, 4.

⁵² Records of the Past, vol. ii, p. 6, line 6.

⁵³ De Rougé, Recherches, p. 129.

⁵⁴ Records of the Past, vol. ii, p. 4.

⁵⁵ See M. de Rougé's Recherches, pp. 130-1, where the inscription is given at length.

⁵⁶ Or "head of the entire sacerdotal order," as De Rougé explains (id. p 132).

⁵⁷ Records of the Past, vol. ii, p. 7.

⁵⁸ Ibid.

⁵⁹ Sixty cubits long by thirty wide, according to Brugsch (History of Egypt, vol. i, p. 105, 1st ed.).

⁶⁰ Records of the Past, vol. ii. p. 8. Dr. Birch is of opinion that this implies some considerable difference in the condition of the Nile waters about the site of the First Cataract in ancient and modern times (Ancient Egypt. p. 54).

⁶¹ Denkmäler, pt. ii. pl. 116 b. Compare De Rougé, Recherches. p. 135.

⁶² Birch, Ancient Egypt, p 53.

⁶³ See De Rougé, Recherches. p. 108.

⁶⁴ Denkmäler, pt. ii, pl. 116 a (right-hand compartment).

⁶⁵ De Rougé, Recherches, p. 129.

⁶⁶ *Denkmäler*, pt. ii. pl. 116 *a* (right-hand compartment). The female figure with a lotus must, I think, represent Ankhnes-Merira herself.

⁶⁷ The Manethonian statement, that Binothris of the second dynasty made a law allowing females to succeed to the throne, cannot be regarded as of much weight, more especially as no practical result is said to have followed.

⁶⁸ Ap. Syncell. *Chronograph.* vol. i, p. 58, B.

⁶⁹ Herod. ii, 100.

⁷⁰ See the note of Wilkinson on the above passage in the author's *Herodotus*, vol. ii. p. 142, 2d edit. Compare De Rougé, *Recherches*, p. 108.

⁷¹ Lenormant, *Manuel d'Histoire Ancienne*, vol. i, p. 345; Brugsch, *History of Egypt*, vol. i, pp. 107-9, 1st ed.; Birch, *Ancient Egypt*, p. 54.

⁷² Ap. Syncell. *Chronograph.* l.s.c.

⁷³ Herod. ii, 134.

⁷⁴ See above, vol. i, p. 96; and compare Brugsch, *History of Egypt*, vol. i, p. 108, 1st ed.

⁷⁵ As those of Sahura and Ranuser (supra, pp. 39 and 40-1).

⁷⁶ Herod. l.s.c. Compare Vyse, *Pyramids of Gizeh*, vol. ii, p. 120.

⁷⁷ Brugsch, *History of Egypt*, vol. i, pp. 107, 108, 1st ed.

⁷⁸ Manetho's numbers furnish the sole basis for any measurement at all; but these are at this point in a deplorable condition. Eusebius and Africanus differed with respect to them to the extent of 355 years!

⁷⁹ Lenormant says of these: "L'art primitif avait atteint son apogée sous la sixième dynastie. C'est dans les tombes exécutées alors que l'on trouve ces belles statues élancées, au visage rond, à la bouche souriante, au nez fin, aux épaules larges, aux jambes musculeuses, dont le Musée du Louvre possède un des plus remarquables échantillons dans la figure d'un scribe accroupi que l'on a placée au centre d'une des salles du premier étage" (*Manuel d'Histoire Ancienne*, vol. i, p. 346). Birch remarks: "Sculpture is admirably shown in the statues of the period" (*Ancient Egypt*, p. 53).

⁸⁰ As, for instance, in the sepulchral tablet, numbered 832, in the Egyptian Gallery of the British Museum.

⁸¹ See particularly the *Denkmäler*, pt. ii, pls. 105 and 111 *b*.

⁸² Birch, *Ancient Egypt*. p. 55: "No temples of the period remain."

⁸³ See the *Denkmäler*, pt. ii, pls. 105-111.

⁸⁴ Ibid. pls. 106, 107.

⁸⁵ See the representation in vol. i, of this work (pl. lxxvii. fig. 198), which is from a tomb of this period.

⁸⁶ *Denkmäler*, pt. ii. pl. 108. In the pyramid period we find one dog only, which stands high on its legs and has a stiffly curled tail (supra, pl. i, fig. 2, vol. i; pl. iii. No. 2).

⁸⁷ *Denkmäler*, l s.c.

⁸⁸ As in a statue of the period, now in the British Museum, No. 55.

⁸⁹ *Records of the Past*, vol. viii, p. 151.

⁹⁰ The writer of the "Praise of Learning" mentions, besides scribes or men of letters, the employments of the blacksmith, the carpenter, the stonecutter, the barber, the boatman, the agricultural laborer, the builder, the gardener, the farmer, the weaver, the armorer, the courier, the dyer, the sandal-maker, the washerman, the fowler, and the fisherman. Representations occur in the tombs of goldsmiths, glass-blowers, potters, tailors, upholsterers, boatbuilders, sculptors, musicians, professional dancers, brickmakers, domestic servants, etc. Embalmers also were, we know, a separate class.

⁹¹ See Dr. Birch's "Introduction" (*Records of the Past*, vol. viii, p 146).

⁹² *Records of the Past*, vol. ii, pp. 3-8.

⁹³ For a copy of the inscription, and a sketch of the altar itself, see the *Transactions of the Society of Biblical Archæology*, vol iii, pls. 1-3, opp. p. 112.

⁹⁴ See above, vol. i, p. 159.

⁹⁵ *Transactions of Bibl. Arch. Society*, vol. iii, p. 114.

⁹⁶ Supra, vol. i, pp. 164-7.

⁹⁷ Ibid. pp. 182-3.

⁹⁸ Ibid. pp. 169-170.

⁹⁹ The earthly and the infernal—"Thoth in the house of selection," and "Thoth at the balance" (supra, vol. i, p. 175).

¹⁰⁰ Sabak, for instance, is worshipped in five cities, Horus or Harmachis in nine, Anubis in three, Athor in three, etc.

¹⁰¹ Supra, vol. i, p. 189.

¹⁰² Ibid. p. 185-6.

¹⁰³ Ibid p. 187-8.

¹⁰⁴ *Denkmäler*, vol. iv, pt. ii, pl. 115 *c*.

¹⁰⁵ Compare above, pp. 21-2 and 46.

CHAPTER XVI.

¹ Wilkinson in the author's *Herodotus*, vol ii. pp 338, and 346, 347; Stuart Poole in Dr. Smith's *Dictionary of the Bible*, vol. i, p. 508

² See above, page 54.

³ M. Mariette says: "Quand, avec la onzième dynastie, on voit l'Egypte se réveiller de son *long* sommeil, les anciennes traditions sont oubliées. Les noms propres usités dans les anciennes familles, les titres donnés aux fonctionnaires, l'écriture elle même et jusqu'à la religion, tout en elle semble nouveau." (See Lenormant, *Manuel d'Histoire Ancienne*, vol i, p. 349.)

⁴ Bunsen, *Egypt's Place*, vol. ii, p 243.

⁵ Eighteen names of kings are given by Dr. Brugsch (*History of Egypt*, vol. i, p. 110, 1st ed.) as belonging to these dynasties. They are taken from the "New Table of Abydos," set up by Seti I. The general character of the names

accords with those of the fourth, fifth, and sixth dynasties. The most frequent is that of Neferkara.

⁶ According to Africanus, Manetho assigned to the seventh dynasty 70 days, to the eighth 146 years, to the ninth 409 years, to the tenth 185 years—total, 740 years and 70 days. According to Eusebius, his numbers were: for the seventh dynasty, 75 days; for the eighth and ninth, 100 years each; for the tenth, 185 years—total, 385 years, 75 days. By an arbitrary correction and combination of these two accounts, M. Lenormant produces for the period a total of 436 years (*Manuel d'Histoire Ancienne*, vol. i, p. 321), which Dr. Birch adopts (*Ancient Egypt*, p. 57). Bunsen, following Eratosthenes, and bending Manetho's numbers into accordance, reckons the actual length of the interval at 166 years (*Egypt's Place*, vol. ii, pp. 217-216).

⁷ *Manuel d'Histoire Ancienne*, vol. i, p. 346.

⁸ *Ancient Egypt*, l.s.c.

⁹ *Manuel*, vol. i, p. 347.

¹⁰ Ibid.

¹¹ Manetho's numbers, as reported by Africanus, are—

	Years
For the fourth dynasty,	274
" fifth "	248
" sixth "	203
Total . . .	725

But the items of the reigns in the fifth dynasty produce the number 218 instead of 248. The substitution of this number would bring the sum total within the period of seven centuries.

¹² See above, vol. i, p. 8.

¹³ Brugsch, *History of Egypt*, vol. i, pp. 112-15, 1st ed.

¹⁴ Wilkinson, *Topography of Thebes*, pp. 415-421.

¹⁵ Ibid. pp. 415-16; Brugsch, *History of Egypt*, vol. i, p. 112, 1st ed.

¹⁶ Wilkinson, p. 420.

¹⁷ Birch gives the hieroglyphic form as 𓉼𓂓𓏺 (*Dictionary of Hieroglyphics*, in Bunsen's *Egypt*, vol. v, p. 584). The phonetic part of this group would be properly rendered by Apt or Apet.

¹⁸ So Wilkinson in the author's *Herodotus*, vol. ii, p 3, note ⁵.

¹⁹ Herod. ii, 166; Plin. *H. N.* v, 9; Ptol. *Geograph.* iv, 5; etc.

²⁰ See the passage from Mariette, quoted ch. xvi, note ³.

²¹ In the time of Amasis, it was said that the number of inhabited cities in Egypt was 20,000 (Herod. ii, 177). This, no doubt, is a rhetorical exaggeration, but from fifty to sixty well-known cities might be numerated.

²² All the epitomes agree in this statement.

²³ Lenormant (*Manuel d'Histoire Ancienne*, vol. i, p. 348) reckons to this dynasty six kings only. Birch (*Ancient Egypt*. p. 58) makes the number eight. Dr. Brugsch avoids a definite statement, but distinctly mentions only five (*History of Egypt*, vol. i, pp. 110-18, 1st ed.).

²⁴ Brugsch, *History of Egypt*, vol. i, pp. 115-117, 1st ed. Sankh-ka-ra is not acknowledged by either Dr. Birch or M. Lenormant; but M. Chabas seems to have established positively both his existence and his place in the eleventh dynasty.

²⁵ Leemans, *Lettres à Salvolini*, pp. 28 et seqq ; Bunsen, *Egypt's Place*, vol. ii, p. 23..

²⁶ The diadem was of gold, and its royal character was marked by the uræus. It is now in the Leyden Museum.

²⁷ Birch, *Ancient Egypt*, p. 58. The coffin is in the British Museum.

²⁸ See the inscription upon his tomb, which is given by M. Mariette in his *Monuments Divers*, pl. 49.

²⁹ See the *Monuments Divers*, pl. 49. A copy of this plate appeared in the *Transactions of the Society of Biblical Archæology*, vol. iv, opp. p. 172, accompanied by a very instructive commentary, the work of Dr. Birch.

³⁰ *Ancient Monarchies*, vol. ii, pp. 74, 90, and 211, 2d ed.

³¹ *Ancient Egypt*. p. 58.

³² Brugsch. *History of Egypt*. vol. i, p. 111, 1st ed.; Birch, l.s.c.

³³ Birch, *Ancient Egypt*, p. 59.

³⁴ Brugsch, *History of Egypt*, vol. i, p 113, 1st ed.

³⁵ Brugsch, *History of Egypt*, vol. i, p. 113, 1st ed.

³⁶ See the *Records of the Past*, vol. x, p. 3.

³⁷ Ibid. p. 4.

³⁸ See Lepsius, *Königsbuch*, Taf. x, No 156.

³⁹ Birch, *Ancient Egypt*. pp. 59-60. One of the commissioners says: "His holiness ordered me to go to this *beautiful* mountain, with the soldiers and principal persons of the whole country."

⁴⁰ Brugsch, *History of Egypt*, vol. i, p. 110, 1st ed.

⁴¹ *Records of the Past*. vol. x, pp. 11-19; Birch, *Ancient Egypt*, p. 83; Lenormant. *Manuel d'Histoire Ancienne*, vol. i, p. 378; etc.

⁴² *History of Egypt*, vol. i, p 114, 1st ed.

⁴³ Ibid.

⁴⁴ *Records of the Past*, vol. x, p. 14; Birch, *Ancient Egypt*, l.s.c.

⁴⁵ Brugsch. *History of Egypt*. vol. i, pp 115-16, 1st ed. A transcript of the original will be found in the *Denkmäler*, pt. ii, pl 150 a.

⁴⁶ Wilkinson, *Topography of Thebes*, p 421; Belzoni, *Researches*, map opp. p. 185.

⁴⁷ On the early commerce of Bahrein, see Sir H. Rawlinson's "Notes on Cap-

tain Durand's Report," in the *Journal of the Royal Asiatic Society* for 1879, pp. 13-39.
[48] Brugsch, *History of Egypt*, vol. i, p. 117, 1st ed
[49] See *Records of the Past*, vol. x, pp. 13, 19.
[50] Brugsch, *History of Egypt*, vol. i, p. 115, 1st ed.
[51] Brugsch, *History of Egypt*, vol. i, p. 115, 1st ed , and compare for a fuller account the French version published by Brugsch himself in the year 1875, p. 82, where Hes is called "la divinité de la joie, de la musique et des plaisirs, celui qui chasse le mal," and where his connection with the toilet tables of *grandes dames* is noticed. It is certainly remarkable how often cases for stibium, mirror handles, and other toilet articles are shaped into the image of this hideous god (Birch, *Guide to Museum*, pp. 28, 31, etc.)
[52] *Records of the Past*, vol. ii, p. 12, note [5].
[53] Brugsch, *History of Egypt*, vol. i, p. 122, 1st ed.
[54] *Records of the Past*, vol. ii, p. 12, § 5, ad fin.
[55] Lenormant, *Manuel d'Histoire Ancienne*, vol. i, p. 318.
[56] Brugsch, *History of Egypt*, vol. i, p. 111, 1st ed.
[57] *Records of the Past*, vol. ii, p. 11, § 11.
[58] Herodotus says that he omits the names of certain kings, since "they left no memorial of themselves," and are therefore not worth mentioning (ii, 101-2).
[59] The famous "Labyrinth," of which some account will be given in the next chapter.
[60] See the "Stelé of Iritisen" (*Records of the Past*, vol. x, pp. 3, 4); and compare Brugsch, *History of Egypt*, vol. i, pp. 121-2, 1st ed.
[61] Birch, *Guide to Galleries*, pp. 17-19.
[62] See Mariette, *Monuments Divers*, pl. 49; and compare below, p. 76.
[63] Mariette, *Monuments Divers*, pl. 50.
[64] See the preface of Professor Maspero, in the *Records of the Past*, vol. x, pp. 1, 2.
[65] There is an *Amen-en-hat* who was employed under Mentu-h tep II to convey his sarcophagus from the valley of Hammamât to the capital (supra, p. 71). There is also an *Amen-sat*, the wife of a sculptor of the time, in one of the sepulchral tablets of the British Museum (Birch, *Guide to Galleries*, p. 33). The *Amen-em-hat* who became king must have received his name under the eleventh dynasty.
[66] See Brugsch, *Histoire d'Egypt*, p. 125.
[67] Mentu, Khem, and Neith are represented together on a tablet set up by Mentu-hotep II. at the island of Konosso (*Denkmäler*, pt. ii, pl. 150 c). The sepulchral tablets of the British Museum show a *Mentu-aa*, a *Mentu-sa*, and a *Mentu-em-hat* among the names of the period (Birch, *Guide to Galleries*, pp. 19, 26, 29).
[68] *Denkmäler*, pt. ii, pls. 149 c, 150 b, c, and d.
[69] *Records of the Past*, vol. vi, p. 3; Birch, *Guide to Galleries*, p. 20, No. 462.
[70] See the *Denkmäler*, pt. ii, pls. 145 c, 147 b, and 148 d. Dr. Birch holds that "shoes were unknown" in ancient Egypt (*Ancient Egypt*, "Introduction," p. xv). But they have been found at Thebes (Wilkinson, *A. E.*, vol. ii, p. 337, ed. of 1878), and certainly the representation in the *Denkmäler*, pt. ii, pl. 149 c. is of shoes and not sandals.
[71] *Denkmäler*, pt. ii, pls. 145 d and 148 a.
[72] Ibid. pls. 147 a and 148 c, d.
[73] Compare Dr. Birch s article in the *Transactions of the Society of Bibl. Archæology*, vol. iv, pp. 172 et seqq.

CHAPTER XVII.

[1] *Records of the Past*, vol. ii, p. 11, § 2.
[2] " As for myself," says Amen-em-hat, " I have given to the humble, and made the weak exist;" and again, "I have made the afflicted ones to be no longer afflicted, and their cries to be heard no more" (ibid. pp. 11-12, §§ 3 and 5).
[3] See Brugsch, *History of Egypt*, vol. i, p. 122, 1st ed.
[4] Supra, p. ch. xvi. note [65].
[5] *Records of the Past*, vol. ii, pp. 12-13, §§ 6 and 7.
[6] Ibid. vol. vi, pp. 137-8.
[7] Ibid. vol. ii, p. 14, § 12.
[8] Ibid.
[9] Ibid , and compare an inscription found by Dr. Lüttge, near Korosko, which is to this effect: "In the twenty-ninth year of King Amen em-hat—long may he live—he came here to beat the inhabitants of the land of Uauat." (See Brugsch, *History of Egypt*, vol. i, p. 123, 1st ed)
[10] In the "Story of Saneha" the following account is given of the prowess of Usurtasen in his early youth:

Moreover, he is a valiant man.
Doing deeds of strength with his sword,
There is not his equal
Behold him going up against the Petti;
He suppresses violence; he chastens pride;
He abases regions; his enemies rise not up again;
That which is before him stands not,
But bows the knee. . . .
He is joyful when he sees multitudes,
He lets not his heart remain behind,
He is cheerful when he sees contest;
He rejoices when he goes up against the Petti.

(*Records of the Past*, vol. vi, p. 137.)

[11] *Records of the Past*, vol. ii, p. 14, § 10.
[12] *Records of the Past*, vol. ii, p. 14, § 10.
[13] Ibid. vol. vi, p. 135, ll. 23-4.
[14] Brugsch, *History of Egypt*, vol. i, p. 125, 1st ed.; and compare the map which accompanies his second volume.
[15] Ibid. p. 124; and compare the French edition (p. 85), which is fuller.
[16] Ibid.
[17] Birch, *Ancient Egypt*, p. 61.
[18] Brugsch, *History of Egypt*, vol. i, p. 124, 1st ed.
[19] Birch, l.s.c.
[20] Brugsch, l.s.c.
[21] *Records of the Past*, vol. ii, pp. 14-15, § 13.
[22] Brugsch, *History of Egypt*, vol. i, p. 124, 1st ed.
[23] *Records of the Past*, vol. ii, p. 14, § 12.
[24] See above, vol. i, p. 34.
[25] Ibid. p. 255.
[26] Herod. ii, 70.
[27] *Records of the Past*, vol. ii, p. 13, § 8.
[28] This fact is glanced at, without being distinctly stated, in the "Instructions," §§ 4, 8. It is seen very clearly in the "Story of Saneha," where the royal dignity of both father and son and their joint participation in governmental acts are apparent (*Records of the Past*, vol. vi, pp. 137-42).
[29] So Brugsch, *History of Egypt*, vol. i. p. 127, 1st ed. Dr. Birch makes the joint reign one of the seven years only (*Ancient Egypt*, p. 60).
[30] The "Instructions" have been translated and published in the *Records of the Past*, vol. ii, pp. 11-16.
[31] The text of § 15 of the "Instructions" is both mutilated and corrupt; so that its meaning is obscure; but to me it seems to have had the intention expressed above.
[32] The name, Khepr-ka-ra, is assigned to him by the author of the "Story of Saneha," while Amen-em-hat is still living (*Records of the Past*, vol. vi, p. 142).
[33] De Rougé, *Recherches*, p. 78.
[34] Mariette, *Monuments Divers*, pl. 50 a.
[35] The height of the obelisk of Antef is no more than 3½ mètres, or less than eleven feet.
[36] *Description de l'Egypt*, "Antiquités," vol. i. p. 229.
[37] For a good representation of this obelisk and its inscriptions, see the *Denkmäler*, pt. ii, pl. 118. The translation given in the text is taken in the main from Dr. Brugsch (*History of Egypt*, vol. i, p. 131, 1st ed.).
[38] See above, vol. i, p. 112.
[39] 1 Kings vii, 21.
[40] See the measurements in the *Denkmäler*, pt. ii, pl. 119, which, added together, amount to 12-62 mètres, or 41 ft. 4 in.

[41] See above, vol. i, pp. 154-6 and compare Wilkinson, *Topography of Thebes*, pp. 177-8.
[42] Brugsch, *History of Egypt*, vol. i, p. 133; vol. ii, p. 181; 1st ed.
[43] Ibid. vol. i, p. 140.
[44] Ibid. pp. 141-2.
[45] Wilkinson in the author's *Herodotus*, vol. ii, p. 348, 3d ed.
[46] Brugsch, *Histoire d'Egypte*, p. 91; Lenormant, *Manuel d'Histoire Ancienne*, vol. i, p. 353.
[47] Brugsch, l.s.c.; Lenormant, p. 350.
[48] Birch, *Ancient Egypt*, p. 61; Brugsch, *History of Egypt*, vol. i, p 138, 1st ed. The Wady Halfa memorial is now in the Museum of Florence.
[49] Supra, pp. 56-8.
[50] *Records of the Past*, vol. ii, p. 14, § 12.
[51] The sign for "gold" in Egyptian is ⌐ or ⌐, which is read as *neb* or *nub*. Nubia is written

⌐⌐⌐ = Nubi.

[52] Brugsch, *History of Egypt*, vol. i, pp 136-8, 1st ed.
[53] Such is the latest reading of the names (Brugsch, p. 139). Formerly they were read as Semit, Hesaa, Chaat, and Arqin (see the French version, p. 91).
[54] Birch, *Ancient Egypt*, p. 62.
[55] Brugsch, *History of Egypt*, vol. i, p. 136, 1st ed.
[56] Birch, l.s.c.
[57] "Mentu-hotep remplissait à la fois les fonctions de ministre de la justice, de l'intérieur, des travaux publics, du culte, et peut-être aussi celles de ministre des affaires étrangères et de la guerre" (Brugsch, *Histoire d'Egypte*, p. 92).
[58] Brugsch, *History of Egypt*, vol. i, p. 141, 1st ed. Compare Esther iii, 2.
[59] Brugsch says "three" (*History of Egypt*, vol. i, p. 120, 1st ed.), Birch (*Ancient Egypt*, p. 64), "four years."
[60] Birch speaks of "the forty-fourth year of Amen-em-hat II." (ib. p. 65); but Manetho gave him thirty-eight years only; and Brugsch (l.s c.) obtains the same number from the monuments.
[61] Lenormant, *Manuel d'Histoire Ancienne*, vol. i. p. 350; Brugsch, *History of Egypt*, vol. i, p. 144, 1st ed.
[62] Birch, *Ancient Egypt*, p. 65.
[63] This king, not otherwise known, is thought to have belonged to the disturbed time between the eleventh and twelfth dynasties, and to have been among the ancestors of the Usurtasens and Amen-em-hats (Brugsch, *History of Egypt*, vol. i, p. 146, 1st ed.).
[64] Ibid p. 147.
[65] See the *Denkmäler*, pt. ii, pls. 123-33.
[66] Brugsch, *History of Egypt*, vol. i, pp. 148 and 150, 1st ed.
[67] The name is given as Kha-ka-ra in the English translation of Brugsch's

Egypt (p. 147); but it is Kha-*khepr*-ra in the French edition of 1875, and also in Bunsen (*Egypt's Place*, vol. ii, p. 622), who follows Lepsius (*Königsbuch*, Taf. vii. No. 181).
[68] *Denkmäler*, pt. ii, pls. 131, 133. Compare the descriptions of Birch (*Ancient Egypt*, pp. 65-7) and Brugsch (*History of Egypt*, vol. i, pp. 155-7).
[69] Compare Bunsen (*Egypt's Place*, vol. ii p. 288; Birch, *Ancient Egypt*, p. 65; Brugsch, *History of Egypt*, vol. i, p. 157, 1st ed.; Cook in the *Speaker's Commentary*, vol. i, p. 450.
[70] *History of Egypt*, vol. i, p. 120.
[71] *Ancient Egypt*, p. 67.
[72] Ap. Syncell. *Chronograph.* vol. i, p. 60, D.
[73] De Rougé, *Revue Archéologique* for 1847, vol. iv, pp. 478 et seqq ; Bunsen, *Egypt's Place*, vol. ii, p. 291; Birch, *Ancient Egypt*, p. 67; Brugsch, *History of Egypt*, vol. i, pp. 162-4. 1st ed.; Wilkinson, *Topography of Thebes*, pp. 500-2.
[74] Brugsch, *History of Egypt*, vol. i, p. 159.
[75] Ibid. p. 160. See the *Denkmäler*, pt. ii, pl. 136 i.
[76] Brugsch, p. 161; *Denkmäler*, pt. ii. pl. 136 h.
[77] Bunsen, *Egypt's Place*, vol. ii, pp. 290-1.
[78] Brugsch, *History of Egypt*, vol. i, p. 100, 1st ed.
[79] Birch says that he "set up his statue on the spot" (*Ancient Egypt*, p. 67); but the inscription quoted by Brugsch (*Histoire d'Egypte*, p. 102) merely states that he had given permission for its erection.
[80] Lepsius, *Denkmäler*, pt. ii, pl. 136 a. Compare Brugsch, *History of Egypt*, vol. i, p 165, 1st ed.
[81] *Denkmäler*, pt. ii, pl. 136 b.
[82] Ibid. pl. 136 c.
[83] Manetho substituted the name of Sesostris for that of Usurtasen, according to both Eusebius and Africanus (ap. Syncell *Chronograph.* vol. i, p. 59, D, and p 60, c), and assigned him the actions which Herodotus ascribes to that monarch (ii, 102-3). He called the father of Rameses II., not Sesostris, but Sethos.
[84] Brugsch, *History of Egypt*, vol. i, p. 161, 1st ed.
[85] Job xix. 24.
[86] Herod. ii, 110.
[87] Wilkinson, *Topography of Thebes*, p. 501; Bunsen, *Egypt's Place*, vol. ii, p. 291; Brugsch, *History of Egypt*, vol. i, pp. 162-4, 1st ed.
[88] Manetho ap. Syncell. *Chronograph.* l.s.c.
[89] Herod. ii, 103-6. The sculptures in Asia Minor ascribed by Herodotus to Sesostris are thought by Mr. Sayce to be Hittite. They are certainly not Egyptian.
[90] Ibid. ii, 103.
[91] Ibid. ii, 108-10.

[92] *Manuel d'Histoire Ancienne*, vol. i, p. 351.
[93] As to Men-kau-ra, Men-kau-hor, Amen-em-hat II., Nefer-hotep II., and others.
[94] Brugsch, *History of Egypt*, vol. i, p. 171, 1st ed.
[95] Ibid.
[96] See above, vol. i, p. 10.
[97] On Egyptian famines, see the *Description de l'Egypte*, vol. vii, p. 332; and compare Brugsch. *History of Egypt*, vol. i, pp. 263-4, 1st ed ; Birch, *Ancient Egypt*. p. 68; Rawlinson, *Historical Illustrations of the Old Testament*, pp. 51-2.
[98] Compare above, vol. i. p. 85; and see Brugsch, *History of Egypt*, vol. i, p. 165, 1st ed.; Birch, *Ancient Egypt*, p. 68; Lenormant, *Manuel d'Histoire Ancienne*, vol. i, p. 352.
[99] The desert generally is considerably above the level of the valley of the Nile; the lower part of the Fayoum is 130 feet below it.
[101] Herod. ii, 101, 149; Diod. Sic. i, 66; Strab. xvii, 1, § 37. The old notion that the Birket-el-Keroun represents the Lake Mœris, though supported by the important authority of Jomard (*Description de l'Egypte*, "Antiquités," vol. i, pp. 79-114), is now pretty generally exploded. The investigations of M. Linant de Bellefonds, embodied in his work, *Mémoire sur le lac Mœris* (Alexandria, 1843), satisfied Wilkinson (Rawlinson's *Herodotus*, vol ii, p. 226, note 7, 3d edit) and even Bunsen (*Egypt's Place*, vol. ii, pp. 328-50); and his conclusions have been adopted by almost all recent critics. They are, however, curiously misrepresented by Dean Blakesley (*Herodotus with a Commentary*, vol. i, pp. 303-8).
[101] See the map, Fig. 16, which follows M. Linant de Bellefonds, and compare Herod. ii, 149, which gives the lake this direction. The Birket-el-Keroun runs nearly from east to west.
[102] Linant de Bellefonds, *Mémoire*, p. 20.
[103] Ibid. p. 13.
[104] Herod ii, 149; Strab. xvii. 1, § 37. The calculations of M. Linant de Bellefonds (pp. 22-24) show that the waters of the lake, besides irrigating the northern and western portions of the Fayoum, would have sufficed for the supply of the whole western bank of the Nile from Beni-Souef to the embouchure at Canopus during one half of the year.
[105] Towards the north the width of the embankment, according to M. de Bellefonds (p. 19), was *sixty* mètres, or nearly 200 feet; but this could be only at the base.
[106] M. Lenormant observes, with justice, that the works constructed by Amen-em-hat III. were as vast as those of the fourth dynasty, and considerably more useful (*Manuel d'Histoire Ancienne*, vol. i, p. 351).

107 Diod Sic. i. 52 § 2; Strab. l.s.c.
108 Brugsch, *History of Egypt*, vol. i, p. 167, 1st ed.
109 Ibid. Compare Birch, *Ancient Egypt*, p. 69.
110 See vol. i, note 89, ch. I.
111 Herod. ii, 148; Manetho ap. Syncell. *Chronograph* vol. i, pp. 59-60; Diod. Sic. i. 61; Strab. xvii, 1, § 38; etc.
112 See Plin. *H. N* xxxvii, 13, where the work of Amen-em hat is compared with that ascribed to Dædalus in Crete.
113 Wilkinson in the author's *Herodotus*. vol. ii, p 226, note 2, 3d ed.
114 Herod. ii, 148.
115 Ibid.
116 Bunsen, *Egypt's Place*, vol. ii, opp. p. 634
117 *Denkmäler*. pt. ii, pl. 136.
118 Brugsch. *History of Egypt*, vol. i, p. 171, 1st ed.
119 Ibid.
120 Birch. *Ancient Egypt*, p. 69.
121 *Records of the Past*, vol. viii, p. 50.
122 Ap. Syncell. *Chronograph*. vol. i, p. 60, A.
123 *Denkmäler*. pt. ii, pl. 140. Compare Brugsch. *History of Egypt*, vol. i, p 174, 1st ed.; Birch. *Ancient Egypt*, p. 73.
124 Birch. p. 72; Bunsen, *Egypt's Place*. vol. ii. p. 373.
125 Herod. ii, 149. Herodotus probably beheld Lake Mœris from the site of the Labyrinth. At the horizon, between seven and eight miles off. he would see the pyramids of Biamo crowned with their statues (Bunsen, *Egypt's Place*, vol. ii. pl. xx. opp. p. 373). The lake would form his horizon on either side of the pyramids, and he would not be able to see that it did not extend beyond Biamo.
126 Bunsen. vol. ii. p. 354.
127 Birch. *Ancient Egypt*, p. 73.
128 The *mafka* of the hieroglyphical inscriptions is regarded by Dr. Brugsch as "the turquoise" (*History of Egypt*, vol. i, p 172, 1st ed.).
129 Lenormant. *Manuel d'Histoire Ancienne*. vol. i. p. 353.
130 Supra, p. 74, 75.
131 Brugsch. *History of Egypt*. vol. i, p. 157, 1st ed.; Birch, *Ancient Egypt*, p. 66.
132 Gen. xxxvii, 25
133 See the *Denkmäler*, pt. ii, pls. 131-3. The six-stringed lyre carried by one of the immigrants (pl. 133) is of a form quite new in Egypt at the period.
134 *Records of the Past*, vol. ii, pp. 14-15. § 13
135 Ibid. p. 12. § 6.
136 Herod. ii, 148. Allowing for a large amount of exaggeration. we must still conclude, from the account given by this writer, that the number of apartments in the palace, known as "the Labyrinth." was prodigious.
137 *Denkmäler*. pt. ii, pl 134, *b, d, e*.
138 Ibid. pls. 128 and 129.
139 Ibid. pls. 129-132.

140 Ibid. pl. 128, upper line.
141 A lion is represented as wounded by two arrows in one of the scenes depicted upon the tomb of Khuumhotep (*Denkmäler*, pt. ii. pl. 132). That kings hunted the lion at this period appears from the "Instructions of Amen-em-hat" (*Records of the Past*, vol. ii. p. 14).
142 Birch in *Transactions of the Society of Biblical Archæology*, vol. iv, p. 177. Compare the *Denkmäler*, pt. ii, pl. 131; and for other varieties of the canine species see pls. 132 and 134.
143 *Denkmäler*, pt. ii, pl. 126. For a representation, see above, vol. i, pl. 76, fig. 195.
144 See above. vol. i, pl. 39, Fig. 96; and compare *Denkmäler*, pt. ii, pl. 126, upper line.
145 Brugsch, *History of Egypt*, vol. i, pp 6 and 175, 1st ed.
146 Herod. ii, 148.
147 On the early date at which the form of the obelisk was known to the Egyptians, see above, p. 31.
148 Herod. ii, 149. It is clear that a pyramid must have been truncated to allow of the superimposition of a colossal statue. The combination can scarcely have been very satisfactory. (See Bunsen's attempted restoration of the two pyramids of Biamo, *Egypt's Place*. vol. ii. pl. 20.)
149 *Records of the Past*, vol. ii. p. 15.
150 Probably it had been greatly added to by later kings before the time of Herodotus's visit.
151 Wilkinson in the author's *Herodotus*. vol. ii. p. 226, note 2, 3d ed.
152 See above, vol. i, p. 103.
153 Brugsch. *History of Egypt*, vol. i. p. 134. 1st ed.; Lenormant, *Manuel d'Histoire Ancienne*, vol. i, p. 353.
154 See especially the tomb of Khnumhotep, represented in the *Denkmäler*, pt. ii, pls. 126-132.
155 Lenormant. l.s.c.
156 Brugsch, *History of Egypt*, vol. i, p. 178, 1st ed.
157 Supra, p. 81. Ammon holds the first place in the highest compartment on this monument.
158 See Brugsch, *History of Egypt*, vol. i, pp. 135, 146. 1st ed.; Birch, *Guide to Galleries*, pp. 20, 27, 32, 33, 34, etc.
159 Sabak is represented in the third line of the Fayoum obelisk, and is placed on a par with Thoth, and before Kneph, Sati, Shu, Athor, Khem, and Horus (*Denkmäler*. pt. ii, pl. 119). His name becomes an element in royal and other appellations (Brugsch, *History of Egypt*. vol. i, p. 174, 1st ed.; Birch, *Guide to Galleries*, pp. 25, 26, 27, 31, etc.).
160 Compare above. p. 74.
161 Brugsch, *History of Egypt*, vol. i, p. 136, 1st ed.
162 *Records of the Past*, vol. vi, p. 137.
163 Ibid. p. 145.
164 Ibid. p. 148.
165 Brugsch, *History of Egypt*, vol. I, p. 150, ll. 75, 76, 1st ed.

CHAPTER XVIII.

¹ Brugsch, *History of Egypt*, vol. i, p. 184, 1st edit.; Bunsen, *Egypt's Place*, vol. ii, pp. 424-7; Lenormant, *Manuel d'Histoire Ancienne*, vol. i, pp. 358-60; Wilkinson in the author's *Herodotus*, vol. ii, pp. 349-51, 3d edit.
² Xoïs is the modern Kasit (Egypt, Khasan) in the lower portion of the tract between the Damietta and Rosetta mouths, about lat. 31° 6'. It lay northeast of Sais and northwest of Sebennytus.
³ Manetho ap. Syncell. *Chronograph.* vol. I, p. 61, A.
⁴ See Brugsch, *History of Egypt*, vol. i, p. 188, 1st ed.
⁵ Ibid. pp. 185-6. Compare Lenormant, *Manuel d'Histoire Ancienne*, vol. i, p. 359.
⁶ Brugsch, vol. i, pp. 184-5, 1st ed.
⁷ Ibid. p. 186. I do not, however, find the sense of "servant" among the meanings of *hotep* in Birch. (See the *Dictionary of Hieroglyphics*, in Bunsen's *Egypt*, vol. v, pp. 404-5.)
⁸ As Dr. Brugsch supposes (*History of Egypt*, vol. i, p. 189, 1st ed).
⁹ *Denkmäler*, pt. ii, pl. 151 c.
¹⁰ Brugsch, p. 192; Birch, *Ancient Egypt*, p. 74.
¹¹ Brugsch, *Histoire d'Egypte*, pp. 120-1.
¹² Ibid. p. 132.
¹³ *Denkmäler*, pt. ii, pl. 151 *f*.
¹⁴ Ibid. pl. 151 *h*.
¹⁵ Ibid pl. 151 *g*.
¹⁶ Birch, *Ancient Egypt*, p. 74; *Denkmäler*, pl. 151 e.
¹⁷ Brugsch, *History of Egypt*, vol. i, p. 192, 1st ed.
¹⁸ Ibid.
¹⁹ Kurtz, *History of the Old Covenant*, vol. ii, p. 2.
²⁰ Ex. i. 1; Kurtz, *History of the Old Covenant*, vol. ii, p. 149; Dean Payne Smith, *Bampton Lectures* for 1869, pp. 79 et seq.
²¹ Supra, p. 84.
²² As Migdol ("a tower"), whence the Greek Magdolon; Succoth ("tents"); Etham ("a fort"), etc.
²³ Brugsch, *History of Egypt*, vol. i, pp. 210-11, 1st ed.
²⁴ Ibid. pp. 212-13.
²⁵ Birch, *Ancient Egypt*, p. 66.
²⁶ See the list of kings in Brugsch, *History of Egypt*, vol. i, p. 188, 1st ed. After Mennefer-ra Ai (the twenty-ninth king of the dynasty) no monarch is said to have reigned more than three years and a month or two.
²⁷ Lenormant, *Manuel d'Histoire Ancienne*, vol. i, p. 359.
²⁸ Manetho ap. Syncell. *Chronograph*, vol. i, p. 61, A.

CHAPTER XIX.

¹ Ap. Syncell. *Chronograph*. vol. i, p. 61, B; Joseph. *Contr. Apion*. i, 14.
² See Bunsen, *Egypt's Place*, vol. ii, pp. 416-18.
³ Birch, *Ancient Egypt*, pp. 74-77, Lenormant, *Manuel d'Histoire Ancienne*, vol. i, pp. 359-65; Bunsen *Egypt's Place*, vol. ii, pp. 424-36; Wilkinson in the author's *Herodotus*, vol. ii, pp. 350-2; Brugsch, *History of Egypt*, vol. i, pp 227-60, 1st ed ; Stuart Poole in *Contemporary Review* for February, 1879, pp. 576-81; etc.
⁴ The one on stone is the inscription of Aahmes which exists in a rock-tomb at El Kaab (Eileithyia), and which has been published *in extenso* by Lepsius (*Denkmäler*, pt iii, pl 11) and translated by M. Le Page Renouf and others. (See *Records of the Past*, vol. vi, pp. 7-10; Brugsch, *History of Egypt*, vol. i, pp. 248-51, 1st ed.; De Rougé, in the *Mémoires de l'Institut*. Prem. Série, vol. iii; etc.) The document on papyrus forms the first fragment of what is called the "First Sallier Papyrus." It is given in the fifth volume of Bunsen's *Egypt*, pp. 630-1, and has been translated by Dr. Lushington in the *Records of the Past*, vol. viii, pp. 3-4.
⁵ See above, vol. i, p. 20.
⁶ See above, p. 27.
⁷ Supra, p. 149.
⁸ So Brugsch, *History of Egypt*, vol. i, p. 221, 1st ed.; Birch in *Records of the Past*, vol. viii, p. 46.
⁹ See above, vol. i, p. 55.
¹⁰ Brugsch, *History of Egypt*, vol. i, pp 215-16, 1st ed.
¹¹ Brugsch, *History of Egypt*, vol. i, pp. 221-2, 1st ed.
¹² Supra, p. 98.
¹³ Supra, p. 99.
¹⁴ Manetho says that at Xoïs there were seventy-six kings in either 484 or 184 years. Even if we take the larger of these numbers, it gives little more than six years as the average of the kings' reigns. And there is more authority for 184 than 484, which would reduce the average to two years and a half.
¹⁵ "Ησαν δὲ Φοίνικες ξένοι βασιλεῖς ἕξ (Man. ap. Syncell. *Chronograph*. vol. i, p. 61, B).
¹⁶ Manetho ap. Joseph. *Contr. Apion*. i, 14. It must be admitted that this statement is qualified by the clause τινές δὲ λέγουσι. But it is the only suggestion of nationality reported by Josephus.
¹⁷ Herod ii, 128. The "shepherd Philition," to whom the Egyptians ascribed the pyramids when Herodotus visited them, must have been the individualization of a belief that Egypt had been ruled by Philistine shepherds.
¹⁸ See Bunsen, *Egypt's Place*, vol. ii, p. 421; Brugsch, *History of Egypt*, vol. I, p. 225, 1st ed; Lenormant, *Manuel d'Histoire Ancienne*, vol. i, pp 360-2.
¹⁹ "C'était un ramassis de toutes les hordes nomades de l'Arabie et de la Syrie" (Lenormant, *Manuel d'Histoire Ancienne*, vol. i, p. 361).

²⁰ Birch. *Ancient Egypt*, p. 75.
²¹ Ap Joseph. *Contr. Apion*. (l.s.c.); τὸ ΣΩΣ ποιμὴν ἐστι καί ποιμένες κατὰ τὴν κοινὴν διάλεκτον. There is no evidence that Manetho knew anything of the Shasu, or in any way connected the Hyksos with them.
²² See the author's "Essay on the Early Migrations of the Phœnicians." in his *Herodotus*, vol. iv, pp. 236–244, 3d ed.
²³ See the author's *Herodotus*, vol. iv, pp. 238–40.
²⁴ On the Hittite worship of Set or Sutech, see *Records of the Past*, vol. iv, pp. 31-2.
²⁵ Ibid. vol. viii, p. 3.
²⁶ The names Set (Saïtes), Bnon, Pachnan or Apachnas, Staan, Archles, Apepi, have nothing Babylonian about them. Set or Sutech has no representative in the Babylonian Pantheon.
²⁷ Παραδόξως ἐκ τῶν πρὸς ἀνατολὴν μερῶν, ἄνθρωποι τὸ γένος ἄσημοι, καταθαρσήσαντες ἐπὶ τὴν χώραν ἐστράτευσαν, καὶ ῥᾳδίως ἀμαχητὶ ταύτην κατὰ κράτος εἶλον (Manetho ap. Joseph. *Contr. Apion*. i, 14).
²⁸ Ibid.
²⁹ Πᾶσι τοῖς ἐπιχωρίοις ἐχθρότατά πως ἐχρήσαντο, τοὺς μὲν σφάζοντες, τῶν δὲ καὶ τὰ τέκνα καὶ τὰς γυναῖκας εἰς δουλείαν ἄγοντες. Τὰς πόλεις ὡμῶς ἐνέπρησαν, καὶ τὰ ἱερὰ τῶν θεῶν κατέσκαψαν (ib.)
³⁰ See the preceding note, and especially the emphatic word κατέσκαψαν.
³¹ Lenormant says: "Dire ce que durant ces ... ans l'Egypte eut à subir de bouleversements est impossible. Le seul fait qu'il soit permis de donner comme certain, c'est que pas un monument de cette époque désolée n'est venu jusqu'à nous pour nous apprendre ce que devint, sous les Hyksôs, l'antique splendeur de l'Egypte" (*Manuel d'Histoire Ancienne*, vol. i, p. 360).
³² See above, p. 69.
³³ Lenormant, p. 363: "La civilisation égyptienne, d'abord comme *anéantie* par l'invasion," etc.
³⁴ Lenormant, p. 362: "Les Pasteurs dans la Basse-Egypte, comme les Tartares en Chine, se laissaient conquérir par la civilisation supérieure de leurs vaincus."
³⁵ Brugsch. *History of Egypt*, vol. i, pp. 230–7, 1st ed
³⁶ See Lenormant's *Frammento di statua di uno dei Pastori di Egitto*, p. 11, and plate.
³⁷ This appears from the remains, which are of Syenite stone (ibid.).
³⁸ *Records of the Past*, vol. viii, p 3.
³⁹ Brugsch, *History of Egypt*, vol. i, p. 237, 1st ed.
⁴⁰ *Records of the Past*, vol. iv, p. 36; Bunsen, *Egypt's Place*, vol. v, p. 734, bottom line. (Compare Birch, *Ancient Egypt*, pp. 76 and 126.)
⁴¹ Brugsch, l s.c.
⁴² Stuart Poole in the *Contemporary Review* for February, 1879, pp. 580–1.
⁴³ See above, p. 198, 199.

⁴⁴ The only exception to this was the Theban k ngdom, which continued a distinct, though subject, monarchy under the Hyksos; but as this was the exact power which expelled the Shepherds, all authority became at once fixed in a single centre.
⁴⁵ Ap. Joseph. *Contr. Apion*. i. 14.
⁴⁶ So the Manetho of Josephus. It is certain that Assyria Proper was not at this time in a condition to make exj editions into Syria (*Ancient Monarchies*, vol. ii, pp. 48–49. 2d edit.); but the "Assyrians" of Manetho may perhaps represent the Babylonians, who had made themselves felt in Syria and Palestine long before this time. (See Gen. xiv, 1–12; and compare the author's *Herodotus*, vol. i. pp. 446–7, 3d edit.)
⁴⁷ Bunsen. *Eg. Place*, vol. v, pp. 734–5; *Records of the Past*, vol. iv. p 36.
⁴⁸ See above. pp. 23, 30–31, 33, 46.
⁴⁹ De Rougé, *Recherches*, p. 45.
⁵⁰ Joseph, l.s.c.; Manetho ap. Syncell. *Chronograph*. vol. i, p. 61, B.
⁵¹ Bunsen, *Eg. Place*, vol. ii, p. 425; Brugsch, *History of Egypt*, vol. i. p. 229, 1st ed. Lenormant, however, prefers the reading Anon (*Manuel d'Histoire Ancienne*, vol. i, p. 362).
⁵² Gen. xxxv, 18.
⁵³ Forty years, according to Eusebius (ap. Syncell. *Chronograph*. vol. i, p. 62, A): forty-four, according to Josephus (l s.c.) and Africanus (ap. Syncell. *Chronograph*. vol. i, p 61, B).
⁵⁴ The latter number, which is given by Josephus (l.s.c.), seems preferable from its exactness, but is perhaps the time of the sole reign, while the other includes the period of association.
⁵⁵ See below, p. 108. The war of liberation almost certainly grew out of the demands made by Apepi on Ra-Sekenen. It was concluded by Aahmes, the first king of the eighteenth dynasty, in his sixth year. Unless, therefore, we suppose the war to have lingered on through several reigns, we must place Apepi and the Ra-Sekenen to whom he sent his messages almost immediately before Aahmes.
⁵⁶ Ap. Syncell. *Chronograph*. vol. I, p. 61, B.
⁵⁷ Africanus himself gave this as the total length of the dynasty (ibid).
⁵⁸ As are the reigns of the kings belonging to the twelfth dynasty in the Turin papyrus (Brugsch, *Hist. of Egypt*, vol. i, p 119, 1st ed).
⁵⁹ If each king associated a successor after he had reigned two years, the length of the *sole* reigns would be as follows:—

	Years
Set (Saïtes)	19
Bnon	27
Pachnan	35
Staan	17
Archles	34
Apepi (Apophis)	29
Total	161

THE MIDDLE EMPIRE.

The entire duration would thus be 161 years.
[60] See above, p. 107.
[61] *Records of the Past*, vol. viii, p. 3.
[62] Brugsch, *History of Egypt*, vol. i, pp 245-7, 1st edit.
[63] M Chabas has argued that the Ra-Sekenen contemporary with Apepi, and mentioned in the sailer papyrus, was the *first* of the name (see *Contemporary Review* for February 1879, p. 579); but I agree with Dr. Brugsch that it is better to regard him as Ra-Sekenen III.
[64] That Sutech represented the sun in the Hittite system appears from the terms of the treaty of peace concluded by the Hittites with Rameses II. (See *Records of the Past*, vol. iv. p. 28, § 8).
[65] Lushington in *Records of the Past*, vol. viii, p. 4, § 5. Chabas takes the same view (*Les Pasteurs en Egypte*, p. 18).
[66] Brugsch, *History of Egypt*, vol. i, p. 241, 1st edit.
[67] *Records of the Past*, vol. viii, p. 4, §§ 2, 3.
[68] Brugsch, *History of Egypt*, vol. i, p. 245, 1st edit.; Birch, *Dictionary of Hieroglyphics*, in Bunsen's *Egypt*, vol. v, p 414.
[69] Brugsch, *History of Egypt*, vol. i, pp. 247, 253, 1st edit.
[70] So Josephus, who professes to follow Manetho (*Contr. Apion.* i. 14). But the number is suspicious for many reasons.
[71] Josephus, *Contr. Apion.* i. 14.
[72] *Records of the Past*, vol. vi, p. 7.
[73] Ibid. pp. 7, 8.
[74] Ap Joseph. *Contr. Apion.* l.s.c.
[75] *Records of the Past*, vol. vi, p. 8, § 14.
[76] Josh. xix, 6.
[77] *Chronographia*. vol. i. p. 62, B: Ἐπὶ πᾶσι συμπεφώνηται ὅτι ἐπὶ Ἀπώφεως ἤρξεν Ἰωσὴφ τῆς Αἰγύπτου. Bunsen limits this to "all Christian chronographers" (*Egypt's Place*, vol. ii, p 433); but quite arbitrarily.
[78] Birch, *Ancient Egypt*, p. 76, Lenormant, *Manuel d'Histoire Ancienne*, vol. i, p 363; Brugsch, *History of Egypt*, vol i. pp. 260-70. 1st ed.
[79] Brugsch, p. 265.
[80] See above, p. 105.
[81] Gen. xl, 2.
[82] Ib. xli, 40.
[83] Ib. verse 43. This fact, and Joseph's "chariots and horsemen" (Gen. l, 9). sufficiently prove that Joseph was not anterior to the Hyksos.
[84] Ib. xli, 42.
[85] Gen xlvii, 26.
[86] Ib. xlvii, 22.
[87] Ib. xlvi, 34.

CHAPTER XX.

[1] Brugsch. *History of Egypt*, vol. i, p. 273. 1st ed.
[2] Ibid. vol. i, pp. 252-3, 1st ed.; Lenormant, *Manuel d'Histoire Ancienne*, vol. i. p 369.
[3] See especially the inscription on the tomb of his officer, Aahmes, son of Abana (*Records of the Past*, vol. vi, pp. 7-9.
[4] Birch, *Ancient Egypt*, p. 78.
[5] That the Hyksos kings introduced the horse and chariot into Egypt is generally admitted. No wheeled vehicles appear in the monuments prior to the eighteenth dynasty. The employment of chariots in the war of liberation appears in the *Records of the Past*, vol. vi, p. 7. The use of cavalry at this time is uncertain.
[6] This capture may have been the work of Ra-Sekenen III. There is no allusion to it in the inscription of Aahmes.
[7] Supra, p. 109.
[8] *Records of the Past*, vol. vi, pp. 7-8.
[9] Birch, *Ancient Egypt*, p. 80; Lenormant, *Manuel d'Histoire Ancienne*, vol. i. p 368.
[10] *Records of the Past*, vol. vi, p. 8.
[11] *Records of the Past*, vol. vi, pp. 8-9.
[12] Brugsch, *History of Egypt*, vol. i, p. 276, 1st ed. M. Chabas considers Teta-an to be the name of a people rather than that of a chieftain (*Les Pasteurs en Egypte*, p. 46).
[13] See the *Denkmäler*, vol. v. pt. iii, pl. 3 a ; and compare Birch, *Ancient Egypt*, p. 80, and Brugsch, *History of Egypt*, vol. i. pp 276-7, 1st ed.
[14] Brugsch, *History of Egypt*, vol. i, p. 277, 1st ed.
[15] 1 Kings vi, 18; vii, 13-45; 2 Chr. ii, 13-16; etc.
[16] Manetho ap. Syncell. *Chronograph*. vol. i, pp. 62. c, and 69, c.
[17] Joseph. *Contra Apion.* i, 15. Josephus gives the name the wrong form of Tethmosis; but clearly means Amosis (Aahmes), the first king of the eighteenth dynasty.
[18] She is called " the daughter, sister, wife, and mother of a king" (Brugsch, *History of Egypt*, vol. i, p. 279, 1st ed.).
[19] Ibid p 278.
[20] See the *Denkmäler*, vol. v, pt iii, pl. 1. Brugsch denies that this is always the case; but Wilkinson (in the author's *Herodotus*, vol ii, p. 355). Birch (*Ancient Egypt*, p. 81), and Canon Trevor (*Ancient Egypt*, p. 77) agree in regarding Nefertari-Aahmes as a black.
[21] So Birch (l s.c.) and Trevor (l s.c.).
[22] Birch, l s c
[23] Brugsch, *History of Egypt*, vol. i, p. 279. Wilkinson renders the expression used by "Goddess wife of Ammon" (Rawlinson's *Herodotus*, vol. ii, p 355, 2d ed.).
[24] *Denkmäler*, vol. v, pt. iii, pl. 3.
[25] Brugsch, l.s.c.
[26] Ap. Syncell. *Chronograph*. vol. i, pp 70 A, 72 A.
[27] This is the view generally taken

(Brugsch, *History of Egypt*, vol. i, p. 280, 1st ed ; Birch, *Ancient Egypt*, p. 81). But there is no appearance of extreme youthfulness in the representations of Amenôphis.

[28] *Denkmäler*, vol. v, pt. iii, pl. 1.
[29] Ibid. pl. 4 e.
[30] *Records of the Past*, vol. iv, p. 7; vol. vi. p. 9. Amen-hotep also employed himself in the enlargement of the great temple at Karnak.
[31] See the *Denkmäler*, vol. v, pt. iii, pl. 12 a.
[32] Thothmes means "Child of Thoth," and is nearly equivalent to Aahmes, "Child of the Moon," since Thoth was a Moon-god (see vol i, pp 369-71).
[33] Ap. Syncell. *Chronograph.* vol. i, p 70 A. Strictly speaking, it is Chebros who is given this short reign. But Chebros, as the second king of the eighteenth dynasty, must represent Amen hotep I.
[34] *E.g.* Chedor-laomer, whose two expeditions are mentioned in the fourteenth chapter of Genesis; and Kudur-mabuk, who calls himself *Apda Martu*, or "Ravager of Syria" (about B.C. 1600). See the author's *Herodotus*, vol. i, pp. 447, 450, 3d ed.
[35] Ibid. pp. 448-9.
[36] See the *Records of the Past*, vol. iv, p. 7; vol. vi. p. 10.
[37] Brugsch, *History of Egypt*, vol. i, p. 250, 1st ed.; *Records of the Past*, vol. vi, p. 10.
[38] Brugsch, l s.c.
[39] Brugsch, *History of Egypt*, vol. i, p. 285.
[40] A representation of the memorial is given in the *Denkmäler*,vol.v, pt. iii, pl 5; and a translation of the inscription upon it will be found in Brugsch's *History of Egypt*, vol. i. pp. 285-6. 1st ed.
[41] See Brugsch, *History of Egypt*, vol i, p. 284. 1st ed.
[42] See *Records of the Past*, vol. iv, p. 7, par. 9.
[43] Ap Joseph. *Contr. Apion.* i, 14, 26.
[44] That the Hyksos introduced the horse into Egypt, though doubted by M. Chabas (*Etudes sur l'Antiquité Historique*, p 415), is the general conclusion of Egyptologists. The employment of horses in war by the Egyptians as early as the reign of Aahmes appears from the inscription of Aahmes, son of Abana (*Records of the Past*, vol. viii, p. 7, par. 6).
[45] On the employment of cavalry by the Egyptians to a certain extent, see M. Chabas' *Etudes*, pp. 425-30; and compare above, vol. i, pp. 449-50.
[46] See 1 Kings x. 28, 29; 2 Chr. i, 16, 17.
[47] Brugsch, *History of Egypt*, vol. i, p. 295, 1st ed.
[48] Brugsch, *History of Egypt*, vol. i, p. 296, 1st ed.
[49] See above, vol. i. p. 108.
[50] For representations of these obelisks see Rosellini, *Monumenti Storici*, pls. xxx-xxxiv, and Lepsius, *Denkmäler*, vol. v, pt. iii, pl. 6.

[51] Birch, *Ancient Egypt*, p. 83
[52] Ap. Syncell. *Chronograph.* vol. i, p. 71, c.
[53] Brugsch, *History of Egypt*, vol. i, p. 296, 1st ed.
[54] The reading Hasheps, or Hashepsu, seems generally preferred by Egyptologists (Birch, *Ancient Egypt*, p. 88; Brugsch, *History of Egypt*, vol. i, pp. 301-14, 1st ed.; Chabas *Etudes*, pp. 101-76, etc.). Professor Dümichen, however, still uses the form Hatasu. (See *Records of the Past*, vol. x. pp. 13-19.)
[55] *Records of the Past*, vol. iv, p. 8.
[56] Brugsch, *History of Egypt*, vol. i, p. 300, 1st ed.
[57] See above, vol. i, pp. 104, 106.
[58] See the *Denkmäler*, pt. iii, pl. 17, b. c.
[59] *Denkmäler*, pt. iii, pls. 14 and 15.
[60] Brugsch, *History of Egypt*, vol. i, p. 302, 1st ed. Birch (*Ancient Egypt*, p. 83) says: " Probably one of these revolting conspiracies and family quarrels of the palace is veiled behind the fact of the short and inglorious reign of Thothmes II." (Compare p. 86.)
[61] See the *Denkmäler*, pt. iii, pls. 15 and 21.
[62] Ibid. pls. 22 and 23.
[63] Ibid. pls. 19 b, 22-4.
[64] Compare Chabas, *Etudes*, pp. 161-2: "On remarquera que cette reine ... affecte continuellement de se servir des titres masculins; elle est appelée *le roi* et non *la reine*, quoique les pronoms personnels et possessifs qui la représentent dans les textes soient généralement du féminin; ces prétentions masculines donnent lieu à des formules très-singulières; c'est ainsi que, dans l'expression *Sa Majesté elle-même*, les termes *Sa Majesté* sont le possessif masculin, et ils sont suivis du pronom féminin *elle-même;* l'anglais *His Majesty herself* rend bien compte de cette anomalie."
[65] Brugsch, *History of Egypt*, vol. i, p. 303, 1st ed.
[66] Ibid. p. 302. Compare Dümichen, *Flotte einer ägyptischen Königin*, p. 17.
[67] *Denkmäler*, pt. iii, pls. 22-4.
[68] Dümichen, l.s.c.; Brugsch, *History of Egypt*. vol. i, p. 301, 1st ed.
[69] *Denkmäler*, pt. iii, pl. 25 d, e.
[70] Ibid. pl. 25 bis, q. Here she calls herself "the beloved of Sati and Khumu" (*i.e.* Kneph).
[71] Brugsch, *History of Egypt*, vol. i, p. 302, 1st ed.
[72] The valuable work of Dr. Dümichen, *Die Flotte einer ägyptischen Königin* (Leipzig, 1868), has given a celebrity to this achievement of Queen Hatasu, which it might not otherwise have obtained. This work, important though it be, is unfortunately incomplete, several of the scenes connected with the expedition not being represented in it. (See Chabas. *Etudes sur l'Antiquité Historique* l.s c.) The résumé of Dr Dümichen's work in the *Records of the*

Past (vol. x, pp. 13-20) falls very far short of the original.
73 See Dümichen's *Flotte, etc* , pl. 1.
74 The troops are not represented in the reliefs; but they are mentioned in the accompanying inscriptions (pl. 1, 4, etc.).
75 On the doubt as to the position of Punt, see above, pp. 71, 72. Dr. Dümichen's connection of the word with the name of the Phœnicians (Pœni, Punici) can scarcely be admitted
76 It is unfortunate that the "Introduction" to Dr. Dümichen's translation of the legends accompanying the reliefs in the *Records of the Past* (vol. x, pp. 11-12) should speak of "naval engagements," and of the "subjugation" and "conquest" of the land of Punt as now effected. Dümichen himself gives no ground for these expressions.
77 *Records of the Past*, vol. x, p. 19; Brugsch, *History of Egypt*, vol. i, p. 304, 1st ed.
78 Dümichen's *Flotte, etc.*, pl. 15.
79 Ibid. pls. 2 and 3.
80 *Records of the Past*, vol. x, p. 14; Brugsch, *History of Egypt*. vol. i, p. 308, 1st ed.
81 Birch, *Ancient Egypt*, p. 84; Chabas, *Etudes*, p. 158.
82 Brugsch, *History of Egypt*, vol. i, p, 306, 1st ed.
83 Dümichen, *Flotte, etc.*, pls. 4 and 5.
84 Ibid. pls. 6 and 11.
85 *Records of the Past*, vol x, p. 17; Brugsch, *History of Egypt*, vol. i, p. 312, 1st ed.
86 *Denkmäler*, pt. iii, pl. 28.
87 Ibid. pl. 19.
88 Thothmes III. began to reign in the fifteenth year of his sister, which he counted as his own fifteenth year (Brugsch, *History of Egypt*, vol. i, p. 314, 1st ed.). His sole reign appears to have commenced seven years afterwards, in what he called his twenty-second year (ibid. p. 320).
89 Ibid. p. 316.
90 On the sacred character of the scarabæus or beetle, and the symbolism which connected it with the sun, see vol. i, pp. 345, 347, 411, etc.
91 Brugsch, *History of Egypt*, vol. i, p. 316, 1st ed.
92 The *name* Sesostris no doubt comes from Sesortosis, a Grecized form of Usurtasen. The ideal figure was composed by uniting in one the actions of all the chief Egyptian conquerors. As the greatest of these Thothmes III. furnished the most traits.
93 Thothmes I. crossed the Euphrates into Mesopotamia and fought battles there, but retained no hold of the region. Thothmes III. seems to have conquered the entire tract as far as the Khabour, and to have left it to his successors, who held it down to the time of Amenôphis IV. The later Egyptian monarchs made raids into Mesopotamia; but no permanent result followed from them.

94 See above, p. 121.
95 Dr. Birch identifies Garu with the later Heroöpolis (*Ancient Egypt*, p. 87). But the identification is very uncertain.
96 See the inscription given by Brugsch (*History of Egypt*, vol i. p. 320, 1st ed) and also in the *Records of the Past*, vol. ii, p 38.
97 Brugsch, *History of Egypt*, vol. i, p. 321. 1st ed.
98 The exact site of this Kadesh is uncertain. Dr. Birch suggests that it occupied the position of the modern Hems. which is enclosed between two branches of the Orontes. (See his *Ancient Egypt*, p 116.)
99 *Records of the Past*, vol. ii. pp. 53-5.
100 Ibid. p. 21; Brugsch, *History of Egypt*. vol. i, p. 329, 1st ed.
101 Given by Brugsch in his *History*, vol. 1, pp. 353-6, 1st ed.
102 No doubt portions of the country were occupied by the very ancient races of the Rephaim. Anakim, Zamzummim, and the like, mentioned in Scripture; but these races do not appear in the inscriptions, and must have sunk into insignificance. The Amorites are sometimes mentioned as possessing parts of the country north of Palestine; and the Edomites hold the tract between the Dead Sea and the Gulf of Akabah. The name "Canaan" also occurs; but the Hittites are the only Canaanitish nation of the Egyptian records.
103 *History of Egypt*, vol. i, pp. 221-4, 1st ed.
104 Brugsch, *History of Egypt*, vol. i, p. 222, 1st ed.
105 See the frontispiece to the first volume of Brugsch, *History of Egypt*, and compare the *Denkmäler*, pt. iii, pl. 116 *a*.
106 *Records of the Past*, vol. ii, p. 21.
107 Ibid. pp. 21-2.
108 Brugsch, *History of Egypt*, vol. i, pp. 334, 342, etc., 1st ed.
109 *Records of the Past*. vol. iv, p. 31.
110 As at Boghaz-Keui, Eyuk, and Karabel on the old road between Ephesus and Sardis (See a paper by Mr. A. H. Sayce, published in the *Proceedings of the Society of Biblical Archæology* for July, 1880)
111 *Records of the Past*, vol. ii, p. 69.
112 Ibid. p. 71.
113 As may be gathered from their tribal and personal names.
114 See the author's *Ancient Monarchies*. vol. ii, pp. 372-3.
115 *Records of the Past*. vol. ii, pp. 21-2; Brugsch, *History of Egypt*. vol. i, pp. 329 30.
116 *Records of the Past*, vol. ii, p. 22, par. 8.
117 Ibid. par. 9.
118 Brugsch, *History of Egypt*, vol. i, p. 331, 1st ed.
119 Birch says with truth: "The inscriptions do not disclose to us in any instance places with a large population in this part of Asia" (*Ancient Egypt*, p. 91).

120 Brugsch, *History of Egypt*, vol. i, p. 333. 1st ed.
121 Ibid.
122 One on the east bank of the Euphrates, at the place of passage, opposite a tablet set up by his father, Thothmes I ; the other near the city called Ni or Nini (*Records of the Past*, vol ii, p. 24).
123 As Wilkinson (in the author's *Herodotus*, vol ii, p. 302, 3d ed.) and Birch (*Ancient Egypt*, p. 104). Brugsch combats the opinion (*History of Egypt*, vol. i, p. 358, 1st ed.), and even seems inclined to place Ni in the country *west* of the Euphrates. But was this ever Naharaīn?
124 Brugsch, *History of Egypt*, vol. i, p. 329, 1st ed.
125 *Records of the Past*, vol. ii, p. 25. Senkara has been identified with Singar or Sinjar, the present name of the low range which crosses Mesopotamia in about the latitude of Nineveh (Wilkinson), and again with Senaar or Shinar, the Hebrew term for the lower Mesopotamian country (Brugsch); but it is quite possible that the modern Senkareh may be intended.
126 Wilkinson in the author's *Herodotus*, vol. i. p. 253; vol. ii, p. 302, 3d ed. Compare *Records of the Past*. vol. ii, p. 27, note 1, where it is admitted that "bitumen" is the subtance spoken of as furnished by the Asi.
127 The Egyptian remains found at Arban on the Khabour (Layard, *Nineveh and Babylon*, pp. 280-2), which contain the cartouches of Thothmes III. and Amenôphis III., indicate most probably a prolonged occupation of that post by an Egyptian garrison
128 See *Records of the Past*. vol. ii, p. 62; and compare Brugsch, *History of Egypt*, vol. i, p. 355. 1st ed.
129 Distinct record is found of expeditions in the thirty-fourth, thirty-fifth, thirty-eighth, and thirty-ninth years (Brugsch, pp. 335, 337, 339, 340); and others appear to have belonged to the thirty-sixth, thirty-seventh, and fortieth (?)
130 For the particulars, see *Records of the Past*, vol. ii, pp. 21-52, and Brugsch, *Hist. of Egypt*, vol i, pp. 326-44, 1st ed.
131 Brugsch, *Hist. of Egypt*, vol. i, p. 334. 1st ed.
132 Brugsch, *History of Egypt*, vol. i, pp. 367-8, 1st ed.
133 See Lenormant, *Manuel d'Histoire Ancienne*, vol. i. pp. 325-6; Brugsch, *History of Egypt*, vol. i, p 387, 1st ed.; Devéria, *Nouvelle Table d'Abydos*, p. 6 (Paris, 1865); etc
134 Brugsch, *History of Egypt*, vol. i, p. 389, 1st ed.
135 See above. pp. 81, 82.
136 The nave of Canterbury Cathedral is 134 feet in length. and, excluding the aisles, forty feet in breadth, so that its area is 5,360 feet. Add one half, and the result is 8,040 square feet. The area

of the Hall of Thothmes was 7,865 square feet.
137 See above, vol. i, pp. 151, 152, and compare Fergusson, *History of Architecture*, vol. i. pp. 106-7. 1st ed.
138 Brugsch, *History of Egypt*, vol. i, p. 286, 1st ed. 70.
139 As the Lateran obelisk, which is only 105 feet high, has been estimated to weigh 450 tons (*Description de l'Egypte*, "Antiquités," vol. i, p. 239, note), the weight of one *more than half as high again* could not be less than half as much again (675 tons), and would probably be considerably more than that, as there is always a certain proportion between the height and the size at the base.
140 See above, vol. i. p. 70.
141 Brugsch, *History of Egypt*, vol. i, p. 404. 1st ed.
142 Ibid. pp. 389-90. This writer speaks of "the indescribable dignity and the kingly mien of the remaining statues of standing or sitting Pharaohs and deities," wherewith Thothmes adorned the great temple (ibid. pp. 387-8).
143 Birch. *Ancient Egypt*, p. 103.
144 The two obelisks known as "Cleopatra's needles" were originally set up by Thothmes III at Heliopolis Augustus transferred them to Alexandria, where they remained till recently. At present (July, 1880) one ornaments the Thames Embankment, while the other is on its way to the United States of America.
145 The obelisk brought to England by the Duke of Northumberland, and long an ornament of Sion House, belonged originally to this locality.
146 See Wilkinson in the author's *Herodotus*, vol. ii, p. 357, 3d ed.; Brugsch, *History of Egypt*, vol. i, pp. 396-7, 1st ed.; Birch, *Ancient Egypt*, p. 102.
147 As will be seen by consulting the *Denkmäler*, pt. iii, pls. 47-59. On the other hand, little is left of the temple built by Thothmes at Elephantiné, which, in the time of the French expedition, was magnificent and nearly complete. (See Brugsch, *History of Egypt*, vol. i, p. 395, 1st ed.)
148 Wilkinson in the author's *Herodotus*, l s c.
149 See above, page 128.
150 *Denkmäler*, vol. v, pt. iii, pl. 40. A reduced drawing of the scene is given in the author's *Herodotus*, vol. ii, p. 214, 3d ed.
151 Brugsch, *History of Egypt*, vol. i, p. 376.
152 As Rosellini, *Monumenti Civili*, vol. ii, p. 249; Hengstenberg. *Aegypten und Mose*, p. 80 (E. T); Kurtz, *History of the Old Covenant*, vol. ii, p. 152; Kalisch, *Comment on Exodus*, p. 9; Palmer, *Egyptian Chronicles*, vol. i, Introduction, p. xix.
153 Ex. i, 14.
154 See Birch, *Ancient Egypt*, p. 98;

Brugsch, *History of Egypt*, vol. i, pp. 375 6, etc., 1st ed. Wilkinson took the same view (Rawlinson's *Herodotus*, vol. ii, p. xv).

[155] See the representation in the *Denkmäler*, pt. iii. pl 40.

[156] Deut xxvi, 5.

[157] Ps. cxiv, 1.

[158] See above, pp. 110, 111.

[159] See Brugsch's map accompanying the second volume of the English translation of his *History*.

[160] Gen. xlvii, 6.

[161] Manetho ap. Syncell. *Chronograph*. p. 61. B

[162] Gen. xlii, 6.

[163] Ex. i, 7.

[164] Ibid. verse 8.

[165] Gen. xv, 13.

[166] The generations from Apepi to Thothmes III. are five, which would probably amount in Egypt to 125 years. The traditional numbers up to the accession of Thothmes II. are $(61 + 25 + 13 + 21 =)$ 120 years. The reign of Thothmes II. was short, probably not exceeding five or six years.

[167] *Records of the Past*, vol. ii, p. 34, par. 22; Brugsch, *History of Egypt*, vol. i, p. 363, 1st ed.

[168] Brugsch, *History of Egypt*, vol. i, p. 362, 1st ed.

[169] *Manuel d'Histoire Ancienne*, vol. i, pp. 386-7.

[170] Herodotus says nothing about the "working of the mines," and does not even notice the existence of mineral treasures in the Colchian territory. According to him, the colony which Sesostris left behind him consisted of soldiers who had accompanied him on an expedition by land against Scythia and Thrace (Herod. ii. 103).

[171] See above, p. 120; and compare Brugsch, *History of Egypt*, vol. i, pp. 335, 336, and 338, 1st ed.

[172] Herod ii, p. 182.

[173] As Birch and Brugsch, who know of no such extensive maritime dominion Birch supposes that Thothmes exercised authority over some of the islands of the Archipelago (*Ancient Egypt*, p. 100); Brugsch confines his maritime sway to Cyprus and the Phœnician coast.

[174] Lenormant, *Manuel d'Histoire Ancienne*. vol. i. p. 385.

[175] See the author's *Herodotus*, vol. iv, p. 202, 2d ed.

[176] *History of Egypt*, vol. i, pp. 371-2, 1st ed

[177] The Mathen or Maten of the fifth stanza are regarded by Dr. Birch as representing Asia Minor generally (*Records of the Past*. vol. ii, p. 33. note *; *Ancient Egypt*, p. 100). They are perhaps the Matieni of Herodotus (i. 72), who adjoined on Cappadocia and Phrygia: but their locality cannot at this time have been so far inland. Probably they held possession of the Cilician coast.

[178] Brugsch, *History of Egypt*, vol. i, p. 405, 1st ed : "We will here bid farewell to the greatest king of Egyptian history."

[179] It appears from his annals that Thothmes insisted on his soldiers taking an oath that none of them would precede him in his attacks upon the enemy, or even "step aside before the king," so as to afford him protection. (See Brugsch, *History of Egypt*, vol. i, p. 324, 1st ed.)

[180] Valery ascribes this obelisk to Thothmes II. (*Travels in Italy*, p. 537, E. T.); but it is undoubtedly the work of his successor (Brugsch, *History of Egypt*, vol. i, p. 404, 1st ed.).

[181] Birch, *Guide to Museum*, p 76.

[182] Brugsch, *History of Egypt*, vol. i, p. 406.

[183] See the "Inscription of Amen-em-heb" in the *Records of the Past*, vol. ii, p. 63, line 36.

[184] That is to say, counting his accession to have taken place upon the death of his brother, and thus including in his own reign all the years of Hatasu.

[185] Birch, *Ancient Egypt*, p. 104.

[186] See the *Denkmäler*, vol. v. pt. iii, pl 38 *a*, *b;* where Hatasu-Merira sits behind her husband on a throne, attired as a goddess, with whip, *ankh*, and tall plumes.

[187] Ibid. pt. iii, pl. 20 *b*, *c;* Lepsius, *Königsbuch*, Taf. xxvi, No. 351.

[188] Amenôphis is the name given him by Manetho (ap. Syncell. *Chronograph*. vol. i, p. 72, A, D).

[189] The seventh year of Amenophis II is mentioned upon his monuments. (Birch, *Ancient Egypt*, p. 105). His reign is supposed to have terminated shortly after this date; but its exact duration is uncertain.

[190] Brugsch, *History of Egypt*, vol. i, p. 407, 1st ed.

[191] Birch. *Ancient Egypt*, p. 104; Brugsch, *History of Egypt*, vol. i, p. 408, 1st ed.

[192] Brugsch, p. 410.

[193] On the frequent occurrence of this kind of representation, see above, vol. i, p. 487, note ³. The earliest specimen is, I believe, that of Amenôphis II. at Koummeh, which is given in the *Denkmäler*. vol. v, pl. 61.

[194] Brugsch, *History of Egypt*, vol. i, p. 411, 1st ed.

[195] Ibid p 412.

[196] See the *Denkmäler*, vol. v, pt. iii, pls. 66, 67.

[197] *Denkmäler*, vol. v, pt. iii, pls. 63 and 64.

[198] Ibid. pl. 62 *b*.

[199] Brugsch, *History of Egypt*, vol. i, p. 412. 1st ed.

[200] Ibid. p. 416

[201] On this identification see above, p. 58, note ⁵.

[202] Brugsch. *History of Egypt*. vol. i, pp. 415-17, 1st ed.; *Denkmäler*, pt. iii, pl. 68.

203 Brugsch, p. 418.
204 Brugsch, p. 413.
205 Ibid, p. 414.
206 See the inscription of Amen hotep on a tablet now in the British Museum.
207 *Denkmäler*, pt. iii, pl. 69 e.
208 Brugsch, *History of Egypt*, vol. i, p. 415, 1st ed.
209 The seventh year of Thothmes IV. is recorded on a tablet in the island of Konosso (Birch, *Ancient Egypt*, p. 105). No later year appears on the monuments. Manetho, however, seems to have given him nine years (ap. Syncell. *Chronograph*. vol. i, p. 72, A. D).
210 Brugsch, *History of Egypt*, vol. i, p. 419, 1st ed.; *Denkmäler*, pt. iii, pls. 70 *bis*, and 74 c.
211 Wilkinson in the author's *Herodotus*, vol. ii, p. 359, 3d ed.; Birch, *Ancient Egypt* p. 107.
212 *Denkmäler*, pt. iii, pl. 72; Birch, l.s.c.; Brugsch, *History of Egypt*, vol. i, p. 440, 1st ed.; etc.
213 She is represented on the monuments with a pale pinkish skin, such as is never given to Egyptians.
214 Amenôphis III. instituted a new festival in honor of the Solar Disk, on the sixteenth of the month Athyr (October 4); and assigned a prominent part in the procession to the Boat of the Solar Disk (*Aten-nefru*). He also placed solar disks on the heads of his crio-sphinxes, and similarly adorned the statues of Pasht or Sekhet. (See Brugsch, *History of Egypt*, vol. i, p. 427, 1st ed.)
215 I cannot agree with Dr. Brugsch in placing Amenôphis III. "*on a level with the great Thothmes*" (*Hist. of Egypt*, vol. i, p. 419); or with M. Lenormant, that "t..e epoch *of great wars* recurs with him" (*Manuel d'Histoire Ancienne*, vol. i, p. 389). There is no evidence that he engaged in any military expeditions excepting towards the south; and there his negro slave-hunts were certainly not " great wars "
216 See his inscription in the temple of Soleb in Nubia, quoted by Birch (*Ancient Egypt*, p. 108); and remark the occurrence of his name on the remains found at Arban in Central Mesopotamia (Layard, *Nineveh and Babylon*, p. 281)
217 *Denkmäler*, pt. iii, pls. 82 a, 87 d, and 88; Brugsch, *History of Egypt*, vol. i, pp. 420-3, 1st ed.; Birch, l.s.c.
218 " Il faut avouer," says M. Lenormant, " que les expéditions de ses troupes n'étaient pas toujours fort che valeresques, et semblent avoir eu souvent pour but (surtout celles que l'on faisait dans le Soudan) la chasse aux esclaves" (*Manuel d'Histoire Ancienne*, l.s.c.)
219 Brugsch, *History of Egypt*, vol. i. p. 421, 1st ed ; Birch, *Ancient Egypt*, 106.
220 M Lenormant (l.s c.) observes with truth: " Amen-hotep III., durant son long règne, fu tun prince *essentiellement bâtisseur*."

221 Brugsch, *History of Egypt*, vol. i, p. 427, 1st ed.
222 See the description in Fergusson, *History of Architecture*, vol. i, pp. 108-9, 1st ed.
223 Brugsch, l.s.c. Compare the *Denkmäler*, pt. iii. pl. 90 a, b, c.
224 Brugsch, p. 437.
225 Wilkinson in the author's *Herodotus*, vol. ii, p. 360, 3d ed.
226 See the *Denkmäler*, pt. iii, pls. 81 g, h, 82 a, 89, etc ; and compare Wilkinson, l.s.c.; Birch, *Ancient Egypt*, pp. 106-9; Brugsch, *History of Egypt*, vol. i, pp. 420, 421, etc.
227 Brugsch, vol. i, p. 429.
228 Wilkinson, l.s c.
229 Brugsch, p. 430.
230 Ibid. p. 426, note. In the *Quarterly Review* for April, 1875 (No. 276) the height is given as no more than fifty-four feet.
231 Brugsch, l.s.c. The " forty cubits" of Amen-hotep's inscription (reckoning the Egyptian cubit at 1 ft. 8½ in.) would give a height of 68 ft. 4 in.
232 See the work of Letronne. *La Statue l'ocale de Memnon, considérée dans ses rapports avec l'Egypte et la Grèce*; and compare *Quarterly Review*, No 276, p 533-5.
233 Strab. xvii, 1. § 46; Pausan. i, 42; Tacit. *Ann* ii, 61; Plin. *H. N.* xxxvi, 7, § 11 ; Juv. *Sat.* xv. 5; Lucian, *Toxar*, 27; etc.
234 Sir David Brewster is said to have first given this explanation in the *Quarterly Review* for Jan., 1831 (No. 88). It has been adopted by M. Letronne, Dr. Brugsch, M. Lenormant, and others.
235 As by Humboldt, Jomard, De Rosière, etc.
236 Pausan. l.s.c.: Τὸν ἦχον μάλιστα εἰκάσει τις κιθάρας ἤ λύρας ῥαγείσης χορδῆς.
237 *Eastern Life*, vol. i, pp. 84 and 289.
238 Brugsch, *History of Egypt*, vol. i, pp. 425-6, 1st ed.
239 Brugsch, *History of Egypt*, vol. i, p. 436, 1st ed.
240 Birch says 110 (*Ancient Egypt*, p. 107); Brugsch, 210 (*History of Egypt*, vol. i p. 420. 1st ed).
241 Brugsch, *History of Egypt*, vol. i, p. 437, 1st ed.
242 See above, vol. i, p. 195.
243 See the *Denkmäler*, pt. iii, pls. 2 b, c, 76 b, 77 c, 100 b, etc.
244 See above, vol. i, pt. lviii.
245 Herod iv, 191; Leo African, ix, p. 294. It is true that lions were at no time very abundant in Egypt; but they were to be found in the deserts on the Egyptian borders, and were perhaps more numerous than is generally imagined
246 See above. pl. xiv.
247 *Ancient Monarchies*, vol. ii, pp. 318, 404; *Transactions of Society of Biblical Archæology*, vol. v, pp. 324-5.
248 See the *Denkmäler*, pt. iii, pls. 72, 74 a, 84 b, 85 b, and 86 a.

[249] Brugsch, *History of Egypt*, vol. i, pp. 432-5, 1st ed.
[250] Ibid. p. 437.
[251] Ibid. p. 438.
[252] Ibid. p. 439.
[253] Wilkinson remarks strongly on the foreign cast of his countenance. (See the author's *Herodotus*, vol. ii. p. 359, 3d ed.) The statues in the British Museum (especially No. 6) show the prognathous character of the face better than the above illustration.
[254] The thirty-sixth year of Amenôphis III. appears in a tablet at the Sarabit-el-Khadim (Birch, *Ancient Egypt*, p. 109).
[255] *Denkmäler*, pt. iii, pl. 75 *a* and *b*.
[256] Brugsch, *History of Egypt*, vol. i. p. 440, 1st ed.
[257] Tii appears on the monuments of Amenôphis IV. as still living (*Denkmäler*, pt. iii, pls. 100 *c*, 101, 102).
[258] See pt. xiv, and compare the *Denkmäler*, pt. iii, pls. 91-110. Brugsch speaks of the "soft *womanish* traits of his countenance" (*History of Egypt*, vol. i, p. 412, 1st ed.).
[259] Brugsch, l.s.c.
[260] Brugsch, l.s.c. For illustrations, see the *Denkmäler*, pt. iii, pls. 91, 99, 100, etc.
[261] M. Lenormant even ventures to suggest that the form of religion established by Amenôphis IV. stood in a close relation to that professed at the time by the Israelite portion of his subjects, which had been, he thinks, materialized during their sojurn in Egypt (*Manuel d'Histoire Ancienne*, vol. i, p. 393).
[262] Hence in the imagery of Scripture our Lord is called "the sun of righteousness" (Matt. iv, 2), and His Church represented as "a woman clothed with the sun" (Rev. xii, 1).
[263] See Brugsch, *History of Egypt*, vol. i, p. 449, 1st ed.
[264] Brugsch, *History of Egypt*, vol. i, p. 450, 1st ed.
[265] Brugsch, *History of Egypt*, vol. i, p. 412, 1st ed.
[266] See the *Denkmäler*, pt. iii, pls. 91-111.
[267] Brugsch, *History of Egypt*, vol. i, p. 414, 1st ed.
[268] Birch, *Ancient Egypt*, p. 110.
[269] *Denkmäler*, pt. iii, pl. 103.
[270] Brugsch, *History of Egypt*, vol. i. pp. 450-1, 1st ed.
[271] Ibid. p. 452.
[272] Brugsch calls them "a garland of seven princesses" (p. 443); and gives their names as Meri-Aten, Mak-Aten, Ankh-nes-Aten, Nofru-Aten, Ta-shera, Nofru-ra, Sotep-en-ra, and Bek-Aten. (Compare Lepsius, *Königsbuch*, Taf. xxix.) In one of the tombs at Tel-el-Amarna all the seven are represented (*Denkmäler*, pt. iii, pl. 106 *b*).
[273] See the *Denkmäler*, pt. iii, pls. 99 *b* and 109.
[274] Ibid. pl. 93.
[275] Brugsch, *History of Egypt*, vol. i, p. 455.

[276] Brugsch, l.s.c.
[276] Ibid.
[277] Brugsch gives the three next successors of Amenôphis IV. in the order of Sa'anekht, Tut-ankh-amen, Ai; Birch in that of Sa'anekht, Ai, Tut-ankh-amen.
[278] Sa'anekht was married to Mi-aten or Meri-aten, one of Khuenaten's daughters; Tutankhamen had for wife Ankh-nes-amen, another of them. Ai was the husband of Tii, the nurse of Khuenaten (Brugsch, *History of Egypt*, vol. i. pp. 456, 460, 1st ed.).
[279] Birch, *Ancient Egypt*, p. 111. Compare the *Denkmäler*, pt. iii. pl. 110.
[280] Brugsch, *History of Egypt*, vol. i, p. 462, 1st ed.
[281] Ibid. pp. 457-9; *Denkmäler*, pt. iii, pls. 115-18.
[282] M. Lenormant says that Tutankhamen "received an embassy from the *Assyrians*" (*Manuel d'Histoire Ancienne*, vol. i. p. 394); but the embassy alluded to came from the Ruten, a people of Syria.
[283] The Egyptian objects found by Sir H. Layard at Arban in no case dated later than the reign of Amenôphis III.
[284] Birch, *Ancient Egypt*, p. 111.
[285] Brugsch, *History of Egypt*, vol. i, p. 461; *Denkmäler*, pt. iii, pl. 114 *g*.
[286] Birch, *Ancient Egypt*, p. 112; Lenormant, *Manuel*, l.s.c.; Brugsch, *History of Egypt*, vol. i. p, 473, 1st ed.
[287] So Brugsch, *History of Egypt*, vol. i, p. 463. M. Lenormant believes that he was Khuenaten's youngest brother (*Manuel*, l.s.c.), but Dr Brugsch regards him as merely an Egyptian of good repute whom Amenôphis III. had honored with his confidence (*History of Egypt*, vol. i, pp. 462-3, 1st ed.).
[288] Birch, *Ancient Egypt*, pp. 112-13.
[289] *Denkmäler*, pt. iii, pls. 119 *e*, *g*, *h*, 122 *a*. *c*.
[290] Ibid. pls. 120 *c*, 122 *b*.
[291] See Brugsch, *History of Egypt*, vol. i, pp 464-8, 1st ed.; *Records of the Past*, vol. x, pp. 29 et seqq.
[292] On the meaning of this phrase, see above, p. 78.
[293] Brugsch, *History of Egypt*, vol. i. p. 467, 1st ed.
[294] See above, p. 85.
[295] *Denkmäler*, pt. iii, pl. 121.
[296] Brugsch, *History of Egypt*, vol. i, p. 471, 1st ed.; Birch, *Ancient Egypt*, p. 112; Lenormant, *Manuel d'Histoire Ancienne*, vol. i, p. 394.
[297] Brugsch, p. 289; Birch, l.s.c.
[298] See the inscription in Brugsch's *History*, vol. i. p. 473, 1st ed.
[299] The number is twenty-eight in the Armenian Eusebius, thirty-six in the Eusebius of Syncellus, and thirty-eight in the same writer's *Africanus*.
[300] When an Egyptian personal name begins with the name of a god, it is uncertain whether the god's name was pronounced first or last. Hence Egyptologers vary between Neferka-Sokari

and Sokari-neferka. Amonrud and Rudamon, Mut-uotem and Notem-mut, and the like.
301 Birch, *Ancient Egypt*, p. 113. M. Lenormant, however, supposes him to have had at least one daughter, from whom he regards Rameses I. as deriving his claim to the succession (*Manuel d'Histoire Ancienne*, vol. i, p. 396).
302 Birch, l s.c.
303 "Il y a là," says M. Lenormant, "des obscurités encore impénétrables dans l'état actuel de la science, et que la découverte de nouveaux monuments pourra seule un jour dissiper."

CHAPTER XXI.

[1] Lenormant supposes him to have been a grandson of Horemheb, through his mother (*Manuel d'Histoire Ancienne*, vol. i, p 396). Birch lays it down (*Ancient Egypt*, p. 113) that Horembeb had no family, and says: "Perhaps the wife of Horus survived that monarch, and Ramses may have married either the widow of his predecessor, or her daughter"(*i.e.*, her daughter by a second husband). Brugsch suggests that Rameses I was "the son, son-in-law, or brother of Horemheb" (*History of Egypt*, vol. ii, p. 8, 1st ed.). According to Wilkinson, (in Rawlinson's *Herodotus*, vol. ii, p. 308) "he was of a different family from Horus," and "restored the original and pure line of the Diospolites," tracing his descent from Amenôphis I. and Queen Nefertari-Aahmes.
[2] The name Rameses may not have been previously unknown in Egypt; but it was at any rate new as a royal name. It is analogous to the earlier forms, Aah-mes and Thothmes, and means "Child of Ra," as they mean respectively "Child of the Moon" and "Child of Thoth." (See Chabas, *Recherches pour servir à l'histoire de l'Égypte au temps de l'Exode*, p. 76)
[3] Rameses I. took the throne name of Ra men-pehti, or Men-pehtira,

◯ ⨀⨀⨀⨀ ⦿. a name modelled on the throne-name of Aahmes, was Ra-nebpehti, or Neb-pehti-ra. The element *pehti* had not been used in any throne-name since the time of Aahmes.
[4] The worship of Set had been discontinued upon the expulsion of the Hyksos. It had revived under Thothmes III. (*Denkmäler*, pt. iii, pls. 33 *a*, 34 *c*, 35 *b*, etc.); but had remained in the condition of a minor and little esteemed cult. Rameses I., by calling his son "Seti," placed him under Set's protection, and gave the greatest possible stimulus to Set-worship.
[5] *Contr. Apion* i. 15. This, of course, becomes a year in the epitomists. (Syncell *Chronograph*, p. 72, B).
[6] Brugsch, *History of Egypt*, vol. ii, p.

9, 1st ed.: Birch *Ancient Egypt*. p. 113; Lenormant, *Manuel d'Histoire Ancienne*, vol. i, p. 397.
[7] See the "Treaty of Peace between Rameses II. and the Hittites" published in the *Records of the Past*, vol. iv, pp. 28-9.
[8] Brugsch. *History of Egypt*, l.s.c.
[9] This was the general rule of the Assyrian, Babylonian, and even the Persian monarchs. (See *Ancient Monarchies*, vol. ii, p. 529; vol. iii. pp. 496-7; vol. iv, p 418; Herod. iv, 204; vi, 20 and 119.)
[10] Brugsch, l.s.c.
[11] *Denkmäler*, pt. iii, pl. 124.
[12] Ibid. pl. 123 *b*.
[13] Ibid. pl. 123 *a*.
[14] Ibid.
[15] Brugsch, *History of Egypt*, vol. ii, p. 23, 1st ed.
[16] See above, p. 123.
[17] Lenormant, *Manuel d'Histoire Ancienne*, vol. i, p. 396; Brugsch, *History of Egypt*, vol. ii, p. 3, 1st ed.
[18] Brugsch, *History of Egypt*, vol. ii, p. 11. 1st ed.
[19] See the inscription quoted by Brugsch (*History of Egypt*, vol. ii, p. 13, 1st ed.).
[20] Ex. xiii, 20; Num. xxxiii, 6, 7.
[21] Brugsch, *History of Egypt*, l.s c.; *Transactions of Society of Biblical Archæology*, vol. vi p. 511.
[22] Ibid. Compare Birch, *Ancient Egypt*, p. 114.
[23] Birch, p. 115.
[24] Brugsch, *History of Egypt*, vol. ii, p. 14, 1st ed Compare the *Denkmäler*, pt. iii, pl 126 *b*.
[25] Brugsch, l.s c.; *Transactions of Society of Bibl. Archæology*, l.s c.
[26] Birch, *Ancient Egypt*, p. 115.
[27] Brugsch, l.s.c.
[28] See above, p. 126.
[29] See the article on the AMORITES in Smith's *Dictionary of the Bible*, vol. i, pp. 61-2; and for their occupation of Kadesh at this period, see Brugsch; *History of Egypt*, vol. ii, p. 15, 1st ed.
[30] *Denkmäler*, pt. iii, pl 127 *a*; Brugsch, *History of Egypt*, vol. ii, p. 15, 1st ed.
[31] Brugsch, l. s. c.
[32] *Denkmäler*, pt. iii, pl, 130 *a*.
[33] I follow the translation of Dr. Brugsch (see his *History*, vol. ii, p. 16). Dr. Lushington has given a somewhat different version in the *Transactions of the Society of Biblical Archæology*, vol. vi, p. 516.
[34] Brugsh, l.s.c.
[35] See the *Records of the Past*, vol. iv. pp. 28-9.
[36] Sixty-five are represented in one bas-relief (*Denkmäler*, pt. iii, pl. 129).
[37] Ibid. pt iii, pl. 128 *a*.
[38] Brugsch, *History of Egypt*, vol. ii, p. 17; Birch, *Ancient Egypt*, p. 114.
[39] *Ancient Monarchies*, vol. ii, p. 527, note [10]; Layard, *Nineveh and Babylon*, p. 644
[40] Brugsch, l.s.c.

⁴¹ See Rosellini, *Monumenti Storici*, pl. 46.
⁴² Birch, *Ancient Egypt*, p. 115.
⁴³ See the inscription of Seti quoted by Brugsch (*History of Egypt*, vol. ii, p 17). Compare *Transactions of Society of Biblical Archæology*, vol. vi. p. 518.
⁴⁴ Brugsch, *History of Egypt*, vol. ii, p. 19, 1st ed. The Khita are placed first, Naharaïn is second.
⁴⁵ *Denkmäler*, pt. iii, pl. 127 b.
⁴⁶ Brugsch, *History of Egypt*, vol. i, p. 5; vol. ii, p. 20.
⁴⁷ As particularly by Amenôphis II. (supra, p. 264).
⁴⁸ Birch, *Ancient Egypt*, p. 117.
⁴⁹ Birch, l.s.c.; Brugsch, *History of Egypt*, l.s.c. Compare Herod. iv, 191, where a custom of this kind is assigned to the nation which he calls "the Maxyes."
⁵⁰ Rosellini, *Mon. Storici*, pl. 55.
⁵¹ Brugsch, *History of Egypt*, vol. ii, p 20.
⁵² Birch, *Ancient Egypt*, p. 117.
⁵³ Herod. iv, 183; Strabo, xvi, 4, § 17; xvii, 1, § 53.
⁵⁴ Birch, *Ancient Egypt*, p. 119. Compare the story told by Herodotus of the Psylli, who went out to war against the South Wind (iv, 173).
⁵⁵ Brugsch, *History of Egypt*, vol. ii, p. 26.
⁵⁶ See above, vol. i. p. 125.
⁵⁷ Brugsch, *History of Egypt*, vol. ii, p. 27.
⁵⁸ Ibid. p. 28.
⁵⁹ Ibid.
⁶⁰ Birch, *Ancient Egypt*. p. 118.
⁶¹ Brugsch, *History of Egypt*, l.s.c.
⁶² B rch, *Ancient Egypt*, p. 119.
⁶³ Ibid.
⁶⁴ Brugsch, *History of Egypt*, vol. ii, p. 25
⁶⁵ Brugsch, *History of Egypt*, vol. ii, p. 26. Compare Wilkinson in the author's *Herodotus*, vol. ii. p 309. 2d ed.
⁶⁶ Brugsch, *History of Egypt*, vol. ii, p. 26.
⁶⁷ See the *Denkmäler* pt. iii, pls. 131–41.
⁶⁸ Ibid. pl. 137.
⁶⁹ See a paper by M. Edouard Naville in the *Transactions of the Society of Biblical Archæology*, vol. iv, pp. 1–19; and compare the *Records of the Past*, vol. iv, pp. 105–112.
⁷⁰ Wilkinson in the author's *Herodotus*, vol. ii, p. 309, 2d ed.; Brugsch, *History of Egypt*, vol. ii, p. 32.
⁷¹ Birch, *Ancient Egypt*, p. 119.
⁷² Birch, *Ancient Egypt*, p. 118; Brugsch, *History of Egypt*, vol. ii, p. 30.
⁷³ Lenormant, *Manuel d'Histoire Ancienne*, vol. i, p. 403: Séti ordonna, la neuvième année de son règne, d'y creuser un *puits artésien*"
⁷⁴ Birch, *Ancient Egypt*, l s.c.
⁷⁵ Lenormant, l.s.c.; Birch, *Ancient Egypt*, p. 117.
⁷⁶ St. Hilaire, *Egypt and the Great Suez Canal*, p. 4.
⁷⁷ I have given the number as seventy-

seven (see note 5, chapter 13); but this number is only reached by including the figures and cartouches of Seti himself and his son, Rameses II., which are also represented.
⁷⁸ See pp. 15, 26–42, and 54–60.
⁷⁹ The names are given in Brugsch's *History of Egypt*, vol. i, p. 110. vol. ii, p. 313, 1st ed.
⁸⁰ Supra, p. 70.
⁸¹ See above, p. 129.
⁸² See the *Denkmäler*, pt. iii, pls. 124–41. Ammon is represented ten times; Horus and Isis five times; Osiris and Athor four; Set, Tum, Ma, Sabak, and Maut twice; the remainder once each.
⁸³ Brugsch, *History of Egypt*, vol. ii, p. 23.
⁸⁴ An inscription quoted by Brugsch (*History of Egypt*, vol. ii, p. 24) says: "Thou wast raised to be a governor of this land when thou wast a youth, and countedst ten full years." But Brugsch himself thinks that "when Rameses II. ascended the throne he may have been about twelve years old, or a little more" (ibid. p. 25).
⁸⁵ At first, Rameses says, he was "left in the house of the women and of the royal concubines, after the manner of the damsels of the palace" (Brugsch, *History of Egypt*, vol. ii, p. 24). But it was not long ere important functions were assigned him (note 88).
⁸⁶ He would no doubt do so as early as possible. If he married Tuaa soon after his accession, and she bore him Rameses in the course of the next year, he may have associated that prince as early as his eleventh year.
⁸⁷ Lenormant, *Manuel d'Histoire Ancienne*, vol. i, p. 402; Brugsch, *History of Egypt*, vol. ii, p. 15; Birch, *Ancient Egypt*, p. 128.
⁸⁸ Manetho's statements that Seti reigned fifty-one or fifty-five years (ap. Syncell. *Chronograph*. pp. 72. B; 73, B), and Rameses II. sixty-one or sixty-six years (ibid.), have but little weight. He may, however, have been rightly informed with regard to Rameses.
⁸⁹ See Chabas, *Recherches*, etc., p. 79; and compare Lepsius, *Königsbuch*, Taf. xxxi, No. 420. The names were spelt in a vast variety of ways, as may be seen in the last-quoted work, Tafeln xxxii and xxxiii.
⁹⁰ See Brugsch, *History of Egypt*, vol. ii, p. 24.
⁹¹ In proof of this, see especially Tacit. *An.* ii, 60. The entire series of conquests assigned commonly to the mythic Sesostris were attributed to Rameses by the informants of Germanicus.
⁹² See below, p. 168.
⁹³ Brugsch, *History of Egypt*, vol. ii, pp. 100–1.
⁹⁴ Birch, *Ancient Egypt*, p. 119.
⁹⁵ Wilkinson in the author's *Herodotus*, vol. ii, p. 312, 2d ed.

[96] Brugsch, *History of Egypt*, vol. ii, p. 76.
[97] Ibid. p. 77. Compare Birch, *Ancient Egypt*, p. 120.
[98] Brugsch, *History of Egypt*, vol. ii, p. 63, 1st ed.
[99] See *Records of the Past*, vol. iv, p. 28. Rameses does not give the name of his adversary in the great Hittite war; and it is possible that Khitasir had not yet ascended the throne.
[100] Birch, *Ancient Egypt*, p. 125.
[101] Birch, *Ancient Egypt*, p. 120. Compare Brugsch, *History of Egypt*, vol. ii, p. 50, 1st ed.
[102] See the "Poem of Pentaour," as given by Dr. Brugsch (*History of Egypt*, vol. ii, p 54, 1st ed.).
[103] *Records of the Past*, vol. ii, p. 69. The Masu are thought to be the people of the Mons Masius, the Airatu those of Aradus: the Patasu may perhaps be the Assyrian Patena; the Leka are thought by Dr. Brugsch to be the Lycians. Khirabu is probably Helbon or Chalybon, the ancient name of Aleppo.
[104] See above, p. 123.
[105] See the "Poem of Pentaour" (Brugsch, *History of Egypt*, l.s.c.).
[106] The story of the spies is told in an inscription repeated several times on the walls of the temple of Abydos, and translated by Dr. Brugsch, *History of Egypt*, vol. ii, pp. 50-2, 1st ed.
[107] Brugsch, *History of Egypt*, vol. ii, p. 47.
[108] *Records of the Past*, vol. ii, p. 68, ll 9-11.
[109] Brugsch, *History of Egypt*, vol. ii, p. 55, 1st ed. In describing the "battle of Kadesh, "I have throughout followed this authority. Dr. Birch takes a somewhat different view of the engagement (*Ancient Egypt*, pp. 120-1).
[110] *Records of the Past*, vol. ii, p. 68, l. 4.
[111] This seems to me the only reasonable account of the position in which Rameses found himself; but it must be confessed that Pentaour's narrative is here very hazy.
[112] Brugsch, *History of Egypt*, vol. ii, p. 57, 1st ed.
[113] Lenormant, *Manuel d'Histoire Ancienne*, vol. i. p. 411; Brugsch, *History of Egypt*, vol. ii, p. 45, 1st ed.
[114] See the *Denkmäler*, pt. iii. pls. 164 b and 165. Compare Brugsch, *History of Egypt*, vol. ii, p. 48, 1st ed.
[115] Birch, *Ancient Egypt*, p. 121.
[116] See the "Poem of Pentaour" in Brugsch's *History*, vol. ii, pp. 60-1, 1st ed. According to this writer, there was a short renewal of the battle on the morrow, or rather a continuation of the butchery, after which Khitasir, at the request of his troops, sent the embassy.
[117] Brugsch, *History of Egypt*, vol. ii, p. 64, 1st ed.; Birch, *Ancient Egypt*, p. 122.
[118] The places attacked and taken in the eighth year are Shalama (Salem in the Jordan valley), Tapur (Dabir at the foot of Mount Tabor), Maram, or Merom, Beth-anath, etc. Ascalon revolted, and was retaken about the same time.
[119] Brugsch, *History of Egypt*, vol. ii, pp. 63-4, 1st ed.
[120] Tacit, *Ann*. ii. 60.
[121] Brugsch, *History of Egypt*, vol. ii, p. 34, 1st ed.
[122] Lenormant, *Manuel d'Histoire Ancienne*, vol. i. p. 421.
[123] Brugsch, *History of Egypt*, vol. ii, p. 65, 1st ed. The true identification of Singara is still uncertain. I have supposed it to be Senkareh, south of Babylon (supra, p. 127); but it may be the modern Sinjar. I think there can be no doubt that it was in Mesopotamia.
[124] Birch, *Ancient Egypt*, p. 129.
[125] Lenormant, l.s.c.
[126] Supra, p. 164.
[127] For a condensed account of the treaty, see *Records of the Past*, vol. iv, pp. 27-32. The full text is given by Brugsch, *History of Egypt*, vol. ii, pp. 68-74, 1st ed. It is a mistake, however, of this writer to call the treaty an "offensive and defensive alliance," since union for offensive purposes is certainly not contemplated.
[128] The geographical position of the Hittite country cut off Egypt from Mesopotamia, unless by the line of Damascus and Tadmor, which is only fitted to be a caravan route.
[129] Brugsch, *History of Egypt*, vol. ii, p. 75, 1st ed.
[130] See the inscription given by Brugsch (ibid. 86).
[131] On this people, see Herod. iv, 191; and compare Hecat. Fr. 304, and Steph. Byz. ad voc.
[132] Infra, p. 177.
[133] Brugsch, *History of Egypt*, vol. ii, p. 78, 1st ed.
[134] See the frontispiece to Brugsch's *History*, vol. i. 1st ed., where this cast of countenance is very noticeable.
[135] Lenormant, *Manuel d'Histoire Ancienne*, vol. I, pp. 423-4.
[136] Lenormant says (l.s.c.) that he was the first to introduce the system; but I have already shown reason for thinking that he was anticipated in the adoption of if by his grandfather (supra. p. 295).
[137] Brugsch, *History of Egypt*, vol. ii, p. 100, 1st ed.; Birch, *Ancient Egypt*, p. 124.
[138] Grote. *History of Greece*, ch. xix (vol. ii. p. 475; edit. of 1862).
[139] Supra, p. 28.
[140] See *Records of the Past*, vol. ii, pp. 11-12; and compare above, pp. 146-7.
[141] As would appear by the letter of Amenemau to Pentaour, quoted above (vol. i, p. 480).
[142] *Transactions of Society of Bibl. Archæology*, vol. I, pp. 357, 359, and 367.
[143] This is a point on which much has been written. M. Chabas regards the

identity of the Aperu with the Hebrews as certain (*Mélanges Egyptologiques*, ii, p. 118; *Recherches pour servir à l'histoire de la 19me Dynastie*, pp. 99-105); Dr. Brugsch, *History of Egypt*, vol. ii, pp 128-9, 1st ed.), Dr. Eisenlohr (*Transactions of Society of Bibl. Archæology*, vol. i, pp. 356-7), and M. Maspero are of the directly contrary opinion. Dr. Birch throws a doubt on the identification (*Ancient Egypt*, p. 128).
[144] Brugsch, *History of Egypt*, vol. ii, p. 88, 1st ed.; Ex. i, 11-14.
[145] Ex. xii, 37.
[146] Brugsch, *History of Egypt*, vol. ii, p. 100. 1st ed.
[147] See above, p. 165.
[148] Birch, *Ancient Egypt*, p. 125.
[149] Ibid. Compare Ex. i. 11.
[150] Lenormant, *Manuel d'Histoire Ancienne*, vol. i, pp. 426-8; Birch, *Ancient Egypt*, p. 129; Brugsch, *History of Egypt*, vol. ii, p. 114, 1st ed.
[151] See above, p. 161.
[152] Wilkinson in the author's *Herodotus*, vol. ii, p. 205, note 2, 2d ed.
[153] Ibid. p. 206, note 4.
[154] Herod. ii, 158.
[155] See the essay of M. Rozière in the *Description de l'Egypte*, "Antiquités," vol. i, pp. 140-4.
[156] Brugsch, *History of Egypt*, vol. ii, pp. 43 and 93, 1st ed.
[157] Brugsch, pp. 90, 98-9, etc.; Birch, *Ancient Egypt*, pp. 124-5
[158] See the "Letter of Panbesa," translated by Mr. Goodwin in the *Records of the Past*, vol. vi, pp. 13-16. and by Dr. Brugsch in his *History of Egypt*, vol. ii, pp. 96-98, 1st ed.
[159] See above, vol. i, p. 106.
[160] For representations see the *Denkmäler*, pt. iii, pl. 185 b, and Roberts's *Egypt and Nubia*, vol. i, vignette on title-page.
[161] *Denkmäler*, pt. iii, pls. 185 et seqq
[162] Brugsch, *History of Egypt*. vol. ii, pp. 90-1. 1st ed. In his concluding remarks, the writer appears to have forgotten that his own glory was, at any rate, the object *mainly* sought by Rameses in his erection of this edifice. Four colossi *of himself* form the façade; and in the interior he associates himself as a god with Ammon, Phthah. and Horus.(*Denkmäler*, pt.iii. pl, 190 c; Brugsch, *History of Egypt*, vol. ii. p. 91, 1st ed.). We cannot ascribe to him any very elevated or intense religious feeling.
[163] *History of Architecture*, vol. i, p. 113, 1st ed.
[164] Fergusson,*History of Architecture*, vol. i, p. 107; Brugsch, *History of Egypt*, vol. ii, p. 89, 1st ed.
[165] See the inscription translated by Brugsch. (*History of Egypt*, vol. ii, pp. 34-42, 1st ed.).
[166] Birch, *Ancient Egypt*, p. 127; Fergusson, *History of Architecture*, vol. i, p. 109. 1st ed.
[167] Brugsch, *History of Egypt*, vol. ii, p. 87, 1st ed.

[168] Ibid. pp. 88, 90, 93, 94, etc
[169] Fergusson, *History of Architecture*, vol. i, p 113, 1st ed.
[170] Fergusson, *History of Architecture*, vol. i, pp. 113-14, 1st ed.
[171] Brugsch, *History of Egypt*, vol. ii, p. 93, 1st ed.
[172] Ibid. p. 89.
[173] See the *Description de l'Egypte*, "Antiquités," vol i. p. 229. Mr. Fergusson makes its height 77 ft. (*History of Architecture*, vol. i. p. 117); M. Chabas closely agrees with this measurement (*Records of the Past*, vol. iv, p. 17).
[174] *Records of the Past*, vol. iv, pp. 19-24.
[175] Supra, p. 172.
[176] See above. vol. i. p. 107.
[177] *History of Egypt*, vol. ii, p. 89, 1st ed.
[178] Brugsch. *Hist. of Egypt*. vol. ii, p. 87. 1st ed. Compare vol. i, p. 44.
[179] Ibid. vol. ii, pp. 34, 88, etc.
[180] Ibid. pp. 87-8.
[181] See the *Denkmäler*, pt. iii, pl. 190 c; and compare Brugsch, *History of Egypt*, vol. ii. p. 91, 1st ed.
[182] For a representation. see the *Denkmäler*, pt. iii, pl. 192 b.
[183] See above, pp. 162-163.
[184] Birch says (*Ancient Egypt*, p. 129); "Rameses exhibits in his features the refined Asiatic, different from the Nigritic type of the kings of the eighteenth dynasty." But no writer, so far as I am aware, has called attention to the nobility and beauty of the face, especially as represented in some of the statues.
[185] Brugsch, *History of Egypt*, vol. ii, p. 111, 1st ed.
[186] "Though men be so strong that they come to fourscore years." (Ps. xc, 10).
[187] Supra p 163.
[188] Brugsch, *History of Egypt*, vol. ii, p. 110, 1st ed.; Lenormant, *Manuel d'Histoire Ancienne*, vol. i p. 404; Birch, *Ancient Egypt*, p. 128. Here, for once, Manetho gave the right number of years (*Fragm. Hist. Gr.* vol. ii, p. 533).
[189] Brugsch, *History of Egypt*, vol. ii, Appendix. Table ii.
[190] Ibid. p. 111 This would allow the concubines an average of five children each, which is quite as many as would be at all probable.
[191] See above, vol. i, p. 259; and compare Herod. ii, 92, with Wilkinson's note (Rawlinson's *Herodotus*, vol. ii, p. 127, 2d ed.).
[192] Birch uses the former (*Ancient Egypt*, p. 129), Brugsch the latter form (*History of Egypt*, vol. ii. p. 111, 1st ed.).
[193] Brugsch. l.s.c.
[194] See above. vol. i, p. 301, note 500.
[195] Nor a description and plan of the Serapeum, see M. Mariette's *Choix de Monuments et de dessins découverts ou exécutés pendant le déblaiement du Sérapéum de Memphis*, Paris, 1856.
[196] See the inscription in the temple of

Abydos translated by Brugsch (*History of Egypt*, vol. ii, pp. 31-42, 1st ed.), where Rameses says of himself: "His breast had a tender feeling towards his parent, and his heart beat for him who brought him up" (p. 34). And again: "The most beautiful thing to behold, the best thing to hear, is a child with a thankful breast, whose heart beats for his father; wherefore my heart urges me to do what is good for Menephthah" (p. 36).

[197] Brugsch, *History of Egypt*, vol. ii, p. 41, 1st ed.

[198] See above, pp. 173-78.

[199] As Usurtasen III., by Thothmes III. (supra, p. 131).

[200] See the *Denkmäler*, pt. iii, pl. 190 c.

[201] Lenormant says: "Ce n'est qu'avec un véritable sentiment d'horreur qu'on peut songer aux milliers de captifs qui durent mourir sous le bâton des gardes-chiourmes, ou bien victimes des fatigues excessives et des privations de toute nature, en élevant en qualité de forçats les gigantesques constructions auxquelles se plaisait l'insatiable orgueil du monarque égyptien. Dans les monuments du règne de Ramsès II., il n'y a pas une pierre, pour ainsi dire, qui n'ait coûté une vie humaine" (*Manuel d'Histoire Ancienne*, vol. i, p. 423).

[202] Birch, *Ancient Egypt*, p. 125; Brugsch, *History of Egypt*, vol. ii, pp. 98-9, 1st ed.; Lenormant, *Manuel*, l.s.c.; Chabas, *Recherches pour servir à l'histoire de l'Egypte aux temps de l'Exode*, pp. 147-8, etc.

[203] So Brugsch, *History of Egypt*, vol. ii, p. 111, 1st ed. Birch (*Ancient Egypt*, p. 129) says the "thirteenth."

[204] Ap. Syncell. *Chronograph*. pp. 72, B, and 73. B.

[205] Birch, l.s.c.

[206] M. Chabas thinks that he was formally associated (*Recherches*, etc., p. 83.)

[207] *I e*, "soul of Ra."

[208] Birch, *Ancient Egypt*, p. 132; Brugsch, *History of Egypt*, vol. ii, p. 118, 1st ed.

[209] See the *Denkmäler*, pt. iii, pl. 200 a.

[210] Chabas, *Recherches pour servir à l'histoire de l'Egypte aux temps de l'Exode*, p. 82.

[211] Brugsch, *History of Egypt*, vol. i, p. 115, 1st ed. M. Chabas' attempt to contravene this statement (*Recherches*, etc., pp. 80-3) completely justifies it.

[212] Brugsch, l.s.c.

[213] Brugsch, *History of Egypt*, vol. i, p. 116, 1st ed. Compare Chabas, *Recherches*, etc., p. 82.

[214] Chabas, p. 87; Brugsch, *History of Egypt*, vol. ii, p. 119, 1st ed.; *Records of the Past*, vol. iv, p. 43.

[215] Brugsch, *History of Egypt*, vol. ii, pp. 127-8, 1st ed.

[216] Ibid. pp. 136-7. Compare Chabas, *Recherches*, etc., pp. 95-7.

[217] On this date, see Brugsch, *History of Egypt*, vol. ii, p. 123, 1st ed.; and compare his work *On the Libyan Peoples in the Fourteenth and Fifteenth Centuries before Christ*.

[218] *Records of the Past*, vol. iv, p. 42; Birch, *Ancient Egypt*, p. 131; Chabas, *Recherches*, etc., p. 86; Brugsch, *History of Egypt*, vol. ii, p. 118, 1st ed.; Lenormant, *Manuel d'Histoire Ancienne*, vol. i, p. 429.

[219] Brugsch, *History of Egypt*, vol. ii, pp. 123-4, 1st ed.

[220] Dr. Brugsch identifies the Akausha with the Achaeans *of the Caucasus*, the Shartana with the Chartani, the Tursha with the Taurians, the Luku with the Ligyes. He also suggests that the Ushash of the time of Rameses III. are the Ossetes, and the "Qaqasha" the "Caucasians!" (See his *History of Egypt*, vol. ii, p. 124.)

[221] *Revue Archéologique* for 1867, pp. 167 et seqq.

[222] The date of Menephthah is probably about B.C. 1350. The Trojan war took place about B.C. 1250, according to Herodotus, Thucydides, and the author of the Life of Homer.

[223] As M. Chabas, *Études sur l'Antiquité historique*, pp. 187-98, and *Recherches pour servir à l'Histoire de l'Egypte*, p. 84; Lenormant, *Manuel d'Histoire Ancienne*, vol. i. p. 429; Birch, *Ancient Egypt*, p. 130; etc.

[224] See Mr. Gladstone's *Juventus Mundi*, p. 144; and his *Homeric Synchronism*. pp. 139-43.

[225] As the slain and the captives together exceeded 18,000, while very many escaped with Marmaiu, the smaller estimate of the text would be the least possible, while the larger would be a highly probable number.

[226] Brugsch, *History of Egypt*, vol. ii, p. 118, § 13, 1st ed.

[227] Ibid p. 117, § 4.

[228] The nome of Prosôpis lay between the Canopic and Sebennytic branches of the Nile, commencing at the point of their separation.

[229] *Records of the Past*, vol. iv, p. 41, § 6.

[230] Brugsch, *History of Egypt*, vol. ii, p. 119, § 29, 1st ed.

[231] Ibid. p. 120, § 33; *Records of the Past*, vol. iv, p. 44.

[232] Brugsch, *History of Egypt*, vol. ii, p 120, § 35, 1st ed. M. Chabas omits the "sandals" (*Recherches pour servir*, etc., p. 88).

[233] Chabas. p. 89; Brugsch, l.s.c.

[234] There is some difficulty in making out the number of the slain, owing to omissions and repetitions. Birch estimates it at 12,535 persons (*Ancient Egypt*, p. 131). But the number of the hands and members brought in is given as 8181 only. (See Brugsch, *History of Egypt*, vol. ii, p. 122, 1st ed.)

[235] The exact number is given as 9376 (Brugsch, l.s.c.).

[236] See the "Annals of Rameses III." in the "Great Harris Papyrus" (*Records of the Past*, vol. viii, p. 45).

²³⁷ The eighth year of Menephthah is the latest found upon the monuments. He may have reigned some time longer; but the twenty years of Africanus (ap. Syncell. *Chronograph*, p. 72, D) are probably in excess.
²³⁸ Ex. v, 1.
²³⁹ Ibid. v, 6–19.
²⁴⁰ Ex. xii, 37.
²⁴¹ Ibid. xiv, 9.
²⁴² The belief of the Egyptians is indicated by Polyhistor, who quotes the opinion of the *men of Memphis*, that Moses watched the ebb of the *tide* which could only be on the southern side of the isthmus (*Fragm. Hist. Gr.* vol. iii, p. 223). The Hebrew tradition appears by the fact that the *Yam Suph* in the later Scriptures is always the Red Sea, never a portion of the Mediterranean (1 Kings ix, 26; Jer. xlix, 21, etc.). It is also sufficiently proved by the uniform rendering of the LXX.
²⁴³ Dr. Brugsch's paper read before the International Congress of Orientalists in 1874, and published in the second volume of the English version of his *History of Egypt* (pp. 333–68, 1st ed.), is beyond a doubt exceedingly ingenious, but it has failed to convince more than a select few.
²⁴⁴ Ex. xiv, 21.
²⁴⁵ Ibid xv, 1–5.
²⁴⁶ Kalisch (*Comment on Exodus*, pp. 192–3) and others argue from Ex. xvi, 28, and xv, 9–12, that the Pharaoh perished; but I agree with Wilkinson (*Ancient Egyptians*, vol. i, p. 54) that "there is no authority in the writings of Moses for supposing that the Pharaoh was drowned." On the contrary, it seems to me that the omission of any reference to the Pharaoh's death is the strongest possible indication that he survived.
²⁴⁷ Brugsch, *History of Egypt*, vol. ii, p. 130, 1st ed. The monuments leave the history of this period in much obscurity; and it must be granted to be uncertain whether Amon-mes revolted against Menephthah, or against his son, Seti II. I have been induced to place Amon-mes *directly* after Menephthah chiefly by his position in Manetho's lists (ap. Syncell. *Chronograph.* pp. 72, c, and 73, D.)
²⁴⁸ Eisenlohr in the *Transactions of the Society of Biblical Archæology*, vol. i, p. 377; Lenormant, *Manuel d'Histoire Ancienne*, vol. i, p. 433.
²⁴⁹ Manetho omits Seti-Menephthah altogether. His name is sometimes found with marks of erasure upon his monuments. (See Birch, *Ancient Egypt*, p. 135).
²⁵⁰ See the "Great Harris Papyrus," translated in the *Records of the Past*, vol. viii. p. 46, § 3; and compare *Transactions of the Society of Biblical Archæology*, vol. i, pp. 359–60, and Chabas, *Recherches pour servir*, etc., pp. 9–15.
²⁵¹ Ap. Syncell. *Chronograph.* p. 73, D.

²⁵² So Manetho, according to Africanus (Syncell. *Chronograph.* p 72, c). Eusebius gives Manetho's number as 26 (*Chron. Can.* pars. i, ch. xx, § 4).
²⁵³ See Chabas, *Recherches*, p. 77.
²⁵⁴ Birch, *Ancient Egypt*, p. 136; *Denkmäler*, pt. iii, pl. 202 c.
²⁵⁵ Seti II.'s monuments are found at Thebes, at Silsilis, and at Ipsambul in Nubia. There is also evidence of his rule being acknowledged in the extreme northeast (Brugsch, *History of Egypt*, vol. ii, p. 132, 1st ed.).
²⁵⁶ Birch, *Ancient Egypt*, p. 135.
²⁵⁷ Ibid.
²⁵⁸ *Denkmäler*, pt. iii, pl 204 e.
²⁵⁹ Bai says, in an inscription, that he "put away falsehood and gave honor to the truth, inasmuch as he set the king upon his father's throne" (Brugsch, *History of Egypt*, vol. ii, p. 134, 1st ed.; Chabas, *Recherches*, p 128).
²⁶⁰ Brugsch, l s.c ; Eisenlohr in the *Transactions of the Society of Biblical Archæology*, vol. i. pp. 377–8.
²⁶¹ Eisenlohr, l.s.c.
²⁶² Lenormant. *Manuel d'Histoire Ancienne*, vol. i, p. 434.
²⁶³ Chabas, *Recherches*, p. 77.
²⁶⁴ Lenormant says categorically: "Siphtah, pour légitimer son pouvoir, épousa une fille de Méreupptah I., la princesse Taouser" (*Manuel*, vol. i, pp 433–4). But this is elevating a conjecture into an historical fact.
²⁶⁵ See the *Denkmäler*, pt iii, pl. 201 a.
²⁶⁶ Ap Syncell. *Chronograph.* p. 73, c; Euseb *Chron. Can.* l.s c.
²⁶⁷ Ibid.
²⁶⁸ *Denkmäler.* pt. iii. pl. 201 a and b.
²⁶⁹ See the authorities quoted above (note ²⁵⁰), and compare Brugsch, *History of Egypt*, vol. ii, p 137, 1st ed. Amid much diversity in details, there is a general agreement that a time of anarchy and confusion is described, when there was no central authority, and the gods were treated with neglect.
²⁷⁰ Nearly two centuries, according to the Manetho of Eusebius (*Chron. Can.* l.s.c.. ap. Syncell. *Chronograph*, p. 73, c); but this is certainly an overestimate. (See above, p. 8.)
²⁷¹ Fergusson, *History of Architecture*, vol i, p. 108, 1st ed.
²⁷² Ibid. p. 106.
²⁷³ Ibid. p. 113.
²⁷⁴ See W. Palmer's *Egyptian Chronicles*, vol. i, "Introduction," p. xv; Stanley, *Sinai and Palestine*, "Introduction," pp. xxxv–xliii, etc.
²⁷⁵ The "Great Pyramid" of Ghizeh covers an area of 543,696 square feet, the "Second Pyramid" one of 499,849 square feet. The area covered by the Palace-Temple of Karnak is estimated at 430,000 square feet (Fergusson. *History of Architecture*, vol. i, pp. 85 and 106.
²⁷⁶ Dean Stanley, quoting "Herodotus and others" as his authorities, expresses a belief that the "smooth outsides of the Pyramids were covered

with sculptures" (*Sinai and Palestine*, "Introduction," p. liv). But the stone casing of the Second Pyramid, which still in part exists, shows no trace of any such ornamentation; and Herodotus speaks of nothing but a short legend in the hieroglyphic character on one of the Pyramids (ii, 125).

[277] On Egyptian painting as subsidiary to architecture, see above, vol. i, pp. 117-118 and p. 134.

[278] What Mr. Fergusson says of Egyptian architecture generally, in summing up its characteristics, is especially true of the period here spoken of: "Taken altogether, we may perhaps safely assert that the Egyptians were the most essentially a building people of all those we are acquainted with, and the most generally successful in all they attempted in this way. The Greeks, it is true, surpassed them in refinement and beauty of detail, and in the class of sculpture with which they ornamented their buildings, while the Gothic architects far excelled them in constructive cleverness: but, with these exceptions, no other styles can be put into competition with them. At the same time, neither Grecian nor Gothic architects understood more perfectly all the gradations of art and the exact character that should be given to every form and every detail. Whether it was the plain flat-sided pyramid, the crowded and massive hypostyle hall, the playful pavilion, or the luxurious dwelling,—in all these the Egyptian understood perfectly both how to make the general design express exactly what he wanted and to make every detail and all the various materials contribute to the general effect. They understood also, better than any other nation, how to use sculpture in combination with architecture, and to make their colossi and avenues of sphinxes group themselves into parts of one great design, and at the same time to use historical paintings, fading by insensible degrees into hieroglyphics on the one hand, and into sculpture on the other,—linking the whole together with the highest class of phonetic utterance. With the most brilliant coloring, they thus harmonized all these arts into one great whole, unsurpassed by anything the world has seen during the thirty centuries of struggle and aspiration that have elapsed since the brilliant days of the great kingdom of the Pharaohs" (Fergusson, *History of Architecture*, vol. i, p. 126, 1st ed.).

[279] Stanley, *Sinai and Palestine*, "Introduction," p. xxxvi.

[280] Ibid. p. xxxv.

[281] See above. p. 144-145.

[282] Stanley, *Sinai and Palestine*, "Introduction," p. xxxvi.

[283] Fergusson, *History of Architecture*, vol. i, p. 113.

[284] Brugsch, *History of Egypt*, vol. ii, p. 90, 1st ed.

[285] Ibid. p. 91.

[286] *Denkmäler*, pt. iii, pls. 63 *a*, 64 *a*, 76 *b*, 77 *c*, etc.

[287] Ibid. pls. 126 *a*, 130 *a*, 145 *c*, 154, 155, 158, etc.

[288] See above, vol. i, pl. lvii. The representation given is only about one-fourth of the actual scene upon the monument.

[289] Rosellini, *Monumenti Storici*, pl. cxxxi. The date of this scene is a little later than the time here assigned to it, since it belongs to the reign of Rameses III.

[290] Birch, *Ancient Egypt*, p. 129; Lenormant, *Manuel d'Histoire Ancienne*, vol. i, p. 426. The latter writer says: "Les monuments de Ramesès II. nous font assister à une *décadence radicale* de la sculpture égyptienne, qui se précipite avec une incroyable rapidité à mesure qu'on s'avance dans ce long règne. Il débute par des œuvres dignes de toute admiration, qui sout le *nec plus ultra* de l'art égyptien; mais bientôt l'oppression universelle, qui pèse sur toute la contrée comme un joug de fer, tarit la source de la grande inspiration des arts. . . . A la fin du règne, la décadence est complète."

[291] Birch, *Guide to Galleries*, p. 17.

[292] Lenormant, l.s.c.

[293] Supra, p. 142.

[294] See above, vol. i, p. 184.

[295] Supra, pp. 46 and 65.

[296] If there is any exception, it is in the reign of Thothmes III., who seems to have had a considerable regard for Set, and represents him not unfrequently on his monuments (*Denkmäler*, pt. iii, pls. 33 *g*, 34 *c*, 35 *b*, 36 *b*).

[297] See above, vol. i, p. 299, note [272].

[298] *Denkmäler*, pt. iii, pl. 125 *a*.

[299] Ibid. pl. 124 *d*.

[300] As Seti II., Setnekht, Seti, and Setem-ua, sons of Rameses II., and others.

[301] *Denkmäler*, pt. iii, pls. 30 *a*, 33 *b*, 46 *a*, 55 *b*, 56 *a*, 58, 65 *d*, 72, 74 *a*, 82 *c*, 124 *d*, 151 *a*, etc.

[302] Ibid. pl. 36 *b*.

[303] Ibid. pls. 37 *a* and 169.

[304] *Records of the Past*, vol. ii, pp. 43, 71, 72, 75, 76, etc.

[305] Ibid. vol. ii, pp. 38, 40, 43, etc., vol. iv, p. 44, etc.

[306] See above, pp. 94, 95.

[307] The only exception, so far as I know, was the appointment of priests, from a very early date, for the cult of the kings, in connection with their burial-place; but this seems to have been a domestic arrangement, and to have belonged to the general worship of ancestors, of which we have spoken supra. vol. i, p. 200-201.

[308] *Denkmäler*, pt. iii, pls. 47, 59.

[309] Ibid. pls. 54 *a* and 57 *a*.

[310] Ibid. pt. iii, pl. 67.

[311] Ibid. pls. 147 *a*, 151 *b*, 199 *d*, etc.

[312] Ibid. pl. 143 *c*.

THE TWENTIETH DYNASTY.

³¹³ See above, ch. xxi, note 162.
³¹⁴ Dean Stanley well says in reference to Rameses II.: "His image carries one back to the days when there were giants upon the earth. It shows how the king, in that first monarchy, was the visible god upon earth. The only thing like it that has since been seen is the deification of the Roman emperors. No pure monotheism could for a moment have been compatible with such an exaltation of the conquering king" (*Sinai and Palestine*, "Introduction," p. xxxvi).
³¹⁵ See the *Denkmäler*, pt. iii, pl. 1.
³¹⁶ Supra, plate xxi, fig. 35.
³¹⁷ *Denkmäler*, pt. iii, pl. 2 d.
³¹⁸ Ibid, pl. 69 a.
³¹⁹ Ibid. iii, pl. 92.
³²⁰ Ibid. pls. 92 and 93.
³²¹ *Denkmäler*, pt. iii, pls. 8 and 203 e.
³²² Ibid. pl. 77 c.
³²³ Ibid. pl. 115.
³²⁴ See woodcut, fig. 40.
³²⁵ See the *Denkmäler*, pt. iii, pl. 95. Compare Rosellini, *Monumenti Civili*, pl. lxix.
³²⁶ *Denkmäler*, pt. iii, pl. 63 a.
³²⁷ See above, vol. i, p. 229.
³²⁸ Rosellini, *Monumenti Civili*, pls. xliv, xc-xcii; Wilkinson, *Ancient Egyptians*, vol. ii, pp. 190-201; *Denkmäler*, pt. iii, pl. 12, etc.
³²⁹ Rosellini, *Monumenti Civili*, pl. lxxiv; *Denkmäler*, pt. iii, pl. 208 a.
³³⁰ Rosellini, *Monumenti Civili*, pls. xc and xci; Wilkinson, *Ancient Egyptians*, frontispiece to vol. ii.
³³¹ *Denkmäler*, pt. iii, pls. 2 b, c, 76 b, 100 b, 121. etc.
³³² Ibid. pl. 208 a.
³³³ Ibid. pl. 118. (See p. 188.)
³³⁴ See above, vol. i, plate lviii. Rosellini, *Monumenti Civili*, pl. cxxi, Nos. 23 and 26; *Denkmäler*, pt. iii, pls. 165, 187 c, etc.
³³⁵ *Denkmäler*, pt. iii, pls. 115 and 127 b.
³³⁶ Ibid. pl. 76 a.
³³⁷ See the *Transactions of the Society of Biblical Archæology* vol. vi, pp. 510, 520; *Records of the Past*, vol. ii, p. 75, etc. Brugsch holds that a *pair* of horses had sometimes one name between them (*History of Egypt*, vol. ii, pp. 13 and 16, 1st ed.).
³³⁸ Wilkinson, *Ancient Egyptians*, vol. i, p. 345.
³³⁹ See above, vol. i, plate lviii.
³⁴⁰ Ibid. Compare the *Denkmäler*, pt. iii, pls 92, 128 a, 153, 166, and 187 d.
³⁴¹ Supra, pp. 127-128. and 141.
³⁴² Supra, pp. 49-50, 64, etc.
³⁴³ *Records of the Past*, vol. ii, pp. 9-16.
³⁴⁴ Brugsch, *History of Egypt*, vol. ii, p. 131, 1st ed.
³⁴⁵ Ibid. p. 45.
³⁴⁶ Lenormant, *Manuel d'Histoire Ancienne*, vol. i, p. 425.
³⁴⁷ The actual "Book of the Dead," as we have it, is taken from a papyrus of the twenty-sixth dynasty; but all the oldest papyri, by means of which the "Book" was conveyed on and preserved, belong to the eighteenth. (See Bunsen, *Egypt's Place*, vol. v, pp. 130-1.)
³⁴⁸ See above, pp. 176-177.
³⁴⁹ Ex. i. 11-14, v, 6-19.
³⁵⁰ See the letter of Ameneman to Pentaour, quoted in vol i, pp. 494-5, which belongs to this period.
³⁵¹ The application of the bastinado to men has been already noticed; and indeed represented in vol. i, l.s.c. For the application of the stick to women, see the *Denkmäler*, pt. iii, pl. 153.
³⁵² See the sculptures, *passim*; and compare above, vol. i. p. 222.
³⁵³ *Denkmäler*, pt. iii. pl. 128.
³⁵⁴ See above, vol. i, p. 222.
³⁵⁵ Supra, p. 139.
³⁵⁶ *Records of the Past*, vol. ii, p. 140, vol. iv, pp. 143-5, vol. vi, pp. 153-6.

CHAPTER XXII.

¹ See above, p. 183.
² Rameses II. (See above, plate xxvii, fig. 60.)
³ "Evidemment," says M. Chabas, speaking of the account of this period given in the Great Harris Papyrus, "il s'agit de discordes civiles, qu'il est possible d'attribuer à une compétition entre des prétendants à la couronne, dont aucun ne réussit à triompher de ses adversaires. L'autorité se trouva fractionnée (*Recherches pour servir à l'Histoire*, etc., p. 136).
⁴ Chabas, p. 17; Eisenlohr, in *Transactions of Society of Biblical Archæology*, vol. i, p 368.
⁵ Supra, p. 183.
⁶ There is a general agreement as to the meaning of this phrase not always found among the various translators of the papyrus. (See Chabas. p. 21; Birch. *Ancient Egypt*, p. 137; Brugsch, *History of Egypt*, vol. ii, p. 137, 1st ed.)
⁷ "Nous ignorons absolument l'origine de Set-nekht" (Chabas, *Recherches*. p. 136).
⁸ Brugsch, *History of Egypt*, vol. ii, pp. 133-4, 1st ed.: "After his (Seti II.'s) death the sovereignty passed in regular succession to *his son*. Set-nakht."
⁹ See the *Denkmäler*, pt. iii, pls. 212 and 213 a.
¹⁰ Seti II.'s throne name was *Ra-user-khepru-meri-amon*; Set-nekht's *Ra-user-shau-meri-amon*, one element only being changed.
¹¹ Eisenlohr (*Transactions of Society of Biblical Archæology*, vol. i, p. 371). Brugsch translates "the person of Set" (*History of Egypt*, vol. ii. p. 137, 1st ed.); Birch, "Kheper and Set" (*Ancient Egypt*, p. 137); but the rendering of Dr. Eisenlohr seems preferable.
¹² Brugsch, l.s.c. Chabas and Birch agree nearly.
¹³ See the *Denkmäler*, pt. ii, pl. 201 a, b. Compare Brugsch, *History of Egypt*,

314   NOTES TO HISTORY OF ANCIENT EGYPT.   [CH. XXII.

vol. ii. pp. 135-6, 1st ed., and Eisenlohr, in *Transactions of Soc. of Biblical Archæology*, vol. i, p. 376.

[14] Brugsch, *History of Egypt*, vol. i, p. 133, 1st ed.

[15] *Records of the Past*, vol. viii, p. 47; Brugsch, *History of Egypt*, vol. i, p. 138, 1st ed.

[16] See the *Denkmäler*, pt. iii, pl. 206 d.

[17] I.e. the sole monument of his erection. There is a tomb at Abydos which was sculptured in his reign, and which has an inscription containing his name, together with that of his wife. Tiimeri hesi, a personage otherwise unknown. (See M. Mariette's *Monuments d'Abydos*, p. 439.)

[18] Brugsch, *History of Egypt*, vol. ii, p. 139, 1st ed. Brugsch says that the fact is "proved by the monuments," but adduces no proof. No doubt Rameses III. has for one of his titles *nefer neter*, but *[?]* this title is common to all the kings from a very early period.

[19] Herod. ii, 121, § 1.

[20] Brugsch, p. 140. Compare Birch, *Ancient Egypt*, p. 137, and Chabas, *Recherches*, pp. 28-30.

[21] It is evident that the classification of Rameses cannot comprise the whole of the population, since it excludes the entire agricultural and the entire mercantile class. It was, I think, a classification of those who were regarded as in some sense functionaries.

[22] Gen. xlv, 8.

[23] Brugsch, l.s.c. I should incline to give the word a wider meaning, and regard it as including all *high* functionaries of whatever kind.

[24] Birch. *Ancient Egypt*, p. 138. Chabas, *Recherches*, p. 31: "Il semble que les guerres de Ramsès soient introduites, non pas dans leur ordre chronologique, mais dans celui de leurs résultats glorieux."

[25] Birch. l.s.c.

[26] *Records of the Past*, vol. viii, p. 48.

[27] *History of Egypt*, vol. ii, p. 140, 1st ed.

[28] Gen. xxxvi. 8, 9.

[29] The hieroglyphic name is read by Dr. Brugsch as *Ashita*, by M. Chabas (*Recherches*, p. 52) as *Sabzta*. Asbita would well express the Asbystæ, who are called by Pliny (*H. N.* v, 5) Hasbitæ.

[30] In the original *Hasa*, which is well compared with Auseis (Herod. iv, 180).

[31] *Records of the Past*, vol. viii, p. 48.

[32] Chabas, *Recherches*, p. 52.

[33] *Records of the Past*, vol. viii, p. 49; Brugsch, *History of Egypt*, vol. ii, p. 141, 1st ed.

[34] Birch, *Ancient Egypt*, p. 138; Chabas, *Recherches*, p. 52.

[35] See Note B in the Appendix.

[36] So Rameses, in the inscription translated by Brugsch (*History of Egypt*, vol. ii. pp. 147-8, 1st ed.).

[37] Ibid. p. 148.

[38] See the representation of the engagement in the *Description de l'Egypte*, "Antiquités," vol. ii, pl. x. Compare Rosellini, *Monumenti Storici*, pl. cxxxi.

[39] Brugsch, *History of Egypt*, vol. ii, p. 149, 1st ed.

[40] Ibid. p. 150. Compare Birch, *Ancient Egypt*, p. 143.

[41] See above, p. 180.

[42] Birch, *Ancient Egypt*. pp. 142-3.

[43] Ibid. p. 144; Brugsch, *History of Egypt*, vol. i, pp. 150-1, 1st ed. The "king of the miserable land of Kush" appears at the head of a series of fourteen captured princes in the sculptures of Medinet-Abou (*Denkmäler*, pt. iii, pl. 209).

[44] Brugsch. *History of Egypt*, vol. ii, p. 152, 1st ed.; *Records of the Past*, vol. vi, p. 20.

[45] Wilkinson in the author's *Herodotus*, vol. ii, pp. 372-3. 3d ed.

[46] Birch, *Ancient Egypt*, p. 145; Brugsch. *History of Egypt*, vol. ii, p. 143. 1st ed.

[47] Brugsch, *History of Egypt*, vol. i, p. 155. 1st ed.

[48] See *Description de l'Egypte*, "Antiquités," vol. ii. pls. 9, 10; Rosellini, *Monumenti Storici*, pl. cxxxi.

[49] Dümichen, *Historische Inschriften*, pt. iv, pls. 30-4; Birch, l.s.c.

[50] Brugsch, *History of Egypt*, vol. ii, p. 156, 1st ed.

[51] Ibid. p. 155.

[52] Ibid. pp. 154-5.

[53] Ibid p. 157.

[54] *Records of the Past*. vol. viii, p. 49, § 7.

[55] Birch *Ancient Egypt*. p. 144.

[56] Brugsch. *History of Egypt*, vol. ii, p. 141, 1st ed.

[57] Brugsch. *History of Egypt*, vol. ii, p. 143. 1st ed. Compare *Records of the Past* vol viii, p. 50, § 8.

[58] *Records of the Past*, vol. viii, pp. 50-1.

[59] Ibid. p. 50, § 6. "There were brought to me," says the monarch, "marvels of real turquoises in numerous bags carried before me, not to be seen again while there are kings."

[60] *Records of the Past*, vol. viii, p. 50, §§ 1-5.

[61] Ibid. p. 49, §§ 8-13. Compare Brugsch, *History of Egypt*, vol. ii, p. 142. 1st ed.

[62] The catalogue of temple gifts offered by Rameses occupies fifty-one pages in the *Records of the Past*, vols. vi and viii.

[63] *Records of the Past*, vol. viii, p. 51, § 2.

[64] Ibid. § 5.

[65] Lenormant, *Manuel d'Histoire Ancienne*, vol. i, p. 442. Compare Rosellini, *Mon. Civili*, vol. ii, pp. 182-7,

⁶⁶ See Virg. *Ecl.* v, 80; Hor. *Epod.* xvii, 76; Juv. *Sat.* vi, 611; Tacit. *Ann.* ii, 69; etc.
⁶⁷ Brugsch, *History of Egypt*, vol. ii, p. 164, 1st ed. Many of the *formulæ* are given in the *Records of the Past*, vol. vi, pp. 121-6, and vol. x, pp. 137-58.
⁶⁸ The hieratic text of the Turin papyrus which contains the account of this trial was first translated into French by M. Devéria in the *Journal Asiatique* for 1865. Since then a translation into English has been made by M. Le Page; Renouf (*Records of the Past*, vol. viii, pp. 57-65); and one into German by Dr. Brugsch. The latter has been done into English by the late Mr. Danby Seymour, and will be found in the translation of Dr. Brugsch's work so often quoted in these volumes (vol. ii, pp. 158-63).
⁶⁹ Brugsch, *History of Egypt*, vol. ii, p. 165, 1st ed.
⁷⁰ Ibid. p. 164.
⁷¹ Brugsch, *History of Egypt*, vol. ii, pp. 158-9, 1st ed. Compare *Records of the Past*, vol. viii, pp. 57-8.
⁷² No doubt it was also an institution at Athens, and may claim, so far, to be compatible with civilization and enlighteument.
⁷³ On the employment of punishments of this kind in ancient times, see the author's *Ancient Monarchies*, vol. iii, p. 247, 2d ed.
⁷⁴ *Records of the Past*, vol. viii, p. 65, § 1 and note.
⁷⁵ Ibid. §§ 2-7.
⁷⁶ Brugsch, *History of Egypt*, vol. ii, p. 166, 1st ed.
⁷⁷ The names are quite unlike Assyrian names, and have not even any clear Semitic derivation.
⁷⁸ Brugsch, l.s.c.
⁷⁹ Lepsius, *Königsbuch*, Taf. xxxviii, No 504.
⁸⁰ *Description de l'Egypte*, "Antiquités," vol. ii, pls. 10, 12; *Denkmäler*, pt. iii, pls. 210, 211.
⁸¹ See above, plate xii, fig. 27, and plate xv, fig. 33.
⁸² Birch, *Ancient Egypt*, p. 145.
⁸³ See Lenormant, *Manuel d'Histoire Ancienne*, vol. i, p. 443.
⁸⁴ Brugsch, *History of Egypt*, vol. ii, p. 167, 1st ed.
⁸⁵ The calendar set up by Rameses III. at Medinet-Abou is thought to prove that he ascended the throne in B.C. 1311 (Lenormant, *Manuel d'Histoire Ancienne*, vol. i, p. 444). If this be so, and he died in his thirty-second year, his death would fall into B.C. 1279 or 1280. The astronomical date of B.C. 1240, three reigns after this (Birch, *Ancient Egypt*, p. 147), is in accordance.
⁸⁶ See above, p. 85.
⁸⁷ Herod. ii, 179.
⁸⁸ *Records of the Past*, vol. ii, pp 109-116. On the date of the "Travels," see Brugsch, *History of Egypt*, vol. ii, p. 104, 1st ed.
⁸⁹ Aristot. *Rhet.* ii, 15.

⁹⁰ Brugsch, *History of Egypt*, vol. ii, pp. 178, 191, 1st ed.; Lenormant, *Manuel d'Histoire Ancienne*, vol. i, pp. 446-7.
⁹¹ Brugsch, *History of Egypt*, vol. ii, p. 172, 1st ed.
⁹² Ibid. p. 167; Lepsius, *Königsbuch*, Taf. xxxviii, and Taf. xxxix, Nos. 504 and 504 *bis*.
⁹³ Brugsch, *History of Egypt*, vol. ii, pp. 167-71, 1st ed.; Birch, *Ancient Egypt*, p. 147.
⁹⁴ *Denkmäler*, pt. iii, pls. 220-222.
⁹⁵ We must except also his tomb in the Biban-el-Moluk, which is a work of some importance. (See Lepsius, *Grundplan des Grabes König Ramses IV.*, Berlin, 1867.)
⁹⁶ Lepsius, *Königsbuch*, Taf. xxxix, No. 505.
⁹⁷ Brugsch, *History of Egypt*, vol. ii, Table ii, at end of volume.
⁹⁸ Ibid. pp. 171-2; *Denkmäler*, pt. iii, pl. 223 *b*.
⁹⁹ Brugsch, *History of Egypt*, vol. ii, pp. 172-3, 1st ed. Others place Meri-Tum between Rameses VIII. and Rameses IX. (Birch, *Ancient Egypt*, p. 147).
¹⁰⁰ Birch, *Ancient Egypt*, p 147; Brugsch, *History of Egypt*, vol. ii, p. 173, 1st ed. The date rests upon the calculations of the French astronomer, Biot.
¹⁰¹ Brugsch, *History of Egypt*, vol. ii, p. 174-7, 1st ed.
¹⁰² Ibid. Table ii, at end of vol. ii.
¹⁰³ Lepsius, *Königsbuch*, Taf. xl, No. 512.
¹⁰⁴ The nineteenth year of Rameses IX. is found upon the monuments (Birch, *Ancient Egypt*, p. 148).
¹⁰⁵ Brugsch, *History of Egypt*, vol. i, p. 247, 1st ed. Compare Chabas, *Mélanges Egyptologiques*, 3me série, vol. i, pp. 60-106.
¹⁰⁶ Brugsch, vol. ii, p. 182.
¹⁰⁷ Birch, *Ancient Egypt*, l.s.c.
¹⁰⁸ Brugsch, *History of Egypt*, vol. ii, p. 178, 1st ed. Compare Chabas, *Mélanges Egyptologiques*, 3me série, vol. ii, pp. 1-2; Birch, *Ancient Egypt*, p. 153; Lenormant, *Manuel d'Histoire Ancienne*, vol. i, p. 446. The position of the priests of Ammon at this time has been compared to that of the Mayors of the Palace under the later Merovingian kings of France.
¹⁰⁹ Brugsch, l.s.c.
¹¹⁰ Ibid. p. 179.
¹¹¹ Ibid. pp. 180-1.
¹¹² Supra, p. 211.
¹¹³ Lepsius, *Königsbuch*, Taf. xl, No. 517.
¹¹⁴ Ibid. Taf. xli, No. 518.
¹¹⁵ Ibid. Taf. xli. No. 519.
¹¹⁶ Rameses XIII. was known as Menma-ra Sotep en-phthah, as Shaemuas, and as Neter-hak-on. See Lepsius, *Königsbuch*, Taf. xli, No. 522.
¹¹⁷ *Records of the Past*, vol. iv. p. 60, § 28; Brugsch, *History of Egypt*, vol. ii, p. 186, 1st ed.; Birch, *Ancient Egypt*, p. 153.

118 Brugsch, *History of Egypt*, vol. ii, p. 189, 1st ed.
119 For the full narrative, see *Records of the Past*, vol. iv, pp. 55–60; or Brugsch, *History of Egypt*, vol. ii, pp. 184–7, 1st ed.
120 So Birch, *Ancient Egypt*, p. 149. I conclude from this that the word used is not that commonly (and rightly) rendered by Naharaïn, which is

𓈖𓌉𓏤𓏏 ⟨symbols⟩

121 This is the earliest case of "possession" on record. That of Saul (I. Sam. xvi. 14) was above a century later.
122 In the twenty-sixth year of Rameses XII. (about B.C. 1140).
123 Requests for gods were not unusual in the ancient world (Herod. v, 67; viii. 64, etc). The god was identified with his image, or at any rate supposed to work through it. A special power was thought to attach to some images.
124 For a representation, see Dr. Birch's *Ancient Egypt*, p. 151.
125 *Records of the Past*, vol. iv, p. 59, § 17.
126 Ibid. § 22.
127 So Brugsch (*History of Egypt*, vol. ii, p. 186, 1st ed.) Dr. Birch, in the *Records of the Past*, vol. iv, p. 60, § 24, makes the period one of "three years, four months, and five days."
128 The phrase used—*em ua neh-neh*—like one paralyzed"—is doubtful. It has been translated "lame"—"agitated"—"agitated and convulsed," etc. According to the general use of *neh*, no physical affection would be intended.
129 *Records of the Past*, vol. iv, p. 60, § 28.
130 So Lenormant (*Manuel d'Histoire Ancienne*, vol. i, p. 447).
131 Bagistan by M. de Rougé, Ecbatana by Dr. Brugsch; but the latter writer has retracted his conjecture (*History of Egypt*, vol. ii, p. 187, 1st ed.).
132 Brugsch, *History of Egypt*, vol. ii, p. 187, 1st ed.
133 Mr. D. Haigh in the *Zeitschrift für ägyptische Sprache* for 1874, p. 65.
134 The capital city of Tiglath-Pileser I. was called "Asshur," as well as his country.
135 *Inscription of Tiglath-Pileser I.* in *Records of the Past*, vol. v, p. 19, par. 27. It is questioned, however, whether the Mizr or Muzr of this passage really represents Egypt.
136 See above, p. 195.
137 Judg. iii, 8.
138 Lepsius, *Königsbuch*, Taf. xli, No. 522; Brugsch, *History of Egypt*, vol. ii, p. 187, 1st ed.
139 *Denkmäler*, pt. iii, pl. 238.
140 They occur at Karnak (ibid, pl. 237), El-Kaab (ib. pl. 236 b), Abd-el-Qurna (ibid pls. 235, 236), and the Biban-el-Moluk (ibid. pl. 234).
141 Fergusson, *Handbook of Architec-*

ture, vol. i, p. 244. The tomb of Seti I. has five pillared chambers, and one "large and splendid chamber with a coved" or arched "roof" (ib. pp. 243–4).
142 Lenormant, *Manuel d'Histoire Ancienne*, vol. i, p. 426.
143 See the *Denkmäler*, pt. iii. pls. 212 a, 219 b, 220 b, e, 221 d, f, g, 223 c; and compare Rosellini, *Monumenti Civili*, pl. cxxv, Nos. 4, 5, 6, which belongs to the reign of Rameses IX.
144 Birch, *Guide to Galleries*, p. 17.
145 See above, p. 193.
146 Brugsch, *History of Egypt*, vol. ii, p. 172, 1st ed.
147 See *Records of the Past*, vol. viii, pp. 57–65; Chabas, *Mélanges Egyptologiques*, 3me série, vol. i, pp. 47–173; vol. ii, pp. 3–26; etc.
148 Brugsch, *History of Egypt*, vol. ii, pp. 158, 169, 179, etc., 1st ed.
149 *Records of the Past*, vol. vi, pp. 24–70, vol. viii, pp. 14–45.
150 Brugsch, *History of Egypt*, vol. ii, pp. 171–2, 188, 1st ed.; *Records of the Past*, vol. vi, pp. 22–4, vol. viii, pp. 6–14.
151 Brugsch calls these tables "the most valuable contribution to astronomical science for all times" (*History of Egypt*, vol. ii, p. 173, 1st ed.); but I am not aware that they have been of any service as yet.
152 Brugsch, *History of Egypt*, vol. ii, pp. 174–5, 1st ed.
153 Ibid. pp. 180 and 189.
154 The "Book of Hades," as recently set forth (*Records of the Past*, vol. x, pp. 85–134), though taken principally from the tomb of Seti I., is in part derived from that of Rameses VI. It is wholly mystical. So also is the "magical Papyrus," which is pronounced to be "a work of the nineteenth or *twentieth* dynasty" (ib. p. 136).
155 Supra, p. 204.
156 Brugsch, *History of Egypt*, vol. ii, p. 164, 1st ed.
157 Lenormant, *Manuel d'Histoire Ancienne*, vol. i, p. 443.
158 See above, pp. 211.
159 See Chabas, *Mélanges Egyptologiques*, 3me série, pp. 47–173.
160 Wilkinson, *Ancient Egyptians*, vol. i, pl. x (opp. title page), and p. 419, No. 189.
161 Rosellini, *Monumenti Civili*, pls. cv, No. 2; cvii, and cviii. These vessels, which belong to the time of Rameses IV., have gayly patterned sails, gilded cabins ornamented with figures of men, and steerage oars gayly painted and terminating in the head of the god Horus, or of the king.
162 Wilkinson, *Ancient Egyptians* (ed. Birch), vol. i, pl. xi, *bis* (opp. p. 436); *Denkmäler*, pt. iii, pl. 236.
163 See the *Denkmäler*, pt. iii, pls. 214, 233, 234.
164 See the woodcut fig. 64.
165 See the *Denkmäler*, pt. iii, pl. 240 d.
166 See the *Denkmäler*, pt. iii, pl. 236.

CHAPTER XXIII.

1 Ap. Syncell. *Chronograph.* p. 73, c.
2 See above, p. 105.
3 Supra, p. 212. We should therefore have expected each successive highpriest to have been a Theban.
4 See Lepsius, *Ueber die XXII. ägyptische Königsdynastie*, p. 259; Brugsch, *History of Egypt*, vol. ii, p. 191, 1st ed.
5 So Lepsius, l.s c. Brugsch (p. 192) suggests that he drove Rameses XIII. into banishment.
6 *Denkmäler*, pt. iii, pls. 243–248.
7 Birch, *Ancient Egypt*, p. 154. Brugsch calls Her-hor's veracity in question, and suggests that he "conferred on himself the honorary title of conqueror of the Ruten, to which he had no right" (*History of Egypt*, vol. ii, p. 193, 1st ed.). But I see no ground for this supposition.
8 Her-hor seems to have had nineteen sons, and an equal number of daughters. (*Denkmäler*, pt. iii, pl. 247 a, 5).
9 So Birch, l.s.c. Yet he gives *netem*,

, as an Egyptian word signifying "sweet" in his *Dictionary of Hieroglyphics*. (See Bunsen's *Egypt*, vol. v, p. 453.)
10 Lenormant, *Manuel d'Histoire Ancienne*, vol i, p 450.
11 Lepsius, *Königsbuch*, Nos. 533 to 551.
12 Lepsius, *Ueber die XXII. Königsdynastie*, p. 287. Compare above, pp. 186–7.
13 *Denkmäler*, pt. iii, pls. 243, 244 a, 245 b, c, 246 a, b.
14 Ibid. pls. 244 b, 246 c.
15 See fig. 49, and compare Rosellini, *Monumenti Storici*, pl. x, No. 40.
16 Bunsen, *Egypt's Place*, vol. ii, pp. 576-7; Brugsch, *History of Egypt*, vol. ii, table iv, at the end.
17 I am not aware of any monument erected by Piankh. His name is found, almost exclusively, on monuments erected by his son. (See *Denkmäler*, pt. iii. pl. 249 c, d; pl. 250 a; pl. 251 a, b; Rosellini, *Mon. Storici*, pl. cxlvii, No. 3).
18 So Birch, *Ancient Egypt*, p. 154. The fact is, however, disputed.
19 Brugsch, *History of Egypt*, vol. ii, p. 194, 1st ed.
20 Brugsch, *History of Egypt*, vol. ii, pp. 194–7, 1st ed.
21 *Denkmäler*, pt. iii, pl. 251 i, k.
22 *Denkmäler*, pt. ii, pl. 251 i.
23 Brugsch, *History of Egypt*, vol. ii, pp. 197–202.
24 Lepsius, *Ueber die XXII. Königsdynastie*, p. 284; *Königsbuch*, Taf. xliii; Birch. *Ancient Egypt*, p. 155.
25 1 Kings iii, 1; vii, 8.
26 Ibid. x. 29.
27 Ibid. xi. 18–20.
28 1 Kings xi. 40.
29 Ap. Syncell. *Chronograph.* p. 73, c.

CHAPTER XXIV.

1 Brugsch, *History of Egypt*, vol. ii, pp. 197–206, 1st ed.
2 See the author's *Ancient Monarchies*, vol. ii, p. 81, 2d ed.
3 See the author's *Ancient Monarchies*, vol. ii, p. 66, 2d ed.
4 Ibid. p. 89.
5 Assyria appears as Assura, , in the inscriptions of Thothmes III. (See above, pp. 241–2.)
6 Brugsch, *History of Egypt*, vol. ii, pp. 192–3, 1st ed.
7 The names on which special reliance is placed are those of Takelot, Osarkon, and Namrut, which are identified with Tiglath, Sargon, and Nimrod. Sheshonk is parallel with the mystic name of Babylon, Sheshach (Jer. xxv, 26, li, 41); and a name, Nebnesha, among those of the ancestors of Sheshonk, is read as Nabonasi,' and called Chaldæan or Babylonian. Now, of these, Tiglath, *alone*, is never an Assyrian name, and could not be, since it means "adoration," and requires a suffix—"adoration to some one," *e.g.* Ninip, Pal-tsira, etc. Nimrod is never *found* as an Assyrian name, and indeed is a word whereof it is difficult to find any representative either in Assyria or Babylonia. Sargon, it is true, was an old Babylonian name, and came into use in Assyria about B.C. 720. But is Osarkon Sargina or Sargon? If so, why the unnecessary prefix, Ua or O, , which is not at all common at the beginning of words in Egyptian? Sheshonk, as Lepsius has shown (*Ueber die XXII. Königsdynastie*, p. 288, is more likely the Jewish proper name Shishak (1 Chr. viii, 14, 25) than the mystical city name Sheshach (which is Babel spelt mystically by reversing the letters of the alphabet). Nebnesha, read as Nabonasi, has a Babylonian look, but, read as Nebnesha, is not even necessarily Semitic. Dr. Birch, who is an advocate for the Semitic origin of the Sheshonks, yet allows that they were possibly "Libyans" and not Semites (*Ancient Egypt*, p. 155).
8 See above, p. 104.
9 Ap. Syncell. *Chronograph.* p. 74, B.
10 Ibid. p. 75, c.
11 Ibid. p. 73, D.
12 Osarkon II. and Sheshonk III. See below, pp. 228 and 229.
13 The early history of the Sheshonk family is made known to us by one of the Apis stelæ discovered by M. Mariette. (See his work *Le Sérapéum de Memphis*. p. 22.) An excellent comment on this inscription will be found in the

small *brochure* of Lepsius, *Ueber die XXII. Königsdynastie*, pp. 265 et seq.
¹⁴ Her rank is shown by the prefix.

suten sat. 🦆 ⚫ which occurs before her name (Lepsius, p. 268, line 11).

¹⁵ Lepsius uses the first, Brugsch the second, of these forms. Mehtenhout was probably a daughter of Menkheprra or Pasebenshu (Psusennes).
¹⁶ So Wilkinson (in the author's *Herodotus*, vol. ii, p. 374. 3d ed.) and Lenormant (*Manuel d'Histoire Ancienne*, vol. i. p. 452).
¹⁷ *Denkmäler*, pt. iii. pls 252–4; Rosellini, *Mon. Storici*, pl. cxlviii.
¹⁸ 1 Kings xi, 28.
¹⁹ 1 Kings xi, 40.
²⁰ See the apocryphal additions to the First Book of Kings contained in the Septuagint, where Jeroboam is said to have married a daughter of Sheshonk. Compare Syncellus (*Chronograph.* p. 184, A).
²¹ 1 Kings xii. 6–20.
²² See above, ch. xxiv, note ⁷.
²³ See 2 Chron. xii. 3. The "twelve hundred chariots" of this passage are a number not incredible; but it is difficult to believe that Egypt ever mustered "sixty thousand horsemen." One is inclined to suspect a corruption of "six" into "sixty."
²⁴ Birch, *Ancient Egypt*, p. 156.
²⁵ 2 Chron. xii, 4. Compare 1 Kings xiv, 25.
²⁶ 2 Chron. xi, 5–12.
²⁷ As Shoco (or Socoh), Adullam, Azekah, Gath, Mareshah, Ziph, Tekoa, Hebron, etc.
²⁸ 2 Chron. xii. 4.
²⁹ 1 Kings xiv. 26; 2 Chron. xii, 9.
³⁰ This is implied in the expressions, "they shall be *his servants*"—"that they may know my service, *and the service of the kingdoms*" (2 Chron. xii, 8).
³¹ 2 Chron. xi, 13–14.
³² See the remarks of Mr. R. Stuart Poole in Smith's *Dictionary of the Bible*, vol. iii. p. 1294.
³³ Ibid. p. 1293.
³⁴ *Denkmäler*, pt. iii, pls. 253 *b, c,* 254 *c,* etc.
³⁵ Ibid. pl. 253 *a*.
³⁶ Ibid. pl. 252. Compare Rosellini, *Monumenti Storici*, pl. cxlviii.
³⁷ Grammatical objections may be taken to both the proposed translations of "Yu'reh-Malk"—"Judah, a king down," and "Judah's king." But Mr. Stuart Poole has shown that the former rendering, at least, is a possible one (Smith's *Dictionary of the Bible*, vol iii. p 1293).
³⁸ Brugsch, *History of Egypt*, vol. iii, p 210, 1st ed.
³⁹ *Denkmäler*, pt. iii, pl. 254 *c*.
⁴⁰ Ap. Syncell. *Chronograph.* pp. 73, D, 74, D.

⁴¹ Brugsch, *History of Egypt*, vol. ii, p. 213. 1st ed.
⁴² Ibid. p. 212.
⁴³ *Denkmäler*, pt. iii, pl. 257 *b, c*.
⁴⁴ Ap. Syncell. i.s.c.
⁴⁵ This was the view of Dr. Hincks. M. Lenormant places the expedition in the reign of Osarkon I., but without identifying him with Zerah (*Manuel d'Histoire Ancienne*, vol. i, p. 453).
⁴⁶ 2 Chron. xiv, 9–13.
⁴⁷ Jeroboam fled to Shishak soon after Solomon began to build Millo (1 Kings xi. 27), which was in the twenty-fourth year of his reign (ib. vi, 1; ix, 10, 24). He must have remained at the court of Shishak some fourteen or fifteen years. The expedition was not till more than four years afterwards (ib. xiv, 25). Thus it can scarcely have been earlier than Sheshonk's eighteenth year.
⁴⁸ *Denkmäler*, pt. iii, pl. 257 *b, c*.
⁴⁹ *Monumenti Storici*, pl. xii, No. 46.
⁵⁰ Brugsch, *History of Egypt*, vol. ii, p. 214, 1st ed. The monuments are so few and scanty for this period that historians are tempted to spin their narratives respecting the dynasty out of very unsubstantial materials. I confess I see no sufficient ground for Dr. Brugsch's "contest between the two brothers."
⁵¹ Manetho allowed twenty-five years only for the three kings who followed after Osarkon I. (ap. Syncell. *Chronograph.* p. 73. D). As one of them (Osarkon II.) reigned at least twenty-two years, very little time indeed is left for the two others. Of course, Manetho may have been mistaken; but the want of monuments for the reigns of Takelut I. and Sheshonk II. tends to confirm him.
⁵² Lepsius, *Ueber die XXII. Königsdynastie*, pp. 268–9. Compare Mariette, *Le Sérapéum de Memphis*, p. 22.
⁵³ An Apis died after he had entered on his twenty-third year (Mariette, *Sérapéum*, p. 18).
⁵⁴ *Denkmäler*, pt. iii, pl. 254 *c*.
⁵⁵ There is no proof of this, and it is only thrown out as a conjecture; but the name is a new and strange one, certainly not Egyptian.
⁵⁶ Asa's revolt is indicated by his fortification of his strongholds (2 Chron. xiv, 6–7).
⁵⁷ 2 Chron. xiv, 9–13. As Zerah's chariots were only 300, it is unlikely that his army was as numerous as that of Shishak, whose chariots were 1200. The "thousand thousand" of the author of Chronicles probably means only "very numerous."
⁵⁸ Lepsius, *Königsbuch*, Taf. xlv, Nos. 589, 591, and 597.
⁵⁹ Brugsch, *History of Egypt*, vol. ii, p. 215, 1st ed.
⁶⁰ Mariette, *Sérapéum de Memphis*, l.s.c.
⁶¹ See 2 Chron. xiv, 9–13. The arguments there used apply equally to the reigns of Takelut I. and Sheshonk II.

⁶² See Lepsius, *Ueber die XXII. Königsdynastie*, Taf. i, at the end of the treatise. Dr. Birch, however, suggests that Takelut II. was the nephew, and not the son, of Sheshonk II. (*Ancient Egypt*, p. 158).
⁶³ Ap. Syncell. *Chronogr.* p. 73, D.
⁶⁴ Lenormant, *Manuel d'Histoire Ancienne*, vol. i, pp. 454–6; Brugsch, *History of Egypt*, vol. ii, pp. 219–24, 1st ed.
⁶⁵ Birch, *Ancient Egypt*, p 157; Brugsch, *History of Egypt*, vol. ii, p. 217
⁶⁶ This dynasty appears to have consisted of three kings, Pet-si-bast (Petubastes), who is given by Manetho forty years; Osarkon, who is given nine years, and Psimut (Psammus), who is given ten. Manetho adds a Zet (Seti?), of whom there is no trace in the monuments, and assigns him thirty-one years.
⁶⁷ The most important of the reliefs are given in the *Denkmäler*, pt. ii, where they occupy no more than six of the plates (pls. 252–259).
⁶⁸ See Mariette, *Sérapéum de Memphis*, pls. 23 et seqq.
⁶⁹ Two statues only belonging to the time are mentioned in the *Denkmäler* (pt. iii, pls. 256 *h* and 259 *c*). The British Museum has, I think, none.
⁷⁰ As one of a king (No. 2277) in the "First Egyptian Room" of the British Museum, and a statuette represented by Lepsius in the *Denkmäler*, pt. iii, pl. 256 *e*.
⁷¹ See Brugsch, *History of Egypt*, vol. ii, pp. 210–13, and 230–2, 1st ed.
⁷² The "Magical Papyrus," translated by Dr. Birch in the *Records of the Past*, vol. vi, pp. 115–26. "appears to have been written between the twenty-first and the twenty-sixth dynasties" (ibid. p. 144). The "spells in the tomb of Boken-ranf" belong to the same form of literature, and approach to, or come within, the period.
⁷³ *Records of the Past*, vol. vi, p. 115.
⁷⁴ Brugsch, *History of Egypt*, vol. ii, p. 212, 1st ed.
⁷⁵ Ibid. p. 221, 1st ed.

CHAPTER XXV.

¹ See vol. i, pp. 37–8, and 114–15.
² See Dr. Smith's *Dictionary of Greek and Roman Geography*, vol. i, p. 57.
³ Herod. iii, 19–22; Strab. xvii. 1, § 3; Diod. Sic. i, 30–3; iii, 32–3; etc.
⁴ Herod. ii, 146; Ptol. *Geograph*. vi, 7.
⁵ These limits must be understood as indicating *about* the extent of the kingdom of Meroë, not as its actual limits at all times, or indeed perhaps at any time.
⁶ See the articles on MEROE and NAPATA in the *Dictionary of Greek and Roman Geography;* and compare Wilkinson in the author's *Herodotus*, vol. ii, pp. 41–2, note ⁵, 3d ed.

⁷ Diod. Sic. iii. 6.
⁸ This is very strongly marked in the Egyptian wall sculptures, where the Egyptians are painted dark-red, the Ethiopians jet-black.
⁹ Gen. x, 6.
¹⁰ See above, pp. 143–144.
¹¹ Brugsch, *History of Egypt*, vol. ii, p. 227, 1st ed.
¹² See Mr. Bunbury's article on MEROE in Smith's *Dictionary of Greek and Roman Geography*, vol. ii, p. 330.
¹³ Baker, *Nile Tributaries*, p. 25. One tribe of Ethiopians was called the Chelenophagi, or "Turtle-eaters."
¹⁴ Dio Cass. liv, 5.
¹⁵ Brugsch, *History of Egypt*, vol. ii. p. 226, 1st ed. Except the name Piankhi, common to the Ethiopians with the family of Her-hor, and the special devotion to Ammon of the Ethiopian Piankhi, there is little to prove any connection of the kind postulated. But even the conjectures of *experts* have a value.
¹⁶ Isaiah xix, 13; Ezek. xxx. 13, 16, etc.
¹⁷ Brugsch, l.s.c. Compare Table iv, at the end of his second volume.
¹⁸ See Mariette, *Monuments Divers*, pl. 1; *Records of the Past*, vol. ii, p. 81; Brugsch, *History of Egypt*, vol. ii, 231, 1st ed.
¹⁹ Compare the *strategi* under the Persian system, who are quite independent of the satraps (Rawlinson's *Herodotus*, vol. ii, pp. 556–7).
²⁰ The *great* efforts of warlike princes were almost always made in their early years. Youth is the time for vigorous effort; and the desire of military glory is then strongest. Upstart princes were under a special temptation to rush into war with the object of consolidating their power.
²¹ This date must not be regarded as exact, but approximate. It depends on the following considerations: Sabaco's first year must, by his synchronism with Hoshea (2 Kings xvii. 4), have been as early as B.C. 723 or 724. Bocchoris, who preceded him, reigned (at least) six years,—say B.C. 730–724. Piankhi had reigned twenty-one years before the revolt, and must be presumed to have continued on the throne some years after it. A moderate estimate for his reign would be twenty-five years. This would make his first year B.C. 755
²² *Records of the Past*, vol. ii, p. 82, § 3.
²³ Hasebek (Crocodilopolis) is mentioned as one of the first places which Tafnekht occupied (ibid. § 4). According to Brugsch, *History of Egypt*, vol. ii, p. 247, 1st ed.), it was one of the last to make its submission to Piankhi.
²⁴ *Records of the Past*, l.s.c.
²⁵ Brugsch, *History of Egypt*, vol. ii, p. 832, § 5, 1st ed.
²⁶ Ibid. § 7.
²⁷ Called Wuapat by Canon Cook,

Uaput by Dr. Birch, but the same name with that of the eldest son of Sheshonk I., which is commonly read as Aupot.

[25] *Records of the Past*, vol. ii, p. 83, § 8; Brugsch, *History of Egypt*, vol. ii, p. 232, 1st ed.

[26] Ibid. p. 324, § 22, 1st ed.

[30] Ibid. p. 235.

[31] Brugsch, *History of Egypt*, vol. ii, p. 236, § 29. Compare *Records of the Past*, vol. ii, p. 88.

[32] Some doubt whether this is intended literally, but both Brugsch and Birch so understand the passage.

[33] See Mariette, *Monuments Divers*, pl. 1, from which the accompanying woodcut is taken.

[34] *Records of the Past*, vol. ii, p. 93, §§ 85-6. Piankhi promised indeed that "only the rebels against the god (*i.e.* himself), the vile, and the worthless should be executed;" but no one could tell that he might not be included in this wide category.

[35] Ibid. p. 95, § 92. Compare Brugsch, *History of Egypt*, vol. ii, p. 241, 1st ed.

[36] *Records of the Past*, vol. ii, p. 98, § 105.

[37] Birch, *Ancient Egypt*, p. 162. Brugsch thinks that he had merely fled to one of the Nile islands (*History of Egypt*, vol. ii, p. 246, § 129, 1st ed).

[38] Brugsch, *History of Egypt*, vol. ii, pp. 246-7, 1st ed.

[39] The inscription of Piankhi terminates as follows: "When his Majesty sailed up the river, his heart was glad; all its banks resounded with music. The inhabitants of the west and east took to make melody at his Majesty's approach. To the notes of the music they sang: 'O king, thou conqueror! O Piankhi, thou conquering king! Thou hast come and smitten Lower Egypt; thou madest the men as women. The heart of thy mother rejoices, who bore such a son; for he who begat thee dwells in the vale of death. Happiness be to thee, O cow who hast borne the bull! Thou shalt live for ever in after ages. Thy victory shall endure. O king and friend of Thebes!'" (Brugsch, l.s.c.; De Rougé, *Inscription Historique du Roi Pianchi-Mériamoun*, p. 15.)

[40] Diod. Sic. i, 79-94; Manetho ap. Syncell. *Chronograph*, p. 74, B.

[41] The statement of Diodorus to this effect (i. 45, § 2) receives some confirmation from the stélé of Piankhi, which makes Tafnekht king of Saïs a little before the time of Bocchoris.

[42] The name of Bocchoris (Bek-en-ranf) has been found nowhere but at the Serapeum of Memphis, where it appeared on several stelae in one of the Apis tombs, and was also traced in black on one of the walls (Mariette, *Sérapéum de Memphis*, p. 24. and pl. 34).

[43] See Diod. Sic. i, 79, §§ 1-3; 94, § 5.

[44] Ap. Syncell. *Chronograph*. p. 74, B.

[45] Mariette, *Sérapéum de Memphis*, p.

[24] The authority of Eusebius is always weak, compared with that of Africanus. Here his number (forty-four) is exceptionally suspicious from its repetition.

[46] The names Shabak, Shabatok, Tahrak, are genuine Ethiopian, terminating in the Ethiopic article. Shabak is "the tom-cat;" Shabatok, "the son of the tom-cat." Shabak has also a genuine Ethiopian countenance, prognathous, and with lips thicker than the later Egyptians. (See plate xxiv, fig. 52.)

[47] Herod. ii, 137. Herodotus says those whom he thus employed were "criminals;" but the forced labor of the really criminal population would scarcely have sufficed to raise conspicuously all the embankments of all the towns. Shabak probably regarded as "criminals" all the disaffected.

[48] Manetho ap. Syncell. *Chronograph*. p. 74, B.

[49] So Bunsen, *Egypt's Place* vol. ii, p. 597, and Stuart Poole in Smith's *Dict. of the Bible*, vol. iii, p. 1337. Recent writers on Egypt do not notice the fact; and Dr. Birch even speaks of his being "supposed" to have reigned only eight years (*Ancient Egypt*, p. 163).

[50] Herod. ii, 139. Piankhi had, it is evident, resided at Napata.

[51] Shabak's "name is found on the monuments of Karnak" (Birch, *Ancient Egypt*, l.s.c.). It occurs also in the Serapeum of Memphis (Mariette, *Sérapeum*, p. 26) and on a slab of stone now in the British Museum, which must have belonged to the great temple of Phthah at Memphis (Chabas, *Mélanges Egyptologiques*, 3me série. vol. i, p. 248), Rosellini has some representations of his sculptures (*Monumenti Storici*, pl. cli, Nos. 2 and 3), but does not say where they were set up.

[52] Hoshea's embassy cannot have been sent later than B C. 723, since it preceded the commencement of the siege of Samaria by Shalmaneser, which was, at the latest, in that year. It was most probably sent in B.C. 724, which I incline to regard as the year of Sabaco's accession.

[53] Supra, p. 127.

[54] See the author's *Ancient Monarchies*, vol. ii, pp. 83-133, 2d ed.

[55] *Ancient Monarchies*, vol. ii, pp. 142-5, 2d ed.

[56] Layard, *Nineveh and Babylon*, p. 156.

[57] *Ancient Monarchies*, vol. ii, pp. 145-7.

[58] Isaiah xx, 1.

[59] Oppert, *Inscriptions des Sargonides*, p. 27.

[60] It is not necessary to suppose that he really went to *Assyria*. The Assyrian kings often held courts for the express purpose of receiving homage at provincial towns in their dominions. Tiglath-Pileser held such a court at Damascus, where Ahaz did homage (2 Kings xvi, 10).

[61] This is the length of reign that Manetho gave him, according to Africanus (ap. Syncell. *Chronograph.* p. 74, B). It is adopted by Bunsen (*Egypt's Place*, vol. ii, p. 597). Chronological considerations seem to me to require the number.
[62] *Monumenti Storici*, pl. cli, No. 5.
[63] *Monuments Divers*, pl. 29, No. e, 2.
[64] Brugsch, *History of Egypt*, vol. ii, p. 269, 1st ed. Compare Mariette, *Monuments Divers*, pl. 29, No. e, 1.
[65] Supra, ch. xvi, note [5].
[66] Supra, p. 42. There is a slight modification here, the king of the fifth dynasty having been named Tatkara.
[67] Ap. Syncell. *Chronograph*. l.s.c.
[68] Strab. i, 3, § 21.
[69] See 2 Kings xviii, 21. At any rate it was Tirhakah who moved to his relief (ib. xix, 9), and who must have been lord-paramount of Egypt at the time.
[70] See the author's *Ancient Monarchies*, vol. ii, pp. 150-60, 2d ed.
[71] 2 Kings xviii, 13-16.
[72] Ibid. verses 17 et seqq.
[73] So Herodotus ii, 141. Pelusium was the usual point at which Egypt was entered from the northeast.
[74] The names, Shabatok and Sethos, are too remote to be properly regarded as identical. Moreover, Sethos is said to have been high-priest of the Memphian Phthah, a title never given to Shabatok. It must be remembered that Egypt at this time was full of sub-kings. (Compare Is. xix, 1, 11, 13).
[75] As caused by the simoom, by a pestilence, or by the direct visitation of God.
[76] Mariette, *Monuments Divers*, pl. 79.
[77] Ibid. pl. 85.
[78] Ibid pl. 87.
[79] Mariette, *Sérapéum de Memphis*, pp. 26 and 28.
[80] Rosellini, *Monumenti Storici*, pl. cl.
[81] Megasthenes. Fr. 20.
[82] See the author's *Ancient Monarchies*, vol. ii, pp. 186-96.
[83] Herod. iii, 7-9.
[84] Birch, *Ancient Egypt*, p. 166.
[85] *Ancient Monarchies*, vol. ii, p. 193. This fact was first brought forward, and the names of the princes and their cities were first deciphered by Sir H. Rawlinson, whose paper on the subject in the *Transactions of the Royal Society of Literature*, New Series, vol. vii, pp. 136 et seqq., has priority over all others, whether published in England or abroad.
[86] Herod. ii, 152.
[87] The fifty-four years of the reign of Psamatik I commence, according to the view now generally taken, in B C 667 or B C 666 (See Brugsch, *History of Egypt*, vol. ii, p. 277; and compare Wiedemann, *Geschichte Aegyptens von Psammetich I.*, p. 121, who makes the date B C. 664, and Stuart Poole in Smith's *Dictionary of the Bible*, vol. iii, p. 1514, who makes it B.C. 669.
[88] *Ancient Monarchies*, vol. ii, p. 195.

[89] Ibid. p. 201.
[90] *Ancient Monarchies*, vol. ii, p. 202.
[91] G. Smith, *History of Asshurbanipal*, pp. 47, 52, etc.
[92] Birch, *Ancient Egypt*, pp. 170-171. Compare Lenormant, *Manuel d'Histoire Ancienne*, vol. i, pp. 464-5. Dr. Brugsch makes Miammon-Nut succeed Piankhi (*History of Egypt*, vol. ii, p. 248, 1st ed.).
[93] The close connection of Miammon-Nut with Tirhakah is strongly exhibited in the sculptures and inscriptions of the Phthah-Osiris temple at Memphis, which Tirhakah probably began, but which must have been completed by Miammon-Nut In one sculpture they are represented as if they were both reigning together. Tirhakah in Lower and Miammon-Nut in Upper Egypt (Mariette, *Monuments Divers*, pl. 83).
[94] See *Records of the Past*, vol. iv, p. 81. Compare Brugsch, *History of Egypt*, vol ii, p. 230, 1st ed.
[95] The serpent (*cobra de capello*), *ur*, 𓆑 was the hieroglyphic for "crown" or "kingdom," whence the interpretation.
[96] *Records of the Past*, vol. iv, p. 81, §§ 5, 6.
[97] So Brugsch, *History of Egypt*, vol. ii, p. 230, § 7, 1st ed Maspero translates "1,100,000 men" (*Records of the Past*, vol. iv, p. 82, note ¹); but this number is scarcely a possible one.
[98] Brugsch, *History of Egypt*, vol. ii, p. 252, § 16, 1st ed.
[99] Ibid. p. 251, §§ 14-15.
[100] *Records of the Past*, vol. iv, p. 83, § 17.
[101] See Mariette, *Monuments Divers*, pls. 79-84.
[102] Brugsch, *History of Egypt*, vol. ii, p. 252, §§ 19-21, 1st ed.
[103] Brugsch, *History of Egypt*, vol. ii, p. 254, 1st ed.; *Records of the Past*, vol. iv, p. 86.
[104] From about B.C. 750 when Piankhi established himself as king. (See above, p. 223.)
[105] The court added to the temple of Medinet-Abou by Tirhakah is the highest effort of the Ethiopians. It is not without merit, but cannot be said to possess real artistic excellence.

CHAPTER XXVI.

[1] See Hom. *Il.* ix, 381-4; Herod. ii, 3, 143; Hecat. Fr. 276; Diod. Sic. i, 31, 45; Strab. xvii, 1, § 46.
[2] Nahum iii, 8-9.
[3] See above, p. 235.
[4] G. Smith's *History of Asshurbanipal*, p. 311. The exact date given is B.C. 652-1.
[5] G. Smith's *History of Asshurbanipal*, p. 155. Egypt is undoubtedly intended, though the word used is Milukha (Meroë or Ethiopia).

6 As related by Herodotus (ii, 151) and Diodorus (i, 66).
7 G. Smith, *History of Asshurbanipal*, p. 66, ll. 24-7.
8 Ibid. p. 66, l. 28.
9 So Herodotus (ii, 152), who, however, knows nothing of their having been sent by Gyges.
10 Gyges had taken the Ionian city of Colophon (Herod. i, 14), and had thus Ionian subjects, whom he could force to serve. His Carian troops were probably mercenaries. (See the author's *Herodotus*, vol. ii, p. 200, 2d ed.)
11 Diod. Sic. i, 66.
12 Lepsius. *Ueber die XXII. ägyptische Königsdynastie*, p. 291.
13 Inaros was the son of a Psamatik (Herod vii, 7, ad fin.)
14 Supra, pp. 179, 198, 200-201.
15 See plate xxii, fig. 47, which is taken from a votive table in the British Museum.
16 Or Shepuntepnt, as Lepsius renders the original, which is 𓊪 𓈖 𓏏 𓊪
(See the treatise of this writer, *Ueber die XXII. ägyptische Königsdynastie*, p. 302, and Tafel ii, at the end of the work.)
17 Ibid., and compare Birch, *Ancient Egypt*, p. 173.
18 Herod ii, 154.
19 Ibid. ii, 30. Mr. Grote supposed that the "camps" of the Greeks and Carians near Bubastis superseded the Pelusiac garrison (*History of Greece*, vol. ii, p. 497, ed. of 1862). But this is nowhere stated.
20 The latest writer on this period (Dr. Wiedemann) pronounces the entire story of the revolt and desertion of the warriors to be "unhistorical" (*Geschichte Aegyptens von Psammetich I. bis auf Alexander den Grossen*, p. 137). But this would seem to be an excess of scepticism. The narrative, in its general outline, is accepted as true by Wilkinson, Grote, Lenormant, Birch, Trevor, and others. I see no reason to doubt it.
21 Herod. ii, 30.
22 Ibid. He makes the number of the deserters 240,000.
23 Diod. Sic. i, 67. He says they exceeded 200,000.
24 This is the only place within the limits of Ethiopia where the course of the Nile is from west to east. (See Herod. ii 31.)
25 Pomp. Mel. iii, 10; Plin. *H. N.* vi. 35, § 191; Steph. Byz. ad voc. Αὐτόμολοι. Strabo, however, gives them the name of Sembritæ (xvii, 1, § 2).
26 Herod. ii, 28.
27 Dumb, not by nature, but by command; being forbidden to utter a word in presence of the children.
28 Herod. ii, 2.
29 Ibid ii, 154.
30 There is some question as to whether Psamatik I., or Amasis, first threw Egypt open to the foreigner. I agree with Mr. Grote that "the establishment of the Greek factories and merchants at Naucratis may be rather considered as dating in the reign of Psammetichus" (*History of Greece*, vol. ii. p. 496).
31 Herod. ii, 179.
32 Strab. xvii, p. 801.
33 Herod. ii. 178.
34 Charaxus, the brother of Sappho, traded in wine between Lesbos and Naucratis (Strab. xvii, p. 807). On the large quantity imported, see Herod. iii, 6.
35 Herod. ii, 185.
36 See *Ancient Monarchies*, vol. ii, pp. 504-6.
37 Herod. ii, 157.
38 The latest date assigned to Psammetichus by modern writers is B C. 610 (Weidemann, *Geschichte Aegyptens*, p. 121). Brugsch (*Hist of Egypt*, vol. ii, p. 277, 1st ed.) makes the date of his last year B C. 612. Others (as Lenormant) carry it back to B.C. 618. If this view is correct, three years only would have elapsed between his establishment of himself as king of all Egypt and his first attack on Ashdod. If the date of Brugsch be preferred, the interval would have been one of nine years.
39 Ashdod, אַשְׁדּוֹד, is probably derived from a cognate root with, the Arabic *shedeed*, "strong." Compare Hebrew שַׁדַּי.
40 The ten years' sieges of Troy and Veii have been rejected as of impossible duration (Grote, *History of Greece*, vol. i, p. 248; Niebuhr, *History of Rome*, vol. ii. p. 468, E. T.); but the far longer and more incredible siege of Azotus has met with ready acceptance (Grote, *History of Greece*, vol. ii, p. 498; Lenormant, *Manuel d'Histoire Ancienne*, vol i. p 470). Wiedemann, however, suggests a doubt (*Geschichte Aegyptens*, p. 131) which is certainly well-founded.
41 The Egyptian wars, like those of the Orientals generally, consisted, for the most part, of a series of spring or summer campaigns, begun and ended in the course of a few months, and continued year after year till the enemy was exhausted, and submitted.
42 Wiedemann, *Geschichte Aegyptens*, l.s.c.
43 Compare *Ancient Monarchies*, vol. ii, pp. 508-16
44 Herod. i, 104.
45 The description in Ezek. xxxviii, may have a general bearing on the struggle between good and evil (see *Speaker's Commentary*, vol. vi, p. 157); but its more striking features are probably derived from the Scythic invasion with which the prophet was contemporary. Gog is made to say: "I will go up to the land of *unwalled villages*; I will go to them that are at rest, and

that dwell safely, *all of them dwelling without walls and having neither bars nor gates,* to take a spoil and to take a prey, to turn thine hand upon the desolate places that are now inhabited, and upon the people that are gathered out of the nations, which have gotten cattle and goods, that dwell in the midst of the land" (verses 11, 12).

[46] Judg. i, 18, xiv, 19; Xanth. Lyd. Fr. 25; Herod. i, 105.

[47] Compare Justin, ii, 3. § 14, with Herod. l.s.c.; and, for the nature of the malady which came on the Scythians at Ascalon, see Hippocrat. *De Aere, Aqua, et Locis,* vi, 108.

[48] It is suspected that they made a settlement at this time in the Jordan valley, occupying Beth-shan, which from them took its later name of Scythopolis (Syncell. *Chronogr.* p. 214, c).

[49] Herod. ii, 153. Three courts had been made, and three gateways built on three sides of the temple previously (ib. 101, 121, § 1, and 136). The south side alone remained without a separate approach.

[50] Ibid. For a representation of the court see the frontispiece to vol. i of Sir G. Wilkinson's *Ancient Egyptians.*

[51] Birch. *Ancient Egypt,* pp. 175-6.

[52] Wiedemann, *Geschichte Aegyptens,* p. 127.

[53] Wiedemann. l.s.c.

[54] Rosellini, *Monumenti Storici,* vol. iv. p. 169.

[55] Birch, *Ancient Egypt,* p. 175; Wiedeman, l.s.c. Among the works of Psammeticbus at Heliopolis was the " elegant obelisk of red granite" which now adorns the piazza of the Monte Citorio at Rome (Valéry, *Travels in Italy,* p. 561). This monument was transported to Rome by Augustus, and set up there originally in the Campus Martius, where it formed the gnomon of a gigantic sundial (Plin. *H. N.* xxxvi. 14).

[56] Birch. *Ancient Egypt,* p 177.

[57] Lepsius, *Ueber die XXII. ägyptische Königsdynastie,* p. 304, and Tafel II, at the end of the work.

[58] Wiedemann speaks of another son, Hor .s, of whom there is a statue in the museum of the Louvre (*Geschichte Aegyptens,* p. 145).

[59] Lepsius, l.s.c. Dr. Wiedemann suspects that Psammetichus himself took his daughter, Nitocris, as a secondary wife, in order to strengthen his title to the throne (*Geschichte Aegyptens,* pp. 143-4); but his ground for this, that she is called " royal wife," as well as " royal daughter," on a tomb (*Denkmäler,* pt. iii, pl. 270 *b*) where the only king mentioned by name is Psammetichus does not seem to me sufficient to establish such an improbability.

[60] Psammetichus cannot have been less than seventy at his death, since he must have been fourteen or fifteen *at least* when he was associated by his father (supra, p. 311). Probably he was as much as seventy-four or seventy-five His *eldest* son would most likely have been fifty by that time.

[61] The Pharaohs of the eighteenth dynasty had constantly been supported in their Syrian invasions by fleets. (See above, pp. 127, 135, etc.) Cambyses took care to be accompanied by one when he attacked Egypt (Herod. iii, 1, 13). It was the loss of his fleet in the battle of the Nile that forced Napoleon I. to abandon the idea of holding Egypt and Syria.

[62] Herodotus makes the canal attempt anterior to the construction of the fleets (ii, 159). But probability is against this. I agree with Wiedemann, who says: "Seine *erste Sorge,* nachdem er den Thron der Pharaonen bestiegen hatte, war . . . eine (Flotte zu grunden" *Geschichte Aegyptens,* p. 147).'

[63] Herod. l.s.c.

[64] See above, vol. i, p. 250.

[65] *Ancient Monarchies,* vol. ii, p. 176, 1st ed.

[66] Thucyd. i, 13.

[67] Herod. ii, 154.

[68] Ibid 159.

[69] So Wiedemann, *Geschichte Aegyptens,* p 147. I have long been of the same opinion.

[70] Supra, pp 161 and 171.

[71] Herod. ii, 158.

[72] Ibid.

[73] It is not likely that the idea embodied in the supposed oracle would have presented itself to the mind of any Egyptian until the attempt of Neco was carried to a successful issue by Darius.

[74] Wilkinson in the author's *Herodotus,* vol. ii, p. 207, note [7], 2d ed.

[75] Herod. l.s.c.

[76] Ibid. iv, 8.

[77] So Herodotus (iv, 42). The fact of the circumnavigation has been much disputed; but it is accepted by Grote (*History of Greece,* vol. ii. p. 499), Junker (*Forschungen aus der Geschichte des Alterthumes,* No. 3), Wiedemann (*Geschichte Aegyptens,* p. 149), Birch (*Ancient Egypt,* p. 178), and others.

[78] Neco's accession is placed by the best authorities between B.C. 612 and 610. His attack on Syria seems to have been certainly in B.C. 608.

[79] Herod. ii, 159.

[80] That the land force consisted to a large extent of the Greek and Carian mercenaries, especially the former, is indicated by the fact that Neco sent the armor in which he fought at Megiddo to be hung up as a thank-offering in the Grecian temple of Apollo at Branchidæ, near Miletus—the first offering which any Egyptian monarch had made to a Greek shrine. (See Herod. l.s.c., and compare trab. xvii, p. 634.)

[81] The ordinary coast route proceeded northwards as far as Dor, when it bent inland to avoid the *detour* round the base of Carmel, and crossed the spur

joining Carmel to the Samaritan highland. Here Megiddo was situated. On the mistake of Herodotus in substituting Magdolon for Megiddo, see the author's note in his *Herodotus*, (vol. ii, p. 208, note 1, 2d ed.)

[82] 2 Kings xxiii, 15-19; 2 Chron. xxxiv, 6-9.

[83] 2 Kings xxiii, 29.

[84] 2 Chron. xxxv, 21.

[85] Ibid. The Egyptian kings generally ascribed their wars to divine direction. Sometimes visions were seen, as by Menephthah (*Records of the Past*, vol. iv, pp. 43-4); sometimes the king claimed that God spoke to him by an internal voice. (See the "Inscription of Pianchi" in vol. ii of the above-cited work, p. 91, § 69, ad fin.)

[86] See 2 Chron. xiv, 12; xvi, 8.

[87] Ibid. xxxv. 24.

[88] This is evident both from 2 Kings xxiv, 7, where we hear of Nebuchadnezzar retaking "from the river of Egypt unto the river Euphrates all that pertained to the king of Egypt," and also from Berosus (ap. Euseb. *Chron. Can.* i, 11, § 2), where we find an account of this re-conquest.

[89] This appears from the three months' reign of Jehoahaz (2 Kings xxiii, 31), who was made king when Josiah died of his wound, and deposed on the return of Neco from Carchemish.

[90] 2 Kings xxiii, 33 and 34.

[91] Jehoahaz, the people's choice, was Josiah's second son, Eliakim, Neco's choice, his eldest. (See 2 Kings xxiii, 31 and 36; 2 Chron. xxxvi, 2 and 5.)

[92] 2 Kings xxiii, 35.

[93] Ibid. xxiv, 1.

[94] Nebuchadnezzar was distinctly regarded as "king of Babylon" at this time by the Jews (2 Kings xxiv. 1; Jer. xlvi, 2; Dan. i, 1). That his father was still alive appears from Berosus (l.s.c.).

[95] Jerem. l.s.c.: "The army of Pharaoh-Necho, king of Egypt, which was by the river Euphrates in Carchemish."

[96] Jer. xlvi, verse 8, with the comment of Dean Payne Smith in the *Speaker's Commentary*, vol. v, p. 532.

[97] Jerem. xlvi, 9. Mr. Stuart Poole has suggested that the "Ludim" of this passage may represent the Greek and Carian mercenaries (*Dictionary of the Bible*, vol. ii, p. 150); but the Ludim are elsewhere always an African people (Gen. x. 13; 1 Chron i, 11; Is. lxvi, 19; Ezek. xxx. 5).

[98] Jer. xlvi, 15.

[99] Ibid. verse 5.

[100] Ibid. verse 16.

[101] Ibid. verse 17.

[102] Dan. i, 1, 2; 2 Chron. xxxvi, 6, 7. It was at this time that Daniel and his companions were carried off, to be eunuchs in the royal palace at Babylon.

[103] Berosus ap. Euseb. *Chron. Can.* l.s.c.

[104] Josephus, *Ant. Jud.* x. 6, § 2; Winer, *Realwörterbuch*, sub. voc. Jehoiakim. The instigation of Neco is glanced at in 2 Kings xxiv, 7.

[105] 2 Kings xxiv, 1.

[106] Before Nebuchadnezzar's seventh year (Josephus, *Contr. Apion.* i, 21), which was B.C. 598.

[107] Alex. Polyhist. Fr. 24.

[108] Compare 2 Chron. xxxvi, 6, with Josephus, *Contr. Apion.* l.s.c. Both sieges seem to have commenced in B.C. 598.

[109] Josephus, l.s.c. Compare Ezek. xxix, 18, where the severe "service" which Nebuchadnezzar served against Tyre is mentioned.

[110] Wiedemann, *Geschichte Aegyptens*, p. 155.

[111] Birch, *Ancient Egypt*, p. 180.

[112] *Denkmäler*, pt. iii, pl. 273 a, b.

[113] Wiedemann, *Gesch. Aegyp.* p. 154.

[114] Ibid. p. 156.

[115] Birch, l.s.c.

[116] Ibid. Compare Wiedemann, *Geschichte Aegyptens*, p. 153.

[117] *Ueber die XXII. ägyptische Königsdynastie*, Tafel ii, at the end of the work.

[118] Wiedemann, l.s.c. Compare Birch, l.s.c.

[119] Herod. ii, 159. Manetho called him Psammûthis (ap. Syncell. *Chronograph.* p. 75, c.)

[120] Lepsius, *Königsbuch*, Taf. xlvii, No. 644.

[121] The Apis and other stelæ show that the six years of Manetho (l.s.c.) and Herodotus (ii, 161) must be cut down to five years and a half (Wiedemann, *Geschichte Aegyptens*, pp. 117-19).

[122] Psamatik II. probably reigned from B.C. 596 to B.C. 591 or 590. Nebuchadnezzar's siege of Tyre lasted from B.C. 598 to B.C. 585.

[123] Herod. ii, 161.

[124] See Wiedemann, *Geschichte Aegyptens*, p. 158.

[125] See the author's *Herodotus*, vol. ii, p. 44; and compare Böckh, *Corp. Inscript. Gr.* No. 5126; Lepsius, *Denkmäler*, pt. vi, pls 98 99, etc.

[126] Wilkinson in Rawlinson's *Herodotus*, vol. ii, p. 45. The indentification is barely possible, since the King Amasis outlived the expedition by at least sixty-three years.

[127] See Wiedemann, *Geschichte Aegyptens*, p. 157, note 2

[128] Wiedemann, l s c.

[129] See Mariette, *Fouilles en Egypte*, pl. 16 bis, b; *Abydos*, pl. 2 b; Lepsius, *Denkmäler*, pt. iii, pl. 274 d.

[130] Wiedemann, *Geschichte Aegypten*, p. 159.

[131] Obelisks were almost always set up in pairs. The obelisk of Psamatik II. still stands in Rome, and is known as the "Obeliscus Campensis" (Wiedemann, *Gesch. Aegypt.* p. 160).

[132] Ibid. pp. 160-1.

[133] Ibid. l.s.c.

[134] Ibid. p. 161: "Eine *schöne*, reich mit Inschriften geschmückte Statue,"

[135] See Lepsius, *Ueber die XXII. ägyptische Königsdynastie*. p. 304, and Taf. ii, at the end of the work.
[136] The Ankhnes-Ranofrehet of Lepsius (ibid. p. 305), called Anchens-Ranefer-ab by Wiedemann (*Geschichte Aegyptens*, p. 196).
[137] Herod. ii, 161.
[138] Manetho ap. Euseb. *Chron. Can.* i, 20, p. 105; Syncell. *Chronograph.* p. 225, c; p. 227, B. The same, or nearly the same, form was used by the LXX.
[139] See above, p. 257.
[140] Ezek. xvii, 15: "He (Zedekiah) rebelled against him in sending his ambassadors into Egypt that they might give him horses and much people."
[141] 2 Kings xxv, 1; Jer. lii, 4.
[142] Jer. xxxvii, 5: "Then Pharaoh's army was come forth out of Egypt; and when the Chaldeans that besieged Jerusalem heard tidings of them, they departed from Jerusalem."
[143] Ibid. xlvii, 1. I agree with Rashi, and the author of the *Seder Olam*, that the capture of Gaza by Apries was probably on this occasion.
[144] See verse 5 of the same chapter, where Gaza and Ascalon are coupled together.
[145] Dean Payne Smith says (*Speaker's Commentary*, vol. v, p. 503) that the more literal interpretation of Jer. xxxvii, 7 would be that he retired without fighting; and so P. Smith, *Ancient History*, vol. i. pp. 186, 234; Lenormant, *Manuel d'Histoire Ancienne*, vol. i, p. 308; and others. But the words of Jeremiah really leave the question an open one.
[146] Joseph. *Ant. Jud.* x. 7. § 3.
[147] 2 Kings xxv, 2–21; 2 Chron. xxxvi, 17–20.
[148] See the author's *Ancient Monarchies*, vol. iii, p. 54, 2d ed.
[149] We cannot suppose Nebuchadnezzar to have been less than twenty-four or twenty-five when he undertook the war against Neco in B.C. 605. If he was born in B.C. 630, he would have reached the age of forty-five in B.C. 585. That is an age at whi h repose becomes very dear to orientals.
[150] Berosus. It is true that we have only fragments of this writer's work, so that the argument *à silentio* loses some of its force.
[151] Some historians place the Phœnician war of Apries immediately before the last siege of Jerusalem by Nebuchadnezzar (P. Smith, *Ancient History*, vol. i, p. 134; Wiedemann, *Geschichte Aegyptens*, pp. 163–4); but they appear to forget that exactly at this time Tyre was being besieged by Nebuchadnezzar, and was probably in alliance with Egypt, certainly advancing Egyptian interests.
[152] Herod. ii, 161.
[153] Diod. Sic. i, 68.
[154] Herod. ii, 169.
[155] Ezek. xxix, 3, 9.
[156] Jeremiah had prophesied (ab. B.C.

585): "Thus saith the Lord, Behold, I will give Pharaoh-Hophra king of Egypt into the hand of his enemies, and into the hand of *them that seek his life*" (Jer. xliv. 30).
[157] Herod. ii, 161–9. Diodorus (l.s.c.) simply repeats Herodotus, and cannot be regarded as a separate witness.
[158] Joseph. *Ant. Jud.* x. 9, § 7.
[159] The sole reign of Apries terminated B.C. 571; but he lived probably six years longer, sharing the royal palace with Amasis, and being by some regarded as still king (B.C. 571–565). See Herod ii, 169; Wiedemann, *Geschichte Aegyptens*, p. 167.
[160] Wiedemann in the *Zeitschrift für ägyptische Sprache* for 1878, pp. 2–6, and 87–9. Compare his *Geschichte Aegyptens*, pp. 168–9.
[161] Supra, p. 257.
[162] Joseph. *Ant. Jud.* x, 6. I cannot see that his account of the execution of Jehoiakim by Nebuchadnezzar is inconsistent with Scripture.
[163] Herod. ii, 169.
[164] One single fragment of a statue of Apries is all that remains to us. It is now in the British Museum (No. 600).
[165] Wiedemann, *Geschichte Aegyptens*, pp. 171 and 175.
[166] *Denkmäler*, pt. iii, pl. 274 *h*, *i*.
[167] Valéry's *Italy*, p. 549.
[168] Wiedemann, *Geschichte Aegyptens*, p. 174.
[169] Valéry, l.s.c.
[170] See Wiedemann's careful enumeration in his *Gesch. Aegypt.* p. 171–5.
[171] *Denkmäler*, pt. iii, pl. 274 *k*.
[172] Ibid. pt. 274 *m*.
[173] Ibid pl. 274 *l*.
[174] Champollion, *Notices Descriptives*, p. 616.
[175] *Denkmäler*, pt. iii, pl. 274 *f*.
[176] *Geschichte Aegyptens von Psammetich I.* pp 171-2.
[177] Herod. ii, 172. Plato (*Tim.* p. 21, E) makes him a native of Saïs itself.
[178] See above note [126].
[179] Herod. ii, 174.
[180] Ibid. ii, 172–3.
[181] Commencing about B.C. 561, at the death of Nebuchadnezzar.
[182] Herod. ii, 177. Theocritus, writing under the Ptolemies, exaggerates still more, making the number of cities in Egypt 33,333 (*Idyll.* xvii, 81–4). One pardons, however, anything to a poet.
[183] Herod. l.s.c.
[184] Ibid. ii, 178.
[185] Ibid. ii, 181. The dealings of Amasis with Cyrênê spoken of by Plutarch (*De virtut. Mulier.* ii, p. 260) and Polyænus (*Strateg.* viii. 41) come to us with too little authority to be regarded as authentic against the silence of Herodotus.
[186] Herod. ii, 154.
[187] Ibid. ii, 180.
[188] Ibid. ii, 182.
[189] See above, pp. 135–137.
[190] Herod. ii, 182 ad fin. Compare Diod. Sic. i, 68.

191 Such evidence as exists is rather the other way. By a cuneiform inscription recently brought from Babylon it appears that "the people of the Lower Sea," or Mediterranean—i.e., the Syrians and Phœnicians—remained subject to Nabonidus, king of Babylon, up to the last year of his war with Cyrus, which was B.C. 538. In that year they revolted, and probably reclaimed their independence. (See the *Transactions of the Society of Biblical Archæology,* vol. vii, p. 143.)

192 As Dr. Wiedemann does (*Geschichte Aegyptens von Psammetich I.* pp. 179-80): "Er zog in Asien gegen Syrien zu Felde, machte sich zum Herrn der phönizischen Städte," etc.

193 Herod. i. 77.

194 Ibid. i, 80-81. The account of Herodotus is that Crœsus first called in the help of his allies on his return to Sardis from Pteria; that he summoned them then to appear *in the fifth month;* that his envoys had scarcely taken their departure, when the army of Cyrus appeared before Sardis, gave the Lydians a second defeat, and took the city within a fortnight. No Egyptians are mentioned, and it is plain that they could not have arrived in the time.

195 Xen. *Cyrop.* vi, 2. § 10; vii, 1. §§ 30-45. The completely unhistoric character of the *Cyropædia* has been sufficiently exposed by Mr. Grote (*History of Greece,* vol. ii, p. 415; vol. iii, p. 157).

196 Herod. iii, 1-2.

197 Ibid. i, 201-14; Ctes. *Pers. Exc.* §§ 6-8.

198 *Behist. Inscr.* col. i. par. 10. Compare Ctes. *Pers. Exc.* § 10.

199 Herod. iii, 10; Manetho, ap. Syncell. *Chronograph.* p. 75, c. Diodorus (ii, 68) gave him forty-five years, counting in probably the six months of Psamatik III.

200 Herod. ii. 175. On the present condition of Saïs, and the site of the temple of Neith, see Wilkinson's plan at the end of the vol. ii of the author's *Herodotus.*

201 Birch (*Ancient Egypt,* p. 182) estimates the weight at "about 500 tons."

202 See Wilkinson in the author's *Herodotus,* vol. ii, p. 263, note 3, 3d ed.

203 Herod. ii. 176.

204 Strab. xvii. 1, § 31.

205 Herod. l.s c. The height of these was only twenty feet.

206 Wiedemann, *Geschichte Aegyptens von Psammetich I.* p. 188.

207 Ibid. p. 187.

208 Ibid. p. 188.

209 Birch. *Ancient Egypt,* l.s.c.; *Denkmäler,* pt. iii, pl. 275 *a–d.*

210 Wiedemann, *Geschichte,* etc., p. 194.

211 Ibid. pp. 198-9.

212 Herod. ii, 182.

213 See above, p. 262.

214 In the author's *Herodotus,* vol. ii, p. 271, note 9, 3d ed.

215 Plin. *Hist. Nat.* xxxv, 3, vii, 56.

216 Wiedemann adds another, whom he calls Cha-teb-ti-ari-bet, and of whom he finds evidence in Mariette's *Monuments Divers,* pls. 95, 96, and in Brugsch's *Recueil,* pl. vii, No. 2. Birch says: "Aahmes married at least three, and apparently four, wives during his lifetime" (*Ancient Egypt,* p. 183). Mariette calls this fourth wife Kheteb-nit-ar-bet.

217 Supra, p. 262.

218 Lepsius. *Ueber die XXII. äguptische Königsdynastie,* p. 309; Wiedemann, *Geschichte.* etc., p. 196.

219 See the *Denkmäler,* pt. iii, pls. 273 *e–h,* 274 *a, b, c, o.*

220 Wiedemann, *Geschichte,* etc., p. 197.

221 Birch, *Ancient Egypt,* p. 183.

222 Herod. ii. 169.

223 Ibid. iii, 16.

224 The remains of Saïs are altogether scanty and insignificant; and the site of the Temple and the royal sepulchres can only be guessed. (See Wilkinson in the author's *Herodotus,* vol. ii, p. 255, note 9.)

225 Herod iii, 14; Manetho ap. Syncell. *Chronograph.* p. 75, D.

226 Herod iii, 10.

227 Ctes. *Exc. Persic.* § 9.

228 They had perhaps been employed against Tyre (Herod. ii, 161), and had certainly served against Cyrēnē (ib. iv, 159). They had also, according to Herodotus (ii, 169), on one occasion engaged the Greek and Carian mercenaries, and defeated them. But their services had not often been required, and during the long reign of Amasis they had probably never crossed swords with an adversary.

229 Egypt had no strong positions, the Nile valley being never less than two miles in width, till considerably above Thebes, and the tracts on either side being through want of water indefensible. Thus the fate of Egypt has been almost always decided by a single battle.

230 Under Artaxerxes Longimanus Memphis (or at least its citadel) stood a siege of considerably more than a year, even though communication with the sea was cut off. (See Diod. Sic. xi, 74-7.)

231 Herod. ii, 1; i, iii, 19, 44.

232 Ibid. iii, 13.

233 Ibid. iii, 11.

234 Herodotus believed that it was the intention of Cambyses, on quitting Egypt, to leave Psamatik as tributary king. But it is very questionable whether he would have done so. Cyrus did not so treat either Crœsus or Nabonidus.

235 On the doubtfulness of all Egyptian history before Seneferu, see above, p. 31-2.

236 Birch. *Ancient Egypt,* p. 165; Lenormant, *Manuel d'Histoire Ancienne,* vol. i, p. 475.

[237] See the author's *Ancient Monarchies*, vol. iv, pp. 451-5, 487-90, 498-9, 534-8, 1st ed.
[238] Lenormant, *Manuel*, vol. i, p. 469; Brugsch, *History of Egypt*, vol. ii, p. 283, 1st ed.
[239] See Herod. ii, 153, 169, 175, 176, and, for the obelisks, see Palmer's *Egyptian Chronicles*, vol. i, "Introduction," p. lxxiv.
[240] On the other hand, some are unpleasing. The "columnar slab, which, raised to about four feet, linked column to column, and kept the view of the sacred shrine from the eyes of the profane vulgar" (Birch, *Ancient Egypt*, p. 177), may have been proper under the circumstances of the time, but cannot be pronounced satisfactory artistically.
[241] Brugsch, *History of Egypt*, vol. ii, p 283, 1st ed.
[242] Brugsch, *History of Egypt*, vol. ii, p. 282.
[243] Wiedemann, *Geschichte Aegyptens von Psammetich I.* p. 128.
[244] Brugsch, *History of Egypt*, l.s.c.
[245] The photographs of M. Mariette, on the other hand, leave nothing to be desired. (See his *Monuments Divers*, pl. 35.)
[246] Brugsch, *History of Egypt*, vol. ii, p. 282, 1st ed.
[247] Ibid.
[248] Birch, *Guide to Galleries*, p. 17.
[249] Lenormant, *Manuel d'Histoire Ancienne*, vol i, p. 469.
[250] *History of Egypt*, vol. ii, pp. 283-4, 1st ed.

[251] See the *Transactions of the Society of Bibl. Archæology*, vol. iii, pp. 425-9.
[252] Brugsch, *History of Egypt*, vol. ii, p. 284, 1st ed.
[253] See Mariette, *Sérapéum de Memphis*, p. 28; and compare Brugsch, *History of Egypt*, vol. ii, pp. 285-8, 1st ed.
[254] Birch, *Ancient Egypt*, p. 176. Diodorus says (i, 84) that the cost was sometimes a hundred talents, or 24,000l.
[255] Mariette (*Choix de Monuments*, p 9), speaking of these sarcophagi, says: "Tous sont de granit poli et luisant."
[256] Herod. ii, 35; Soph. *Œd. Col.* 339-41.
[257] Herod. l.s.c.
[258] "Les rois Saïtes avaient cru vivifier l'Egypte et rendre un peu de jeune sang à la vieille monarchie fondée par Ménès, en permettant au grand courant d'idées libérales, dont la Grèce se faisait déjà l'instigatrice, de se répandre dans son sein. Sans le savoir, ils avaient par là introduit sur les bords du Nil un nouvel élément de décadence. Exclusivement constituée pour la durée, pour conserver ses traditions en bravant les siècles, la civilisation égyptienne ne pouvait se maintenir qu'en demeurant immobile. Du jour où elle se trouva en contact avec l'esprit de progrès, personnifié dans la race et dans la civilisation grecque, elle devait forcément périr. Elle ne pouvait se lancer dans une voie nouvelle, qui était la négation de son génie, ni continuer son existence immuable" (Lenormant, *Manuel d'Histoire Ancienne*, vol. i, p. 475).

APPENDIX.

[1] See his work, *Theologische Schriften der alten Aegypter nach dem Turiner Papyrus zum ersten Male übersetzt*, Gotha, 1855.
[2] Lepsius has arranged the fragments in his *Königsbuch der alten Aegypter*, zweite Abtheilung, Berlin, 1858.
[3] Wilkinson's work on the Turin papyrus is of the most elaborate character. He not only represents in *fac-simile* the face of the MS., containing the names and length of reigns of the kings, but gives the back also, which contains writing on an entirely different subject, but of great value towards determining the true position of many of the fragments. Another *fac-simi'e* edition, which I have not seen, was published by Pleyte and Rossi in 1869-76.
[4] Chabas, *Recherches*, pp. 35-50; Birch, *Ancient Egypt*, pp. 139-42; Eisenlohr in *Records of the Past*, vol. viii, p. 47. M. Lenormant agrees, so far as the Danaans, Sardinians, Sicilians, and Tuscans are concerned (*Manuel d'Histoire Ancienne*, vol. i, p. 440).
[5] Chabas, *Recherches*, p. 39.
[6] Herod. i, 170, v, 106, etc.; Scylax, *Peripl.* § 7; Strabo, v, 2, § 5, etc.

[7] Mr. Bunbury in the *Dictionary of Greek and Roman Geography* (vol. ii, p. 907) gives Σαρδῶος as the only Greek ethnic form. But Σαρδόνιοι is found in Herodotus (vii. 165).
[8] This objection holds good also in the cases of the S*h*aruten, Tulus*h*a, and Uas*h*ash.
[9] Chabas, *Recherches*, p. 47.
[10] Dionys. Hal. *Antiq. Rom.* i, 30.
[11] As Niebuhr argued (*History of Rome*, vol. i. p. 66, E. T.) on the authority of the grammarian Festus (ad. voc. *Oscum*).
[12] As they expressed Gozan by Qazautana, Megiddo by Maketu, Gaza by Qazata, Migdol by Maktal, etc.
[13] So Lenormant, *Manuel d'Histoire Ancienne*, vol. i, p. 438.
[14] These are well pointed out by M. Chabas (*Recherches*, pp. 40-7).
[15] Herod. vii, 20. Compare v, 13.
[16] *History of Egypt*, vol. ii, p. 147, 1st ed.
[17] Ibid. p. 140.
[18] Ibid.
[19] Ibid. p. 151.
[20] Ibid. pp. 123-5.

INDEX.

AAHMES, reign of............................ii. 112
Acantha (*Mimosa Nilotica*)...........i. 27
Accoucheurs...............................i. 247
Aemhetp....................................i. 179
Africa and Asia, long struggle for pre-
  dominance..............................ii. 116
Africa the nursery of lions............ii. 146
African explorers.........................i. 4
  invasion of Egypt....................ii. 179
Agricultural implements................i. 81
Agriculture................................i. 79
Albert Nyanza.............................i. 5
Alexandrian canal, loss of life in con-
  struction...............................ii. 252
Amasis, career...........................ii. 261
  crown a Babylonian feudatory....ii. 261
  affection for the Greeks............ii. 262
  joius alliance against Persia......ii. 263
  fosters art.............................ii. 264
Amen-em-hat, accession...............ii. 77
  defensive policy......................ii. 78
  political wisdom......................ii. 80
Amen-em-hat II., unimportant reign..ii. 84
Amen-em-hat III., engineering skill..ii. 88
Amen-hotep I............................ii. 115
Amen-hotep III..........................ii. 142
  architectural and sculptured
  works.............................ii. 143-145
Amen-hotep IV., personal appear-
  ance..................................ii. 147
  builds a new capital..............ii. 149
Ameni, general of Usurtasin..........ii. 83
Amenôphis II., accession of.........ii. 138
Amenôphis IV., successors of.......ii. 151
Amenti, the four genii of..............ii. 187
Ammon, identity with Zeus or Jupi-
  ter......................................i. 153
  form under which worshipped....i. 153
  mythic names........................i. 154
  great temple of.......................ii. 82
  becomes head of the Pantheon..ii. 93
  worship restored....................ii. 151
Ammon-Ra, address to.................i. 191
Amou. *See* Ammon.
Amu, tribes of the...............i. 56; ii. 56
Amusements........................ii. 48, 92
Animal worship, origin of.............i. 197
Animals, domestic, of ancient
  Egypt...................i. 37, 90; ii. 21, 48
  sacred and sacrificial........i. 193, 195
  sculptured............................i. 126
  wild, indigenous in Egypt.........i. 33
Ancestors, worship of..................i. 200
Anointing oils...........................ii. 82
Antef the Great..........................ii. 70
Anubis, conductor of the dead......i. 187
Anuka, companion of Kneph.........i. 181
Apepi, last Hyksos monarch.........ii. 108
Apis, sacred bull of Memphis........i. 196
  worship......................ii. 176, 269
Apophis, original principle of evil....i. 186
Appendix.................................ii. 271
Apries, accession and military opera-
  tions..................................ii. 258
Arch in Egyptian architecture........i. 121
Archers...........................i. 217, 219

Architect....................................i. 241
Architecture................................i. 51
  different origins......................i. 91
  sepulchral..............................i. 92
  temple-building.......................i. 104
  effectiveness of columns..........i. 114
  forms of capitals....................i. 115
  caryatid piers........................i. 116
  domestic................................i. 118
  Egyptian dislike of uniformity...i. 122
  earliest of the arts................ii. 18
  decline of.............................ii. 75
  new features.........................ii. 93
  highest perfection...................ii. 184
Arithmetic.................................i. 137
Armies......................................i. 212
Arms. offensive..........................i. 216
  manufacture of......................ii. 64
Arsenoïte nome, the....................i. 17
  See also Fayoum.
Art, Egypt and Ethiopia compared...i. 49
  mimetic.................................i. 52
  religious censorship of............i. 127
  reaction in eighteenth dynasty....i. 136
  birth and development............ ii. 18
  Greek and Eyptian compared...ii. 45
  turned into new channels.........ii. 75
  decline of............................ii. 217
  under the Sheshonks..............ii. 230
  Greek, introduced..................ii. 249
  under Ethiopians and Syrians....ii. 268
Artisan class of early period.......ii. 25
Artists, social status..................i. 242
Arts of life, advance..................ii. 47
Ascacolon taken by barbarians.....ii. 250
Ases-kaf, reign of....................ii. 36
Ashdod the key of Syria.............ii. 250
Asia and Africa, line of communica-
  tion......................................i. 22
Asp, "Egyptian cobra"................i. 44
Ass, as a beast of burden............i. 38
Assessors, the forty-two.............i. 188
Asshur, the Assyrian capital.......ii. 124
Assyria pays tribute to Thothmes
  III....................................ii. 127
  ascendency of......................ii. 238
Assyrian conquest of Egypt........ii. 241
Assyrians, weakness of.............ii. 223
Astrology................................i. 143
Astronomy...............................i. 130
Ataka, a copper-producing country..i. 203
Atbara, character of the river......i. 10
Aten, the disk of the sun............i. 172
Athor, goddess of lower world....i. 173
Atum. *See* Tum.
Automoli, the soldier class........ii. 248
Avaris, the city of the shepherds ii. 104, 113
  the siege of..................ii. 110, 113

BABYLONIA, revolt against Assyrian
  yoke..................................ii. 246
Babylonian astronomy...............i. 141
Babylonians besiege Jerusalem...ii. 255
Bacis, sacred bull of Hermonthis...i. 197
Bahr el Azrek..........................i. 7
  See Blue Nile.

Banquets...................................i. 258; ii. 51
Barley, cultivation of................i. 31, 83
Bast, feast at Bubastis.................i. 199
  See also Pasht.
Bastinado, the use of...................i. 52
Bas-reliefs....................i. 123, 127; ii. 187
Battering-rams..........................i. 220
Beasts of burden........................i. 90
Belzoni's tomb.........................ii. 160
Benno (Ardea bubulcus)...............i. 41
B s, god of death......................i. 186
Birds, remarkable varieties.......... i. 39
Boat-building..........................i. 236
Boats as transports....................i. 221
  ordinary, of Nile..................i. 237
  very early use.....................ii. 48
"Book of Respirations"..........i. 72, 176
Boundaries of Egypt....................i. 2
Bows...................................i. 217
British enterprise in Africa...........i. 4
Bronze, manufacture of.................i. 235
Brugsch quoted.........................i. 143
Bubastis, feast of Bast................i. 199
Builders...............................i. 248
Building material......................i. 46
Bull, the sacred.......................i. 196
Bureaucracy, powerful and numerous....................................i. 206
Burial places..........................i. 91
  preparing bodies for..........i. 238, 239

CALASIRIES, the, a military body....i. 211
Cambyses, Persian monarch...........ii. 264
  defeats last of the Pharaohs.....ii. 267
Camel, commercial importance.........i. 38
Canal from Nile to Red Sea...........ii. 171
  from Nile to Bitter Lakes and Gulf of Suez...........................ii. 252
Canals, elaborate Nile system.........i. 84
  fearful mortality in construction, ii. 252
Capitals, forms in architecture.......i. 115
Caravan routes........................i. 22
Caricature in tomb-scenes.............i. 132
Carts, rare use.......................i. 90
Carvings, ornamental.................ii. 192
Caryatid piers........................i. 116
Castor-oil tree.......................i. 28
Cats, highly esteemed in Egypt........i. 39
Cattle, breeding and rearing..........i. 87
  wild, pursuit of...........i. 254; i. 214
Cavalry...............................i. 214
Chairs................................i. 229
Chameleon, the........................i. 44
Chariot-making........................i. 220
  service............................i. 214
Chase of wild beasts..........i. 253; ii. 49
Cheops, sarcophagus of................i. 98
  See also Khufu.
Chephren, temple of...................i. 104
  See also Shafrn.
Chronology, early Egyptian...........ii. 1
Circumcision, the rite of.............i. 209
Circumnavigation of Africa..........ii. 253
Civilization, Egyptian and modern,
  coincidence........................i. 203
  advance in..........................i. 47
  development from new centre...ii. 58
  second Egyptian....................i. 74
  practical form from eleventh dynasty............................i. 92
Class distinctions..........i. 204, 249; ii. 47
Classification of officers............ii. 97
Clubs..................................i. 216
Coach-building. *See* Chariot-making
Cœle-Syria, valley of..................i. 21
Coloring, primitive aspect.............i. 117
Colossi twin, impressive appearance............................ii. 144
  of Rameses II.....................ii. 174
Colossus of the Rameseum..............i. 107
Column, effective in architecture.....i. 114
"Columns, Hall of "...................ii. 159

Commerce, encouraged..........ii. 73, 74
  under Rameses III................ii. 203
Conjugation o. tenses..................i. 65
Conjunctions, rarity of................i. 66
Copper.................................i. 47
  ore, importation of...............ii. 203
Coptic, the legitimate descendant of
  Egyptian language..................i. 58
Corn, great abundance..................i. 79
Cotton, cultivation of............i. 32, 84
Cows, wh te, sacred....................i. 197
Crocodile, habits and nature.....i. 34, 177
  chasing and spearing....i. 255; ii. 64. 79
Cuirasses.............................i. 213
Cushite race. the.................ii. 53, 82
Customs...............................i. 203
Cyprus, reduction by Amasis..........ii. 262
Cyréné, unsuccessful expedition of
  Apries............................ii. 260

DÆMONES. *See* Genii.
Daggers...............................i. 216
Dancing...............................i. 245
Dashoor, Southern stone pyramid of..i. 102
Daughters, hereditary rights.........ii. 34
Dead, preservation of the.............i. 100
Decoration, colored...................i. 117
Deification of created beings.........i. 149
Deity sometimes incarnate in animals............................i. 196
Delta, great plain of..................i. 14
  augmentation of....................i. 16
  Eastern, Semitic invasion.........ii. 99
  Western, revolt of................ii. 99
Demonology..........................ii. 269
Demotic writing.......................i. 58
Desert tract of Africa and Asia.......i. 1
Disk-worship..........................i. 172
  becomes state religion..........ii. 147
Dock-yards established by Neco.....ii. 251
Dogs, Egyptian varieties...............i. 39
  domestication and breeding...ii. 64, 92
Domestic animals of Egypt....i. 37; ii. 48
Doora, cultivation and harvest.......i. 82
Dress....................i. 250; ii. 23, 92, 190
Drum..................................i. 224
Drunkenness...........................i. 53
Duck, Egyptian (*Anas Nilotica*).......i. 40
Dwelling-houses, Egyptian.......i. 118, 120
Dyes...................................i. 85
Dykes..................................i. 85
Dynasties, contemporaneous...........ii. 95
Dynasty, sixth, the...................ii. 53
  four chief kings..................ii. 55
  thirteenth, obscurity of..........ii. 96

EASTERN DESERT, geological formation
  ....i. 17
Eating, Egyptian customs..............i. 258
Ecclesiastical literature of Egyptians.ii. 70
Eclipses, observations by the Egyptians................................i. 139
Eels of the Nile.......................i. 42
Egypt, geography and boundaries......i. 4
  ancient, area......................i. 4
  inundations of the Nile...........i. 10
  borders of.........................i. 19
  historical connection with Asia...i. 21
  struggle for national supremacy...i. 21
  climate............................i. 23
  rarity of rain.....................i. 24
  vegetable productions..............i. 25
  wild animals.......................i. 33
  domestic animals...................i. 37
  remarkable birds...................i. 39
  fish...............................i. 41
  minerals...........................i. 46
  ethnology..........................i. 48
  intellectual progress..............i. 51
  literature.........................i. 51
  ancient granary of the world......i. 79
  tenure of land.....................i. 80
  military force....................i. 212

INDEX. 331

Egypt, monumental history..........ii. 10
  decline following sixth dynasty..ii. 67
  internal improvements in eleventh
    dynasty......................ii. 74
  extends its boundaries..........ii. 83
  sought by emigrants............ii. 84
  threatened with invasion from
    east.........................ii. 99
  conquered by the Hyksos........ii. 100
  fascination upon Asiatic mind...ii. 102
  effects of disintegration.......ii. 103
  ultimate advancement under
    Hyksos........................ii. 106
  upper dynasty of native princes.ii. 108
  African invasion................ii. 173
  threatened with destruction in
    reign of Rameses III...........ii. 199
  strength in isolation and unity..ii. 208
  causes of decline...............ii. 208
  two silent centuries............ii. 209
  asylum for political fugitives...ii. 222
  relations with Ethiopia.........ii. 231
  divided into seven kingdoms.....ii. 234
  under Ethiopian yoke...........ii. 234
  under Assyrian yoke.............ii. 241
  Ethiopian and Assyrian struggle
    for supremacy..................ii. 242
  regains its independence........ii. 214
  influx of Asiatic Greeks........ii. 248
  trade with Asiatic Greece.......ii. 249
  threatened by Tartars...........ii. 250
  difficulties of labor...........ii. 252
  war with Persia.................ii. 266
Egyptian belief in future life.....ii. 99
  civilization, coincidence with
    modern........................ii. 203
  court, corruption ....ii. 204
  idea of present life............ii. 91
  prayers, deficiency in..........i. 192
  prevalence of murder and vio-
    lence.........................ii. 63
  races and tribes................i. 50
  religion........................i. 146
  temple-building.................i. 104
  territory, fivefold division....i. 18
  year, the.......................i. 142
Egyptians ancient physical character-
    istics.........................i. 48
  intellectual status.............i. 51
  invasion of Syria and Mesopo-
    tamia.........................ii. 115
  manners and customs.............i. 203
  military genius.................i. 220
  Pharaonic times.................ii. 139
  theories regarding origin.......i. 48
Egyptology, h w regarded..........ii. 133
Elephant-hunting..................i. 255
El-Tij.............................i. 20
Embalmers.....................i. 237-239
Embalming, process and cost....i. 237, 238;
                       ii. 22
Emblems borne in procession.......i. 210
Emerald mines, region of.......i. 18, 47
  region of Gebel Zubara..........ii. 69
Emigration, foreign...............ii. 92
Empire middle.....................ii. 8
  new, the.......................ii. 7
  old, the.......................ii. 10
  beginnings.....................ii. 13
Employments, ill-paid.............i. 248
Endowments, system of.............i. 207
Engineering science of Egyptians..i. 144
Engravings........................i. 227
Entertainments, grand.............i. 257
Epic poems........................i. 72
Epitaphs, ante mortem.............i. 192
Esarhaddon, son of Sennacherib...ii. 241
  attempts conquest of Egypt.....ii. 241
Esculent plants...................i. 29
Estates, descent from father to son. ii. 47
Ethiopia, former extent...........i. 19
  subdued by Usurtasen...........ii. 85
  geography of...................ii. 231

Ethiopia, proper..................ii. 232
Ethiopian race. *See* Cushite.
  civilization....................i. 49
Ethiopians a formidable power.....i. 55
  Caucasian origin...............i. 55
  modern representatives.........i. 55
Eunuchs, shamelessness and trick-
    ery..........................ii. 204
European races in history, first appear-
    ance.........................ii. 61
Evil spirits, expulsion...........ii. 179
Explorations in Africa.............i. 4

Faience...........................i. 232
Fanaticism........................i. 52
Farmer, peasant, trials of........i. 225
Fast-days.........................i. 209
Fayoum, the, curious basin of.....i. 16
  irrigation of..................i. 85
Fellahin, agricultural laborers, con-
    dition........................i. 224
Female influence..................ii. 61
Fertility of soil.................i. 79
Festivals, religious..............i. 199
Field sports.....................ii. 92
Fish, abundance of................i. 41
Fishing...........................i. 252
Fish-spear........................i. 252
Flax, cultivation of.........i. 32, 84
Flowers, use at banquets..........ii. 55
Food, character and variety......ii. 51
Foreign trade.....................i. 226
Fowl, domestic....................i. 51
Fowling.....................i. 253; ii. 49
Frost, absence of.................i. 24
Fruit-trees of Egypt..............i. 28
Funereal ritual, the..............i. 70
Furniture.....................ii. 24, 92

Galleys used in war...............i. 220
Games.............................i. 209
Geckos, small lizards.............i. 43
Genii, definite offices of........i. 187
Gentleman, occupations of........i. 252
  daily life of..................i. 256
Geometry of the Egyptians.........i. 138
Ghizeh, three great pyramids of...i. 94
  second pyramid.................i. 96
  first or great pyramid.........i. 97
Glass, invention..................i. 230
  uses of........................i. 230
  increased elegance ....ii. 76
  blowing........................i. 230
Glazing...........................i. 233
Goats, use of.....................i. 88
God, the nature of................i. 148
  the crocodile-headed...........ii. 96
Gods, hideous forms in sculpture..i. 131
  mere attributes of deity.......i. 149
  names and descriptions......i. 153-186
  minor divinities..........i. 176, 188
  triad worship of...............i. 190
  classification.............i. 189; ii. 65
  expansion and multiplication ..ii. 64
Gold mines........................i. 46
  ornaments......................i. 234
Goldsmiths........................i. 234
  vases..........................i. 234
Glyptic art......................ii. 21
  decline of....................ii. 216
Grain cultivated by ancient Egyp-
    tians.........................i. 31
Grammar, Egyptian.................i. 63
Granite...........................i. 46
Grasses cultivated for fodder.....i. 31
Great pyramid of Ghizeh, construc-
    tion.........................ii. 28
Greece, Asiatic, intercourse with
    Egypt........................ii. 248
Greeks in Egypt..................ii. 248
Guitars...........................i. 244
Gum-arabic........................i. 27

HAIR-DRESSING of ancient Egyptians.i. 50
Hak. *See* Heka.
Hammamât, valley of..............ii. 69, 71
Harmarchis. *See* Horus.
Harness of horses...................i. 216
Harps..............................i. 243
Hatasu, sister of Thothmes II.......ii. 118
 ambition and achievements.....ii. 119
Hebrew race, interest attaching to..ii. 133
Heka, goddess of the tombs..........i. 183
Heliopolitan obelisk of Usurtasen...ii. 81
Heredity of official posts...........i. 206
Heresy, absence of..................i. 207
Her-hor, the first priest-king......ii. 219
Hermotybies, the, a military body...i. 211
Herodotus, chronological scheme....ii. 3
Herusha, the.................ii. 56, 58
Hieratic writing....................i. 58
Hieroglyphic writing........i. 58; ii. 25
High-priest,officebecomeshereditary,ii. 212
Hippopotamus-hunting............i. 255
History, birth of..................ii. 64
Hittite empire, ascendency of......ii. 169
 invaders of Egypt...............ii. 104
Hittites, enlarged dominion........ii. 156
Hoe, Egyptian, the.................i. 82
Hor-em-beb, reign of ....ii. 151
Horses................i. 90 ; ii. 48; 117, 192
Horus, Harmarchis.................i. 171
 representations and titles......i. 171
Hospitality, necessity of...........i. 257
Houses, early Egyptian............ii. 19
 become more luxurious.......ii. 191
Hunting.............................i. 253
Hydraulic works....................i. 85
Hyena, striped, the................i. 84
Hyksos, conquest of Egypt.........ii. 100
 rule in Egypt..................ii. 105
 kings..........................ii. 107
 length of dynasty..............ii. 108
 driven from Egypt.............ii. 109
"Hymn to the Nile," extract........i. 191
"Hymn to Tum"....................i. 166

IBIS, two varieties.................i. 40
Ichneumon (*Viverra Ichneumon*)....i. 35
Iguanas..............................i. 43
Immigration to Nile valley........ii. 84
Infantry...........................i. 212
Insects, abundance of..............i. 42
Intaglios....................i. 123, 127
Interpreters, introduction of.....ii. 248
Ipsambul, rock-temple of.........ii. 172
Iron..................................i. 47
 uses of...........................i. 235
Irrigation system in the Fayoum, ii. 89, 92
Isis, wife of Osiris............i. 169, 173
 as commonly figured.............i. 174
 titles............................i. 174
Isolation, policy of................ii. 208
Israelites in Egypt.................ii. 133

JAVELIN............................i. 217
Jeroboam takes refuge in Egypt....ii. 224
 elected king of Israelites......ii. 225
 the ally of Sheshonk I.........ii. 226
Jerusalem taken and plundered by
 Sheshonk I......................ii. 226
 taken by Nebuchadnezzar........ii. 256
 siege and fall..................ii. 258
Jewish race, life and character.....ii. 133
Jews, last remnant led into captivity..................ii. 258
Joseph probable minister of Apepi..ii. 110, 133
Josiah, king of Judah, defeated by
 Neco............................ii. 254
Judæa revolts against Babylon......ii. 258

KHAMSEEN wind, the................i. 24
Karnak, Great Temple of.....i. 105, 107–113; ii. 159

Kharn, probably the Syrians........ii. 101
 country of the..................ii. 125
Khem, god of vegetable world......i. 157
 titles............................i. 158
Khepra...............................i. 164
Khitu, great land of the............i. 125
Khitasir, Hittite leader against Rameses II..........................ii. 165
Khons, a moon-god..................i. 174
 form assigned...................i. 175
 temple in Thebes................i. 175
 ordinary titles.................i. 175
Khonsu, the ark of.................ii. 214
 See also Khons.
Khu-aten, new city of..............ii. 149
Khufu, accession of................ii. 27
 ambition, egotism, vanity......ii. 30
 See also Cheops.
Kings, early, table of..............ii. 15
 absolute divinity..............ii. 94
King-worship......................ii. 189
Kish or Kush. *See* Ethiopians.
Kneph, god of Elephantiné..........i. 155
 figured appearance............i. 156

LABOR, demand for..................i. 248
 the division of.................ii. 64
Laborers, agricultural.............ii. 224
Laboring classes...................ii. 52
Labyrinth, the.....................ii. 90
Lakes of the Delta.................i. 15
Landed property hereditary........ii. 23
Language, analogies of..............i. 48
 of the Egyptians................i. 57
Lasso, used in hunting cattle......i. 254
Lead..........................i. 47, 235
Lebanon, the forests of...........ii. 158
Leopard-skin, priestly rank denoted
 by.........................i. 208, 210
Libya, extent and geographical character...........................i. 19
 authority of Egypt.............ii. 135
Libyans, origin and ultimate absorption...............................i. 53
 Egyptian victory...............ii. 180
Libu. *See* Libyans.
Limestone...........................i. 46
Linen, general use of...............i. 33
 exquisite character.............i. 228
Lion as symbol of royalty..........i. 146
 hunt rarely indulged.....i. 255 ; ii. 79
 employed in the chase....i. 34, 254
Literature...........................i. 51
 general character................i. 68
 variety and extent..............i. 69
 as an amusement................ii. 49
 as a profession................ii. 64
 decline of.....................ii. 217
Literary activity..................ii. 193
Litters.............................i. 250
Lizards.............................i. 43
Lyres...............................i. 243
Lyrical poems.......................i. 74
Locust plagues......................i. 45
Loom, Egyptian.....................i. 229
Lotus, varieties of.................i. 29
Lower orders, condition...........ii. 52
 rebellion......................ii. 77
Luxurious living, results..........ii. 53
Luxury, advance of................ii. 51

MA, Egyptian goddess of truth......i. 182
Maces...............................i. 216
 cylindrical......................i. 244
Magic, belief in..............ii. 204, 269
Mail, coats of......................i. 213
Malouli. *See* Merula.
Mammeisi, a kind of temple........i. 113
Man, ultimate destiny........i. 149, 150
Manetho, chronological scheme.....ii. 4
Manners............................i. 203
Manufacturers......................i. 226

INDEX. 333

Manuscript, most ancient in the world.................................ii. 42
Marmain, African chief.................ii. 178
Masonry, exact, in the pyramids.....ii. 33
Maut, wife of Ammon Ra...............i. 160
 titles..................................i. 160
Maxyes, invasion during reign of Rameses III.............................ii. 201
Meats....................................ii. 51
Mechanical skill .... i. 226
Medical practitioners....................i. 246
 writings................................i. 78
Medicinal plants.........................i. 32
Medicine, Egyptian proficiency........i. 143
Medinet-Abou, temple at.................i. 105
Memnon, vocal, the.....................ii. 144
Memnonium. See Rameseum.
Memphis, great seat of Egyptian Empire...................................ii. 53
 re-establishes independence........ii. 67
 captured by the Hyksos.............ii. 104
 besieged by Piankhi................ii. 236
Mencheres. See Menkaura.
Menephthah succeeds Rameses II....ii. 177
 reverses and disasters..............ii. 177
 foreign relations...................ii. 178
Menh or Menhi.........................i. 183
Menkaura, succession..................ii. 34
Mentu, deity presiding over the sun.................................i. 167
 worshipped at Hermonthis...........i. 167
 feast at Paprenis...................ii. 199
 ruling tribe of the copper-mines..ii. 42
 the defeat of.......................ii. 56
Mentu-hotep, official of Usurtasen...ii. 83
 reign of............................ii. 70
Mentu-hotep II........................ii. 71
Mercenaries, employment of............ii. 247
Meri-s-ankh, wife of Shafra............ii. 34
Merseker, goddess of silence..........i. 183
Merula worshipped in Nubia............ii. 178
Mesopotamia invaded by Egyptians..ii. 117
 decline of Egyptian power........ii. 215
Mesopotanian Empires ....i. 56
Metallurgy........................i. 233; ii. 25
Metals, deficiency of..................i. 46
Metempsychosis a feature in Egyptian writing..............................i. 76
Meydoun, pyramid of..........i. 93; ii. 20
Mi-ammon-nut, accession..............ii. 242
Military class........................i. 211
Mimetic art......................i. 123, 135
Minerals...............................i. 46
Mining under Rameses III..............i. 203
Mnevis, sacred bull of Heliopolis.....i. 197
Mœris, Lake, formation by Amen-emhat III............................ii. 88
Mohammedan misrule in Egypt.......i. 12
Mokhay' (Cardia myxa) the..........i. 27
Monarchs doubtful of sixth dynasty..ii. 55
Monarchy, Egyptian disintegration of....................................i. 63
Monotheism of Egyptians...............i. 148
Monumental history...................ii. 10
Monuments, ethnological value.......i. 49
Moon-gods, the.........................i. 174
Moral code, requirements............ii. 52
Morals.................................i. 52
 decline of.........................ii. 217
Mosaic antique described..............ii. 21
Moses leads his people out of Egypt..ii. 181
Mummies..............................ii. 22
 worship of........................ii. 201
Murket, royal architect..............i. 247
Music..................................i. 49
Musical instruments...................i. 243
Musicians..............................i. 242
Mysteries, Egyptian..................i. 201
Mythology, gods of....................i. 148
 Egyptian, apparent confusion....i. 201

NABOPOLASSAR, king of Babylonia...ii. 254
Nahsi, or *Nahasu*......................i. 54

Napata, important city of Ethiopia..ii. 232
Nations bordering upon Egypt........i. 54
Natron Lakes, valley of................i. 19
Natrum...............................i. 47
Naucratis founded by Greeks........ii. 249
Naval tactics..........................i. 221
Nebta, or Nebtel. See Nephthys.
Nebuchadnezzar, son of Nabopolassar................................ii. 254
 military expeditions.........ii. 254, 259
 joins battle with Neco.............ii. 255
Neco, accession of....................ii. 251
 seeks to unite his navies........ii. 252
 subjection of Syria...............ii. 253
 his expedition circumnavigates Africa...........................ii. 253
 defeated by Nebuchadnezzar....ii. 255
Nefer-hetp. See Khons.
Nefer-hotep, reign of.................ii. 97
Nefert-ari-Aahmes, wife of Aahmes..ii. 114
Negro tribes subject to Egypt.........ii. 56
 re-establish independence........ii. 113
Negroes of Nile Valley.................i. 54
Nehemao titles.........................i. 184
Neith, goddess of Saïs, titles.........i. 162
 feast at Saïs......................i. 199
Nelumbium (*Nymphœa nelumbo*).....i. 30
Nephthys, sister of Isis................i. 180
Netpe. See Nut.
Nobility, early Egyptian...............ii. 9
" Noph, the princes of "..............ii. 233
 protectorate over Egyptian kingdoms..............................ii. 233
Nile, fertilizing influence.............i. 1
 valley of............................i. 2
 source and course................i. 5-10
 White, the.........................i. 7
 Blue, the..........................i. 7
 tributaries of.....................i. 7
 inundation of..............i. 10; ii. 88
 system, the........................i. 12
 boats as transports................i. 221
 and canals for transportation...ii. 48
 lower, rich valley of.............ii. 68
 valley, mineral wealth...........ii. 69
 flotilla built by Aahmes.........ii. 112
Nilometer mentioned ....ii. 89
Nitocris, probable accession......ii. 62
Novels, Egyptian.......................i. 75
Nubi or Nubti..........................i. 185
Nubia, Northern, permanently attached to Egypt....................ii. 85
Nubians, commerce with Egyptians..ii. 92
Nut, mother of Osiris..................i. 180
 goddess of the firmament........i. 180
Nyanzas. See Albert and Victoria...i. 5

OBELISK, invention of ....i. 105
 purely Egyptian....................i. 112
 architectural use..................i. 112
Obelisks erected by Usurtasen.......ii. 81
 removed to London and New York.............................ii. 138
Occultations of planets by moon, noted by Egyptians.....................i. 140
Officials of the kingdom..............i. 206
Oils used in anointing................i. 32
Olive-cultivation in the Fayoum....i. 85
Olyra. See Doura.
Onuris, the Egyptian Mars............i. 178
 See also Mentu.
Ornament in architecture............ii. 19
Ornaments of gold and silver...i. 234, 235
Osarkon I.............................ii. 227
 successors of......................ii. 229
Osirid legends.........................i. 170
Osiris, chief god of Egypt............i. 168
 judge of souls....................i. 168
 myths connected with.............i. 169
 usual representation..............i. 169
 feast in honor of..................i. 199
 devotees of........................ii. 188
Ox, Indian or humped..................i. 38

PACIS. *See* Bacis.
Painting, Egyptian ignorance of. ...i. 132
  the mechanism of..............i. 133, 240
Palace temples......................i. 113
  Theban..........................ii. 185
Palestine invaded by Thothmes III..ii. 123
  friendly relations with Egypt....ii. 222
Palm, date, the.....................i. 26
  dom, the........................i. 25
Pantheistic nature of Egyptian religion.............................i. 198
Pantheon, formation of..............i. 152
Papremis, feast of Mentu............i. 199
Papyrus, the........................i. 29
  Turin.........................ii. 2, 16
  of the kings...................ii. 271
Pasht, wife of Phthah...............i. 179
Peasant, Egyptian, condition of.....i. 80
Pectoral plates.....................i. 232
People, homogeneous................ii. 208
Pepi, army levy....................ii. 56
  supremacy of...................ii. 57
  titles assumed by..............ii. 59
Persea (*Balanites Ægyptiaca*).......i. 28
Persia, war with Egypt........ii. 264, 266
Persian invasion...................ii. 266
  soldiery.......................ii. 266
Perso-Medic power, rise of.........ii. 263
Petroleum...........................i. 47
Pharaoh of Joseph, the..............i. 111
Phœnician, confusion arising from
  name...........................ii. 104
  and Greek vessels..............ii. 251
Phonetic character of hieroglyphics..i. 61
Phrygians, antiquity of............ii. 248
Phthah, physical creator of universe.i. 158
  forms and titles............i. 158, 159
  temple at Memphis..............i. 160
Piankhi, reign of..................ii. 233
  suppresses revolt of Tafnekht..ii. 235
Picture-writing.....................i. 59
  of the Khita..................ii. 126
Pigs, prejudice against.......i. 249; ii. 51
Planetary motion, study of..........i. 140
Plough, Egyptian....................i. 81
Poetry..............................i. 68
Political system..................ii. 209
Polygamy............................i. 259
  decline of morals.............ii. 217
Polytheistic system, gradual growth.i. 152
Ponds...............................i. 252
Population, varying estimates.......i. 53
Porcelain...........................i. 232
Pottery.............................i. 231
  increased elegance............ii. 76
Poultry.............................i. 89
Prayers, deficiency in..............i. 192
Prepositions, declension of.........i. 66
Princes, status and home-life.......i. 240
Priest-class under Apries.........ii. 261
Priestesses.........................i. 210
Priestly succession.................i. 205
Priests, dress of...................i. 209
  food...........................i. 209
  marriage among.................i. 209
  obligations and habits.........i. 208
  power and organization...i. 206; ii 209
  revenues.......................i. 208
Prisoners, treatment of.....i. 221; ii. 13
Procession, triumphal..............ii. 224
Processions, conspicuous feature of
  ritual.........................ii. 200
Produce, transportation of..........i. 90
Professions, learned................i. 245
Pronouns, use of....................i. 64
Prophets............................i. 206
Proto-Doric columns................ii. 98
  tombs..........................i. 103
Psammetichus establishes power over
  all Egypt.....................ii. 246
  of Libyan descent.............ii. 247
  experiment to discover primitive
  race..........................ii. 248

Psammetichus' aggressive policy toward Syria........................ii. 250
  attention to art and architecture.ii. 250
Psammetichus II., patron of art....ii. 257
Psamatik III., defeated and put to
  death by Cambyses.............ii. 267
  short reign...................ii. 266
Punt, geographical location........ii. 72
  fertility and products.........ii. 72
  in Egyptian tradition..........ii. 73
  naval expedition of Hatasu....ii. 120
Pyramid building....................i. 92
  at Saccarah....................i. 93
  of Meydoum.....................i. 93
  germ of.......................ii. 20
Pyramid kings, the.................ii. 26
  extent of dominion............ii. 54
Pyramids, three great, of Ghizeh....i. 94
  object and adaptation..........i. 99
  architectural merits...........i. 100
  mechanical skill displayed.....i. 101
  brick..........................i. 102
  grandeur of...................ii. 43

QUARRIES of Hammamât valley......ii. 71
Queen's chamber of Great Pyramid.i.. 98

RA, God in the sun.................i. 163
  figure and emblems.............i. 163
  distinguished from Osiris......i. 164
  universal worship..............i. 164
Ra-Sekenen III., war with Apepi...ii. 109
Race differences....................i. 49
Races distinct......................i. 50
  relative antiquity............ii. 248
Rain in Egypt.......................ii. 24
Rameses I., accession of..........ii. 154
  Syrian war....................ii. 155
Rameses II., accession of.........ii. 163
  campaigns.....................ii. 164
  Syrian wars...................ii. 165
  treaty with Hittites..........ii. 167
  marries daughter of Khitasir..ii. 169
  large number of captives......ii. 170
  subject races under...........ii. 171
  cities built..................ii. 172
  wonderful architectural works.ii. 173
  institutes polygamy...........ii. 175
  proofs of Semitic origin......ii. 175
  character.....................ii. 176
  introduction of the harem....ii. 204
Rameses III., accession..........ii. 197
  wars..........................ii. 198
  war with African nations.....ii. 199
  constructions................ii.[202
  sympathy with his people.....ii. 203
  conspiracy against...........ii. 204
  trial of the conspirators....ii. 205
  personal description.........ii. 206
  legitimate wife..............ii. 206
  tomb of.....................ii. 207
Rameses IV.......................ii. 209
Rameses V........................ii. 210
Rameses IX......................ii. 211
  trial of sacrilegious malefactors.ii. 211
Rameses XII., story of the ark of
  Khonsu......................ii. 213
Rameseum at Thebes..............ii. 105
  Temple of the...............ii. 160
Rameside *physique*, decline of...ii. 209
Ranuser, reign of................ii. 40
Red Sea, crossing of the Israelites.ii. 182
Rehoboam fortifies Judæa.........ii. 225
Religion..........................i. 146
  popular and metaphysical phases.i. 148
  sacred animals................i. 194
  animal-worship................i. 197
  outward aspect................i. 198
  Pantheistic nature............i. 198
  worship of ancestors..........i. 200
  of primitive period..........ii. 22
  advance of...................ii. 45
  of the eleventh dynasty......ii. 76

INDEX. 335

Religion of the Hyksos...............ii. 105
  changes............................ii. 188
Religious writings of Egyptians.....i. 70
Reptiles.............................i. 43
Reservoir built by Rameses III......ii. 203
Ribu. See Libyans.
"Ritual of the Dead," origin..........ii. 22
  first appearance of cardinal doctrine............................ii. 35
Roads, non-existence of..............i. 90
Rock-sepulchres......................i. 102
Rock-temple of Ipsambul.............ii. 172
Rock-tombs, pictorial representations...............................i. 119
Roman transportation of obelisk....i. 112
Romances. *See Novels*...............i. 75
Rut-ammon, stepson of Tirhakah...ii. 242
Ruten, the, appearance of civilization............................ii. 125

SABAK. *See Savak.*
Saccarah pyramid, the................i. 93
Sacrifice, two kinds.................i. 193
Sahura, reign of.....................ii. 38
Sais, feast of Neith.................i. 199
Salt.................................i. 47
Sandals, use of......................i. 251
Sands in Nile valley.................i. 3
Sandstone............................i. 46
Sankh-ka ra, traffic with Punt.....ii. 72
Sarcophagus in Ghizeh pyramid.....i. 95
  varieties of........................i. 239
Sargon, founder of last Assyrian dynasty...........................ii. 230
Sati, wife of Kneph..................i. 161
Savak, crocodile-headed god........i. 177
Schools..............................i. 246
Science, Egyptian....................i. 137
Scorpion (*Scorpio crassicauda*).....i. 45
Scribes, importance of...............i. 215
  government..........................i. 246
Sculptors............................i. 240
Sculpture, Egyptian, purpose of.....i. 126
  its defects......................i, 124-127
  mechanical process..................i. 240
  of pyramid period...................i. 44
  increased excellence...............ii. 93
Sculptured tomb-scenes..............ii. 132
Scythic tribes of Na ha-rain........ii. 126
Sea-service..........................i. 220
Semitic origin of Egyptian language.i. 57
  influence, spread of................i. 99
Senefru, reign of....................ii. 26
Sennacherib, Assyrian monarch..ii. 240, 241
  menaces Judæa......................ii. 246
  destruction of his army............ii. 240
Sepulchral chambers as temples.....ii. 22
Sepulchres, earliest.................ii. 19
Serapeum, necropolis of the bulls...ii. 176
Set, the principle of evil............i. 169
  conspires against Osiris............i. 169
  father of Osiris....................i. 177
  brother of Osiris...................i. 184
  worship of.........................ii. 188
Set, first known monarch of Hyksos.ii. 107
Seti, accession of...................ii. 155
  campaign against Syrians...........ii. 156
  wars in south and west.............ii. 158
  architectural works................ii. 159
  inscriptions of....................ii. 161
  personal appearance................ii. 162
Seti II..............................ii. 182
Set-nekht, accession of.............ii. 196
Sexes, relations of..................i. 259
Shabak, reign of....................ii. 239
Shabatok, son of Shabak............ii. 239
Shafra, accession, personal appearance............................ii. 32
  titles assumed.....................ii. 33
Shasu, the, identity with the Hyksos.i. 56
  nomadic people from region of Dead Sea.............................ii. 101
Shaving..............................i. 250

Sheep-breeding.......................i. 88
Shepherd kings, period of...........ii. 8
  innovations of.....................ii. 106
Sheshonk I., accession...............ii. 224
  expedition into Palestine..........ii. 225
Shields..............................i. 213
Ship-building on both seas.........ii. 291
Shoes supersede sandals............ii. 76
Shu, light of the sun................i. 166
  special office.....................i. 167
Sieges, mode of conducting..........i. 219
Silver...............................i. 46
  ornaments..........................i. 235
Sinaitic Peninsula, Egyptian dominion...............................ii. 61
Siphthah, usurpation of.............ii. 183
Sistrum, or rattle...................i. 244
Slain in battle, treatment of........i. 222
Slave-labor..........................i. 80
Slaves..............................ii. 52
Slingers.............................i. 213
Snake, horned, the...................i. 44
Snow, absence of.....................i. 24
Society under the Pharaohs..........i. 259
Soda, subcarbonate of................i. 47
Soil of Egypt........................i. 2
Soldiers, class rank of..............i. 211
Solomon, reign in Palestine........ii. 222
Solpuga, a variety of spider.......i. 45
Sont. *See Acanthus.*
"Sothiac Cycle" of Egyptians........i. 142
Soul after death.....................i. 150
Spears...............................i. 216
Sphynx, Great, of the Pyramids.....i. 127
Spider, *solpuga*....................i. 45
Standards, war......................ii. 218
Stars, fixed, Egyptian tabulation....i. 141
Statuary, negative and positive defects...........................i. 125
  under Psamatik II.................ii. 257
Statues, Egyptian, peculiarities of..i. 124
  portrait............................i. 240
Statuettes, porcelain................i. 233
Stone in architecture...............ii. 19
Stone-cutting..................i. 227 ;iii. 25
Sun, Egyptian worship of......i. 162 ; ii. 142
Sun-gods, the........................i. 162
Superstitions of Asia...............ii. 269
Sutech. *See Set.*
Swallow, sea (*Sterna Nilotica*).....i. 41
Swine................................i. 88
Swineherds..........................ii. 249
Swords, straight.....................i. 216
Sycamore, Egyptian, the..............i. 26
Symbolism in religion................i. 198
Symphony, triple, the................i. 245
Syntax, Egyptian, chief points.......i. 67
Syria, chief strategic features......i. 22
  as a political power...............i. 22
  Egyptian maps in..................ii. 127
  overrun by Egyptians..............ii. 115
Syrians, commerce with Egypt......ii. 92

TABLE, luxuries of, fondness for....i. 258
Tables...............................i. 229
Tafné, daughter of Ra................i. 182
Tafnekht, revolt of..................i. 224
Tuhal, the, country of..............ii. 125
Tambourines..........................i. 243
Taour, or Taourt. *See Taouris.*
Taouris, feminine counterpart of Set................................i. 185
Tartars threaten to invade Egypt...ii. 250
Taxation of lower orders............ii. 194
  priestly exemption.................i. 207
Tekaru, identification with the Teucri.............................ii. 274
Temple, Egyptian, oldest existing...ii. 21
Temples, Egyptian...................ii. 104
  dedication of......................ii. 190
  receptacles of vast wealth.........i. 208
Terra-cotta..........................i. 231
Teta-an, a Nubian chief.............ii. 113

Teucri. *See* Tekaru.
Theban dynasty, first.................ii. 74
  kings, qualified sovereignty.......ii. 105
  palace-temples...................ii. 185
Thebes, Amon, the great god of.......i. 153
  rise of..........................ii. 69
  becomes a free city..............ii. 69
Thoth, moon-god.....................i. 175
  titles and appearance............i. 175
  legend of........................i. 176
  revealer of God's will...........i. 176
  object of universal reverence....i. 176
Thothmes I., aggression upon Asia...ii. 106
Thothmes II........................ii. 118
Thothmes III., important reign.....ii. 122
  aggressive wars with Asiatic nations...........................ii. 123
  elaborate details of his campaigns.
    ii. 128
  maritime successes..............ii. 135
  songs of victory................ii. 136
  personal appearance.............ii. 138
Thothmes IV.......................ii. 140
Threshing, described...............i. 83
Ti, the tomb of...................ii. 41
Tiles, glazed.....................i. 232
Tirhakah, sole ruler of Egypt......ii. 240
Tombs, remarkable.................i. 92
  Proto-Doric.....................i. 103
  earliest, construction..........ii. 19
Tools used in stone-cutting........i. 223
"Tour in Palestine," extract.......i. 75
Towns, early existence............ii. 23
Trade under the Pharaohs..........i. 226
  with Punt......................ii. 72
Trades, most important............i. 226
Traditions regarding early monarchs.
    ii. 17
Tree-planting in reign of Rameses III.
    ii. 208
Trees of Egypt....................i. 25
Trinity, doctrine of..............i. 151
Troops, transportation of.........i. 223
Trumpet..........................i. 224
Tum or Atum......................i. 165
  the setting sun................i. 165
  titles and forms...............i. 165
  house of, at Heliopolis........i. 166
Turin Papyrus..............ii. 2, 16, 271
Turquoise mines of Sarabi-tel-Khadim.
    ii. 208
Turtle of the Nile, the...........i. 43
Tyre, siege of...................ii. 256
  surrenders to Nebuchadnezzar...ii. 258

UPHOLSTERY........................i. 229
Uua, official and historian of Pepi.
    ii. 57, 69
Unity of God......................i. 151
Usurkaf succeeds Aseskaf..........ii. 37
Usurtasen, brilliant reign........ii. 80
Usurtasen III., conqueror of Ethiopia.
    ii. 85
  forts built by..................ii. 86

VASES........................i. 232, 234
Vegetables cultivated..........i. 31, 84
Vegetation of Egypt...............i. 25
Vessels, different types.........ii. 251
Veterinary art....................i. 88
Victoria Nyanza...................i. 5
Vine, wide-spread cultivation.....i. 86

WADY-MAGHARAH tablet.............ii. 30
Wagons, absence of................i. 90
Wall decorations.................i. 134
"Wall, Great" the...............ii. 171
War-chariot......................i. 215
War tactics......................i. 218
Water system of African interior..i. 4
  communication..................i. 90
  -carriage for heavy commodities.ii. 48
Weapons of defence...............i. 213
Weaving..........................i. 228
Wheat, varieties of...............i. 31
  methods of cultivation..........i. 83
"Wilderness of the Wanderings." *See*
  El-Tij.
Wilkinson, Sir G., "Manners and Customs".........................i. 204
Wine an important produce of the
  farm..........................ii. 48
Witchcraft......................ii. 269
Women, dress....................i. 251
  sacred........................i. 210
  degradation of................ii. 270
Wool, general use................i. 88
Worship and gods, local.........i. 152
  of animals, origin............i. 197
  of ancestors..................i. 200
  of reigning monarch...........i. 23
Writing, Egyptian.............i. 57, 58
  common among educated classes.i. 245
  enchorial or demotic invented..ii. 251
Wood, early architectural use....ii. 19

Zea. See Doera.

www.ingramcontent.com/pod-product-compliance
Lightning Source LLC
Chambersburg PA
CBHW020302240426

43673CB00039B/673